Land Law

Land Law

Sixth edition

J G Riddall MA (TCD)
of the Inner Temple, Barrister at Law
formerly Senior Lecturer in Law, University of Leeds

Butterworths
London, Edinburgh, Dublin
1997

United Kingdom	Butterworths a Division of Reed Elsevier (UK) Ltd, Halsbury House, 35 Chancery Lane, LONDON WC2A 1EL and 4 Hill Street, EDINBURGH EH2 3JZ
Australia	Butterworths, SYDNEY, MELBOURNE, BRISBANE, ADELAIDE, PERTH, CANBERRA and HOBART
Canada	Butterworths Canada Ltd, TORONTO and VANCOUVER
Ireland	Butterworth (Ireland) Ltd, DUBLIN
Malaysia	Malayan Law Journal Sdn Bhd, KUALA LUMPUR
New Zealand	Butterworths of New Zealand Ltd, WELLINGTON and AUCKLAND
Singapore	Reed Elsevier (Singapore) Pte Ltd, SINGAPORE
South Africa	Butterworths Publishers (Pty) Ltd, DURBAN
USA	Michie, Charlottesville, VIRGINIA

A CIP Catalogue record for this book is available from the British Library.

First edition 1974
   Reprinted 1977
Second edition 1979
   Reprinted 1982
Third edition 1983
   Reprinted 1986
Fourth edition 1988
   Reprinted 1990, 1991, 1992
Fifth edition 1993

ISBN 0 406 99612 1

Cover photograph: Cookham, Berkshire

Printed by Redwood Books, Trowbridge, Wiltshire

Preface

In speaking, in previous editions, of the changes made by the 1925 legislation, we said that at midnight on 31 December 1925 the windows rattled, lightning flashed and the ground shook but the lawyer's client slept undisturbed in his bed. The same thing can be said of midnight on 31 December 1996, when the Trusts of Land and Appointment of Trustees Act came into force – when again the windows rattled, and the client slept on, undisturbed. Not since 1925 has there been such an upheaval in the law. But, as with the 1925 legislation, the changes have little or no noticeable impact on a lawyer's client.

So great were the changes made to the structure of English and Welsh land law by the Act that its passage alone would have been sufficient to warrant a new edition of this book. There have, though, been two other Acts which, although of less radical overall importance, would have required a new edition, namely the Landlord and Tenant (Covenants) Act 1995 and the Land Registration Act 1997.

These three Acts have caused a more substantial re-writing of the text than in any edition since the first appearance of the book in 1974. Chapter 7 on Strict Settlements and Chapter 8 on Trusts for Sale have been reduced in length, a short new chapter added on Bare Trusts, and a new chapter added on the Trusts of Land and Appointment of Trustees Act 1996. The latter Act has necessitated amendments to the text throughout the greater part of the book. The chapter on Covenants in Leases, now Chapter 22, has been largely rewritten. Changes have been required also by the Family Law Act 1996.

The attempts by the courts to undermine the intention of the legislature in the field of adverse possession (see page 469) have continued, albeit at a lower key (see *Pulleyn Hall Aggregates (Thames Valley) Ltd* (1993) 65P & CR 276, page 471).

Such attempts at what the Law Reform Committee regarded as amounting to a 'judicial repeal of the statute' have, incidentally, been paralleled in the field of public law, by the adoption by the Court of Appeal of the bizare notion that the phrase 'as of right' in section 31 of the Highways Act 1980 and in section 22(1) of the Commons Registration Act 1965 (see *R v Suffolk County Council, ex p Steed* (11 July 1996)) requires a belief by users that their use was in the exercise of a legal right – a notion introduced *per curiam* by Tomlin J in *Hue v Whitely* in 1929, and propounded without a shred of authority and contrary to the history of the law and the rationale on which it rests (see [1997] Conv 29). The way in which the courts 'openly exult in the defeat of squatters' claims' ((1980) 96 LQR 333) is thus now witnessed in the defeat of claims for public rights based on twenty years' use under the 1965 and 1980 Acts.

At a late stage in the preparation of this edition, I concluded that one difficulty facing students of land law may be that, although they understand what they read as they go along, it may sometimes be hard to recognise the structure of the subject – to see the wood for the trees. To provide assistance, a summary of each of the principal chapters has been added. Where, on the final page, space has permitted (without re-typesetting the entire book) this is where the summary appears. Where this has not been possible, the summary appears in Appendix II.

In the light of the changes that have occurred in the scope and extent of the book over its successive editions, it will be noted that the words 'Introduction to ...' have been dropped from the book's title.

I express my thanks to the University of Sheffield for use of the University's Crookesmoor Library, without which it would have been very difficult for this edition to be produced. I am most grateful to the University and to the staff of the library for their help.

The publishers have once again been their efficient and friendly selves. I am very conscious of the amount of detailed work that goes into the sub-editing of the text, the preparation of the tables of cases and statutes and the index; and I am grateful also for the thought that went into the selection (after much discussion and deliberation!) of the picture for the front cover of this edition.

My deepest debt is once again to my wife, for her encouragement and support, for the many hours spent reading proofs, and for her patience at my long absences at my desk.

My intention has been to state the law as at 1 June 1997.

J G Riddall
Hills View Cottage
Bradwell
Hope Valley
Derbyshire

Contents

Table of Statutes

References in this Table to *Statutes* are to Halsbury's Statutes of England (Fourth Edition) showing the volume and page at which the annotated text of the Act may be found.

Table of cases

PAGE

PAGE

PAGE

CHAPTER 1

What is Land Law all About?

What is land law about? It is, we suggest, very broadly about four things. First, it is about what, for our present purposes, may be termed 'ownership'. Ownership has various sides to it. Important among these is *title*, a term which may (again for present purposes) be regarded as indicating the legal right to land. Suppose that A owns a house, Rose View. A sells the house to B and B leaves it in his will to C. In this case the title to the property passes from A, to B, to C. It passes, that is, if the transactions involved are carried out in the way required by the law. For example, for A to convey the title to the land to B, he must execute the transaction in a document termed a deed.[1] If A fails to execute a deed, the legal title remains with A. If the title does pass to B, then whether the title passes from him to C will depend on whether B makes a legally valid will. If he does so, then the title passes to C.

If B fails to make a valid will[2] then, the will being null, B's property will devolve on his death as if he had died intestate, and therefore pass to B's next of kin, whom, let us say, is X. Suppose that this is what has happened, and that X dies shortly afterwards, leaving a will in which he made gifts of specified property to certain named individuals and 'the residue of my property' to Y. In this case, the title to the house will have passed under X's will to Y. Y discovers what has happened and claims the house from C, who, unaware of the defect in his title, has been living contentedly at Rose View since B's death. Whether Y has any remedy is a question with which we shall deal in a later chapter. For the present, the point to note is that one aspect of ownership is concerned with the title to land, and, in particular, with chains of title, chains along which title passes like an electric current to light a bulb at the last link. (In the last example, the light flashing on Y, not, to his chagrin, on C.) Matters concerning title occur throughout the book.

Another aspect of ownership is concerned with the question – what, physically, does 'land' consist of? For example, when A bought Rose View, did he buy at the same time a vein of fluorspar that lies 200 feet beneath the surface, and, associated with this question, what rights did A acquire and to what obligations did A become subject, as a result of his ownership of the land? Matters relating to these aspects of ownership are considered in Chapter 4.

---

1   Prior to the Law of Property (Miscellaneous Provisions) Act 1989 for a document to be a deed it was required to be sealed by, in the example, A. After the Act, for a document to be a deed it must be declared to be a deed and be witnessed by two people. See Chapter 15.
2   Ie, if the requirements of the Wills Act 1837 are not complied with, eg if the will is not witnessed as required by s 9 of the Act.

Another aspect of ownership is concerned with the periods of time for which land may be granted by one person to another. For example, suppose that G now owns Rose View. His wish is that on his death the house should go to his wife, Anne, for her life time, and on her death to their daughter, Beatrice. So in his will he leaves the land to Anne for her life and then (or, as we say, 'with remainder to') Beatrice. Here Anne does not have full ownership of the land, she has it only for her life time: she has, we say, a *life interest*. On her mother's death, Beatrice becomes the full owner. Or it might be that G left the land to Anne (A) for her life time, then to Beatrice (B), for her life time, and then to a son, Charles (C). Here ownership would have been divided up between A, and B, and C: it would have been divided up in time, a chunk of time of ownership being given to A, a chunk of time to B, and then on B's death, full ownership to C. What we have called a 'chunk of time' English law terms an 'estate' in the land. Estates in land are the particular subject of Chapter 3.

Another sphere of land law is concerned with interests in land held by persons other than the owner. To explain what we mean by this suppose that G owns Greenacre, a cottage with a large garden. One morning, a group of people assemble outside the gate. Conversation develops between them and it transpires that each has some involvement with G's land. V explains that G has allowed him to lay drain-pipes under Greenacre from his, V's, recently built bungalow on the far side of G's land to the road on which the group is standing. W tells the others that G has given him an undertaking that Greenacre will be used only for residential purposes (and would therefore not be turned into, for example, offices). It was only because of this undertaking given by G, W explains, that he recently bought an old coach house from G that stood at the far end of Greenacre and converted it into his present home. X says that he is the manager of a local bank. Recently he agreed that the bank should lend G a sum of money, which Greenacre as security for the loan, ie that G had mortgaged the land to the bank as security for the loan. Y mentions that some weeks previously G had agreed to sell him a piece of Greenacre in order to enable him, Y, by increasing the size of his adjoining garden, to construct a tennis court. The piece of land had not actually been conveyed to him yet, Y explains, but G had signed the contract agreeing to the sale. Y was looking forward to becoming owner of the land so that he could begin work on the tennis court. Z opens the gates and begins to go through. 'Oh, its all right', he says, "G's getting on a bit you know. He's allowed me to take over the vegetable garden. He's let me have it for three years. I've put a shed there to keep my tools in.'

So V has his pipes. W has his promise from G about the use of Greenacre, X's bank has the mortgage, Y has the contract signed by G, and Z has the vegetable garden for three years. None of them is the *owner* of the land, G is, but they all have some form of *interest* in the land. V watches to see that G does not interfere with his pipes, W watches to see that the house is not turned into offices, X watches G's repayments of the loan (ready to claim the land if he fails to keep up the payments due), Y is waiting to get the land he wants for his tennis court, Z is on the look out for G helping himself to the vegetables that Z has grown (or even trying to get Z off the land). All of them have an interest to protect against any default by G, and if G does infringe the interest of any of them, then they would no doubt consider taking legal proceedings against him

−V − to seek an injunction to restrain G from interfering with his pipes, W to seek an injunction to prevent the conversion of the house into offices, X to seek an order requiring G to give up possession so that the land could be sold, Y to seek a decree of specific performance to compel G to execute the conveyance, and Z to seek an injunction restraining G from stealing his vegetables (or from trying to prevent him from using the land).

Thus V, W, X, Y and Z all have rights enforceable against G, the owner of the land. The law relating to the various forms of interest held by V, W, X, Y and Z is explained in various later chapters in the book.

The next day, the same group are again by the gate. 'Have you heard?' says V, "G's sold up.'

'What!' exclaims W, 'sold Greenacre?'

'Yes', explains V. 'Sold up and gone. There was a furniture van here last night. He's gone to South America. He'll be on the 'plane now.'

'And who has bought the place?' asks W.

'P has', V tells them.

They look at each other anxiously.

'What about my pipes?' thinks V.

'What about the house being turned into offices?' thinks W.

'What about the mortgage on the house?' thinks X.

'What about my tennis court?' thinks Y.

'What about the vegetable patch? Will I still be able to use it?' thinks Z.

What indeed. The matter that worries each of the group by the gate constitutes a major strand in English land law; if A holds an interest in B's land, and B transfers the land to C, does A's interest bind C? The question arises throughout this book. Indeed, in terms of both practical importance and of the extent of the law that has been evolved in giving an answer, the issue is probably the most important in English land law. The issue first arises in Chapter 5, on trusts, and it arises again in most subsequent chapters. It is the subject specifically of Chapter 25, on Registration of Incumbrances, and is a matter of major importance in Chapter 26, on Registered Land.

Land law is concerned, then, first with various aspects of *ownership* of land, and secondly with *interests in land* and, particularly, with the question whether such interests in land are binding on a subsequent holder of the land.

A third aspect of land law is concerned with restrictions placed, on grounds of public policy, on certain forms of disposition of land. For example, because of the principle that land should be freely transferable, the law does not permit a grant to be made to another person subject to a condition that he never sells it. (A condition such as this, one which places a restraint on the free transfer of land, is void. The matter is considered in Chapter 4.) Another example of a restriction on the form of disposition that a landowner can validly make − one that restricts how far into the future he can legally decree to whom his land is to pass after it has left his hands − is examined in Chapter 14.

A fourth aspect of land law may be regarded as being concerned with the machinery of the law. Suppose that a layman goes to his lawyer and says, 'I wish to leave my property in such and such a way'; or, 'I wish to allow this land to be used for a school, but if the school closes down I want the land back'; or, 'I wish to mortgage my land to X'; or 'I wish my land to go to my son, but only if he gets married'; or, 'I wish to sell my land to P'; or 'I wish to grant my neighbour a right to cross my land'; or, 'I wish to ensure that if I sell part of my land to W, the land will not be used for anything except a private dwelling'. In each of these cases, the lawyer will say, 'Yes, certainly. This can be done. I will draw up the necessary document.' The law provides the machinery by which the transactions may be effected and a legally binding relationship brought into existence. It is here that we enter what we may call the lawyer's side of land law, the side that is concerned with the machinery, the technicalities of the law, the way things are done.

We can give an example of what we mean by the machinery of land law. Suppose that a man, a widower, G, wishes his land to go on his death to his son, but his son is only seven. It would be inappropriate for the boy to be responsible for the management of the property. He would not know what to do and others might take advantage of him. It was, in part, to cater for such a situation that there evolved the machinery of a trust, an arrangement under which one or more persons could be made responsible for the management of property, whilst another was given the benefit of it. So that, in our example, G could leave the land to trustees for his infant son. The trust is thus one example of the way in which the law has developed forms of machinery for giving effect to a property owner's needs.

It was with regard to the machinery of land law that radical changes were made by five statutes enacted in 1925, statutes which have come to be referred to collectively as 'the 1925 legislation'. We shall meet the statutes concerned, in particular the Law of Property Act 1925, throughout this book. Indeed, we shall often say, 'Before 1926 ... ' such and such was the position; 'after 1925, the position was ... '. But it must be stressed that by far the largest part of the 1925 legislation involved the technical structure of the law. It was only in a few, exceptional, instances that the actual substance of the law was changed. For the lawyer, at the stroke of midnight on 31 December 1925, the windows rattled, lightning flashed, the ground shook, but the layman noticed nothing. The client, the landowner, slept undisturbed. For him, nothing was different on 1 January 1926. He had the same rights, the same obligations as on the previous day. He might later learn from his legal advisers that on 1 January 1926 conveyancing had, by the legislation, been 'simplified'. It is unlikely though, that he noticed any change in the time that it took his solicitor to carry out conveyances, and there is no evidence that he would have found his solicitor's bills for this work to be any lower.[3] Yet, so fundamental, so complex, so wide-ranging were the changes made by the 1925 legislation, that lawyers have, since that time, sometimes tended to treat 1925 as some kind of watershed, a revolution even, in English property law. It was no such thing. The character of the 1925 legislation has been misunderstood. The present writer has heard an eminent academic (though no property lawyer, and now retired) refer to there being 'no need to go back before 1925', as if the 1925 legislation constituted some sort of codification of the land law. It was nothing of the kind. The legislation made changes of immense importance to the structure,

3   See (1984) CLP 63 (S. Anderson).

but the structure was not replaced. English land law has evolved over nine centuries. The 1925 legislation was a hiccup, and by no means the biggest hiccup,[4] in the course of its long development.

Another upheaval occurred in 1996 with the passage of the Trusts of Land and Appointment of Trustees Act. But here too, what was primarily affected was the machinery, not the substance, of the law. At midnight on 31 December 1996, the windows again rattled, and the client again slept undisturbed.

The aspects of law we have considered so far have been, in the main, private in nature, in the sense of relating to the needs of private persons; but there is also a sphere of land law that lies in the public domain, being concerned with the regulation of certain matters affecting land, designed to give effect to the economic, or social, or environmental policies of the state.

If we look at a text book on land law written at the end of the last century, we find that the law expounded is concerned solely with what we have spoken of as private law. When we look at textbooks published in the second half of this century, we find that increasing amounts of space are devoted to matters lying in the public realm. Of particular importance among these are the subjects of rent control, compulsory purchase, planning, and housing. In each of these spheres, the state, acting in what is deemed to be the public interest, imposes schemes of regulation on the physical or economic use of land.

These schemes of regulation are of great practical importance. If a student has taken a lease of a house, it may well be a matter of much moment to him whether his landlord can put up his rent, or evict him if his declines to pay a higher rent; whether the local authority goes ahead with a scheme to compulsorily purchase the land, demolish the house, and build a motorway; whether, if he becomes homeless, the local authority is under any obligation to house him.

In writing a book on land law, a decision has to be made as to what proportion of the book should be devoted to the first three aspects of land law we have described, the private aspects of the subject, and what proportion to the public aspects. In this book, the greater attention is paid to the private sphere. The reason for this is that, whilst a student of land law should be aware of subjects such as planning law, and its place in the structure of land law as a whole, any satisfactory treatment of planning law – a sphere of law which is itself the subject of books a great deal longer than this – can, we believe, only be achieved at the cost of such a reduction in the space devoted to the private sphere that the treatment of the latter becomes inadequate. (Indeed, the law within this private sphere is so extensive that in practice it very often takes all a student's efforts to grasp the multifarious elements within the year that is commonly allocated to the study of the subject.) The public domain of land law in this book is therefore relegated to the side lines: not because of its lack of importance, but because the principal object of the book is to explain the working of the private law.

Enough of preliminaries. We must turn to the meat. In the next three chapters we deal with matters relating to 'ownership'. In the course of so doing,

4   The Statute of 1290 was profoundly more important. See Chapter 2.

we shall learn that although in this chapter we have spoken to ownership of land, there is, in fact, no such thing as 'ownership' of land in any absolute sense or, at any rate, that only one person truly *owns* land, the Crown.

Readers approaching the subject of land law for the first time may already have acquired a knowledge of the working of the British constitution as a result of studying British history, or the constitution itself. In either case they will realise that in order to understand the present constitution, it is necessary to have at least some knowledge of how it has evolved. (Indeed, without such a knowledge, some branches of the subject would probably appear barely credible.) Thus, even if it is the purpose of a writer to describe the modern constitution, and no more, he will find himself driven at various points to say, 'It is like this because ... ' of what happened at such and such a time in the past. Someone writing on land law finds himself in a similar position. Although it may be his purpose to confine himself solely to a description of the modern law, at various points he finds himself driven to say 'The law is this, because ...' of what happened in the past.

In order to understand the nature of modern English land law the need to know how the present law evolved is thus unavoidable. This does not mean that there is any necessity to delve into history for its own sake. All that is required is an understanding of the background of those principles which constitute the framework of the law today. The next two chapters are concerned with two such principles: tenure and estates. The law described in the two chapters is therefore set in a historical framework. This treatment will incidentally enable certain historical matters to be explained once and for all, thus avoiding the need to return to matters of history in later chapters. For example, in the next chapter, the description of the English manor includes an explanation of the origin of 'rights of common'. When, later, rights of common are considered separately (in Chapter 19) there will be no need to deal again with the historical background to the matter.

Tenure, the subject of the chapter that follows, was the foundation of the feudal structure of land holding and this structure was, in turn, the foundation on which English land law has been built.

Although certain forms of tenure are discernible in Saxon England, the starting point for its later evolution is generally regarded as the Conquest of 1066.

CHAPTER 2

Tenure

LAND HOLDING AFTER THE CONQUEST

When William, Duke of Normandy, invaded England in the Autumn of 1066 he brought with him a large army. The barons who accompanied William and helped him wrest England from Harold expected something in return for their assistance. They wanted land: land with which to reward their own followers, and to form themselves estates in the defeated kingdom. Immediately after the Battle of Hastings William began the process of rewarding the chief men among his followers with grants of land in England.

William can have known little about his new kingdom – he had only been in England once before[1] – but the distribution of land could not await a detailed survey of the conquered territories: that had to come later. So what William did was to grant to each of his most important followers the land of one or more Englishmen who had resisted him, either at Hastings or later, and whose resistance had ended in flight or death, and whose lands now, as a consequence, lay at the disposition of the new king.[2]

It became established, however, that in return for a grant of land, a tenant was required to undertake to render certain services to the king. The most common form of service consisted of the provision of a certain number of knights for a certain number of days in each year. The knights provided in this way made up the largest part of the king's army. Various other forms of service also existed.

By means of granting land the king was able to provide himself with the greater part of his army, to garrison his castles, to fill the great offices of state, to provide for the principal servants of his household, and to obtain supplies of various provisions.

A baron who had received a grant of many manors would not retain all of them in his own hands. If Henry, a baron, had undertaken to provide the king with, say 30 knights, in order to be able to provide the knights required, he might himself make grants of land to tenants of his own in return for the promise of the supply of a certain number of knights (see page 11). If Henry received 40 manors from the king he might grant 15 manors to Roger in return for the promise of 11 knights, 18 manors to Michael in return for the promise of 14 knights and the remaining knights would be made up of Henry himself and four knights hired by him for money, perhaps from among the younger

---

1   Anglo-Saxon Chronicle, MS D (1052); (1953) EHR 526 (D.C. Douglas).
2   Stenton, p 57.

sons of other noblemen. Of the seven manors which Henry had not yet granted away, he might grant one manor to the Priory of St Peter at Siddlemouth in return for the promise that a mass would be said every Tuesday and Friday for the salvation of his soul, and the remaining six manors he might retain in his own hands in order to provide food and supplies for his household.

Of the 15 manors granted to Roger, Roger might himself, in return for the promise of services, grant six to Bertram, four to Hubert, one to Andrew and retain four in his own hands. Similarly Michael, who is also Henry's man, might grant away a certain number of manors to Brian and Robert, and retain the remainder in his own hands.

Those who received grants of land direct from the king were tenants-in-chief. Thus, in our example Henry was a tenant-in-chief. King William granted land to about two hundred tenants-in-chief. Most of these in their turn granted away lands to inferior tenants, who themselves made grants to tenants of their own, and so the process (known as *subinfeudation*) was repeated down the scale. The system of land holding after the Conquest thus came to resemble a vast pyramid, at the apex of which stood the Crown.

Andrew holds one manor, the manor of Dale, from his lord, Roger. Roger does not have possession of the land, but merely has the rights of overlordship: he is said to hold the *seignory*. Henry similarly, holds a seignory as Roger's lord. Henry and Roger, standing as they do between the King and the person holding the land are termed *mesne* lords.

It is now necessary to examine the working of a typical manor, such as the manor of Dale, in order to appreciate more fully certain aspects of the modern law.

The manor of Dale

Andrew holds the manor of Dale, from his lord, Roger. The land on one side of the village is ploughed; on the other side it lies fallow, and cattle are grazing. These two tracts of land are the two 'open fields' of the manor. In any year, one of the fields is under cultivation. The other is left uncultivated and the cattle graze on the stubble of the previous year's crops and the self-sown grass and weeds. The following year the field which had been left fallow the year before is ploughed, and the field which had raised a crop the year before is left fallow.[3] Each of the open fields is divided into long strips, about 16 feet wide and occupying about half an acre.

Beyond the open fields, on one side of the manor lies woods and scrubland with pigs rooting in the undergrowth. On the other side the ground rises up to the moor where there are sheep. All this made up the 'waste', and stretches as far as the boundary of the manor. Within the manor there is the manor house, near which is an orchard and a paddock. In the paddock Andrew keeps his

---

3   In the majority of manors a three-field system of crop rotation evolved from the two-field system.

horse. After his suit of armour, this horse is the most valuable thing he owns. Andrew does not regard himself as owning the land of the manor. He merely holds this of Roger, just as Roger holds it of Henry, who holds it of the king. Thus no subject considers himself as 'owning' land: he merely holds it as a tenant from whoever is his lord.

From the manor Andrew obtains supplies for his household. In order to provide food he retains some of the lands of the manor in his own hands. The remaining lands he grants to tenants of his own within the manor.

The unit of distribution of land within the manor is the strip. Thus to Alfrec, Andrew grants 20 strips, ten lying in the North Field, and ten in the South Field. The strips which Andrew does not grant to tenants in the manor, he retains. The strips which Andrew retains, together with his orchard and paddock, make up the lord of the manor's *demesne.*

Just as Andrew is bound to render services to his lord, so it is natural that he should require his own tenants to perform services in return for the land they have been granted.[4] Andrew's principal need is for men to work on the lands of his demesne. So the services that he demands from his tenants will usually be of an agricultural nature. For example, Alfrec, who, as we have seen, was granted land by Andrew, is bound to do 14 days' ploughing a year on the lord's land. Other tenants might be obliged to perform a certain number of days' labour in the year but without the nature of the work being fixed in advance, the work being decided, when the day came, by Andrew's bailiff. Thus Wilfric is obliged to render four days' labour a week throughout the year; Wulfston two days' labour a week; and so on.

Thus the pyramid-like structure of landholding, with the king as its apex, does not end with Andrew as lord of the manor, but stretches down within the manor. The foundations of the pyramid were the peasant farmers holding their strips in the open fields.

FORMS OF TENURE

In this account of how land was held in England we have seen that a tenant might hold land for one of a variety of kinds of service. But whatever the nature of their services, all tenants had one thing in common, namely that they all held lands of a superior lord. Each one was in possession of land by virtue of *tenure*, a word derived from the Latin 'tenere', meaning 'to hold'. Tenure thus connotes not merely the holding of land but also the holding of land from a superior lord, and furthermore that the land is held in return for certain services by the tenant to his lord.

As time went on tenures came to be classified according to the kind of service rendered to the lord. (See the chart on page 11.)

---

4   As, in many cases, would the Saxon lord who had held the manor before the Conquest.

Tenures in chivalry

KNIGHT SERVICE

A tenant who held by the tenure of knight service was originally obliged to provide his lord with a specified number of fully armed horsemen. By the middle of the twelfth century the obligation to provide men had largely been commuted for a fixed money payment, termed *scutage*. By the end of the Middle Ages, with the decline in the value of money, scrutage had largely ceased to be collected.

GRAND SERGEANTY

A tenant who held by the tenure of grand sergeanty did so in return for performing some service of an honourable character; for example, holding an office of state, such as that of chamberlain.

Spiritual tenures

DIVINE SERVICE

When Henry granted a manor to the Abbey of St Peter at Siddlemouth in return for the promise of specified spiritual services, namely the saying of a mass every Tuesday and Friday for the salvation of his soul, the Abbey held the manor by the spiritual tenure of divine service. The spiritual service might take other forms, for example, giving specified sums of money to the poor every Shrove Tuesday.

FRANKALMOIGN

If the Abbey had been required to undertake no specified spiritual services, but merely to pray for the soul of Henry, then it would have held by the spiritual tenure of frankalmoign.

There were differences between the two forms of spiritual tenure with regard to the way in which each could be enforced.

Socage tenures

PETTY SERGEANTY

When the king granted land to a tenant in return for services of a non-personal nature, such as carrying his letters, or feeding his hounds or hawks, or providing him with arrows, or straw for his bed, then the tenant held by the tenure of petty sergeanty.

COMMON SOCAGE

The service most commonly rendered under this form of tenure was of an agricultural character, both the nature (eg ploughing) and the amount (eg 20

THE FEUDAL STRUCTURE OF LAND HOLDING (See p 7)

FORMS OF TENURE (See p9)

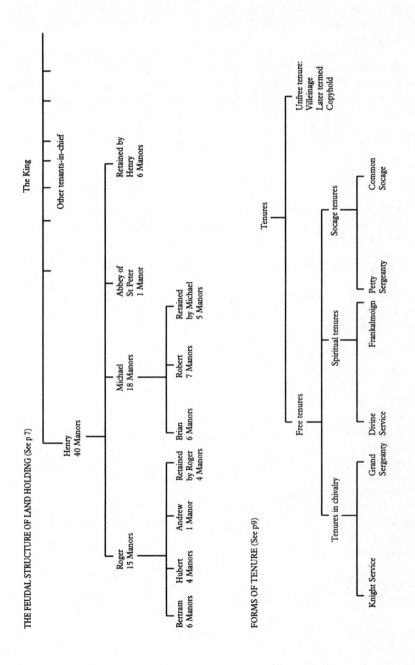

days a year) being fixed. But the services were not necessarily of an agricultural nature, and many other kinds are recorded. In towns a form of common socage existed under which money rents were rendered instead of services. This form of common socage is termed burgage tenure.

Common socage was a residuary class of free tenure: if a free tenure was not provided to be one of the others, then it was held to be common socage.

By the end of the fifteenth century the services rendered in connection with common socage had largely been commuted into money payments, sometimes called *quit rents* (by which the tenant became quit of his services). Like scutage, by the end of the Middle Ages quit rents had largely ceased to be collected.

Villein tenure

When describing the manor of Dale we saw that Wilfric held land in the manor and was bound to work for four days a week throughout the year on the lord's demesne. We saw that the nature of his work was not fixed in advance. What he had to do could be decided when the day came by Andrew's bailiff. The fact that the *amount* of work, ie four days a week, but not the *nature* of the work, was fixed in advance established that Wilfric holds his land by villein tenure. Whereas Alfrec (see page 9) is a free tenant (holding by the free tenure of common socage) Wilfric is not: he holds by the unfree tenure of villeinage.

INCIDENTS OF TENURE

We have seen that the tenures were distinguished by the forms of service in return for which land was granted to tenant by his landlord, but it became established that the services rendered by a tenant were not the only rights to which a lord was entitled. In addition, certain other matters evolved, some being in the nature of obligations on the tenant and some in the nature of rights belonging to the lord, which together are termed the *incidents* of tenure.

When considering the free tenures, we find that the list of incidents which relate to the socage tenure does not coincide with that relating to tenures in chivalry. This is one reason why it was necessary to distinguish between tenures in chivalry and socage tenures. Another difference lay in the relative prestige of each class.

Incidents relating to tenures in chivalry

Suit of Court

When a lord granted land to a tenant, one of the obligations on the tenant was to attend his lord's court and assist in its deliberations. He owed his lord *suit of court*.

Each lord thus had his own court. The jurisdiction of the court of any lord included the right to hear any dispute as to who had the better right to hold land as the lord's tenant.

AIDS

On certain occasions the tenant was obliged to make a payment (an 'aid') to his lord. Originally the occasions on which such payments could be demanded varied, as did the amounts of the payments. Magna Carta 1215 limited the occasions to (i) the ransom of the lord, (ii) the knighting of his eldest son and (iii) the marriage of his daughter.

DISTRESS AND FORFEITURE

If Bertram (see page 11) failed to perform the services to Roger which were the condition of his tenure, then Roger's remedy, given him by feudal law, was to seize chattels (for example, horses, oxen and stores of wheat) on Bertram's land and to hold them until Bertram performed the services which he owed to Roger. This was the remedy of *distress*. Roger *distrained* on Bertram's goods. In addition, if, when Roger granted the land to Bertram, he had expressly reserved the right to forfeit the land in the event of the services not being performed, then if the services were not performed, Roger could *forfeit* the land.

There was another form of forfeiture. If any person was attainted (ie found guilty) of high treason, then the king had the right to seize and keep his lands. The king had this right of forfeiture regardless of whether the person held as a tenant-in-chief, or held of a mesne lord. This right arose from the royal prerogative, and was not properly an incident of tenure, but, like the incidents proper, it was a liability to which the tenant might be subject, and for convenience it is included in the list of incidents of tenure.

ESCHEAT

We have learned that Roger granted the manor of Dale to Andrew. But we have not considered for how long the manor was granted to Andrew. It was possible that Roger might grant the manor to Andrew for his (Andrew's) life time. In this case, when Andrew died the manor of Dale reverted to Roger. Roger could then retain it in his own hands, or grant it afresh to another tenant.

If Roger granted the land to Andrew for his (Andrew's) life, then on Andrew's death to whom should Roger grant the land? What better tenant could Roger find than Andrew's eldest son, Arnold? Arnold has grown up on the manor of Dale and knows the tenants. It would seem natural that Arnold should follow his father as lord of the manor. So Roger could grant the manor of Dale to Arnold, son of Andrew.

So natural did it seem that the eldest son should follow his father (or, if there was no son, that the nearest relative should succeed) that from early times we find grants being made in the form 'to Andrew, *and his heirs*'. In this case, when Andrew died, his son Arnold succeeded to the land. When Arnold died, his son succeeded; and so on, for ever, but the word 'heir' (whatever meaning may be attached to it in common parlance), did not mean only the eldest, or only, son; though if there was such a person, he was the heir. The word 'heir' meant the nearest blood relative ascertained according to certain rules. A person's heir was to be found not only among his issue (ie children, grandchildren, great grandchildren, etc) but also by looking to his collaterals (ie his brothers and sisters). A female could be heir only if no male blood relative of the same degree existed. A wife, not being a blood relative, was not her husband's heir;[5] for the same reason a relation-in-law was not an heir. During the Middle Ages intricate rules were devised for determining who was the heir of a dead person. If a tenant died without an heir the tenancy came to an end and the land *escheated* to the lord.

Whenever a tenancy came to an end, in fact, the land escheated to the lord. The two most common forms of escheat were:

(a) *propter defectum sanguinis* (on account of failure of blood). This was escheat on the death of a tenant without an heir, discussed above; and

(b) *propter delictum tenentis* (on account of the tenant's crime). This occurred if a tenant was convicted and sentenced to death ('attainted') for felony.

With the passage of time it came to be accepted that if no mesne lordship could be proved to which the land could escheat, the land was deemed to be held directly from the crown. It is for this reason that, except in relatively rare cases where a mesne lord can still prove his right of seignory, all land in England is today deemed to be held of the Crown.

It is convenient at this point to mention that in modern law there may be other instances of escheat. For example[6] (continuing the list above):

(c) if a person owes more money to his creditors than he can pay, he may be declared bankrupt. Whatever property[7] he has passes to an official called the trustee in bankruptcy, who distributes it (or if it is in a form other than money, sells it and distributes the proceeds) among the creditors. But the trustee in bankruptcy has the right to disclaim property if acceptance of the property will incur more financial liability than benefit. If the property is land, and if it is disclaimed by the trustee in bankruptcy, then the land escheats; today, as we have seen, normally to the Crown;

(d) if land is held by a corporation which is not incorporated under the Companies Act 1985[8] (eg a corporation established by a royal charter, such as the Hudson Bay Company) and the corporation is dissolved, any land which it held escheats to the Crown.[9]

---

5 Provision was made for a landholder's widow by her right, subject to certain conditions, to hold one-third of her husband's land for her life time. (The interest was not terminated by her remarriage. On her death the one-third passed to her husband's heir.) This was the right of dower. The allocation of the land was made by the landholder's heir. In the event of dispute, appeal lay to the sheriff. A widower was entitled, subject to certain conditions, to a life interest in the whole of his deceased wife's land. This was the right of curtesy. Rights of dower and curtesy were later much restricted. Their remaining vestiges were abolished in 1925.

6 For other instances in which land may escheat, see 9 *Halsbury's Laws* (4th edn) para 787.

7 Subject to limited exceptions; see Insolvency Act 1986, s 283.

8 Section 654.

9 *Re Wells* [1933] Ch 29.

Escheat, then, is the right of a superior lord to receive back the land on the termination of a tenancy.[10]

HOMAGE

When Andrew received the manor of Dale from Roger he became Roger's man, and made an oath of homage, by which a spiritual bond between lord and man was created.

FEALTY

A tenant also made an oath of fealty. By this he swore to carry out his obligations to his lord faithfully. By the oath of fealty a temporal link was created between lord and man.

RELIEF

Roger grants the manor of Dale to Andrew and his heirs. When Andrew dies his son, Arnold, succeeds him as Roger's tenant. If Arnold is of full age (at that time, 21) then Roger is entitled to a payment termed relief. The payment represents the price paid by Arnold for the right to succeed as tenant.

WARDSHIP

Relief was payable if Arnold, Andrew's heir, was of full age. If Arnold was an infant (ie under 21) Roger had the right to manage the land until Arnold was 21 and to take the proceeds until Arnold reached that age, subject to paying for Arnold's upbringing and education. This right was the incident of wardship.

MARRIAGE

If Andrew's heir, Arnold, was an infant at Andrew's death then Roger also had the right to select a wife for Arnold to marry. If Arnold refused to marry the woman Roger had chosen, then he had to pay Roger a fine. Thus the incident of marriage was of financial value to the lord.

Incidents relating to socage tenures

The incidents relating to the socage tenures (ie petty sergeanty and common socage) were suit of court, aids, forfeiture, escheat, fealty and relief; but not wardship, marriage and homage.

Incidents of villein tenure

These were as follows:

---

10   Ie, on the termination of a feudal tenure, not a lease. Leases are considered in Chapter 17.

1.   FEALTY

As in the case of the free tenures, by this oath a villein tenant undertook to perform his obligations to his lord faithfully.

2.   SUIT OF COURT

Wilfric, the villein tenant, as well as Alfrec, the free tenant, owes suit of court to Andrew, but the court which Alfrec attends, and the court which Wilfric attends, are not the same. The free tenants owe suit of court to the Court Baron of the manor. The villein tenants owe suit of court to the Court Customary of the manor.

3.   FORFEITURE

If a villein tenant failed to perform his services or committed certain other offences, then the lord was entitled by custom to forfeit the land.

4.   HERIOT

When a villein tenant died, the lord of the manor was entitled to take his best beast, or some other chattel.

5.   ESCHEAT

It became customary for the lord to permit the heir of a villein tenant to succeed to the land. If a villein tenant died without an heir the land escheated to the lord of the manor.

6.   RELIEF

When the heir of a villein tenant succeeded to the land, then (as in the case of land held by a free tenure) a payment termed a relief was payable to the lord.

7.   FINES

These were payable to the lord by a tenant who transferred the land he held to another.

8.   The lord of the manor might by custom have:

   (a) rights to mines and minerals beneath the land of the manor;
   (b) sporting rights, for example to hunt over the open fields;
   (c) the right to hold a market or fair in the manor.

9.   The villein tenant might be liable to contribute to the upkeep of dykes, ditches, sea walls, bridges and such like.

10. The lord might be liable for the upkeep, or to contribute to the upkeep, of dykes, ditches, sea walls, bridges and such like.

11. The tenant might by custom have:

   (a) rights to mines and minerals;
   (b) the right to pasture beasts on the waste land of the manor.

Manorial incidents of common socage

The incidents listed under 8, 9, 10 and 11 above might by custom relate also to the tenure of common socage. Thus Alfrec, who held land in the open fields by the free tenure of common socage, might, like Wilfric the villein tenant, have the right to keep pigs in the wood. Alfrec as well as Wilfric might be obliged to contribute to the upkeep of the bridge over the stream.

THE LATER HISTORY OF TENURES

Later history of villein tenure

Originally a villein tenant had no legal right to his land, and he had no access to the royal courts. He held his land at the will of his lord. If ousted by his lord, he had no redress.

The legal position of the villein tenant later improved. Even in early times, what mattered to the villein tenant was what happened in practice rather than what may have been the legal theory. And in practice what mattered was the custom of the manor. If it was the custom of the manor that, on Wilfric's death, his son and heir Wilfrid should succeed to his father's holding, and that Wilfrid should pay a relief on half a groat, then whatever the legal rights of the lord of the manor might be, he would be flying in the face of the custom of the manor if he refused to permit Wilfrid to succeed to the land, or demanded a higher sum by way of relief. As the strength of the custom of the manor became more deeply entrenched it came to be accepted that a villein tenant held his land 'at the will of the lord and according to the custom of the manor'.

By the end of the fifteenth century the position of the villein tenant had improved further. The royal courts[11] had by then become willing to assist a villein tenant who had been ousted from his land by his lord otherwise than in accordance with the custom of the manor (for example, otherwise than for failing to perform the services he owed). Thus the custom of the manor became accepted by the common law as being legally binding on lord and tenant.

With the improved position of the villein came a change in the name by which the tenure was known. The new name derived from the method by which it was customary for a villein tenant to transfer his land to another. If Robert, a villein tenant, wished to transfer his land to Edward, then the first step was for Robert to surrender his land to his lord in the manorial court, at the same time nominating Edward as the intended transferee. In early times the lord could decide whether to permit Robert to surrender his holding, and whether to accept Edward as the new tenant. Later he became bound by the custom of the manor both to accept Robert's surrender and to accept whoever Robert nominated as the new tenant. The lord then admitted Edward as the

---

11   At first Chancellor's court (see Chapter 5) and later the courts of common law. See C.M. Gray *Copyhold, Equity and the Common Law* (1963).

new tenant. This method of transfer is termed 'surrender and admittance'. The transaction was recorded on the court roll, and the new tenant was given a copy of the relevant entry as proof of his title. The new tenant came to be regarded as holding 'by custom of the manor and by copy of court roll', and for this reason the tenure came to be called 'copyhold'.

Reduction in the number of tenures, and in the number of incidents of tenure

In the twelfth century there were at least six forms of tenure, and at least 16 types of incident. Today there is only one form of tenure, common socage, and the incidents of tenure have virtually ceased to exist.

The number of tenures was reduced in two stages:

A. In 1660, by the Tenures Abolition Act, which abolished grand and petty sergeanty and knight service.
B. At the end of 1925, by the Law of Property Act 1922,[12] which abolished copyhold tenure; and by the Administration of Estates Act 1925[13] which abolished frankalmoign.

Grand and petty sergeanty and knight service had greatly altered by the time of their final abolition and frankalmoign ceased to be living tenure many centuries before 1925. But copyhold continued to be living tenure right up until the end of 1925.

We have seen that the only tenure to exist is common socage. Any incidents which exist today thus relate to this tenure. The incidents which relate to this tenure today fall, in the main, into two categories:

(1) incidents of a tenure which has been abolished, the incidents being expressly preserved by the Act which abolished the tenure itself. The following incidents fall into this category:
 (a) the honorary services of grand sergeanty. These were preserved by the Act of 1660 which abolished the tenure of grand sergeanty. These are of no more than historical interest;
 (b) certain of the incidents of copyhold. When copyhold was abolished at the end of 1925 (by the Law of Property Act 1922), the incidents of copyhold tenure which still survived at that time were divided into three classes:
  (i) Those in the first class were abolished from 1 January 1926. This class included: fealty, suit of court and escheat for want of heirs.
  (ii) Those in the second class were abolished at the end of 1925, but the lord of the manor was given the right to compensation from the tenant for their loss. The date for claiming compensation has long since passed. The incidents in this class included: relief, forfeiture to the lord, heriots, quit rents, rights of the lord to timber.

12   Section 128 and Sch 12, para 1.
13   Sch 2, Pt 1.

(iii) Those in the third class were preserved and continue indefinitely unless abolished by agreement between the lord of the manor and the tenant (or by statute).[14] The incidents in this class include:

(a) any rights of the lord or tenant to mines and minerals;

(b) any rights of the lord in respect of fairs, markets and sporting;

(c) any tenants' rights of common (eg to pasture beasts on the waste land of the manor). These rights are now regulated by the Commons Registration Act 1965;

(d) any liability of the lord or tenant for the upkeep of dykes, ditches, sea walls, bridges and the like.

(2) Those which had always related to common socage, and which have not been abolished by any Act. There are six incidents in this class:

(a) Fealty.

(b) Suit to court.

(c) Forfeiture to the lord.

(d) Relief.

These incidents still technically exist but are of no practical importance and are now no more than curiosities.

(e) Escheat other than escheat *propter delictum tenantis* (which was abolished by the Forfeiture Act 1870) and escheat *propter defectum sanguinis* (which was abolished by the Administration of Estates Act 1925). If a tenancy comes to an end for any other reason, for example for either of the two reasons cited on p 14 then the land still escheats. As we have seen, escheat today will almost invariably be to the Crown.

(f) In 1922 some land held by common socage still had annexed to it certain rights and liabilities of a manorial origin.[15] These were treated by the Law of Property Act 1922 in the same way as the corresponding incidents of copyhold tenure and were placed in the same three categories set out above. The incidents of manorial origin relating to common socage fell, in the main, into the third category and are therefore preserved permanently unless extinguished by agreement between the lord of the manor and the tenant.

Let us illustrate the incidents[16] of common socage which can exist today by three examples.

---

14 Eg Coal Industry Act 1975, s 3.
15 See p 17.
16 In addition to the incidents of tenure which may still exist, in rare cases it is still possible that tenure may be evidenced by an obligation to render a service (eg a payment of money) to a superior lord. For example, in Blaxhall in Suffolk those who hold certain allotments, known as 'Common yards' (which, it seems, were taken out of the common land of the manor and granted to villagers under the Allotments Act of 1832) are obliged to pay a yearly rent of 6d to the lord of the manor. Whether the land had been held by the allotment holders before 1926 as copyholders or as socage tenants, their relationship with the lord of the manor would continue after 1925 to be that of lord and tenant under the old framework of tenures. (I am obliged to the Clerk of the Blaxhall Parish Council for confirming that (in 1975) these rents continued to be paid.)

1. Mr Smith holds Bluebell Cottage. In theory his land is still subject to the incidents of fealty, suit of court, forfeiture and relief. Of more importance is the fact that if Mr Smith becomes bankrupt and for some reason the trustee in bankruptcy disclaims the land, then the land escheats to Mr Smith's superior feudal lord – today the Crown, because no mesne lordship can in his case be proved to exist.[17]

2. Simon Galton holds Quebec Farm. It is an incident of his tenure that he has a right of common to pasture 60 sheep on the hills above Dale.

3. Marcus Holly holds Copyhold Farm. As in the case of the many farms bearing this name, the land was originally held by copyhold tenure. As an incident of the common socage tenure by which the land is now held, Marcus Holly, as the holder of the land, is under an obligation to contribute a certain proportion of the cost of maintaining a drain adjoining his land.

CONCLUSION

The main threads which can be traced in the history of tenures are as follows:

1. There was a gradual commutation of services rendered into money payments.
2. With the decline in the value of money, these money payments ceased to be worth collecting.
3. Where there were other incidents valuable to the lord (eg marriage and wardship in the case of the free tenures and various incidents of a manorial character in the case of copyhold tenure) the fact of tenure continued to be of importance.
4. The number of types of tenure was reduced. By the beginning of the twentieth century only common socage and copyhold survived as living tenures. Since the end of 1925 the only form of tenure has been common socage.
5. Tenure continues as a legal fact today. The reason for its continued existence has been, as this chapter has shown, that 'Our law has preferred to suppress one by one the practical consequences of tenure rather than to strike at the root of the theory of tenure itself'.[18] Thus all land (except that occupied by the Crown) is in law still held from the Crown,[19] either directly or (most commonly) through mesne lords, whose identity has in the great majority of cases long ceased to be known.

Commonhold

In 1996 the government proposed a bill, the Commonhold Bill, that would have introduced a new form of land holding. In the event, the Bill was not

---

17   See *Re Lowe's Will Trusts* [1973] 2 All ER 1136, [1973] 1 WLR 882.
18   Megarry and Wade, p 37.
19   *A-G of Ontario v Mercer* (1883) 8 App Cas 767 at 772.

proceeded with. If a bill along the lines proposed does pass into law, it may happen that land affected comes to be referred to as being held by 'commonhold tenure'. Whatever the nature of commonhold, as proposed, may be (the matter is treated in a later chapter[20]), it is not a tenure in the sense that that word is properly used in property law and as described in this chapter.

20   See Chapter 22.

CHAPTER 3

Estates

THE MEANING OF AN 'ESTATE' IN LAND

Suppose that Roger (R), who holds the seignory of the manor of Dale,[1] is asked 'For how long did you grant the manor to Andrew (A)?' R might reply, 'I have granted the manor to A for his life' or, 'I have granted the manor to A and his heirs.' In either case R's answer would indicate the duration, or at any rate the maximum possible duration, of the time before which the tenancy would come to an end. (In the case of a grant 'to A and his heirs' the tenancy could last for ever.)

The duration of a tenancy of land (ie the maximum time before which the tenancy must come to an end) is termed the *estate* for which the tenant holds the land. Thus, instead of being asked 'For how long did you grant the land to A?' R could have been asked 'For what estate did you grant the land to A?'

Thus the answer to the question:

'In return for what services (or on what conditions) is land held?' tells us the tenure by which the tenant holds the land.

The answer to the question:

'For how long is the land held?' tells us the estate for which the tenant holds the land.

Just as there have been various forms of tenure, so also are there various forms of estate. These vary according to the various durations for which land can be granted.

We have met two forms of estate. We saw[1] that R might have granted Dale to A 'for life'. In this case A would hold a *life estate* in the land. We saw, too, that R might have granted Dale to A 'and his heirs'. In this case A would have held what is now termed a *fee simple* estate. There are only two other forms of estate that have existed; the *fee tail* and the *term of years*. These will be discussed later.

To recapitulate, A did not own the manor of Dale, but held it of his lord R. To ascertain the nature and extent of A's interest in the land we need to know the tenure by which he held the land, and the estate for which he held the land.

Thus:

X might have held Blackacre by the tenure of knight service for a life estate; Y might have held Greenacre by the tenure of common socage for a fee simple estate (or, as we say, for an estate in fee simple);

Z might have held Redacre by the tenure of grand sergeanty for an estate in fee simple; and so on.

1 See Chapter 2.

Villein tenants did not, in law, hold any estate in their land. Nevertheless, by the custom of their manor, villein tenants often came to hold the equivalent of an estate in their land. Thus Wilfric might hold (for purposes of succession on death) the equivalent of a fee simple estate; and, in this case, the land would descend to his heir. Later, with the development of copyhold, the common law came to recognise the legal existence of estates in land held by copyhold tenure.

We shall now examine in outline the nature of each of the four types of estate. There is a chart showing the forms of estate on page 47.

The fee simple estate

THE NATURE OF A FEE SIMPLE ESTATE

The word *fee* indicates that land held for this estate is capable of being inherited. We have seen that this is so. We have seen that when land was granted to A and his heirs, then on A's death the land was inherited by his heir. Having said this, three qualifications must be made:

1. In early times it became possible for the holder of a fee simple estate in land to transfer the land to someone else (eg by gift or by sale) during his lifetime. If A, the holder of a fee simple estate, transferred the fee simple to B during his (A's) lifetime, then on A's death the land could not pass to A's heir: it had already passed to B. (It would then be B who held the fee simple in the land. If B did not transfer the land to someone else, then on his death the land passed to *his* heir.)
2. From about the fifteenth century it became possible for the holder of a fee simple estate in land to leave his interest in land in his will to a stranger, ie to someone other than his heir. How it became possible for a person to leave land by will (to *devise* land), we shall see later.

    If A did devise the land to someone other than his heir, then his heir was thereby excluded from inheriting the land. So the land only passed to A's heir provided that A had either made no will (provided that he had died *intestate*) or that he made a will but had omitted to devise the land in the will (ie that he had died intestate in respect of the land).

    So the position we have reached is this: on the death intestate of the holder of a fee simple estate (who had not transferred the land to another during his life time) the land passed to his heir.
3. We have seen a person's heir could be found amongst his issue (his children, grandchildren, etc) and if he had no issue, amongst his collaterals (ie his brothers and sisters), the male taking before the female. These were the principles developed in early law. The position was changed by the Inheritance Act 1833[2] which enacted that a person's heir is to include,

---

2   Section 6.

after his issue, his ancestors; ie his father, grandfather, mother, grandmother, etc. The male in this case too takes before the female (eg a grandfather takes before a mother). If there are no issue or ancestors the heir is to be sought among collaterals.

Important changes were made by the Administration of Estates Act 1925.

The first change is the provision that after 1925 if a person dies intestate his land is to pass not to his heir but (together with all his other property) to persons determined according to rules laid down in the Act.[3] The first persons to benefit under these rules are the deceased's spouse and children. If the deceased left no spouse or children, the parents are entitled; if there are no parents, any brothers and sisters take, followed by other relatives in a list which ends with half uncles and aunts. The persons entitled under the Act are sometimes colloquially termed the 'next of kin',[4] and we shall use this term. (It should be noted that it is *not* correct to say that if today a person dies intestate his property passes to his 'heir'.)

The second change is the provision[5] that after 1925, if an intestate is not survived by relatives listed in the Act, the land is to pass to the Crown as 'bona vacantia' (goods having no owner). (This seldom makes any difference in practice because, as we have seen, by the twentieth century, when land escheated on the extinction of a tenancy, it usually escheated directly to the Crown.)

The word 'simple' in 'fee simple' indicates that the fee is an ordinary fee, as opposed to a special form of fee, the fee tail. (This is considered later.)

In practice, to hold a fee simple estate for the tenure of common socage (the only tenure that now exists) is today virtually equivalent to being the owner of the land. If A 'owns' Bluebell Cottage then in law he holds the land by the tenure of common socage for an estate in fee simple.

The transfer of land held in fee simple inter vivos

Let us suppose that A has granted Blackacre to B to hold by the tenure of common socage for an estate in fee simple. B wishes to see (or give) the land to C. Before 1290 he could do this in one of two ways.

1.   SUBINFEUDATION

As we saw in the last chapter, B could[6] grant the land to C to hold of him as his tenant. In this case B *sub-infeuds* the land to C and thus a new link in the feudal chain is formed.

---

3   AEA 1925, ss 45, 46, amended by the Intestates' Estates Act 1952.
4   Strictly 'next of kin' are those persons who were entitled to an intestate's personalty before 1926, as determined by the Statutes of Distribution 1670 and 1685. Next of kin under those Acts included provision for the spouse.
5   AEA 1925, s 46(1)(vi).
6   Provided that subinfeudation was not prohibited in the grant of the land to B. Bracton ff 45b-46b.

2. SUBSTITUTION

The other method by which B might transfer land to C was by the method termed *substitution*. In this case when B granted the land to C, C held the land as tenant, not of B, but of B's lord, A.

Thus C replaced B as A's tenant. C stepped into B's shoes. What had been B's obligations to A were assumed by C. C took over B's place in the feudal structure and B dropped out of the picture.[7]

B might have sold the land to C for £40. (In addition to paying B the £40, C would have to render the services of the tenure to A. Thus, if he held by common socage he might have to pay A a quit rent of £1 pa.) Alternatively, B might have granted the land to C, not in return for a lump sum of £40, but in return for C agreeing to paying him, B, an annual rent of £1.

A rent payable by a tenant to his lord is termed a rent '*service*'. Thus the quit rent payable to A under C's socage tenure is a rent service. A rent *charge* (by convention spelt as one word, rentcharge), is a rent payable otherwise than by a tenant to his lord. As we have seen, in the case of the annual payment by C to B, B is not C's lord (A is); thus the payment which C makes to B is a rentcharge. The two forms of rent which C has to pay may be illustrated thus,

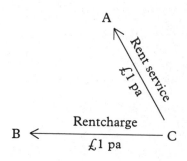

One reason why it is necessary to distinguish between a rent service and a rentcharge is that the remedies available to A if C fails to pay the rent service were different from the remedies available to B if C failed to pay the rentcharge.

Before the grant to C, B held the fee simple, so the grant by A to B must have been to B and his heirs. This being so, how could B cut off his heir, D, from succeeding to the land? Before about 1200 it seems that he was not, in fact, able to do so. If B granted the land to C, C held it only until B's death, then D succeeded. (Only if B obtained D's consent to the transfer was C's interest not cut short by B's death.)

---

7   Bracton, writing prior to 1257, opposed such form of transfer unless the lord consented, or unless the original grant had been to B 'and his assigns'. Bracton, ff 13, 17b, 30. But as the importance attached to the idea of homage declined, and the relationship of lord and tenant came to be of a less personal nature, tenants began to transfer their land without the permission of their lord. The statute Quia Emptores, 1290, authorised transfer by a tenant 'at his own pleasure', ie without his lord's consent.

What interest did C take on the grant to him by B? By 1306 it had become accepted that C would take the full fee simple.[8] Thus on C's death it would pass to *his* heir, and, furthermore, if during his lifetime, C transferred the land to E then E would take the full fee simple, and on E's death, it would pass to his heir, and so on.

THE STATUTE QUIA EMPTORES 1290

Suppose that A granted land to B in fee simple to hold of him by the tenure of knight service. If B died leaving an infant son, A would enjoy the benefit of the incidents of marriage and wardship, the latter giving him the right to the proceeds of the land until B's heir attained 21. If, before he died, B had subinfeuded the land to C, then on B's death A would benefit from the incident of marriage (with regard to B's heirs), but he would derive no advantage from the incident of wardship, since the land was in the hands of C. The process of subinfeudation in this way caused loss to superior lords, including, of course, the supreme feudal lord, the king. In 1290 it was therefore enacted by the Statute Quia Emptores that henceforth, when the holder of a fee simple transferred his land to another in fee simple, it should be by way of substitution, and not by way of subinfeudation. Thus the process of subinfeudation, which had formed one of the principal characteristics of the structure of land holding since the Conquest, was cut short. After the Statute, if B granted Blackacre to C in fee simple, C could not hold the land as tenant of B, he held it as tenant of B's lord, A. The Statute provided that C should hold the land from A for the same service as that for which it had been held by B.

The statute did not prevent the king from granting land to tenants to hold of him as lord. Indeed, the king could not transfer land by means of substitution, as there was no lord above the king.

Before the Statute, if B granted Blackacre to C in fee simple, and in return C was obliged to pay B £1 a year, then, as we have seen, if the transfer had been by way of subinfeudation, the rent was a feudal rent service; if it was by way of substitution, it was a rentcharge. If B granted the fee simple in Blackacre to C *after* the passing of the Statute, and C was obliged to pay B £1 a year, this rent was necessarily a rentcharge. It could no longer be a rent service.

The transfer of land held in fee simple by will

Originally, at common law, land could not be devised. On the death of a fee simple tenant the land devolved on his heir. If he purported to leave it to someone else in his will the disposition had no effect. There are four stages in the story of how it became possible for land to be devised:

1. By the fourteenth century it had become possible for land to be devised by means of a device known as a '*use*' (later to be called a 'trust'). We shall

---

8   Holdsworth, iii, p 106.

consider later the nature of the 'use' (or 'trust') and how land could be devised by means of it.

2. In 1535 the Statute of Uses abolished, or at any rate partially abolished, trusts. People thought that it was no longer possible for them to devise land. There was an outcry. As a result:

3. In 1540 the Statute of Wills enacted that it should be permissible for a person to devise up to two-thirds of land which he held by the tenure of knight service, and all land which he held by a socage tenure.

4. In 1660 the Tenures Abolition Act converted all land held by knight service into land held by common socage. The effect was thus to make all land freely devisable.

Meaning of 'alienation' and 'to alienate'

To alienate property means, broadly, to transfer it to someone else. In the case of property which is capable of being inherited, for example, a fee simple estate in land, to alienate the interest carries the further meaning of diverting the property from the course of devolution (ie the path it would normally follow) if it had not been alienated.

Thus if, before 1926, B held the fee simple in Blackacre, on his death intestate the land devolved on his heir. If, in his will, he left the land to someone else, he alienated the land: he alienated the property by will. Similarly, after 1925, if B leaves the land to someone other than his next of kin, he has alienated the property by will.

Further, if, during his lifetime, B sells the land or gives it away, thus diverting the property – before 1926 from his heir, or after 1925 from his next of kin – he has alienated the property inter vivos.

The life estate

THE NATURE OF THE LIFE ESTATE

B, who holds Blackacre in fee simple grants the lands to C for his (C's) lifetime: he grants the land 'to C for life'. C then holds a life estate in the land. C becomes a 'tenant for life'. When C dies his interest comes to an end, and the land reverts to B. Since C's interest ends on his death, he cannot devise his interest to anyone; nor, if he dies intestate, is there anything to be inherited – before 1926 by his heir, after 1925 by his next of kin. The estate is therefore not one which is capable of being inherited: it is not an estate '*in fee*'.

We have said that B granted the land to C for life. Do we mean that B granted the land to C to hold as B's tenant? Or do we mean that B granted the land to C to hold as tenant of B's lord, A? Ie, is the grant by way of subinfeudation or by substitution?

Is the position this?   or this?

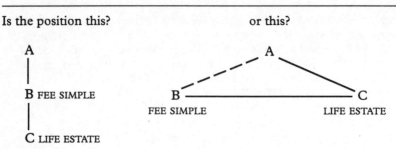

A

B FEE SIMPLE

C LIFE ESTATE

A

B ———————————— C
FEE SIMPLE   LIFE ESTATE

The answer is that either was possible, and this remained true even after 1290. The Statute Quia Emptores referred only to subinfeudation by way of grants in fee. The Statute did not prohibit subinfeudations by way of grants of a life interest. So, even after 1290, B could have granted the land to C for life, to hold him, B, as his feudal tenant. Whether or not this was the case depended on the circumstances of the grant.

With the decline in the importance of tenure it became rare for a life tenant to hold the land as feudal tenant of the grantor. Thus when B, the holder of a fee simple in Blackacre in the fifteenth century, granted land to C for life, C generally held the land as tenant of A.

There is one case, however, when a person who has been granted a life estate cannot hold other than as the feudal tenant of the grantor. This occurs when the grantor is the king. Thus if the king grants Blackacre to B for life, B holds the land as feudal tenant of the Crown.

Nevertheless, when speaking of estates we can from now on, for most purposes, forget about tenure, and about a tenant's feudal lord. Tenure remained the framework within which estates operated, but it is a framework which had an increasingly shadowy existence.

So when B, the holder of the fee simple in Blackacre, grants the land to C for life, the pattern that concerns us is merely this:

B   C
Fee Simple ————————→ For life

Alienation of the life estate

If B grants Blackacre to C for life, can C alienate Blackacre inter vivos? The answer is that C can transfer his interest in the land, say to D, but since C cannot transfer to D more than he, C, himself has, D's interest in the land will only last as long as C's interest in the land would have done if it had not been transferred to D. So, when C dies, D's interest comes to an end, and the right to possession of the land reverts to B.

The life estate *pur autre vie*

What estate did D hold? His interest lasts only for as long as C's life. So D holds a life estate – but the life is that of C, not of himself. So D holds a life estate for the life of another (C). D holds what is termed a life estate *pur autre vie* (for the life of another).[9]

WASTE

Types of waste

Suppose that A grants Dale Manor, a house and its surrounding estate, to B in fee simple. B,

(a) allows the house to fall into disrepair;
(b) fells a plantation of fir trees and sells the timber;
(c) opens a quarry, and extracts all the reserves of sand and gravel;
(d) strips the lead from the roof; and
(e) chops down a row of ornamental poplars lining the drive.

Assuming that B has obtained planning permission for (c) and that no restrictions[10] affect (b), (d) and (e), no objection can be raised in law to what has occurred, but if A had granted the land to B for life and thereafter to C, C would have cause to feel aggrieved. For example, by felling all the timber B would have obtained all the benefit and C would be left with tree stumps; and by extracting all the sand, C would be left with no more than a hole in the ground. It is the function of the doctrine of waste to provide a degree of protection for the interests of C in a situation such as have been described.

Acts or omissions that result in a change in the land are in law termed *waste*. Thus all the matters set out above are examples of waste. Waste falls under one of four headings.

1.   PERMISSIVE WASTE

This consists of allowing land (including the buildings on it) to deteriorate for want of attention (eg allowing the house to fall into disrepair[11]). Other examples of permissive waste include failure to repair sea walls,[12] or to clean out a moat so as to prevent foundations becoming rotten.[13] B, the tenant for life, is not liable for permissive waste (which might therefore perhaps be better termed 'permitted' waste).

---

9   If a person on whose lifetime continuation of a life estate *pur autre vie* depends (C) 'remains beyond the seas, or elswhere absent themselves in this realm, by the space of seven years together, and no sufficient and evident proof be given that he is alive, he is to be accounted as naturally dead.' Cestui que Vie Act 1666. See *Chard v Chard (otherwise Northcott)* [1956] P 259 at 267.
10   Eg designation of the house as a 'listed building'; existence of a Tree Preservation Order. See Chapter 4.
11   *Powys v Blagrave* (1854) De GM & G 448.
12   *Griffith's Case* (1564) Moore KB 69.
13   *Sticklehorne v Hatchman* (1585) Owen 43.

2.   VOLUNTARY WASTE

This consists of acts which alter land to its detriment (eg felling the fir trees[14]), but which fall short of mere wanton destruction. To open a mine or quarry on the land is an act of voluntary waste.[15] B is liable for voluntary waste.

3.   EQUITABLE WASTE

This consists of acts of wanton destruction (eg stripping lead off the roof[16] and chopping down the trees planted for ornament[17] along the drive). Pulling down a house[18] and felling trees planted to provide shelter[19] are the other examples of acts of equitable waste. B is liable for equitable waste.

4.   AMELIORATING WASTE

We have said that waste consists of any act or omission which results in a change in the land. If B makes an improvement to the land, for example if he repairs old stone buildings and converts them into houses,[20] he alters the nature of the land and thus commits an act of waste. Alterations to land which improve the value of land are termed ameliorating waste. It might seem unlikely that C would wish to raise any objection to B improving the value of the land, but it could happen that C objected to a particular change proposed by B, eg converting a farm into a market garden[1] (notwithstanding that the change would increase the value of the land) and would therefore wish to restrain B from making the alteration.

B is not liable for ameliorating waste in that, since the value of the land will have increased, no damages are recoverable.[2] Further, if C seeks an injunction to restrain B from making the change, then unless the change will affect the whole nature of the land (perhaps, for example, building a holiday camp on a wild stretch of coast) the courts will be unlikely to grant the remedy sought.

Remedies

If B commits an act of waste (and here we are speaking of forms of waste other than ameliorating waste), C can bring an action for damages against him. If B derives a profit from the act (eg selling the lead he has stripped from the roof) C can claim the profit. Further, C can seek an injunction requiring B to desist from committing waste already begun; or to refrain from committing waste not yet begun.

14   *Honywood v Honywood* (1874) LR 18 Eq 306.
15   *Campbell v Wardlaw* (1883) 8 App Cas 641.
16   *Vane v Lord Barnard* (1716) 2 Vern 738; (M & B).
17   *Marker v Marker* (1851) 9 Hare 1.
18   *Williams v Day* (1680) 2 Cas in Ch 32.
19   *Weld-Blundell v Wolseley* [1903] 2 Ch 664; *Turner v Wright* (1860) 2 De GF & J 234; (M & B).
20   *Doherty v Allman* (1878) 3 App Cas 709; (M & B).
 1   *Meux v Cobley* [1892] 2 Ch 253.
 2   *Jones v Chappell* (1875) LR 20 Eq 539 at 541.

Liability

We have said that B is not liable for ameliorating or permissive waste, and that he is liable for voluntary and equitable waste. This is what the common law presumes A's intention to have been, and in the absence of any indication to the contrary, this is the liability which will be imposed on B. But A can impose whatever liability he wishes on B. Thus he can, if he so wishes, provide that B is not to be liable for equitable waste, or for voluntary waste, or for both forms of waste. Or A can, if he wishes, provide that B is to be liable for permissive waste.[3] Such a provision places a burden on B, but he is not obliged to accept the gift. He can, if he wishes, disclaim the gift (in which case C will become entitled to the land).

It is rare for a grant to make a tenant for life not liable for equitable waste, but it is not uncommon for a grant to make him not liable for voluntary waste. (If a tenant for life is made not liable for 'waste', without specifying for what kind of waste he is not to be liable, then he is deemed to be not liable for voluntary waste, but liable for equitable waste.[4])

These are the basic principles. Special rules, however, apply in the case of trees, and minerals, eg the sand and gravel from the quarry.

Trees

In law, trees are of two kinds: timber and non-timber trees. Timber trees are oak, ash and elm, which are at least 20 years old, together with any other trees by which the custom of the locality rank as timber, eg birch is timber in Yorkshire, beech is timber in Buckinghamshire. All other trees are non-timber trees.

A tenant for life who is made not liable for waste (ie voluntary waste) can fell any trees, whether timber or non-timber, and keep all the proceeds for himself, provided that he does not commit equitable waste, eg cutting down trees planted for ornament or shelter. (If he is made not liable for equitable as well as voluntary waste he can cut down even trees planted for ornament or shelter.)

A tenant for life who is liable for voluntary waste (as he is unless the grant expressly makes him not liable) can fell the following trees:

1. Trees which are not, and cannot, irrespective of their age, become timber trees[5] (eg willows or larches), other than fruit trees in an orchard or garden.[6]
2. Young trees which, when mature, will become timber trees, but which need to be cut for the purpose of thinning, in order to allow the proper development of others.[7]

---

3   *Woodhouse v Walker* (1880) 5 QBD 404; (M & B). Leaving agricultural land uncultivated is not permissive waste: *Hutton v Warren* (1836) 1 M & W 466 at 472. So B is not liable if he does this even if he is made liable for permissive waste. (He will only be liable if he is specifically made liable for this failure.)
4   LPA 1925, s 135.
5   *Re Harker's Will Trusts* [1938] Ch 323, [1938] 1 All ER 145.
6   Co Litt 53a.
7   *Bagot v Bagot* (1863) 32 Beav 509 at 518. As to the distribution of proceeds of sale, see *Earl Cowley v Wellesley* (1866) LR 1 Eq 656.

3. Timber trees which are part of a timber estate (an estate cultivated for the produce of saleable timber, where the timber is cut periodically in accordance with a regular cycle of afforestation[8]) and which it would be normal forestry practice to fell. Such trees are regarded as forming part of the income from the land. On the sale of the trees B is entitled to the net income, after providing for the replanting and other expenses incurred in the proper course of management of the estate.[9]

4. Any trees which are required for 'estovers', ie for certain customary purposes such as repairing a house or burning as fuel in the house ('house-bote'), or repairing fences ('hay-bote') or repairing agricultural implements ('plough-bote').[10]

5. Dead trees.

Minerals

To open a new mine (or quarry) is an act of voluntary waste.[11] To work one which is already open at the commencement of the life interest is not any form of waste.[12] Thus a tenant for life who, by the grant, has been made not liable for waste is subject to no restrictions with regard to the extraction of minerals. He can work an existing mine or open a new one. A tenant for life who is liable for waste can work a mine which had been opened before his life interest began, but he cannot open a new one. (The Settled Land Act 1925 introduces modifications.[14])

'Impeachable'

In the context of waste the word '*impeachable*' is sometimes used in place of 'liable'; eg as in the statement 'A tenant for life is impeachable for voluntary waste unless the settlement makes him unimpeachable'.

ESTATES IN POSSESSION, IN REMAINDER AND IN REVERSION

B holds Blackacre in fee simple. B therefore has the right to possession of the land. B grants Blackacre to C for life. C thus has a life estate in the land. This now gives C the right, during his lifetime, to possession of the land. When C dies his interest in the land comes to an end and the right to possession of the land reverts, ie goes back, to B.

---

8   *Honywood v Honywood* (1874) LR 18 Eq 306.
9   *Re Trevor-Bayte's Settlement, Bull v Trevor-Bayte* [1912] 2 Ch 339.
10 Co Litt 41b, 53b.
11 *Campbell v Wardlaw* (1883) 8 App Cas 641.
12 *Dashwood v Magniac* [1891] 3 Ch 306 at 360; (M & B).
13 Section 66.
14 See Chapter 7.

It will be noted that when B, the holder of the fee simple, granted the land to C for life, he did not thereby deprive himself of the fee simple. He deprived himself, it is true, of the right to possession of the land during C's lifetime, but he still held the fee simple, even though he did not have the right to possession of the land until C had died and the right to possession reverted to him. This is expressed by saying that while C is alive B holds the fee simple *in reversion*. Before he granted the life estate to C, we say that B held the fee simple *in possession*. Then, as we have just seen, during C's lifetime B holds the fee simple in reversion. On C's death, B's fee simple becomes, once again, a fee simple in possession.

What is the position if B dies before C does? Who does the land go to when C dies? The answer is that it reverts to the holder of the fee simple, but B, who was the holder of the fee simple, is dead; so who does the land go to? The answer lies in the nature of a fee simple. What happens to the fee simple on B's death depends on whether or not he made a will. If B made a will the land reverts to whoever B devised the land to in his will; if he died intestate, then before 1926 it passed to his heir, and if there was no heir it escheated. After 1925, it passes to his next of kin; if there is no next of kin, it passes (by statute) to the Crown as *bona vacantia*. So there is always someone for the land to revert to on C's death.

Now let us suppose that B wishes the land to go to C for his life, and on C's death, for the land to go to C's brother, D, for his life. In this case, C has a life estate in the land, and so too has D. But D does not acquire the right to possession of the land until C's death. In this case we say that D has a life interest *in remainder*. B's grant takes the form,

'to C for life, with remainder to D for life'.

D is termed a *remainderman*.

Since C has the immediate right to possession of the land, we say that C has a life interest in possession. When C dies and D becomes entitled to the land, D's life interest ceases to be a life interest in remainder and becomes a life interest in possession (or, as we say, the life interest 'falls into' possession). While C and D are alive B's fee simple is in reversion. When D dies, B's fee simple ceases to be in reversion and falls into possession. There can be any number of successive life interests, strung together like beads on a piece of string.

Now suppose that B grants Blackacre,

'to C for life, with remainder to D in fee simple'.

Here C has a life interest in possession. D has, this time, a fee simple in remainder. Once B has granted away the fee simple to D, he has parted with the fee simple completely. He has, as we say, parted with the 'entire estate', meaning his entire interest in the land. So when D dies the land will not revert to B. Thus, having granted Blackacre to C for life with remainder to D in fee simple, B has no interest in the land whatsoever.

What is the position if Blackacre is granted (as before),

'to C for life with remainder to D in fee simple',

and D dies *before* C, so that when C dies, D is no longer alive for the fee simple to fall into possession in his hands? The answer lies in the fact that from the moment of B's grant D's fee simple in remainder is his property. So, as it is his property, he can leave it in his will to whoever he chooses. And if he dies intestate the land passes (after 1925) to his next of kin.

There is another consequence of the fact that D's fee simple in remainder is his property. Since it is his property he can sell it (or give it away) during his lifetime. This is so notwithstanding that the fee simple is still in remainder. A purchaser might, for example, want Blackacre so much that he was prepared to wait until C died. Another reason is that a purchaser might make some money out of the deal. For example, suppose that Blackacre is worth £40,000, that C is 97 (and ill), and that D needs money. E may approach D and say 'I will buy your fee simple in remainder for £37,000', D agrees. D gets the money he needs. E is happy since C dies six months later and he makes a substantial profit (£3,000 less the interest which the £37,000 would have earned if he had left it invested for six months between the sale and C's death). Of course E takes a risk. C may recover and live to 103; and E would have been better off by leaving his money invested, but E employs a good actuary who has the chances and the figures carefully calculated.

From this can be seen that, from the moment of B's grant, D's fee simple in remainder is just as much an item of his property as his watch. The remainder (as we call it for short) is his property now, notwithstanding that he does not have the right to possession of the land until some time in the future (ie when C dies). The remainder thus constitutes a present right to the future enjoyment of property.

We know that if B grants Blackacre,

'to C for life with remainder to D in fee simple',

there can be no reversion to B, since he has parted with the entire fee simple estate. For the same reason, there can be no grant of a remainder after the grant of a fee simple. For example, in the case of a grant in the form,

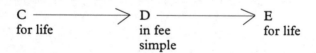

the gift to E (whether for life or for any other interest) has no effect. Having given the fee simple (in remainder) to D, B has parted with the entire estate. E gets nothing. There can therefore be neither a remainder nor a reversion after the grant of a fee simple.

The fee tail estate

The year is 1280. B, eldest son of A, is about to be married. A wishes to give Blackacre Castle to his son, as his son's new home. A holds Blackacre Castle in fee simple. The land has been in his family since the time of the Conqueror. 'I shall go to live on my manor at Greenacre,' A thinks, 'and B will have Blackacre. When he dies, Blackacre will pass to his eldest son; and when that son dies it will pass to his eldest son, and so on. The family name will be linked with Blackacre for ever.' A thought then strikes him 'But what if B sells Blackacre? What if B becomes burdened by debt and has to sell the land? Or if he decides to live in Ireland and doesn't want to retain Blackacre? Blackacre won't pass to future generations of our family then. If I grant Blackacre to B and his heirs, this sounds satisfactory, but I know that, as holder of the estate that this grant will give him, he can part with the land as soon as he chooses. What I want is a form of grant that really will convey the land to B *and his heirs* – and by heirs I mean the line descending through his eldest son, and that son's eldest son, and so on, for ever.'

If A attempted to make his intention more clear by granting the land to B 'and the heirs of his body', even this would not have the effect that he desired since it had been decided by this time that a grant in this form would give B initially a life estate. If he had no children, then on his death the land would revert to A, but if he had a child, B could sell the land, or give it away, the transferee receiving a full fee simple, A's intention thus being frustrated. A's wish to be able to grant land in such a way that it would pass down from one generation to the next was shared by other great land holders. In 1285, to meet their wishes, the Statute De Donis Conditionalibus was passed. The Statute made no bones about the wrong that the Statute was intended to put right:

> ' ... and where one giveth land to another and the heirs of his body ... it seemed very hard ... to the givers ... that their will being expressed in the gift, was not heretofore, nor yet is observed: ... after issue [had been] born ... heretofore such feoffees [the persons to whom the land had been granted] had power to aliene the land so given, and to disinherit their issue ..., contrary to the minds of the givers, and contrary to the form expressed in the gift.'

To the great land owners of the time, an undesirable situation indeed.

To remedy the matter the Statute continued:

> 'Our lord the King, perceiving how necessary and expedient it should be to provide a remedy in the aforesaid cases, hath ordained, that *the will of the giver, according to the form in the deed of gift* manifestly expressed, *shall be* from henceforth *observed*; so that *they to whom the land was given* [ie in a form such as 'to X and the heirs of his body'] *shall have no power to aliene the land* so given, but it shall remain unto the issue of them to whom it was given after their death ....'[15]

---

15   The italics are added.

Thus if, after the passing of the Statute, A grants Blackacre 'to B and the heirs of his body', B will not have the power to alienate[16] the land; on his death it will pass to his heir, and the heir must be found among his issue (his children or his children's children, etc). (The land could not pass to an heir found among collaterals, because the Statute had expressly provided that it would 'remain unto the *issue* of them to whom it was given ... ')

If B had no issue, or if in the future there came a time when there was no heir to succeed to the land, the Statute provided that the land was to revert to the grantor (ie A) or if by then he was dead, his heir. (If B's issue were extinct this did not necessarily mean that A, his father, would have no heir, because A might have had other children besides B, all of whom would be capable of being his heir on the extinction of B's line, and, further A's heir could be sought among not only his issue but also his collaterals.)

Let us suppose that in 1320 A grants Blackacre 'to B and the heirs of his body'. B has a son, C, and then dies. C has one child, a daughter, D, and then dies, D marries and has one son, E, and then dies. E, when three years old, is drowned. No other issue of B are alive. If A had been alive, the land would have reverted to him, but since he had died, it reverts to his heir, his grandson X (the son of A's son, Y, who is also dead). This sequence of events can be illustrated thus:

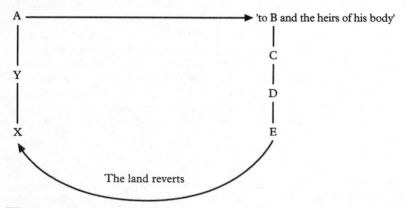

What estate in the land did B receive when the land was granted to him? The Statute did not create any new estate by name, but the interest which B received came to be known as a *fee tail* estate. Thus, as a result of the statute, there developed what came in time to be accepted as a new estate. So we may speak of A, the holder of the fee simple estate in Blackacre, granting the land to B for a fee tail estate; or we can say that he granted it to B for an estate *in fee tail*; or simply to B *in fee tail*; or, even, to B *in tail*.

As has been seen, if B's issue die out the land reverts to A. There is therefore always a possibility that the land will revert to A. Thus A has not parted with his interest in the land completely. If B's issue die out A will once again hold

---

16   If B transferred the land inter vivos, the interest of the grantee ended on B's death and the land passed to B's heir.

the fee simple in possession. The interest which A retains after the grant of the land to B is therefore a fee simple in reversion.

We saw that if B, the holder of the fee simple in land, granted the land to C for life, B retained the fee simple in reversion. We now learn that the same principle applies in the case of the grant of a fee tail: the grantor retains the fee simple in reversion. The reason is that a life estate and a fee tail estate are each something less than the fee simple. They can be 'carved out' of the fee simple, in such a way that the grantor still retains something[17]. In the case of a grant of a life estate, what remains with him is the certainty that the life estate will come to an end at some time, and that the land will then revert; in the case of the grant of a fee tail, what remains with him is the possibility that the fee tail will come to an end, and that the land will then revert to him.

Just as there could be a succession of life estates, so there could equally be a succession of fee tail estate, as in a grant,

'to B in fee tail with remainder to C in fee tail with remainder to D in fee tail'.

Or there could be a grant consisting of a succession of life and fee tail estate,[18] as in a grant by A,

'to B for life, with remainder to C in fee tail, with remainder to D for life, with remainder to E in fee tail'.

Let us trace an imaginary devolution to this last grant:

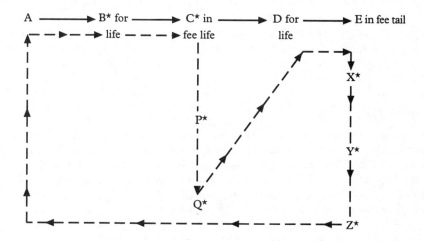

On this diagram an asterisk against a person's name indicates that he or she held the land. When Q died without issue (and all C's other issue being

---

17 Subject to what is said later.
18 For an example, see *Blathwayt v Lord Cawley* [1976] AC 397, [1975] 3 All ER 625.

extinct), the fee tail granted to C came to an end. It would then have passed to D, but by this time he was dead. So too was E. So the land passed to X in fee tail. When Z died, all E's issue being extinct, the land reverted to A who throughout this time had held the fee simple in reversion. The land having reverted to him, he holds once again the fee simple in possession. (If A had in the meantime died the land will pass to whoever he left the fee simple in reversion to in his will. If he died intestate the fee simple will pass to his heir.)

While B was alive he held a life interest in possession. C held a fee tail in remainder, D a life estate in remainder and E a fee tail in remainder. When B died, C's fee tail ceased to be a fee tail in remainder and became a fee tail in possession. What interest in the land at that point did C's eldest son P hold? The answer is that he held no interest in the land. It is true that if C died, P, being his eldest son and therefore his heir, would succeed to the land. (He, P, would then hold the fee tail in possession.) But while his father, C, is alive, P cannot claim to be his heir, because a person's heir can only be ascertained on his death. P, therefore, during his father's lifetime has no more than a hope of succeeding to the land; he merely has what is termed a *spes successionis*.

The principal characteristics of the fee tail estate can be summarised thus:

1.   On the death of a tenant in tail the land descends to his heir, the heir being found among his issue only (not collaterals or ancestors).
2.   In the absence of an heir, the land reverts to the grantor.
3.   At common law a tenant in tail cannot alienate the land by will. (It will be seen later that the position was changed by statute in 1925.)

Why fee *tail?* The word tail is derived from the French 'taille', meaning 'cut down to size'. The fee tail is thus a fee, an estate of inheritance, which has been cut down by the various restrictions on alienability which we have described.

Barring the fee tail

For about two hundred years after the Statute De Donis 1285, land held for an estate of fee tail devolved generation by generation to the lineal heir. By 1472,[19] however, it had become possible because of the willing connivance of the courts for a fee tail to be broken ('barred') and converted into a full fee simple by means of a collusive action termed a 'common recovery'. By this means, if Z held Blackacre in fee tail, and he wished to sell the land to a purchaser, P, and he wished P to receive the full fee simple in the land (thus cutting out his, Z's, heirs), Z brought proceedings, known as suffering a common recovery,[20] before the court, and the judgment resulted in Z obtaining the land in fee simple; but this process could only be employed by a tenant in tail if he was either (a) a tenant in tail in possession, or, (b) if, as tenant in tail in remainder, he had the consent of the freehold tenant in possession at the time.

19   *Taltarum's Case* (1472) YB 12 Edw 4 fo 19 pl 25.
20   For an explanation of the mechanics of the processess of suffering a common recovery and levying a fine (post), see Hargreaves, Chapter 8.

Thus if a grantor (G) granted Blackacre to A for life, with remainder to B for life, with remainder to C in fee tail, and C wished to convert his fee tail in remainder into a fee simple in remainder, he needed the consent of A (or if A was dead, that of B), in order to do so. If A and B had both died, with the result that C's fee tail had fallen into possession, he could employ the common recovery to produce a fee simple without the consent of anyone. If C died without barring the entail and the land passed to C's heir, D, D could similarly bar the entail by a common recovery without needing anyone's consent.

If the freehold tenant in possession refused to consent to a tenant in tail in remainder barring the fee tail, then the tenant in tail, being unable to employ a common recovery, was driven to employ another device, that of the 'fine'. This was another form of collusive action before the court. Its use became established by 1540.

A fine had the advantage that the consent of the freehold tenant in possession was not required; but it had a serious drawback: the estate that was produced from its use was not a full fee simple, but a modified form of fee simple, termed a 'base fee'.

The base fee

A base fee has the same characteristics as a fee simple, except that its duration lasts only as long as the fee tail (from which it was produced) would have lasted if it had not been barred. We can illustrate this by an example. G grants land to A for life, with remainder to B in fee tail, with remainder to X in fee simple. B proposes to sell his interest (which is still in remainder) to P. A declines to concur in B barring the entail. B can therefore only bar the entail by means of a fine. This he does. The estate that P acquires will be a base fee in remainder. Let us suppose that the following events (illustrated below) then occur. (1) A dies (P will then hold the base fee in possession). (2) P sells the land to Q. (3) B dies leaving an only son, C. (4) Q gives the land to U. (5) C dies leaving a daughter, D. (6) U dies and the land passes under his will to V. (7) D dies, childless. No other issue of B remain alive.

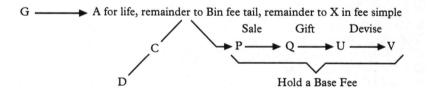

At that moment B's fee tail, if it had not been barred, would have come to an end. At the same moment, therefore, the base fee comes to an end, and the land passes to X, the original remainderman (or if he is dead, his estate). If there had been no remainder after the grant to B, the land would have reverted to G (or his estate).

A base fee was thus of less value than a fee simple, since the holder had constantly to be looking over his shoulder, as it were, to see whether the original fee tail tenant's issue were likely to become extinct. The greater the number of possible heirs there were alive, the more closely the value of the estate would approach that of a full fee simple.

Fines and Recoveries Act 1833

The old collusive actions employing the recovery and the fine were slow, cumbersome and expensive. The need to use these contrivances was removed by the Fines and Recoveries Act 1833. Under this Act it became possible for the holder of a fee tail to bar the entail by executing a document making an inter vivos transfer of the interest. The document concerned (termed a 'disentailing assurance') had to be made or evidenced by a deed, and had to be enrolled within six months at the Court of Chancery.[1]

Thus if X held Blackacre in fee tail and he wished to convey the land in fee simple to Y, X executed a disentailing assurance in Y's favour. If X wished to hold the fee simple himself, he conveyed the land to a trustee on trust[2] for himself.[3]

The old principles were, however, preserved. Thus a tenant in tail in possession could create a full fee simple, as could a tenant in tail in remainder who had the consent of the feehold tenant in possession (termed by the Act, the 'protector'), but a tenant in tail in remainder who executed a disentailing assurance without the protector's concurrence created only a base fee.

It should be noted that the Act did not enable X to bar the entail by will. Thus if X did not execute any disentailing assurance during his life, and in his will he left Blackacre to his friend Y, on his death the devise to Y was ineffective and the land passed (still in fee tail) to X's heir.

Law of Property Act 1925

It was not until the Law of Property Act 1925 came into operation that it became possible for a fee tail to be barred by will, and then only if certain conditions are fulfilled. Under this Act,[4] if X holds Blackacre in fee tail and in his will he devises the land to Y, then provided that:

1. X's will is made, or confirmed by codicil, after 1925; and
2. X is of full age; and
3. X is tenant in tail in possession at his death; and
4. X's will refers to Blackacre specifically,[5] or refers to X's entailed property generally, or refers to the instrument under which X had acquired Blackacre (eg 'I devise to Y all land that I acquired under the will of my father, W'),

---

1   Later, enrolment was at the Central Office of the Supreme Court.
2   Trusts and trustees are examined in Chapter 5.
3   After 1925 it was possible for X to execute the disentailing assurance in his own favour; ie to convey the land to himself (LPA 1925, s 72(3)) thus avoiding the need to employ a trust.
4   Section 76.
5   See *Acheson v Russell* [1951] Ch 67, [1950] 2 All ER 572.

then the entail is barred and Y takes the land in fee simple. If any condition is not satisfied, Y receives nothing and the unbarred fee tail passes to X's heir.

The Law of Property Act further provided that after 1925 personalty (which before 1926 could not be entailed, because of the wording of the Statute De Donis) should be capable of being granted in fee tail.

Enlargement of a base fee into a fee simple

A base fee could,[6] however, be enlarged into a full fee simple. If G granted Blackacre to A for life with remainder to B in tail, with remainder to C in fee simple, and B conveyed his interest to Q without A's concurrence, this conferring on Q a base fee, Q's base fee would be enlarged into a full fee simple if:

1. B executed a fresh disentailing assurance in favour of Q, this time with A's concurrence.[7]
2. B executed a fresh disentailing assurance in favour of Q after A's death.
3. Q acquired C's fee simple in remainder (eg by buying it from C, or inheriting it under C's will).[8]
4. Q remained in possession of the land for 12 years after the death of A.[9]

Trusts of Land and Appointment of Trustees Act 1996

The Act provides[10] that where a person purports by an instrument coming into operation after the commencement of the Act to grant to another an entailed interest in real or personal property, the instrument does not create an entailed interest but 'operates, instead, as a declaration that the property is held in trust absolutely for the person to whom an entailed interest in the property was purportedly granted'.

The meaning of 'held in trust' will be explained in a later chapter.[11] For the present it is sufficient to note that the Act prevents the creation of new fee tail estates, but that estates in fee tail in existence at the time of the Act continue to run their legal course.

---

6   With certain exceptions. For example:
    1. When land was given to the Duke of Wellington in 1814 as a reward for his services, the Act conferring the land on him did so in fee tail, and provided that the entail should be unbarrable.
    2. If land was granted to A 'and to the heirs of his body begotten on Susan', such a fee tail is termed a 'tail special' and the land descended to issue born to Susan alone. If Susan died during A's lifetime without leaving issue, there could then be no heir to succeed to the land on A's death. In this situation A was termed 'a tenant in tail after possibility of issue extinct'. Such a tenant could not bar the entail, and on his death the land passed to the remainderman or, if none, reverts to the grantor.
7   Fines and Recoveries Act 1833, ss 19, 35.
8   Ibid, s 39.
9   Limitation Act 1980, s 27, replacing Limitation Act 1939, s 11.
10 Section 2, Sch 1, para 5.
11 Chapter 10.

'Heir' in modern law

If the holder of a fee tail (in existence at the date of the commencement of the Trusts of Land and Appointment of Trustees Act 1996) does not bar the entail (either inter vivos or by will), then the land descends to his heir, found among issue, ascertained under the old rules of descent. This is one of the only two instances in which it will today be necessary to refer to the old rules for ascertaining a person's heir. The other is where a testator leaves property expressly to his 'heir'[12] (in which case the heir may be found among issue, or ancestors, or collaterals).

ESTATES OF FREEHOLD

The fee simple, the fee tail and the life estate constitute the three freehold estates. They are freehold estates because originally only a person who held by a free tenure could hold one of these estates in land. Later, as we have seen, the law came to recognise the existence of estates in land held by copyright tenure, but freehold estates continued to be confined to the fee simple, fee tail and life estate.

Besides the fact that they could all originally only be held by a person who held land by a free tenure, the three freehold estates have another thing in common: they are all of indefinite duration. There is no knowing, at the time of the grant, when an estate of freehold will end.

A person who held a freehold estate in land was termed a 'freeholder'. Since the end of 1925 the term 'freeholder' has had a more limited meaning and now refers to a person who holds a fee simple estate in land.

The leasehold estate or term of years

The nature of a lease

Let us suppose that L (which in this section will represent 'landlord'), a merchant in Lincoln, inherits from his father in 1230 the fee simple[13] in Greenacre, some agricultural land outside the city. L has no interest in farming. What should he do with the land? He could sell it; that is, transfer the fee simple to another, but it so happens that he does not want to part with the land, because his son, aged 14, has shown more interest in farming than in a merchant's life. Perhaps, when he is older, the son would like to take over the land and farm it. So L does not want to part with the fee simple.

---

12   As in *Re Bourke's Will Trusts* [1980] 1 All ER 219, [1980] 1 WLR 539.
13   Since at this date the fee tail had not yet come into existence it is strictly anachronous to speak of the fee *simple*. To be accurate we should speak of L transferring the land 'in fee', but since we are speaking of the estate that later came to be called the fee simple we shall, for the sake of simplicity, refer to it as the fee simple.

T (which in this section will represent 'tenant'), the younger son of a villein tenant, is 30 years old. He helps his father work the strips which his father holds in the open fields outside the city. T would like to farm his own land, and be free of his father's control. T would be glad to farm the land which L has inherited.

For the reasons we have seen, L would not be prepared to grant the land to T in fee simple. Nor would it suit him to grant the land to T for life. T might live for another 60 years or more. L wants to have the land in his own hands in seven years' time when his son reaches 21.

So L is willing to let T occupy the land for seven years, but no more. T is willing to accept this arrangement. L and T therefore make an agreement by which L permits T to occupy the land for seven years, and T promises to pay L a rent of 8s a year.

This arrangement suits T well. If L had offered to sell him the land he would have had to refuse as he does not have the purchase money, but T reckons that with hard work and reasonable harvests he should have no difficulty in paying the rent.

The arrangement is doubly convenient to L. First, as we have seen, he can be sure of being able to reoccupy the land in seven years' time. Secondly, and quite apart from any wish to reoccupy the land, L decides that it would not be in his best interests to sell the land. If he did sell the land, he could demand a lump sum in return, but what would he do with this money? It so happens that he has no immediate need for a large lump sum. What L needs is an addition to his regular income. If L sold the land for a lump sum, the money could be used on sundry items but it would gradually be frittered away. By agreeing that T should occupy the land in return for an annual rent L augments his income and, at the same time, preserves intact the wealth which the land represents.

It would be possible for L to achieve the object of augmenting his income by granting the fee simple to another in return for a rentcharge or a (feudal) rent service, but once the amounts of these had been fixed they could not be changed, and with the decline in the value of money, the value of the payments, whether by way of rent service or rentcharge, would decline, until they ceased to be worth collecting. As we have noted, the arrangement that L makes with T has the advantage for L that T's right to occupy the land comes to an end in seven years' time. L can then either reoccupy the land or make a fresh arrangement (either with T or with someone else) at a new rent that takes account of the fall in the value of money since the last rent had been fixed.

We have said that L made an arrangement with T. The arrangement was intended to be legally binding on both of them. It thus constituted a contract between them, and the arrangement was no more than a contract. L had granted T neither a fee simple estate, nor a life estate, in the land. He granted T no *estate* in the land. Nor did T hold the land by any tenure known to the law – he did not hold by knight service or common socage, nor by any other feudal tenure. It was L who held the land by a recognised tenure, that of common socage; and it was L, not T, who held by a recognised estate, that of fee simple.

As far as the law relating to land was concerned, T held nothing. All that he had was the contract between himself and L. T thus stood outside the recognised boundaries of the land law. T held no recognised interest in the land whatsoever.

L had granted T a right to occupy the land for a period of seven years. It was said that he had granted him the right to occupy it for a term of years. It was said that he granted T '*a term of years*'. A 'term of years' later came to be called a *lease*. A person who grants a lease is termed a *lessor*, a person who holds a lease, a *lessee*. (An old name for lessee is 'termor'.)

Leasehold becomes an estate

T takes possession of the land, ploughs it, and sows wheat. What difference does it make to him that he holds no interest in the land and that his right to be there rests merely on the contract which he made with L?

The matter becomes important if T is ousted from the land. Let us suppose that S (which in this section represents 'stranger') throws T off Greenacre and starts to reap the wheat which T had sown. What action can T take?

If T seeks a writ to obtain redress before the royal courts, he finds that he is asked, 'What estate in the land do you hold which entitles you to recover the land?' and he must answer, 'None', and when he is asked, 'Who is the legal holder of the land?' T must answer, 'L'. He is told, 'Then it is for L to take proceedings to recover the land, not you.'

Thus the advantage of holding a recognised estate in land was that the holder of the estate was able to recover possession of the land. T, not holding a recognised estate, was not able to recover possession.

If L took action to recover the land from S, all well and good, but if L chose to ignore S's intrusion, T had no means of recovering the land. He might sue L for breach of the contract between them, but even if he was successful in this action, all he would get would either be money (and not the value of the land, but merely compensation for loss of the lease), or the offer of some other land, perhaps many miles from Lincoln and unsuited to his needs.[14] What he would not get was what he wanted, namely Greenacre.

The situation which we have just considered might be exploited by L. Suppose that L decides that his son will never want the land; that he, L, could do with the money which he would get from selling the land. And let us suppose that P (which in this section represents 'purchaser') offers a good price for the land. So L sells the land to P, transferring the fee simple to him. P then ousts T from the land. What is T's position then? He cannot sue P, for the same reason that we saw prevented him from suing S: namely, he has no legal interest in the land.

T's only action lies against L, under the contract between them. T may recover damages from L, but he will not recover what he wants, namely, possession of Greenacre. L, for his part, may not be bothered at having to pay compensation to T if (as he has planned) the price he obtains from P is more than sufficient to pay this compensation and leave a substantial sum over. For L to refuse to take action against S might be unfair to T, but for L to *sell* the fee

14   Pollock and Maitland, II, p 107.

simple to P was an even graver injustice. To strike at this abuse a remedy was made available in 1283 by which a lessee (T) could recover possession of the land from a purchaser (P) from the lessor (L). The remedy was the writ *Quare ejecit infra terminum*. By means of this writ T could compel P to allow him to occupy the land during the remaining years of the lease, but if T was ousted, not by P, the purchaser from L, but by S, a stranger, then T still had no means of recovering the land if L chose to take no action against S.

By the end of the thirteenth century, however, T was able to sue S for trespass (in the action commenced with the writ of trespass *De ejectione firmae*), and to recover damages from him. Thus, the position, by about 1400, was that if he was ousted by P, T could recover possession of the land; if ousted by S he could recover damages.

The final development came when it was decided, in 1499, that in an action under the writ *De ejectione firmae* (an action of 'trespass in ejectment', or 'ejectment', for short), T could recover the land itself from S, and not, as previously, merely money damages only. When that state was reached T was at last able to recover the land from anyone who dispossessed him.

The lease had by now acquired two important characteristics of an estate in land – first, it indicated the duration of the holder's interest in the land; and, secondly, the holder was able to recover the land from anyone who dispossessed him. This being so, it was no longer possible to deny that a lease was a true estate in land, and leases were therefore admitted to the company of estates, but owing to the late date at which it attained the status of estate, it was set apart from the old freehold estates (the fee simple, fee tail and life estates) and placed in a category of its own. To distinguish it from the old freehold estates, the lease was classified as a non-freehold estate.

Leasehold as a form of tenure

If T now held a true estate in the land, by what tenure did he hold the land? When L permitted T to occupy Greenacre, the relationship between them, whilst in law based on contract, resembled, in practice, the relationship of lord and tenant. Anyone who saw T ploughing Greenacre and knew that T paid money to L, might well think 'L has granted Greenacre to T, to hold of him for a money rent. L is T's lord; T is L's tenant'.

So closely did the relationship of lessor and lessee resemble that of lord and tenant as it existed in the context of tenures that, by the time a lease had come to be accepted as a true estate, it had also been accepted that leasehold constituted a form of tenure.[15]

Thus, by the end of the Middle Ages, leasehold was regarded as both a tenure and an estate. Indeed, there was nothing unreasonable in this, since a lease had the characteristics of both a tenure and an estate. Tenure is concerned with the holding of land from a superior lord in return for certain services; and T holds Greenacre of L in return for a money rent. Estate is concerned with the duration of the holder's interest, and T holds Greenacre for seven years.

15   Co Litt, ii, 93a.

Since leasehold was a form of tenure it was natural for some of the terminology of tenure, in particular the words 'lord' and 'tenant', to be applied to the relationship of lessor and lessee. L came to be termed the lord (or land lord) and T the tenant, and today the terms landlord and tenant are used as alternatives to lessor and lessee.

Leaseholds have, however, been regarded primarily as being a form of estate, and in the classification of tenures and estates, it is among the latter that leaseholds appear. This is why we were able to say that the only form of tenure that exists today is common socage.

Rent service

When we discussed rents in the context of the feudal tenures, we said that a rent paid by a tenant to a superior lord was termed a rent service (since the rent formed the service to the lord). On the other hand, if B transferred Blackacre to C by way of substitution (the only means possible after 1290[16]), and if B made it a condition of the transfer that C should pay him an annual rent, this was a rentcharge.

Because the relationship between L and T was accepted as that of lord and tenant, any rent which T paid was classed as a rent service.

Distress[17]

Since the rent which T paid was classed as a rent service, the remedy of distress, which was available to a feudal lord in the event of his tenant failing to perform his services, was made available to L, the lessor, if T, his tenant, failed to pay his rent. This meant that if T failed to pay the rent due, L could enter Greenacre and seize and take away sufficient of T's possessions[18] to cover the cost of the rent outstanding: L had the right to *distrain* on T's goods. Originally L had no right to sell the goods, but in 1689 the Distress for Rent Act provided that if a lessee failed to pay the rent within five days of distress being levied, and if the lessor gave notice to the lessee of his intention to sell the goods, then the lessor had the right to sell them.[19]

Leasehold reversions

The notion of a reversion, considered above,[20] was applied to leases. If L grants a lease for three years then at the end of the three years the right to possession of the land reverts to L. During the existence of the lease, L holds the reversion.

It is not true to say that L holds the fee simple in reversion. The reason is that he continues to hold the fee simple throughout the continuance of the lease. L may not be in possession of the land during the continuance of the

16   See p 25.
17   See Law Commission Working Paper No 97, *Distress of Rent.*
18   Certain goods came to be protected against distress. See Megarry and Wade, p 682.
19   [1983] Conv 444 (A. Hill-Smith).
20   See p 32.

lease (T is) but L still continues in possession of the fee simple. It is by virtue of holding the fee simple that L receives the payments of rent from T.

It must therefore be emphasised that the term 'fee simple in possession' does not mean that the holder of this interest is necessarily entitled to possession of the land. If he had granted a lease, then he is entitled to the rents instead. During the continuance of the lease he is in possession, not of the land, but of the right to receive the rents.

When B granted Blackacre to C for life, B was entitled to nothing until C's death. In this case B did hold the fee simple in reversion. When L granted a lease, L continued to hold the fee simple in possession. L's 'reversion' was merely the right to repossession of the land at the end of the lease. To distinguish this right from a fee simple in reversion, we refer to L's reversion as a *leasehold reversion*.

Terminology

As regards the granting of a lease, the term 'to demise' is sometimes used as an alternative to 'to lease'. Similarly, as regards the interest granted, a lease is sometimes termed a 'demise'. A lease may also be termed a 'tenancy'. Generally, 'tenancy' is used in connection with a shorter period (eg weekly or monthly tenancy); 'lease' for a longer period (eg a seven-year lease), but a lease, a demise, and a (leasehold[1]) tenancy are in law all the same creature.

CLASSIFICATION OF ESTATES

From what has been said so far it will be appreciated that estates are classified in the following way.

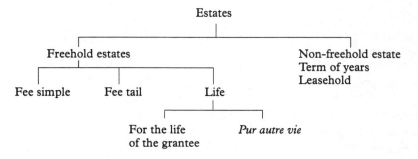

WORDS OF LIMITATION

In the last chapter we saw that B might grant land to C 'for life', or to C 'and his heirs', and we saw that if he granted the land to C 'and his heirs', C acquired

---

1 Ie, as opposed to a feudal tenancy, eg socage tenure.

an estate in fee simple. The words 'and his heirs' mark out what kind of estate had been granted to C. The words 'and his heirs' are termed *words of limitation*. Similarly, the words 'and the heirs of his body', in the grant of a fee tail estate are words of limitation. Words of limitation are thus words which delimit the estate granted to some person previously mentioned.

There are two ways in which the subject of words of limitation may arise:

1.   One is concerned with the question, 'a grantor (or testator) wishes to grant such-and-such an estate, *what words are needed* to produce this estate?'
2.   The other is concerned with the question, 'a grantor (or testator) has used such-and-such words in his grant, *what estate is produced* by these words?'

Whichever way the subject arises, to ascertain the relevant answer it is necessary to find out;

(a)   the date of the disposition; and
(b)   whether the grant is by deed or will.

The subject of words of limitation was of more importance under the old law than it is today. The matter will therefore be treated briefly.

At common law

The old law rested on the assumption that a person did not intend to give away more than he indicated that he wished to give away. In granting away land the smallest estate that can be granted is a life estate. So, before 1926, if B granted Blackacre,

'to C',

all that C received was a life estate, since B had not indicated that C was to receive more than a life estate.

If B wanted to grant C an estate in fee simple, then he had to use the correct words to convey this estate to C. In order to grant Blackacre to C in fee simple, B had to grant the land,

'to C and his heirs'.

These were the only words which would suffice. No departure from them was permitted. If the grant had been to,

'to C and his heir', or
'to C and heirs',

C did not make a fee simple estate, but merely a life estate.

If B had in fact intended to grant a fee simple to C, then he could put the matter right by making a fresh grant, but if the grant to C had been in B's will, in this case it would be too late for B to put the matter right. For this reason, in the case of grants by will, the strict rule requiring use of the words 'and his heirs' was relaxed, and it sufficed if some words such as 'for ever' or 'absolutely' were used which showed an intention to pass a fee simple estate, but if even words such as these were lacking, then C took only a life estate.

The same principles governed the grant of a fee tail. In the case of an inter vivos grant, the rule was that only certain words would pass a fee tail estate. We have seen[2] that a grant,

'to B and the heirs of his body',

created a fee tail estate, and these were the words usually used. Some other expression would, however, suffice provided that it included the words 'heirs', and restricted the heirs to those found among lineal descendants. Thus, a grant,

'to B and the heirs from him proceeding',

since it complied with this requirement, would pass a fee tail to B. But if the requirement was not met, then B took only a life estate.

In the case of grants by will, the strictness of the rule was (as with the fee simple) relaxed. If the words used showed an intention to create a fee tail, then a fee tail was created. Thus if in his will B devised Blackacre,

'to C and his issue', or
'to C and his descendants',

C received a fee tail.

Changes made by statute

In the nineteenth century certain changes were made in the rules governing words of limitation:

1. In the case of an inter vivos grant of a fee simple or of a fee tail, the Conveyancing Act 1881[3] provided that the two estates could be created by use of the words 'in fee simple' and 'in tail', respectively. These statutory words were provided as optional alternatives to the strict common law words.
2. In the case of grants by will, the Wills Act 1837[4] provided that a fee simple was to pass unless a contrary intention was shown. Thus, after 1837, if B devised Blackacre 'to C', C received a fee simple, since B had shown no intention to grant him any other interest.

The assumption that the grantor intended to grant a fee simple unless he showed an intention to the contrary was extended to inter vivos grants by the Law of Property Act 1925,[5] and this is the principle that underlies the present law concerning words of limitation. Thus if, at the present day, B grants Blackacre,

'to C',

then regardless of whether the grant was inter vivos or by will, C obtains a fee simple.

---

2 See p 35.
3 Section 51.
4 Section 28.
5 Section 60(1).

If B wants to grant a life estate to C he must make this intention clear, as by granting the land,

'to C for life'.

The Trusts of Land and Appointment of Trustees Act 1996[6] prevented the creation of fee tail estates in real or personal property[7] (but did not affect fee tail interests in existence at the date of the coming into operation of the Act). After the Act, words that would previously have created a fee tail operate[8] to convey an absolute interest; ie in land, a fee simple absolute in possession.

The position today is therefore as follows. In the case of a grant by deed or by will:

1. To create a life estate, an intention to create a life estate must be shown. If the intention is not shown a fee simple passes.
2. To create a fee simple estate, no special words need be used. The use of no words, or any words that show an intention to create a fee simple, or words that would, before the Trusts of Land and Appointment of Trustees Act 1996, have created a fee tail estate, all today result in the creation of a fee simple.

CLASSIFICATION OF PROPERTY IN ENGLISH LAW

If S (which in this section represents 'stranger') takes the land of O (which in this section represents 'owner'), O can bring an action against S and claim, as of right, the return of the land. The court does not have any discretion to order that S should, for example, either give up the land or pay O its value. O has an action to recover the 'thing' (the *res*) itself: we say that he has an action *in rem*, or a *real action*. A real action is thus one in which the plaintiff has a claim as of right to the return of his property.

In early law a real action lay in respect of the three freehold estates in land only. In the case of all other property (O's horse, his furniture, his clothes, his sword, etc), whilst the owner had a right to bring an action against a person who had dispossessed him, the remedy he could obtain was an order that the defendant should either give up the property to O or pay O its value (as the defendant chose). O has no claim as of right to the return of the thing itself. His action, which was directed not so much against the 'thing', but rather against the person of the defendant, was termed a *personal action* or an action *in personam*.

Property in respect of which a real action lay (ie the three freehold estates) came to be termed *real property*, or *realty*. Property in respect of which only a personal action lay came to be termed *personal property* or *personalty* or *chattels* (from an older word meaning cattle, originally the most important form of chattel).

---

6   Schedule 1, para 5.
7   For the distinction between real and personal property, see infra.
8   The manner in which the words operate is considered further in Chapter 10.

Thus if O held Blackacre for an estate in fee tail and he was dispossessed by S, since an estate in fee tail was realty, O had an action in rem against S for the recovery of Blackacre. If S took O's horse, since a horse was personalty, O had only a personal action against S, and an order by the court would direct S either to give up the horse or pay O its value (as S chose).

We have seen that a lease came to be accepted as an estate in land and that by 1499 a tenant was able to recover the land from anyone who ousted him from it, but a lessee's action (by the writ *ejectionae firmae*) was not one of the ancient real actions invented to protect the freehold estates in land, and by the time a lease was accepted as a fully-fledged estate in land, the gates of real property had been closed for too long for them to open to admit the new estate. So leaseholds stayed outside, and since they could not be classed as real property, they could only be classed as personal property. It might seem odd that a lease, an interest in land, should be classed under the same head as that which included pots and pans, but that is where leaseholds were placed, and that is where they have remained to this day. However, it was recognised that a lease was a special form of chattel; and for this reason it was termed a 'chattel real'; that is, a chattel, but a chattel that, since it relates to land, has affinities with real property. All other chattels are termed 'pure chattels'.

The principles we have described apply today subject to two modifications:

1. It became accepted that not only the three freehold estates but all interests in land (other than leases) were real property.[9] Thus easements and profits, which are met later in this book, are items of real property.
2. The Common Law Procedure Act 1854[10] gave the court a discretion to order specific restitution of chattels. Thus if today S takes O's horse, O can ask the court to exercise its discretion to order S to restore the horse to him (and only in exceptional circumstances would the court be likely to decline so to order): but S still has no claim as of right to such an order.[11]

RENTCHARGES

In this chapter the nature of rentcharges has been explained, and there will be occasion to refer to rentcharges at various points in the remaining chapters of the book. It will be convenient at this point to explain, however, that by the Rentcharges Act 1977:[12]

---

9   By the middle of the nineteenth century it had become accepted that copyhold was a form of real property. This was confirmed in *Re Sirett* [1968] 3 All ER 186, [1969] 1 WLR 60.
10   Section 78.
11   The Torts (Interference with Goods) Act 1977 entitles O to seek an order from the court for (a) delivery of the horse; (b) delivery of the horse or the payment of its value, as S elects; (c) damages. An order under (a) is made at the discretion of the court. Thus the Act does not disturb the ancient principle that O has no claim as *of right* to demand the return of the horse.
12   Enacted follwing the Law Commission's report, *Transfer of Land, Report on Rentcharges* (Law Com No 68, 1975).

1. with certain exceptions,[13] no new rentcharges may be created after 22 August 1977;[14]
2. with certain exceptions,[15] existing rentcharges are to be extinguished at the expiry of 60 years from the passing of the Act (22 July 1977) or the date on which the rentcharge became payable, whichever is later;[16]
3. holders of land subject to a rentcharge are enabled to discharge their land from the rentcharge by paying compensation to the rentcharge holders, calculated according to a formula set out in the Act.[17]

SUMMARY

An estate in land refers to the duration of time for which the land is to be held.

Since 1290, alienation of the fee simple has been by substitution, not by sub-infeudation. If a rent is reserved it is a rentcharge, not a rent service.

Since 1660, the fee simple has been freely alienable inter vivos or by will.

After 1925, if the holder of a fees simple estate dies intestate the land passes to his 'next of kin'.

A life estate can be alienated. The transferee receives a life estate *pur autre vie*.

Waste is the term for acts or omissions that alter land. Waste is of four kinds.

An estate in land may be in possession, in remainder or in reversion.

There can be no remainder or reversion after the grant of a fee simple.

The fee tail estate was one that passed to the grantee's heir found among issue only. On failure of issue the land reverted to the grantor. The grantor of a fee tail retained a fee simple in reversion.

Means were devised by which a fee tail could be barred.

Under the Law of Property Act 1925 a fee tail could be barred by will.

No new fee tail can be created after the 1996 Act.

Under a lease a person holds land for a specified period of time.

The grantor of a lease retains the fee simple.

Leases began as contracts. Later they came to be accepted as being also a form of estate, a non-freehold estate.

Real property is that in respect of which a real action may be brought.

Personal property is that in respect of which only a personal action is available. Leases are personal property.

Words of limitation mark out the estate that a grantee is to receive.

After the 1996 Act, a fee simple passes unless an intention is shown to pass a life estate.

13   Section 2(3).
14   Section 2(1).
15   In particular, 'estate rentcharges', defined (s 2(4)) as ones 'created for the purpose: (a) of making covenants to be performed by the owner of the land [see Chapter 21] affected by the rentcharge enforceable by the rent charge owner against the owner for the time being of the land; or (b) of meeting or contributing towards the cost of the performance by the rent owner of covenants for the provision of services, the carrying out of maintenance or repairs ... ' [1988] Conv 99 (S. Bright).
16   Section 3.
17   Sections 4-10. These provisions replace those in the Law of Property Act 1925 (ss 191and 192).

CHAPTER 4

Ownership of Land – the Fee Simple Estate

'OWNERSHIP' OF LAND

We know already, and as will be more fully appreciated after reaching the later stages of this book, there is no such thing in English law as absolute ownership of land. One reason for this (explained in Chapter 2) is that all land[1] is held (however small the consequence), from the Crown, by tenure.[2] Nevertheless, for all practical purposes, the holder of the fee simple is today treated as being the equivalent of the owner of the land; but the term 'owner' has not (except in common parlance) replaced the term 'holder of a fee simple'. This is because use of the term 'fee simple' serves to indicate the manner in which land is held. It indicates that we are speaking of what is still an *estate* in land, an estate with the specific characteristics we noted in the last chapter (in particular with regard to the devolution of the land on the death of the fee simple holder). Thus to say that A holds a fee simple in Blackacre, tells us what we need to know about the manner in which the land is held.

What is 'land'?

Whether we choose to speak of A as owning the land or A as holding the fee simple in land, the question arises: what *is* land, of what is *land* comprised?

At common law the maxim is *cuius est solum eius est usque ad caelum ad inferos*: he who owns the surface owns everything up to the heavens and down to the depths of the earth. There have, however, come to be many exceptions to this rule:

1. Ownership of certain minerals such as coal and petroleum have been vested in the Crown or in a public corporation.[3]
2. At common law, coin, bullion, or manufactured artefacts made of gold or silver (or containing a substantial[4] amount of gold or silver) found hidden

---

1   Other, of course, than that in the hands of the Crown.
2   Another reason will be explained in Chapter 24.
3   Petrol in strata is vested in the Crown; Petroleum (Production) Act 1934.
4   *A-G of the Duchy of Lancaster v G E Overton (Farms) Ltd* [1982] Ch 277, [1982] 1 All ER 524 (hoard of Roman coins found buried, containing only a small amount of silver, held not to be treasure trove). See (1981) 44 MLR 178 (N.E. Palmer).

(not merely lost of abandoned) in or on land, or in a building on land, the owner being unknown, were *treasure trove* and belonged to the Crown, not to the fee simple owner. The common law of treasure trove was superseded by the Treasure Act 1996[5] under which ownership of all 'treasure' as defined[6] by the Act vests[7] in the Crown (as part of the hereditary revenues of the Crown[8])[9] and may be transferred, or otherwise disposed of, in accordance with directions given by the Secretary of State (eg by deposit in a museum). 'Treasure' includes things that would have been treasure trove before the Act together with certain coins;[10] objects at least 300 years old when found and which are not coins, of which at least 10 per cent is gold or silver; and objects of at least 200 years old of a class designated by the Secretary of State as being of outstanding historical, archaeological or cultural importance. When treasure is transferred to a museum the Secretary of State is required to determine whether a reward is paid (by the museum) to the finder, the occupier or a person who had an interest in the land.[11]

3   Gold and silver found in a gold or silver mine at common law belong to the Crown.[12]

4. It has been suggested that the ownership of airspace above the surface extends no further than the height of the atmosphere;[13] and statute provides that no action shall lie in trespass or in nuisance in respect of aircraft which fly over land at a reasonable height in all the circumstances.[14]

Fixtures

A further maxim of common law is *quicquid plantatur solo, solo credit*: whatever is attached to land, becomes part of the land. Thus land includes any buildings on the land. This aspect of the *quicquid plantatur* principle received confirmation in the Law of Property Act 1925: '"Land" includes ... buildings or ... parts of buildings (whether the division is horizontal, vertical or made in any other way[15]) ...'[16] Thus, a brass front door knocker, when bought at a shop, is a chattel. When in place on the front door it becomes part of the house, and hence part of the land. An object which was originally a chattel, but which has become part of the land (ie, part of a building) is termed a 'fixture'.

---

5   [1996] Conv 321.
6   Section 1.
7   Section 4.
8   Section 6.
9   Or, if there is one, a franchisee in right of treasure trove for the place where the treasure is found (eg the Duke of Cornwall). Section 4(1)(*a*).
10 Section 1(a)(ii), (iii); s 3(2).
11 Section 10.
12 *Mines Case* (1567) 1 Plowd 310; Royal Mines Act 1688.
13 *R v Trent River Authority, ex p National Coal Board* [1969] 2 WLR 653 at 658, per Lord Denning.
14 Civil Aviation Act 1949, s 40(1).
15 See p 58.
16 Section 205(1)(ix).

The possibility of disputes over whether or not a chattel has become a fixture will be recognised. A puts a sun dial in his rose garden. Later, he sells his house to B. When B takes possession of the land the sun dial has been removed. Was A entitled to take the sun dial? If it was a fixture, ownership of the sun dial passed with the land to B, who can recover it from A; if it was not a fixture, A was entitled to remove it.

Originally, whether a chattel became a fixture was regarded as depending on whether the chattel had been physically fixed to the land, eg by nails, or screws, or cement. Since the second half of the nineteenth century[17] it has come to be accepted that whether a chattel has become a fixture depends on the purpose for which the chattel was brought on to the land. If a chattel is placed on land with a view to it being enjoyed in its own right, for example, as an ornament, or an object of utility, then it remains a chattel, irrespective of the fact that it might have been necessary for the chattel to be secured to the land in order to be properly enjoyed or utilised. On the other hand, if a chattel is placed on land with the intention that it should form an integral part of the structure of a building, or part of the architectural design of a building or grounds, then, irrespective of whether it rests by its own weight or is in some way fixed, it becomes a fixture and thus part of the land. The test, it will be noted, seeks to give effect to the intention of the person who introduced the chattel on to the land.

Applying the test of 'purpose', the courts have held the following to be fixtures:

1. statues, figures and vases, being part of the architectural design of a house; and stone seats, being part of the design of the grounds;[18]
2. moveable dog grates (for fire places) which had been substituted for fixed grates;[19]
3. garden ornaments, including a stone statue, a lead trough and patio lights;[20]

(In none of these three cases were the items fixed in any way, but rested by their own weight.)

4. fitted carpets; light fittings attached to the property (but not lampshades); gas fires in the form of mock coal fires, of an appropriate size for the aperture of the fireplace and fed by fixed gas pipes; towel rails, soap fittings and tap fittings; kitchen units and sink; white goods (eg refrigerators) fixed into standard size holes, being part of an overall fitted kitchen and physically fixed and plumbed or wired in, and not easily removed from a fitted kitchen as a whole; curtains matching a fixed pelmet and made specifically for the windows they covered;[1]
5. tip-up seats bolted to the floor inside, and advertising panels fastened to a wall outside, a cinema.[2]

---

17   The modern test can be seen emerging in *D'Eyncourt v Gregory* (1866) LR 3 Eq 382.
18   *D'Eyncourt v Gregory* (1866) LR 3 EQ 382.
19   *Monti v Barnes* [1901] 1 KB 205.
20   *Hamp v Bygrave* (1982) 266 Estates Gazette 720.
 1   *TSB Bank plc v Botham* [1995] EGCS 3.
 2   *Vandeville Electric Cinemas Ltd v Muriset* [1923] 2 Ch 74.

The following have been held not to be fixtures:

1. tapestries attached to the wall of a house;[3]
2. a collection of stuffed birds in glass-fronted cases fixed to the walls of a gallery of a country house;[4]
3. chairs, on temporary hire, in a theatre, fixed to the floor (by screws) in order to comply with a local authority's regulations;[5]
4. a corrugated iron shed, laid on a concrete floor, the framework of the shed being secured to the concrete base by bolts fastened to iron straps and fixed in the concrete;[6]
5. pictures fixed into the recesses in the panelling of a room[7] (' ... interest focused attention not on the design of the room but on the pictures themselves. They were put in place on the wall to be enjoyed as pictures'[8]);

(all these, it will be noted, were fixed in some way to the land)

6. printing machines standing by their own weight on the floor of a factory;[9]
7. greenhouses, standing by their own weight on dollies not attached to the land;[10]
8. a statue of a Greek athlete resting by its own weight on a plinth in a garden (the plinth being a fixture, the statue being the last of a number of different items that had rested on the plinth).[11]

Whilst it is the purpose for which a chattel is placed on or fixed to land that determines whether it becomes a fixture, the question whether a chattel is physically fixed to land is nevertheless relevant in that the answer determines the burden of proof: if something is fixed to the land, then prima facie it is a fixture, with the result that the burden of proof rests with the party who is seeking to show that it is not a fixture: if he fails to discharge this burden, the item is held to be a fixture. If something is not fixed, then prima facie it is not a fixture and the burden of proof rests with the party seeking to show that it is a fixture. The degree of attachment thus provides the prima facie result; the purpose for which the thing was brought on to the land provides the conclusive result.

A dispute as to whether something is or is not a fixture may arise between a vendor (claiming that the item is not a fixture, with the consequence that he may remove it) and a purchaser (claiming that it is a fixture, with the

---

3   *D'Eyncourt v Gregory* (1866) LR 3 Eq 382; *Leigh v Taylor* [1902] AC 157; cf *Whaley* [1908] 1 Ch 615 (tapestries, fixed as part of a general scheme of decoration and not for their better enjoyment, held to be fixtures).
4   *Viscount Hill v Bullock* [1897] 2 Ch 482.
5   *Lyon & Co v London City and Midland Bank* [1903] 2 KB 135.
6   *Webb v Frank Bevis Ltd* [1940] 1 All ER 247.
7   *Berkley v Poulett* (1977) 241 Estates Gazette 911; (M & B).
8   Per Scarman LJ.
9   *Hulme v Brigham* [1943] KB 152, [1943] 1 All ER 204.
10 *Dibble Ltd v Moore* [1970] 2 QB 181, [1969] 3 All ER 1465; see also *Deen v Andrews* (1986) 52 P & CR 17.
11 *Berkley v Poulett* (1977) 241 Estates Gazette 911; (M & B).

consequence that it has become his property along with the land).[12] The same issue may be the subject of dispute between a person entitled to a testator's real property and one entitled to his personal property.

A dispute on the same issue may also arise on the expiry of a lease, between the lessee (claiming that something he has brought on to the land has not become a fixture) and the lessor (claiming that it has become part of the land and so cannot be taken away by the lessee).

The hardship that a tenant would suffer as a result of an item he has installed (eg a coke stove) becoming, as a fixture, part of the land and so the lessor's property, is mitigated by the common law rule that a lessee is permitted to remove a chattel notwithstanding that it has become a fixture, provided that it is either (a) a trade fixture, or (b) a domestic or ornamental fixture which can be removed without causing substantial damage. Examples of (a) have included the fittings of a public house,[13] shrubs planted by a market gardener,[14] petrol pumps at a filling station[15] and fluorescent light fittings and carpeting secured to the floor by gripping rods.[16] Examples of (b) have included an ornamental chimney piece,[17] stoves, grates, kitchen ranges[18] and panelling.[19] Trade fixtures must be removed before the expiry of the lease.[20] Domestic and ornamental fixtures must be removed before the expiry of the lease or within a reasonable time thereafter.[1] (Unless he is entitled to remove an item on the ground that it is a tenant's fixture, a tenant loses the benefit of any improvement that he has made to the land.[2])

Division of land

Land can be divided vertically, as where a person buys a plot of land (the line dividing the plot from other land extending from the boundary upwards into the sky and downwards towards the centre of the earth). Or land can be divided both vertically and horizontally, as where a person buys a flat[3] (the vertical division consisting of the outer limits of the flat, and the horizontal divisions being those dividing the flat from the properties above and below); or where a person buys a vein, eg of lead, beneath the surface of the earth.

For example, suppose that A sells one flat in his house to B, another flat to C, and a mineral vein beneath the surface to D.

12 As in *Phillips v Lamdin* [1949] 2 KB 33, [1949] 1 All ER 770.
13 *Elliott v Bishop* (1854) 10 Ex Ch 496.
14 *Wardell v Usher* (1841) 3 Scott NR 508.
15 *Smith v City Petroleum Co Ltd* [1940] 1 All ER 260.
16 *Young v Dalgety plc* (1987) 281 Estates Gazette 427, CA.
17 *Leach v Thomas* (1835) 7 C & P 327.
18 *Darby v Harris* (1841) 1 QB 895.
19 *Spyer v Phillipson* [1931] 2 Ch 183.
20 See [1987] Conv 253 (G. Kodilinye).
 1 For agricultural fixtures, see Agricultural Tenances Act 1995, s 8.
 2 For proposals by the Law Commission that would require a landlord to compensate a tenant for improvements made by him with the landlord's concurrence, see Law Com 178 (1989).
 3 See Tolson 'Land'Without Earth – Freehold Flats in English Law' (1950) 14 Conv (NS) 350; M. Vitoria, *New Square, Lincoln's Inn and its Flying Freeholds* (1977) 41 Conv (NS) 11.

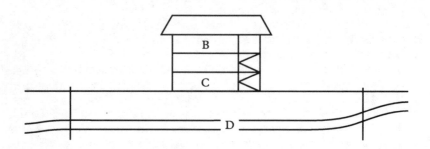

It will be seen that in this example A is left with the land surrounding the building, the middle flat, the stairs and the shell of the building, including the roof (and the air above), and all the ground beneath the surface except for that sold to D.

In practice, however, although instances exist in which a flat is held for a fee simple estate, such instances are rare. The reason for this is that a person who holds a flat in fee simple does not (for reasons that will become clear in a later chapter) possess any effective legal means by which he can compel the person who owns the remainder of the property (eg the outside walls and the roof) to abide by any undertakings that that person may have given with regard to the proper management of the property as a whole, for example repairing leaks in the roof, cleaning the stairs and landings, and maintaining the surrounding gardens.

It has been because of the absence of any means of enforcing such undertakings that the practice has been for flats to be held for a leasehold estate, the landlord holding the fee simple in the building, with each flat being let to a tenant. Where a person holds under a lease he *is* (for reasons that will become clear in a later chapter) able to enforce undertakings of the kind mentioned against the landlord.

The drawback, however, is the wish by people to own their flat absolutely, not hold under a lease, an interest the value of which decreases with each year that passes. It was to enable a person who holds the fee simple in a flat to enforce undertakings relating to the management of the property against the owner of the whole structure that a new form of land holding, termed commonhold, has been proposed. The matter is considered further in a later chapter.[4]

4   Chapter 22.

Land covered by water

In the case of land covered by water, for example a river, the bed of the river belongs to the fee simple owner of the land through which the river passes. Where the river forms the boundary between two plots belonging to two different fee simple owners, the presumption is that each owner is the owner of the bed up to the middle line. Similar principles apply in the case of a lake.

What has been said about the beds of rivers and lakes applies to all non-tidal water. The bed of all tidal water belongs to the Crown.

Land by the sea

A person who holds land by the sea, owns the land down to the high-water mark of medium tides. Land lying between the high- and low-water mark,[5] which is termed the foreshore, belongs to the Crown.[6] The public have a right of navigation and fishing[7] over the foreshore under common law (subject to local byelaws). Recreation by the public over the foreshore is permitted by the Crown as a privilege.

Gradual[8] accretions[9] to land,[10] and alluvial land formed by the gradual recession of the sea,[11] belong to the person who owns the land adjacent to the sea. (The principle that accretions belong to the owner of the adjacent land applies also to land by the side of inland water[12] (ie where the bed of the water is in other ownership).)

Wild animals

Ownership of land does not carry with it ownership of wild animals on the land, since wild animals are not capable of being owned:[13] they are *res nullius*: things without an owner. However, a land owner has a right[14] to catch and kill wild animals on his land. Once wild animals are caught or killed (whether by the owner or anyone else, including a trespasser[15]) they become the property of the owner of the land.

---

5   *Anderson v Alnwick District Council* [1993] 3 All ER 613.
6   *Re Hull and Selby Rly Co* (1839) 5 M & W 327.
7   Including the right to dig for bait to be used in the exercise of the right to fish: *Anderson v Alnwick District Council* [1993] 3 All ER 613.
8   Sudden accretions belong to the Crown.
9   [1986] Conv 247 (W. Howarth).
10   *Gifford v Lord Yarborough* (1828) 5 Bing 163. Cf *Baxendale v Instow Parish Council* [1982] Ch 14, [1981] 2 All ER 620. See [1982] Conv 208, 'Movable Fees' (R.E. Annand).
11   *Government of State of Penang v Beng Hong Oon* [1972] AC 425, [1971] 3 All ER 1163.
12   *Southern Centre of Theosophy v State of South Australia* [1982] AC 706, [1982] 1 All ER 283.
13   *The Case of Swans* (1592) 7 Co Rep 15b at 17b.
14   Subject to what is said below.
15   *Blades v Higgs* (1865) 11 HL Cas 621.

Rights attaching to ownership

At common law the ownership of land brings with it certain rights.

Riparian rights

We have seen that the bed of non-tidal water belongs to the fee simple owner of the land adjacent to the water. (Such an owner is termed a 'riparian' owner.) Ownership of the bed carries with it certain rights concerning the water. These are termed riparian rights.

NAVIGATION[16]

The riparian owner has the exclusive right of navigation on the water that overlies his land. The public will, however, acquire rights of navigation if either (a) the riparian owners dedicate the water as a public highway, or (b) if statutes confer such rights on the public.

Over tidal water the public has a right of navigation, but this may be restricted by statute.[17]

FISHING

A riparian owner has an exclusive right of fishing.[18] He may grant the right to fish to another person or persons but the public cannot acquire any right to fish the water, even if it has fished the water over a long period, and even if it has a right of navigation over the water.[19] In tidal water the public has the right to fish unless the Crown has granted the exclusive right to a particular person or persons.

ABSTRACTION OF WATER

At common law a riparian owner had the right to extract percolating water without any restriction as to the amount he took. He could extract water which flowed through a defined channel (eg a river) for certain purposes and subject to certain restrictions.

The extraction of water from any source of supply (ie whether percolating water, eg from a well, or water flowing through a defined channel, eg a river) is not controlled by the Water Resources Act 1991[20] under which no person may[1]

---

16   [1985] JPEL 440 (S.E. Foster).
17   Eg under National Parks and Access to the Countryside Act 1949, s 20. See *Evans v Godber* [1974] 3 All ER 341, [1974] 1 WLR 1317.
18   See *Fothringham v Kerr* (1984) 48 P & CR 173.
19   *Pearce v Scotcher* (1882) 9 QBD 162.
20   Section 24, replacing Water Resources Act 1962.
 1   Except in the case of abstractions of small quantities (up to specified maxima) in particular circumstances, eg where the abstraction is for domestic purposes of the occupier's household or for agricultural purposes other than spray irrigation; section 27.

extract water from any source of supply unless he is permitted to do so by licence from what is now the Environment Agency.

The question whether a landowner has a right to take water (with or without a licence, as the case may be) must be distinguished from the question whether a landowner will be liable in tort if he causes subsidence to his neighbour's land by the extraction of water.[2]

FREEDOM FROM POLLUTION AND INTERFERENCE WITH FLOW

A riparian owner has a right to receive a flow of water unaltered in quality by higher riparian owners. Thus if a riparian owner pollutes the water by discharging chemicals into it, he infringes the rights of the lower riparian owners. Any of these can bring an action against him seeking an injunction to restrain him from further polluting the water, and for damages.

A riparian owner also has the right to receive a flow of water unaltered in quantity[3] by a higher riparian owner. Thus if a riparian owner diverts a river, or dams it, the lower owners have an action against him.[4]

We shall see in a later chapter, however, that it is possible that a riparian owner may *acquire* a right as against the lower owners to pollute the water or to alter the quantity of the flow, but even if the lower owners are for this reason prevented from taking action against him, steps may be taken against him under the Water Resources Act 1991 to prohibit him polluting the water, and under the same Act, to prevent him from altering the flow of water by extracting water or by building a dam otherwise than in accordance with the provisions of the Act.

Support

A landowner, O, has a right to have his ground supported both from beneath and from the side. For example, as regards support from beneath, if O sells a mineral vein beneath his land to N, and N mines the vein, N must maintain the support for the surface.[5] If N's operations cause the surface to sink, then O has an action (for the tort of nuisance) against N for any damage caused by the subsidence. As regards support from the side, if O and N own adjacent plots of land and N digs a quarry (or undertakes any other operation) on his

---

2 See *Bradford Corpn v Pickles* [1895] AC 587; *Langbrook Properties Ltd v Surrey County Council* [1969] 3 All ER 1424, [1970] 1 WLR 161; *Stephens v Anglian Water Authority* [1987] 3 All ER 379, [1987] 1 WLR 1381, [1988] LQR 183 (J. G. Fleming), [1988] Conv 175 (M. Harewood).

3 See *Tate and Lyle Industries Ltd v Greater London Council* [1983] 2 AC 509, [1983] 1 All ER 1159.

4 If the higher owner has obtained a licence under the Water Resources Act 1991, this is a defence to the action.

5 *Backhouse v Bonomi* (1861) 9 HL Cas 503; *Jordeson v Sutton, Southcoates and Drypool Gas Co* [1899] 2 Ch 217 (excavation on defendant's land penetrated underground stratum of quick-sand extending under plaintiff's land; drainage of quicksand by defendant caused subsidence of plaintiff's land: defendant liable).

land, and this causes O's land to subside, then here, too, O has a right of action against him for the removal of support.[6]

If there is a building on O's land, and it is damaged as a result of the withdrawal of support by N, then the position is that if (1) O's land would have subsided (by reason of the withdrawal of support) even without the added weight of the building on it, and if (2) the damage which would have been caused to O's land without a building on it would have been more than merely slight, then O can recover damages for the cost of damage to the buildings as well as to the land,[7] but if these conditions are not satisfied, O cannot claim for the damage to the building. Thus, if it was the additional weight of the building on the land that caused the land to subside, and the land would not have subsided if there had been no building on it, then O cannot claim for the damage to the building. This is because O's right extends only to having his land, not his buildings, supported. The reason why he can claim for damage to his building in the situation referred to above is that the damage to his building results from the infringement of his right to have his land supported.

If O has a right of action against N for infringement of his right of support then O can claim damages, and he can seek an injunction restraining N from the further withdrawal of support. He may also be able to obtain an order requiring N to restore the support which has been withdrawn, but where N has acted neither wantonly nor unreasonably, and the cost of restorative work would be out of all proportion to the advantage of the restoration to O, the court may refuse to make an order and will limit O's remedy to damages.[8]

If support for O's land is withdrawn as a result of natural causes on N's land (eg rain eroding N's land), O has no right of action against N for any damage which he, O, suffers. Thus O cannot require N to make good natural erosion of N's land. Nor has O any right of action if the damage to his land is caused by N abstracting percolating water from beneath his, N's, land, since at common law this is something that N is entitled to do.[9]

Restrictions on the freedom of the holder of a fee simple

We have seen that certain rights are by common law conferred on a holder of land. But the law also imposes certain restrictions. We can illustrate these restrictions by the following examples. Let us suppose that A holds Greenacre.

---

6   *Dalton v Angus* (1881) 6 App Cas 740.
7   *Stroyan v Knowles* (1861) 6 H & N 454.
8   *Redland Bricks Ltd v Morris* [1970] AC 652, [1969] 2 All ER 576.
9   *Popplewell v Hodkinson* (1869) LR 4 Exch 248; *Langbrook Properties Ltd v Surrey County Council* [1969] 3 All ER 1424, [1970] 1 WLR 161; *Stephens v Anglian Water Authority* [1987] 3 All ER 379, [1987] 1 WLR 1381, [1988] LQR 183, (J. G. Fleming), [1988] Conv 175 (M. Harwood).

1. If A makes a practice of burning motor car tyres on his land and this causes disturbance to his neighbour's enjoyment of his land (or if he commits any other act which constitutes the tort of nuisance) then his neighbour may sue him for damages, or seek an injunction to restrain him from committing the nuisance (or seek both remedies).

2. If A stores water in a reservoir on his land and the water escapes and damages his neighbour's land, his neighbour may sue him for damages in tort under the rule in *Rylands v Fletcher*.[10] (Under this rule a landowner is liable for damage caused by the escape from his land of anything which he has caused to be brought on to his land and which is likely to do mischief if it escapes.)

3. If A acts in a way which infringes a right of an owner of adjacent land (eg removing support from his neighbour's land), then he is liable in tort to the other landowner.

4. A may not kill certain types of bird on his land (eg golden eagles); others he may not kill during the close season (eg certain species of duck)(Wildlife and Countryside Act 1981). A may not use certain devices for the killing of deer on his land, and may not kill deer during the close season (Deer Act 1991). Various other animals are protected by other Acts; eg badgers by the Badgers Act 1973.

5. If A wishes to build a house on one of his fields (or to make any material change in the use to which the land is put) he must first obtain planning permission from the local planning authority (Town and Country Planning Act 1990).

6. If some of the buildings on A's land are in a dilapidated condition he may be ordered by the local authority to repair them. If they are insanitary he may be ordered to demolish them (Housing Acts 1957 to 1988).

7. If A leases a building or part of a building on his land, the maximum rent he charges may be subject to the provisions of the Rent Acts.[11] The same Acts may affect A's ability to eject a tenant, either at the end of a tenancy, or during a tenancy (eg for non-payment of rent).

8. If A dumps rubbish on his land he can be required to clear it by the local authority (Town and Country Planning Act 1990). If he dumps old cars (and certain other forms of refuse) on his land, he commits an offence and can be prosecuted (Civic Amenities Act 1967).

9. If A wishes to erect a sign saying 'Horses for Hire. Apply at the Farm' (or to erect any other notice or advertisement on his land which is visible to the public) then the sign must comply with the requirements (eg as to size, colour, etc) of the Town and Country Planning (Control of Advertisements) Regulations 1992.

10. If a local authority wishes the public to have a right of access to A's land, then failing a voluntary agreement between A and the authority, the authority has power to compel A to permit the public access to a specific part of the land, by making an 'access order' under powers conferred by the National Parks and Access to the Countryside Act 1949.

---

10   (1868) LR 3 HL 330.
11   See Chapter 17.

11. As we have seen, A may not extract water (either in the form of water flowing through a defined channel or in the form of percolating water), except in certain specified circumstances, unless he has a licence from a river authority. Nor ⸱may he build a well or a dam without a licence (Water Resources Act 1991).

12. If A's land lies within an area designated as a Conservation Area, then A may fell no tree nor demolish any building without consent from the local planning authority (Town and Country Planning Act 1990).

13. If the local authority has made a tree preservation order in respect of any tree on A's land the tree may not be felled without the consent of the local planning authority (Town and Country Planning Act 1990).

14. If any building on A's land has been included in the list of buildings of special architectural or historic interest drawn up (under the Town and Country Planning Acts) by the Secretary of State for the Environment, then the building may not be demolished or altered or extended without the consent of the local planning authority.

15. If A owns land by the sea and he extracts gravel or sand from the shore, then if A's activity has caused, or there is reason to fear that A's activity will cause erosion or encroachment by the sea,[12] the local authority has power to make an order under the Coastal Protection Act 1949. The effect of the order is to require A to apply for a licence from the local authority before continuing further extraction, thus enabling the authority to control the rate of extraction and impose any conditions it considers necessary to safeguard the coast.

16. If aircraft[13] fly over his land, A can bring no action either for trespass to his airspace or for nuisance, provided that the flight is at a height which is reasonable under the circumstances, and the relevant regulations are observed (Civil Aviation Act 1982).

17. The ownership of certain matters in the land (eg coal, petroleum) is vested in the Crown or in certain public bodies.

18. If the route of a proposed motorway lies across his land, A can be compelled to sell the land under a compulsory purchase order. There are a wide variety of purposes for which certain government departments, public authorities (particularly local authorities) and utility bodies (public and private) are given power to purchase land compulsorily. Compensation for land purchased compulsorily is, broadly, based on the value of the land according to its use prior to the compulsory purchase.

It will be seen that some of these restrictions arise from common law and the others from statute. It will be seen, too, that the restrictions range from what may be of little importance (eg 1) to the ultimate restriction – loss of the land itself (eg 18). (Some of the restrictions are of such importance, and the law relating to them of such complexity and extent that they form the subject of distinct branches of law: for example, planning law, the law of compulsory purchase, the law relating to public health, and to rent control and security of tenure.)

12   *British Dredging (Services) Ltd v Secretary of State for Wales* [1975] 1 WLR 687.
13   Including an aircraft which is being flown over A's land for the purpose of taking aerial photographs of A's land, with a view to offering the photographs for sale to A: *Baron Berstein of Leigh v Skyviews and General Ltd* [1978] QB 479, [1977] 2 All ER 902.

Modified fee simples

In dealing with the fee simple estate it remains to be explained that a fee simple may, in addition to existing in its normal form, exist in one or other of three modified forms. One of these we have already met, the base fee. This, it will be recalled, is a fee simple that ends when the fee tail from which it was derived would have ended if it had not been barred.[14] The other forms of modified fee simple are the determinable fee simple and the conditional fee simple. They share with the base fee the characteristic that they are fee simples that may be cut short before what would otherwise be their natural termination.[15]

The difference between a conditional and determinable fee simple can be explained in the following way. Suppose that a client, G, goes to his solicitor and says that he wishes to give land, Blackacre, to A on condition that A remains a JP, and that if A ceases to be a JP then he, G, should have the right to recover the land (by re-entering it) and that if he exercises this right, the fee simple should come to an end and become again vested in G. The solicitor makes out a conveyance which spells out the grant in the form that G has stipulated, the grant containing the words, ' ... to A in fee simple on condition that ... ' etc. The fee simple received by A is termed a conditional fee simple.

Now suppose that G tells his solicitor that he wishes to grant Greenacre to B in fee simple until B ceases to be Vicar of Wye, and that if B ceases to be the incumbent of this parish then at that moment the fee simple should (regardless of any action by G, regardless even of whether G has knowledge of the event) become vested again in G (with the result that if the land had been leased by B to a tenant, any rent due after B had ceased to be incumbent would be the property of G, not B). The solicitor makes out a conveyance which spells out the grant in the form that G has stipulated, the grant containing the words ' ... to B until ... etc'. The fee simple received by B is termed a determinable fee simple.

Originally, whenever a conditional or a determinable fee simple was granted, the full terms of the grant would have been spelled out. In the course of time, however, it became acceptable that words such as, 'on condition that ...', 'but if ... ', 'provided that ...', words that have the effect of latching a condition onto an otherwise complete fee simple, create a conditional fee simple (ie an estate that gives the grantor a right, in the circumstances specified, to bring the grantee's interest to an end by re-entering); and that words such as 'until ...', 'for as long as ...', 'during the continuance of ...', 'so long as .... ', words that specify the limit, the duration of the estate, the point of its termination, create a determinable fee simple (ie an estate that terminates automatically, and reverts to the grantor, on the occurrence of the event stipulated).

During the evolution of the doctrine of estates in land, conditional and determinable fees have become subject to different rules. It will be convenient

---

14   See p 39.
15   Ie on the death of a holder intestate and without statutory next of kin. See p 23.

at this point to set out the differences and similarities between the two estates in the form of the following tabulation. The first mentioned is included by way of recapitulation.

NATURE

Conditional fee simple	*Determinable fee simple*
A conditional fee simple is one that has some condition attached to it by which the fee simple estate may be cut short mid-flight.	A determinable fee simple is one that determines automatically on the happening of some event (which by its nature may never happen[16]). The event specified marks the boundary, the limit, of the estate.
A conditional fee simple is created not only by the words 'on condition that', but also by such words as 'provided that' or 'but if'.	A determinable fee simple is created not only by the word 'until', but also by such words as 'during', 'while', or 'as long as'; as in such grants as for 'as long as the church of St Paul shall stand';[17] for 'so long as the premises are used for the purpose of a public library';[18] to a school 'so long as it shall continue to be endowed with a charity';[19] to the incumbent of a church for 'as long as he shall permit all the sittings ... to be occupied free'.[20]
What matters is the effect of the words, taken in the context of the instrument in which they are used. If their effect is to introduce a *separate condition* which, if fulfilled, cuts short the estate granted, they created a conditional fee simple.	
Turning to the differences between the two forms of grant, we find that in the case of a conditional fee simple the courts have adopted strict rules as to the conditions they will accept as being valid.	If the words used *mark the limit* of the estate which has been granted, they create a determinable fee simple. In the case of a determinable fee simple, the courts have adopted a less stringent attitude.[1]

RESTRAINTS ON ALIENATION

In the case of a conditional fee simple, a condition that cuts short the fee simple on the holder alienating the land is void. Thus in a grant 'to E in fee simple on condition that he does not sell the land', the condition is void.[2] So too are conditions such as 'on condition	In the case of a determinable fee simple, on the other hand, a restraint on the holder alienating the land is valid.[3] Thus grants 'to A in fee simple until he sells the land'; or 'to A in fee simple until, during the lifetime of X, he sells the land'; or 'to A in fee simple until he

---

16   Challis, p 251.
17   *Walsingham's Case* (1579) 2 Plowd 547 at 557.
18   *Hopper v Corpn of Liverpool* (1943) 88 Sol Jo 213.
19   *A–G v Pyle* (1738) 1 Atk 435.
20   *Re Randell* (1888) 38 Ch D 213.
 1   *Brandon v Robinson* (1811) 18 Ves 429.
 2   *Re Wilkinson* [1926] Ch 842.
 3   *Hood v Oglander* (1865) 34 Beav 513 at 322.

Conditional fee simple	*Determinable fee simple*
that he does not sell the land during X's life';[4] or 'that he does not sell the land to anyone but X'; or, 'that he does not make a devise of the land'; or 'that he does not mortgage the land'.[6] These conditions are all void. However, some conditions which amount to only a partial restraint on alienation have been held to be valid; for example, a grant of land to X 'on condition that he never sells out of the family', was held[8] to be valid.	sells the land to anyone other than X'; or, 'to A in fee simple until he mortgages the land', would all be valid.

RESTRAINTS ON DEVOLUTION

Similarly, in the case of a conditional fee simple, a condition cutting short the fee simple in the event of the land following a course of devolution prescribed by law is void.	In the case of a determinable fee simple, the law here too takes a more tolerant view, and restraints against a course of devolution prescribed by law are valid.

For example, if land is granted to E, and E dies intestate, the law prescribes that the land should pass to E's next of kin. Thus a grant 'to E in fee simple on condition that if E dies intestate the fee simple shall come to an end', attempts to place a restriction on the course of devolution prescribed by law. The condition is therefore void.[9]

RESTRAINTS ON BANKRUPTCY

Similarly, if E holds land and he goes bankrupt, the law prescribes that the land is to pass to his trustee in bankruptcy (who will sell the land and distribute the money among E's creditors). Thus a condition in a grant 'to E in fee simple on condition that he does not commit an act of bankruptcy', is void.[10]	A grant 'to E in fee simple until he commits an act of bankruptcy', on the other hand, is valid.

RESTRAINTS ON MARRIAGE

Following the same pattern, in the case of a conditional fee simple, a restraint on the holder marrying is void. Thus in a grant 'to E in fee simple on condition that he never marries', the condition is void. However, what amount to only partial restraints have been held to be valid.	In the case of a determinable fee simple, the law again takes a more tolerant view, and restraints against marriage, whether partial or total, are valid. Thus a grant 'to E in fee simple until he marries', is valid.[11]

4   *Re Cockerill* [1929] 2 Ch 131.
5   *Re Brown* [1954] Ch 39, [1953] 2 All ER 1342; (M & B).
6   *Re Jones* [1898] 1 Ch 438.
7   *Ware v Cann* (1830) 10 B & C 433.
8   *Re Macleay* (1875) LR 20 Eq 186.
9   *Re Dixon* [1903] 2 Ch 458.
10   *Re Machu* (1882) 21 Ch D 838.
11   *Morley v Rennoldson* (1843) 2 Hare 570 at 580.

Conditional fee simple

For example, conditions against marrying a particular person,[12] or a Roman Catholic,[13] or a Scotsman,[14] were all held to be valid. Further, a condition that a donee should lose his interest on marriage (or re-marriage) will not be void if the purpose of the gift is to provide for the donee while single (or while a widow or widower).[15]

PUBLIC POLICY

A condition in a conditional fee simple is void if it is contrary to public policy. Thus a condition in a grant to W (a wife separated from her husband) in fee simple 'on condition that she never returns to her husband' is void.[16] So also is a condition against undertaking public office,[17] or entering one of the armed forces.[18]

CERTAINTY

Further, the condition in a conditional fee simple is void if the meaning of the words used is not sufficiently certain. For example, a grant to a donee on condition that he continued 'to reside in Canada' was held to be void because of the uncertainty attaching to the word 'reside'.[19] The reason for this rule is that it must be possible to ascertain from the moment of the creation of the fee simple what event will constitute the occurrence of the condition specified,[20] but if the meaning of the words used is clear, then the mere fact that there may in practice be difficulty in determining whether the condition has been fulfilled will not disturb the validity of the condition.[1] (In the event of doubt, a ruling can be obtained from the court.)

Determinable fee simple

A determinable fee simple is similarly void if it is contrary to public policy. Thus a grant 'to W (a wife separated from her husband) until she returns to her husband', is void.

Similarly, the grant of a determinable fee simple is void unless there is certainty as to what terminates the estate.[2]

---

12 *Re Hanlon* [1933] Ch 254.
13 *Duggan v Kelly* (1848) 10 I Eq R 295.
14 *Perrin v Lyon* (1807) 9 East 170. See also *Jenner v Turner* (1880) 16 Ch D 188.
15 *Jones v Jones* (1876) 1 QBD 279; *Re Hanson* [1928] Ch 96. See also *Re Hewett* [1918] 1 Ch 458.
16 See *Re Johnson's Will Trusts* [1967] Ch 387, [1967] 1 All ER 553.
17 *Re Edgar* [1939] 1 All ER 635.
18 *Re Beard* [1908] 1 Ch 383.
19 *Clavering v Ellison* (1859) 7 HL Cas 707.
20 *Sifton v Sifton* [1938] AC 656, [1938] 3 All ER 435; but use of the word 'reside' (or 'residence') will not necessarily entail invalidity due to uncertainty (*Re Gape's Will Trusts* [1952] Ch 743, [1952] 2 All ER 579), particularly where the word is used in connection with a particular house: *Re Coxen* [1948] Ch 747, [1948] 2 All ER 492.
1   Similarly, a clause in a will that provided that a beneficiary's interest should end if she married a person 'not of Jewish parentage and of the Jewish faith' was held to be void for uncertainty. *Clayton v Ramsden* [1943] AC 320, [1943] 1 All ER 16. Cf *Blathwayt v Baron Cawley* [1976] AC 397, [1975] 3 All ER 625, in which the phrase 'be a Roman Catholic' was found not to be void for uncertainty. See also *Tepper's Will Trust* [1987] Ch 358, [1987] 1 All ER 970.
2   *Re Gape's Will Trust* [1952] Ch 743, [1952] 2 All ER 579 (continuance of gift dependent on 'permanent residence is England' held to be valid).

Conditional fee simple	*Determinable fee simple*

RESULT OF VOIDNESS

In the case of a conditional fee simple, if the condition is void (for any of the reasons set out above) then the condition is struck out leaving the fee simple free of the condition.

In the case of a determinable fee simple, if the determining event is void then the *whole grant* is void. This is because the duration of the estate cannot be ascertained. (Just as it is not possible to have a field without a boundary, so it is not possible to have an estate without a limit marking its extent.)

Thus in the case of the grant on condition that the donee continues 'to reside in Canada', the condition is struck out leaving the donee with a fee simple free of any restriction.[3]

In the case of a grant 'to E until he ceases to reside in Canada', the whole grant is void, and E gets nothing.

OCCURRENCE OF THE SPECIFIED EVENT

Regarding the result if the determining event occurs, if R grants land 'to E in fee simple on condition that he continues to be enrolled as a solicitor', and E is struck off the roll, then the fee simple does not end automatically, but continues until R re-enters the land.[4] Originally there had to be physical re-entry by R, but now the re-entry can be made by written notification by R to E.

In the case of a determinable fee simple, if the determining event occurs (ie *reverter* occurs), then the fee simple ends automatically and reverts to R (or, if R is dead, to his estate), without any step being taken at all.[5]

Regarding the significance of the way in which the fee simple comes to an end, if (using the example above) E holds a conditional fee simple, and he is struck off the roll and R does not discover this until six months later, and only then re-enters, any rent paid in respect of the land during that six months belongs to E, not R. R only obtains the right to the rent from the time he re-enters.

If R grants E a determinable fee simple and E leases the land to T at £100 a month then, from the moment the fee simple is cut short, the rent paid is the property of R. (If T pays the rent to E, E must hand it over to R.)

IMPOSSIBILITY

If it becomes impossible for the condition specified to occur, the fee simple becomes absolute. For example, if R grants land 'to E in fee simple on condition that he does not marry X' and X dies, the fee simple becomes absolute.

Similarly, if it becomes impossible for the determining event to occur, the fee simple becomes absolute.[6]

---

3   *Sifton v Sifton* [1938] AC 656, [1938] 3 All ER 435.
4   Challis, pp 252, 260. *A-G v Shadwell* [1910] 1 Ch 92; *Re Rowhook Mission Hall, Horsham* [1985] Ch 62, [1984] 3 All ER 179, not following *Re Clayton's Deed Poll* [1980] Ch 99, [1979] 2 All ER 1133.
5   *Manning's Case* (1609) 8 Co Rep 94b at 95b.
6   *Re Leach* [1912] 2 Ch 422 at 429.

| Conditional fee simple | Determinable fee simple |

ALIENATION OF THE FEE SIMPLE

A conditional fee simple may be alienated inter vivos or by will but, since the grantee or devisee can receive no more than the grantor or devisor held, the grantee or devisee will hold a conditional fee simple, ie a fee simple which can be brought to an end on the occurrence of the event specified.

Similarly, a determinable fee simple may be alienated inter vivos or by will, the recipient then holding the determinable fee simple.

THE INTEREST RETAINED BY THE GRANTOR

If R grants E a conditional fee simple, the interest retained by R is termed a right of re-entry.

If R grants E a determinable fee simple the interest retained by R is termed a *possibility of reverter* or a *right of reverter*. E is termed a *revertee*.

At common law, a right of re-entry was not alienable inter vivos; nor was it alienable by will. When R died it passed to his heir. A right of re-entry became alienable by will under the Wills Act 1837,[7] and alienable inter vivos under the Real Property Act 1845.[8]

At common law, a possibility of reverter was not alienable inter vivos, nor was it alienable by will. When R died it passed to his heir. A possibility of reverter probably became alienable by will under the Law of Property Act 1925,[9] and possibly alienable inter vivos under the same Act.

ADDITION OF REMAINDERS

Before 1926 it was not possible to add a remainder after a conditional fee simple, though after the Real Property Act 1845 there was nothing to stop the grantor of the conditional fee simple granting away the right of re-entry, and thus, in effect, creating a remainder.
Under the Law of Property Act 1925[10] it became possible to grant away the right of re-entry at the same moment as the grant of the conditional fee simple. The effect is that it is now possible to add a remainder to a conditional fee simple, eg a grant 'to E in fee simple, but if he ceases to be enrolled as a solicitor, to George'.

In the case of a determinable fee simple it is possible to grant an interest following the determinable fee. Thus there can be a grant 'to E in fee simple until he ceases to be a solicitor, and then over to George'. The gift to George is termed a 'gift over' (not a 'remainder').

The following further points call for attention.

1. A grant to A in fee simple 'until A dies' confers on A not a determinable fee simple, but a life estate. Where the grant is to A in fee simple until the death of B, then A receives a life estate *pur autre vie* (ie for the life of B).

7   Section 3.
8   Section 6.
9   Section 4(2).
10   Section 4(3).

2. Where G grants land to A in fee simple until the happening of some event which is fixed in point of time[11] (eg to A in fee simple until the date of the tercentenary of the founding of the University of Adney), A receives a term of years, ie a lease for the period concerned.

3. In view of (1) and (2) above it will be seen that the event that terminates a determinable fee simple must be one that by its nature may never happen. If the event is one that is bound to happen, eg the death of a specified person, or the arrival of a certain date (eg the date of the tercentenary of the founding of the University of Adney), then no determinable fee simple is created, since 'it is an essential characteristic of all fees, that they may possibly endure for ever'.[12] However, whilst the law takes a realistic view of human mortality (regarding it as certain that all humans are bound to die), it is less realistic about the endurability of material objects. Thus in the case of a grant in fee simple for as long as a certain tree stood, although it could be argued that it was in reality certain that the tree would not stand for ever (with the result that no estate in fee, ie no determinable fee simple, would pass) the grant was none the less accepted[13] as conferring a valid determinable fee simple.[14]

4. The limitations of determinable and conditional interests relate to the *ending* of the interest granted, once it has begun. An interest that is determinable or conditional must be distinguished from the grant of an interest that is subject to a condition *precedent*, ie a condition that must be satisfied before the interest begins: eg to 'A in fee simple if he attains 21'; to 'the first son of A to marry for life'; to 'A in fee simple when he is called to the Bar'. An interest that is subject to a condition precedent may, in addition, be made conditional or determinable: thus there could, for example, be a conditional life interest subject to a condition precedent; or a determinable fee simple subject to a condition precedent; eg 'to A in fee simple when he attains 21', 'until the land ceases to be used for agricultural purposes'. When distinguishing a condition which relates to the ending of an interest from a condition precedent, the condition is referred to as 'a condition subsequent'.[15] Conditions precedent are considered further in Chapter 13.

5. The Sites for Schoolrooms Act 1836 was enacted in order to encourage and facilitate the granting of land to trustees for the purpose of enabling elementary schools for the poor to be established. The 1836 Act was replaced by the School Sites Act of 1841, the provisions of which were amended and supplemented by the School Sites Acts of 1844, 1849, 1851 and 1852. Under the 1841 Act, if A holds a fee simple absolute, or a life estate, or a fee tail, and he grants land of up to one acre in extent to trustees on trust to provide a site for a school, the trustees receive a full fee simple in the land.[16] (If A holds a life interest or a fee tail, the consent of the person next entitled to the land is

---

11 Challis, p 252.
12 Challis, p 251.
13 *Idle v Cook* (1705) 1 P Wms 70 at 75.
14 Similarly, a grant in fee simple 'as long as the Church of St Paul shall stand' created a valid determinable fee simple. *Walsingham's Case* (1579) 2 Plowd 547 at 557.
15 (1990) 106 LQR 185 (G. H. Treitel).
16 Section 2.

required.) The Act provides that upon the land granted ceasing to be used for the purpose specified in the grant, it reverts to the person entitled as if the grant had not been made.[17] (If that person has died, the interest passes to his estate.) The legislation thus provides for the creation of a determinable fee simple.[18]

In order to deal with the problem[19] of reverters becoming exercisable very many years after the original grant[20] (when the identity of the person entitled to the reverter might not be known), the Reverter of Sites Act 1987[1] (as amended[2]) provides[3] that where a reverter arises under a relevant enactment,[4] the land is to be held by the person in whom it was vested before the reverter, as trustee, on trust for the persons 'who but for this Act would from time to time be entitled to the ownership of the land by virtue of its reverter with a power, without consulting them, to sell the land' and hold the proceeds for those persons (but with no entitlement for them to occupy the land).

With regard to the identity of the person or persons entitled under the Act, suppose that G grants a plot of land on his country estate for use as a school. G later sells the estate to P. The school closes. Who, under the Act, is entitled to the land? Is it G (or, if he has died, the person to whom he devised the reverter), or is it P (or if he no longer holds the estate, the person who does now hold it)? In *Marchant v Onslow* [5] it was held that in the circumstances set out above, ie where the land granted was carved out of a larger land holding, it is the current holder of the surrounding land who is entitled. Where the land granted was not so carved out of a larger estate, it is the grantor (or the person to whom the grantor assigned the reverter or, if the grantor has died, the person to whom the reverter passed under the grantor's will or intestacy) who is entitled. The devolution of property on the termination of the determinable fee simple therefore depends on the evidence before the court as to whether the land granted is or is not to be regarded as having been carved out of a larger estate, evidence that may include, for example, maps and plans drawn up a century or more earlier. The decision represents a departure from the principle of English law that the devolution of property is determined by rules of law, not by matters of evidence, as to the proper interpretation of which opinions may differ.

---

17   Ibid. No words are required to create the reverter. All that is required is the presence of an intention to make a grant under the Act. See *Imperial Tobacco v Wilmott* [1964] 2 All ER 510, [1964] 1 WLR 902.

18   The provisions of the School Sites Act were followed in relation to the provision of sites for libraries and museums by the Literary and Scientific Institutions Act 1854, and for churches and chapels by the Places of Worship Sites Act 1873.

19   [1980] Conv 186 (C. J. Allen, S. Christie).

20   As in *Re Clayton's Deed Poll* [1980] Ch 99, [1979] 2 All ER 1133 and in cases cited therein.

1   Enacted after consideration by the Law Commission: *Property Law: Right of Reverter* (Law Com No 111, 1981).

2   By the Trusts of Land and Appointment of Trustees Act 1996, s 5, Sch 2.

3   Section 1.

4   See n 18, supra.

5   [1994] 2 All ER 707, [1974] 3 WLR 607; [1994] Conv 489 (J. Hill).

Where, at the date of the Act, the claim of the person entitled was statute barred[6] (ie because he had failed to claim the land within twelve years from the date of his becoming entitled to do so) the trustee holds the land for the purpose of securing a scheme, to be made by the Charity Commissioners, under which the land is to be held for the charitable purpose specified in the scheme. Where the claim is not statute barred, the trustee has power (for example, if he is unable after reasonable enquiries to trace the person entitled) to apply for a scheme which extinguishes the reverter holder's interest and provides for the land to be held for a charitable purpose specified in the scheme.[7]

6. Any fee simple which is not modified in any way is termed a fee simple *absolute*. A fee simple that is not absolute is termed a *modified* fee simple. Conditional and determinable fee simples are thus two forms of modified fee simple. Another form of modified fee simple is the 'base fee' (derived from a fee tail), considered in the last chapter. Fee simples can thus be classified as follows:

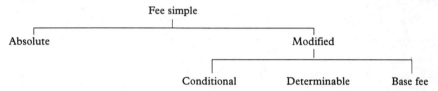

It should be noted that the classification of fee simple (explained in Chapter 3) into fee simple in possession, in remainder and in reversion is distinct from the classification – absolute, conditional, determinable. If A grants Blackacre to B for life with remainder to C in fee simple, C's fee simple is a fee simple in remainder, but it is not modified in any way – it is not conditional or determinable, so it is fee simple absolute in remainder; but unless there is a need to distinguish a fee simple absolute from a modified fee simple, we omit the word 'absolute' and speak of a 'fee simple'.

Similarly, if we have no need to distinguish between a fee simple in possession and a fee simple in remainder (or in reversion), we leave out the words 'in possession' and just speak of a fee simple. Thus where we speak of 'a fee simple', without adding further words, the implication is that the fee simple is both absolute and in possession.

7. Interests other than a fee simple can exist in a conditional or determinable form. For example, there can be a conditional or determinable life interest.

The rules considered in the case of the fee simple apply equally to a determinable life interest, the only variations stemming from the nature of a life interest. Thus,

---

6　See Chapter 24.
7　Section 2. If the reverter holder objects within five years he is entitled to receive compensation for the loss of his interest.

A grant 'to A for life, on condition that he never marries' would (since the condition is void) confer on A a life interest free from the condition.

A grant 'to A for life or until he marries' would (since the restraint is here valid) confer on A a determinable life interest.[8]

Thus a grant 'to E for life, but if he ceases to be enrolled as a solicitor, then over to X', creates a conditional life interest.

A grant 'to E for life until he ceases to be enrolled as a solicitor, then over to X', creates a determinable life interest.

RECAPITULATION

To get matters straight, what, again, just *is* a fee simple? It is a period of time during which land is held from the Crown, the period (since 1926) enduring until a holder of the land dies intestate and without having a relative in the list set out in the Administration of Estates Act 1925,[9] the land at this point reverting to the Crown.

SUMMARY

A fee simple is a period of time during which land is held from the Crown, the period (since 1925) enduring until a holder of the land dies intestate and without having a relative in the list set out in the Administation of Estates Act 1925, the land at this point reverting to the Crown.

At common law, cuius est solum eius usque ad caelum ad inferos. There are exceptions.

A fixture is something that, formerly a chattel, has become part of the land. The degree of annexation decides the burden of proof. The purpose of annexation determines the result.

Land may be divided horizontally as well as vertically.

Certain (principally common law) rights attach to ownership of land, and certain (principally statutory) restrictions limit what an owner may do.

Modified fee simples comprise conditional fee simples, determinable fee simples and base fees.

A conditional fee simple is one to which a condition is attached by which the estate may be cut short.

A determinable fee simple is one that determines on the occurrence of a specified event.

Rules relating to restraints on alienation, restraints on devolution, the result of voidness, and occurrence of the specified event differ as between conditional and determinable fee simples.

Rules relating to public policy, certainty, impossibility and alienation apply to conditional and determinable fee simples alike.

The Reverter of Sites Act 1987 deals with the problem of reverters that become exercisable long after the grant.

8   Challis, p 256.
9   Section 46, as amended by the Intestates' Estates Act 1952, the Administration of Justice Act 1977 and the Statute Law (Repeals) Act 1981.

CHAPTER 5

Trusts and Equitable Interests

THE NATURE OF A TRUST

The year is 1300. A is going to Italy. He expects to be away for two years. He leaves behind him his young wife, B. Who is to manage his land, Blackacre, while he is away? A bailiff can be appointed to look after the day to day running of his farm but who is to take important decisions? Who is to take any necessary legal proceedings? A decides to ask his brother, T (which in this chapter represents 'trustee'), to look after his land while he is away. T agrees. A therefore transfers the fee simple in Blackacre to T to hold the land on trust for B until such time as he should return from Italy, and then to transfer the fee simple back to him, but if he dies to transfer the fee simple to B.

What today we call a trust has been created. A grantor, A, has transferred property, Blackacre, to a person whom today we call a trustee, T, to hold for the benefit of a beneficiary, B, subject to the conditions stated.

It was, in fact, and still is, often the practice when creating a trust to transfer the property to two (or more) trustees. We shall see the reason for this later.

In this book the creation of a trust will be represented like this:

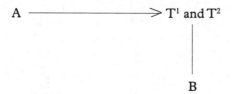

$$A \longrightarrow T^1 \text{ and } T^2$$

$$B$$

Let us consider another example. A is leaving for France. He wishes to give his farm Greenacre to his nephew B before he goes, but B is only seven years old. A therefore conveys the fee simple in Greenacre to two trustees, T^1 and T^2, on trust for B.

If T^1 and T^2 later leased the land and, instead of keeping the rent for B, spent it on themselves, they would be acting in breach of trust, but if B sought a remedy against T^1 and T^2 he would be told by the court: 'A conveyed the fee simple to T^1 and T^2, not to you. T^1 and T^2 are the legal holders of the fee simple. They can therefore do as they wish with the rents they collect. They may be under a moral duty to account to you for the rents, but this court does not enforce moral obligations. This is not a court of conscience. In the eyes of the law you have no interest in the land. This court can give you no remedy.'

A beneficiary under a trust thus originally had no remedy in law if the trustees acted in breach of trust. In the course of time beneficiaries who sought redress began to petition the King and his Council for a remedy, the King being the fountainhead of justice. The King came to refer to such petitions to the Lord Chancellor. The Lord Chancellor heard these petitions and might grant a decree ordering the trustees to carry out their trust. It later became the practice for petitions to be addressed direct to the Lord Chancellor. In the exercise of this jurisdiction, the Lord Chancellor came to be regarded as holding his own court, a court different and distinct from the courts of common law. The Lord Chancellor's court became known as the Court of Chancery.

In hearing petitions from those who were unable to obtain a remedy before the courts of common law, the Lords Chancellor evolved certain principles. At first these were little more than rules of guidance, but by the nineteenth century they had hardened into a rigid and systematic body of law.

Thus the common law courts administered the rules of common law, and the Court of Chancery administered the rules of equity. We can therefore say that at common law trustees of a trust were regarded as the true owners of the property and a beneficiary had no remedy against them if they acted in breach of trust. Equity, on the other hand, compelled the trustees to carry out the trust, ie to account to the beneficiaries for all the benefits of ownership. Equity did not deny that the trustees were the owners at common law, but required them to carry out their trust. If A granted Greenacre to T on trust for B, equity compelled T to allow B to enjoy the benefits of ownership – the rents and profits from the land, or (at T's discretion[1]) occupation of the land itself.

Thus we say that whilst T is the legal owner, holding the legal estate in the land, B is the beneficiary, or equitable owner, holding the equitable estate in the land.

By virtue of holding the legal estate T has the right, indeed the duty, to control and manage the land. If the land is to be leased, then it is T who executes the lease. Thus if T leased the land to X for £10 a year, X would pay the rent to T; and T would hand the rent (as one of the benefits of the land) to B, if he was old enough (originally 21) to receive the money. If he was not, he would retain it for him. (In time there arose a duty to invest the money, so that it earned interest and was not merely lying idle.)

So when we speak of T being the legal owner and B being the equitable owner there is no conflict within the statement; there is merely a description of division of function; management rests with T, enjoyment with B. Any confusion that might be produced by referring to T as the legal 'owner', when we know that the real owner is B, is avoided if we refrain from using the words 'owner' and 'ownership' (words which, as we noted earlier, had no place in the original law) and speak of T holding the legal estate, and of B holding the equitable estate.

What kind of legal estate T holds depends on what kind of estate A granted to him. Normally it would be a fee simple estate that A would have conveyed, but there is no reason why originally it should not have been a life estate or even a fee tail.[2]

---

1   See *Re Earl of Stamford and Warrington* [1925] Ch 162; *Re Bagot's Settlement* [1894] 1 Ch 177.
2   The position is now different. See Chapter 6.

'Equity follows the law'

We have said that the trustee or trustees hold the land 'on trust for B', and that B holds an equitable estate. The kind of equitable estate that B holds depends on the form of A's grant. If the grant had been 'on trust for B' before 1926, since no words of limitation were added,[3] B would have taken merely a life estate. If common law words were used, they were applied strictly in construing what estate was created, but equity did not insist on the use of the strict common law words. For example, 'on trust for B absolutely' gave B an equitable fee simple.

In Chapter 3 we saw that if a person held a fee simple estate then, before 1926, on his death intestate the land devolved to his heir. If A granted land to trustees on trust for B for a fee simple estate, and B died intestate, B's heir would become the beneficiary under the trust, the common law rules regarding estates being borrowed by equity and applied to the interests of beneficiaries under a trust.

Originally trusts were of a simple character, but ultimately it became possible to create a succession of interests under a trust. For example A might grant Blackacre 'to T[1] and T[2] and their heirs (in fee simple) on trust for B for life (a life estate), with remainder to C and the heirs of his body (in fee tail) with remainder to D and his heirs (in fee simple)'. Thus:

T[1] and T[2]   Legal fee simple

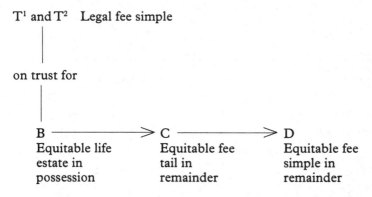

on trust for

B ⟶ C ⟶ D
Equitable life   Equitable fee   Equitable fee
estate in   tail in   simple in
possession   remainder   remainder

Equity applied the common law rules to each of these equitable interests. Thus if C, who held an equitable fee tail in remainder, barred the fee tail without the consent of B (ie he used a fine) and transferred his interest to X, X took a base fee – an equitable base fee. X's equitable base fee would then continue for as long as C's (equitable) fee tail would have continued if it had not been barred.[4]

Further, the common law rules with regard to waste were applied to equitable interests under a trust. Thus if A granted land to trustees on trust for B for life with remainder to C in fee simple, B was subject to the common law rules regarding waste.

---

3   See Chapter 3.
4   Ibid.

Thus with regard to (a) the rules governing the different forms of estate; (b) the rules of waste and (c) the rules applicable to the common law words of limitation (if these were used), equity adopted the rules that had been evolved by the common law, and applied them to the interests of persons entitled under a trust. This is what is meant by the statement 'Equity follows the law', but it should be noted that equity only followed common law rules where it chose to do so, and at various points in the law we meet instances in which equity has elected not to follow the common law: indeed, we have mentioned one already; namely, that equity did not insist on the use of the strict common law words of limitation. Another important divergence between the rules of common law and equity will be met when dealing with mortgages.[5]

Separate devolution of the legal estate and the equitable interests under it

Each of the two forms of estate, legal and equitable, followed its own course of devolution. Suppose that in 1995[6] A conveyed Blackacre to T in fee simple on trust for B for life with remainder to C in fee tail, with remainder to D in fee simple, we can trace an imaginary subsequent devolution of the legal and equitable estates like this:

	1	2	3	4	5
Legal estate	T dies leaving all his property to U; U then holds the legal fee simple			U dies intestate. The fee simple in Blackacre passes to U's heir V	
Equitable estate		B dies. C holds the equitable fee tail in possession	C dies. C's only child, X, holds the equitable fee tail in possession		X dies without issue. D holds the equitable fee simple in possession

The final result[7] is that V holds the legal fee simple on trust for D for an equitable fee simple.

Termination of a trust

The trust does not come to an end automatically at that point. Until the trustee, V, takes the appropriate step the trust continues, V holding on trust for D. The

---

5   See Chapter 23.
6   Ie, prior to the prevention of the creation of interests in fee tail by the Trusts of Land and Appointment and Trustees Act 1996.
7   Subject to what is said in later chapters.

trust ends when the trustee, V, transfers the legal fee simple to D. D will then hold the legal fee simple, with which his previous equitable interest merges.

The rule in *Saunders v Vautier*[8]

This brings us to a rule of fundamental importance in English land law. The rule is this. Where, in the story of a trust, the point is reached when the trustees hold on trust for a person who is of full age and is absolutely entitled, that person can require the trustees to convey the legal estate to him (so ending the trust). 'Absolutely entitled' means holding the entire equitable interest, eg a fee simple absolute (ie not conditional or determinable or subject to a condition precedent). So, in the example above, on X's death D can demand that the fee simple should be transferred to him, and the trust put at an end.

The rule applies equally where two or more persons are of full age and between them absolutely entitled, and it applies to all forms of property, real and personal. So if trustees hold 10,000 shares in a company on trust for A (who is 16) for life, with remainder to B, when A attains 18 he and B (if he too is 18) can, since between them they are entitled to the entire equitable interest, put an end to the trust, requiring the trustees to transfer the shares to them as they direct (eg one-quarter to A and three-quarters to B).

Meaning of 'in possession'

It will be noted that (in the example above) until D called on V to convey the legal estate to him (thus terminating the trust), V would have held a legal fee simple absolute in possession (in possession because it is not in remainder or in reversion). When C's son, X, died and the fee tail ended, D then held an equitable fee simple absolute in possession. There can thus be two fee simples absolute in possession, one legal and one equitable.

How, it may be asked, if V held a fee simple absolute in possession (a legal one) and so did D (an equitable one) could they *both* be in possession – who in fact was in physical possession of the land? Here we stand on the edge of heresy. The words 'in possession' in this context do not necessarily have anything to do with who is in actual possession, ie physical occupation, of the land. The words 'in possession' merely indicate that the estate is not in remainder or in reversion. So when V holds on trust for D, V is in possession of the legal estate, and D is in possession of the equitable estate. Who is in actual physical possession of the land is a different matter: it might be one of various people. If the land had been leased to T, then T would be in possession of the land. If X had been living on the land, when X died D might have moved on to it (as beneficiary he is entitled to the benefits of the land and is entitled[9] to occupy the land).

---

8 (1841) 4 Beav 115.
9 Prior to the Trusts of Land and Appointment of Trustees Act 1996, at V's discretion; after the Act, by a right conferred by the Act, s 12; see Chapter 11.

Beneficial owner

Suppose that A granted land to T on trust for B for life with remainder to C in fee simple. The land produces an income of £100 a year. The money is paid by T to B. B may then think 'I don't need this money. My nephew D needs the money more than I do. I will transfer my right to this money (ie my equitable life estate under the trust) to t [another trustee] to hold on trust for D', and so he does.

What has happened (omitting C's equitable fee simple in remainder) is this:

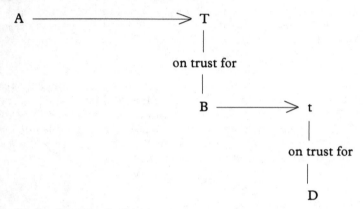

So the final pattern is this:

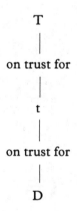

A 'sub-trust', as it were, has come into existence. The interest which t holds is the equitable life interest that B conveyed to him. (Since the life is that of B, it is an equitable life interest *pur autre vie*.) D holds an equitable life interest *pur autre vie* (B's life) also. Thus t is a trustee as well as T, but he holds on trust for D. The ultimate beneficiary is D. D is said to be the *beneficial owner* – since he is the person entitled to the benefit from the land. t is not the beneficial owner, since he holds his interest on trust for D. This is why a person holding an equitable interest (in our example, t) is not necessarily always the beneficial owner.

If a person holds an interest in property, and he holds it free of any trust, then he is the beneficial owner. In the above example, before A granted the fee simple to T on trust for B and C for their respective interests, A was the beneficial owner. When he created the trust, B and C were the beneficial owners, for their respective interests. When B transferred his equitable interest to t on trust for D, D and C were the beneficial owners.

So these statements can be made:

1. The interest of a beneficiary (ie a person entitled under a trust) is always equitable.
2. The interest of a beneficial owner (ie a person who does not hold on trust for anyone else) may be legal, *or* equitable, according to the circumstances.

The word 'benefici*ally*' (which is an adverb describing how a beneficial owner holds property) should not be confused with 'benefici*ary*' (which is a noun describing a person who holds an interest under a trust).

With this in mind, we can go on to say:

1. A beneficiary generally holds beneficially (ie unless there is a 'sub-trust');
2. A beneficial owner is by no means always a beneficiary.

Bare trusts

The meaning of the term 'bare trust' must also be explained. A bare trust is one under which the trustees have no duty to perform (eg no duty to sell the property and invest the proceeds) and under which the beneficiary is of full age and absolutely entitled (or under which the beneficiaries are all of full age and absolutely entitled). For example, if T^1 and T^2 hold on trust for A for life with remainder to B, when A dies, if B is of full age, the trust becomes a bare trust. Under the rule in *Saunders v Vautier*[10] B can put an end to the trust by requiring the trustees to convey the legal title to him.

If, on the other hand, T and T_2 hold property on trust to sell it and hold the proceeds for A for life with remainder to B, and A dies before the property has been sold, the trustees, still having a duty to perform, would not hold on a bare trust for B. B could, however, under the rule in *Saunders v Vautier* require the trustees to transfer the legal title in the property to him since he is (we here assume) of full age, and he is absolutely entitled.

Whenever a bare trust exists, the rule in *Saunders v Vautier* will apply. But the rule in *Saunders v Vautier* is not confined to instances when the trust is a bare trust. (The fact that the trustees are under some form of continuing duty, eg to sell, does not prevent the beneficiaries from being absolutely entitled to the entire equitable interest.)

Whether a trust is or is not a bare trust is only rarely significant. The application of the rule in *Saunders v Vautier* is frequently a matter of importance.

---

10   (1841) 4 Beav 115. See p 79.

THE BONA FIDE PURCHASER RULE

Originally a trust was enforceable only against the trustees who undertook the trust. Thus, if A granted Greenacre Farm to T^1 and T^2 on trust for B, and in breach of the trust (because A had given them no power to sell the land), T^1 and T^2 sold the farm to a purchaser (P), then B could sue T^1 and T^2 and recover damages for breach of trust, but he lost his interest in the farm. (We say that P took the legal fee simple 'free' from B's equitable interest.) However, if:

1. B could find the trustees;
2. if they were solvent (ie they had not spent all the money received from P and all their own money as well); and
3. if B had no special reason for wanting the farm, rather than money instead,

then he did not lose. He could sue the trustees and recover from them the purchase money paid by P.

On the other hand, if the trustees had disappeared, or if they were insolvent, B had no remedy, and even if the trustees were solvent and B could find them, money might be a poor substitute if B had special reasons for wanting Greenacre Farm. 'Alas!' B might think, 'Greenacre Farm – my childhood home – lost for ever', and as he ponders the matter he might think 'Is it right that P should have the farm? T^1 and T^2 held it on trust for me. Surely P now ought to hold it on trust for me?'

Originally equity gave B no remedy against P; that is, equity did not require P to hold the land on trust for B. In the course of time the position changed. 'Why', it might have been argued before a Lord Chancellor in the fifteenth century, 'should P take the land free of B's equitable interest? If P knew that T^1 and T^2 held the land subject to B's equitable interest, why should P escape? He ought to take the land subject to B's equitable interest; that is, he ought to hold the legal fee simple on trust for B, just as T^1 and T^2 had done.'

'If he knew of B's equitable interest,' the Court of Chancery came to say, 'then indeed he ought to take the fee simple subject to B's equitable interest'.[11]

So the rule came to be that if T^1 and T^2 transferred the land in breach of trust to P, and P knew of B's equitable interest, he took subject to B's interest, but if he did not know of B's interest, it came to be established that, provided certain other conditions were satisfied, P took the land free of B's interest (with the result that B's only remedy was a claim against T^1 and T^2 for breach of trust.

The requirements to be satisfied for a purchaser to take free of the trust

These were as follows:

1. P had to be a *purchaser* from T^1 and T^2. 'Purchaser' here has a special meaning which we shall consider shortly, but it includes a 'buyer' in the ordinary sense.

---

11   This point had been reached by about the middle of the fifteenth century.

2. P had to have acted in good faith ('bona fide'), that is, without fraud. So he had to be not merely a purchaser, but a bona fide purchaser.
3. P had to have given consideration to T^1 and T^2 for the land. P had to be a 'purchaser *for value*'. If T^1 and T^2 sold the land to P this condition would be satisfied.
4. P had to be a purchaser of the *legal* estate from the trustees. In our example P bought the legal fee simple from T^1 and T^2 and so this condition was satisfied.

Finally, to complete the picture, the condition we stated first:

5. P had to have taken the land without notice of B's interest.

All five conditions would have to be satisfied for P to take the land free of B's interest. If any one of the conditions was not satisfied, P would take the land subject to B's equitable interest. For example, if the trustees gave the land to P (so that P was not a purchaser for value), then P would take the land subject to B's interest (and, of course, that would not be an undue hardship on P, since he had not paid anything for the land). Again, if P knew that T^1 and T^2 were holding the land on trust for B, he would take it subject to B's interest (regardless of whether he had bought the land from T^1 and T^2 or they had given the land to him). Thus, it was not sufficient for P to be a bona fide purchaser for value of the legal estate if he took with notice. He had to be a bona fide purchaser for value (of the legal estate) *without notice* in order to take free of B's interest.

Notice: actual and constructive

Suppose that A executed a deed in which he granted Greenacre to T^1 and [2] on trust for B, and T^1 and T^2 sold the farm (ie the legal fee simple in the land) to P, and P failed to inquire whether T^1 and T^2 had a good title to the land; and so P never saw the deed executed by A; and so P did not know that T^1 and T^2 held the land on trust for B. In this case P would have no actual notice of B's equitable interest, but 'notice' (in the context of the rule with which we are dealing) came to include not only actual notice but also what is termed 'constructive notice'.[12] A person has constructive notice of all those things which he would have discovered if he had made inquiries a reasonably prudent person would have made.[13] If this were not so, purchasers could 'shut their eyes'.[14]

In the above example, P should have inquired into T^1 and T^2's title to the land; and if P had done so (by looking at the deed executed by A) he would have discovered the existence of B's equitable interest. P thus has constructive notice of B's equitable interest and is therefore bound by it.

12   *Bailey v Barnes* [1894] 1 Ch 25 at 35.
13   See *Re Montagu's Settlement Trusts* [1987] Ch 264. How far back in time inquiries should be made is considered in a later chapter. See Chapter 25.
14   Maitland, *Equity*, p 113.

A person is also deemed to have knowledge of all those things that have come to the knowledge of his agent, for example, his solicitor. This is termed 'imputed notice'. Imputed notice includes matters which a person's agent would have discovered if the agent had made the inquiries he should have made. In practice imputed notice is treated as being a form of constructive notice, so we merely say ' ... without notice, actual or constructive.'

The principles relating to actual and constructive (including imputed) notice were given statutory force by the Law of Property Act 1925.[15]

INSPECTION OF THE LAND

A purchaser is expected not only to investigate the title deeds to the land but also to inspect the land, to see who is in occupation of it. If he finds not the legal owner, but some other person, in occupation, then he is expected to inquire what interest (if any) the occupier holds in the land. If he fails to make this inquiry, he has constructive notice of any interest in the land that the occupier in fact holds.[16]

If P finds that the legal owner is in occupation, then the question arises as to whether the purchaser takes subject to the equitable interests of other persons who are also in occupation. For example, a matrimonial home is occupied by a husband and wife (H and W). The house was conveyed into the name of H alone. In fact (perhaps for reasons that will be considered later in this chapter), H holds the house on trust for himself and W. H, not revealing the existence of W's equitable interest, sells the property to P. Does P have constructive notice of W's equitable interest (and so take subject to it)? In *Caunce v Caunce*,[17] in 1969, it was held that since W's presence was in no way inconsistent with H holding the legal title free of any trust, P was not fixed with constructive notice of W's equitable interest. In *Williams and Glyn's Bank Ltd v Boland*,[18] in 1980, however, in the same circumstances, but due to reasons stemming from registration of title under the Land Registration Act 1925 (reasons that will be explained in Chapter 26) P took subject to W's equitable interest.

Statement of the rule

We are now in a position to state the bona fide purchaser rule. It can be stated from B's viewpoint, and from P's; thus:

---

15   Section 199(1)(ii).
16   Eg the rights of a tenant under a lease; *Hunt v Luck* [1902] 1 Ch 428.
17   [1969] 1 All ER 722, [1969] 1 WLR 286.
18   [1981] AC 487, [1980] 2 All ER 408.

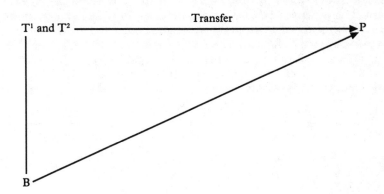

The holder of an equitable interest (B) can enforce the trust against anyone (P) who acquires the trust property, except a bona fide purchaser for value of the legal estate without notice.

A bona fide purchaser for value of a legal estate without notice, actual or constructive, of an equitable interest to which the property acquired is subject (P), takes free of that interest (ie the interest of B).[19]

Legal interests bind all the world

Suppose that T^1 and T^2 held Greenacre on trust for B, who was seven, and they leased to land to X. X would hold a legal lease (nothing equitable about it – nothing on trust for X – so the lease is a legal lease). In this case the land would be subject to B's equitable interest, and X's legal interest (see below). If T^1 and T^2 then sold Greenacre to P, a bona fide purchaser without notice of either B's or X's interest, the question would arise as to whether P was bound by X's legal lease.

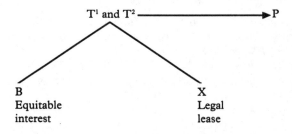

---

19   *Pilcher v Rawlins* (1872) 7 Ch App 259; (M & B).

The position is that the bona fide purchaser rule refers only to equitable interests. There is no rule than enables a person to take free of legal interests.[20]

So the saying is 'legal interests are valid against all the world' – meaning legal interests (such as X's legal lease) are binding on anyone who acquires the property (Greenacre) that was subject to the legal interest. Thus if T^1 and T^2 sell it to P, and P gives it to Q, and Q leaves it in his will to R, and R sells it to S, and so on, all these people take the land subject to X's lease.

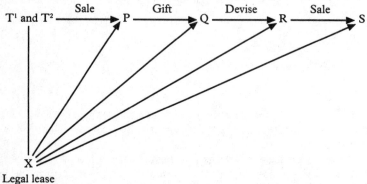

Legal lease

Neither P, nor Q, nor R, nor S, nor anyone else in the world who acquires the land, can put X off the land (until his lease expires) because they take the legal fee simple subject to his legal interest, but, since P was a bona fide purchaser without notice of B's equitable interest, he takes free of the interest. P is therefore bound by X's interest, but not by B's. It should be noted that in the case of a legal interest (eg X's lease) notice is irrelevant – X's interest binds P regardless of whether or not P had notice of the lease.

A person who holds a legal interest (eg X) is thus more secure than a person who holds an equitable interest.

What worried the holder of an equitable interest

Although, as we shall see, the position was changed by legislation in1925, before 1926 a person who held an equitable interest could never be sure that he would not find that the persons who held the legal estate (T^1 and T^2) had conveyed the land to someone who proved to be a bona fide purchaser[1] and who would therefore take the land free from his equitable interest. The holders of equitable interests could therefore never sleep easily at night. This was a major defect of the law. (We shall see later in this chapter that the 1925 legislation took steps towards freeing the holders of equitable interests from this worry by enacting that certain equitable interests should be registrable as *land charges*.)

---

20   Subject to what is said later on registration (Chapter 25).
1   Ie for value without notice.

What worried a purchaser of the legal estate: the onus of proof

A bona fide purchaser could sleep without fear that he would wake up one morning and find that he had taken the land he had purchased subject to B's equitable interest (without fear that he had paid his money only to find himself a trustee for B), provided always that he could be sure that he was a bona fide purchaser. But a doubt might remain that he (or his lawyer) had failed to investigate everything that ought to have been investigated, with the result that he might one day find himself fixed with constructive notice of an equitable interest.

If T^1 and T^2 sell land to P, and B claims that P is bound by his equitable interest, and the case goes to court, the onus of proof is on P to show that he had no notice, actual or constructive, of B's interest. (B, of course, can challenge P's evidence and seek to overthrow P's claim that he took without notice.) If P fails in his attempt to satisfy the court that he took without notice, or if P says nothing, or if he does not appear in court, then B's claim succeeds, notwithstanding that B had given no evidence to show that P took with notice. The onus is thus on P to prove that he is a bona fide purchaser without notice. If he fails to establish this, he is bound by B's interest. (B must, of course, prove the existence of his equitable interest, but if P's claim fails, he need prove nothing further.) The onus on P was thus a heavy one and might be difficult to discharge.

Another of a purchaser's worries was that he could never be certain that someone might not appear who could prove that he had a legal interest in the land, eg a legal lease, which would therefore bind him.

We shall see later that legislation in 1925 went a long way towards removing a purchaser's worries as to the interests by which he would be bound.

Developments of the rule and its status today

The bona fide purchaser rule, with all its ramifications, was something that was evolved gradually over the centuries, its development continuing into the present century.[2] At the outset (as indicated earlier) a beneficiary was able to enforce a trust only against the original trustee. If this trustee parted with the land, by sale or by gift, or if he went bankrupt and the land passed to his creditors, or if he died, and the land passed to his heir, then the beneficiary lost his interest in the land. By stages, however, the Lord Chancellor's court began to require persons to whom land had passed from a trustee to hold the land on trust for the beneficiary. Thus a beneficiary came[3] to be able to enforce the trust against the trustee's heir (ie after the trustee's death); against a donee from the trustee; against a devisee from the trustee; against a person who had purchased the property from the trustee with actual knowledge that it was trust property; against the trustee's creditors[4] (ie in the event of the trust

---

2   *Re Nisbet and Potts' Contract* [1906] 1 Ch 386.
3   The steps are set out by Maitland, *Lectures on Equity*, pp 112, 113.
4   *Finch v Earl of Winchelsea* (1715) 1 P Wms 277.

property passing into their hands on the trustee's bankruptcy); and, finally, against a person who purchased the trust property with constructive notice of the beneficiary's equitable interest. After the trust had become enforceable against all these types of person, the final result was that the only person against whom a trust remained unenforceable was the bona fide purchaser for value of the legal estate without notice, actual or constructive of the beneficiary's interest. The bona fide purchaser rule still operates today, except in certain instances where changes have been made by statute,[5] but no statute has ever abolished the rule and it remains one of the foundations of the law.

We must now turn back to the rule itself and consider more precisely the meaning of some of the terms used.

'purchaser'

If property is transferred from A to B, this may be either:

(a) because A decided to transfer it to B, and B decides to accept it; for example if A sells the property to B, or gives it to him, or leaves it to him in his will. In these cases the transfer is 'by act of the parties', namely A and B; or

(b) because the law requires (regardless of the wishes of A and B) the property to be transferred from A to B. For example, if A goes bankrupt, and B is the trustee in bankruptcy, A's property vests in B as the trustee in bankruptcy. It vests in B because the law so provides. In this case the transfer is not by act of the parties, but 'by operation of law'. Another example of a transfer by operation of law would be if A died intestate and B was his next of kin.

A 'purchaser' in land law is a person who receives property otherwise than by operation of law. So if A sells land to B, or if he gives it to B, or if he leaves it to B in his will (so that B is respectively a buyer, a donee or a devisee), in all these cases B is a purchaser. If A died intestate and B received his property as his next of kin, B would not be a purchaser. (It will be seen that since a donee is a purchaser, the words 'for value' in the phrase 'purchaser for value' are of significance.)

'for value'

'Value' includes any form of consideration (including money) that would be valid consideration in the law of contract. So if A gives land to Miss B in return for Miss B's promise of marriage, Miss B is a purchaser for value. In addition, payment of an existing debt (which is not consideration in contract) is 'value'.[6]

To be a purchaser for value, a purchaser does not have to give full value. As in the law of contract, the actual value of the consideration is irrelevant. If

---

5   See p 95.
6   *Thorndike v Hunt* (1859) 3 De GF & J 563.

A conveys Blackacre to B in return for a peppercorn, B is a purchaser for value.[7]

A person who gives no consideration for property he receives is termed a 'volunteer'. So if A gives land to B, or A leaves land to B in his will, in both these cases B is a volunteer. It will be noted that a donee and a devisee are none the less purchasers, because they take otherwise than by operation of law. A purchaser can thus be a volunteer.

'of the legal estate'

We said that in order to take free of B's equitable interest, P must be a bona fide purchaser for value of the *legal estate*. If P bought the legal fee simple from T^1 and T^2 this condition would be satisfied.

Suppose that A grants land to T^1 and T^2 on trust for B, and B transfers his equitable interest to t on trust for C. Suppose that t then sells the equitable interest which he holds to P. Like this:

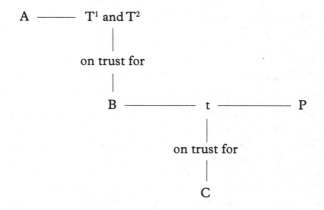

The question then arises: does P hold the interest he has acquired subject to, or free from, C's equitable interest? Since we are determining whether a purchaser (P) takes free from an equitable interest (C), we apply the bona fide purchaser rule, and whilst P may be a bona fide purchaser, and for value, and without notice of C's equitable interest, he is not a purchaser of the legal estate. What he acquired was an equitable interest, because that is all that B

---

7   The meaning of 'value' in the context of the Land Charges Act 1972 was the subject of examination in *Midland Bank Trust Co Ltd v Green* [1981] AC 513, [1981] 1 All ER 153; (M & B). The case is considered in Chapter 25.

transferred to him. P is therefore not a bona fide purchaser of a legal estate and so he takes subject to C's interest. The result will be as follows:

T¹ and T²

on trust for

P

on trust for

C

Any proceeds from the land which T¹ and T² hand to P, P must hold on trust for C.

Conflicts between two equitable interests

It will be seen in the above example that C and P each hold an equitable interest. Where there is a conflict between two persons each holding an equitable interest (C saying 'You hold your interest on trust for me, P', and P saying 'I take my interest free from yours, C') the rule is 'first in time, first in right'. Since C's equitable interest was in existence before P's, C *takes priority*.[8] This, however, is merely another way of reaching the conclusion which was reached by saying that since P is not a purchaser of the legal estate, he takes subject to C's equitable interest. The two approaches lead to the same result.

Why equity allowed a bona fide purchaser to take free of equitable interests

What we have just considered raises the question, if equity did not allow P to take free of C's equitable interests (since he was a bona fide purchaser of an equitable interest), why did equity allow a bona fide purchaser of the *legal* estate to take free of equitable interests? The answer is that equity recognised that if a buyer of land was always to take the land subject to equitable interests, no one would be safe in buying land. So equity recognised, in order to make it practical for land to be bought and sold, that if a person satisfied the

8   *Rice v Rice* (1854) 2 Drew 73.

requirements of the bona fide purchaser rule, he should take free of any equitable interests that happened to exist.

If T^1 and T^2 held land on trust for B and they sold the land to P, and P was a bona fide purchaser, then equity was faced with two innocent parties – B and P. Notwithstanding that B's interest had arisen before P's, equity said in effect, 'We are sorry B, but we must allow P to take the fee simple free of your interest, otherwise the buying and selling of land would be almost impossible. All we can do is help you to get damages for breach of trust from T^1 and T^2. If you bring T^1 and T^2 before this court we shall make them pay you.'

Equity was, however, able to help the holders of equitable interests by extending the scope of the rules relating to constructive notice. As a result of these extensions, it became increasingly difficult for a purchaser to prove that he had taken without notice of an equitable interest. As equity cast the net of notice ever wider, fewer purchasers escaped its trammels, and, being ensnared, were fixed with notice, and so took subject to the equitable interests concerned.

The only person, as we have learned, whom equity permitted to escape its net was the bona fide purchaser for value of the legal estate without notice. But we do not view the history of land law correctly if we regard the bona fide purchaser as 'equity's darling'. Equity did not love the bona fide purchaser. It did no more than grudgingly allow him his position, and for the sole reason that conveyancing would have been hamstrung if he was bound by equitable interests of which he had no notice.

Persons claiming through a bona fide purchaser

So far we have been speaking about T^1 and T^2 conveying the legal fee simple to P, and we have discussed the rule in the context of whether or not P was a bona fide purchaser. But suppose there was a chain of transactions – suppose that P gave the land to Q, Q devised it to R, R sold it to S, S gave it to X.

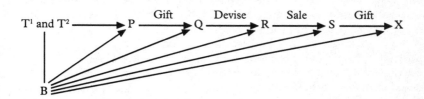

In order to be a bona fide purchaser (and to take free from B's equitable interest) it is not necessary to be a purchaser from the original trustees. Suppose that, in the above example:

P has notice of B's interest. P is not a bona fide purchaser without notice, and so he is bound by B's interest.
Q is a volunteer. As Q is not a purchaser for value, he is bound also.
R too is a volunteer. As R also is not a purchaser for value, he is bound.
S, however, is a bona fide purchaser for value (of the legal estate) without

notice. He therefore takes free of B's interest. At this point B's interest is
severed from the land, so when S gives the property to X –

X   is a volunteer, but he claims through a bona fide purchaser (S) and so X,
and anyone[9] who subsequently acquires the property, takes free of B's
equitable interest (even if they have notice of B's interest).[10]

Purchaser pro tanto

Suppose that, in the last example, R had not *sold* the legal fee simple to S,
but had leased it to him for, say, 99 years, at a rent of £25 a year. Whether or
not S would take the lease subject to, or free from, B's equitable interest
would depend on whether S, as lessee, was a bona fide purchaser. Since a
purchaser is someone who acquires an interest in property otherwise than by
operation of law, and since S did not acquire the interest by operation of law,
eg on R's bankruptcy or intestacy, S is a purchaser. It is true that S did not
acquire the fee simple and acquired only a lesser interest, but to the extent of
that interest, he is a purchaser. We say that he is a purchaser *pro tanto*. Since
he is obliged to pay rent he is a purchaser for value. Whether he complies
with the other requirements depends on the circumstances. If he does, he
takes free of B's equitable interest. A mortgagee of property (eg a building
society to whom a house is mortgaged as security for a loan) is also a
purchaser[11] pro tanto.

THE NATURE OF EQUITY

Equity acts 'in personam'

In the example above, it will be seen that while the land is in the hands of P, of
Q and of R, they will have to account to B for any profits they receive from the
land. Equity compelled them to hand over the money they had received by
issuing a decree ordering them to do so. Similarly, the Court of Chancery
might issue a decree ordering trustees not to sell the land in breach of trust; or,
if they had done so, and the land had passed into the hands of a bona fide
purchaser, to pay compensation for breach of trust. If a person disregarded a
decree issued by Chancery ordering them to pay compensation, Chancery
could imprison them until they did pay. This constitutes a difference from the
practice of the common law courts. If a defendant failed to pay damages
awarded by a court of common law, then the court sent the sheriff to the
defendant's land. The sheriff took away some or all of the defendant's goods

9   Except for T[1] and T[2]. If they (or one of them) subsequently acquire the property, they take
     it subject to B's equitable interest which is then revived. If this were not so, they would be
     able to benefit from their own breach of trust.
10   *Wilkes v Spooner* [1911] 2 KB 473; (M & B).
11   LPA 1925, s 205 (1)(xxi).

and sold them. The proceeds were used to pay the damages awarded. This practice was not used by Chancery.

It is sometimes said that damages were a common law remedy. This is only half the story. Monetary compensation was awarded by equity also: the difference between common law and equity lay in the means of *enforcing* the remedy. Since equity brought pressure to bear on a defendant by imprisoning his person, we say that equity acts 'in personam', ie against the person of the defendant. Common law, as we have seen, acted against the defendant's goods.

We may note here that the phrase 'in personam' has a number of meanings in English and Welsh law, and the meaning intended in any instance can only be elucidated from the context in which the phrase appears. We have so far met two meanings: these are where the words appear:

(i) (as above) in the phrase 'Equity acts in personam'; ie equity enforces its remedies by imprisoning someone who disregards its decrees (as opposed to enforcing its remedies by the method used by the common law); and

(ii) in the phrase 'an action in personam'; ie an action for the recovery of an item of personal property (as distinguished from a 'real action' for the recovery of an item of real property).

Equitable remedies

Another difference between legal (ie common law) and equitable remedies lies in the forms of remedy available. We have seen that common law and equity both award monetary compensation. In addition, equity issued the decrees of specific performance and injunction. A decree of specific performance is an order to a person to carry out a specified act or acts; for example, to perform his side of a contract. An injunction is an order to a person either (a) to refrain from doing some act, for example committing a nuisance by digging a quarry which causes his neighbour's land to subside or (b) to put right something already done, for example restoring the neighbour's land to its previous condition.

The jurisdiction of equity

Equity thus supplemented the common law by providing remedies not available at common law. If S contracted to sell B a cow for £100, and S refused to carry out the contract, B could either:

(i) claim damages for breach of contract in a court of common law; or

(ii) seek a decree of specific performance in the Court of Chancery ordering S to hand over the cow; or

(iii) claim both damages (for the delay in receiving the cow) and an order of specific performance, but originally if he had required both forms of remedy he would have had to start separate proceedings before a court of common law and before a court of equity.

The position was therefore as follows:

	Contract and tort	Trusts
Common law courts	The courts could grant damages for breach of contract, and damages for tort	The courts had no jurisdiction
Court of equity	The court could grant decrees of specific performance and injunction (but originally[12] not monetary compensation)	The court could grant compensation for breach of trust, and decrees of specific performance and injunction

The courts of common law and equity were reorganised under the Judicature Act 1873, but the principles of common law and equity remained, and to this day remain, distinct.

Equity's remedies discretionary

One final difference between common law and equity remains to be mentioned. If, to take the last example, S failed to perform his contract with B, and B sued S, then since S was in breach of contract, at common law B was entitled to damages as of right: a court of common law had no alternative but to award B damages.[13] The remedies awarded by equity were awarded at the discretion of the court. If B had been guilty of some sharp practice, or if there was any other reason why the court considered that B did not deserve the remedy he sought, or if the court considered that it would be inequitable to S for B to be granted a remedy, then equity would not grant the decree which B sought. Thus all equitable remedies were (and still are) discretionary.

The differences between equity and common law can be summarised thus:

1. The spheres of jurisdiction of equity and common law were different. Equity had exclusive jurisdiction in the field of trusts, and a jurisdiction which supplemented that of the common law courts by providing additional remedies.
2. These additional remedies were the decrees of specific performance and injunction.
3. Equitable remedies were awarded at the discretion of the court. The common law remedy of damages was awarded as of right.

---

12   Until the position was changed by the Chancery Amendment Act 1858 (Lord Cairns' Act) Section 2 provided that in any case where the Court of Chancery had jurisdiction to grant an injunction or a decree of specific performance, the court had discretion to award damages in addition to or in place of such decrees. The Act has been repealed but the jurisdiction is now conferred by the Supreme Court Act 1981, s 2. For examples of the exercise of the jurisdiction, see *Bracewell v Appleby* [1975] Ch 408, [1975] 1 All ER 993; *Biggin v Minton* [1977] 2 All ER 647, [1977] 1 WLR 701. See [1981] Conv 286 (T. Ingman and J. Wakefield).
13   Similarly, if S occupies O's land, and O seeks an order for possession against S, the court has no discretion to suspend the operation of the order: it must take effect immediately: *Department of the Environment v James* [1972] 3 All ER 629, [1972] 1 WLR 1279.

4. Equity enforced its decrees by the sanction of imprisonment. Common law enforced an award of damages by seizure of a defendant's goods.

It will be noted that all the above four matters relate to procedure and remedies rather than to substantive rules of law. As regards the rules of law, the principal differences between equity and the common law lies in the fact that whilst legal rights are valid against all the world, equitable rights are valid against all the world except a bona fide purchaser. This had been described as the 'polar star of equity'.[14] It could well be described as the polar star of English and Welsh land law.

MODIFICATION OF THE OLD RULES BY STATUTE: REGISTRATION OF ENCUMBRANCES

In this chapter we have learned that legal interests are binding on all the world (ie on any purchaser) and that equitable interests are binding on any purchaser except a bona fide purchaser. This is the starting point. But these two principles have been modified by statute. The Land Charges Act 1972 (which replaced the Land Charges Act 1925) provides that certain interests (in the main equitable interests but including a small number of legal interests) bind a purchaser if they are registered in the central register of Land Charges (which is at Plymouth), and do not bind a purchaser if they are not so registered.[15] Thus, in the case of interests that are registrable, the statutory provisions relating to registration replace the old rules relating to legal interests and equitable interests. An example of an equitable interest that is registrable (and in respect of which the old bona fide purchaser rule therefore no longer applies) is an equitable easement. In later chapters we shall meet various other matters that are registrable under the Land Charges Act 1972. A summary of all these appears in Chapter 25, which deals with registration of encumbrances (encumbrances being matters that have an adverse effect on, that encumber, land).

DEVELOPMENT OF THE MODERN TRUST

When considering how it became possible to transfer land by will we saw[16] that by the fourteenth century it had become possible to devise land by means of a 'use'. (A 'use' was an earlier name for a trust; a trustee held land 'to the use of' a beneficiary.[17]) What happened was this. Suppose that A did not wish all his land to pass on his death to his heir, but wished one part of it, Greenacre, to pass to his daughter, C. To achieve this, sometime during his lifetime A

---

14 *Stanhope v Earl Verney* (1761) 2 Eden 81 at 85 per Henley LC.
15 Subject to what is said in Chapter 25.
16 See Chapter 3.
17 Maitland considered that the word 'use' was derived, through French medieval law, from the word 'opus' in the seventh century use of the Latin word in the phrase 'ad opus', meaning 'on behalf of'.

would transfer the legal fee simple in Greenacre to trustees to hold on trust for himself, A, during his lifetime and on his death on trust for whoever A should designate in his will. In his will he named C as the person for whom the trustees were to hold the land on his death. By this arrangement A had the benefit of the land for the rest of his life; on his death C became entitled to call on the trustees to convey the legal fee simple to her. On their so doing the trust came to an end and C, as A had wished, received the legal fee simple.

There were other purposes for which trusts were employed. For example, payment of feudal dues, such as relief, which were payable on the death of a land holder, could be avoided. If on A's death a sum of 300s was payable by way of relief to A's superior lord, A could evade this payment having to be made by transferring the legal fee simple, during his lifetime, to T^1 and T^2 to hold on trust for himself for the rest of his life and then for whoever A wished to receive the land – including, if A so wished, his heir. When A died no relief was payable since the legal fee simple was then vested in T^1 and T^2, and they were still alive. T^1 and T^2 then transferred the legal estate to whomsoever A had directed. No relief was payable because no holder of the legal estate had died. The same means was used to evade other feudal incidents.

Since the Crown was the ultimate loser by the evasion of feudal incidents, in 1535 the King secured the passage of the Statute of Uses. We saw earlier that the public outcry following the Statute led to the passing, in 1540, of the Statute of Wills which permitted land to be devised at common law, ie without the need to employ a trust. But it was believed that the Statute of Uses had made it impossible (except in a limited number of instances) to create a trust.

Ultimately, ways were discovered of evading the Statute of Uses.[18] Neither the mechanics of the Statute nor the means of evading it need concern us here and it will be sufficient for our purpose to say that a grant that employed the words 'unto and to the use of' T^1 and T^2 on trust for B for life (or for whatever equitable interests were to be granted), were sufficient to create a trust which was unaffected by the operation of the Statute.

The Law of Property Act 1925 repealed the Statute of Uses 1535, and the need to use the words 'unto and to the use of' the trustees (or to employ any other means of evading the Statute of Uses) disappeared. Thus today a trust can be created merely by using the words ' … to T^1 and T^2 on trust for … '

IMPLIED TRUSTS

The trusts we have spoken of so far in this chapter are ones that have arisen as a result of the express intention of a settlor; they are *express trusts*. In addition to arising by the express intention of a settlor, a trust may come into existence as a result of what is inferred as having been some person's intention; such trusts are termed *implied trusts*. For example, A provides the purchase price of a house. He directs the vendor to convey the property into the name of B. Here the law infers that it was A's intention that B should hold the property on

18   See M & W, Appendix 3.

trust for him, A; B holds the legal estate on an implied trust for A.[19] But (and this is the case in all implied trusts) if B can rebut the presumption by producing evidence that A intended to make a gift of the property to him, then B will take the property, not as a trustee, but beneficially.[20] (In certain instances the court will presume that A's intention was to make a gift to B, for example, where A was B's father. In these instances it would be for A to provide evidence showing that he had *no* intention of making a gift to B. If A satisfies the court on this score – if he rebuts the presumption of gift – then B will hold on trust for A.)

Implied trusts can be of importance in connection with disputes over ownership of the matrimonial home. Suppose that a husband (H) and wife (W) acquire a house as their matrimonial home. Both contribute to the purchase price. The property is conveyed in H's name alone. The result will be that H holds the legal fee simple on trust for himself and W.[1] The law in this field is examined further when dealing with co-ownership in Chapter 10.

An implied trust under which the trustees hold the trust property on trust for the settlor is termed a *resulting trust*. For example, if A conveys property to T on trust for B for life, with no mention of any remainder, it is inferred that it is A's intention that on B's death the land should be held on trust for him, A. The trust is an implied trust, and, at the same time, a resulting[2] trust, because the property is held for the settlor.

CONSTRUCTIVE TRUSTS

In some circumstances – the categories of which are by no means closed – the court may hold that irrespective of the intention of anyone a trust has nevertheless come into existence. Here the court constructs a trust in order to produce an equitable result between certain parties: the court requires someone holding certain property to hold it not beneficially, but as a trustee for a specified beneficiary or beneficiaries. Such a trust is termed a *constructive trust*. For example, if T holds property on trust for B, and T, in breach of trust, sells the property to P, and P is not a bona fide purchaser without notice, then, as we know, P holds the property on trust for B. The position of trustee is imposed by equity on P: thus P holds under a constructive trust for B. A constructive trust may also come into existence as a means of preventing fraud.[3] For example, if a trustee makes use of his position as trustee to make some profit for himself, he holds the profit on a constructive trust for B.[4]

SUMMARY

See Appendix II, p 567.

---

19 *Dyer v Dyer* (1788) 2 Cox Eq Cas 92.
20 As in *Fowkes v Pascoe* (1875) 10 Ch App 343.
 1 *Cook v Cook* [1962] P 235, [1962] 2 All ER 811.
 2 From the Latin, *resultare*, to spring back.
 3 As in *Bannister v Bannister* [1948] 2 All ER 133; (M & B).
 4 *Williams v Barton* [1927] 2 Ch 9.

CHAPTER 6

The Reduction in the Number of Legal Estates

LEGAL AND EQUITABLE INTERESTS BEFORE 1926

In previous chapters, we have learnt about the various forms of estate that could exist – the fee simple, the fee tail, and so on. We have seen, too, that the freehold estates may be classified according to whether they are in possession, in remainder, or in reversion, and also as to whether they are absolute or modified (ie conditional of determinable).

By way of introduction to this chapter, let us set out some of the forms of interest in land that could exist before 1926, and which can still exist at the present day:

Fee absolute in possession	Life estate (absolute) in possession
Fee simple absolute in remainder	Life estate (absolute) in remainder
Fee simple absolute in reversion	Life estate (absolute) in reversion
Conditional fee simple in possession	Conditional life estate in possession
Conditional fee simple in remainder	Conditional life estate in remainder
Determinable fee simple in possession	Determinable life estate in possession
Determinable fee simple in remainder	Determinable life estate in remainder
Fee tail[1] in possession	Term of years (ie lease)
Fee tail[1] in remainder	

Before 1926 any of these interests could exist in a legal or in an equitable form. An interest was legal if it was not held under a trust. Thus if A held the legal fee simple in Blackacre and he granted the land to B for life with the remainder to C in fee simple until he committed an act of bankruptcy, B took a legal life interest in possession, and C took a legal determinable fee simple in remainder. If, on the other hand, A had conveyed the legal fee simple to trustees[2] to hold on trust for B for life with remainder to C in fee simple until he committed an act of bankruptcy, then B would have held an equitable life interest in possession and C an equitable determinable fee simple in remainder.

---

1 Although not common, there is no reason why there should not have been conditional and determinable fee tails.
2 Using words that evaded the effect of the Statute of Uses; see Chapter 5.

We must stress that before 1926 any of the interests listed above (and any others that can be thought of by juggling with the various possible combinations) could exist either as a legal interest (not under a trust) or as an equitable interest (under a trust). So it was possible – to take a couple of interests at random – to have a legal conditional life estate in remainder or an equitable conditional life estate in remainder; it was possible to have a legal fee tail in possession or an equitable fee tail in possession; and so on.

LAW OF PROPERTY ACT 1925, SECTION 1

The two legal estates

As a result of the Law of Property Act 1925, since 1925 it has no longer been possible for all interests in land to be either legal or equitable, according to the circumstances. Section 1 of the Act provides that after 1925 only two of the interests that we listed above can exist in a legal form. These are the fee simple absolute in possession and the term of years – the first and the last on the list on the previous page. The result is that all the others, since they are not one of the two that can be legal, must be equitable.

So if today A grants Blackacre to B for life, B takes an equitable interest. It must be equitable, since a life interest is not one of the two interests that can be legal. Furthermore, it is equitable even though A did not convey the land to trustees on trust for B for life. However, since B's interest is equitable, it must exist under a trust. This raises the question, if A did not set up a trust, where does the trust come from? The answer, broadly, is that A will hold the legal fee simple on trust for B. A thus in effect constitutes himself trustee of the land for B; so a trust does, in fact, come into existence. If A does not want to make himself the trustee, he could[3] grant the legal estate to trustees to hold on trust for B for life (with remainder to himself, on B's death).

To illustrate and emphasise the effect which s 1 of the Law of Property Act 1925 had, let us set out a number of interests in land, as follows:

Legal	Fee simple absolute in poss- ession	Fee simple absolute in re- mainder	Fee simple in reversion	Con- ditional fee simple	Deter- minable fee simple	Fee tail	Life estate	Term of years (lease)
Equit- able	Fee simple absolute in poss- ession	Fee simple absolute in re- mainder	Fee simple in reversion	Con- ditional fee simple	Deter- minable fee simple	Fee tail	Life estate	Term of years (lease)

This table illustrates the position before 1926 when all these interests could exist either as legal interests (top row) or as equitable interests (bottom row).

---

3   Subject to what is said in Chapter 7.

Now let us show the effect of s 1:

Legal	Fee simple absolute in poss-ession							Term of years (lease)
Equit-able	Fee simple absolute in poss-ession	Fee simple absolute in re-mainder	Fee simple in reversion	Con-ditional fee simple	Deter-minable fee simple	Fee tail	Life estate	Term of years (lease)

It will be seen that, on the top row of the above table, only the fee simple absolute in possession and the term of years remain. All the other interests on the top row are omitted because, since the end of 1925, they cannot exist as legal interests.

It will also be seen from the table above, that s 1 did not strike out any equitable interests. Any interest in land could be equitable before the Law of Property Act 1925, and s 1 made no change in this position. Any kind of interest in land can therefore still exist as an equitable interest today.

Thus s 1 did not provide that the fee simple absolute in possession and the term of years can only exist as legal estates. What s 1 provided was that *only* the fee simple absolute in possession and the term of years can exist as legal estates. This being so there is nothing to prevent these two estates being equitable.

The result is, therefore, that the fee simple absolute in possession and the term of years are the only estates that can exist in either a legal or an equitable form. All others can exist only in an equitable form.

After 1925, by convention, the word 'estate' is reserved for the two legal estates, namely the fee simple absolute in possession and the term of years. What could previously be called equitable 'estates' are, after 1925, referred to as equitable 'interests'. So if today A holds a fee tail, we speak of his holding an equitable interest, not an equitable estate, in the land.

We have said that the term of years is one of the two estates that can exist as legal estates. In practice, s 1 speaks of the 'term of years *absolute*' as being one of the two estates that can be a legal estate. This raises the question as to what is meant by 'absolute' in this context. We have noted earlier that in relation to freehold estates, 'absolute' means not conditional or determinable, but this cannot be the case here, since the Act,[4] in defining a 'term of years absolute', includes within the definition a lease that is 'liable to determine by notice, re-entry, operation of law ... or in any other event', thus including within the definition a lease that is conditional or determinable. It seems, therefore, that the word 'absolute' in the term 'term of years absolute' carries no intelligible meaning.

---

4   LPA 1925, s 205(1)(xxvii).

'Interests in the land of another'

Section 1, in addition to reducing the number of estates that could exist as legal estates, also reduced to five the number of interests in the land of another that could exist as legal interests. We can explain the meaning of 'interests in the land of another' by an illustration. Suppose that A owns Redacre and Y owns a piece of land, Greenacre, which lies between A's land and a road. Y grants A a right of way across Greenacre, so that A may have direct access to the road.

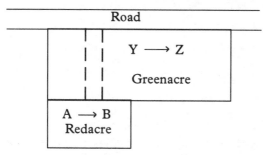

Further, let us suppose that the arrangement is such that if A sells the land, say to B, B (as the new owner of Redacre) will enjoy the right to cross Greenacre; and that if Y sells Greenacre, say to Z, then Z will be bound to permit A (and later B) to cross Greenacre, and so on, with the result that whoever owns Redacre has a right of way across Greenacre. A right of way having these characteristics is termed an *easement*. Easements may take various forms; the right may be a right, not to cross Greenacre, but to put pipes under Greenacre or to have electricity wires running across Greenacre supported by pylons standing on Greenacre. A does not, of course, own any part of Greenacre; but he does own the easement across Greenacre. We say that A has an interest in Greenacre. An easement is thus an example of an interest in the land of another.

Easements can be of various durations. For example, Y might have granted the easement to A for 21 years, in which case the easement would be enjoyed by whoever owned Redacre (A, B, etc), until 21 years had expired. Or Y might have granted the easement to A until A died or parted with Redacre. In this case A would hold the easement for the equivalent for a determinable life interest. Or Y might have granted the easement to A for the equivalent of a fee simple interest: in this case the easement would last as long as the fee simple in Redacre lasted – ie perhaps for ever. So an easement might be granted for the equivalent of a term of years, or for life, or for the equivalent of a fee simple, and in the last case, it might be granted for the equivalent of a fee simple absolute, or of a determinable fee simple, or of a conditional fee simple.

Having seen that various durations of easement can exist, we must go on to explain that an easement can be a legal easement or an equitable easement. The creation of equitable easements is considered later, but briefly we can say here that if Y is to grant A a legal easement, the grant by Y must be contained in a deed. If Y does not use a deed, then, provided certain other conditions are satisfied, A may nevertheless obtain an equitable easement.

Now suppose that Y grants a legal easement to A to cross Greenacre and an equitable easement to Q (equitable because no deed was used) to run a pipe under Greenacre, like this:

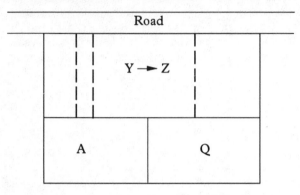

What difference would it make that A holds a legal easement and Q an equitable one? The answer is that while Y holds Greenacre, virtually none,[5] but if Y sells Greenacre to Z, the question arises as to whether Z takes subject to, or free from, A's and Q's easements. Since A's easement is legal, and since legal interests are valid against all the world, Z takes Greenacre subject to A's legal easement (irrespective of whether he had notice of it), but in the case of Q's equitable easement, if Z was a bona fide purchaser (without notice of Q's easement) he would take free of the easement (and so could block or dig up the pipe).[6] If he was not a bona fide purchaser, then he would take Greenacre subject to Q's equitable easement.[7]

Now let us retrace our steps. We have seen that easements could be of various 'durations', ie equivalent to various forms of estate. Before 1926, an easement of any 'duration' could be either legal or equitable. We can set the matter out like this.

Legal	Easement equivalent to a fee simple absolute	Easement equivalent to a conditional fee simple	Easement equivalent to a determinable fee simple	Easement equivalent to a life estate	Easement equivalent to a term of years
Equitable	Easement equivalent to a fee simple absolute	Easement equivalent to a conditional fee simple	Easement equivalent to a determinable fee simple	Easement equivalent to a life estate	Easement equivalent to a term of years

Section 1 of the Law of Property Act 1925 provided that an easement could be a legal easement only if it was an easement equivalent to a fee simple absolute in possession, or equivalent to a term of years absolute.

5   One difference is that if Q brings an action against Y for infringing his easement, since Q's easement is equitable, the remedies available to Q are awarded at the court's discretion. See Chapter 5.
6   Subject to what is said in Chapters 18 and 25.
7   Ibid.

The change which s 1 made can be shown thus:

Legal	Easement equivalent to a fee simple absolute			Easement equivalent to a term of years
Equitable	Easement equivalent to a fee simple absolute	Easement equivalent to a conditional fee simple	Easement equivalent to a determinable fee simple	Easement equivalent to a life estate	Easement equivalent to a term of years

Thus, after 1925, if A granted an easement to Y for seven years (a grant for the equivalent of a term of years) and he did so in a deed, this would create a legal easement, but if A granted Y an easement to last for as long as A lived then (regardless of whether or not the grant was in a deed), the easement, being for life, was necessarily equitable (because it was not one of the two forms of easement which could be legal).

Having illustrated the meaning of 'an interest in the land of another' by means of an easement (and having seen the effect of s 1 on the forms of easement that can, after 1925, exist as legal easements) we are now in a position to return to the point where we stated that s 1, in addition to reducing to two the estates that could exist as legal estates, reduced to five the interests in the land of another that could exist in a legal form.

The first of these five interests we have already considered, namely:

1.　'AN EASEMENT, RIGHT OR PRIVILEGE IN OR OVER LAND FOR AN INTEREST EQUIVALENT TO AN ESTATE IN FEE SIMPLE ABSOLUTE IN POSSESSION OR A TERM OF YEARS ABSOLUTE'.[8]

The others on the list are as follows:

2.　'A RENTCHARGE IN POSSESSION ISSUING OUT OF OR CHARGED ON LAND BEING EITHER PERPETUAL OR FOR A TERM OF YEARS ABSOLUTE'.[9]

We saw earlier[10] that a rentcharge was a rent payable otherwise than by a tenant to his lord. A rentcharge is an item of property and since under the old law a real action was available to enforce payment of the rent, it is classified as an item of real property.

3.　'A CHARGE BY WAY OF LEGAL MORTGAGE'.[11]

We shall be considering the meaning of this phrase later, in the chapter on mortgages, but for the present we can say that in order to be a 'charge by way

---

8　LPA 1925, s 1(2)(a).
9　LPA 1925, s 1(2)(b). For the effect of the Rentcharges Act 1977, see Chapter 3.
10　See Chapter 2.

of legal mortgage' the mortgage must be in a certain form and the document used to create the mortgage must be a deed.

4.   'LAND TAX, TITHE RENTCHARGE, ANY OTHER SIMILAR CHARGE ON LAND WHICH IS NOT CREATED BY AN INSTRUMENT'.[12]

This group consisted of certain charges imposed on land by statute. Land tax and tithe rentcharge have now been abolished, and although one charge[13] on land still exists which comes under this heading, the group is now of little importance.

5.   'RIGHTS OF ENTRY EXERCISABLE OVER OR IN RESPECT OF A LEGAL TERM OF YEARS ABSOLUTE, OR ANNEXED, FOR ANY PURPOSE, TO A LEGAL RENTCHARGE'.[14]

In a lease there is commonly a provision under which the landlord has the right to re-enter (ie and re-occupy) the land if the tenant fails to carry out his obligations, for example if he fails to pay the rent. This is what is referred to in the phrase 'exercisable over or in respect of a legal term of years'.

Following the same pattern that we have seen before, a right of entry may be equitable. For example, if the lease was an equitable lease, then since the right of entry would in this case not be 'exercisable over or in respect of a legal term of years', the right of entry would necessarily be equitable.

Now we must consider the second limb of the item we are discussing, namely a right 'of entry ... annexed, for any purpose, to a legal rentcharge'. Suppose that in 1976[15] A transferred the fee simple in Blackacre to B subject to a rentcharge of £100 payable for 25 years. In order to enforce payment of the rentcharge, A may convey the land to B for an estate in fee simple subject to a proviso that if the rentcharge is not paid within so many days of such and such a date each year, the fee simple shall come to an end. In this case, A will have granted B a conditional fee simple. As we saw earlier a person who grants a conditional fee simple retains a right of entry. In our example A therefore has a right of entry. Since it is annexed to a rentcharge, and since, let us assume, the rentcharge is a legal one, then A holds a right 'of entry ... annexed ... to a legal rentcharge'. This, then, is the other form of right of entry that can exist as a legal one.

This completes our survey of the five interests in the land of another that can, under s 1, exist as legal interests. Any interest which does not come within one of these five heads is necessarily equitable.

THE LAW OF PROPERTY (AMENDMENT) ACT 1926

In Manchester and Bristol, and certain other places, it was[15] for long a common practice to make sales of land subject to a rentcharge. So the seller received

---

11   LPA 1925, s 1(2)(c).
12   LPA 1925, s 1(2)(d).
13   Tithe redemption annuity.
14   LPA 1925, s 1(2)(e).
15   Ie before the Rentcharges Act 1977. See Chapter 3.

both a lump sum (the purchase price) and a continuing payment (the rentcharge). Payment of the rentcharge was usually secured by a right of entry held by the owner of the rentcharge.

When the Law of Property Act 1925 came into operation on 1 January 1926, the position was this: the fee simple was subject to a right of entry. This meant that the fee simple could be brought to an end if the rentcharge was not paid. This meant that the fee simple was a conditional fee simple. This meant that the fee simple was not a fee simple absolute. This meant that the fee simple was not a 'fee simple absolute in possession'. This meant that, as a result of s 1 of the Law of Property Act 1925, the fee simple could not be legal, and so had to be equitable. Thus in Manchester and other places, thousands of householders who had up till then held the legal fee simple in their land found that their interest was now equitable. This was an effect not foreseen by those who had drafted the 1925 legislation.

To put matters right, the Law of Property (Amendment) Act 1926[16] provided that the following words should be added to s 7 of the Law of Property Act 1925; 'a fee simple subject to a legal or equitable right of entry or re-entry is for the purposes of this Act a fee simple absolute'. The effect of the provision is that a fee simple subject to a right of entry is to be deemed to be absolute *for the purposes of the Act*. Since it is thus a fee simple absolute for the purposes of s 1 it is therefore capable of being a legal estate, notwithstanding that it is in fact a conditional fee simple. (The words did not convert conditional fee simples into fee simples absolute. Conditions attached to conditional fee simples remained unaffected.)

So the result was that all the people who before 1926 had held a legal fee simple subject to which a right of entry was annexed, were, by the Act of 1926, confirmed in their legal status.[17]

THE PURPOSE OF SECTION 1

One question remains. Why did s 1 of the Law of Property Act 1925 reduce the number of estates and interests that could exist as legal estates and interests? The customary answer is that the change was made to facilitate conveyancing, but this explains nothing until one can see how the change did facilitate conveyancing, and this is something that will not be understood until nearly the end of this book has been reached. So, for the present, it will have to be accepted that there were good reasons for the change, and that these will be appreciated later.

SUMMARY

See Appendix II, p 568.

---

16   Section 7 and Sch.
17   The result achieved by the Law of Property (Amendment) Act 1926 with regard to a conditional fee simple (ie that it is to be deemed to be absolute for the purpose of s 1 of the Law of Property Act 1925), is obtained for a fee simple coming into existence under the School Sites Act (see p 71) by s 7(1) of the Law of Property Act 1925.

CHAPTER 7

Strict Settlements

SETTLEMENTS

A person *settles* property if, when alienating it, he settles how the property is to be held after the transfer has taken place. Thus if G grants land to A for life with remainder to B, we say that A has *settled* the land on A for life with remainder to B. Similarly, while if G makes an outright gift of land to his adult son, S, we do not say that he has settled the land on S, if the grant is to S, an infant son, provided that S attains the age of 18, or if he grants the land to the son until the son commits an act of bankruptcy, here G, having settled in advance how the land is to be held, does settle the land on the son, according to the terms of the grant. A person who settles property is said to create a *settlement*. A person who settles property is termed the *settlor*. Property subject to a settlement can be realty or personalty.

Since a grant for a succession of interests – to A for life with remainder to B – is, as indicated above, a settlement, it transpires that we have already met settlements at various points earlier in this book.

Originally, a settlement might be created by direct grant – to A for life with remainder to B – but after the development of the trust it became the practice for settlements to be created under the machinery of a trust, the legal estate being vested in trustees on trust for the beneficiaries named for the interests stated in the grant.

A settlor's intention in creating a settlement is most commonly to make provision for his family, either provision for them after his death or during his life time for some such purpose as making provision for a son or daughter on their marriage, and for children of the marriage (and perhaps for their children also). During the eighteenth and nineteenth centuries settlements for family provision often came to be of great length and complexity, with elaborate arrangements designed to provide for the settlor's widow and children in addition to the eldest son, and to cover a range of possible eventualities (' ... but if B dies before attaining the age of 21 then over to C in tail with remainder to ... ' and so on).

Where a settlor owned land and he wished the provision for the beneficiaries to be in the form of money, to achieve this he could leave the land to trustees imposing on them a duty to sell the land and hold the proceeds of sale for the beneficiaries. In such a case, where the grant was to A for life with remainder to B, the trustees would invest the proceeds of sale and pass the income (eg from investments in stocks or shares, or in government securities) as it arose to A, and on A's death transfer the capital, ie the investments, to B. A trust in which this duty is imposed is termed a *trust for sale*, the settlor granting the land to the trustees 'in fee simple absolute in possession *on trust for sale* for ...'. Settlements in which no duty to sell the land was imposed, ie when the intention that it was the land that should pass down the family to future generations, came to be called *strict settlements* – settlements that were intended strictly to be settlements of land. Statutes were passed in 1882 and 1925 that regulated the form in which strict settlements were to exist and today the term 'strict settlement' is used exclusively to mean a settlement that is subject to the later Act, the Settled Land Act 1925.

In 1996 the Trusts of Land and Appointment of Trustees Act laid down that after the coming into force of the Act no settlement under the Settled Land Act 1925 could (except in certain limited instances) be created, all trusts of land after the Act being required to be in a new (and much simplified) form prescribed by the Act. But strict settlements in existence at the date of the Act were not affected, and continue their existence, as before, under the provisions of the Settled Land Act 1925. In time, however, as settlements under the 1925 Act come to an end, this form of settlement will become extinct. But this may not be for a considerable time.

Since strict settlements in being at the time of the Act continue to exist (and even, in limited circumstances, can still be created); since reports of cases prior to the 1996 Act contain numerous references to settlements under the 1925 Act; and since the strict settlement has formed so central an element in the law's development that a proper understanding of land law is not possible without a knowledge of its nature and structure, the subject of strict settlements continues to have a place in a book on land law. As a result of the 1996 Act, however, the subject can be dealt with in less detail than in previous editions of this book.

Settlements after 1925

In the last chapter we saw that as a result of s 1 of the Law of Property Act 1925, a life interest and fee simple in remainder can no longer exist as legal interests. They are thus necessarily equitable and can only exist under a trust. So the first method of creating a settlement mentioned above (ie, by direct grant) became impossible after 1925 and since that time a settlement has only been capable of being created under a trust.

Nothing in the 1925 legislation altered the previous position that a settlement of land could be created by means of a trust for sale. On the contrary, the Law of Property Act 1925 contained provisions that not only regulated but also facilitated the operation of trusts for sale.

A major change in the law relating to settlements of land was the provision, introduced by the Settled Land Act 1882[1] and confirmed by the Settled Land Act 1925, that if a settlement of land did not exist under a trust for sale it

---

1   For the effect of the Act, see p 126.

could only exist under a special form of trust, a form laid down in the statutes. So the position was this:

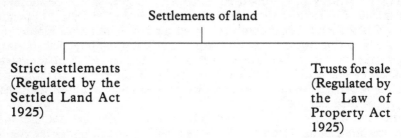

Settlements of land

Strict settlements
(Regulated by the
Settled Land Act
1925)

Trusts for sale
(Regulated by
the Law of
Property Act
1925)

Since a strict settlement is a special form of trust, we would expect the grantor to convey the legal estate in the land to a trustee to hold on trust for specified beneficiaries, and this is the position. Who the trustee is we shall see shortly. The beneficiaries are the people whom the settlor intended to benefit under the settlement. For example, in a settlement on A for life, with remainder to B for life, with remainder to C in fee simple, A, B, and C are the beneficiaries under the trust, each having an equitable interest in the land. A, for example, has an equitable life interest in possession, and so on. The position we reach is this:

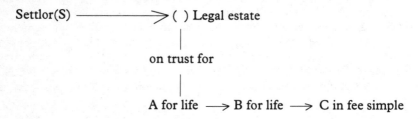

Settlor(S) ————————> ( ) Legal estate

on trust for

A for life ——> B for life ——> C in fee simple

Under the machinery of the Act of 1882 the legal estate could be held by anyone whom the settlor chose to name as trustee, but the Settled Land Act 1925 provided that after 1925 the legal estate had to be vested in A, as the first person entitled in possession to the land, ie the first person in the chain of interests.

A is thus in a dual position, holding two interests: the legal estate, which he holds as a trustee; and his own beneficial, equitable, life interest. In his capacity as a trustee he is termed the *tenant for life* of the settlement.

So the position is this:

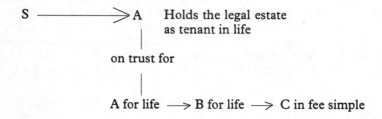

S ————————> A   Holds the legal estate
                as tenant in life

on trust for

A for life ——> B for life ——> C in fee simple

As regards his own 'private' life interest, A is literally a tenant for life, since he holds a life interest under the trust. But it is vital to distinguish between the term 'tenant for life' as it refers to A's own equitable interest under a strict settlement, and the term 'tenant for life' as it is used in the Settled Land Act 1925, when it refers to the holder of the legal estate in the land. In this book, in order to distinguish between the two uses of the phrase we shall use a capital 'T' when referring to the statutory 'Tenant for life', the person who under a strict settlement under the Settled Land Act 1925 holds the legal estate on trust for the persons entitled (himself included) under the settlement.

The Tenant for life holds what S conveyed to him, namely the legal fee simple[2] absolute in possession and he holds this on trust[3] for the equitable interests under the settlement: in our example, for himself for an equitable life interest in possession, with remainder to B for life, with remainder to C in fee simple.

Another provision of the Act was that in order to create a strict settlement two documents had to be used.[4] In a settlement created inter vivos they were (and in the rare and exceptional cases where strict settlements can still come into existence, still are):

1. A vesting deed.
2. A trust instrument (which is also a deed)

The function of the vesting deed is to convey the legal estate from S to the Tenant for life, A.[5] In essence it is thus no more than a conveyance. But a vesting deed contains items which do not appear in a normal conveyance. For example, it must contain a statement that the land is subject to a strict settlement. What the other items are we shall see later.

The principal function of the trust instrument is to name the beneficiaries under the settlement (A for life, etc).[6] The trust instrument has other functions, one being to appoint the trustees of the settlement,[7] whose principal function is to supervise the trust and to see that A does not take advantage of his position to act to the detriment of those who will follow after him, namely B and C. (They have other and more specific functions that we shall see later.)

The position we reach, therefore, is this"

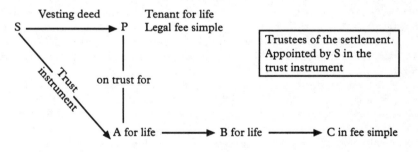

2   Settled leasehold land is considered at the end of the chapter.
3   SLA 1925, ss 16(1)(i), 107(1).
4   SLA 1925, s 4(2).
5   SLA 1925, s 4(2).
6   SLA 1925, 4(3)(a).
7   SLA 1925, s 4(3)(b).

It is important to distinguish between the Tenant for life who by authority of the vesting deed is trustee of the settled land and holds the legal fee simple, and the trustees of the settlement who are appointed by the trust instrument but hold no interest or estate in the land whatsoever.

In the light of what has been said so far, what was the position in the event of a conveyance after 1925 (and before the Trusts of Land Act and Appointment of Trustees Act 1996) by a settlor to trustees, T_1 and T_2, on trust for A for life with remainder to B in fee simple? The answer is that (i) land was settled on persons by way of succession: (ii) the land was not held on trust for sale; therefore (iii) the land was subject to a strict settlement; so (iv) the legal estate ought to have been vested in A as Tenant for life (not in T_1 and T_2) and two documents (a vesting deed and a trust instrument) ought to have been used; thus (v) the settlement was in a form that was no longer permitted to exist. If, notwithstanding this, a settlor did in fact create a settlement in the form and by the means stated, the Act provided machinery for ensuring that the settlement was converted into the form in which it should, under the 1925 Act, have been created.[8]

We may note here that a settlement might be created not only by a settlor (S) conveying the legal estate to the Tenant for life, A, on trust for himself, A, for life with remainders over, but also, where S wishes to retain a life interest in the land himself, by S settling the land on trust for himself for life with remainders over. Here S converted himself from being beneficial owner of the legal fee simple into being (as Tenant for life) a trustee of the legal fee simple. But where this occurred it was not sufficient for S merely to declare that he held Blackacre on trust for himself for life with remainders over. As in all other instances where a strict settlement arose, two documents had to be used.[9] S had to execute a vesting deed declaring that he held the land as Tenant for life under the Settled Land Act 1925, and a trust instrument, setting out the equitable interests (ie including his own).

SALE OF THE LAND BY A TENANT FOR LIFE

The purpose of the Settled Land Act 1925 was to prevent land from being 'tied up' in the future by enabling the Tenant for life to dispose of the land, eg to sell it. The Act gave (and, in the case of strict settlements in existence at the date of the 1996 Act, continues to give) him power to sell the land (ie to sell the legal fee simple) provided that he complied with certain conditions. For example, he must obtain the best price reasonably obtainable.

When an intending purchaser, P, examines the vesting deed (ie of a strict settlement created before the 1996 Act), he will see that the land is held subject to a strict settlement. So he will be aware of the existence of equitable interests. This originally would have caused him to refuse to purchase the land, since he would take subject to them. The Settled Land Act 1925 provides, however, that a purchaser of settled land will take the land free of the equitable interests provided that he pays the purchase money, not to A, but to the trustees of the

---

8   For how this was achieved, see p 120 of the previous edition.
9   Section 4(1).

settlement (whose names appear in the vesting deed) and obtains a receipt signed by at least two trustees or a trust corporation[10] (ie a corporation authorised by law to undertake trust business).[11] This provision constitutes a major exception to the bona fide purchaser rule,[12] since the purchaser takes free of the equitable interests notwithstanding that he has notice of their existence.

It is true that A, B and C lose their interest in the land. But what happens is that when the land is sold, the trustees then hold the purchase money on trust for those entitled under the settlement. So the interests of the beneficiaries from then on are in money, instead of being in land. The trustees will invest the purchase money, and the income as it arises will be handed over to A. On A's death the trustees will pay the income as it arises to B. When B dies, and C becomes absolutely entitled, the trustees will transfer the capital to C. At this point the trust will come to an end.

So when a Tenant for life sells the land, the equitable interests of the beneficiaries (including himself) are detached from the land and attach instead to the purchase money that P paid to the trustees. We express this by saying that the interests of the beneficiaries are '*overreached*'. Thus 'overreaching' means 'being detached from the land'.

By requiring a purchaser to pass the purchase money to the trustees the beneficiaries are protected against misappropriation of the money by the Tenant for life. We shall see later that common law and statute combine to prevent the Tenant for life from exploiting the land itself to the detriment of the beneficiaries while he is in possession of it.

It may be helpful to summarise the ground covered so far:

1. After 1925, if a settlement of land was not created under a trust for sale it had to be created in the form of a strict settlement.
2. A strict settlement had to be created by two documents. In the case of an inter vivos settlement, these were a vesting deed and a trust instrument.
3. The legal estate had to be vested in the Tenant for life, who was (subject to what is said later) the first person entitled to possession of the land under the settlement.
4. The trustees of the settlement were persons appointed as such by the settlor in the trust instrument.
5. The Tenant for life is given power by the Act to sell the land.
6. On sale of the land the purchaser must pay the purchase money to the trustees of the settlement.
7. Provided that the purchaser pays the purchase money to the trustees and ensures that they are at least two in number or a trust corporation, he takes free of the equitable interests of the beneficiaries under the settlement. The equitable interests are detached from the land and attach instead to the purchase money. This process is termed overreaching.

---

10 SLA 1925, s 18(1)(b).
11 See LP (Am) Act 1926, s 3. Public Trustee (Custodian Trustee) Rules 1926 (SR & O 1926, 1423 L 37).
12 See Chapter 5.

8. The trustees then hold the money on trust for the beneficiaries under the settlement.

Having outlined the principal features of the Settled Land Act 1925, we must now turn to consider a number of aspects of the Act in more detail.

'SETTLED LAND'

The Act provided that the machinery of a strict settlement was to apply whenever land was 'settled land'. The Act provided[13] that land was 'settled land' whenever it was subject to a 'settlement' as defined by the Act. By the definition of a settlement in s 1 of the Act, a settlement would come into existence in each of the following seven instances:

1. Where S granted land to A for life *with remainder* to B in fee simple.[14] (This is the example of a settlement that we have used so far in this chapter.)
2. Where S granted land to F for an estate in *fee tail.*[15]
3. Where S granted land 'to H in fee simple (or for life) but if H dies without issue then over to J' (ie for a *conditional interest*).[16] A fee simple that was conditional by reason of the grantor having a right of re-entry in the event of non-payment of a rentcharge was not settled land.[17]
4. Where S granted land 'to K in fee simple (or for life) until K commits an act of bankruptcy' (ie for a *determinable interest*);[18] similarly, where the grant is to permit K to reside on (or occupy) the land for as long as he desires to do so[19] (or for as long as he desires to do so and remained unmarried[20]), and thereafter for Z.
5. Where S granted land 'to the first son of M to be called to the Bar' (ie for the grant of a *contingent interest*).[1]
6. Where S granted land to Q in fee simple, but *charged* the land with the payment of £50 per annum to S's widow during her lifetime (with the result that whoever holds the fee simple is responsible for paying the £50 to S's widow, the land forming the security for the annual payments); or where S granted land to N in fee simple subject to a charge of £50 per annum to a named charity, for ever.[2]
7. Where S granted land in fee simple to V, and V was an *infant.*[3]

---

13   Section 2.
14   Section 1(1)(i).
15   Section 1(1)(ii)(a).
16   Section 1(1)(ii)(c) and 117 (1)(iv).
17   See p 105.
18   Section 1(1)(ii)(c). Fee simples that are determinable by reason of the operation of the School Sites Acts 1841-1852 are generally regarded as not being settled land under the Settled Land Act 1925. See Law Com No 111 (*Rights of Reverter*) para 15.
19   *Re Carne's Settled Estates* [1899] 1 Ch 324; *Re Baroness Llanover's Will* [1903] 2 Ch 16. See also *Re Paget's Settled Estates* (1885) 30 Ch D 161.
20   *Re Boyer's Settled Estates* [1916] 2 Ch 404.
 1   Section 1(1)(iii).
 2   Section 1(1)(v).
 3   Section 1(1)(ii)(d). For the present position with regard to land held by an infant, see p 149.

It will be seen that in the case of 1, 2, 3, and 4 above a succession of interests was, or might be, involved. In the case of 2, on F's death the land passed to F's heir, and on F's heir's death it passed to his heir, and so on. In the case of 3, the land was transferred to H, but it might later pass to J. In the case of 4, the land was transferred to K, but if the determining event occurred, then S became entitled.

In the case of 5, if S has directed that until the gift vested the income from the land was to be given to, say N, then there was an element of succession involved (first N, then M's son), but if S made no such direction, the income which arose while the gift was contingent accumulated and went to whichever son of M (if any) became entitled to the land. In this case no succession of interests was involved; but the land is settled land nevertheless because the Settled Land Act 1925 provided[4] that land granted for a contingent was to be subject to a 'settlement'.

Similarly in the case of 6 and 7, here too the land is settled land because the Act provided[5] that in these situations the land was to be subject to a 'settlement'.

Regarding 6, the land was only settled land if the charge was created 'voluntarily or in consideration of marriage or by way of family arrangement'.[6] So if the person in whose favour the charge was created (in our example S's widow) gave consideration (other than marriage), then the land was not settled land.

Trustees of the settlement

The Act provided[7] for the trustees of the settlement to be:

1. The persons (if any) who, under the settlement, were trustees with power to sell the land.
2. The persons, if any, declared by the settlement to be trustees of the settlement for the purpose of the Settled Land Act 1925, ie the persons appointed by the settlor.

If trustees of the settlement were not expressly appointed by the settlor, the Act provided that certain other persons were to be the trustees of the settlement. There were five heads under which trustees of the settlement were to be found, the first two being those set out above.[8] If no trustees were obtained under one head, it was necessary to pass on to the next. If no trustees were obtained under any of the five heads and the settlement was created by will the Act provided that the settlor's personal representatives[9] were to be the trustees of

---

4   Section 1(1)(iii).
5   Section 1(1)(v) and 1(1)(ii)(d).
6   Section 1(1)(v).
7   Section 30.
8   For the other three heads, see p 105 of the previous edition.
9   The persons responsible for administering the estate of a dead person. Those appointed by a testator are termed executors; those authorised to act in the case of an intestacy are termed administrators. There can be a sole personal representative.

the settlement.[10] In the absence of trustees under any of the above heads, the court had power to appoint trustees.[11]

The Tenant for life

The Tenant for life was, as we have said, the first person entitled to the land under the settlement (and where settlements under the Settled Land Act 1925 existed at the date of the 1996 Act, this person still is Tenant for life under the 1925 Act). But in some situations in which land was subject to a settlement there was no one capable of being the Tenant for life, eg as in case 5 – 'to the first son of M to be called to the Bar': until a son of M qualifies, no one is entitled to the land and so there was no Tenant for life. Let us first, however, look at the situations when there was a Tenant for life, and so no problem arose.

INSTANCES WHEN THERE WAS A TENANT FOR LIFE

In case 1 above we know (because it is the example we started with) that A was the Tenant for life.[12] In 2, F, who had an equitable fee tail, was the Tenant for life. (A Tenant for life by no means necessarily always held an equitable *life* interest under the settlement.) In the case of 3, H, who held a conditional interest, was Tenant for life. In 4, K, who held a determinable interest, was Tenant for life.

In 6, Q was the Tenant for life. He held a legal fee simple on trust for himself for an equitable fee simple subject to the charge in favour of S's widow. If he sold the land the purchaser had to pay the purchase money to the trustees of the settlement in the way we have described. The trustees would buy an annuity of £50 for S's widow. The balance of the proceeds of the sale of the land they would give to Q. The Act thus enables the land to be sold free of the charge, and yet protected the interest of S's widow.

INSTANCES WHEN THERE WAS NO TENANT FOR LIFE

We have noted that if S made a grant, as in 5 above, 'to the first son of M to be called to the Bar' there would be no Tenant for life. Another situation when there was no Tenant for life was case 7 – where S granted land to an infant, V. Since an infant could not (and cannot) hold a legal estate in land, an infant cannot be a Tenant for life. Another situation in which there would be no Tenant for life would be a variation of 6: if S did not grant the fee simple to Q, but merely directed that certain land was to be charged with the payment of a certain sum to S's widow.

---

10   Section 30(3).
11   Section 9(3).
12   Further, if the interest granted amounted, in effect, to a life interest, then the grantee becomes Tenant for life. *Re Carne's Settled Estates* [1899] 1 Ch 324 (house held on trust to allow a woman to occupy it for as long as she wished, rent free: woman held to be Tenant for life.)

POSITION IF THERE WAS NO TENANT FOR LIFE: THE STATUTORY OWNER

The Act provided[13] that if there was no Tenant for life, the settlor was required to convey the legal estate to the 'statutory owner'.

The statutory owner was the person who (being of full age) the settlor directed should have the powers of Tenant for life. Suppose that a settlor wished to give land to V, who was seven, and directed that X should have the powers of Tenant for life, and he appointed Y and Z as trustees of the settlement, the position would be this:

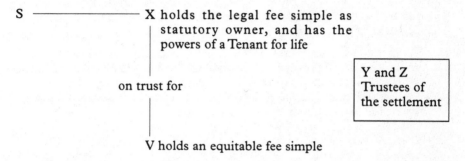

S ————————— X holds the legal fee simple as statutory owner, and has the powers of a Tenant for life

on trust for

Y and Z
Trustees of
the settlement

V holds an equitable fee simple

If X sold the land, the purchaser, P, would have to pay the purchase money to the trustees of the settlement, Y and Z, who would then hold the purchase money on trust for V.

If there was no Tenant for life and if the settlor did not confer on any person the powers of Tenant for life, the trustees of the settlement were the statutory owners,[14] to whom the settlor would have to convey the legal estate. But he conveyed the legal estate to them as statutory owners, not as trustees of the settlement. So if, in the last example, the settlor had not conferred the powers of Tenant for life on X, the position would have been this:

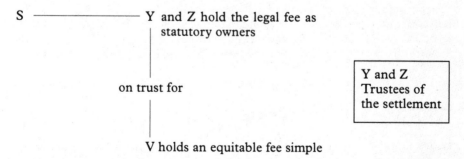

S ————————— Y and Z hold the legal fee as statutory owners

on trust for

Y and Z
Trustees of
the settlement

V holds an equitable fee simple

If the land was sold to P, it was sold by Y and Z in their capacity as statutory owners, and the purchase money was paid to them in their capacity as trustees of the settlement.

---

13 Sections 4(2), 23(1), 117(1)(xxvi).
14 Section 117(1)(xxvi).

If there was no Tenant for life, no statutory owners were appointed, and no trustees were appointed, then it was necessary for trustees to be found, if necessary, as we have seen, by appointment by the court. Once trustees existed they acted not only as trustees but also as statutory owners. Thus, one way or another, there was always someone to hold the legal estate and exercise the powers of Tenant for life.

Infants and settled land under the Settled Land Act 1925

The question of land being granted to an infant might have arisen in two ways in the context of settled land:

1. The first was where S granted land to A, an infant, for an estate of fee simple absolute in possession. The Settled Land Act 1925 provided[15] that in this case, although no succession of interests was involved, the land was to be settled land. For the reasons we have seen, the infant could not be Tenant for life. As there was no Tenant for life, the legal fee simple was vested in the statutory owner.[16]
2. Where S granted land to A, an infant, for life, with remainder to B in fee simple. Here the land was settled land by virtue of the fact that it was granted for a succession of interests. Since A was an infant he could not be the Tenant for life. So here too the legal estate was vested in the statutory owner.

In 1, when A attained full age he could require the statutory owner to convey the legal fee simple to him absolutely and the settlement came to an end. In 2, when A attained full age he could require the statutory owner to transfer the legal fee simple to him, and he thereupon became the Tenant for life.

Settlements created by will

When a settlor died the whole of his property vested in his ordinary personal representative, who conveyed the land in the settlement to the person qualified to be the first Tenant for life (or statutory owner).[17] He did this by a vesting assent which replaced the vesting deed. The will operated as the trust instrument.[18]

POWERS OF A TENANT FOR LIFE

Let us suppose that in his will S, who died in 1994, left his farm Greenacre to his son, A, for life with remainder to A's son, B. S did not leave the farm on

15   Section 1(1)(ii)(d).
16   In the case of a settlement created by will, pending the vesting of the legal estate in the statutory owner, the settlor's personal representative has all the powers of a Tenant for life and of trustees of the settlement: SLA 1925, s 26(1).
17   SLA 1925, s 6(b).
18   SLA 1925, s 6(a).

trust for sale for his son and grandson, so a strict settlement arose. A became (and remains) Tenant for life. By virtue of his own equitable life interest, A is entitled to the farm during his lifetime. The Settled Land Act 1925 confers on him certain powers.

Power to lease the settled land

Suppose that Greenacre Farm (see above) includes a paddock. Some years before his death, A's father, S, had leased the paddock to N for 21 years. On succeeding to the land, the annual rent paid by N forms part of the income from the land and so belongs to A. (A receives the rent as Tenant for life because in that capacity he holds the legal fee simple and so is N's landlord. He receives the rent as trustee, and hands it over to himself as beneficiary.) When the lease expires, N asks A if he will grant him a fresh lease for a further 21 years. Without the intervention of statute, A would have been able to grant a lease to N, but it would only have been binding until A's death.

The Settled Land Act 1925 provides[19] that A, as Tenant for life, has power to grant leases that are binding on the land beyond the time of his death, ie which will be binding on B, the remainderman, but the power only enables the Tenant for life to grant leases for certain maximum periods: a building lease may not exceed 999 years; a lease for the purpose of mining may not exceed 100 years; and a lease for any other purpose may not exceed 50 years.

For the valid exercise of the power, the Tenant for life must give written notice to the trustees of his intention to grant the lease;[1] the lease must be for the best rent reasonably obtainable in the circumstances, regard being had to any fine taken;[2] and the lease must take effect in possession (ie the tenant must have the right to move in) not more than one year after the date of the grant of the lease.

When a lease is granted, the rent normally belongs to A, but in the case of a mining lease, A is entitled to only a proportion of the rent. What this proportion is and who is entitled to the balance, we shall see later.

Power to sell the settled land[3]

A Tenant for life's power of sale[4] extends to the whole or any part of the settled land.

---

19 Section 41.
20 A building lease is one in which a tenant agrees to undertake certain building work, eg adding a new building or improving an existing one.
 1 If the lease is for not more than 21 years, then subject to two conditions being satisfied (see SLA 1925, s 42(5)) no notice need be given.
 2 A fine is an initial lump sum payment in consideration of which a lower rent will be payable. A fine becomes capital money.
 3 SLA 1925, s 38.
 4 See *Wheelwright v Walker* (1883) 23 Ch D 752; (M & B).

The Tenant for life must give notice to the trustees of his intention[5] to sell and he must obtain the best price reasonably obtainable.[6] (There is no requirement that the land must be auctioned.)

In order that the purchaser may take free of the equitable interests under the settlement he must, as noted above, pay the purchase money to the trustees.[7]

Power to exchange the settled land for other land

If A, as Tenant for life, decided to part with the paddock to P, and P owned a field which would make a useful addition to Greenacre Farm, A has power under the Act[8] to exchange the paddock for P's field.

Any difference in value would be adjusted according to the relative values of the two properties, a difference due to A being paid into, and a difference due from A coming from, the capital money.

Power to grant options[9]

A Tenant for life has power to grant by writing (with or without consideration) an option to another to purchase or lease the settled land. Notice must be given to the trustees.

CAPITAL MONEY

This is money held by the trustees of the settlement. It can come from a variety of sources: for example, from sale of the settled land (or part of it), from a fine on the grant of a lease, from consideration on the grant of an option, or from the sale of timber.[10]

Capital money:

either   (a)   is invested and produces income which goes to the person entitled in possession under the settlement, ie A, during his lifetime;

or   (b)   may be used for certain specified purposes, for example making up the difference on an exchange of land. Another is to meet the whole or part of the cost of making improvements.

Power to make improvements[11]

A Tenant for life does not need a power conferred by statute to make improvements if he is prepared to pay for them out of his own pocket, but in

---

5   SLA 1925, s 101.
6   SLA 1925, s 39.
7   SLA 1925, s 18(1)(b).
8   Section 38.
9   SLA 1925, s 51. The option must be made exercisable within a period not exceeding ten years.
10   See p 120, infra.
11   Sections 83-87.

some circumstances the Act authorises the trustees to pay for improvements out of capital. What is commonly termed a Tenant for life's 'power to make improvements' would therefore more correctly be termed his 'power to have improvements paid for out of capital'.

For some kinds of improvements, listed in Part I of the Third Schedule to the Settled Land Act 1925, the whole cost is payable out of capital money. These are improvements that are likely to be of permanent benefit and so likely to benefit B when he becomes entitled to the land. B will receive that much less capital, but the land will have been that much improved.

Part II of the Third Schedule includes such matters as the restoration of buildings damaged by dry rot, and additions or alterations to existing buildings. For these the trustees of the settlement may (and, on a court order, must) require A to repay the money advanced out of capital, by not more than 50 half-yearly instalments.

Improvements listed in Part III include the installation of electric power and light and the purchase of such farming aids as motor lorries, traction engines and combine harvesters. For these the trustees must require repayment by A, by not more than 50 half-yearly instalments.

Power to mortgage the settled land

The Act[12] gives the Tenant for life power, on notifying the trustees, to mortgage the land for one of a specified list of purposes. One is paying for an improvement listed in the Third Schedule of the Act. Another is to pay any difference when settled land is exchanged for other land.

But money borrowed has to be repaid. If no capital money is available, A is personally liable to repay the loan. If capital money is available and the money has been borrowed to make up the difference in an exchange of land, capital money can be used to repay the loan.

Distinct from A's statutory power to mortgage the legal fee simple is his right to mortgage his own equitable interest. Since this is less valuable than the fee simple he will be able to borrow less; but he can use the money for any purpose he pleases. He alone is responsible for repaying the loan.

Power to dispose of the principal mansion house[13]

Hitherto we have regarded the Tenant for life as someone who has the right to dispose of the whole or any part of the settled land merely on giving notice to the trustees. In the case of the principal mansion house, however, in certain circumstances[14] he requires their consent. ('Dispose' includes selling, leasing, exchanging or mortgaging.)

---

12 Section 71.
13 Section 65.
14 See p 112 of the previous edition of this book.

The principal mansion house is any house occupied as the main residence unless it is occupied as a farm house or unless the house and its grounds occupy not more than 25 acres.[15]

Power to effect other transactions under an order of the court

The Act[16] confers jurisdiction on the court to make an order authorising a Tenant for life of settled land to effect any transaction concerning the settled land that could have been validly carried out by an absolute owner and which, in the opinion of the court, would be for the benefit of the land or the beneficiaries under the settlement; for example, the granting of a lease for a period longer than that permitted[17] by the Act.[18]

TIMBER

The principles relating to waste were explained in Chapter 3. Under the Act a Tenant for life who is impeachable for waste may fell timber trees with the consent of the trustees of the settlement (or the court), but he may retain only one-quarter of the proceeds, three-quarters becoming capital money. (A Tenant for life who is not impeachable for waste can, by common law, fell timber and keep all the proceeds.)

RENT FROM MINING LEASES

The 1925[20] Act empowers a Tenant for life to grant mining leases for periods not exceeding 100 years, but he does not take the whole of the proceeds. If his lessee opens and works a new mine a Tenant for life who is impeachable for waste will take only one-quarter of the rent, three-quarters going to the trustees of the Settlement. In other cases the Tenant for life takes three-quarters, the trustees one-quarter.

Summary of a Tenant for life's powers

Powers exercisable on giving notice to the trustees	Powers exercisable with the consent of the trustees	Powers exercisable without notice to, or consent of, the trustees
Sale	Cut timber	Make improvements
Lease	Dispose of the	
Exchange	principal mansion	
Mortgage	house (if consent	
	is expressly required)	

15   Section 65(2).
16   Section 64.
17   Under s 41.
18   *Re Rycroft's Settlement* [1962] Ch 263, [1961] 3 All ER 581; (M & B).
19   Section 66.
20   Section 41.

How capital money arises

It will be noted that capital money may arise in the following ways:

1. From the sale of all or any of the settled land.
2. When settled land is exchanged for other land, and the settled land is worth more than the other land.
3. From a fine paid under a lease.
4. From a proportion of the proceeds of sale of timber.
5. From a proportion of the rent under a mining lease.

Statutory powers and the provisions of the settlement

A settlor was able to extend the statutory powers[1]. For example, he might confer a power to grant leases beyond the periods prescribed in the Act[2]. Thus the powers conferred by the Act and those given in the settlement are cumulative.

But the statutory powers could not be excluded, nor could they be restricted. Any provision in the settlement which purported to exclude or restrict a statutory power was void.[3]

MISCELLANEOUS MATTERS

Death of a Tenant for life

The procedure here depends upon whether the settlement continues to exist or comes to an end.

Consider a settlement on A for life with remainder to B for life with remainder to C in fee simple. On A's death the legal fee simple will vest not in his general, or ordinary, personal representative (normally his executor) as it would in the case of settled land, but in his *special personal representatives* – who are the trustees of the settlement,[4] acting in a further capacity. The legal fee simple is then transferred[5] to the next Tenant for life (in our example, B) by a *vesting assent*,[6] which fulfils the same functions and contains the same details as a vesting deed.

The settlement continues with B as Tenant for life. But on B's death, since C is now absolutely entitled, the settlement comes to an end, and the land must[7] be vested in C by B's ordinary personal representative using a simple

---

1 Section 109(1).
2 See ante.
3 Section 106. For examples, see p 113 of the previous edition.
4 AEA 1925, s 22(1).
5 SLA 1925, s 7(1).
6 Assent: a document by which personal representatives, having completed the administration of the estate, transfer land to the appropriate beneficiary. (They *assent* in writing to the transfer.)
7 SLA 1925, s 7(5).

(ordinary) assent. C now holds the legal fee simple absolute in possession free of any trust. If he wishes to sell the land the simple assent by which the land has been conveyed to him will establish his title, and satisfy a purchaser that the settlement no longer exists.[8]

The curtain principle

The Act provides[9] that a purchaser of land from a Tenant for life is not entitled to inspect the trust instrument. This is withheld from his view 'behind the curtain'.

Two advantages accrue from what is termed the 'curtain' principle. If a Tenant for life proposes to sell the land, the interests of the beneficiaries, which are likely to be of a private, personal, nature are not disclosed to an outsider. Secondly, the purchaser is saved the trouble of reading what may be a lengthy recital of equitable interests. All that the purchaser needs to know is whether the vendor (the Tenant for life) has a good legal title, and this the vesting deed or vesting assent makes clear.

On the sale of the settled land the vesting deed is handed over (with the other title deeds) to the purchaser. The trust instrument is retained by the trustees.

Contents of a vesting deed and trust instrument

We have mentioned, in the course of this chapter, some of the contents of a vesting deed and a trust instrument. We are now in a position to set out the contents of the two documents, and to see the reason for each item.

THE VESTING DEED

Item	*Purpose*
1. Describes the settled land.	So that those concerned know what land is involved.
2. Declares that the settled land is vested in the person (or persons) to whom it is conveyed, upon the trusts affecting the settled land.	This: 1. Conveys the legal estate to the Tenant for life (or statutory owner). 2. Warns a purchaser that the land is settled land (so that he knows he must pay his money to the trustees of the settlement).
3. States the names of the trustees of the settlement.	So that a purchaser knows to whom to pay his money.
4. States the names of any persons empowered (in the trust instrument) to appoint new trustees of the settlement.	So that if one or more of the original trustees is dead or has retired, a purchaser can find out the names of the new trustee or trustees.

---

8 *Re Bridgett and Hayes' Contract* [1928] Ch 163; (M & B).
9 SLA 1925, s 110(2).

Item	*Purpose*
5. States any extension of the statutory powers or additional powers conferred (in the trust instrument) on the Tenant for life (or statutory owner), eg a power to grant leases of up to 100 years.	So that if A proposed to lease Greenacre Farm to T for, say, 80 years, T will know whether he has power to do this.

THE TRUST INSTRUMENT[10]

1. Declares the trusts affecting the settled land, eg to A for life, with remainder to B, etc.	This declaration creates the equitable interests under the settlement.
2. Appoints the trustees of the settlement. (They must be expressly stated to be appointed as trustees 'for the purposes of the Settled Land Act 1925'.)[11]	This is the appropriate document in which to appoint the trustees.
3. (May) confer a power to appoint new trustees (eg the power may be given to a surviving trustee or to some other person or persons).	So that if one or more trustees dies or retires fresh trustees can be appointed in their place.
4. (May) extend the Tenant for life's statutory powers, or confer on him additional powers.	(If the settlor so wishes.)

Precedents for a vesting deed and for a trust instrument are set out under Forms No 2 and 3 in the First Schedule of the Settled Land Act 1925.

Functions of the trustees of a strict settlement

We are now in a position to collect together the various functions which the trustees of the settlement perform:

1. Where S (incorrectly) conveys a legal estate to someone other than the Tenant for life (or the statutory owner) or (b) uses only one document, the trustees execute a vesting deed.
2. Where a Tenant for life dies and the settlement continues after his death, the trustees act as special personal representatives.
3. Where there is no Tenant for life, the trustees act as statutory owner holding the legal fee simple, and have the powers of a Tenant for life for the purpose of managing the land.[12]
4. They must be given notice if the Tenant for life intends to exercise his statutory powers of sale, exchange, leasing or mortgaging.

---

10 SLA 1925, s 4(3).
11 SLA 1925, s 30(1)(ii).
12 SLA 1925, s 102.

5. They must give their consent in order that the Tenant for life may be able to exercise certain statutory powers.
6. They receive capital money and hold it on the trusts of the settlement.
7. If the Tenant for life wishes to acquire an interest in the legal estate for his own benefit, the trustees exercise the relevant powers of the Tenant for life for the purpose of the transaction.
8. If the Tenant for life parts with his equitable interest under the settlement and he either unreasonably refuses to exercise his powers or to consent to the trustees exercising them, the court may order that the Tenant for life's powers shall be exercisable instead by the trustees.

Settled leasehold land

It is not only a fee simple estate but also a leasehold estate that may be the subject of a strict settlement. Suppose that S held Greenacre Farm, not for an estate of fee simple, but for a legal lease of 999 years, of which 99 have expired. When S created a strict settlement, he assigned the lease (ie the unexpired portion of 900 years) to A as Tenant for life. A held this on trust for himself for life with remainder, let us say, to B. When A died the settlement came to an end. The legal estate (ie the lease) vested in A's ordinary personal representatives who, by an assent, assigned the legal title to the lease to B.

So, strictly, we should not say that in a settlement under the Settled Land Act 1925, the Tenant for life holds the legal fee simple (though this may be the more common situation), but we should say instead that the *legal estate* in the land is vested in the Tenant for life. In that way we are correct, irrespective of whether the settled land is held for a fee simple or a leasehold estate.

It will be noted that the holder of the fee simple (S's, then A's, then B's landlord) remains outside, and unaffected by, the settlement.

Settled land after the Trusts of Land and Appointment of Trustees Act 1996

At the present day, ie after the 1996 Act, land is subject to the Settled Land Act 1925 (is subject to a 'strict settlement') only if:

1. the settlement was made before the coming into operation of the 1996 Act; or,
2. the settlement was created after the coming into operation of the Act 'on the occasion of an alteration in any interest in, or of a person becoming entitled under a settlement' which was in existence at the commencement of the Act or derives from such a settlement, and no provision is made in the settlement that the settlement is not to be a settlement for the purposes of the Settled Land Act 1925.[13]

---

13   Trusts of Land and Appointment of Trustees Act 1996, s 2(1).

Strict settlements and the purpose of the Settled Land Acts[14]

As noted earlier, a 'strict settlement' is the name given to the type of settlement that evolved during the eighteenth century, reaching its fullest form in the nineteenth, and that had as its object the retention of land within a settlor's family. In its fullest form a strict settlement might be of great complexity, property being 'allowed to be moulded according to the circumstances and wants of every family'.[15] In essence, however, a strict settlement took the form of a grant by a settlor (S) to himself for life with the remainder to his eldest son (A) for life, with remainder to A's (as yet unborn) eldest son (B) in tail.[16] How did this secure the continuance of the land within the family? After S had died and when B attained 21, he could, with his father's concurrence, bar the entail and turn it into a full fee simple in remainder. Father and son could then (under the principle in *Saunders v Vautier*) divide the land between them in whatever proportion they agreed. Sometimes, particularly where the family was impoverished, this might happen. But what often happened (and what S relied on happening) was that a number of years would elapse between S's death and B attaining his majority. During this intervening period, A would live as master in the great house. After dinner he would stand and, mellow with port, survey the deer park and the woods beyond. Gradually, he would come to have the same wish as his father – that the estate should remain within the family, that it should pass to B, and B's son, and so on, for ever. So A ceased to think of the settlement being broken when B attained 21.

Young B, deep in debt, had no such feelings for the great house and its lands. What B wanted was ready cash to pay his debts and lead a fast life in London. If his father would agree, B could bar the entail, and convert the fee tail in remainder into a fee simple in remainder. This would be a commodity that would be readily saleable, or one that B could mortgage as security for the money he needed to pay off his creditors. But, without his father's consent, all B would be able to obtain if he barred the entail would be a base fee, and the value of this would be small – too small to be worth giving up entitlement to succession to the estate on his father's death. But B's father, now having grown sentimental about his broad acres and dreaming of a grandson succeeding to the estate, would not consent to the disentailment.

'Let's be practical', A would say to B, 'what you need is money, and you need it now. What we can do is this. I will consent to you barring your fee tail in remainder if, in exchange, you agree that the land is – by the same deed – resettled on me (A) for life, with remainder to you (B) for life, with the remainder to your eldest son in fee tail. And, what is more, as part of the arrangement you will receive, as a charge on the land, an income of 1,000 guineas a year until you succeed to the land on my death.' B is in no position to refuse, and the

---

14 B. English and J. Saville *Strict Settlements: A Guide for Historians* (1983).
15 Fourth Report of the Real Property Commissioners, 1833, p 6, see Manchester, p 335.
16 Provision would be made also for the settlor's wife on his death, in the form of a charge on the land to provide income for her life time (a *jointure rentcharge*), and for the settlor's younger children on his death, in the form of lump sums (*portions*).

land is resettled in the way A proposes. Some years later A dies. B then holds the land for life with remainder to his newly born son, C, in fee tail. 'When C attains 21', B thinks, 'we shall be able to break the entail and divide the land between us.' C, who becomes a bigger gambler even than his father, would be glad to do this. But years pass and by the time C attains 21, B has matured. He has himself now come to love the deer park and the woods beyond. 'Now', B says to C, 'what you need is money, and you need it fast. What we can do is this ... '. And the arrangement is repeated. It was in this way that great estates remained in the same families for many generations.

It has been estimated that possibly as much as half of land in nineteenth century England was subject to some form of strict settlement.[17] Economic disadvantages might attach to the subjection of so much land to the fetters constituted by a settlement. In particular, the existence of the settlement might lead to under-capitalisation and poor management of the land. For example, where land needed drainage, the life tenant would be able to carry out the work only if he could find the money out of his own pocket – perhaps from rents already at a low level. Unless the settlor had conferred the power on the life tenant, capital money, if it existed, could not be used for improvements to the land.

Further, unless express powers were conferred on the trustees or the life tenant, no lease for longer than the life tenant's life could be granted. But, without the certainty of being able to hold the land for a reasonable period, few tenants would be likely to manage the land with an eye to its long-term benefit, and rents from leases for the uncertain duration of a life would be lower than could be demanded for leases for a fixed period.

The extent to which the existence of settlements contributed to the decline in the fortunes of the great landed estates in the last century has been the subject of debate. In recent years, the tendency has been to regard the economic detriment caused by settlements as having been exaggerated.[18] It has been pointed out that very many settlements did confer powers necessary for good management, such as leasing, on the trustees or on the tenant for life, and that, where no powers existed in the settlement or where they were inadequate, these powers could be obtained by private acts – and that hundred of such acts were so obtained. Further, a number of public Acts during the century conferred a variety of powers necessary for good management of land on trustees or tenants for life of settled land; in particular, the Settled Estates Drainage Acts 1840 and 1845, the Settled Estates Act 1856 and the Improvement of Land Act 1864.

No public Act, however, conferred a power to sell the whole of the settled land. It was this step that was taken by the Settled Land Act 1882.[19] Thus it was this Act, culminating the earlier legislation, that finally enabled a settlement

---

17   English and Saville, op cit, p 31; F.M.L. Thompson *English Landed Society in the Nineteenth Century* (1963) pp 65-68.
18   Or even, indeed, invented by writers of law texts seeking a rationale for the changes of 1925. See 'Land Law Texts and the Explanation of 1925', S. Anderson [1984] CLP 63.
19   See the speech of Ear Cairns on presenting the Bill, Manchester, p 340.

to be broken by the sale of the land (with the conversion of the beneficial interests from interests in land to interests in money). In addition to conferring a power to sell the settled land, the Act conferred powers of leasing, mortgaging, exchanging and improving (from capital money) the land broadly similar to those that were later contained in the Settled Land Act 1925.

The significance of the Act of 1882 lay in two directions. First, it undermined the psychological device that lead to the resettlement of land at each new generation. To revert to our example, when S died, A did not have to wait until B attained his majority before the land could, after the barring of B's entail, be sold. The land could be sold as soon as A succeeded as life tenant. (Indeed, the land could be sold by the settlor during his life tenancy if he so decided.) Secondly, even if there was no wish to sell the whole of the land, the Act, by enabling any part of the land to be sold, provided a means by which capital money could be provided for the improvement of the remainder.[20]

The Act of 1882 did not, however, alter the structure of a settlement; the legal estate remained in the trustees, the tenant for life continued to hold only an equitable interest. The Act achieved its object by conferring on the tenant for life *power* to execute transactions with regard to the legal estate: although holding only an *equitable* interest, he had power under the Act to sell, lease or mortgage, the *legal* fee simple. The significance of the 1925 Act, it will now be appreciated, lay not in powers it conferred on a life tenant (although the powers it conferred were in fact wider than under the 1882 Act[1]), but in changes it made to the structure of a settlement, requiring the legal estate to be vested, no longer in trustees, but in the first person entitled in the chain of interests, the statutory Tenant for life. After 1925, when A sold the land he sold what he actually held (ie as Tenant for life), namely, the legal estate.

In the development of the English land law two forces can be seen at work. On the one hand there are those who have been in favour of it being possible for land to be tied up for generations to come. In this class we find owners of estates who wish to ensure that land is retained after their deaths within their own families. Opposed to them are those who consider that restraints on free alienation of land are against the public interest. In the latter class we find, amongst others, those who inherit land for a limited interest, eg a life interest, who would prefer the land to be sold so that they could have the money instead; and those who want to buy land but find that a restraint of the kind we have been considering prevents its sale.

Much of the history of English land law is concerned with the struggle between these two groups. The sympathy of the courts have been pulled in both directions: on the one hand the courts have recognised that a grantor should, within limits, be permitted to frame his grant in the terms he wishes. Support for this attitude has come from the principle that for liberty to be served, restrictions on an individual's actions should not be imposed without

20 SLA 1882, ss 25-29.
1 Eg under the 1882 Act the maximum duration for which building leases could be granted was 99 years; for mining leases, 60 years; for other leases 21 years (compared with 999, 100 and 50 years respectively under the Act of 1925).

due cause, and from the principle that there is no demerit in a person being permitted to make provision for his family's welfare after his death. On the other hand, the courts have accepted that undue restraints on alienation of land may be contrary to the public good. Support for this attitude is to be derived from the recognition that the freedom of one generation to prescribe the course of devolution of property in the future entails the removal of the same freedom from the generations that follow.[2] In this book we meet several ways in which the courts have countered such restraints on alienation. For example, in Chapter 4 we saw that in the case of a conditional fee simple, certain types of restraint on alienation were void. In Chapter 3 we saw how the courts accepted the collusive actions of fines and recoveries by which the fee tail could be barred. In Chapter 12 we shall see that if the period of uncertainty before a gift vests might be too long, the gift may be void. All these constitute attacks by the common law on the ability of a landowner to grant land in a form that predetermines to whom the land is to pass after it has left the grantor's hands.

But the greatest attack was made, not by the courts, but by the legislature, with the passing of the Settled Land Act 1882. This Act was, we know, replaced by the Settled Land Act 1925, but the purpose of the two Acts, whilst their mechanics differed, was the same – to free settled land from the fetters imposed on it by a settlor.

The irony, however, lies in the fact that by the time the Settled Land Act 1882 was passed, as a form of disposition of land strict settlements were falling from favour. Until about the middle of the nineteenth century land had been the primary source of wealth in the country. And land not only produced income, it gave power, and conferred status. Bankers, merchants and traders might have their wealth in other forms, but the supreme badge of social position was the holding of land. So for a person of position to wish his wealth to devolve to his issue, was for him to wish that his land should pass to his issue. But following the industrial revolution, ownership of capital invested in industry, in commerce and in banking came to exceed in economic importance the holding of land. So men of property who wished their wealth to pass to their descendants were concerned less with settlements of land than with settlements of personalty. The family estate might still be settled to descend to future generations, but relative to other forms of wealth, the settlement of land ceased to have its earlier importance. Another reason for the decline in the significance of settlements of land was concerned with the fiscal disadvantages, after the introduction of estate duty in 1894, attached to forms of disposition (of both land and personalty) that entailed a succession of life interests. Under the scheme of taxation introduced by the Finance Act 1894, if S settled land on A for life, with remainder to B for life, with remainder to C in fee simple, tax was levyable on the death not only of C, but also on the deaths of the preceding life tenants, A and B. With the introduction of the principle that no estate duty was payable on the death of a spouse with a life interest, the furthest that a settlor would generally wish to limit the devolution of his property would be in

---

2   See Morris and Leach, 15; L. M. Simes (1954-55) 103 Univ of Pennsylvania LR 707. See Chapter 12.

the form of a gift to his widow for her lifetime, with remainder to his children absolutely. In making such a grant a settlor lost the satisfaction of knowing that the land would (assuming that no advantage was taken of the Settled Land Act 1882) pass through the hands of the person he named in the settlement, but he gained the consolation of knowing that he had not saddled his descendants with a disposition that would result in the diminution (through taxation) of the value of the settled property on the death of each successive life tenant.

In the twentieth century settlements of land under the Settled Land Act 1925 declined in favour even where the settlement was merely in the form of a gift to a spouse for life with the remainder to the children. The principal reason was the cumbersome machinery established by the Act. If it was wished that land should go to a widow for her life, with remainder to the children, a simpler and equally effective form of disposition was to be found in the trust for sale.

SUMMARY

A disposition that creates a succession of interests is termed a settlement.

After 1925, if a settlement of land was not created as a trust for sale, it was subject to the Settled Land Act 1925 (and was 'settled land' subject to a 'strict settlement').

Under a strict settlement the legal estate is vested in the first person entitled as the statutory Tenant for life, who holds the legal estate on trust for those entitled (himself included).

A settlement created inter vivos was created by a vesting deed and a trust instrument.

The Tenant for life has power to sell the land and effect transactions specified in the Act.

On sale of the land, the purchase price is payable to the trustees of the settlement (appointed in the trust deed), whereupon the equitable interests are overreached and attach to the purchase money.

The Settled Land Act 1925 laid down seven situations in which land was, if not subject to a trust for sale, to be settled land under the Act, including when land is conveyed to an infant.

If there is no one to act as Tenant for life, the legal estate is vested in the trustees of the settlement.

With a limited exception, no new settlement under the Settled Land Act 1925 can come into existence after the Trusts of Land and Appointment of Trustees Act 1996.

CHAPTER 8

Trusts for Sale

Trusts in which the trustees are under a duty to sell the land conveyed to them and hold the proceeds on trust for the beneficiaries named have existed since at least as early as the sixteenth century. The Trusts of Land and Appointment of Trustees Act 1996 made radical changes in the effect of a grant to trustees on trust to sell the land subject to the trust, that is, on the operation of a trust for sale. In order to understand the nature of these changes, and to understand the myriad earlier cases in which trusts for sale are featured, it is necessary to understand how a trust for sale operated prior to the Act. But at this point it should be noted that, great as the changes effected by the 1996 Act were, the Act did not *abolish* the trust for sale. On the contrary, the Act made express provision with regard to the operation of trust for sale. So there is nothing today that prevents a settlor from framing a disposition in the form of a trust for sale and, indeed there may well be circumstances in which it may be appropriate for him to do so.

In the last chapter we saw that before 1926 a settlement of land could:

1. be created by a direct grant without employment of a trust; or
2. exist under a trust; the trust being either (a) a trust for sale; or (b) a trust under which the trustees were under no duty to sell the land.

We saw also that nothing in the 1925 legislation prevented settlements continuing, after 1925, to be created under the machinery of a trust for sale. So a settlor, if he wished, could continue to create a settlement by granting the legal fee simple to trustees on trust for sale for, say, A for life with remainder to B in fee simple.

If trustees have got to sell the land, it cannot be said that the *land* has been settled on A for life with remainder to B in fee simple. If anything, it is money that has been settled on A and B. However, the Law of Property Act 1925[1] conferred on trustees for sale a statutory power to postpone the sale of the land, and if they postponed the sale, then until the sale took place they in practice held the land on trust for the beneficiaries specified.

If a house was settled on A for life with remainder to B, and the settlement was created under the machinery of a trust for sale, what happened in practice might have been the same under a trust for sale (eg A lived in the house during his lifetime and when he died, B got it) as under a strict settlement. But there were major differences in the structure of the two arrangements. Under a strict

---

[1] Section 25. The power exists unless a contrary intention appears. See post.

settlement, A would be Tenant for life and could sell the house. Under a trust for sale, if the house was sold the sale would be by the trustees.

If S left land in his will to trustees on trust for sale for A for life with remainder to B, this might be because he genuinely wanted the land to be sold and money held on trust first for A and then for B; or because he wanted to create a settlement of land without using the machinery of a strict settlement.

If the latter was his wish, he could not be certain of preventing the trustees from carrying out the duty imposed on them to sell the land. But he was entitled to direct that the trustees should not sell the land without the consent of a specified person or persons. He could, for example, direct that the trustees were not to sell the land without the consent of A. In this case, if A wanted to live on the land, or for the land to be retained for some other reason, then (unless A changed his mind and gave consent) the land could not be sold.

A trust was still a trust for sale notwithstanding that the trustees were required (either expressly or impliedly[2]) not to sell without obtaining certain consents, since the Law of Property Act 1925 expressly provided[3] that this was to be so.

We have said[4] that a settlement was capable of being created under a trust for sale; but the machinery of a trust for sale might be used for other purposes. Suppose that T wanted to leave his property between his three favourite charities. In his will he could direct that all his property, including his land, was to be sold and distributed between three charities. On T's death the land was then subject to a trust for sale. (The trustees in this case would have been the executors appointed in the will.)

Thus after 1925 settlements were able to exist under a trust for sale or under the machinery of a strict settlement, and trusts for sale were able to be employed for the purpose of creating a settlement, or for other purposes.

A trust for sale arose not only when a grantor expressly so directed but also in certain circumstances in which statute provided that land was to be held under a trust for sale. Examples of such circumstances are given later.

Structure of a trust for sale

The structure of a trust for sale was (and, where after the 1996 Act a settlor chooses to adopt this form of disposition, still is) as follows: the settlor (or grantor) conveys the legal estate to trustees on trust for sale for the beneficiaries. The advantage of a trust for sale over a strict settlement was that there was no 'Tenant for life', no separate 'trustees of the settlement', no 'statutory owner' and no 'special personal representatives', as may exist in a strict settlement. A trust for sale was, in fact, so simple that in time few people bothered with the

---

2 As in *Re Herklots' Will Trusts* [1964] 2 All ER 66, [1964] 1 WLR 583; (M & B) (direction that a person holding life interests under a trust for sale had permission to reside in the property during her lifetime, or as long as she wished, construed as requiring her consent to sale); and in *Ayer and Benton* (1967) 204 Estates Gazette 359.
3 Section 205(1)(xxix).
4 See Chapter 7.

elephantine structure of a strict settlement. But strict settlements sometimes came into existence by accident. For example, S, in his home-made will, left his house to his widow for life and on her death to his daughter. On A's death, a strict settlement came into existence since the land had been limited in trust for persons by way of succession and the machinery of a trust for sale had not been used.

Sale of the land

When the trustees sold the land they conveyed the legal estate to the purchaser. The purchaser paid the purchase money to the trustees. The trustees then held the proceeds of sale on trust for the beneficiaries, according to their respective interests. (In this respect, the 1996 Act made no change.)

As far as the purchaser was concerned, provided that he ensured that he got a receipt signed by not less than two trustees (or on behalf of a trust corporation), he took the land free from the equitable interests of the beneficiaries.[5] The effect thus corresponds to what occurred when land was sold by a Tenant for life under a strict settlement: the purchaser took the land free of the equitable interests, the interests of the beneficiaries being transferred to the purchase money.

Trusts for sale imposed by statute

In certain circumstances prior to the 1996 Act, a trust for sale was imposed by statute. These included:

1. If land was held after 1925 by more than one person.[6] Thus if G conveyed (or devised) the legal fee simple in Blackacre 'to A and B', a trust for sale arose. Who the trustees were, and who the beneficiaries were, will be considered in a later chapter.
2. If X dies intestate, his property vests[7] in a person termed an 'administrator' (A). It is A's duty to distribute X's estate among X's next of kin according to the laws of intestacy. The Administration of Estates Act 1925 laid down that A held X's property on trust for sale.[8] So A would sell the property and distribute the money to the next of kin.
3. If trustees lent money to R, and as security for the loan R mortgaged his house to the trustees, and R failed to repay the loan according to the agreement, and the trustees realised their security and so obtained the house, they held the house on trust for sale.[9]

---

5   LPA 1925, ss 2, 27; LP (Am) A 1926, Sch.
6   LPA 1925, ss 34 and 36.
7   See Chapter 11.
8   AEA 1925, s 33(1).
9   LPA 1925, s 31.

4. If trustees for sale of land sold the land and invested the proceeds in the purchase of other land, the land so purchased was held by them on trust for sale.[10]

Documents used to create a trust for sale under the Law of Property Act 1925

By will

On the settlor's death the legal title to his property vested in his personal representative. The personal representative then conveyed the legal estate in the land to the trustees of the trust for sale by means of a simple assent, ie not a vesting assent. (A *vesting* assent relates only to a strict settlement.) The will was treated as the trust instrument, and so two documents came into existence; namely, the assent, and the will treated as a trust instrument.

If T left land on trust for sale for B and he appointed X and Y as his executors and as the trustees for sale, since the legal estate vested automatically in X and Y as T's personal representatives, there would be only one document in existence, namely T's will. He could not hold property in some other capacity (eg as a trustee) without making a written assent vesting the property in himself in that other capacity. So X and Y had to execute an assent that transferred the legal title from themselves as personal representatives to themselves as trustees for sale. Two documents would then have come into existence – the will and the assent.

Inter vivos

When a trust for sale was created inter vivos for the purpose of settling land it was customary for two documents to be used: (1) the settlor conveyed the legal estate to the trustees by deed (ie by ordinary conveyance; not by a vesting deed, since the land was not settled land); (2) the settlor set out the equitable interests in a trust instrument. The use of two documents had the same advantages that we saw accrue in the case of a strict settlement – a purchaser could take the conveyance as one of the title deeds, and the trustees could retain the trust instrument; the privacy of the settlement was ensured, and so on. But there was no legal requirement that when a trust for sale was created inter vivos two documents had to be read.

The powers of trustees for sale under the Law of Property Act 1925

Suppose that S conveyed Blackacre to T_1 and T_2 on trust for sale for A for life with remainder to B. If the land had been settled land the legal estate would have been vested in A as Tenant for life, and he would have had all the powers of management which were conferred by the Settled Land Act. But in the case

10 LPA 1925, s 32(2).

of a trust for sale the legal estate was in the trustees, and it is they who were responsible for the management of the land. What powers did they have? The Law of Property Act 1925 provided[11] that trustees for sale were to have all the powers conferred by the Settled Land Act 1925 on a Tenant for life and on the trustees of a strict settlement. Thus if trustees for sale wished, say, to lease the land, they could do so subject to the same limitations as to the length of lease, etc as apply in the case of a lease granted by a Tenant for life under a strict settlement. And they would not need to give notice to anyone, since they also has the powers of trustees of a strict settlement, who would be the persons to whom notice would have to be given by a Tenant for life if he intended to lease the land.

As in the case of a strict settlement, a settlor could confer powers on trustees of a trust for sale that were additional to those conferred by statute.

THE POWER TO POSTPONE SALE

Where a trust for sale existed and the trust property was land,[12] the trustees had (as noted at the beginning of the chapter) a statutory power (under the Law of Property Act 1925[13]) to postpone the sale. If the trustees exercised this power, it might happen that the land was never sold.[14] For example, if land was conveyed to T_1 and T_2 on trust for sale for A for life with remainder to B for life with remainder to C in fee simple, and the trustees postponed sale throughout the life times of A and B (eg because first A and then B wished to live on the land), and on the death of B, C called on the trustees to convey the legal fee simple to him, then C would receive the land, not the proceeds of sale of the land.

The statutory power to postpone sale existed by reason of the fact that the Act provided that 'A power to postpone sale shall, in the case of every trust for sale, be implied ... ' But the provision continued ' ... unless a contrary intention appears'. Thus a settlor could, if he so wished, exclude the power to postpone sale by directing that the trustees were not to have this power. Or the power might be excluded impliedly by some indication that this was the settlor's intention. For example, where a testator directed that on the death of a life tenant certain land was to be sold and the proceeds distributed among those of a specified class of relatives who were living at the completion of the sale, it was held that this direction showed an intention that the statutory power to postpone sale was to be excluded.[15]

Where the statutory power to postpone sale was, expressly or impliedly, excluded, then, in the absence of a direction requiring the consent by some person to the sale and the refusal of this consent, or of any provision of statute requiring the trustees to abide by the wishes of the beneficiaries,[16] the land

---

11   Section 28(1).
12   Including a leasehold interest in land: LPA 1925, s 205(1).
13   Section 25(1).
14   By LPA 1925, s 25(3) it is provided that trustees are to incur no liability if they postpone sale indefinitely.
15   *Re Atkin's Will Trusts* [1974] 2 All ER 1, [1974] 1 WLR 761.
16   Eg LPA 1925, s 26(3) as amended by LP(Am)A 1926, Schedule. See post.

had to be sold. Thus under the Law of Property Act 1925, if S conveyed land to trustees on trust for sale to A for life with remainder to B in fee simple, and S excluded the statutory power to postpone sale, the land had to be sold.

If trustees were obliged to sell the land (because the statutory power[17] had been excluded) they had to do so within a reasonable period. A year was usually considered a reasonable period in this context.[18]

EXERCISE OF THE POWER TO POSTPONE SALE

It is a principle of law that if two or more persons have a power conferred on them, then in order to exercise the power they must all agree that the power should be exercised: they must be unanimous for the power to be exercised. In the case of a trust for sale, the starting point was that the trustees were under a duty to sell, but they had a power conferred on them by statute to postpone sale. So in order to retain the land, they had to be unanimous in agreeing that the power to postpone should be exercised. If the trustees were not unanimous in agreeing to exercise the power to postpone the sale, sale could not be postponed and so the land had to be sold (ie notwithstanding that a majority might have wished it to be retained).[19]

CONSULTATION

There were two circumstances in which, in the case of a trust for sale prior to the 1996 Act, the trustees were under a duty to consult the beneficiaries and abide by their wishes. These were (1) where a trust for sale was created expressly, and the settlor expressly imposed this duty on the trustees; (2) where a trust for sale was created by statute, the Law of Property Act 1925[20] imposed on the trustees a duty with regard to any of their powers to 'consult the persons of full age beneficially interested in possession' and 'so far as was consistent with the general interest of the trust' to 'give effect to the wishes of such persons, or in the case of dispute, to the majority' by value of them.

Consents

In addition to a direction to the trustees to consult there was another way in which a settlor could give the beneficiaries a measure of control over the exercise of their powers by trustees. A settlor could direct that trustees were not to exercise their powers, or one of more specified powers, unless the consent of certain persons had been obtained.[1] For example he could direct that land was not to be sold without the consent of the person entitled in possession under the trust. If this person declined to give his consent, the land could not be sold.

---

17 By analogy with the 'executor's year' (the period within which an executor should sell property in respect of which a duty to sell exists); *Re Petrie* [1962] Ch 355, 3 All ER 1067.
18 *Re Petrie*, ante.
19 *Re Mayo* [1943] Ch 302, [1943] 2 All ER 440; (M & B).
20 Section 26(3), as amended by LP(Am)A 1926, Schedule.
 1 LPA 1925, s 28(1), s 205(1)(xxix).

There was no limit to the number of persons whose consent to sale (or to any other disposition by the trustees) a settlor could require to be obtained. If some of these people could not be found, or if they unreasonably refused to give consent, the court had power[2] to authorise the trustees to act without their consent.

The nature of a trust for sale

It will have become apparent that a trust for sale as it existed prior to the Trusts of Land and Appointment of Trustees Act 1996 could take a number of different forms. At one extreme a settlor could exclude the power to postpone the sale, so that land would have to be sold. At the other extreme a settlor could direct the trustees to consult the beneficiaries and give effect to their wishes and he could direct that the land was not to be sold without the beneficiaries' consent. In this case, if the beneficiaries wanted the land (and not money) the land would almost certainly never be sold. This may seem to have been more of a 'trust not to sell' than a trust for sale. But there was one factor that was shared by every trust for sale, namely, that the starting point was that the trustees were under a *duty* to sell. It was this duty that underlay the doctrine of conversion.

The doctrine of conversion

Suppose that S conveyed Blackacre to T^1 and T^2 on trust for sale to A for life with remainder to B. The trustees did not sell the land. B made a will in which he left all his real property to his sister, R, and all his personal property to his sister, P. A week later B died. A week after that A died. To whom did B's interest in Blackacre pass, to R or to P? Since Blackacre was real property, it might be thought that B's interest would have passed to R, but this was not the case. It passed to P. The following chain of argument explains why:

1. The land was subject to a trust for sale.
2. The trustees were therefore under a duty to sell the land.
3. If they had carried out their duty and sold the land at the instant the trust for sale was created, the trust property would have consisted of money (and so, as personalty, would pass to P).
4. One of the maxims of Equity is that 'Equity looks on that as done which ought to be done'.
5. Acting under this maxim, since the trustees ought to have sold the land at the moment of the creation of the trust, Equity looked on the land as in fact having been sold.
6. In the eyes of Equity the land therefore was money.
7. The land was therefore to be treated as if it was money for the purpose of devolution under B's will.

---

2   LPA 1925, s 30.

8. Thus, since the land had been notionally converted into money by the creation of the trust for sale, it passed to P, as the person entitled to B's personalty.[3]

If B had in fact wanted Blackacre to go to R, he could have arranged this in his will. He could have said 'I leave my personal property, excluding my interest in Blackacre, to P; and I leave my interest in Blackacre and my real property to R.'

The reason for the existence of the doctrine stemmed from the unfairness that could arise without it. Consider what could happen without the doctrine in the example above. If the trustees sold the land one day before B's death, B's interest (now money) would go to P; if they sold one day after B's death it would go to R (since at B's death the property would still have been land). So the devolution of B's interest in Blackacre would depend not on his will, but on when the trustees happened to sell the land. The doctrine of conversion prevented this anomaly from arising. From the moment of the creation of a trust for sale, the beneficiaries' interests were deemed to be personalty, irrespective of whether or not the land had been sold. Any uncertainty as to whether a beneficiary's interest under the trust was in realty or personalty was therefore removed. A beneficiary knew that his interest was personalty and he could make his arrangements, for example the terms of his own will, accordingly.

The doctrine of conversion operated not only where land was held on trust to be sold (and so turned into money) but also, conversely, where money was held on trust to be invested in land. In the latter case the trust property, although in fact still money, was deemed (eg for the purpose of devolution) to be realty.[4]

The doctrine of conversion was, as we shall see in Chapter 10, abolished (in the context of trusts for sale of land) by the Trusts of Land and Appointment of Trustees Act 1996.

Comparison with strict settlements

At this point it may be useful to make a comparison between the principal features of a strict settlement and of a trust for sale as these existed before the 1996 Act.

Strict settlements	**Trust for sale**
1. The legal estate was vested in the Tenant for life or statutory owner.	The legal estate was vested in the trustees.
2. Two documents had to be used to create a strict settlement.	Two documents, though sometimes convenient, were not essential for the creation of a trust for sale inter vivos.
3. The holder of the legal estate had a power of sale.	The holders of the legal estate were under a duty to sell.
4. The doctrine of conversion had no place in strict settlements.	The doctrine of conversion operated under trusts for sale.

3   *Re Kempthorne* [1930] 1 Ch 268.
4   *Re Duke of Cleveland's Settled Estates* [1893] 3 Ch 244.

5. A settlor could not restrict the power of the holder of the legal estate to sell the settled land.	A settlor could place certain restrictions on the exercise by the trustees of their duty to sell the land.
6. Strict settlements were controlled primarily by the Settled Land Act 1925.	Trusts for sale were controlled primarily by the Law of Property Act 1925.

Origins of trusts for sale

Trusts for sale first appear in the fourteenth century. They were a means by which a testator arranged for the payment of his debts, property being left to the executor on trust to sell it and use the proceeds to pay the testator's creditors. In the early stages of its development a purchaser only took free of the equitable interests under the trust if he ensured that the proceeds of sale were applied as the settlor had directed. Later it became the practice for a settlor to include an express direction that a purchaser should take free of the equitable interests provided that he paid the purchase money to, and obtained a receipt from, at least two trustees. Statute made this the position (subject to contrary indication by the settlor) in 1859,[5] and the Law of Property Act 1925[6] confirmed that. The use of trusts for sale for family settlements dates, in the main, from the nineteenth century.

Keeping equitable interests 'off the title'

It has for long been the aim of conveyancers that equitable interests should, as far as possible, be kept 'off the title'. Keeping equitable interests 'off the title' means keeping any statement of equitable interests out of any document of title relating to the legal estate. Thus if there is a series of documents making up the title deeds to a piece of land,[7] there will be no reference in any of them to the equitable interests of the beneficiaries. In the case of a strict settlement equitable interests were kept off the title by the requirement of the Settled Land Act 1925 that two documents had to be used, a vesting deed that conveyed the legal estate and a trust instrument that set out the equitable interests. In the case of trusts for sale, equitable interests were kept out of the title by the practice of using two documents, a conveyance and a trust instrument. It might be apparent, of course, if a document of title consisted of a conveyance to trustees on trust for sale, or a vesting deed or vesting assent, that equitable interests did exist, but they were nowhere set out in any of the title deeds: they were kept 'off the title'.

SUMMARY

To recapitulate, after 1925 and prior to the Trusts of Land and Appointment of Trustees Act 1996:

---

5   Law of Property Amendment Act 1859, s 23.
6   Sections 2(1)(ii), 27(1).
7   Assuming that in the case of any trust for sale created inter vivos, two documents are used.

1. A trust for sale was one of the two forms in which land could be held for a succession of interests.
2. Trustees for sale had a statutory power to postpone sale.
3. The statutory power to postpone sale was excluded if the settlor so directed.
4. In order to exercise the statutory power to postpone sale the trustees had (as in the case of exercise of any power) to be unanimous. Thus, in the event of disagreement, the land had to be sold.
5. Trustees for sale had all the powers of a Tenant for life and the trustees under strict settlement under the Settled Land Act 1925.
6. Where a trust for sale was imposed by statute or where the settlor so directed, the trustees were required to consult, and (so far as was consistent with the interests of the trust) abide by, the wishes of the beneficiaries of full age interested in possession before selling the land (or exercising any other power).
7. Trustees could be required (by the settlor) to obtain the consent of specified persons before selling the land.
8. Where a trust for sale existed, the doctrine of conversion applied.
9. Although trustees were under a duty to sell the land, land under a trust for sale might in practice (because of 2, 6 or 7) never be sold.
10. In the event of the land being sold, the purchaser, if he obtained a receipt for the purchase money from at least two trustees or a trust corporation, took free of the equitable interest under the trust.

We have considered the nature of a trust for sale as it existed prior to the Trusts of Land and Appointment of Trustees Act 1996 in part because of the importance of the trust for sale in the evolution of English and Welsh land law, and in part because the effect of the 1996 Act cannot be understood without knowing what it was that the Act changed. In the chapter after next we shall learn, however, that although certainly not abolished, trusts for sale became, after the 1996 Act, no more than a shadow of what they had hitherto been. (Further, before the notion of a trust for sale is dismissed as today an irrelevance, it should be noted that the 1996 Act did not affect the operation of a trust for sale of property that consists entirely of personalty.)

CHAPTER 9

Bare Trusts

As was seen in Chapter 5, a bare trust is one in which the trustees have no duty specified by the settlor to perform (eg to sell land and invest the proceeds) and under which the beneficiary is (or beneficiaries are) of full age and absolutely entitled.

A bare trust may come into existence in various ways. If S wishes that his nephew, A, who is of full age, should have the benefit to Blackacre, he may decide (because A is in Africa) not to convey the land to A, but, since the land will continue to need to be managed (eg rents collected), to declare himself trustee of the legal estate for A. Since A is of full age and absolutely entitled (and S had not declared that he held the land on trust for sale or subject to any other specific duty), a bare trust arises. Or a shareholder who wishes to conceal his identity as the owner of the shares may transfer the shares to a nominee, for example a bank or a company set up for the purpose, to hold the legal title to the shares on trust for him beneficially.

In practice, however, it has been through the decision of the courts that the existence of a bare trust has commonly come to attention. For example, in *Hodgson v Marks*[1] a woman, A, orally agreed to transfer the title to her house to B, a lodger, the agreement being that beneficial ownership was to remain with A. The transfer took place. A and B continued to live in the house. Later, B (holding the legal title) sold the house to C, who mortgaged the property to D, a building society. When A learned of the sale of the house to C, she sought a declaration that C held the legal title on trust for her absolutely and that (under the rule in *Saunders v Vautier*[2]) C should transfer the legal title to her, and that the transfer should be free of the mortgage to D. The court upheld A's claim. B had held the legal estate on a bare trust for A and for this reason (coupled with a reason explained in a later chapter) she was entitled to the declaration sought.

From the previous two chapters it has been learned that it was one of the major objectives of the 1925 legislation that where land was held on trust, in the event of the legal estate in the land being sold, the purchaser should not be concerned with the equitable interests that existed under the trust, taking free of these if he obtained a receipt for the purchase money from two trustees or a trust corporation. How did the 1925 legislation achieve this objective in the case of a bare trust? It failed to do so. The trust is not a trust for sale, and since in a bare trust no element of succession exists, the trust did not fall into any of

1 [1971] Ch 892, [1970] 3 All ER 513.
2 (1841) 4 Beav 115; see Chapter 5.

the categories in which the Settled Land Act 1925 provided that a strict settlement under the Act was to arise. So a bare trust (due, it seems, to an oversight by those who drafted the legislation) fell outside the 1925 scheme.

The loser, or potentially the loser, from this failure to bring bare trusts within the 1925 scheme was a purchaser of the legal estate in the land from the trustee. Where a strict settlement or a trust for sale existed, a purchaser was made aware that the land was held on trust by the document that vested the legal estate in the person who was selling the land to him – in the case of a strict settlement by the fact that the document was a vesting deed (or vesting assent), in the case of a trust for sale by the fact that the document stated that the land was held by trustees for sale. Thus forewarned, a purchaser knew that he was safe if he obtained a receipt as required by the legislation.

In the case of a bare trust, not having the protection afforded by the Settled Land Act 1925 or the Law of Property Act 1925 to those who complied with their requirements as to the purchase money, a purchaser was subject to the bona fide purchaser rule. If, in the example above, the uncle who declared himself trustee of Blackacre for his nephew sold the land to P, unless P could show that he was a bona fide purchaser without notice, actual or constructive, of the nephew's interest, he took subject to it, with the result that the nephew could, under the rule in *Saunders v Vautier*[3] call on P to convey the legal estate in the land to him (P's remedy lying against the uncle, if he could find him and if the uncle was not insolvent).

It having been the purpose of the 1925 legislation to remove the hindrance to conveyancing caused by a purchaser never being sure that he would not be bound by constructive notice, the fact that a bare trust lay outside the 1925 scheme constituted a defect that came to be seen as one that required rectification. The matter was considered by the Law Commission in its report on overreaching[4] and, in line with recommendations by the Commission, the Trusts of Land and Appointment of Trustees Act 1996 contained provisions that gave a purchaser of land held under a bare trust protection of kind corresponding to that previously enjoyed by a purchaser of land held under a strict settlement or a trust for sale. How this was achieved will be seen in the next chapter.

SUMMARY

A bare trust is one in which the beneficiaries are of full age and absolutely entitled and in which the trustees have no specified duty to perform.

A bare trust may be created expressly or may arise from a decision of the court that one person holds property on trust for another.

A bare trust fell outside the machinery of the 1925 legislation with the result that purchasers from bare trustees did not have the protection afforded by the overreaching provisions of that legislation.

Bare trusts were brought within the fold with regard to overreaching by the Trusts of Land and Appointment of Trustees Act 1996.

3   Supra.
4   Law Com No 181.

CHAPTER 10

Trusts of Land[1]

In 1996 the Trusts of Land and Appointment of Trustees Act made important changes in the law relating to trusts of land. The essential feature of the Act is that it confers powers and imposes duties on trustees of what the Act refers to as a 'trust of land'. The starting point, therefore, in understanding the effects of the Act is to note the meaning of a 'trust of land'. Section 12 of the Act states:

> 1.–(1)   In this Act–
>   (a) 'trust of land' means (subject to subsection (3)) any trust of property which consists of, or includes land, and
>   (b) 'trustees of land' means trustees of a trust of land.
> (2) The reference in subsection (1)(a) to a trust–
>   (a) is to any description of trust (whether express, implied, resulting or constructive), including a trust for sale and a bare trust, and
>   (b) includes a trust created, or arising, before the commencement of this Act.

The section concludes with an exception: (3) The reference to land in subsection (1)(a) does not include 'land which ... is settled land' (ie under the Settled Land Act 1925).[2] Dealing further with settlements under the Settled Land Act 1925, section 2 states, 'No settlement created after the commencement of this Act is a settlement for the purposes of the Settled Land Act 1925, and no settlement shall be deemed to be made under that Act after that commencement'. The effect of these provisions is as follows.

(a) Settlements under the Settled Land Act 1925 in existence at the date of the Act are unaffected and continue to operate under the 1925 Act – the legal estate continues to be vested in the statutory Tenant for life, who continues to have the powers conferred on him by, and to be subject to the requirements of, the Settled Land Act 1925.

(b) No new settlement under the Settled Land Act 1925 can come into existence (with limited exceptions[3]) after the date of the 1996 Act. Thus

---

1   The Trusts of Land and Appointment of Trustees Act 1996, P. Kenny and A. Kenny (1997); [1996] Conv 401 (A.J. Oakley), [1996] Conv 411 (N. Hopkins).

2   Also excepted by section 1(3) is land to which the Universities and Colleges Estates Act 1925 applies.

3   The only settlement under the Settled Land Act 1925 that can come into existence after the 1996 Act is one 'created on the occasion of an alteration in any interest in, or of a person becoming entitled under a settlement which, (a) is in existence at the [date of the Act], or (b) derives from a settlement within paragraph (a)' (section 2(2)), and no provision is made in the document creating the settlement that the settlement is not a settlement for the purpose of the Settled Land Act 1925 (section 2(3)).

strict settlements in existence at the date of the Act continue for the course of their natural lives until, eventually, no settlements under the Settled Land Act 1925 will remain.

We know, from Chapter 7, that if in 1990 (ie before the 1996 Act) S transfers land 'to T_1 and T_2 on trust for A for life with remainder to B', the result is that since (a) the land has been granted for a succession of interests; and (b) the settlement has not been created under a trust for sale, the land is subject to the Settled Land Act 1925 and (notwithstanding that the grant is in an incorrect form) a strict settlement under the Act came into existence. What is the result if a grant in the same terms is made after the 1996 Act? The answer is as follows.

(a) Because of section 2 of the 1996 Act, the settlement cannot be a strict settlement under the Settled Land Act 1925.
(b) There is nothing in the 1996 Act that requires the grant of land for a succession of interests to be made under a trust for sale.
(c) Thus there is nothing that prevents the grant of the legal estate to trustees on trust for the beneficiaries specified from taking effect in the form that the grant was made - 'to T_1 and T_2 on trust for ... '
(d) Since the trust is one the subject matter of which is land, the trust comes within the definition of a 'trust of land' in section 1 of the 1996 Act.
(e) Thus, as a 'trust of land' under the 1996 Act, the trustees have the powers conferred, and are subject to the duties imposed, on them by the 1996 Act.

Before proceeding further it must be stressed that with the exception of settlements in existence at the date of the Act,[4] all trusts the subject matter of which is land are trusts of land within the definition of the 1996 Act, irrespective of whether the trusts are created expressly (inter vivos or by will) or arise as implied (including resulting) or constructive trusts.

We now turn to consider the features of a trust that comes within the Act's definition of a trust of land. Hereafter in this chapter a 'trust of land' and 'trustees of land' mean respectively a trust of land within the definition of the Act and trustees of such a trust. The phrase 'the date of the Act' means the date of the coming into force of the Act (1 January 1997). The principal matters requiring attention are these.

1. What are the powers of trustees of a trust of land? Can a settlor exclude all or any of the powers conferred?
2. Are the trustees obliged, in the exercise of their functions, to consult the wishes of the beneficiaries?
3. What rights are conferred on the beneficiaries with regard to occupation of the land?
4. Are trustees of a trust of land able to delegate their functions to beneficiaries?
5. What effect did the Act have on trusts for sale, in particular with regard to postponement of sale, the doctrine of conversion, and trusts for sale previously imposed by statute?

---

4   And settlements within the exception in section 2(2), (3). See note 3.

6. How did the Act affect the way in which land is held by infants?
7. How did the 1996 Act affect land held on charitable (and ecclesiastical and public) trusts?
8. What is the position of a person who purchases land from the trustees of a trust of land?
9. What provision is made for the ending of a trust of land?
10. What provision is made for applications to the court?
11. Did the 1996 Act create a new form of trust?
12. Did the 1996 Act continue the policy of the Settled Land Acts of 1882 and 1925 that land held for a succession of interests had to be capable of being sold (ie and not able to be 'tied up' for years into the future)?

THE POWERS OF TRUSTEES OF A TRUST OF LAND

Section 6 of the Act confers on the trustees of a trust of land all the powers of an absolute owner. Thus none of the limitations that restricted the powers of a Tenant for life under the Settled Land Act 1925 (and hence of a trustee of a trust for sale) find a place in the 1996 Act - trustees of land can grant leases of any length, they can mortgage the land to raise money for purposes not permitted by the Settled Land Act, and they can fell timber, pay for improvements out of capital and sell the principal mansion house free from the restraints that existed in the case of settlements of land before the Act.

In addition to conferring on trustees of land all the powers of an absolute owner, the Act confers on them certain specific powers:

(a) a power to purchase a legal estate in any land in England or Wales, for the purpose of investment, or occupation by any beneficiary or for any other purpose,[5] and,
(b) a power, where the beneficiaries of full age are absolutely entitled to land subject to the trust, to partition the land and convey the partitioned land in severalty (ie in separate parcels) to the beneficiaries according to their interests.[6]

LIMITATION OF POWERS UNDER THE ACT

Although the scope of their powers is unlimited, the exercise of the powers set out above is, or may be, subject to crucial restrictions.

1. In conferring on trustees all the powers of an absolute owner, the Act provides that the exercise of the powers must be 'for the purpose of exercising their functions as trustees' – as *trustees*.[7] Thus trustees would be in breach of trust if their motive was one extraneous to the purpose of the trust (for example if their motive in selling the land was to assist in a development scheme in which they had an interest).

5 Section 6(3), (4).
6 Section 7.
7 Section 6(1).

2. In exercising the powers set out above, trustees are required to have regard to the rights of the beneficiaries.[8]

3. Trustees are prohibited from exercising the powers set out above in contravention of any other enactment or rule of law or equity (or contrary to any restriction or condition imposed in any other enactment that confers a power on trustees).[9] Thus the fact that the trustees have all the powers of an absolute owner, the conferment of this power does not, for example, free them from the restrictions on the manner in which trust money may be invested that are imposed by the Trustees Investment Act 1961; nor from such rules of equity as those that require proper accounts to be maintained; or that prohibit a trustee from making a profit from his position as a trustee; or that require a trustee not to put himself in a position in which his duty as trustee and his personal interest conflict.

4. Subject to certain exceptions, which will be treated later, trustees are required in the exercise of their functions to consult the beneficiaries of full age who are entitled to an interest in possession in the land and, as far as is consistent with the general interest of the trust, to give effect to their wishes.[10]

5. If the disposition creating the trust requires any consent (ie of a beneficiary of any other person) to be obtained before a power is exercised, the power may not be exercised without that consent.[11]

6. The powers conferred by the Act set out above are exercisable by the trustees only to the extent that the powers have, or any particular power has, not been excluded by the settlor in the disposition creating the trust.[12] Thus if a settlor provides that the powers conferred by the 1996 Act (as set out above) are excluded, the trustees have no power to dispose of the land (by sale) or of an interest in the land (by lease or mortgage).

CONSULTATION

Trusts created or arising after the Act

In the case of all trusts expressly created, and all implied and constructive trusts arising, after the 1996 Act, the Act[13] imposes on the trustees a duty in the exercise of any function relating to land subject to the trust, so far as practicable, to consult the beneficiaries of full age and beneficially entitled to an interest in possession in the land, and so far as consistent with the general interests of the trust, to give effect to the wishes of those beneficiaries, or (in the case of dispute) of the majority (according to the value of their combined interests). Where after the Act a trust is created expressly, the duty may be excluded by the settlor.[14]

---

8 Section 6(5).
9 Section 6(6), (8).
10 Section 11.
11 Section 8(2), 10.
12 Section 8.
13 Section 11.
14 Section 11(2)(a).

Trusts in existence at the date of the Act[15]

In the case of implied and constructive trusts, the duty to consult is imposed by the Act. In the case of express trusts, created by will, no duty to consult is imposed by the Act; in the case of express trusts created inter vivos, no duty to consult is imposed by the Act unless the settlor executes a deed declaring that the duty introduced by the Act is to apply.

OCCUPATION

The 1996 Act[16] confers on a beneficiary who is beneficially entitled to an interest in possession of the land[17] an entitlement to occupy the land if:

(a) the purposes of the trust are held by the trustees to include making the land available for his occupation; and

(b) the land is available; and

(c) the land is suitable for occupation by him.[18] (It might be that A holds a life interest in land, and so satisfies the requirement as to having an interest in possession in the land but, being 16, the trustees regard a four bedroom house as not being suitable for occupation by him.)

The right of a beneficiary under a trust of land to occupy the land is considered further in a later chapter.[19]

DELEGATION

The 1996 Act[20] confers power on trustees of land to delegate to any beneficiary or beneficiaries of full age and beneficially entitled to an interest in possession in land subject to the trust any of their functions which relate to the land. Thus if trustees hold land on trust for A for life with remainder to B in fee simple, if A is of full age the trustees can delegate to him responsibility for the management of the land together with all or any of the powers conferred on trustees of land by the Act. (It will be appreciated that where the trustees delegate the exercise of their powers to a life tenant under the trust, the life tenant will be in a position in some respects similar to that of a statutory Tenant for life under the Settled Land Act 1925.)

Delegation must be by power of attorney, which must be given by all the

---

15   Section 11(3).

16   Section 12.

17   It seems that the right of occupation is therefore not conferred by the Act where the interest of the beneficiary is not in land but is expressly stated to be in the proceeds of sale. See p 149, infra.

18   Or for the occupation of beneficiaries of a class of which he is member or of beneficiaries in general. Section 12(1)(a).

19   Chapter 11.

20   Section 9.

trustees jointly.[1] The power of attorney (which cannot be an enduring power) can be revoked by any one of them.[2]

Beneficiaries to whom functions have been delegated are in the same position as trustees, and subject to the same duties and liabilities.[3]

The power of attorney delegating functions to a beneficiary is revoked on (a) the appointment as a trustee of a person other than those by whom the power was given;[4] or, (b) a beneficiary to whom functions are solely delegated ceasing to be entitled to an interest in the land (eg if the grant is to T^1 and T^2 on trust for A for life until he commits an act of bankruptcy, and A commits an act of bankruptcy).

TRUSTS FOR SALE

Power to postpone sale

The 1996 Act[5] confers on trustees of a trust for sale, irrespective of whether the trust for sale was created before or after the Act, a power to postpone a sale. The power to postpone a sale conferred by the Act is not capable of being excluded by the direction of the settlor (as was the power to postpone sale conferred by the Law of Property Act 1925). Thus if in 1995 G grants land to T_1 and T_2 on trust for sale for specified beneficiaries and directs that the power to postpone sale conferred by the Law of Property Act 1925 is not to apply, and at the date of the 1996 Act the trustees have not yet sold the land, they cease to be obliged to do so, by reason of the power to postpone sale conferred on them by the 1996 Act.

CONVERSION

It will be recalled that, under the doctrine of conversion, if G grants land to T_1 and T_2 on trust for sale for A for life with the remainder to B, and B dies leaving all his realty to R and all his personalty to P, on the death of the life tenant, A, it would be P who was entitled under B's will, on the ground that, the trustees having been under a duty to sell the land, the trust property was to be deemed to be personalty (ie the proceeds of sale) from the date of the creation of the trust, notwithstanding that the land had not in fact yet been sold.

The 1996 Act abolished the doctrine of conversion *to the extent* of its provision that 'Where land is held by trustees subject to a trust for sale, the land is not to be regarded as personal property'.[6] The change applies in the

---

1 Under the Enduring Powers of Attorney Act 1985.
2 Unless expressed to be irrevocable and given by way of security: section 9(3).
3 Section 9(7).
4 But not on a person by whom the power was given dying or otherwise ceasing to be a trustee: section 9(3).
5 Section 4. See (1997) LQR 207 (P.H. Pettit)(demolition of the erroneous view that the Act 'abolished' trusts for sale).
6 Section 3(1). The subsection continues, 'and where personal property is subject to a trust for sale in order that the trustees may acquire land, the personal property is not to be regarded as land'. See (1997) LQR 207 (P.H. Pettit)(no abolition of conversion within the terms of section 3.

case of trusts created before or after the Act[7] with one exception: the doctrine continues to apply in the case of trusts for sale created by will where the testator died before the Act[8] (and so before he had had a chance to amend the terms of his will to take account of the effect that the Act would have on the devolution of his estate). Thus, in the example above, if the date of A's death was before the 1996 Act, B's interest in remainder would, under the doctrine of conversion, go to P. If A dies after the Act came into force, B's interest in remainder, as an interest in realty, goes to R.

Trusts for sale previously imposed by statute

It will be recalled (from Chapter 8) that in certain instances statute imposed a trust for sale. For example, the Administration of Estates Act 1925 laid down that where a person died intestate his estate should be held by the administrator on trust for those entitled under the intestacy. The 1996 Act amended statutory provisions that had in certain circumstances[9] imposed a trust for sale with effect that in those circumstances there should instead be a trust of land (without a duty to sell).[10]

Trusts for sale after the 1996 Act

From what has been said so far in this Chapter it might be thought that while the 1996 Act did not prohibit the creation of a trust for sale (on the contrary, the Act made express provision with regard to trusts for sale), no purpose would now be served in creating a trust for sale since under the Act, trustees of a trust for sale have a power to postpone that is not capable of being excluded. Indeed, is there in fact any difference between a grant of Blackacre to T_1 and T_2 on trust for specified beneficiaries (a trust under which the trustees have a power of sale conferred by the Act, a power that may in practice never be exercised) and a grant of the land to T_1 and T_2 on trust for sale for beneficiaries specified (a trust under which the duty to sell may be postponed indefinitely)? In either case, it would seem, the trustees are able to decide whether to sell the land or retain it. A difference does, however, exist, one that stems from the principle that in order to exercise a power trustees must be unanimous. Consider the position where one trustee proposes sale and the other trustee proposes retention.[11] In the case of a grant to the trustees *on trust*, since the trustees are not unanimous in exercising the power of sale, the land will be retained. In the case of a grant to the trustees on trust *for sale*, since the trustees are not unanimous in exercising the power to postpone the sale, the land must be sold.

---

7 Section 3(3).
8 Section 3(2).
9 Including those listed in Chapter 8, p 132.
10 Section 5, Sch 2.
11 And there is no beneficiary whom the trustees are under a duty to consult, or if there is such a beneficiary, he expresses no opinion.

It seems that a further difference between a trust of land that is in the form of a trust for sale and one that is not, lies in the fact that where a trust for sale is in a form that expressly provides that it is in the proceeds of sale that the equitable interests exist (eg, where the grant is not of Blackacre to T_1 and T_2 on trust for sale for A, but is a grant to T_1 and T_2 on trust to sell Blackacre and hold the proceeds of sale for A) then the right of occupation which is conferred[12] by the Act on beneficiaries who are entitled to an interest in possession of *land* may not apply.[13]

INFANTS

Under the Law of Property Act 1925[14] an infant is not capable of holding a legal estate in land. Any interest of an infant in land is therefore necessarily equitable. Before the 1996 Act the trust under which an infant's beneficial interest was held could be either a trust for sale or a strict settlement under the Settled Land Act 1925, in the latter case the legal estate being held by the statutory owner.[15] (Where a disposition purported to grant a legal estate in land to an infant, the land became settled land under the 1925 Act.[16])

The 1996 Act made no change to the position that an infant cannot hold a legal estate in land. After the Act, the trust under which the infant's equitable interest is held is necessarily a trust of land under the Act.[17]

LAND HELD ON CHARITABLE, ECCLESIASTICAL OR PUBLIC TRUSTS

Section 29 of the Settled Land Act 1925 provided that all land vested in trustees for charitable, ecclesiastical or public purposes was to be deemed to be settled land under the Act and that the trustees of such trusts were to have all the powers of a statutory Tenant for life and the trustees of a settlement. The 1996 Act[18] repeals section 29 of the 1925 Act and provides[19] that no land held for charitable, ecclesiastical or public purposes shall be deemed to be settled land. Land subject to such trusts therefore becomes subject to trust for land under the 1996 Act. The 1996 Act provides[20] that in case of trusts for charitable, ecclesiastical or public purposes the powers conferred on trustees of a trust of land shall not be capable of being excluded.

---

12 By section 12.
13 See p 146.
14 LPA 1925, section 1(6).
15 Normally the trustees of the settlement. See p 115.
16 LPA 1925, section 1(1)(ii)(d).
17 No settlements under the Settled Land Act 1925 now being capable of being created (subject to n 3, p 142) after the 1996 Act.
18 Sch 4.
19 Section 2(5).
20 Section 8(3).

SALE OF THE LAND

Protection of purchasers

If land is held on trust for certain beneficiaries and the trustees sell the land, the purchaser takes free from the equitable interests of the beneficiaries only (as learned in previous chapters) if either he can show that he is a bona fide purchaser for value without notice of the equitable interests, or statute provides that on his compliance with certain conditions he will take free of the equitable interests notwithstanding that he has knowledge that such interests exist. In the case of a trust for sale, under the Law of Property Act 1925 a purchaser took free if he paid the purchase price to the trustees and obtained a receipt signed by at least two of them or on behalf of a trust corporation; in the case of a settlement under the Settled Land Act 1925, he took free if the money was paid to the trustees of the settlement. Where a bare trust existed, no statute applied and a purchaser took free of the equitable interests only if he could show that he was a bona fide purchaser under the old rule.

To enable land held under a trust of land within the meaning of 1996 Act to be sold free of the equitable interests, the 1996 Act[1] applies[2] the overreaching provision of the Law of Property Act 1925 (payment of the purchase money to two trustees or a trust corporation) to trusts of land under the Act (including now, therefore, bare trusts).

Obtaining a receipt from two trustees or a trust corporation will operate to overreach the equitable interests on the transfer of the legal estate to the purchaser. But ensuring that the equitable interests are overreached is not the first matter as to which a purchaser must satisfy himself. He must first ensure that the transfer will be effective to convey the legal estate from the trustees to himself. (If he fails to receive the legal estate, overreaching is irrelevant.)

In order that the legal estate is transferred to the purchaser, the trustees must have power to sell the land. Does a purchaser have to ascertain whether they have this power before he can safely pay the purchase price? A purchaser knows that the 1996 Act confers on trustees of a trust of land all the powers of an absolute owner, thus a power of sale. But he knows, too, that this power can be excluded or restricted. He knows also that trustees of a trust of land may be required to obtain the consent of certain persons before exercising a power, and, further, that they are under a duty to consult the beneficiaries of full age in possession (and abide by their wishes), and, in exercising their power, to have regard to the rights of the beneficiaries. Does he have to satisfy himself that all requisite consents have been obtained and duties, including consultation, observed? If so, the delays in conveyancing would be likely to be considerable. In order to strike a balance between the need to avoid such delays while at the same time sufficiently protectingthe interests of the beneficiaries, the 1996 Act provides as follows.

1. With regard to the power of the trustees to sell the land, the trustees are under a duty to bring to the notice of a purchaser any limitation of their powers.

1   Section 25(1), Sch 3.
2   By amending section 2(1) and (2) and 27 of the Law of Property Act 1925. See [1997] Conv (N. Hopkins).

If a purchaser has notice of a limitation in the trustees' powers (eg that the power of sale is excluded) either from notice of this fact given by the trustees or from any other source (eg from an examination of the document transferring the title to the trustees), he fails to receive the legal title.[3] If he has 'no actual notice of the limitation', 'the limitation does not invalidate' the conveyance, ie he receives the legal title. From the inclusion of the word 'actual' before the word 'notice' it seems that a purchaser does not fail to receive the legal title by reason of having constructive notice of the limitation, ie notice that he would have obtained if he had made all due enquiries. It is, however, unlikely that any purchaser would buy land without inspecting the document of title under which the vendor received the title to the land, and that a purchaser of land from trustees of a trust of land would therefore in this way obtain actual notice of any limitation in the trustees' powers.

2. With regard to consents, the Act provides that where a disposition creating a trust of land requires the consent of more than two persons to the exercise by the trustees of any their functions relating to the land, a purchaser will receive the legal title if he satisfies himself that the consent of any two of those persons has been obtained.[4]

3. With regard to the duty of trustees to consult the beneficiaries and the duty to have regard to the rights of the beneficiaries, the Act provides that a purchaser 'need not be concerned' to see that these requirements have been complied with, ie he will receive the legal estate notwithstanding that they have not.[5]

4. If trustees of a trust of land, in conveying land to a purchaser, do so in contravention of any other enactment or in contravention of any rule of law or equity, the conveyance to the purchaser is valid if he has no actual notice of the contravention.[6] Thus if a purchaser proceeds notwithstanding that he has actual notice of such a contravention, the conveyance is invalid.

Thus if a purchaser satisfies himself that, if consents are required, two at least are obtained, and he has no actual knowledge of the exclusion of (or any restriction on) the trustee's powers to sell the land, and he has no actual knowledge that the conveyance is in contravention of any enactment or rule of law or equity, he will receive the legal title to the land. But, as indicated above, receipt of the legal title represents only one aspect of his concerns. In order to receive the legal title free from the equitable interests he must ensure that he obtains a receipt for purchase money from at least two trustees or a trust corporation.

End of a trust of land: deed of discharge

The rule in *Saunders v Vautier*[7] lays down (as noted in an earlier chapter) that where all the beneficiaries of a trust are of full age and between them absolutely

---

3 Section 16(3).
4 Section 10(1).
5 Section 16(1). The section does not apply to registered land (Chapter 26).
6 Section 16(2). The section does not apply to registered land (Chapter 26).
7 (1841) 4 Beav 115.

entitled to the trust property (whether realty or personalty), they are entitled to require the trustees to convey the legal title to the property to them in such manner (eg in such shares) as they direct.

The 1996 Act provides that where in the case of any trust of land each of the beneficiaries is a person of full age and capacity who is absolutely entitled to the land, the trustees have power to convey the land to the beneficiaries even though the trustees have not been required to do so, and imposes on the beneficiaries a duty to do whatever is necessary to secure that it vests in them.[8] (If they fail to co-operate, they court can order them to do so.)

If, after the 1996 Act, trustees hold land on trust for A for life with remainder to the first son of A to be called to the Bar; and A dies; and B, a son of A, is called to the Bar; and the trustees convey the legal estate in the land to B; and B wishes to sell the land to P, P will wish to satisfy himself as to the final link in the chain of B's title - that the trustees had power to transfer the legal title to B. (They would, without provision to the contrary, need to satisfy themselves that B had been properly admitted to an Inn of Court.) In such a circumstance as this, P is assisted by the provision of the 1995 Act that where trustees of a trust of land convey the legal title in the land to beneficiaries who are of full age and capacity and absolutely entitled, they must[9] execute a deed declaring that they are discharged from the trust. The execution of the deed entitles P (in our example) to assume that the land is no longer subject to the trust, (and thereby frees him from the necessity of assuring himself that B had been of full age and absolutely entitled) unless P has actual notice that the trustees were mistaken that B was of full age and absolutely entitled.

APPLICATIONS TO THE COURT

The 1996 Act[10] repeals section 30 of the Law of Property Act 1925, under which the court previously had jurisdiction to order trustees of a trust for sale to sell land (and enabled consents that could not be obtained to be dispensed with). The jurisdiction was extensively employed, in particular in the case of disputes between two co-owners as to whether a home should be sold. In its place, section 14 of the 1996 Act confers on the court a jurisdiction, wider than that conferred by section 30 of the 1925 Act, to make such orders as it thinks fit with regard to the exercise by the trustees of any of their functions (including an order relieving them of any obligation to obtain the consent of, or to consult, any person in connection with the exercise of any of their functions); or declaring the nature or extent of a person's interest in property subject to the trust.

An application to the court for an order may be made by any person who is a trustee of land or who has an interest in property subject to the trust.

---

8   Section 6(2).
9   Section 16(4)(a).
10   Section 25(2), Sch 4.

DID THE 1996 ACT CREATE A NEW FORM OF TRUST OF LAND?

The Act did not enact that a new form of trust of land should come into existence. What it did was to define a 'trust of land' as consisting of all existing forms of trust of which the subject matter is land other than settlements under the Settled Land Act 1925, and then to make provision, with regard to power and duties, for trusts that come within the definition.

In one limited respect only is it permissible to regard the Act as resulting in the creation of a new form of the trust of land. By removing the statutory measures that previously prevented a trust for a succession of interests from taking effect other than as a trust for sale or a strict settlement under the Settled Land Act, the Act permitted the creation of a trust in a form that had not, prior to the Act, been possible.

In reality, however, the Act did not so much create a new form of trust as to restore the law, with regard to the form that a trust the subject matter of which is land can take to the position before the Settled Land Act 1925 when no bar existed to a grant[11] to T_1 and T_2 on trust for specified beneficiaries. It seems likely, however, that the 1996 Act will come to be regarded as creating a new form of trust of land, notwithstanding that nowhere in the Act is a provision to this effect to be found.

What is not open to dispute is the fact that the Act replaced the previous dual system of conveyancing of land held on trust (ie that operating in the case of trusts for sale, and that operating in the case of strict settlements, when vesting deeds or vesting assents and separate trust instruments were required) with a single, uniform system, that under which trustees of a trust of land convey the land by means of a simple conveyance.

Even if it transpires that the 1996 Act comes to be regarded as having introduced a new form of trust of land, it should never be forgotten that the classification of trusts into express, implied (including resulting) and constructive trusts, remains of significance; and, further, that in the case of trusts expressly created, under the Act such a trust may be either one that does, or does not, take the form of a trust for sale.

WAS THE OBJECTIVE OF THE SETTLED LAND ACTS OF 1882 AND 1925 PRESERVED BY THE ACT OF 1996?

It was one of the principal objects of the Settled Land Acts that land held on trust for a succession of interests (or for an infant) should be capable of being sold, the equitable interests thereafter existing in the proceeds of sale: that land should not be rendered incapable of disposal for years, or even generations, into the future. This object was achieved, as seen in earlier chapters, by requiring land held for a succession of interests to be held under either a trust for sale or a strict settlement, in the latter case, under the Settled Land Act 1925, the

---

11 Employing the words necessary to avoid the effect of the Statute of Uses 1535.

Tenant for life having a power of sale that could not be excluded or restricted by the settlor.

Where, under the 1996 Act, a settlor conveys land to trustees on trust for a succession of interests and[12] excludes the power to dispose of the land that is otherwise conferred by the Act, it seems that the objective of the Acts of 1882 and 1925 is no longer achieved. Whether the court has jurisdiction under section 14 to make an order that authorises the sale of the land notwithstanding an express exclusion of the power of sale is uncertain. Section 14 enables the court to make orders with regard to the exercise by the trustees of any of their 'functions'. Whether it remains a 'function' of trustees to sell the land if they have no power to do so, remains to be seen. (If the jurisdiction to make such an order is held not to exist, it would be open to the trustees to apply to the court for an order under the Variations of Trusts Act 1958, varying the terms of the trust by omitting the exclusion of the power of sale conferred by the 1996 Act.)

SUMMARY

The principal matters accomplished by the Act may be listed as follows.

1. By preventing the creation of new settlements under the Settled Land Act 1925, the Act ensured that settlements under the 1925 Act would not in future be capable of being created by inadvertence (as by land limited for a succession of interests being conveyed to trustees otherwise than on trust for sale).

2. A purchaser from a trustee of a bare trust was enabled (by paying the purchase money to two trustees or a trust corporation) to take free of the equitable interests under the trust notwithstanding that he had no notice of them.

3. The rights of beneficiaries to occupy the land were placed on a more rational and secure basis than previously existed.

4. The previous dual system of conveyancing (ie that for trusts for sale and that for strict settlements) was replaced by a single system.

5. A uniform code with regard to the duties and powers of trustees of a trust the subject matter of which was land, and with regard to the rights of beneficiaries under such a trust, was introduced.

6. By abolishing the requirement (explained in a later chapter) that land held by co-owners must be held on trust for sale, the Act brought the method by which co-owners hold land into line with what is generally the reality of the situation.

12   Under s 6.

CHAPTER 11

Co-ownership I – The Structure[1]

Concurrent interests in land

Under the heading of co-ownership we study the position when two or more persons hold an interest in land in possession at the same time. In a grant to A for life with remainder to B in fee simple, A and B hold interests which are in possession at different times – first A's interest and then B's, but if G grants land 'to A and B in fee simple', this is a case of co-ownership. A's interest and B's interest are *concurrent*.

In this chapter we shall examine the structure of the law. In the chapter that follows we shall see how the law of co-ownership arises in various everyday contexts.

THE BASIC PRINCIPLES

Joint tenancy and tenancy in common

Let us suppose that A and B hold Blackacre in fee simple. They are then both entitled to occupy the land. If the land is let, they are each entitled to a half share of the rent; if it is sold, they are each entitled to a half share of the proceeds of sale. So far, no problem arises. But what happens when one of them, say A, dies? What happens to his half share in the land? One solution would be for the property to pass, if A died testate, to whoever A left the half share in his will and if he died intestate, before 1926, to his heir or, after 1925, to his next of kin. But another solution is possible. It is arguable that when A died he ceased to have any interest in the land, and that this therefore left B as the sole owner of Blackacre. In English law, either of these two arrangements can operate. If the former arrangement exists, we say that A and B hold their interest as *tenants in common*. If the latter exists, we say that they hold as *joint tenants*. (The word 'tenant' in tenant in common and in joint tenant has nothing to do with being a tenant under a lease. It stems from the use of the word 'tenant' in the old context of tenure.)

Which arrangement (ie tenancy in common or joint tenancy) operates in any one case will usually depend on the terms of the grant. If T leases land 'to A and B as joint tenants', they hold as joint tenants. If he leases the land to them as 'tenants in common', they hold as tenants in common. If A and B are buying land from a vendor (V), they will tell V that the conveyance is to convey

1   M. P. Thompson, *Co-ownership* (1988).

the land to them as joint tenants, or as tenants in common, according to how they wish to hold the land.

If land is held by A, B, C, and D as joint tenants, as each co-owner dies, the number of co-owners is reduced until the time is reached when the land is held by a single owner, ie the last survivor. The right of the survivor or survivors under a joint tenancy to succeed to a fellow joint tenant's interest on his death is termed the *right of survivorship (jus accrescendi)*.

When there remains only one sole surviving joint tenant, the property then becomes his sole property, and on his death passes under his will or intestacy in the normal way. (Joint tenancy is a convenient way for a husband and wife to hold the house they live in (the matrimonial home). When one of them dies, the other one automatically gets the house.)

A further distinction between joint tenancy and tenancy in common (ie in addition to that relating to the position on death) relates to the nature of the interest held. Under tenancy in common each co-owner is regarded as holding a share of the property. (Hence an alternative term for tenancy in common, and that used in the Law of Property Act 1925, is the holding of property in 'undivided shares'.) Under joint tenancy, on the other hand, each joint tenant is regarded as owning the whole estate along with his fellow co-owners. Thus while joint tenants have rights against each other, against the outside world, they are in the position of a single owner.[2]

If land is held by co-owners as beneficial joint tenants, it follows from the nature of joint tenancy that if the land is sold the proceeds are divided equally. Thus sometimes[3] the reason for a dispute over whether joint tenancy or tenancy in common exists concerns, not the devolution of the property on a beneficial co-owner's death, but the distribution of the proceeds after the sale of the land, one party claiming that joint tenancy had existed with the result that he is entitled to an equal proportion of the proceeds[4], the other party claiming that tenancy in common had existed, and that he is entitled (eg because of the size of his contribution to the purchase price), to a larger than equal share.

Since, for joint tenancy to exist, the *jus accrescendi* has to be capable of operating, and since the *jus accrescendi* operates on death, and since a corporation never dies, the rule used to be that a corporation could not hold property as a joint tenant: if a corporation was a co-owner, the co-ownership could only be tenancy in common. The position was changed by the Bodies Corporate (Joint Tenancy) Act 1899 which provided that a corporation should be capable of acquiring and holding a property as a joint tenant, in the same manner as if it was an individual.[5] On the dissolution of a corporation holding as a joint tenant, the property passes to the other joint tenant.[6]

2   Williams 143, M & W (5 edn, p 417).
3   As in *Robinson v Robinson* (1976) 241 Estates Gazette 153; *Malayan Credit Ltd v Jack Chai-MPH Ltd* [1986] AC 549, [1986] 1 All ER 711.
4   As in *Goodman v Gallant* [1986] Fam 106, [1986] 1 All ER 311.
5   Section 1(1).
6   Section 1(2).

Co-parcenary and tenancy by entireties

Another form of co-ownership, in addition to joint tenancy and tenancy in common, is co-parcenary. This arises by operation of law on the death of the holder of an unbarred fee tail leaving daughters and no issue through the male line.[7] Its occurrence today is rare (and with the prevention of the creation of new fee tail estates by the Trusts of Land and Appointment of Trustees Act 1996, likely to become rarer). Previously a fourth form of co-ownershiop existed, tenancy by entireties.[8] No new tenancy by entirety was capable of being created after 1882,[9] and tenancies by entireties existing at the end of 1925 were then converted into joint tenancies.[10]

The 'four unities'

In order that co-owners may hold as joint tenants, certain conditions must be satisfied.

1. All the co-owners must hold the same interest in the land. This is expressed by saying that there must be *unity of interest* for a joint tenancy to exist. This requirement would not be satisfied if G granted land to A in fee simple and to B for 21 years, since here A and B would hold different interests, one a fee simple and the other a lease; nor would it be satisfied if land was granted to A and B in fee simple, as to one-third and two-thirds respectively.
2. All the co-owners must acquire their title to the land under the same document. (This is known as *unity of title*.)
3. All the co-owners must acquire their interest at the same time. This is known as *unity of time*. For example, if in his will T left land 'to my sons A, B, and C', this requirement would be satisfied, the interests of A, B and C all vesting at T's death, but the requirement would not be satisfied if T left land 'to my son A, and to my son B (aged six) if he attains the age of 21.' In this case A's interest would vest at T's death, but B's interest would not vest until he attained 21. (But it should be noted that if T left land 'to my

---

7 At common law, if a person dies intestate leaving daughters but no sons, then his heir consists of all his daughters (ie not, as in the case of male issue, the eldest child). The daughters hold the land as co-parceners. Co-parcenary resembles tenancy in common in that there is no *jus accrescendi*, and in that the interests of co-parceners can be of different sizes (eg if, before 1925, A died intestate leaving two daughters, B and C, and C died intestate leaving two daughters, D and E, then B, D and E would be co-parceners of the land, B holding a one-half share, and D and E hold a quarter share each.) Co-parcenary differs from tenancy in common in that it arises only by operation of law.
8 Tenancy by entireties arose where land was conveyed to a husband and wife in a way that would otherwise have created a joint tenancy (eg if no words of severance were employed, or if the land was conveyed to them as 'joint tenants'). Tenancy by entireties resembled joint tenancy in that on the death of one spouse the other took the whole. It differed from joint tenancy in that neither spouse could alienate his or her interest without the agreement of the other. Thus no severance was possible unless both spouses agreed.
9 Married Women's Property Act 1882, ss 1, 5.
10 LPA 1925, Sch 1, Pt VI.

sons A and B', and B was six, then B's interest, like A's, vests at the time of the testator's death and there is no lack of unity of time. The fact that B cannot hold a legal estate estate until he is 18 is here irrelevant.)

If any of these three requirements is not satisfied, then the co-ownership cannot be joint tenancy, but can be tenancy in common.

4.   The fourth requirement is *unity of possession*. This requirement is common to both joint tenancy and tenancy in common. If the requirement is not satisfied, then there is no co-ownership, either joint tenancy or tenancy in common. Unity of possession exists when each co-owner is entitled to possession of the whole of the property: no one co-owner can claim possession of any part to the exclusion of the others.

We have said that if one of the first three unities is lacking, then the co-ownership cannot be joint tenancy and so must be tenancy in common. If all four unities are present this does not, however, necessarily mean that the co-ownership must be joint tenancy. It merely means that the co-ownership is capable of being a joint tenancy. Whether it is or not depends on a variety of factors including, for example, the terms in which the land is conveyed to the co-owners. We shall deal with the other factors shortly.

Many disputes could be avoided if co-owners ensured that in the conveyance to them there was an unequivocal statement as to how they were to hold their beneficial interests.[11]

Severance[12]

Nature

If A, B and C hold land as joint tenants, and one of them, say A, decides that he does not want his share on his death to go to B and C (he wants, let us suppose, to leave his share in his will to X), then A can convert his interest from that of a joint tenant to that of a tenant in common.[13] If he does so, then on his death his share will pass under his will to X. But the fact that A has converted his holding into a tenancy in common does not affect the way in which B and C hold their interests, they remain joint tenants between themselves. The result is that if B dies, since he holds as a joint tenant, his share does not pass under his will or intestacy, but passes automatically to the other joint tenant, C. It should be noted that when A converts his interest from a joint tenancy to a tenancy in common, whilst he obtains the ability to exclude B and C from acquiring his share on his death, he also excludes himself from acquiring B's or C's interests on their deaths. (He cannot have it both ways.)

The term used to describe the conversion of a joint tenancy into a tenancy in common is '*severance*'. In the last example, when A converted his interest

---

11   [1995] Conv 105 (L. Tee).
12   [1986] LS Gaz R 1699 (R. Owen).
13   *Cray v Willis* (1729) 2 P Wms 529; *Williams v Hensman* (1861) 1 John & H 546 at 557; (M & B). The method is explained later.

into that of a tenant in common, we would speak of A severing the joint tenancy, ie he severs the joint tenancy to the extent of his interest. But, as we have seen, as between B and C the joint tenancy remains unsevered, and B and C continue to hold as joint tenants in relation to each other.

If there are three joint tenants, A, B and C, and one of them (A) dies (so that B and C then hold the property) and B then converts his interest into that of a tenant in common, at this point the joint tenancy existing between himself and C comes to an end, since it is not possible for co-ownership to exist consisting of one tenant in common and one joint tenant. Thus when B converted his interest into that of tenant in common, he in effect converted C into a tenant in common at the same time.[14] The result would be that if C died before B, C's share would pass under his will or intestacy, notwithstanding that C had taken no step to sever the joint tenancy.

SEVERANCE BY ALIENATION INTER VIVOS

If A and B hold as tenants in common they can sell their own half share during their lifetimes, or make any other disposition of it.

This raises the question whether, if A and B hold as joint tenants, they can transfer their half share during their lifetimes. (We must, incidentally, be careful about using the term 'share' in the context of joint tenancy. This is because, under joint tenancy (as already seen), each co-owner is regarded as owning the whole of the property. But it is convenient to think of joint tenants (as well as tenants in common) holding a certain share of the property, and this is a notion we shall continue to use in this chapter, the convenience of so doing being permitted to override what is technically an inaccuracy.) The answer to the question we have raised is that if A and B hold as joint tenants, they can alienate their shares inter vivos.

If A, B and C hold as joint tenants, and A transfers his interest to X, X does not hold as a joint tenant (as A had done) along with B and C. This is because, when one joint tenant transfers his share to another person, the transferee must hold his share as a tenant in common since, in the case of the transferee, there is no unity of time, or of title.[15] X therefore holds as tenant in common; B and C continue to hold as joint tenants. The joint tenancy has been severed – to the extent of A's interest. Alienation of his share by a joint tenant thus constitutes one of the ways in which severance may occur. (This was originally[16] the way in which a joint tenant could convert his own interest into that of a tenant in common: what happened was that if A, B and C held as joint tenants, and A wanted to hold as a tenant in common he executed a deed granting his interest to trustees, on trust for himself. The transfer to the trustees severed the joint tenancy with regard to A's interest.[17])

If A transfers his share not to X, but to B, one of the other joint tenants, the same principle applies. The joint tenancy is severed to the extent of A's

14   *Williams v Hensman*, ante.
15   In the case of a transfer by way of sale, severance occurs at the execution of the contract.
16   For a simpler method introduced by the Law of Property Act 1925, s 36(2), see post.
17   *Cray v Willis* (1729) 2 P Wms 529.

interest: B holds the one-third share he received from A as a tenant in common; he continues to hold his original one-third share as a joint tenant. When B dies, the one-third share he received from A passes under his will or intestacy (let us say to D) and B's original one-third share vests in C. D will then hold one-third and C two-thirds. And, as seen above, since D holds as tenant in common, the whole joint tenancy is now severed and C holds as a tenant in common also.

Severance occurs not only where a joint tenant transfers his whole interest (by sale or gift) to another, but also where a joint tenant makes a partial alienation of his interest, as where a joint tenant mortgages his interest, or grants it to another merely for life.[18] Further, severance occurs not only where a joint tenant alienates his interest voluntarily but also where there is involuntary alienation; as where a joint tenant's interest becomes vested in his trustee in bankruptcy on the joint tenant being adjudicated bankrupt.[19]

SEVERANCE BY MUTUAL AGREEMENT

If co-owners hold as joint tenants they can sever the joint tenancy (with the result that they all then hold as tenants in common) by mutual agreement.[20]

SEVERANCE BY A COURSE OF DEALING

Further, the joint tenancy will be severed if, short of actual agreement, there is shown to have been a 'course of dealing' (by the co-owners) 'sufficient to intimate that the interests of all were mutually treated as constituting a tenancy in common', for example, 'negotiations [between the co-owners] which, although not otherwise resulting in any agreement, indicate a common intention that the joint tenancy should be regarded as severed.[1]

Summary

We may now summarise the differences between joint tenancy and tenancy in common which we have met so far.

	A, B, C and D hold as JOINT TENANTS	A, B, C and D hold as TENANTS IN COMMON
1.	On A's death his interest vests in B, C and D. B, C and D then hold a one-third share each as joint tenants.	On A's death, his interest passes under his will; of if he died intestate it passes to his next of kin.

18 *Re Gorman (A bankrupt)* [1990] 1 All ER 717, [1990] 1 WLR 616; *Re Dennis (A bankrupt)* [1993] Ch 72, [1992] 3 All ER 436; *Re Pavlou* [1992] 3 All ER 955, [1993] 1 WLR 1046, *Re Palmer* [1994] Ch 316, [1994] 3 All ER 835 (CN).
19 Where a husband who held property with his wife, holding as joint tenants, purported to convey the property to another by forging his wife's signature, it was held that the husband conveyed no more than his interest and that the joint tenancy was severed: *Ahmed v Kendirck and Ahmed* [1988] 2 FLR 22. Cf *Penn v Bristol and West Building Society* [1996] 2 FCR 729 (joint tenancy not severed where purchaser was cognisant of the forgery and party to the fraud for the purpose of which the forgery was committed).
20 *Williams v Hensman* (1861) 1 John & H 546, per Page Wood VC at 557; (M & B).
 1 Per Sir John Pennycuick, *Burgess v Rawnsley* [1975] Ch 429 at 447.

A, B, C and D hold as JOINT TENANTS	A, B, C and D hold as TENANTS IN COMMON
2. A can transfer his interest inter vivos to X. X would hold A's share as tenant in common. B, C and D would remain joint tenants *inter se*.	A can transfer his interest inter vivos to X. X would hold A's share (as A had done) as a tenant in common. B, C and D remain tenants in common.
3. A could transfer his interest to B. B would then hold A's quarter share as a tenant in common. He would continue to hold his original quarter interest as a joint tenant. C and D would continue to hold a quarter share each as joint tenants.	A could transfer his interest to B. B would then hold A's share, and his own original share, as a tenant in common. B would then hold a half share, C a quarter share and D a quarter share, all holding as tenants in common.
4. A can sever his interest and thereby convert is into an interest held as a tenant in common. B, C and D would remain joint tenants.	A alone could not convert his holding into a joint tenancy. (If he wishes his share to go to B, C and D on his death he could, of course, leave it to them in his will.) (A, B, C and D could together convey the property to themselves as joint tenants, thereby converting the tenancy in common into a joint tenancy.)
5. If C and D are the surviving joint tenants, and C converts his interest into a tenancy in common, then D also holds as a tenant in common. (It is impossible for one of two co-owners to hold as a tenant in common, and for the other to be a joint tenant.) Thus if D dies before C, his interest passes under his will or intestacy, notwithstanding that he was not the co-owner to sever the joint tenancy.	
6. In order to hold as joint tenants, the four unities of – interest time title and possession must be present. If any of the unities of – interest, time, title are missing the co-ownership cannot be joint tenancy but can be tenancy in common.	In order to hold as tenants in common only unity of possession need be present.

In the main, all the principles which we have mentioned in this chapter applied before 1925, and still apply today. Statute has, however, made important changes in the field of co-ownership, and it is to these changes that we must now turn.

CO-OWNERSHIP UNDER THE LAW OF PROPERTY ACT 1925, AS AMENDED

The trust

It was an effect of ss 34-36 of the Law of Property Act 1925[2] that land owned (concurrently) by more than one person, was held subject to a trust for sale. These sections of the 1925 Act were amended by the Trusts of Land and Appointment of Trustees Act 1996 with effect that from the date of the 1996 Act, land held by more than one person is held no longer under a trust for sale, but instead under a trust of land under the 1996 Act.

Since the land is subject to a trust, there must be trustees (just as, before the 1996 Act, there had to be trustees for sale), who hold the legal estate in the land on trust for beneficiaries. We must therefore consider who the trustees are, and who the beneficiaries are, under this trust.

THE BENEFICIARIES

The identity of the beneficiaries presents no difficulty; the beneficiaries are the co-owners to whom the land is granted. So if a grantor (G) conveys the land to A, B, C, D, E and F, all these six persons are beneficiaries (*the beneficial co-owners*) under the trust. Thus:

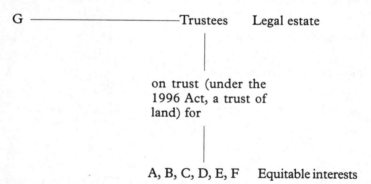

THE TRUSTEES

We shall first consider who the trustees are when the land is granted to the co-owners inter vivos.

INTER VIVOS GRANT

1. If, in an inter vivos grant, G conveys the legal estate to certain named trustees, then the persons so named (provided that they are of full age[3]) become

---

2   For an analysis of the background to the drafting of the sections and the intentions of the draftsmen, see [1990] CLJ 277, 296-301 (C. Harpum).
3   LPA 1925, s 20.

the trustees. If G conveys the legal estate to more than four trustees, only the first four named take the legal estate as trustees.[4]

G may name a co-owner beneficiary as, or among, the trustees. G could therefore convey the legal estate (inter alia) in the following ways:

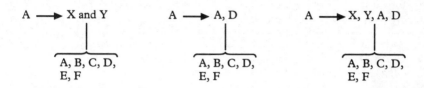

2. If G does not name the persons to be the trustees (if, for example, he conveyed the land 'to A, B, C, D, E and F'), the trustees are the first four named of the co-owners who are of full age. So, if C is six years old, the trustees will be A, B, D and E and they will hold the legal estate for themselves and the other co-owners (including C) like this:

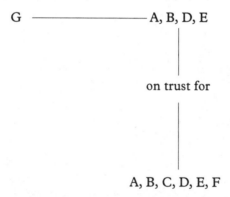

It should be noted that in this case the trust arises automatically,[5] and the legal estate vests automatically in A, B, D and E and the equitable interest vests automatically in A, B, C, D, E and F.

DEVISE

G leaves Blackacre 'to A, B, C, D, E and F' in his will. On his death the land (along with the rest of G's property) vests in his personal representatives, let us say his executors X and Y. They hold all of G's property on trust to give effect to the directions of G's will, but in the case of Blackacre they hold the

---

4   LPA 1925, s 34(2).
5   Ie by virtue of the effect of LPA 1925, ss 34-36, as amended by the Trusts of Land and Appointment of Trustees Act 1996.

land under a trust of land for the co-owners named, the trust being imposed by statute by virtue of the fact that the beneficiaries under the will are co-owners of the land.

If the land is to be retained, it may be decided that it would be more convenient for the legal estate to be held by the devisees. In this event, the personal representatives will (by assent) convey the legal estate to the devisees (up to a maximum of four) whom it has been agreed shall be the trustees, on trust for all the beneficial co-owners.

Thus, whether the land is conveyed to the co-owners inter vivos or by will, we find that a trust of land arises; we know how trustees are ascertained; and we know that the beneficiaries are all the co-owners.

Joint tenancy and tenancy in common

Before 1926 the position was as follows:

1. Co-ownership could exist –
    (a) under no trust (as where G granted land directly 'to A, B, C, D, E and F')
    (b) under a trust (including a trust for sale).
2. Joint tenancy and tenancy in common could exist in a legal or an equitable form.

Thus, if G granted land to three co-owners, A, B and C, the land could be held by them under any of the six arrangements set out below.

1	2	3	4	5	6
ABC Legal joint tenants	ABC Legal tenants in common	ABC Legal tenants in common	ABC Legal tenants in common	ABC Legal joint tenants	ABC Legal joint tenants
	ABC Equitable joint tenants	ABC Equitable joint tenants	ABC Equitable tenants in common	ABC Equitable joint tenants	ABC Equitable tenants in common

From this it will be seen that before 1926 in numbers 1 and 2, A, B and C hold the legal estate as joint tenants and tenants in common respectively without any trust being employed. In numbers 3, 4, 5 and 6 they hold their interest as beneficiaries under a trust. It will also be seen from numbers 3, 4, 5 and 6 that the trustees could hold either as joint tenants or tenants in common; and that the beneficiaries could similarly hold either as joint tenants or tenants in common.

THE CHANGES MADE BY THE LAW OF PROPERTY ACT 1925

These were twofold:

1. After 1925 land held by co-owners was (as already seen) subject to a trust for sale.

2. After 1925 tenancy in common could (and still can) no longer exist in a legal form.[6]

---

6   LPA 1925, s 1(6).

These changes affected the pattern set out as follows.

(i)   As a result of 1 above, numbers 1 and 2 in the table are no longer possible since in numbers 1 and 2 no trust exists.

(ii)   As a result of 2 above, numbers 3 and 4 are no longer possible, since in numbers 3 and 4 the legal estate was held by the trustees as tenants in common, and we have stated in 2 above that since 1925 tenancy in common can no longer exist in legal form.

(iii)   Numbers 5 and 6 can still exist today, since the legal estate is held by the trustees as joint tenants, and not as tenants in common.

(iv)   The trusts shown in numbers 5 and 6 had, under the 1925 Act, to be trusts for sale.

THE CHANGE MADE BY THE TRUSTS OF LAND AND APPOINTMENT OF TRUSTEES ACT 1996.

The trusts shown in numbers 5 and 6 are trusts of land (ie no longer trusts for sale). The result is that, since the 1996 Act when land is held by co-owners:

(a)   the land is held under a trust of land under the 1996 Act.

(b)   the trustees invariably hold the legal estate as joint tenants;

(c)   the beneficiaries can hold the equitable interest *either* as joint tenants *or* tenants in common.

THE TRUSTEES HOLD AS JOINT TENANTS

We have seen that before 1926 if the co-ownership existed under a trust, the trustees could hold either as joint tenants or as tenants in common. But there were disadvantages in trustees holding as tenants in common. For example, let us suppose that T^1, T^2 and T^3 held the legal estate as tenants in common on trust for A, B, C and D, the beneficial co-owners. If T^3 died, since he held as a tenant in common, his share would vest in his personal representative (X) who would then have to transfer this property to T^1 and T^2 (or to a newly appointed trustee, T^4). It would have been more convenient for X not to have become involved with the trust property. This could have been achieved by T^1, T^2 and T^3 holding the trust property as joint tenants. Under the latter arrangement, when T^3 died, his share would vest automatically in T^1, T^2 and X would not become involved in any way. If T^1 and T^2 wished to appoint another trustee, T^4, they could do so,[7] and the property would then become vested in T^1, T^2 and T^4.

This is another example of a use to which joint tenancy can be put and it is the reason why the Law of Property Act 1925 provided (and continues to provide) that after 1925 the only form of legal co-ownership that can exist is joint tenancy.

At this point it should be noted that the statement, 'the trustees hold the legal estate as joint tenants and the beneficial co-owners hold their equitable interest as tenants in common' is a grave but common error. Before 1926 beneficial co-owners could hold as joint tenants or tenants in common. The

7   Under the Trustee Act 1893, s 10. The power now exists under the Trustee Act 1925, s 36(1).

1925 legislation made no change in this position. Thus after 1925 the beneficial owners can still hold as joint tenants or tenants in common.

No severance of a legal joint tenancy

Suppose that:

1. A and D hold the legal fee simple as joint tenants on trust for A, B, C and D as joint tenants.
2. D sells his equitable quarter share to X.
3. D decides that he does not wish to continue to be a trustee. A and D agree that B should be appointed in D's place.[8] A and D transfer the legal estate to A and B.[9]
4. The result is that A and B hold on trust for A, B, C and X.

It will be noted that when D transfers his equitable interest to X, this does not affect D's position as trustee. He remains a trustee holding the legal estate as a joint tenant with A, notwithstanding that he has parted with his equitable interest. D remains a trustee until B is appointed a trustee in D's place. X does not become a trustee unless he is so appointed.

When B becomes trustee in place of D, there is no severance of the legal joint tenancy. This is because (a) no legal tenancy in common can exist after 1925; and (b) the Law of Property Act 1925 provides that 'No severance of a joint tenancy of a legal estate ... shall be permissible'.[10]

Severance of an equitable joint tenancy after 1925

The rules relating to severance of a joint tenancy (considered on p 158) continue to apply unchanged after 1925 in the case of the beneficiaries holding as joint tenants, but with one extension. The Law of Property Act 1925 added to the ways in which a beneficial joint tenancy can be severed by providing[11] that severance of a co-owner's interest occurs if the co-owner gives notice in writing of his intention that the joint tenancy should be severed (ie severed as to his share). In order to be effective, the notice must evince an intention that the severance should occur immediately.[12]

Where the joint tenancy is severed by notice under the Law of Property Act 1925[13] the notice to the other co-owners may state this intention expressly or impliedly, as where A gives notice to B and C of his wish that the property should be sold and that he should be paid his share out of the proceeds of sale.

---

8   Power conferred on trustees to appoint a fresh trustee in place of one who dies, remains out of the United Kingdom for more than 12 months, desires to be discharged as a trustee, or refuses, is unfit or is incapable of acting as a trustee; Trustee Act 1925, s 36.
9   TA 1925, s 40.
10 Section 36(1).
11 Section 36(2).
12 *Harris v Goddard* [1983] 3 All ER 242, [1983] 1 WLR 1203 (prayer in a wife's petition for divorce that the court should order such transfer of property in respect of the matrimonial house as should be just, held not sufficient to constitute notice of severance); (1984) 100 LQR 161; [1984] Conv 148 (S. Coneys).
13 Section 36(2).

With regard to the method by which notice of severance under the Law of Property Act 1925[14] may be given, the Act provides that the notice must be in writing.[15] It is further provided that the notice (and, incidentally, any other notice required to be served by the Act) will be 'sufficiently served' (ie in the event of a denial by another co-owner that the notice was received) if it is left at the 'last-known place of abode or business' of the person to be served or affixed on the land or on any building on it,[16] or if it is sent by post in a registered letter[17] or by recorded delivery[18] and addressed to the person at his last known 'place of abode or business, office or counting house', and the letter is not 'returned through the post office undelivered'.[19]

Section 36(2) of the Law of Property Act 1925 provides that the power to sever by the giving of notice is exercisable 'where a legal estate ... is vested in joint tenants beneficially'. Clearly, taken literally, this condition can never be satisfied, since the legal estate held by co-owners can never be held beneficially. It is held by them as trustees. The meaning has been taken to be that the power to sever by notice is exercisable only where the trustees and the beneficial owners under the trust are the same people. If this is so, then the power to sever by notice is not exercisable where, for example, A and B hold on trust for A, B and C; or A and B for A and C; or A and B for C and D.

If the power to sever by notice is in fact limited in this way then the old method of severance must still be observed wherever the holders of the legal estate are not the same people as the holders of the equitable interest. Under the pre-1926 law an equitable joint tenant (A) who wished to sever his own interest was able to do so by transferring his interest to trustees on trust for himself.[20] The alienation to the trustees severed the interest, but A retained the ultimate beneficial interest, which he then held as a tenant in common. It would follow from this that if (i) X and Y hold on trust for A, B, C and D as equitable joint tenants; (ii) A gives notice in writing to B, C and D of his intention to sever the joint tenancy (ie as to his share); (iii) A dies; (iv) B transfers his interest to trustees on trust for himself; (v) B dies; then the extraordinary result is that although B will have severed his interest, A will not. Thus X and Y would hold on trust, one-third for B's estate, one-third for C, one-third for D (and nothing for A's estate). On the other hand, if the legal estate had been vested in A, B, C and D, and the same events had occurred, then the trustees (C and D) would have held one-quarter for each of A's estate, B's estate, C and D.

The difference in outcome, depending on who holds the legal estate, is, of course, especially paradoxical in view of the fact that it was the aim of the 1925 legislation to rationalise the law. It has been suggested that, in order to

14   Ibid.
15   LPA 1925, ss 36(2) and 196(1).
16   LPA 1925, s 196(3). Whether this was done is a matter of proof.
17   LPA 1925, s 196(4).
18   Recorded Delivery Service Act 1962, s 1.
19   LPA 1925, s 196(4). See *Re No 88 Berkeley Road NW 9* [1971] Ch 648, [1971] 1 All ER 254: notice sent by recorded delivery by A and B, addressed to house owned by A and B. Letter accepted by A in B's absence. Notice sufficiently served on B.
20   See p 159, ante.

avoid the anomaly, 'it might be possible to construe the statutory words "vested in joint tenants beneficially" so as to give them a wider meaning than normally'.[1] It is to be hoped that if the matter came before the court this course would be followed, and an interpretation adopted that permitted severance to be effected by the giving of notice by an equitable joint tenant, irrespective of who happened to be the trustees holding the legal estate at the time.

At one stage it was thought that one joint tenant could sever his interest by adopting a course of conduct from which his intention to sever could be inferred; eg by taking out a summons under s 17 of the Married Women's Property Act 1882 asking for an order that the property should be sold.[2] It has since been established, however, that a unilateral act or course of conduct by one joint tenant cannot be sufficient to sever the joint tenancy.[3] (Nor can a unilateral declaration of itself sever a joint tenancy, though if the declaration is in writing and is delivered to the other joint tenants, this will constitute severance by notice, under the Act.)

However, a particular course of conduct will, as stated earlier, be sufficient to sever a joint tenancy if it indicates a *common* intention between the joint tenants that the joint tenancy should be severed. Thus, in *Burgess v Rawnsley*,[4] a house was transferred into the names of A and B (who were unmarried) 'as joint tenants'. Later B orally agreed to sell her interest in the property to A, but subsequently refused to sell. It was held that the oral agreement (notwithstanding that it was unenforceable due to non-compliance with s 40 of the Law of Property Act 1925) was sufficient to evince an intention by A and B that the beneficial joint tenancy should be severed. Thus when A died, B held the legal estate on trust for herself and A's estate equally.

DO THE BENEFICIAL CO-OWNERS HOLD AS JOINT TENANTS OR AS TENANTS IN COMMON?[5]

In order to determine how beneficial co-owners hold their interests certain tests have to be applied.[6] They are as follows.

1. Are the four unities present? If they are not, then (even if the grantor had stated expressly that A, B, C and D were to hold as joint tenants) there can be no joint tenancy, and A, B, C and D holds as tenants in common. If the four unities are present we proceed to the next test.

---

1   M & W, p 436.
2   *Re Draper's Conveyance* [1969] 1 Ch 486, [1967] 3 All ER 853; (M & B).
3   *Nielson-Jones v Fedden* [1975] Ch 222, [1974] 3 All ER 38; following *Re Wilks* [1891] 3 Ch 59.
4   [1975] Ch 429, [1975] 3 All ER 142; (M & B). Cf *Barton v Morris* [1985] 2 All ER 1032, [1985] 1 WLR 1257 (inclusion of house, held by couple as beneficial joint tenants, in the couple's partnership accounts for tax purposes did not constitute a course of dealing sufficient to show a common intention that the joint tenancy should be severed). [1986] Conv 354 (JEM).
5   For an argument in favour of abolishing equitable joint tenancy, see [1987] Conv 29 (M. P. Thompson); [1987] Conv 273 (riposte by A. M. Pritchard); ibid, 275 (reply by M. P. Thompson).
6   The tests existed before 1926 and were not affected by the changes made by the 1925 legislation.

2. Did the grant expressly state that the co-owners were to hold as joint tenants (as by a grant 'to A and B as joint tenants', or 'to A and B jointly') or as tenants in common? If so, in the absence of fraud or mistake giving rise to a claim for rectification[7] or rescission, the express declaration is conclusive and the parties hold as the grant declares[8]. If the grant gave no such direction, we proceed to the next test.

3. Did the grant use what are termed 'words of severance'? Examples of words of severance are as follows: 'to A and B equally'; 'to A and B share and share alike'; 'to be divided between A and B'; 'to A and B in equal shares'. Words such as these, which indicate that the co-owners are to take a distinct share in the property, are construed as implying that the co-owners are to take as tenants in common.[9] Thus, if words of severance are used, the co-owners take as tenants in common. If no such words are used (and there is no other indication in the gift that tenancy in common is intended) then we proceed to the next test.

4. Are the circumstances of the grant such that equity presumes that the co-owners are to hold as tenants in common? There are three situations in which, in the absence of any indication to the contrary, equity presumes that the co-owners hold as tenants in common. These are as follows.

(A) PURCHASE OF LAND IN UNEQUAL SHARES

If A and B purchase land from V and B contribute the purchase money in unequal shares (eg A pays £3,000 and B pays £6,000), then equity presumes that A and B hold as tenants in common.[10] Thus A and B will hold the legal estate as joint tenants on trust for A and B as tenants in common. If A and B wish to hold their beneficial interests as joint tenants, they will direct V to convey the legal estate to them as joint tenants on trust for themselves as joint tenants. The case we are speaking of only raises a *presumption* of tenancy in common. The presumption can be rebutted if there is evidence to the contrary, ie that joint tenancy was intended. (If a husband and wife contribute in unequal shares to the purchase of their home, it will normally be the presumption that they intend to hold the property as joint tenants in equity.)

If A and B contribute equally no presumption of tenancy in common arises, and (provided that (B) and (C) below do not apply) we would pass to step 5 below.

---

7   *Robinson v Robinson* (1976) 241 Estates Gazette 153 (transfer to X and Y declaring them beneficial joint tenants; transfer not executed by X or Y; Y held not to be estopped from producing evidence that the intention of himself and X had been to hold as tenants in common, and the court could order accordingly).

8   *Pettitt v Pettitt* [1970] AC 777 at 813; *Pink v Lawrence* (1978) 36 P & CR 98 at 101; *Godwin v Bedwell* (1982) Times, 10 March.

9   Where a grant uses words which produce a contradictory result (eg 'to A and B jointly and equally') then (following the rule of construction in a deed) the result produced by the first words prevails; in a will, the result produced by the last; *Slingsby's Case* (1587) 5 Co Rep 18b; *Perkins v Baynton* (1781) 1 Bro CC 118. Thus in 1980 it was held that a conveyance by deed to a husband and wife 'in fee simple as beneficial joint tenants in common in equal shares' created a joint tenancy; *Joyce v Barker Bros (Builders) Ltd* (1980) 40 P & CR 512. But cf *Martin v Martin* (1987) 54 P & CR 238, [1987] Conv 405 (JEA).

10 *Lake v Gibson* (1729) 1 EQ Cas Abr 290; *Bull v Bull* [1955] 1 QB 234, [1995] 1 All ER 253.

(B) Partnership Property

If A and B hold land as partners, whether or not under a formal partnership agreement, there is a presumption that they hold their beneficial interest as tenants in common.[11] For example, A and B might be partners in a firm of solicitors with offices in a town; they hold their beneficial interest in the land as tenants in common. The reason is that it is presumed that in the case of a business relationship, the co-owners would wish their interest in the land on their death to form part of their estate and pass under their will or intestacy, rather than pass to the other partners. (In a case heard by the Privy Council in 1986, it was held that where a lease was granted to two (or more) tenants, the premises being required by them for their business purposes, then (even if the tenants were not partners) there was a presumption that they held their beneficial interests in the lease as tenants in common.[12])

(C) Money lent on mortgage

If A and B lend money to a landowner, R, and as security for the loan R mortgages the land to A and B, then A and B hold their interest in the mortgage as tenants in common. If R fails to repay the loan and A and B obtain the land they hold it (beneficially) as tenants in common.[13] This presumption arises irrespective of whether A and B lent the same or different amounts to R.

If none of these presumptions arises:

5.   The final step is that we can say that the co-owners hold as joint tenants.

Thus if the four unities are present, if there are no express words indicating how the co-owners are to hold the land, no words of severance are used, and none of the equitable presumptions arise, the beneficial co-owners hold as joint tenants.[14] (If a beneficial joint tenant is not content with this position he can, as seen above, convert his interest into that of a tenant in common, by severing the joint tenancy by giving notice to the other beneficial co-owners.)

Since, in the absence of fraud or mistake,[15] an express declaration of beneficial joint tenancy prevails over an equitable presumption of tenancy in common, where A and B contribute in unequal shares to property that is conveyed to them as beneficial joint tenants, then they hold as joint tenants in equity and, accordingly, if the land is sold the proceeds are divided equally.

The sale of land held by co-owners

When land is held by co-owners opinion between them may become divided over whether the land should be retained or sold. Some may wish the land to

---

11   *Lake v Craddock* (1732) 3 P Wms 157.
12   *Malayan Credit Ltd v Jack Chai-MPH Ltd* [1986] AC 549, [1986] 1 All ER 711; [1986] Conv 354 (JEM).
13   *Petty v Styward* (1631) 1 Rep Ch 57; *Re Jackson Smith v Sibthorpe* (1887) 34 Ch D 732.
14   As in *Re Osoba* [1979] 2 All ER 393, [1979] 1 WLR 247, and in *Re Bourke's Will Trusts* [1980] 1 All ER 219, [1980] 1 WLR 539.
15   See p 169, ante.

be sold, because they wish to have the money that a sale would produce; others may wish the land to be retained, perhaps because they wish to continue to occupy the land; or because they consider the land to be a good investment (with regard to the income it produces in the form of rent, or with regard to its potential increase in value, or with regard to both these matters).

Prior to the 1996 Act, whether land was sold or retained depended, in the first place, on whether the trustees were under a duty to consult the beneficiaries and abide by their wishes (or the majority of them). Such a duty existed (a) where an intention was shown in the grant that it should exist, and (b) where the duty was imposed by statute,[16] namely where the trust for sale was created by statute. If the duty to consult existed, then whether the land was sold or retained depended on the wishes of the beneficiaries.

Where no duty to consult existed and the trustees were unanimous in wishing to retain the land (ie unanimous in exercising their statutory power to postpone sale), the land was retained. Where they were not unanimous in this regard, the land had to be sold. A beneficiary who dissented from what was proposed could[17] apply to the court for an order requiring or prohibiting sale, as the case might be.

After the 1996 Act, whether land held by co-owners is retained or sold will depend (as a result of the duty to consult imposed by the 1996 Act) on the wishes of the beneficial co-owners (or the majority by interest of them). In the event of wishes being divided equally (or in the event of the duty to consult having been excluded) the result will be (the trustees not being unanimous in exercising the power of sale conferred by the Act) that the land is retained. It would be open to a trustee (or a beneficial co-owner who is not a trustee) to apply to the court for an order ordering sale. As noted in Chapter 10, the jurisdiction previously conferred by the Law of Property Act 1925 on the court to order sale of land held under a trust for sale (and to make associated orders) has been replaced by a wider jurisdiction conferred by the 1996 Act.[18]

It should be noted that if A, B and C are co-owners and A wishes the property to be sold, and B and C do not, and A applies to the court for an order that the property should be sold, and the court makes the order sought, it would be open to B and C, if they so wished, to buy the property. The result would be that A would receive his one-third share in money from B and C, who would be left as owners of the property. Thus, where a co-owner wishes the property to be sold, he is in effect asking no more than that he should be paid his share of the value of the property. An order by the court that the property should be sold is therefore satisfied if a co-owner who wishes to retain the property pays the one who wants it to be sold for his share.[19] The court may order that if a specified sum is paid by the co-owner not wanting sale to

16 LPA 1925, s 26(3) as amended by LP(Am)A 1926, Schedule.
17 Section 30.
18 Section 14.
19 Similarly, if a matrimonial home is held by H and W on trust for themselves, and W wants the property to be sold, and H wants to remain living there and the court maks an order for sale, the order is satisfied by H paying W for the value of her interest; *Jones v Challenger* [1961] 1 QB 176, [1960] 1 All ER 785.

the other co-owner within a specified period, then the order for sale is not to be enforced.[20]

Distribution of the proceeds of sale

If the court makes an order (ie under the jurisdiction now conferred by the 1996 Act) for sale, the court will direct how the proceeds are to be distributed. If the co-owners hold as beneficial joint tenants then, as noted earlier, the proceeds will be divided equally. If they hold as beneficial tenants in common, any express direction as to how they held their beneficial interests (eg equally[1]) will normally (ie in the absence of fraud or mistake) prevail.[1] If there is no direction as to the proportions in which they hold their interests, it will be presumed that they hold equally.

If the legal estate is vested in A, who holds on an implied trust for A and B then in the older cases, if the contributions of A and B to the purchase of the house were quantifiable, the court would commonly make an order under which the interests of the parties were proportionate to their contributions.[2] For some years, where property, particularly the matrimonial home, had been acquired by the efforts of both parties, in the absence of any reason to the contrary,[3] the courts tended to eschew mathematical calculations, and hold that the intention of the parties (if they had considered the matter) would be most closely given effect to by ordering the beneficial interests to be held equally.[4] More recently the courts have adopted a more flexible approach, but it remains the position that it is what is found by the court to have been the *intention of the parties* that is the deciding factor in the determination of how the equitable interest is to be divided among the beneficiaries.[5]

---

20   As in *Bernard v Josephs* [1982] Ch 391, [1982] 3 All ER 162.
1   *Dennis v McDonald* [1981] 2 All ER 632, [1981] 1 WLR 810.
2   For example, in the following cases the proportions directed to be held for H and W were as stated: *Hazell v Hazell* [1972] 1 All ER 923, [1972] 1 WLR 301, four-fifths and one-fifth; *Heseltine v Heseltine* [1971] 1 All ER 952, [1971] 1 WLR 342, one-quarter and three-quarters; *Muetzel v Muetzel* [1970] 1 All ER 443, [1970] 1 WLR 188, two-thirds and one-third; *Re Nicholson* [1974] 2 All ER 386, [1974] 1 WLR 476 twenty forty-firsts and twenty-one forty-firsts.
3   See *Harvey v Harvey* [1982] Fam 83, [1982] 1 All ER 693.
4   *Smith v Baker* [1970] 2 All ER 826, [1970] 1 WLR 1160; *Rimmer v Rimmer* [1953] 1 QB 63; [1952] 2 All ER 863; *Fribance v Fribance (No 2)* [1957] 1 All ER 357, [1957] 1 WLR 384; *Ulrich v Ulrich and Felton* [1968] 1 All ER 67, [1968] 1 WLR 180; *Hargrave v Newton* [1971] 3 All ER 866, [1971] 1 WLR 1611; *Davis v Vale* [1971] 2 All ER 1021, [1971] 1 WLR 1022; *Lloyds Bank v Rosset* [1991] 1 AC 107, 132; *McHardy and Sons v Warren* [1994] 2 FLR 338; *Halifax Building Society v Brown* [1995] 3 FCR 110. See also *Turton v Turton* [1988] Ch 542, [1987] 2 All ER 641 (beneficiaries' interests are in the proceeds realised by the sale not, as held by McKaney J, in the value of the property at a date, some years earlier, when the co-owners had separated); followed in *Passee v Passee* [1988] 1 FLR 263 (valuation to be an up-to-date one, not one based on the value at the date when the plaintiff went out of possession, some years earlier).
5   *Passee v Passee* [1988] 1 FLR 263; [1988] Conv 361 (J. Warburton).

Powers of trustees for sale in the case of co-ownership before the 1996 Act

Since, before the 1996 Act, the powers of trustees for sale were restricted (being limited to those of the Tenant for life and the trustees of a strict settlement), and since co-owners of land, for example a husband and wife owning the matrimonial home, might wish to effect a transaction outside the powers of trustees for sale, for example to give the house or part of the land on which it stood, to a child, it was the practice for grants to co-owners to confer on them, in the conveyance of the legal estate, all the powers of an absolute owner. A standard form of words was ' ... the trustees for the time being of this deed shall have power to mortgage, charge, lease or otherwise dispose of all or any part of the said property with all the powers in that behalf of an absolute owner'.

Entitlement of co-owners to occupy the land

In Chapter 5 we saw that prior to the 1996 Act, trustees of land had discretion as to whether a beneficiary with an interest in possession should (ie as a means of giving effect to his beneficial interest) be permitted to occupy the land. After the 1996 Act a beneficial co-owner's need to rely on the trustees' discretion in this regard is replaced by the statutory right of occupation conferred by the Act[6] on a person entitled to an interest in possession in the land, subject to the conditions set out in Chapter 10.[7]

No doubt with regard to previous litigation arising from disputes between co-owners as to occupation of the land, the Act provides that where two or more beneficiaries are entitled to occupy land the trustees may exclude or restrict entitlement of any one or more (but not all) of them, and may impose reasonable conditions on any beneficiary in relation to his occupation of land having regard, inter alia, to the purpose for which the land is held. Conditions that may be imposed include one requiring a beneficiary in occupation to pay any expenses in respect of the land, and requiring him to pay compensation to a beneficiary whose right of occupation has been excluded or restricted.

Since disputes as to entitlement to occupy land most commonly arise between a husband and wife (or between unmarried partners), and since, where such couples own their home, they are trustees of the legal estate on trust for themselves as beneficial co-owners, the provisions of the Act concerning the imposition by trustees of conditions as to occupation are likely to be of little practical value because of the dispute, there will be no agreement between the couple as to the conditions to be imposed. And if agreement in this regard exists, a need for the exercise of power to impose conditions will, in practice, not have arisen.

6   Section 12.
7   See p 146.

The reason for the imposition of the statutory trust

Why was land held by co-owners required by the Law of Property Act 1925 to be subject to a trust for sale? Why does the 1996 Act continue to require that land held by co-owners should be held under a trust? Assuming that the co-owners are all of full age, why should they not hold the legal estate as joint tenants or as tenants in common, as they wish? This was possible before 1926. Why was the position changed?

The answer is that the position could be unsatisfactory. Suppose that in 1900 the legal fee simple in Blackacre was held by A, B, C and D as tenants in common, as was then possible. In 1901 A dies leaving all this property between his four children, E, F, G and H. In 1902 B goes to Australia. In 1903, C dies intestate leaving six daughters, I, J, K, L, M and N. In 1905 D, who is in need of money, is offered a good price for Blackacre by P. 'I will gladly sell,' says D, 'but I shall have to get the agreement of my fellow co-owners before the land can be sold.' 'Who are the other owners?' asks P. 'Well,' replies D, 'E, F, G and H each own a one-sixteenth share; B owns a quarter share; and I, J, K, L, M and N each hold a one-twenty-fourth share. I shall have to write to ask them if they agree to the sale.' And he does so. All the replies that he receives are in favour of selling the land; but the letter he sent to B is returned marked 'Addressee deceased'. After enquiries, D learns that B died intestate in 1904, shortly after his fourth marriage had been dissolved, leaving numerous children and grandchildren. D sets about tracing their whereabouts. After three years of letter writing and before tracing all B's children and grandchildren, D learns that C's daughter N had died leaving her property between her 14 nephews and nieces. The land will by now be owned by innumerable persons. D is unlikely ever to be able to trace them all. Or if he could ever trace them, it would take so long that by then P would have lost interest in buying the land.

Even if D was able to trace all the co-owners and they all agreed to the sale, before P could safely pay over his purchase money, he would have to make sure:

(i)   that no *other* co-owners existed – for example, he would have to make sure that C did leave only six daughters;

(ii) that all the say, 180, co-owners were in fact entitled to their share.

This would present difficulties so great that any arrangement that avoided such a situation would seem preferable.

How the imposition of a trust for sale under the Law of Property Act 1925 and now a trust of land under the 1996 Act avoids this kind of situation from arising, can be explained by considering what would happen in the same circumstances today.

1. The legal fee simple in Blackacre is vested in A, B, C and D as joint tenants with A, B, C and D as beneficial tenants in common.

2. When A dies the trustees are B, C and D; the beneficial co-owners are (E, F, G and H) and B, C and D.

3. When C dies, the trustees are B and D; the beneficial co-owners are (E, F, G and H), B, (I, J, K, L, M and N) and D.

4. When B dies, the legal fee simple vested in D; the beneficial co-owners are (E, F, G, and H) (B's next of kin) (I, J, K, L, M and N) and D.

5. In order to sell the land D would have to appoint another trustee. Let us say that D appoints T as second trustee. The legal fee simple is then vested in D and T.

6. In deciding whether to sell the land D and T are obliged to consult the wishes of the beneficiaries, or the majority (in value) of them. If the majority agree, they can sell. If they are unable to obtain the consent of a majority of the beneficiaries, either because they refuse to agree or because they cannot be traced, D and T may apply to the court under s 14 of the 1996 Act for an order authorising them to sell. In the case of land as divided in beneficial ownership as Blackacre, the court would almost certainly make an order directing sale.

7. D and T convey the legal fee simple to P. P pays his money to the trustees, ensuring that they both sign the receipt. P has complied with the provisions of the Law of Property Act 1925 governing the purchase of land from trustees and he therefore takes free of the equitable interests of the beneficial co-owners, whose interests are henceforth in the purchase money.

8. D and T can start distributing the money to those beneficiaries whose identity and share can be ascertained. (D can safely take his quarter share of the purchase money immediately.)

The land could be sold to P within a matter of months of his approach to D. P is content – he acquires the land and he is freed from the ~~~ ~~~se difficulties he would have been faced with prior to 1925. His enquiries into the title to the land will, in fact, be simple. He will need to inspect the conveyance of the legal fee simple to A, B, C and D; the death certificates of A, B, and C; and the instrument appointing T as new trustee and vesting the legal fee simple in him (together with D). These five documents establish D and T's right to sell the land.

It will be noted from this example that the result of the operation of joint tenancy is that on the deaths of A, B and C, the legal fee simple becomes vested in successively fewer people as each death occurs, a purchaser having a smaller number of people with whom to deal as each trustee dies.

If D and T did not get the agreement of the majority of the co-owners (and did not protect themselves by getting an order from the court under s 14), P will nevertheless take a valid legal title free of the equitable interests of the beneficial co-owners.[8] If any of the beneficial co-owners can show that they have suffered loss, their remedy lies against D and T in an action for breach of trust.

TERMINATION OF CO-OWNERSHIP

1.   Sale

If A, B, C and D are co-owners of Blackacre, and the land is sold to P, the co-ownership will come to an end since the land has become vested in a sole owner, P.

---

8   Trusts of Land and Appointment of Trustees Act 1996, s 11.

2.   Partition

Partition consists of the physical division of the land between the co-owners, each co-owner becoming sole owner of the land allocated to him. The power conferred by the Trusts of Land and Appointment of Trustees Act 1996[9] on trustees of a trust of land to partition land was noted in Chapter 10.

3.   Union in a sole owner

The co-ownership may come to an end as a result of the beneficial interests becoming vested in a sole beneficial owner. This may arise in three ways.

(i)   Suppose that A, B and C are legal and beneficial co-owners (holding beneficially either as joint tenants or as tenants in common). A and B transfer their beneficial interest to C. The result is that A, B and C then hold the legal estate as joint tenants on trust for C, the sole beneficial owner. Assuming that C is of full age, he can require the trustees to convey the legal estate to him.

(ii) Suppose that A, B and C are beneficial co-owners holding as tenants in common; A and B bequeath their interests to C. On the deaths of A and B, C will hold the legal fee simple on trust for himself absolutely.

(iii) Suppose that A, B and C are beneficial co-owners holding as joint tenants. On the deaths of A and B, C (the sole surviving legal joint tenant) holds the legal fee simple on trust for himself absolutely.

It will be seen that in (ii) and (iii) the entire legal estate and equitable interest becomes vested in one person, C. It is a principle of law that where the legal and equitable interests in property become vested in one person, then the trust under which the equitable interest existed comes to an end. Thus when the legal and equitable interest in the land vests in C, the trust comes to an end, and C is free to deal with the property as absolute owner of the legal fee simple. He can, for example, if he wishes, sell the land to P.

Sale after union in a sole owner

In the last example ((iii) above), P will, of course, require some proof that C is entitled to sell the land. The document of title which C will be able to show to P will be the conveyance to A, B and C. From this P will know that the land was held on trust. But P could say to C 'You may have been one of the trustees, but where are A and B?' C could then show P A's and B's death certificates. This would prove that A and B were dead and that C must be the sole surviving trustee, but it would not tell P whether C was, in fact, as he claimed, the sole *beneficial* owner; and that is what P needs to know. It would be no use C being the sole surviving trustee if he, C, held on trust for himself and, say, X, Y and

---

9   Section 7, replacing a more limited power under LPA 1925, s 28(3). Previously, under the
    Partition Acts 1539 and 1540, any joint tenant in common had a statutory right, subject to
    certain conditions, to demand partition. The Partition Act of 1868 gave the courts power to
    order that, instead of partition, the land should be sold. See [1982] Conv 415 (R. Cocks).

Z. If C did hold on trust for himself and these people, and P bought the land, and accepted a receipt signed by C alone, then since P would have failed to comply with the statutory condition[10] that enables him to take free of the equitable interests of the beneficiaries, he would find himself holding the land on trust for X, Y and Z (and also, in theory at any rate, for C, although C would not be able to enforce this interest as, having obtained the purchase money, equity would grant him no remedy).

Even if C could point out to P that the land had been held by A, B and C on trust for A, B and C as joint tenants, the evidence of A's and B's death certificates would not guarantee that C was both sole surviving trustee and sole surviving beneficiary, since A (or B) could have transferred[11] his interest *inter vivos* to X. X would then be a beneficial tenant in common. When A and B died C would be left holding the legal fee simple on trust for himself and X. If P bought the land from C alone, he would take the land subject to X's equitable interest (and, again at any rate in theory, subject to C's equitable interest).

Thus, regardless of whether A, B and C had held as beneficial joint tenants or tenants in common, P could not safely purchase the land from C alone.

To be safe, P would have to require C to appoint another trustee (eg D) and then purchase the property from C and D, getting a receipt for the purchase money signed by both of them. P would then be protected: if any beneficial interest existed other than C's, P would take free of it.

If P bought the land from C alone, he would only be safe if he could show that he had no knowledge of any beneficial (equitable) interests other than C's; ie that he was a bona fide purchaser of the legal estate without notice. (It must be remembered that beneath all the legislation we have spoken of in this chapter, and the previous chapters, the principles of the bona fide purchaser rule remain alive.) Thus if P could prove he was a bona fide purchaser, he would take free, in the example we are using, of X's interest. But there is always the danger that X may be able to show that P has constructive notice of his interest, with the result that P will be bound. In practice no purchaser will want to find himself having to rely on the defence that he is a bona fide purchaser. So even if P was confident that he could establish that he was a bona fide purchaser, to be safe he would have to require C to appoint a second trustee, in order that he could get a receipt signed by two trustees. It is, of course, a nuisance for C (assuming that he is in fact now the sole owner) to have to go to the trouble of appointing another trustee merely to enable him to sell the land, and two moves have been made by statute to overcome this difficulty. The first was a provision in the Law of Property (Amendment) Act 1926,[12] the effect of which was that where A, B and C held as beneficial joint tenants, and C was the sole survivor, then C was entitled to deal with the legal estate as it was not held on trust. But this did little more than confirm the position reached by applying the basic principles of law, and whilst the statute gave, and continues to give, C the right to sell the land without appointing

---

10　LPA 1925, s 2(1), as amended by the Trusts of Land and Appointment of Trustees Act 1996, Sch 3.
11　Or severed his own interest, thus converting his interest into that of a tenant in common.
12　Adding words to LPA 1925, s 36(2).

another trustee, this does not mean that P is compelled to buy the land. P can say, 'Either you appoint another trustee to safeguard me, or you can keep the land.' So the problem was not resolved.

Law of Property (Joint Tenants) Act 1964[13]

The second move was made by the Law of Property (Joint Tenants) Act 1964. (The Act was not amended, or its operation affected by the 1996 Act.) The effect of this Act can be explained like this:

1. Suppose that G conveys land by deed to A, B and C as beneficial joint tenants. A, B and C will then hold the legal fee simple, on trust for themselves as beneficial joint tenants.
2. If the beneficial interest of A, B or C is severed (either by A, B or C severing their own interest by notice, or as a result of A, B or C transferring their interest to, say, X), under the provisions of the Act the fact and details of the severance can be recorded in a 'memorandum of severance' on the deed which conveyed the legal estate to A, B and C.
3. If A and B later die, and C wishes to sell the land to P, and P satisfies himself that A and B are dead, and that there is no memorandum of severance on the deed, then notwithstanding that P pays the purchase money to C alone, he will (the Act provides) take free of any equitable interests which in fact exist under the trust, due to severance by A or B (or even C).

Thus, if A proposes to sell his equitable interest to X, it is up to X to satisfy himself before he pays the purchase money that a memorandum of severance has been entered on the deed that conveyed the legal estate to A, B and C. Similarly, if A severs his own interest by giving notice to B and C, it is up to A to see that a memorandum of severance is entered on the deed. If he fails to do so, and he dies leaving all his property to his widow, W, and C eventually sells the land to P, P will take free of the equitable interest that passed to W under A's will.

If P does find that there is a memorandum of severance on the deed, but he nevertheless buys the land, and pays the purchase money to C alone, he will take subject to the equitable interest to which the severance relates. If, in the last example, A had recorded the fact of the severance of his interest on the deed, then P would take the land subject to W's equitable interest as to the one-third share in the property which she acquired under A's will.

The result is that if A, B and C are beneficial joint tenants, and A and B die, and the deed concerned is free from any memorandum of severance, P can safely buy the land from C alone, without requiring him to appoint a second trustee. (If there is a memorandum of severance, P can only safely buy the land if a second trustee is appointed and he takes a conveyance from, and pays the purchase money to, them both.)

---

13   (1966) Conv (NS) 27 (P. Jackson).

Suppose that G conveys land to A, B and C as beneficial *tenants in common*,[14] and on their deaths A and B leave their beneficial interests to C. The result will be that C will hold the legal fee simple (as the sole surviving legal joint tenant) on trust for himself absolutely. The 1964 Act does not enable C to sell the land to P without appointing a second trustee since the Act applies only where A, B and C are beneficial *joint tenants*. In the situation posed, P would have to require C to appoint a second trustee before he could safely buy the land.

The 1964 Act has proved useful: matrimonial homes are often owned by a husband and wife as beneficial joint tenants; when one of them dies and the survivor wishes to sell the house, the 1964 Act enables him or her to do so without having to appoint a second trustee.

Nuisances do, however, remain.

(i) The Act applies only where property is held beneficially by joint tenants. Thus if G conveys land to A, B and C as beneficial tenants in common, A and B die leaving their beneficial interests to C, the result will be that C will hold the legal estate on trust for himself absolutely. But since the 1964 Act does not apply, C will, if he wishes to sell the land, have to appoint a second trustee.

(ii) Consider the example under (i) page 176. Here C ended up with the complete legal and equitable interest. In order to provide a purchaser with a conveyance that establishes C's entitlement to sell the land as sole beneficial owner, the conveyance will have to recite the fact that A, B and C had held as beneficial tenants in common under the trust and that A and B had transferred their interests to C – thus bringing the equitable interests on to the title.

CO-OWNERSHIP OF LEASEHOLDS

In this chapter we have considered the position where the subject of the co-ownership is a freehold estate in land; for example where G conveys the legal fee simple to A, B, C and D as joint tenants to hold for themselves beneficially. The arrangements described in this chapter apply also to leasehold interests in land.[15] Where L grants a lease to two or more tenants (A and B), then A and B hold the legal title to the lease as trustees for themselves in equity, as joint tenants or tenants in common as the case may be. Or it may be that an existing lease held by a sole tenant is assigned to two or more assignees. For example, suppose that L grants a lease for 99 years to G. If G assigns the lease to A, B, C and D (with the result that G will drop out of the picture and A, B, C and D will become L's tenant in G's place) then A, B, C and D will hold the legal lease as joint tenants or tenants in common, according to the circumstances.

Thus if A, B, C and D were beneficial joint tenants of the lease and A died, B, C and D would then hold the legal lease on trust for themselves.

14   Or if land is conveyed to co-owners with no statement as to their beneficial interests but by an equitable presumption they hold as tenants in common; (1975) 94 LN 221 (M. J. Wells).
15   See *Marsh v Von Sternberg* [1986] 1 FLR 526, [1986] Fam Law 160.

All the machinery of a trust (now a trust of land under the 1996 Act) applies. For example, if, after A's death, B, C and D want to sell the lease, ie the part remaining unexpired, then the lease will have to be sold. Supposing that P buys the unexpired portion of the lease, we can illustrate the chain of devolution like this.

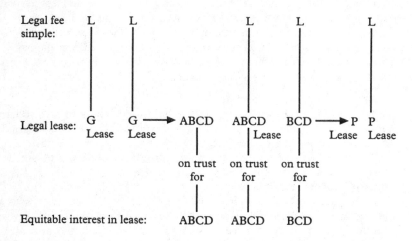

After the sale, B, C and D will hold the purchase money on trust for themselves, so they can share the money out between them, and that is the end of the matter as far as they are concerned. As regards the land, L remains the landlord (as he has done throughout) with P now his tenant under the lease.

ARE THE INTERESTS OF BENEFICIAL CO-OWNERS INTERESTS IN REALTY OR IN PERSONALTY?

Before the Trusts of Land and Appointment of Trustees Act 1996, since the interests of beneficial co-owners existed under a trust for sale, these interests were, as a result of the doctrine of the conversion, personalty. Thus if a beneficial tenant in common of a house died leaving his personalty to P and his realty to R, his interest in the house went to P.[16] (If he had wanted it to go to R, he should have said so.) Yet if H and W owned their own house, to say that they do not own *land* was contrary to what seems manifestly to be the position, and the effect of applying the doctrine of conversion could produce results that ran so contrary to what would appear to have been the intentions of the legislature,

---

16   *Re Kempthorne* [1930] 1 Ch 268.
17   (i)   Section 35(1) of the Administration of Justice Act 1956 provides for the making (as a means of enforcing a court judgment) of a charging order on 'land or any interest in land' of a debtor. In *Irani Finance Ltd v Singh* [1971] Ch 59, [1970] 3 All ER 199, it was held that a charging order under the Act could not be made against two co-owners of land since their beneficial interests were, by the doctrine of conversion, personalty

that in some instances the courts held[17] that for certain purposes (and in certain instances it was enacted[18] that in particular contexts) the interests of beneficial co-owners were to be deemed to be interests in land, not personalty.

Thus, before the 1996 Act, where a trust for sale existed whilst the starting point was that the interests of the beneficiaries were, by the doctrine of conversion, personalty, nevertheless for certain purposes, these interests might be deemed to be interests in land.

It was to remove uncertainties and to bring the legal position into line with the realities of the situation (in particular that the beneficial interest of a co-owner of land was in practice in the land itself not in the proceeds of sale) that the 1996 Act,[19] implementing a recommendation of the Law Commission,[20]

not land. The Charging Orders Act 1979 (enacted following the Law Commission's report on *Charging Orders*, 1976 (Law Com No 74); [1981] Conv 69 (A. Sydenham); G. C. P. Walker, *Charging Orders against Land*) provides that ' ... a charge may be imposed by a charging order ... on (a) any interest held by the debtor beneficially – under any trust ... ' In *National Westminster Bank Ltd v Stockman* [1981] 1 All ER 800, [1981] 1 WLR 67 it was held that the 1979 Act had the effect of enabling a charging order under the 1956 Act to be made against the interests of beneficial co-owners. In *National Westminster Bank Ltd v Allen* [1971] 2 QB 718, [1971] 3 All ER 201n, it had been held that a charging order under the 1956 Act could be made against the *legal* interest in land held by co-owners. This means of enabling the 1956 Act to be applied to land held by co-owners was shown by the decision in *Stockman* to be obviated by the 1979 Act. In *Perry v Phoenix Assurance plc* [1988] 3 All ER 60, [1988] 1 WLR 940; (M & B) it was confirmed that a charging order in respect of the beneficial interest of a co-owner of land was imposed under s 2(1)(b) of the 1979 Act by virtue of being an interest under a trust (not as an interest in land under s 2(1)(a)(i) and (2)). See also *Clark v Chief Land Registrar* [1993] Ch 294, [1993] 2 All ER 936.

(ii) Section 70(1) of the Land Registration Act 1925 provides that 'All Registered land shall ... be deemed to be subject to the following overriding interests as may be for the time being subsisting in reference thereto ... (g), the rights of every person in actual occupation of land ....' The operation of the Land Registration Act 1925 has not yet been explained. For present purposes it is sufficient to note that in *Williams and Glyn's Bank Ltd v Boland* [1981] AC 487, [1980] 2 All ER 408 overruling *Cedar Holdings Ltd v Green* [1981] Ch 129, [1979] 3 All ER 117, CA the House of Lords held that the interest of a beneficial co-owner was an interest 'subsisting in reference' to registered land within the meaning of s 70(1) of the Act and that the interest of a beneficial co-owner who was in actual occupation of the land was therefore an overriding interest under s 70(1)(g). See Chapter 26.

(iii) Section 54(1) of the Land Registration Act 1925 provides that 'Any person interested ... in land ... may lodge a caution with the registrar ...' In *Elias v Mitchell* [1972] Ch 652, it was held that a beneficial co-owner was a 'person interested ... in ... land' for the purpose of s 54(1) and was therefore entitled to lodge a caution. The meaning of this, too, will become apparent in Chapter 26.

18 (i) Section 2 of the Law of Property (Miscellaneous Provisions) Act 1989 requires contracts for the sale or other dispositions of land or 'any interest in land' to be in writing. The definition of 'any interest in land' included (confirming the effect of *Cooper v Critchley* [1955] Ch 431, [1955] 1 All E 520, in relation to s 40 of the Law of Property Act 1925) 'any interest ... in ... the proceeds of sale' of land. Thus the interests of beneficial co-owners are, as 'land' within the meaning of the section, subject to the requirement of the section.

(ii) The Limitation Act 1980. Section 38(1) of the Act (see Chapter 24) defined land as including the proceeds of sale of land.

19 Section 3.

20 Law Com No 181.

abolished the doctrine of conversion as it applied to trusts for sale of land. This step rendered superfluous those statutory provisions that had, to bring interests held under a trust for sale within the meaning of 'land', defined 'land' as including any interest in the proceeds of sale of land, and such provisions were accordingly repealed by the 1996 Act.[1]

SUMMARY

Where land is held by co-owners as joint tenants, on the death of one co-owner his interest vests in the remaining co-owners.

Where co-owners hold as tenants in common, on the death of a co-owner, his interest passes under his will or intestacy.

For joint tenancy to exist, the 'four unities' must be present.

Between the end of 1925 and the end of 1996, land held by co-owners was held on trust for sale. After 1996, land held by co-owners is held under a trust of land under the Trusts of Land and Appointment of Trustees Act 1996.

The trustees are the first four co-owners of full age.

The beneficiaries are all the co-owners.

Since the Law of Property Act 1925 the only form of legal co-ownership that can exist is joint tenancy.

The interests of beneficial co-owners can be held as joint tenancy or as tenancy in common.

A legal joint tenancy cannot be severed.

A beneficial joint tenancy can be severed by alienation or (since 1925) by notice.

To determine whether beneficial co-owners hold as joint tenants or tenants in common four tests are applied.

The 1996 Act imposes on the trustees a duty to consult.

The 1996 Act confers on the trustees a power of sale.

The 1996 Act confers on the beneficial co-owners a right to occupy the land.

Where the legal estate becomes vested in a sole trustee, a purchaser cannot safely purchase the land unless a second trustee is appointed, or advantage is taken of the Law of Property (Joint Tenants) Act 1964.

1   Sch 4.

CHAPTER 12

Co-ownership II – The Practice

In this chapter we shall see how the principles of co-ownership that were examined in the last chapter arise in certain everyday affairs and, in particular, the way in which these principles are relevant in resolving disputes concerning the matrimonial home.

Ownership

CO-OWNERSHIP AND IMPLIED TRUSTS

In Chapter 5, we saw that if A and B purchase property which is conveyed into the name of A, there is a presumption that A holds under an implied trust for himself and B. Since A and B are co-owners in equity how does co-ownership which arises in this kind of circumstance fit into the pattern of the law that was described in the last chapter? The matter arose for decision in *Bull v Bull*[1] in 1955. A mother and her son contributed to the purchase of a house which was conveyed into the son's name. It was held that since the mother and son were in equity co-owners of the property, and since they were tenants in common (having contributed in unequal shares), and since s 36(4) of the Settled Land Act 1925 provides that an 'undivided share [ie a tenancy in common] in land shall not be capable of being created except under a trust instrument or under the Law of Property Act 1925, and shall then only take effect behind a trust for sale',[2] the trust under which they held their equitable interests was a trust for sale.[2] The decision became an established part of the law of co-ownership, and any weakness in the[3] decision's reasoning[4] is more than compensated for

1 [1955] 1 QB 234, [1955] 1 All ER 253.
2 The decision followed that in *Re Rayleigh's Weir Stadium* [1954] 2 All ER 283, [1954] 1 WLR 786, though in this case there was no reliance on s 36(4) of the Settled Land Act 1925. It is not easy to see how it was possible for s 36(4) to be called in aid since no trust instrument existed, and the tenancy in common was not 'created ... under the Law of Property Act 1925'. See (1963) 27 Conv (NS) 51 (B. Rudden); (1982) Conv 213 (M. Friend, J. Newton); [1986] Conv 379 (W. J. Swadling). The decision can only find its authority in the section if this is construed as being intended to enact that an 'undivided share in land ... shall ... only take effect behind a trust for sale.'
3 Eg *Waller v Waller* [1967] 1 WLR 451 at 453; *Taylor v Taylor* [1968] 1 All ER 843 at 846; *Williams and Glyn's Bank v Boland* [1980] 3 WLR 138 at 142, 148; *City of London Building Society v Flegg* [1988] AC 54, [1987] 3 All ER 435; (M & B).
4 See n 2 supra.

by the good sense and convenience of the result it produced[5] – a result that the drafters of the 1925 legislation would, it is suggested, almost certainly have intended had they directed their attention to the situation in which the case arose.

Since the Trusts of Land and Appointment of Trustees Act 1996[5a] catches within its net implied trusts, including those that arose before the Act, where A and B purchase property which is conveyed into the name of A alone (and correspondingly in every other situation in which an implied trust arises), the trust on which the property is held is now no longer a trust for sale but a trust of land under the 1996 Act.

OWNERSHIP OF THE MATRIMONIAL HOME

A married couple set up home together. If they are married and they later divorce, then irrespective of whether the title to the house is in their joint names or in the name of one of them alone, the distribution of their property (eg for the purpose of making provision for the maintenance of the wife) is at the discretion of the court under jurisdiction conferred by the Matrimonial Property and Proceedings Act 1973.[6] In deciding in what terms the order of the court should be framed the present ownership of the home is a matter that will need to be taken into account.

The question of ownership of the home may arise other than in the context of a divorce. For example, W dies leaving all her property, not to her husband, but to, say, a son by a former marriage. What interest, if any, of hers in the home will pass under her will to the son? Or again, if the husband is adjudicated bankrupt, what interest of his, if any, in the home vests in the trustee in bankruptcy (ie and what proportion is left for the wife)? In situations such as these the question of ownership of the home falls to be determined by principles of law evolved by the courts over the years. It is by reference to such general principles of law also that questions of ownership are determined where the parties are a couple who are not married.

We shall here set out the law as it applies to a married couple, noting at a later stage the extent (a limited extent) to which the position may be different where the couple is unmarried.

In situations where the legal title is conveyed into the joint names of the husband and wife, disputes over the beneficial ownership are likely to be rare. If the conveyance is silent as to the proportions in which beneficial ownership is to be shared the presumption is that the parties hold equally. If there is a declaration as to the proportions in which the beneficial ownership is to be shared, then in the absence of fraud or mistake, the declaration prevails.

---

5   See (1995) 19 Conv (NS) 146 (F. R. Crane).
5a   Section 1.
6   Sections 24 and 25.

It is in situations where the legal title to the home is conveyed into the name of one spouse alone that disputes commonly arise, the other spouse claiming a share in the beneficial ownership – ie that the legal title is held on trust for both parties, in whatever proportion is claimed (the claim most often made being that the beneficial ownership is held equally.) Since in such situations it is most frequently the husband who holds the legal title, with the wife as claimant, it is in relation to this situation that the law will here be explained. But it should be borne in mind that the same principles apply where it is the wife who holds the legal title, with the husband being the claimant for a share in the beneficial ownership.

Implied (resulting) trusts under the principle of purchase in the name of another

As seen when dealing with trusts and equitable interests in an earlier chapter, if, when a home (or any other property) is purchased, the wife contributes to the purchase price, the law infers that it was the intention of the parties that the wife should have a share in the beneficial ownership proportionate to her contribution – that the husband holds the legal title on an implied trust for himself and his wife.

In *Ivin v Blake*[7] it was held that indirect contributions to payment of the purchase price by the wife (eg assisting in the running of the husband's business) were not of themselves, in the absence of any agreement with or assurance from, the husband, sufficient to confer on the wife a share in the beneficial ownership of the property.

Constructive trusts

In recent years in disputes as to the beneficial ownership of a home the courts have come[8] to pay less attention to the principle of purchase in the name of another (with its arithmetical working) and instead to base their conclusions on the notion of a constructive trust under which the husband holds the legal title on trust for himself and his wife, in such proportions as the court determines.[9] For such a constructive trust in the wife's favour to arise two conditions must be satisfied.

(i) There must be evidence that prior to the acquisition of the property there had been an arrangement, agreement or understanding between the husband and wife that the wife was to have a share of the beneficial ownership of the home – evidence of what has come to be termed a 'common intention'. The evidence may be circumstantial, as where acceptance of a loan by a couple from one of their parents to pay the deposit on a home was held to be capable

7 [1995] 1 FLR 70, [1996] Conv 462 (A. Lawson).
8 *Grant v Edwards* [1986] Ch 638, [1986] 2 All ER 426, CA; [1986] Conv 291 (J. Warburton); (1986) 45 CLJ 394 (D. Hayton).
9 *Rimmer v Rimmer* [1953] 1 QB 63, [1952] 2 All ER 863, CA; *Ulrich v Ulrich and Felton* [1968] 1 All ER 67, [1968] 1 WLR 180, CA.

of constituting evidence of a common intention that the beneficial ownership should be shared.[10] The agreement must relate specifically to the beneficial ownership of the home. An agreement relating to some other matter connected with the home, for example as to how the property is to be occupied (eg, as a home for the couple and their children) is not sufficient, since this provides no indication as to the parties' intention as to the beneficial ownership.[11]

(ii)   The wife must be able to produce evidence that she acted to her detriment or altered her position to a significant degree, in reliance on the agreement.[12]

Thus it is not sufficient to show a common intention and an act to her detriment. The latter must be performed *in reliance* on the former: the conduct must be of a kind 'which the woman could not reasonably be expected to have embarked on unless she was to have an interest in the home'; the wife must prove that she has acted to her detriment in the reasonable belief that by so acting she was acquiring an equitable interest. Thus 'setting up house together, having a baby and making payments to general housekeeping expenses ... ' will not by themselves be sufficient since these 'may all be referable to the mutual love and affection of the parties' rather than to any agreement that she is to have an interest in the home. The evidence that is most likely to be held as constituting an act to her detriment is evidence of the wife having contributed to the purchase price.

The reasoning behind the requirement that there should be an act to her detriment by the wife is as follows: (a) Section 53(1)(b) of the Law of Property Act 1925 requires a declaration of trust to be 'manifested and proved by some writing' signed by the person able to declare the trust. (b) The dispute will have arisen in the absence of an express written agreement (because if there had been a written agreement, in the absence of fraud or mistake, the agreement would have prevailed), (c) The absence of writing renders the agreement invalid under s 53; (d) But the act to her detriment by the wife, by providing consideration, enables the court to treat the agreement as enforceable under the law of contract and so opens the way for the court to give effect to the agreement by the imposition of a constructive trust. (No account in this chain of reasoning appears to be taken of the provision of s 53(2) that the section is not to affect the creation or operation of, inter alia, constructive trusts.)

SUBSEQUENT CONDUCT

If the wife is not able to produce evidence of a prior agreement showing a common intention as to beneficial ownership, it is open to the court to infer from the *subsequent* conduct of the parties that they must have had, at the time of the purchase, a common intention as to the beneficial ownership of the property and, on the basis of this inferred common intention, to erect a

10   *McHardy and Sons v Warren* [1994] 2 FLR 338 (engaged couple); *Halifax Building Society v Brown* [1995] 3 FCR 110 (married couple).
11   *Lloyds Bank plc v Rosset* [1991] 1 AC 107, [1990] 1 All ER 1111, HL; (1991) 54 MLR 126 (S. Gardner); (1993) 56 MLR 224 (P. O'Hagan).
12   *Midland Bank Ltrd v Dobson and Dobson* [1986] 1 FLR 171, CA.

constructive trust in the wife's favour. (But where this inference is drawn, the inference must be of what the court considers the intention actually to have been, not what the court considers, in the light of their conduct, the parties ought to have intended: it is not 'the function of the court to fill in the gap by doing what the parties as reasonable spouses would have agreed was to happen on the break up had they thought about it'.[13])

The subsequent conduct most likely to enable the court, looking back, to find that there had been a common intention is expenditure by the wife. Such expenditure could include regular contributions to the mortgage instalments, the repayment of part of the mortgage, or the making of a substantial[14] contribution to the family expenses so as to enable the mortgage instalments to be paid.[15]

But subsequent conduct sufficient to constitute evidence of an original common intention is not confined to expenditure. In *Midland Bank v Cooke*[16](a case in which the wife claimed an increase in her beneficial entitlement to 50%) the evidence showed that the couple had agreed to share the profits of the business while it prospered and the risks of indebtedness if it failed, and over the upbringing of the children, and over a home towards the cost of maintenance and improvement of which the wife had contributed. There would, Waite LJ concluded, hardly be a clearer case of an intention to share everything equally, including therefore, the court held, beneficial ownership of the home.

WHY 'CONSTRUCTIVE' TRUST?

Since an implied trust arises from the implied intention of the parties and a constructive trust is one imposed by the court irrespective of the intention of the parties, it may seem strange that the courts should refer to a trust that has as its basis the common intention of the parties, as a 'constructive trust'. There is, though, a respect in which, although based on a common intention, a constructive trust is in fact imposed on the parties. It is this: where an implied trust arises (based on purchase in the name of another), the share of the wife's equitable interest will correspond with the proportion of the purchase price that she contributed. Where a constructive trust arises (based on a common intention together with an act by the wife to her detriment in reliance on this), the division of the equitable interest is at the discretion of the court – the outcome is not a matter of arithmetic, but the court determining, with a 'broad brush',[17] the outcome in whatever way it sees best in order to produce a just result as between the parties.

Cases concerning beneficial ownership of a home have fallen into two categories. In the first fall those instances in which the wife made a contribution to the purchase price. In the second fall instances in which she made no such contribution. In the first category, the wife, having made a contribution, is entitled, under the equitable principle of purchase in the name of another, to

---

13   *Per* Lord Upjohn, *Pettit v Pettit* [1970] AC 777, 816, HL.
14   *Falconer v Falconer* [1970] 3 All ER 449, [1970] 1 WLR 1333, CA.
15   *Burns v Burns* [1984] Ch 317, [1984] 1 All ER 244, CA.
16   [1995] 4 All ER 562; [1997] Conv 66 (M. Dixon).
17   *Per* Peter Gibson LJ; *Drake v Whipp* [1996] 2 FCR 296, CA.

a share in the beneficial ownership in proportion to her contribution to the total cost. In such cases the dispute is not over whether the wife has an entitlement to a share in the beneficial ownership in proportion but over what that share should be, the wife in most such cases claiming to be entitled to a half share. In the second category, the wife's claim is that although she made no contribution to the purchase price, she should nevertheless be entitled to share in the beneficial ownership with her husband.

Thus where the courts look to a constructive trust to provide an equitable remedy to the dispute, in the first category of cases the device of a constructive trust is employed to warrant an increase in the wife's share; in the second category it is employed to give her a share when otherwise she would be entitled to none whatsoever.

'ESTOPPEL'

We may note here that in some instances the courts have referred to the wife's entitlement as arising under the doctrine, not of constructive trust, but under that of proprietary estoppel – the husband being estopped, by reason of the common intention and the wife's act to her detriment, from denying the wife's claim to a share in the beneficial ownership. Whether in this context any distinction between constructive trust and proprietary estoppel needs to be drawn has been the subject of debate.[18] The matter is unsettled. What is clear, however, is that whether the court adopts the term constructive trust or proprietary estoppel (or treats the two terms as alternatives without distinguishing between them), in one respect at least the outcome is the same, namely, that the court is free to impose whatever solution it thinks fit (eg without regard to arithmetical calculations) in order to achieve justice between the parties.

A common intention – but when?

Throughout the treatment of co-ownership in the previous pages a recurring theme has been that beneficial ownership is to be determined according to what is found to have been the common intention of the parties as to the beneficial ownership of the property in the event of separation or divorce. Until relatively recently, the common intention that the courts sought to establish was that which existed when the property had been acquired: ' ... it is the intention of the parties when the property was purchased that is important'.[19] Where W contributed to mortgage repayments this was taken as illustrating a common intention at the outset that if such contributions were kept up, W should acquire, or acquire an increased share of, a beneficial interest.

A change of approach was marked by *Passee v Passee*.[20] In 1965 a house was bought for occupation by a man, M, and a woman, W, and the woman's

18   See P. H. Pettitt, *Equity and the Law of Trusts*, (7th edn, p 142).
19   *Burns v Burns* [1984] Ch 317, [1984] 1 All ER 244, *per* Fox J.
20   [1988] 1 FLR 263; [1988] Conv 361 (J. Warburton).

daughter, D, and conveyed into M's name alone. M provided £515, W £500 and D £250, the balance to be raised by a mortgage. M, W and D lived in the house and all contributed to the outgoings including the mortgage repayments. D died in 1972. W continued to live in the house with M and paid contributions until 1985. M later claimed possession of the property. W counter-claimed that she had an interest in the house on her own behalf and, as D's personal representative, on behalf of D. In the Court of Appeal Nicholls LJ held that in this kind of circumstance what mattered was not the situation that obtained when the property was acquired but when the question of the allocation of the beneficial interest arose for determination, usually when a party wished the property to be disposed of. The Court held that M was entitled to 60% of the beneficial interest, W 30% and D's estate 10%, the valuation being at the date of the proceedings and not, as claimed by M, when W's contributions ended in 1985.

The approach in *Passee v Passee* was followed by the Court of Appeal in *Stokes v Anderson*[1] in 1991, when the court held that it was not so much for the court to *find* a common intention, but rather the court should supply a common intention by reference to what all the material circumstances showed to be fair.

The line taken by the Court of Appeal in these cases has been welcomed as being in accord with social reality[2] and the interests of justice. The result is that not much of the notion of a common intention survives. The decision as to what is fair has to be made by a judge. So at the end of the road what we are left with is not a search for an original common intention as to the division of the beneficial interests, but division of the property being settled by a judge in such manner as he thinks just according to all the events in relation to the property that have occurred (a position that does not equate to, but moves closer to, that which exists when the matter falls to be dealt with in the course of divorce proceedings).

In recent years the distinction between the principles of an implied trust arising from purchase in the name of another and a constructive trust arising from an original common intention have become so intermingled as to begin to cease to be capable of being recognised as principles that in the development of equity have been distinct. For example, it may be that a contribution to the purchase price (which gives rise to an implied trust proportionate to the contribution) is treated as evidence of a common intention that founds a constructive trust under which the beneficial ownership is to be shared equally.

More and more we are driven to conclude that rather than applying established principles of law to the facts presented to them and from these principles drawing their conclusion, instead the courts consider within their own hearts what they consider to be a just solution and then employ whatever principles of law come to mind to support the conclusion that has already been reached, cherry picking along the way from earlier judgments in order to convey the impression that precedent is being followed. This comment is intended as no criticism. What matters is the outcome. Rarely – if ever – it is

1   [1991] FCR 539.
2   [1988] Conv 361 (J. Warburton).

submitted, is a feeling left that a decision fails, in all the circumstances, to achieve a fair solution.

What has been happening, it is clear, is that the law in this sphere has been evolving. At first the only basis for a claim was the long established principle of purchase in the name of another. Then the device of a constructive trust was introduced, with a common intention at the outset and an act in reliance being the precondition necessary for the trust to be found to exist. Then it came to be accepted that subsequent conduct could be adduced as evidence of what the original intention had been. Then there was a shift towards looking at the position, not at the outset, but at the time when the dispute comes before the court. Then we meet a case in which a constructive trust is held to exist on the basis of common intention alone, no act by the claimant in reliance thereon having been, or needing to be, shown.

The evolution of attitudes is illustrated by reference to what at one stage began to be termed 'family assets'. Diplock LJ put the matter thus: 'It comes to this: where a couple, by their joint efforts, get a house and furniture, intending it to be a continuing provision for their joint lives, it is the prima facie inference from their conduct that the house and furniture is a "family asset" in which each is entitled to a share. It matters not in whose name it stands: or who pays for what: or who goes out to work and who stays at home. If they both contribute to it by their joint efforts, the prima facie inference is that it belongs to them both equally: at any rate, when each makes a financial contribution which is substantial.'[3]

The House of Lords rejected the notion. Lord Upjohn expressed the majority view of the House when he said, ' ... we have in this country no doctrine of community of goods between spouses and yet by judicial decision were this doctrine of family assets to be accepted some such doctrine would become part of the law of the land. I do not believe that it accords with what the parties intended even if sub silentio or would regard as common sense ... the expression "family assets" is devoid of legal meaning and its use can define no legal rights or obligations.'[4]

More recently, however, the willingness of the courts to look to the totality of a relationship in seeking grounds for inferring the existence of an original intention indicates, perhaps, a move in the direction of acceptance of the notion that Lord Diplock had expressed.

Any attempt to present a picture of the law relating to the ownership of a home by reference to the law set down in cases decided over the past half century is bound, therefore, to meet with difficulties. A case decided in, say, 1965 represents the law as it had by then evolved. The principle of law on which the decision rests may still hold good, or it may have been eroded or superseded by later decisions.

No criticism can, as indicated above, be levelled at the courts for seeking to perform equity's ancient role of evolving new rules in the quest for a just solution. But a quality needed for a satisfactory system of jurisdiction is

---

3   *Ulrich v Ulrich and Fenton* [1968] 1 WLR 180, 189.
4   At p 817.

predictability: there must be principles by reference to which lawyers can advise potential litigants as to the most likely outcome of a claim. It is therefore to be hoped that attention will be paid by the courts to the continued need in this sphere for a set of principles that form a consistent pattern – a pattern with a greater degree of consistency, it has to be said, than the current state of the law on occasions can be regarded as presenting.

Matrimonial Proceedings and Property Act 1970

A respect in which statute intervened with regard to disputes over the ownership of a home concerns the effect in law of one spouse carrying out improvements to property that is owned by the other. In a number of cases prior to 1970 it was held that improvements to the property by a wife or physical work by her (provided that it was substantial in nature and not merely of a 'do-it-yourself' kind) could result in her acquiring an equitable interest, (or an increased share) in the equitable interest. In *Pettitt v Pettitt*, however, the House of Lords held that 'in the absence of agreement ... one spouse who does works or spends money upon the property of the other has no claim whatever upon the property of the other'.[5]

The effect of the decision was reversed by the Matrimonial Proceedings and Property Act 1970, s 37 of which provides that where a husband or wife contributes in money or money's worth to 'the improvement of real or personal property in which ... either or both of them has or have a beneficial interest, the husband or wife so contributing shall, if the contribution is of a substantial nature and subject to any agreement between them to the contrary express or implied, be treated as having then acquired by virtue of his or her contribution a share or an enlarged share[6], as the case may be, in that beneficial interest of such an extent as may have been agreed or, in default of such an agreement, as may seem in all the circumstances just to any court before which the question of the existence or extent of the beneficial interest of the husband or wife arises (whether in proceedings between them or in any other proceedings)'.

The following points call for attention.

(a)   The section applies irrespective of whether the legal estate is in the husband or the wife, or in them both.

(b)   The section applies to any property, not necessarily the matrimonial home (eg it could apply to a shop or some other business premises).

(c)   As previously had been the principle of the courts, the contribution must be 'substantial'.[7]

(d)   The section relates both to the position where the husband or the wife carries out some work on the property (a contribution in 'money's worth') and also where a spouse[8] makes a financial contribution ('in money') to the work concerned.

---

5   [1970] AC 777, [1969] 2 All ER 385.
6   See *Re Pavlon (A bankrupt)* [1993] 3 All ER 955, [1993] 1 WLR 1046.
7   See *Harnett v Harnett* [1973] Fam 156, [1973] 2 All ER 593.
8   As in *Griffiths v Griffiths* [1974] 1 All ER 932, [1974] 1 WLR 1350.

(e)   The section applies to personal as well as real property, and so would apply, eg to an improvement by W to premises held by H on lease.

And, of particular significance –

(f)   There is no requirement that there must be evidence of prior common intention as to the beneficial ownership.

Couples who are unmarried

To what extent do the principles applicable in the case of disputes between a married couple apply also where the couple is unmarried – to what extent can a (domestic) partner claim a share in the beneficial ownership of a home in the event of a dispute? The answer is that the same principles, with regard to both purchase in the name of another and constructive trust apply in such a situation. A difference exists, however, in that whilst in the case of married couples the evolution of the law has seen a relaxation of the conditions necessary for a constructive trust to exist, no, or little, such relaxation has been apparent where the couples are unmarried: the law is applied in a stricter fashion. Thus where the woman has made a contribution to the purchase price, the contribution is likely to be treated as giving her a proportionate share rather than as indicative of an intention that the property should be shared equally. Where there is no contribution to the purchase price there is likely to be closer scrutiny as to whether there was an original 'common intention'.

But where there is sufficient evidence of an original common intention that the property should be shared equally, coupled with a detrimental act in reliance on this, a constructive trust that gives the woman an equal share will arise. For example, in *Hammond v Mitchell*,[9] a man, H, and woman, M, who began living together in 1977, and who had two children, lived in a bungalow which was conveyed into the name of the man alone. Extensions were made to the bungalow, financed by a loan from a bank, with the bungalow as security. M supported H in his business ventures by acting as an unpaid assistant, and undertook part-time teaching with H's encouragement. The relationship broke down and M claimed (in an action under section 30 of the Law of Property Act 1925) a beneficial interest in the bungalow. The court held that there had been a common intention that the beneficial ownership of the property should be shared and that this had been evidenced (inter alia) by M agreeing, at the time of the bank loan, that the bank's interest in the property should take priority over her own (ie in the event of the loan not being repaid).

By way of contrast, in *Burns v Burns*[10] a woman used her earnings as a driving instructor to pay for household expenses, including rates and, telephone bills, and fixtures and fittings. The court found no evidence of a common intention that she should acquire a beneficial interest in the house and so declined the order sought.

9   [1992] 2 All ER 109, [1991] 1 WLR 1127.
10   [1984] Ch 317, [1984] 1 All ER 244.

What matters in every instance is what is to be inferred in the circumstances as having been the common intention of the parties with regard to the beneficial interests in the property.

In some instances a claim to a beneficial interest in property has been made by a mistress (or some other person other than a spouse, eg a housekeeper) not on the ground of an implied trust, but on the ground that an equitable licence had come into existence (eg by virtue of the principle of estoppel). Equitable licences are considered in Chapter 20.

Disputes over the matrimonial home in the context of divorce proceedings

Where divorce proceedings have been commenced, the court has, as mentioned earlier, jurisdiction under the Matrimonial Causes Act 1973[11] to make such order as it considers just with regard, inter alia, to the matrimonial home.[12] In the exercise of this jurisdiction the court is under a duty to consider all the relevant circumstances[13] having regard to the means of each and the needs of each, with first consideration being the welfare of any children. It is in no way bound by the matter of title.

In seeking a just resolution of disputes over what should happen to matrimonial property in the event of a divorce the courts have followed the principle[14] of the 'clean break', ie that the property should be dealt with once and for all, and arrangements involving any continuing relationship avoided. But the principle is not one necessarily of universal application and there will be departures from it if the circumstances so warrant. For example, in 1991 in *Clutton v Clutton*,[15] it was held, after a divorce, that the wife's beneficial interest was two-thirds, the former husband's interest one-third, but the latter's interest was not to be enforceable until after his former wife's death, remarriage or permanent co-habitation.

Spouses' right of occupation

The question of a spouse's ownership of the matrimonial home is distinct from whether a spouse has a right to occupy the home. If a spouse has a

---

11   Section 24, as amended by the Family Law Act 1996
12   The jurisdiction exists in relation to any 'property' to which one of the parties to the proceedings is entitled. 'Property' includes a leasehold interest, thus including the interest of one tenant in a lease held jointly with the other party to the proceedings; *Newton Housing Trust v Al-Sulaimen* [1997] 2 FCR 33.
13   Section 25; [1981] Conv 404 (M. Hayes and G. Battersby).
14   Given statutory endorsement by the Matrimonial Causes Act 1973, s 25 A (inserted by Matrimonial and Family Proceedings Act 1984, s 3).
15   [1991] 1 All ER 340, [1991] 1 WLR 359.

beneficial interest in the property, she has a right of occupation by virtue of being a co-owner, a right now conferred (and regulated) by the Trusts of Land and Appointment of Trustees Act 1996.

Irrespective of whether or not a spouse has a beneficial interest in the property, a spouse has a right of occupation, by virtue of the fact of being a spouse, conferred by common law, and by statute, under the Family Law Act 1996.[16] The statutory right of occupation conferred by the Act is registrable under the Land Charges Act 1972 as a Class F land charge.[17] In order to bind a purchaser the right must be registered, but the right is valid as against the other spouse irrespective of whether or not it is registered.

Disagreement over whether a home should be sold

In the last chapter we saw that following the Trusts of Land and Appointment of Trustees Act 1996 the outcome of a disagreement between beneficial owners as to whether the property should be sold depends upon whether a duty to consult the beneficiaries exists (and, if it does, on what the majority wish is) and, if there is no duty to consult, whether the trustees are unanimous in agreeing to exercise the power of sale conferred by the Act.

Legal estate held by H and W

Where the legal estate is held by two people on trust for themselves, these principles do not assist since, in practice, where there is disagreement between two co-owners, the property can never be sold since the signature of both will be needed on the conveyance and on the receipt for the purchase money. Suppose that a marriage has faltered. H has gone off with another woman. Wanting money, H wants the house to be sold. W, who wants a roof over her head, refuses to agree. If the property is to be sold, H will have to obtain from the court an order of sale, ie an order requiring W to concur with the sale, by adding her signature to the conveyance and giving up possession (unless, as noted in the last chapter, she is willing and able to buy out H's interest in the property and so become sole owner).

Until about 1977 the tendency was for the court to have regard primarily to the then existing duty of trustees for sale to sell, placing the wish of H for capital above the needs of W and any children to remain in the family home.[18] In 1977, in *Williams v Williams*,[19] the view was expressed that this approach was 'out-dated', and the court declined the order for sale sought by the husband.

16   Part IV, re-enacting with minor amendment, the Matrimonial Home Act 1983.
17   See Chapter 25.
18   As in *Burke v Burke* – [1974] 2 All ER 944, [1974] 1 WLR 1063.
19   [1977] 1 All ER 28 at 30, per Lord Denning.

From that time the courts have taken a wider view than previously and have been guided, inter alia, by looking to see whether the purpose of the trust – to provide a home – is exhausted. In making this decision the fact that there are children of the marriage living in the house is a matter that the courts have taken into account.[20] If the purpose is no longer being served, a sale will be ordered;[1] if the purpose is not yet exhausted, no sale (or immediate sale) will be ordered.[2] The tendency in recent years[3] has been for the court to take account of the position of the parties, and to frame the order made so as to strike a balance between their interests,[4] for example by postponing an order for sale until the youngest child has attained a specified age[5] or completed full-time education; or by suspending an order for sale on the party in occupation agreeing to pay mortgage instalments and other ougoings on the property, and to pay the other party an 'occupation rent'; or by suspending the order for sale for the lifetime of the party in occupation or until she vacated the property or re-married, or became dependent on another man, she paying her former husband an occupation rent in recognition of her occupation of property in which he held a one-third beneficial interest.[6]

Legal estate held by one spouse alone

If H holds the property on trust for himself and W under an implied trust (ie as to W's share), H, as trustee, is now required by the Trusts of Land and Appointment of Trustees Act 1996[7] to consult the beneficiaries, ie himself and W, as to whether the property should be sold. If he fails to consult W and proposes to sell, W can seek an injunction restraining the sale. In determining whether to grant the injunction the court will take into account the same matters as in the case of an application for an order for sale (ie in particular, whether the purpose of the co-ownership still exists). Where the court decides to permit the sale, H will be ordered to appoint a second trustee before making the sale in order to protect W's interest in the proceeds of sale (ie to provide a safeguard against H dissipating, or departing with, the purchase money).

The principles that we have considered concerning the sale of a matrimonial home have been applied also to the homes of those other than married couples.[8]

---

20 *Burke v Burke* [1974] 2 All ER 944, [1974] 1 WLR 1063.
1 *Jackson v Jackson* [1971] 3 All ER 774, [1971] 1 WLR 1539; *Rawlings v Rawlings* [1964] P 398, [1964] 2 All ER 804.
2 *Jones v Jones* [1971] 2 All ER 737, [1971] 1 WLR 396; *Bedson v Bedson* [1965] 2 QB 666, [1965] 3 All ER 307.
3 [1984] Conv 103 (M. P. Thompson).
4 See *Re Evers's Trust* [1980] 3 All ER 399, [1980] 1 WLR 1327; (M & B); [1982] Conv 415 (R. Cock).
5 *Mesher v Mesher and Hall* [1980] 1 All ER 126n.
6 As in *Harvey v Harvey* [1982] Fam 83, [1982] 1 All ER 693.
7 Section 11.
8 *Re Evers's Trust* [1980] 3 All ER 399, [1980] 1 WLR 1327; (M & B) (order for sale postponed indefinitely, with liberty to apply for a sale at a later date); *Bernard v Josephs* [1982] Ch 391, [1982] 3 All ER 162.

In a dispute in such a situation, the application to the court will be under s 14 of the 1996 Act (not under the Matrimonial Causes Act 1973).

We have treated the question of the beneficial ownership of co-owned property separately from the question of whether co-owned property (in particular a home) should be sold. This treatment has been adopted as a matter of convenience, since the legal principles involved are distinct. It will be appreciated, however, that in practice the two matters commonly arise for decision together – M marries or cohabits with W; a house is conveyed into M's name alone. The couple break up; M moves away. M claims that the property is his alone and that it should be sold; W claims that she has an interest in the property and, so that she should be able to stay in it, that it should not be sold.

Sale by a sole trustee under an implied (or constructive) trust

We come now to an important question. Suppose that H holds the legal title to the matrimonial home on trust for himself and W. H, without consulting W, sells the property to P. How is W's interest affected? (We shall speak in this section in terms of H and W, a married couple, but the principles apply in the case of any sole trustee holding for himself and one or more other persons (and to any form of land, not necessarily a home).

It is true that H, as a sole trustee, should not, it has been held, sell the land, and that if an application is made to the court (by W) he can be restrained by injunction from selling until a second trustee has been appointed. But what if no injunction is in force restraining him from selling, eg because W is unaware of what is afoot and so has made no application to the court, or if an injunction is in force but H disregards it? If, after the sale, H holds the proceeds of sale on trust for himself and W then it may well be that the issue never comes before the court, W accepting the sale as a *fait accompli*. But what if W does not accept the proceeds as a substitute for her interest under the trust (perhaps because she wants to keep a roof over her head), or if H disappears with the purchase money, or if he dissipates the money and becomes insolvent (thus making any action by W against H pointless)? In these situations W's only remedy will be to seek to enforce the trust against the purchaser. Can she do so?

It will be recognised that had there been two trustees (for example, if before the sale H had appointed another person as trustee[9]) the question would not arise, since, provided the purchaser obtained a receipt from the two trustees, W's equitable interest would be overreached and would attach to the proceeds of sale, the purchaser thus taking free of her equitable interest under the trust.[10]

---

9   As a trustee has power to do; Trustee Act 1925, s 36.
10   *City of London Building Society v Flegg* [1988] AC 54, [1987] 3 All ER 435.

The situation we are dealing with is one in which the sale is by a sole trustee, so there can be no overreaching. Further, since the trust is implied, not express, there is nothing in the documents of title to warn a purchaser that he should not pay the purchase price until a second trustee has been appointed. So the question we face is this: what if a sole trustee, under an implied trust, sells the property? The answer is that since the purchaser did not obtain a receipt signed by two trustees, he does not obtain the protection afforded by the Law of Property Act 1925.[11] So we are thrown back on the old law: specifically, the principles relating to the bona fide purchaser. If the purchaser can show that he is a bona fide purchaser, without notice of the equitable interest, he takes free of the interest.

This question – the question whether a co-owner's beneficial interest binds a purchaser from a sole trustee – has arisen in a series of important cases in which the purchaser has been a purchaser *pro tanto*, a mortgagee. What has happened has been that H has held land on an implied trust for himself and his wife. H, needing to borrow money, has mortgaged the house. On H failing in the mortgage repayments, the mortgagee bank has sought an order for possession so that it can exercise its statutory power (considered in Chapter 23) to sell the property and recoup what it is owed from the proceeds of sale (passing the balance to the owner). The significance for the bank of W's claim should be noted. If W's claim succeeded she would be entitled, by virtue of her interest, to remain living in the property. In this case, the bank, unable to sell without vacant possession, would not find a purchaser, and so be unable to recoup the money it was owed. Thus, whether or not W's interest binds the bank determines whether or not the bank's security for the loan is of any value. In *Caunce v Caunce*,[12] H and W agreed to purchase property in their joint names. W contributed £479. H, in breach of their agreement, had the house conveyed into his name alone. H then borrowed from a bank a total of £1,200 on the security of three successive mortgages.[13] Two years later H was adjudicated bankrupt. Shortly afterwards he left the home. W claimed that her equitable interest (amounting to the £479) took priority over the mortgagee's, on the ground that the bank took with constructive notice of her equitable interest.

It was held that where a vendor or mortgagor was himself in possession of property, the purchaser or mortgagee was not fixed with notice of the equitable interest of any other person (eg Q) who was resident there, and whose presence was not inconsistent with the vendor or mortgagor being the sole beneficial owner, merely because the purchaser or mortgagee did not make inquiries on the property. Further, it was held that the fact that the property was a matrimonial home did not, where H and W were living in the property, fix a purchaser or mortgagee with constructive notice of any equitable interest which W might have had. Since H and W were living

---

11 Section 2.
12 [1969] 1 All ER 722, [1969] 1 WLR 286; (M & B).
13 On the question whether a sole trustee for sale had power to execute a valid mortgage otherwise than in accordance with powers conferred on trustees for sale by LPA 1925, s 28(1), see [1981] Conv 19 (S. M. Clayton).

together, there was nothing to fix the bank with constructive notice of W's equitable interest in the property. The bank's mortgages thus took priority over W's claim for £479.

In 1980 a case, *Williams and Glyn's Bank Ltd v Boland*,[14] was decided in which the facts were in all essentials the same as those in *Caunce v Caunce*.[15] The House of Lords held that the wife's claim succeeded. The grounds of the decision related to principles concerning the Land Registration Act 1925 (considered in Chapter 26). For the present it is sufficient to note that the Lords recognised that their decision ran counter to the decision in *Caunce v Caunce*, and indicated that if the facts in the latter case came before the courts again, the decision should be in favour of the holder of the equitable interest.

This was the outcome in *Kingsnorth Finance Co Ltd v Tizard*.[16] A home was in the name of a husband, H, alone. After the marriage broke down, W did not sleep at the house but returned during part of each day to care for the two children. H applied to K for a loan, describing himself on the application as 'single'. A surveyor, S, as agent for K, visited the house. H told S of the separation. S's report to K listed the occupants as H and the children but did not mention the separation. K loaned H £66,000 secured by a mortgage of the house. H went abroad and the loan was not repaid. K sought possession. The court held that (1) W was beneficially entitled to a half share in the property; (2) W was in occupation of the house at all material times; (3) H's description of himself as single coupled with S's mention of children should have alerted K to the need for further enquiries. Not having made these, K was fixed with constructive notice of W's interest, which was therefore binding on him.

Bankruptcy[17]

In the sphere of co-ownership various disputes may arise, for example, between co-owners as to whether they hold beneficially as joint tenants or tenants in common; between co-owners as to the proportions in which they hold the property (or, over the same issue, between one co-owner and the trustee in bankruptcy of the other[18]); between co-owners as to whether the land should be sold; whether, if the land is sold by a sole trustee, a co-owner's equitable interest binds a purchaser (including a mortgagee). We now come to another form of dispute.

Suppose that a husband (H) and wife (W) are the beneficial owners of their home. H incurs debts that he cannot pay. He goes bankrupt. Under the

---

14   [1981] AC 487, [1980] 2 All ER 408.
15   Supra.
16   [1986] 1 WLR 783; [1986] Conv 283 (M. P. Thompson).
17   See [1986] Conv 393 (J. G. Miller); (1988) 107 Law Notes 107 (G. Gypps).
18   As in *Re Pavlou (A bankrupt)* [1993] 1 WLR 1046, [1993] 3 All ER 955.

Insolvency Act 1986,[1] H's assets (with limited exceptions, eg his clothes) vest in his trustee in bankruptcy who will sell the assets and distribute the proceeds among H's creditors in proportion to the sums they are owed. But what about what may be H's most valuable asset – his interest in the matrimonial home?

When H is declared bankrupt, his equitable interest vests in the trustee in bankruptcy, but W's equitable interest is not affected[2] and, thus, if the property is sold, W will be entitled to a sum out of the proceeds of sale proportionate to her interest. It may be, however, that W (perhaps because her share of the proceeds will be insufficient for the purchase of other accommodation) declines to leave the property on the ground that her equitable interest entitles her to remain in occupation. In this event, since the property will only find a buyer if it can be sold with vacant possession, the trustee in bankruptcy will have to apply to the court under s 14 of the Trusts of Land and Appointment of Trustees Act 1996 (formerly under section 30 of the Law of Property Act 1925), directing W to give up possession to enable the sale to take place.

The conflict of interest that confronts the court is thus a conflict between a non-bankrupt co-owner who resists sale, and a bankrupt co-owner's creditors (represented by the trustee in bankruptcy) who seek sale.

In exercising its jurisdiction in the making of an order, the court is, in the circumstances we are dealing with, required by the Insolvency Act 1986[3] to make such an order as it thinks just and reasonable, having regard to certain factors set out in the Act. These are (using our example) (a) the interests of H's creditors; (b) the conduct of W so far as it contributed to the bankruptcy; (c) W's needs and her financial resources; (d) the needs of any children of the marriage; (e) all the circumstances of the case other than the needs of H.

Prior to the Act, the question whether an application by a trustee in bankruptcy for an order for sale should succeed, ie the question as to which should prevail, the interests of the wife or the interests of the creditors, came before the court in a number of cases. In all these the courts held that as between the conflicting claims those of the creditors should prevail (with the consequence that sale of property was ordered,[4] W receiving the relevant proportion of the proceeds, but having to leave the house). As Walton J expressed the matter in *Re Bailey* in 1977, 'The voice of the trustee in bankruptcy, reminding the debtor of the obligation to pay one's debts, should prevail as compared with one's obligations to maintain one's wife and family. This may be yet another case where the sins of the father have to be visited on the children, but that is the way in which the world is constructed, and one must be just before one is generous.' It was always clear, however, that whilst the court was strongly influenced by the fact of the trustee in bankruptcy's duty to sell the

---

1 Consolidating earlier legislation, in particular the Insolvency Act 1985, and replacing the Bankruptcy Act 1914.
2 Assuming that W's interest is not affected by an order by the court made under s 339 of the Insolvency Act 1986. See Riddall *Law of Trusts* (5th edn, p 59).
3 Section 336(4).
4 *Re Turner (A bankrupt)* [1975] 1 All ER 5, [1974] 1 WLR 1556; *Re Bailey (A bankrupt)* [1977] 2 All ER 26, [1977] 1 WLR 278; *Re Densham (A bankrupt)* [1975] 3 All ER 726, [1975] 1 WLR 1519; *Re Lowrie* [1981] 3 All ER 353; (M & B).

bankrupt's assets, the decision remained one that was at the court's discretion.[5] Nevertheless, in no case was the discretion exercised in favour of the non-bankrupt co-owner. The furthest that the court was prepared to go was to postpone sale. Thus, in *Re Holliday (A bankrupt)* in 1981,[6] sale was postponed for five years, until the two eldest children of the marriage would be over 17. But the concession was made only because of special circumstances, including the fact that the bankrupt left his wife, the co-owner, for another woman, leaving his wife to provide a home for the children of the marriage, and the fact that the court considered that the postponement would not inflict any undue hardship on the creditors.

In 1982, a committee set up under the chairmanship of Sir Kenneth Cork to review the law of the practice of insolvency (whose report led to the Insolvency Acts of 1985 and 1986) concluded,[7] with regard to the conflicting interests of a bankrupt's family and those of his creditors, that it would 'be consonant with present social attitudes to alleviate the personal hardship to those who are dependent on the debtor but not responsible for his insolvency, if this can be achieved by delaying for an acceptable time the sale of the family home'.[8] The Committee recommended that the courts should have a specific power, having regard to the needs of the bankrupt's family, to postpone a trustee in bankruptcy's power to sell the property. Effect was not given to this recommendation. There is, however, provision in the Act[9] that where, in the case of a home that is a matrimonial home, occupied by the bankrupt and children under 18, 'an application is made after ... one year [from the vesting of] the bankrupt's estate in a trustee, the court shall assume, unless the circumstances are exceptional, that the interests of the bankrupt's creditors outweigh all other considerations'. The intention is that during the year following the bankruptcy,[10] the interests of the creditors should not necessarily be treated as paramount, and that a period of up to a year should be treated as one during which it would be reasonable for the court to postpone sale in order to allow the family to make arrangements for other accommodation, but that sale should not be postponed for longer than one year unless the circumstances of the case are exceptional.

In *Re Citrol*[11] in 1990 the Court of Appeal was not prepared to allow as long a postponement as one year. The case concerned a matrimonial home. At first instance, the court, after finding that the beneficial interest was shared equally between the bankrupt and his wife, postponed an order for sale until the youngest child reached 16. The Court of Appeal held that only in exceptional circumstances, more exceptional than those that were ordinarily the 'melancholy consequences of debt and improvidence', could the interest of a non-bankrupt

---

5   *Re McGarthy (A bankrupt)* [1975] 2 All ER 857, [1975] 1 WLR 807.
6   [1981] Ch 405, [1980] 3 All ER 385; (M & B); (1981) 97 LQR 200 (C. Hand); [1981] Conv 79 (A. Sydenham); [1983] Conv 219 (C. Hand); [1986] Conv 393 (J. G. Miller).
7   *Report of the Review Committee on Insolvency Law and Practice* (1982) Cmnd 8558.
8   Para 199.
9   Section 336(5) with s 335(A) added by TLATA 1996, Sch 3.
10   Ie, the vesting of the bankrupt's property in the trustee.
11   [1992] Ch 142, [1990] 3 All ER 952; (M & B); [1991] Conv 302 (A. M. M. Lawson).

spouse prevail so as to cause an order for sale to be postponed for a substantial period. The circumstances, albeit distressing for the wife and her children, were not exceptional, and the court substituted a period of postponement of six months for that ordered in the court below.

Nor were there found to be exceptional circumstances in *Barclays Bank v Hendricks* in 1995[12] when an application by a wife to postpone an order for the sale of a matrimonial home until the children of the marriage had reached 18 was rejected, the fact that the wife's share of the proceeds of sale would be sufficient to purchase a less pleasant and convenient house being held not to constitute exceptional circumstances. It is clear that the onus of proving the existence of such circumstances is a heavy one.

The Act of 1986[13] made the statutory right of occupation of the matrimonial home conferred on a spouse by the Matrimonial Homes Act 1983 binding (whether registered or not) on a trustee in bankruptcy.[14] Where, therefore, W has registered this statutory right (as a Class F Land Charge), it will therefore be necessary for the trustee in bankruptcy to apply to the court to have the charge removed before the property can be sold.

The 1986 Act provides that applications in connection with a bankruptcy to have a charge registered under the Matrimonial Homes Act 1983 removed from the register,[15] and applications made by a trustee in bankruptcy for an order under s 14 of the Trusts of Land and Appointment of Trustees Act 1996 for sale of a dwelling house,[16] must be made to the court having jurisdiction in relation to the bankruptcy.

In dealing with the claim of a bankrupt co-owner who is not a spouse (ie that the house should not be sold) the courts have followed the same principles as when the co-owners are spouses: the interests of creditors have prevailed, the non-bankrupt co-owner being allowed, at most, and then only exceptionally, a postponement of sale.[17]

We have considered the principles of law that operate the case of a conflict between the trustee in bankruptcy of a bankrupt co-owner (who wants sale) and the other, non-bankrupt, co-owner (who resists sale). It has been held that the same principles with regard to the matters that the court should take into account in deciding whether to order sale (in particular relating to 'exceptional circumstances') apply equally where[18] A and B are co-owners, B mortgages her equitable interest in the property to C, B fails to repay the loan, and C seeks an order for sale of the property (ie between a mortgagor co-owner and a mortgagee seeking sale).

We may mention here that another instance of a conflict between one beneficial co-owner of a home and a creditor of the other co-owner arises when the creditor seeks to have a charging order on the land made absolute

---

12   [1996] 1 FCR 710.
13   Section 336(2)(a).
14   Reversing the position under the Acts of 1967 and 1983. The Act of 1983 is re-enacted in the Family Law Act 1996, Part IV.
15   Section 336(2)(b). The Act of 1983 is re-enacted in the Family Law Act 1996, Part IV.
16   Section 336(3).
17   *Re Evers's Trust* [1980] 3 All ER 399, [1980] 1 WLR 1327; (M & B).
18   *Austin-Fell v Austin-Fell* [1990] Fam 172, [1990] 2 All ER 455, [1990] FD 172.

and this step is resisted by the other co-owner (eg on the ground that matrimonial proceedings involving an application for reallocation of matrimonial property have been commenced)[19] or when a co-owner seeks to have a charging order that has been made absolute set aside.[20]

SUMMARY

Where two (or more) people contribute to the purchase price of property that is conveyed into the name of one of them, that person holds the legal title on trust for both (or all) of them; prior to the Trusts of Land and Appointment of Trustees Act 1996, on trust for sale, after the Act, under a trust of land under the 1996 Act.

Formerly, the trust was treated as an implied trust. More recently the trust has been regarded as a constructive trust.

The holder of the legal estate in land will hold on constructive trust for himself and another where there is evidence of (a) a common intention to this effect; and (b) and act by the other to their detriment in reliance on (a).

Subsequent conduct may be accepted as evidence of the existence of an original common intention.

Under the Matrimonial Proceedings and Property Act 1970, a married person who contributes in money or money's worth acquires a beneficial interest in the property.

Disputes in the context of divorce proceedings are determined under the Matrimonial Causes Act 1973.

A spouse has a right to occupy the matrimonial home (a) at common law; (b) under the Family Law Act 1996; (c) if she has a beneficial interest, under the Trusts of Land and Appointment of Trustees Act 1996.

Where a home is held by a husband on trust for himself and his wife, and the wife is in occupation, (under *Boland*) a purchaser takes subject to the wife's equitable interest.

As between a non-bankrupt beneficial co-owner and the creditors of the other (bankrupt) co-owner, the interests of the latter have generally prevailed.

19 *Harman v Glencross* [1986] Fam 81, [1986] 1 All ER 545 (charging order absolute postponed to any other made by the court in matrimonial proceedings (affecting transfer of husband's property to wife) commenced before charging order nisi was made); [1986] Conv 218 (J. Warburton); cf *First National Securities v Hegerty* [1985] QB 850, [1984] 3 All ER 641 (charging order nisi obtained before matrimonial proceedings commenced, charging order absolute not disturbed); [1985] Conv 129 (P. F. Smith).
20 As in *Abbey National plc v Moss* [1994] 2 FCR 587, CA (Hirst LJ (correctly, it is submitted) dissenting on the principle applicable and, consequently, on the outcome).

CHAPTER 13

Future Interests

A future interest is an interest in property that the owner holds now, but from which he can derive no benefit until some future point in time. We have already met instances of future interests. For example, in Chapter 3 we saw that if A grants land to B for life with remainder to C in fee simple, C has a fee simple in remainder. We saw too that since this fee simple in remainder is C's property now he can dispose of it as he wishes: he can sell it or give it away; and if he dies before B, the fee simple in remainder will pass under his will; or if he dies intestate, it will pass to his next of kin. From the moment of A's grant the fee simple in remainder thus becomes C's property, but he can derive no benefit from the land itself until the fee simple falls into possession on B's death. C's fee simple in remainder is thus an example of a future interest.

Another example of a future interest is provided by a grant of land by A, who holds the fee simple, to B for life. Here A, after making the grant, will hold the fee simple in reversion. This too is a future interest. The interest is A's property now, but he will derive no benefit from it until B's death, when the fee simple once more becomes a fee simple in possession.

Thus if (before the Trusts of Land and Appointment of Trustees Act 1996 prevented the creation of interests in fee tail) A grants land to B for life with remainder to C for life with remainder to D in fee tail with remainder to E in fee simple, then during B's lifetime, C, D and E all hold future interests. On B's death, C's interest will fall into possession; D and E will continue to hold future interests. On C's death D's interest falls into possession and E continues to hold a future interest. On the extinction of the fee tail granted to D, the property will become E's in possession.

Vested and contingent interests

An interest, whether future or in possession, may be vested or contingent. If an interest is not contingent then it is vested. An interest is contingent in either of the following two situations:

1. It is contingent so long as the identity of the beneficiary or beneficiaries is unknown. For example, a grant by A, a bachelor,

'to my first son to be born',

is contingent as, at the time of the grant, the identity of the grantee is unknown.

2. It is contingent so long as any condition attached to the grant remains unfulfilled. For example, a grant,

'to B when he is called to the Bar',

remains contingent until B is called to the Bar. Or a grant,

> 'to C when he attains 21', C being 17,

is contingent until the condition is fulfilled by C reaching the age of 21. In a grant,

> 'to X and Y for their joint lifetimes, with remainder to the survivor in fee simple',

the remainder is contingent until the death of the first to die. In a grant,

> 'to X for life with remainder to Y in fee simple if he survives X',

the remainder is contingent until X's death. In a grant,

> 'to X for life with remainder to his heir',

the remainder is contingent until X's death (because not until then can it be known who is X's heir).

A gift may also be contingent as a result of two particular rules. Thus a grant,

> 'to X for life with remainder to his first daughter to marry in fee simple, with remainder, if X has no daughter who marries, to Y',

the remainder to Y is contingent because of the rule that any gift that follows a gift of a contingent fee simple (ie the gift to X's first daughter to marry) is contingent. And in grants,

> 'to X in fee simple on condition that he remains enrolled as a solicitor, with remainder to Y in fee simple';

and,

> 'to X in fee simple until the Tower of London falls, with remainder to Y in fee simple',

the gifts to Y are in both cases contingent because of the rule that a gift that follows a conditional or determinable fee simple is contingent.

Consider a grant (before the 1996 Act) by A to B for life on his attaining 21, with remainder to C (a bachelor) for life, with remainder to the first son of C in fee tail, with remainder to D for life, with remainder to E in fee tail when he is called to the Bar. Here B has a contingent interest, as a condition has to be fulfilled before B becomes entitled to benefit, namely his attaining 21. C's life interest is vested as there is nothing to make it contingent: we know C's identity and no condition has to be fulfilled for him to become entitled. The interest is a future interest as C does not derive benefit from the land until B's death. The gift to C's first son is a contingent future interest, as we do not yet know the identity of C's first son. If C has a son, the interest will become a future vested interest. D holds a future vested interest. E holds a future contingent interest. If, at some time after the grant, E is called to the Bar, his interest will become a future vested interest. And, to complete the picture, we may add that A holds a future vested interest, ie the fee simple in reversion. It is vested as no condition must be fulfilled in order that A may be entitled: for example, if B, C, D and E all died after the grant, no condition would need to be fulfilled before A became entitled to the land: he would be entitled straight away. An interest in reversion is, in fact, necessarily always a vested interest. (The fact that the interest may never revert is irrelevant.)

CONDITIONS PRECEDENT AND SUBSEQUENT[1]

In Chapter 4 the distinction was noted between conditions precedent, which relate to the commencement of an interest, and conditions subsequent, which relate to the ending of an interest. Thus whilst a grant 'to A in fee simple on his becoming enrolled as a solicitor' is a grant of a fee simple subject to a condition precedent (and A holds a contingent interest), a grant 'to A (a solicitor) in fee simple on condition that he remains enrolled as a solicitor' is a grant of a conditional fee simple. The grant is of a *vested* conditional fee simple, since A's identity is ascertained and no condition has to be fulfilled in order for him to become entitled: the condition relates to the ending of the fee simple, not its commencement.

CERTAINTY

When dealing with the conditional fee simple we learned[2] that the condition that will cut short the fee simple must be defined with sufficient certainty for it to be possible to see what events will cause the fee simple to come to an end[3] (and so give the grantor the right to exercise his right of re-entry). In the case of a condition precedent (ie a condition that will make the interest contingent, eg 'to A if he attains 21') the condition must also be expressed with sufficient certainty for it to be possible to know in what circumstances the grantee will become entitled.

The courts have accepted a less stringent test[4] in the case of a condition precedent than in the case of a condition subsequent[5] but it must nevertheless be possible to ascertain the point in time at which the gift will cease to be contingent and become vested.[6] This principle may be of relevance when a

---

1 (1990) 106 LQR 185 (G. H. Treitel).
2 See Chapter 4.
3 We saw that the event which marks the limit of a determinable fee simple must also be expressed with certainty.
4 See *Re Allen* [1953] Ch 810 at 817.
5 For example, in *Re Abrahams' Will Trust* [1969] 1 Ch 463, [1967] 2 All ER 1175, a testator directed that a beneficiary, G, should obtain a certain benefit under the will on his becoming engaged to 'a person professing the Jewish faith' (a conditon precedent). By another clause in the will G was entitled to a share in other property, but the testator directed that this interest should terminate on his marrying a person not 'professing the Jewish faith' (a condition subsequent). It was held that the words 'professing the Jewish faith', although they might give rise to some difficulty, were sufficiently certain for the condition precedent to be valid; but the same words were not sufficiently certain for the purpose of the condition subsequent, which was therefore void. In *Re Tuck's Settlement Trust* [1978] Ch 49, [1978] 1 All ER 1047, it was held that a direction that a beneficiary should only be entitled if he was married to an 'approved wife' (of the Jewish faith) as defined by the settlor was not void for uncertainty.
6 Or when a contract subject to a condition precedent (eg a contract for the purchase of a house conditional on the purchaser obtaining a mortgage) becomes binding. *Lee-Parker v Izzet* [1971] 3 All ER 1099, [1071] 1 WLR 1688 (contract valid); *Re Rich's Will Trust* (1962) 106 Sol Jo 75; *Lee-Parker v Izzet (No 2)* [1972] 2 All ER 800, [1972] 1 WLR 775 (contracts void).

settlor has given property for a certain class of beneficiaries at a specified time in the future. For example, suppose that a testator leaves property,

> 'to all my grandchildren living 21 years after my death'.

The gift is contingent since the identity of the beneficiaries will not be known until the expiry of the period specified. There is no uncertainty here as to the point in time at which the gift will vest, and so the condition is certain. Similarly, when a testator who died in 1926 left property,

> 'to such of my descendants as are living 21 years after the death of the last survivor of the lineal descendants of Queen Victoria living at my death',[7]

it was held that since, at the testator's death, it was possible to determine who all the lineal descendants of Queen Victoria were, it would be possible to know when the gift vested. The gift was therefore valid with regard to the certainty of the condition that a beneficiary had to fulfil in order to become entitled (ie being alive at the expiry of the period specified).

Why does it matter whether an interest is vested or contingent?

The answer to this question is that if someone holds a vested interest, then he cannot lose it. If he holds a contingent interest, he may or he may not obtain a benefit from the property concerned. This difference can be illustrated by an example. Suppose that (1) A grants Blackacre to B for life with remainder to C in fee simple; and (2) W grants Greenacre to X for life with remainder to Y in fee simple, provided that he attains 25. C (who holds a vested interest) makes a will leaving all his property to D. Y (who holds a contingent interest) makes a will leaving all his property to Z. C and Y (who is not yet 25) then die. Since C's interest was vested, the interest forms part of his property at his death, and so his interest in Blackacre (a fee simple in remainder) passes to D.[8] But since Y's interest was merely contingent Z obtains nothing. The gift to Y fails, and on X's death the land will revert to W.

What we have said with regard to Y's contingent interest failing on his death applies whenever the contingency relates to the grantee personally,[9] eg his attaining a certain age, or marrying, or acquiring a particular qualification or surviving another person. Where, however, the contingency does not relate to the grantee personally, the contingent interest will pass under his will or intestacy. For example, suppose that W gives Greenacre in 1970 to X for life with remainder to Y in fee simple provided that planning permission for a specified development on Greenacre is granted within five years of the gift. Y dies leaving all his property to Z. Z would receive the interest (which would still be contingent) under Y's will. (If the condition was fulfilled within the time specified, Z's interest would become a vested fee simple in remainder; if it was not fulfilled, the remainder would fail.)

---

7   *Re Villar* [1929] 1 Ch 243; (M & B); followed in *Re Leverhulme (No 2)* [1943] 2 All ER 274.
     See also *Pownall v Graham* (1863) 33 Beav 242.
8   *Re Roberts* [1903] 2 Ch 200 at 202.
9   *Re Cresswell* (1883) 24 Ch D 102 at 107.

Thus, with regard to the position on death, a vested interest always passes under the will or intestacy of the holder; a contingent interest does not do so unless the condition is other than one relating to the grantee personally.

We have explained one reason why it matters whether an interest is vested or contingent. There is another reason. If an interest is contingent, then it is subject to the rule against perpetuities.[10] (The content of this rule is examined in the next chapter.) If it is vested, it is not subject to this rule.

Having said that a contingent interest, to be valid, must not infringe the rule against perpetuities, we must go on to explain that when considering whether a particular interest is or is not subject to the rule against perpetuities, an interest is classified as being contingent not only where, (1) the identity of the beneficiary or beneficiaries is unknown; or (2) any condition attached to the grant remains unfulfilled (the two conditions we have met already), but the interest will be contingent also where (3) the size of a beneficiary's share is uncertain.[11] For example, suppose that in a gift by will property is left,

'to all the children of A, born or hereafter to be born',

A being alive at the testator's death and having two children, B and C, at the time of the gift.

If A dies without having any more children, then his two children will take a half share each, but if A has a third child and then dies each child will be entitled to a third share, and so on – as each fresh child is born, the share of the children previously born is reduced. Thus as long as A is alive (and so possibly may have more children) the size of each beneficiary's interest is uncertain. For this reason the property cannot be distributed until A has died. Not until that point can it be known what share each beneficiary is entitled to. So until A has died the gift to B and C (for the purpose we are now speaking of, namely, determining whether the gift is subject to the rule against perpetuities) is contingent. The gift is contingent, be it noted, with regard not only to the interests of any children not yet born, but also with regard to the interests of A's children, B and C. It is true that the identity of B and C is known, and that no condition must be fulfilled for B and C to take, but the size of their shares is, during A's lifetime, uncertain. Only when A dies, as we have said, will this uncertainty come to an end, and the gift become vested. Since the gift is thus, ie for the purpose of the rule against perpetuities, a gift of a contingent interest, it must comply with the rule against perpetuities, the nature of which is to be explained in the next chapter.

It will therefore be seen that a gift may be vested in the context of the law of succession, and it may be contingent in the context of the rule against perpetuities. This will be the case wherever a gift satisfies the first two conditions

10 Two further differences between vested and contingent interests existed in the past. One related to alienation. Vested interests could be alienated at common law from early times. Contingent interests were not alienable at common law. They became devisable under the Statute of Wills 1540; their assignment inter vivos became enforceable in equity in the eighteenth century (*Wright v Wright* (1750) 1 Ves Sen 409) and at common law under the Real Property Act 1845, s 6 (now LPA 1925, s 4(2)). The other difference lay in the fact that contingent remainders were liable, in certain circumstances, to destruction by the tenant in possession. Vested interests could never be destroyed in this (or in any other) way.

set out above, but not the third. By way of illustration consider the interest of C in the example above. We know C's identity, and no condition must be fulfilled for him to become entitled (ie to at least *some* share in the property). Thus for the purpose of succession his interest is vested (notwithstanding that the size of his interest is liable to be diminished). Thus if C dies leaving all his property to Z, then C's interest under the gift will pass on his death to Z. (Z will then have to wait until A dies before he receives his share, ie the share which C would have received.) However, since the size of each beneficiary's interest is not known, the gift to C, for the purpose of the rule against perpetuities, is contingent and so, to be valid, must comply with the rule against perpetuities.[12]

To a study of this rule we now turn.

SUMMARY

Interests are in possession or future.

A future interest is one from which the holder derives no interest until some time in the future.

Interests, both in possession and future, are vested or contingent.

An interest is contingent if:

the identity of a beneficiary is unknown; or,
any condition is unfulfilled; or,
the gift is one that follows a conditional fee simple; or,
the gift is one that follows a determinable fee simple.

The condition in a condition precedent must be sufficiently certain.

The interest of a person whose interest is contingent by reason of a condition that relates to him personally does not pass under his will or intestacy if he dies before the condition is fulfilled.

The interest of a person whose interest is vested passes on his death under his will or intestacy.

A contingent interest is subject to the rule against perpetuities.

A gift is contingent for the purpose of the rule against perpetuities if the share of any beneficiary is uncertain.

11　*Jee v Audley* (1787) 1 Cox Eq 324; *Hale v Hale* (1876) 3 Ch D 643.
12　It will be seen from the next chapter that the whole gift (including the gift to C) complies with the rule and so is valid. If the gift had infringed the rule it would have been void, and so there would have been nothing to pass on C's death to Z.

CHAPTER 14

The Rule Against Perpetuities[1]

Introduction

If a person grants property to a named, living individual, for example:

'to my nephew Tom Jones',

then the law raises no objection. Further, if a person grants property to certain living individuals for their lives, in a grant such as:

'to A for life, with remainder to B for life, with remainder to C for life, with remainder to D in fee simple',

the law again raises no objection. But if a person grants property,

'to my first grandson to be called to the Bar',

then the law pricks up its ears. The reason is that the grant does not identify an actual person who is entitled to the property. The identity of the person who will be entitled to the property is uncertain. It may turn out that the identity of the person entitled to the property remains uncertain for a long time. For example, if the grant,

'to my first grandson to be called to the Bar',

had been made by will, and the testator had died in 1900 leaving a son one month old, and that son grew up, and when he was 60 had a son of his own, and that son, the testator's grandson, was called to the Bar when he was 40, 100 years would have elapsed between the time of the testator's death and the time when it became known who was entitled to the property. During all this time what was to happen to the property would have remained in doubt.

The attitude of the law has been that it is against the public interest for uncertainty such as this to exist for too long. The common law therefore set a limit to the length of time during which uncertainty such as this could be tolerated. The common law imposed a rule which, in effect, said to a grantor, 'You must not frame your grant in such a way that it can remain uncertain for longer than a certain period who is to get the property you are granting. If you break this rule, your grant will be void.' The rule that has this effect is called the rule against perpetuities, or the perpetuity rule.

---

1   J. C. Gray *The Rule against Perpetuities* (4th edn, 1942); R. H. Maudsley, *The Modern Law of Perpetuities* (1981).

The rule in its basic form was a creation of the common law.[2] It was amended by the Law of Property Act 1925 and again by the Perpetuities and Accumulations Act 1964 which came into effect on 16 July 1964.[3] So, when considering whether a grant infringes the rule, it is necessary to consider whether the grant came into effect before 1926; between 1 January 1926 and 15 July 1964,[4] or since 16 July 1964.

The rule applies, and has always applied, to grants of realty and of personalty, to grants inter vivos and by will; and to both legal and equitable interests. Certain forms of interest that are not subject to the rule are set out at the end of the chapter.

We shall first consider the basic, common law, rule and then the modifications to the rule made by statute.

THE PERPETUITY RULE AT COMMON LAW

The rule is that a grant of a contingent interest is void ab initio unless it is certain that the interest will vest, if it vests at all, within a life or lives in being when the grant comes into operation plus a further period of 21 years from the expiry of the last life in being, plus any relevant gestation periods.

The meaning of this will become clear when we have examined the meaning of some of the words and phrases used in the rule.

'contingent'

The rule applies only to a grant of a contingent interest. As we saw in the last chapter, if a grant is not contingent, then it is *vested*. The circumstances in which a grant is contingent for the purposes of the rule against perpetuities were explained in the last chapter.

We may mention here that a class gift is a gift to a group of persons by description, where it is not possible to identify every possible member of the class when the grant comes into operation. So in a gift,

'to all the children of A (a living person) born or hereafter to be born',

is a class gift. So too is a gift by a testator,

'to all my grandsons who attain 21'.

But a gift by a testator,

'to my four sons',

2   The rule reached full develoment in 1833 in *Cadell v Palmer* (1833) 1 Cl & Fin 372 (M & B) but the origins of the rule can be traced to the seventeenth century. An important stage in its evolution was marked by the *Duke of Norfolk's Case* (1681) 1 Vern 163.

3   Following the recommendation of the Law Reform Committee, Fourth Report, 1956, Cmnd 18.

4   For example, in *Re Atkin's Will Trusts* [1974] 2 All ER 1, [1974] 1 WLR 761; (M & B), the case was heard in 1974, but since the case concerned a gift in the will of a testator who died in 1957, it was the law in force before the Act of 1964 that was applied.

is not a class gift as it will be possible to identify every possible member of the class when the grant comes into operation at the testator's death.

'certain that the interest will vest'

Vest means becomes vested. Vested, as we have seen, means not contingent. Thus the rule is that it must be certain that the interest will cease to be contingent within the prescribed period. For example, if the interest was contingent because a condition was attached to the grant, then when the condition is satisfied the gift ceases to be contingent. For example in a grant,

'to A for life with remainder to B when he is called to the Bar',

until B is called to the Bar his interest is contingent. When he is called to the Bar his interest ceases to be contingent and becomes vested.

It will be noted that 'vest' does not necessarily mean 'vest in possession'. In the last example, when B is called to the Bar, his interest ceases to be contingent and so becomes vested; but he is not entitled in possession until A has died. While A is alive B's interest is an interest in remainder, but it is vested nonetheless. (An interest that is vested, but not yet in possession, is sometimes referred to as being 'vested in interest'.)

'within a life or lives in being'

The common law rule is that a contingent interest is void ab initio unless it is certain that it will vest, if it vests at all, within a life or lives in being plus a further period of 21 years.

The phrase 'within a life in being' means within the lifetime of a[5] person – any[6] person – alive when the gift comes into operation. For the purpose of the rule a person is 'in being' during the period between his conception and birth, when he is *en ventre sa mère*[7] (in his or her mother's womb). 'In being' thus means in existence, ie alive, including being alive *en ventre sa mère*.[7]

Lives in being must be the lives of humans.[8] The lives of animals or insects (eg butterflies[9]) are not permitted.

The perpetuity period

The perpetuity period consists of the lifetimes of persons who are alive (ie including those *en ventre sa mère*[10]), when the grant comes into operation, plus

---

5 Gray, at 201.
6 *Pownall v Graham* (1863) 33 Beav 242 at 246, line 15; Maudsley, p 42; L. M. Simes (1953) 52 Mich LR 186. The subject of lives in being is discussed again later.
7 *Long v Blackall* (1979) 7 Term Rep 100.
8 The acceptance of the lives of the testator's horses in *Re Dean* (1889) 41 Ch D 552 is regarded as having been incorrect.
9 See *Re Kelly* [1932] IR 255 at 260; (M & B).
10 Provided that such persons are subsequently born.

a further 21 years, plus any subsequent period of gestation. (How this last period may affect the position will be considered in due course.)

'when the grant comes into operation'

In the case of a gift in a will, the gift comes into operation at the testator's death. In a grant inter vivos, the grant comes into operation at the date of the grant.[11]

How the common law rule is applied

In applying the common law perpetuity rule to any disposition (and by disposition we mean any one part of a gift if the gift consists of two or more parts) there are three steps that have to be taken.

1. First, decide whether the interest granted is contingent. (If it is not, there is no need to proceed further.)
2. Decide when the gift will vest, ie cease to be contingent. This may be when some condition is fulfilled, or when the identity of a beneficiary becomes known, or when the size of the share to which each beneficiary is entitled becomes known (eg when all the members of a class have been born).
3. Next comes the crucial step. It is now necessary to consider whether the vesting of the gift *must* occur (if it occurs at all) within 21 years from the death of some person alive or *en ventre sa mère* at the testator's death.[12] If so, the gift is valid. But if it is found that the gift could conceivably, by any possibility, however remote, vest more than 21 years after the death of any person alive or *en ventre sa mère* at the testator's death, then the gift infringes the rule and is void.[13]

Consider in this connection a gift by will 'to the first son of A to attain 12', where A is alive at the testator's death. Here it is possible to show that the gift must vest, if it vests at all, within 21 years from the death of a person alive or *en ventre sa mère* at the time of the testator's death: the gift must vest, if it vests at all, within 21 years from A's death. A is alive at the testator's death; he is a life in being; therefore the gift is valid. Thus for a gift to be valid it must be possible to postulate, by reference to the life of some actual person (or persons), that the gift must vest, if it vests at all, within the perpetuity period. So the question[14] that must be asked in testing the validity of a gift is: 'Can I point to some person (or persons) alive when the gift takes effect, and say that gift must vest, if it vests at all, within 21 years from that person's death (or the survivor of those persons' deaths)?' If the answer is yes, the gift is valid; if no, it is void.

---

11   Ie in the case of a deed, when the instrument has been signed and delivered.
12   Or date of inter vivos grant.
13   For a vivid explanation of the operation of the rule see S. M. Fetters, 'Perpetuities: The Wait and See Disaster' (1975) 60 Cornell LR 380 at 390-393.
14   This question is a modified version of that by B. Sparks (1955) U of Florida LR 465 at 470.

Who the person or persons pointed to are, it matters not. They can be anyone in the whole world.

If a gift can be shown to be valid it will often be the case (as in the last example) that the life or lives which enable us to show that the gift is valid are the lives of persons mentioned in the gift. So, as a matter of practicalities it is useful, and usual, to consider first whether the gift must vest, if it vests at all, within the lifetimes (plus 21 years) of persons mentioned in the gift. But it must always be remembered that if it cannot be shown that the gift will vest within the lifetimes of people referred to in the gift, this is not the end of the matter. The gift will be valid if it can be shown that it will vest within the lifetime of some other person alive at the testator's death, someone not referred to in the gift. Examples of this will be given later.

ILLUSTRATIONS

Let us see how the rule operates in the case of the following examples. In the course of considering these a number of characteristics and special aspects of the rule will be illustrated.

1. A gift by will,

> 'to A for life, with remainder to A's first son to be called to the Bar in fee simple', A being alive and having two sons, B and C, at the testator's death.

   (i) Is there a grant of a contingent interest? The gift to A is clearly vested, but the remainder is contingent, and so, to be valid, must comply with the rule.

  (ii) When will the gift (ie the remainder) vest? When a son of A (not necessarily B or C) is called to the Bar.

 (iii) Must the gift vest, if it vests at all, within the lifetime of a person who is alive or *en ventre sa mère* at the time of the testator's death plus 21 years? Or can we conceive a situation in which the vesting could occur more than 21 years after the death of every life in being at a testator's death?

The answer is that it is possible that the gift could vest more than 21 years after the death of lives in being. B and C might die the day after the testator. A might have another son, whom we will call D (and who, it will be noted, is not a life in being). A and everyone else in the world alive at the testator's death could then die. Twenty-one years later the perpetuity period would end. Then, some years after that, D might be called to the Bar. Thus, since the gift could vest outside the perpetuity period, the remainder is void. (This will not affect the gift to A. On A's death the property will revert to the testator's estate and pass to the person entitled to the residuary estate.)

2. A gift by will,

> 'to the first son of A to attain 30', where A is alive and has two sons, B and C.

The gift is contingent. The gift will vest when a son of A (not necessarily B or C) attains 30. Must this occur within lives in being at A's death plus 21 years? No. B and C might die. A might have another son, D, who would not be a life in being. A might then die. D might attain 30 more than 21 years from A's death. So the gift is void.

The gift must be bound to vest

In the last example it is, of course, possible that the time of vesting could occur before the end of the perpetuity period. For example, suppose a son, D, was born ten years before A's death. In this case D would attain 30 within 21 years from A's death and so the gift would in fact vest within the perpetuity period. (Or B and C might not die, and one of them might attain 30). Is it possible to say for this reason that the gift is valid? The answer is, no. The rule is that for a gift to be valid, the interest must be bound to vest, if it vests at all, within the perpetuity period.[15] The rule is not that a gift is valid if it *could* vest within the perpetuity rule. If this were the rule, the gift 'to the first son of A to attain 30' would be valid because, as we have seen, it is quite possible for it to vest within the period. But, as we have shown, it is also possible that it could vest outside the perpetuity period; and so, for this reason, it is void.

3.   A gift by deed,

> 'to the first of A's sons to be ordained', A being dead and having two sons, B and C.

The gift is contingent. It will vest when B or C is ordained. Must this occur within the lifetime of someone in being at the date of the gift, plus 21 years? Yes, it must. If B or C is ordained, this can only happen within their own lifetimes, and as they are lives in being the rule is not infringed and so the gift is valid.

'if it vests at all'

It should be noted that it is irrelevant that the gift may never vest at all. Consider the above example. Neither B nor C may ever be ordained (both of them may already be successful agnostic chemists), but this is immaterial. The rule is not that the gift must be bound to vest within the perpetuity period. (If this were

---

15   There have been very few instances of any departure from a rigid application of this rule. One (*Re Atkin's Will Trusts* [1974] 2 All ER 1, [1974] 1 WLR 761; (M & B)) was when a gift by will of land would vest on the completion of the sale by the trustee of the property devised. The trustee was under a duty to sell the land within a year of the testator's death. If the trustee failed in this duty the sale might not have occurred (and the gift thus vest) until after the perpetuity period. But the court, not being willing to allow the interests of the beneficiaries to be defeated by reason of the fact that it was possible that the trustee might fail to sell within a year, disregarded this possibility in considering whether the gift was void under the perpetuity rule, and the gift was held to be valid. But such departures from a strict application of the rule are rare.

the rule, no contingent interest could ever be valid since there is no certainty with regard to what may happen in the future: the world could end tomorrow.) The rule is that the gift must be bound to vest, *if it vests at all*, within the perpetuity period. Thus, although there is no certainty that a son of A will ever be ordained, if a son *is* ordained, it is certain that this will be bound to occur within the perpetuity period (with the result, as we have seen, that the gift is valid).

Express confinement within the perpetuity period

4.   A gift by will,

> 'to all my children, grandchildren and great grandchildren living 21 years after the death of the survivor of my brothers, X, Y and Z'.

The gift is contingent. The gift will vest 21 years after the death of whichever of the testator's brothers is the last to die. Can the gift vest more than 21 years after the death of a life in being? No, it cannot. The testator has expressly limited the gift to vest 21 years after the death of a person (X, Y or Z) who is alive at his death. Therefore the terms of the gift confine the period during which the gift can be contingent to the perpetuity period, and so the gift is necessarily valid. Thus there is no need even to consider whether there are any circumstances in which the gift could vest outside the perpetuity period. The very terms of the disposition bring the gift within the rule. The position is the same in a gift by will,

> 'to the first of my descendants to shake hands with Mr Blair'.

It will be recalled[16] that when considering conditions precedent, we saw that in *Re Villar*[17] a testator, who died in 1926, left property,

> 'to such of my descendants as are living 20 years after the death of the last survivor of the lineal descendants of Queen Victoria living at my death',

and that the gift was held to be valid.[18] We saw that as regards certainty, the court held that the contingency on which the gift vested was sufficiently certain, notwithstanding the difficulties involved in ascertaining when the last of the 120 descendants of the Queen (living at the testator's death) died. We can now understand why the gift complies with the rule against perpetuities: the gift expressly confined the period during which the gift was contingent to a period one year shorter than the perpetuity period, namely the lives in being specified plus 20 years.

Whenever, in fact, a settlor confines the period during which the gift is contingent to ascertained (or ascertainable) lives in being (plus, if he wishes, a period not exceeding 21 years) then the gift cannot infringe the rule against perpetuities. But this does not mean that the gift is therefore necessarily valid. The gift must, as we have seen, also satisfy the requirement that the time of

16   See Chapter 13.

vesting must be capable of being known with sufficient certainty. Thus if a testator today left property in the terms of the will in *Re Villar*[19] the gift would almost certainly be void: not because it infringes the rule against perpetuities (it does not), but because the condition precedent which marks the time of vesting of the gift is uncertain. Thus the gift would be void for uncertainty,[20] not for perpetuity.

'Royal lives' clauses

We may note here that a clause in which a settlor limits the time of vesting of a gift by reference to the lives of certain persons living at his death, whether ascertained (as in the example above, where the lives were those of X, Y and Z) or ascertainable (as in *Re Villar*), the clause is termed a 'royal lives' clause (ie irrespective of whether the lives specified are those of royal persons).

Provided that it would be possible to ascertain without undue difficulty the date of death of the survivor of the persons specified, the use of a royal lives clause will thus always provide an effective means of ensuring the validity of a contingent gift. The next four examples illustrate this.

5.   A gift by will,

> 'to my first grandson to marry', the testator leaving one child, A, at his death, and no other issue.

The gift is contingent. The gift will vest when a grandson of the testator marries. Could this happen more than 21 years after the death of every person alive at the testator's death? Yes, it could. A could have a son, B, who will not be a life in being. A could then die. B could marry many years after 21 years from A's death. So the gift is void.

6.   A gift by will,

> 'to my first grandson to marry before the expiry of 21 years from the death of the last survivor of the lineal descendants of Queen Elizabeth II living at my death'.

Assuming that the condition precedent is certain (as would be likely), the use of the royal lives clause confines the vesting of the gift within the perpetuity period. The gift is therefore valid.

7.   A gift by will of a testator who died last 31 December,

> 'to my first grandson to marry before the expiry of 21 years from the death of the last survivor of the lineal descendants of Queen Victoria living at my death'.[1]

---

17   *Re Villar* [1929] 1 Ch 243; (M & B).
18   The use of the descendants of Queen Victoria was held to validate a gift taking effect in 1944; *Re Warren's Will Trusts* (1961) 105 Sol Jo 511.
19   Supra.
20   *Re Viscount Exmouth* (1883) 23 Ch D 158; *Re Moore* [1901] 1 Ch 936.
 1   Where the testator left children living at his death.

Since it would not now be practicable to find the location (and perhaps even the identity) of all the descendants of Queen Victoria who were alive on 31 December last, it would not be possible to determine the dates of their death (and from this, the time when the gift vests). So the gift is void for uncertainty.[2] It should be noted that the gift is not void because it infringes the rule against perpetuities: it does not infringe the rule, since the gift is limited to lives in being at the testator's death, plus 21 years: it is for uncertainty[3] that it fails.[4]

8.   A gift by will of a testator who died last 31 December,

> 'to my first grandson to marry before the expiry of 21 years from the death of the last survivor of the lineal descendants of Queen Elizabeth II'.

Here the donor has failed (by omitting the words 'living at my death') to limit the gift to take effect 21 years from the death of a life in being at his death. The gift is void for perpetuity as well as for uncertainty.

Gifts vesting on the occurrence of an event unconnected with a person referred to in the gift

The matter which makes a gift contingent will often be a requirement that a beneficiary satisfies some condition, eg marrying, or attaining 21, but the contingency may relate to an event unconnected with any beneficiary or other person referred to in the gift. Whether the gift will be valid or void is to be determined by the application of the rule in the normal way. The next three examples illustrate this.

9.   A testator retained the ownership of minerals under land which had been acquired by a railway company for the purpose of building a railway. In his will he directed that the proceeds of sale of the minerals should be divided equally between his three children,

> 'if the minerals ... should be worked'.[5]

If the gift had been construed as one to take effect if the minerals should be worked during the lifetime of the children, then the gift would have been valid. But the court found that there was no intention that the will was to be construed in this way. The gift to the children was clearly contingent, but since the contingency did not relate to the children personally, when a child died his interest would pass to whoever was entitled under his will or intestacy. For this reason it was possible that the gift would vest (when the minerals began to be worked) more than 21 years after the death of any person alive at the testator's death. The gift therefore infringed the perpetuity rule and was void.

---

2   The dispositions in *Re Moore* [1901] 1 Ch 936, 'until 21 years from the death of the last survivor of all persons who shall be living at my death', was void for the same reason.
3   It is suggested that uncertainty causes the invalidity of a gift by will 'to A's first grandson to marry a woman born before my death', A being alive at the testator's death.
4   *Re Viscount Exmouth* (1883) 23 Ch D 158; 29 Halsbury 288.
5   *Thomas v Thomas* (1902) 87 LT 58. See also *Re Wood* [1894] 3 Ch 381; (M & B) (property directed to be distributed among a class 'when my gravel pits are worked out').

10. A gift by will to,

> 'the first man to swim the North Sea',

would be void on the same grounds.

11. A gift by will to,

> 'the first man to swim the North Sea within 21 years from my death'.

Since it would not be possible for the vesting to occur more than 21 years after the death of someone alive at the testator's death, the gift is valid. Thus whenever the gift requires that the gift must vest (if it vests at all) within a period of not more than 21 years[6] from the time when the gift comes into operation, the disposition must comply with the rule.

Gifts vesting at a specified time after the grant comes into operation

The following three examples provide illustrations of this form of gift. The rule is applied in the normal way.

12. A gift by will,

> 'to all A's children living 30 years after my death', where A is dead.

As A is dead he cannot have any other children subsequent to the gift coming into operation. If any children of A are living 30 years after the testator's death, they will be doing so within the lifetime (their own) of people alive at the testator's death. So the gift is valid.[7]

13. A gift by will,

> 'to all A's sons living 28 years after my death', where A is alive at the testator's death.

The gift is void. Any of A's sons alive at the testator's death could die. A could have another son. A could then die. The perpetuity period would expire 21 years later. The subsequent vesting of the gift (28 years after the testator's death) would occur outside the period. So the gift infringes the rule and is void.[8]

14. A gift by will,

> 'to all my descendants living 50 years after my death',

Descendants (eg grandchildren and greatgrandchildren of the testator) could be born after the testator's death. The lives of these descendants would not be lives in being. When the gift vested in these descendants 50 years after the death of the testator more than 21 years could have elapsed since the death of

---

6   Or, of course, within lives in being plus 21 years.
7   *Lachlan v Reynolds* (1852) 9 Hare 796.
8   *Palmer v Holford* (1828) 4 Russ 403.

persons who were alive when the grant came into operation. Thus, since the gift could vest outside the perpetuity period, it is void.[9]

En ventre sa mère

We have said that a life in being includes the life of a person *en ventre sa mère* when the gift comes into operation. Here is an illustration.

15. A gift by will to,

> 'the child with which my wife A is enceinte for life with remainder to the first son of X to be ordained within 21 years of the birth of my unborn child'.

The remainder is contingent.[10] The gift will vest when a son of X is ordained. By the terms of the will the gift can only vest, if it vests at all, within 21 years of the birth of the unborn child. The unborn child, being *en ventre sa mère*, is treated as a life in being.[11] Thus the gift must vest within the perpetuity period, and so is valid.[12]

Subsequent periods of gestation

Not only is a child which is *en ventre sa mère* at the time the gift comes into operation treated as a life in being but, further, any subsequent gestation period during which a child is *en ventre sa mère* may be added to the perpetuity period.[13] The next example provides an illustration.

16. A gift by will,

> 'to the first of A's sons to attain 21', where A is alive and has two sons, B and C.

The gift is contingent. The gift will vest when a son of A (not necessarily B or C) attains 21. Must this occur within the perpetuity period, extended, as we now learn, by any subsequent gestation period? Yes, it must. Consider these events. B and C die soon after the testator. A's wife conceives another child. A dies. Nine months later the child is born. Twenty-one years later the gift vests. The vesting has occurred within the perpetuity period, which in this case consists of A's lifetime, plus the gestation period during which A's son was *en ventre sa mère*, plus 21 years. So the gift is valid.

No 'wait and see'

Consider the gift set out under 2 above, a gift by will,

---

9   *Speakman v Speakman* (1850) 8 Hare 180.
10   The life interest is also contingent: this part of the gift does not infringe the rule.
11   *Long v Blackall* (1797) 7 Term Rep 100.
12   *Re Wilmer's Trusts* [1903] 1 Ch 874.
13   Gray, p 224.

'to the first son of A to attain 30', where A is alive and has two sons, B and C.

We saw that the gift was void since A could have another son (D) who might attain 30 more than 21 years from the death of A, B and C (and any other life in being at the testator's death). Thus since the gift could vest outside the perpetuity period, it is void. But let us suppose that the testator died on a Monday (and so the gift came into operation on that day) and A had a son who was due to have his 30th birthday on the following Wednesday. Is it not possible, it might be asked, to wait and see whether the son does celebrate his birthday? If he does live until the Wednesday, it might be argued, then the gift will have vested within the perpetuity period. (It will have vested within a life in being – the son himself, who was alive at the time the gift came into operation.) Surely, if the law is prepared to allow gifts to remain contingent for the length of the perpetuity period it ought to be possible to wait and see whether a gift does in fact vest within the perpetuity period?

The answer is that under the common law rule this is not permitted. One may not wait and see whether the gift does in fact vest within the perpetuity period. The gift must be judged at the moment the grant comes into operation; and no matter how probable it is that the gift will vest within the perpetuity period, if it is conceivable, looking at the matter from the time when the grant comes into operation, that the gift may vest outside the period, it is void.[14] Thus even if A had a son who was due to attain the age of 30 one day after the testator's death, since it is possible for that son to die before his birthday, and for A to have another son who would not attain the age of 30 within the perpetuity period, the gift is void.

It is true that if a gift complies with the rule, then it is necessary to wait and see whether the gift vests.[15] But here one is not waiting to see whether the gift is valid or void for perpetuity, one is waiting to see whether the contingency occurs.

Possibilities, not probabilities

Thus the rule is concerned with legal possibilities, not with actual probabilities. The next two examples illustrate this.

17. A gift by will (that set out at 1 above),

> 'to A's first son to be called to the Bar', A being alive and having two sons, B and C, at the testator's death.

We noted earlier that the gift is void, the reason being that A might have another son (D) who would not be a life in being and who might be called to the Bar

---

14   If there is any ambiguity in the terms of the disposition, then the court will lean in favour of a construction that brings the gift within the rule; *Re Deeley's Settlement* [1974] Ch 454, [1973] 3 All ER 1127.

15   Thus 'there has always been this element of Waiting and Seeing with gifts which were valid under the common law rule, but none with void gifts'. Maudsley, p 36.

more than 21 years from the death of someone alive when the grant came into operation. But what if A was a woman who was 70[16] at the testator's death, or if A was a man who had had his reproductive organs surgically removed? In either case, it would not in practice be physically possible for A to have another son and so the gift could only vest, if it vested at all, within the lives of B or C. The common law, however, paid no heed to biological likelihood, or even physical certainty,[17] and the rigid application of the rule caused the gift to be void.[18] (The common law faced without blinking the existence of a 'fertile octogenarian'.[19])

The law does, however, pay regard to what is, and what is not, *legally* possible. Consider the next example.

18. A gift by will of a testator who died before 1970,

> 'to A for life with remainder to such of her grandchildren living at my death or born within five years thereafter who shall attain 21'.

Without the words 'or born within five years thereafter', the remainder would have been valid, since the grandchildren entitled on attaining 21 would, by virtue of the limitation, be lives in being. But the words 'or born within five years thereafter' could result in a grandchild of A attaining 21 outside the perpetuity period. Suppose that A had a child, B, shortly after the testator's death; and that B had a child, C, within five years of the testator's death. C would be a grandchild of A and so entitled to take. But C could attain 21 more than 21 years from the death of a life in being at the testator's death, and so outside the perpetuity period. But for this to occur B would have had to have had off-spring while aged under five. (B would have had to have been a 'precocious toddler'[20]). This is physically impossible.[1]

Is the gift valid or void? It is valid. The reason does not rest on the fact that it is physically impossible for circumstances to occur in which the gift would vest outside the perpetuity period, but on the facts that (a) in a disposition made before 1 January 1970 'grandchild' is construed as meaning legitimate grandchild;[2] (b) a legitimate child can only be born of parents who are married; (c) a marriage of a person under 16 is void;[3] (d) so B could not have a legitimate child. Thus the gift could not vest outside the perpetuity period, and was held[4] to be valid.

---

16 As in *Jee v Audley* (1787) 1 Cox Eq Cas 324. See also *Ward v Van Der Loeff* [1924] AC 653; (M & B); *Re Dawson* (1888) 39 Ch D 155; (M & B); *Figg v Clark (Inspector of Taxes)* [1997] 1 WLR 603.
17 *Re Deloitte* [1926] Ch 56.
18 *Jee v Audley*, ante. *Re Dawson* (1888) 39 Ch D 155; (M & B).
19 W. Barton Leach (1965) 78 HLR 973 at 992.
20 W. Barton Leach, op cit.
 1 Except perhaps in Latin America. See Morris and Leach, p 85.
 2 For the position after 1969, see Family Law Reform Act 1969, s 15(1), which was brought into force on 1 January 1970 (SI 1969/1140).
 3 Marriage Act 1949, s 2; replacing Age of Marriage Act 1929, s 1.
 4 *Re Gaite's Will Trusts* [1949] 1 All ER 459; (M & B).

Gifts valid by reference to a life in being not referred to in the gift

Early in this chapter we saw that a gift is valid if it can be shown that the gift will vest, if it vests at all, within the life of some person – any person[5] – alive when the gift takes effect. In the great majority of cases, if a gift can be shown to be valid it will be by using the life of a person referred to in the gift, and from the illustrations given so far it will be seen that this is so. But to apply the rule correctly, we must test the validity of a gift by considering the lives of all persons alive at the testator's death, not only the lives of persons referred to in the gift. Consider by way of illustration a gift by a testator,

19. 'to all my grandsons', the testator having two sons, A and B, but no grandsons alive at his death.

When will the gift vest? When A and B die and so can have no more sons. At this point the identity of all the beneficiaries will be known. Must the vesting occur within the lifetime of persons alive at the testator's death plus 21 years? Yes, it must. The gift will vest at the death of the survivor of A and B. A and B are lives in being. So the gift is valid. It will be noted that A and B are not referred to in the gift, but this is of no consequence because, as stated above, lives in being are those of anyone in the world, whether referred to in the gift or not, alive at the testator's death.

The distinction between lives in being and validating lives

The term 'lives in being' is capable of bearing two meanings. Much of the confusion that has arisen[6] over the nature of the rule stems from the fact that the distinction between the two meanings has not always been drawn. The first meaning, the true meaning, of the term, is the lives of everyone alive in the world at the time the gift comes into operation (including, perhaps, any who happen to be in space at that time). It is these lives that we survey in order to test the validity of the gift: it is in relation to these lives that we ask the question 'Must the gift vest, if it vests at all, within the lifetime of some person alive at the testator's death?'

The second meaning that can be attached to the term is the lives of persons which enable us to say (if in fact the grant is such that we *are* able to say) that the gift is valid. For example, in a devise 'to the first son of A to attain 21', if we ask, 'Must the gift vest, if it vests at all, within the lifetime of some person in the world alive at the testator's death, plus 21 years?' we answer, 'Yes; the gift must vest, if it vests at all, within 21 years of A's death. A was alive at the testator's death, and so the gift is valid.' Here it is A's life that enables us to show that the gift is valid. A's life is a life in being in the second, narrow, restricted, sense of the term.[7] A life in being in this sense is thus a life by reference to which the validity of the gift can be established. A life in being in

---

5   *Pownall v Graham* (1863) 33 Beav 242 at 246, line 15.
6   See p 247, n 15.
7   A's life is, of course, also a life in being in the first sense.

this second sense can be distinguished by referring to it as a 'measuring life', or a 'validating life', or a 'governing life'.

Bearing in mind these two meanings of the term, consider a devise by T,

'to A's first son to be ordained', where A is alive at the testator's death.

Must the gift vest within a life in being plus 21 years? The answer, as we saw earlier, is no. Here the life of A, and any children of his, his wife, and everyone else in the world, including Mr Foo Chung Ku, who lives in Outer Mongolia, is a life in being in the first sense. But since we are not able to show that the gift must vest, if it vests at all, within any one of these lives, plus 21 years, there is no life in being in the second, restricted, sense of the term. Thus there are always lives in being in the true sense of the term (short of the world being destroyed by cosmic catastrophe at the same second that the gift takes effect), but only lives in being in the second, restricted, sense if the gift is valid.

The two meanings of 'lives in being' can be illustrated by considering a gift that employs a royal lives clause. Take the gift at 6 above. Who are the lives in being in the true sense of the term? The answer is, all persons in the world (including Mr Foo) alive at the testator's death. Who are lives in being in the restricted sense? The answer is, the lineal descendants of Queen Elizabeth II living at the testator's death. In the gift at 8 above, who are the lives in being in the true sense? Again, all the persons in the world alive at the testator's death. Who are the lives in being in the restricted sense? The answer is that as the gift is void, there are none.

Purpose of the rule[8]

We said at the beginning of this chapter that one purpose of the rule against perpetuities was to prevent there being an undue length of time during which there would be uncertainty as to what person, if any, would be entitled to the property granted. The rule has served another rôle. It forms part of the weaponry of the English law designed to prevent grantors being able to predetermine for too many generations ahead the path of devolution that land shall follow after their death: to prevent land being (in common, but well-established,[9] parlance) 'tied up' for longer than is regarded acceptable on grounds of public policy.

There have been two principal grounds on which it has been argued that it is contrary to public policy for owners to be capable of determining for further into the future than a certain period the devolution of their property. One reason is a matter of economics. During the period that the devolution of property is pre-determined by a settlor, the property is inalienable. If it is inalienable it is likely not to be tended with the care that would be bestowed by an absolute owner. If property is not tended, its economic value declines and, to this extent, the nation's wealth is reduced – 'if it were not for this rule, property would be unproductive, and society would have less income'.[10] In the

---

8   See L. M. Simes, *Public Policy and the Dead Hand* (1955); Maudsley, Chapter 9.

9   Marsden, p 32.

10   Simes, op cit, p 36.

case of land this argument has lost much of its weight since land subject to future interests has come by force of statutory provision (ie under the Settled Land Acts 1882-1925 and the Law of Property Act 1925 and the Trusts of Land and Appointment of Trustees Act 1996) to be held under a trust, the legal estate being held by a trustee, or trustees, who have a statutory power to sell the land.[11]

The other argument,[12] one which retains its validity in relation to land, is concerned with justice: to the extent that a person can pre-determine the devolution of his wealth the freedom of his successors to do likewise is removed: what is freedom for one generation is a fetter for the next.[13] Justice between the generations can thus only be achieved by allowing each new generation to alienate its property free from restraints imposed by a generation that has gone before.

We have met instances earlier in this book of rules that strike at attempts to predetermine the devolution of property after it has left a settlor's hands. For example, in Chapter 3 we saw how it became possible for a fee tail to be barred. Now consider the effect of the perpetuity rule in this context. Suppose that a testator, attempting to keep land within his own family after his death devises land to his son A for life, with remainder to A's infant son B for life, with remainder to B's eldest son for life, with remainder to that son's eldest son for life, and so on, for perhaps 20 generations or more. The testator's intention is frustrated by the rule against perpetuities.[14] The gift to A, to B and to B's eldest son is valid but the succeeding remainders are void.

The rule thus not only prevents an undue length of time existing before it becomes known who will be entitled to land but by so doing (and this has throughout its history been its primary purpose) limits the extent that a settlor can predetermine the devolution of wealth after it has left his hands. It will be appreciated that as between the arguments for and against the creation of future interests, the common law reached a compromise: owners could impose their will, but only for the duration of lives in being plus a further period of 21 years. This formula permitted a grantor to settle property on his widow, his children and any unborn grandchildren during their minority[15] – a form of settlement that was considered to strike a reasonable balance between the wishes of settlors and the public interest (although it was also, as we saw in

---

11   In the case of a trust for sale, in the form of a duty to sell coupled with a power to postpone sale. See Chapters 7-10.

12   Mentioned in Chapter 7. See p 127.

13   L. M. Simes, *Public Policy and the Dead Hand* (1955).

14   As it would have been by an earlier rule, the rule in *Whitby v Mitchell* (1890) 44 Ch D 85 (sometimes referred to as the Old Rule against Perpetuities) under which, in a disposition of realty, any remainder to the issue of an unborn person was void. The rule first appears in the sixteenth century. It was abolished by the Law of Property Act 1925, s 161, the rule by that time being superfluous, since the rule against perpetuities had by then come to achieve in a more satisfactory way the object of the older rule.

15   Before the reduction of the age of majority from 21 to 18 by the Family Law Reform Act 1969, s 1(1).

Chapter 7, a form of settlement that could be used in a way that could lead, as the settlor intended, to the re-settlement of land within a family at each succeeding generation).

The common law rule was successful in attaining its objective, but, as a weapon, it was a blunderbus rather than a rifle, and the success of the rule was gained at the expense of many gifts which fell before it without there being any valid ground of public policy why the gift should not have taken effect.[16] In order to curb the severity with which the common law rule might operate, certain modifications to the rule were made by statute. In particular, important changes were made (following recommendations by the Law Reform Committee[17]) by the Perpetuities and Accumulations Act 1964.

STATUTORY MODIFICATIONS

'Wait and see' under the Perpetuities and Accumulations Act 1964

The common law rule, stated briefly, was that:

> The grant of a contingent interest is void ab initio unless it is certain that the interest will vest within the perpetuity period.

We stressed that for a grant not to infringe the rule it had to be certain, at the time the grant came into operation, that the gift would vest within the perpetuity period. It was not permissible to wait and see whether the gift did in fact vest within the perpetuity period. If there was any possibility of it vesting outside the period, then the gift infringed the rule and was void.

This was the rock on which numerous dispositions foundered. For example, in the case of a gift by will,

> 'to the first of A's sons to marry', A being alive at the testator's death,

whilst it is possible that the gift might vest within the perpetuity period, since it is equally possible that the gift might vest outside the period, the gift infringes the common law rule.

Section 3 of the 1964 Act now makes it permissible, subject to certain conditions being satisfied, to wait and see whether a gift does vest within the perpetuity period. We shall consider shortly what the conditions which have to be satisfied are. In the above example it so happens that the requirements of the Act are satisfied, with the result that we are permitted to wait and see whether the gift vests within the perpetuity period. We cannot say at the outset that the gift is valid. All we can say to begin with is that the gift is not void. We must then 'wait and see' whether a son of A does marry within the perpetuity period. If he does, then we can say for certain that the gift is valid. If no son of A has married by the end of the period, the gift is void.

---

16 On the desirability of the reform, see R. Maudsley, 'Perpetuities: Reforming the Common Law Rule – How to Wait and See' (1975) 60 Cornell LR 334. For a contrary view, see S. M. Fetters, 'Perpetuities: The Wait and See Disaster' (1975) 60 Cornell LR 380.

We must now consider the requirements that must be satisfied for us to be allowed to 'wait and see' whether a gift vests within the perpetuity period.

The first requirement is that the instrument should take effect after 15 July 1964. Thus if a testator makes a will in January 1964 and dies in December 1964, this requirement is satisfied. If he had died in June 1964, the requirement would not have been satisfied.

The second requirement is that the grant must be one which, although void at common law on the ground that it is not certain to vest within the perpetuity period, is nevertheless capable of vesting within the period. If the grant is bound to vest outside the perpetuity period, then not only is it void at common law but furthermore the Act of 1964 will not come to its assistance, with the result that it is void.

Thus the Act of 1964 only makes it permissible to wait and see where the gift may vest within the period or may vest outside the period. As we have seen, if the gift does in fact vest within the period, it is valid. If it ceases to be possible for it to vest within the period at that point, it becomes void.

The statutory 'wait and see' period

The position we have reached so far is this: where a grant may, but is not certain, to vest within the perpetuity period, the Act of 1964 makes it permissible to wait and see whether the gift does vest within the perpetuity period.

What is meant by 'does vest within the perpetuity period'? One could be forgiven for expecting that this means merely that the gift vests within the perpetuity period at common law, the perpetuity period which we have dealt with up to now, but this is not so. The Act lays down that where the Act applies and we 'wait and see', we are permitted to 'wait and see' until the end of, not the common law perpetuity period, but the end of a perpetuity period determined in a manner prescribed by the Act.

So our statement above must be amplified to read 'Where a grant may, but is not certain, to vest within the perpetuity period prescribed by common law, the Act of 1964 makes it permissible to wait and see whether the grant does in fact vest within the perpetuity period prescribed by the Act.'

Thus we have two perpetuity periods to contend with: the common law period for the purpose of establishing whether the Act applies; and the statutory period for establishing, if the Act applies, the length of the period for which we are permitted to 'wait and see'.

What is this statutory period? How is it calculated? How does it resemble and differ from the common law perpetuity period? The statutory period resembles the common law period in that it consists of lives in being plus a further 21 years. It resembles the common law period, too, in that the words 'in being' mean living or *en ventre sa mère*.

The statutory period differs from the common law period in that, whereas in the common law period the lives are those of any persons alive when the gift comes into operation, in the statutory period the lives that may be used are the lives only of those persons specifically listed by the Act.

The Act does not refer to a 'statutory perpetuity period'. It merely provides that for the purpose of the 'wait and see' provision, the perpetuity period is to be determined by reference to the lives of the persons listed in s 3(5). It is clear that the Act does, therefore, in effect create, for the purpose of its 'wait and see' provision, a new statutory, perpetuity period.

Who are the persons whose lives the Act says must be the lives in being for the purpose of this statutory perpetuity period? They are:[18]

(a) the donor
(b the donee
(c) the donee's parents or grandparents
(d) the owner of a prior interest.

Let us look at these in more detail.

(A) THE DONOR

'the person by whom the disposition was made'.[19] The life of the donor can only be of use in the case of an inter vivos grant. In the case of a gift by will, since the testator is dead at the moment the grant comes into operation his life can be of no use.

(B) THE DONEE

'a person to whom or in whose favour the disposition was made, ... '[20]

It will, of course, be impossible at the time the grant comes into operation to know for certain who the donee or donees will be. For example, in the case of a grant to an individual, it is likely that there will be one or more conditions attaching to the grant. For example, in an inter vivos grant by a grantor (G),

'to my son A for life with remainder to my first grandson to attain 21',

there is the condition that G has a grandson, and the condition that the grandson attains 21. Until these conditions are fulfilled we do not know the 'person to whom or in whose favour the disposition was made'. (Indeed, if we did know, the gift would be vested and so the question of perpetuity would not arise.)

Similarly, in the case of a grant to members of a class, we do not know, when the grant comes into operation, which members of the class will be entitled to take. (Here, too, if we did know, the gift would be vested and not contingent and no question of perpetuity would arise.)

The Act, however, goes on to make clear that what is intended is a person who is *potentially* a donee. The full wording[1] is:

'(b) a person to whom or in whose favour the disposition was made, that is to say:

---

17 Fourth Report, Cmnd No 18 (1956).
18 Section 3(5).
19 Section 3(5)(a).
20 Section 3(5)(b).
 1 Section 3(5)(b). The quotation given excludes sub-paragraphs (iii) to (v).

(i)   in the case of a disposition to a class of persons, any member or potential member of the class;

(ii)   in the case of an individual disposition to a person taking only on certain conditions being satisfied, any person as to whom some of the conditions are satisfied and the remainder may in time be satisfied.'

Thus in the example above of an inter vivos grant:

'to my son A for life with remainder to my first grandson to attain 21',

if G has a grandson at the time of the grant then that grandson's life may be used as a life in being under (b)(ii) above.

(C)   THE DONEE'S PARENT OR GRANDPARENT

The words[2] of the Act are, 'a person having a child or grandchild within subparagraphs [(i) or (ii)] of paragraph (b) above, (ie a person who has a child or grandchild who is a potential donee under (b) above, 'or any of whose children or grandchildren, if subsequently born, would by virtue of his or her descent fall within those sub-paragraphs;' (ie a person whose child or grandchild would on birth become a potential donee under (b) above.)[3]

Thus (c) includes a person who is the parent or grandparent of a potential donee, and a person who is potentially the parent or grandparent of a potential donee.

(D)   THE OWNER OF A PRIOR INTEREST

The words[4] of the Act are, 'any person on the failure or determination of whose prior interest the disposition is limited to take effect'.

For example in a grant by will:

'to A for life with remainder to the first grandchild of X to marry',

A is a life in being under (d) as the owner of the interest on the determination of which the disposition 'to the first grandchild of X to marry' takes effect; and in a bequest,

'to the first son of A to be ordained [A being dead and having one unordained son, B] but if A had no such son, then to the first grandchild of C [C being alive] to attain 21',

in applying the statutory wait and see provision to the second limb of the disposition (the first limb being valid at common law), B is a statutory measuring life under this head.

The common law required that the lives which may be used in determining the common law perpetuity period must be 'in being' at the time the grant comes into operation. This requirement applies also to the lives which may be used in the statutory period.[5]

---

2   Section 3(5)(c).
3   See (1969) 27 CLJ 285 (M. J. Pritchard); Maudsley, p 132.
4   Section 3(5)(d).
5   Section 3(4)(a).

In the last chapter we noted that where a grantor limits a gift to vest on the death of the survivor of a class of persons (ie he employed a royal lives clause) the common law renders the condition precedent void for uncertainty if it is not reasonably practicable to ascertain who all the lives were. The 1964 Act preserves this principle as regards the lives that may be used for the statutory 'wait and see' period by providing that lives under (b) or (c) may not be used if the number of persons under either group 'is such as to render it impracticable to ascertain the death of the survivor'.[6]

The alternative fixed perpetuity period made available by the 1964 Act

We saw earlier that in order to extend the perpetuity period at common law, use was made of 'royal lives clauses' by which a gift to a testator's descendants was, for example, in one case limited to take effect 20 years after the death of the survivor of all the lineal descendants of Queen Victoria living at the testator's death. Even if a means such as this was used, the length of the perpetuity period could not be extended beyond the span of a person's lifetime plus a further 21 years. One disadvantage of using 'royal lives clauses' is the risk that the disposition might be held to be invalid on the ground that the lives selected were too numerous for it to be reasonably practicable to ascertain who was the survivor. Even if the disposition is not invalid for this reason, another disadvantage might be the expense and trouble to which executors would be likely to be put in discovering when the last life in being expired. To avoid these disadvantages, the 1964 Act provides an alternative to the common law perpetuity period, namely a fixed period not exceeding 80 years.

For the fixed period to become the perpetuity period of a grant, the Act provides that the period must be 'specified in that behalf in the instrument'.[7] This requirement is satisfied where a fixed period is expressly stated to be the perpetuity period for the disposition, as in a gift,

'to my first great-grandson to marry within 50 years of my death, which period I hereby state is to be the perpetuity period for this gift',

or where, although a fixed period is not specified, the period intended is 'unambiguously identified',[8] as where it was directed that the period should be from the testatrix's death until 1 January 2020.[8]

It will be noted that the fixed period does not have to be 80 years. The fixed period merely must not exceed 80 years. So a grantor can select any period he wishes up to and including 80 years.

This fixed perpetuity period can constitute a perpetuity period for the purpose of determining at the outset whether the gift is valid or void. For example in a gift by will,

---

6   Section 3(4)(a). *Re Thomas Meadows & Co Ltd and Subsidiary Companies (1960) Staff Pension Scheme Rules* [1971] Ch 278, [1971] 1 All ER 239.
7   Section 1(1).
8   *Re Green's Will Trusts* [1985] 3 All ER 455; (1986) 49 MLR 258 (R. Warrington).

> 'to A's eldest grandson living 80 years after my death, which period I hereby specify as the perpetuity period for this gift',

it can be seen from the outset that the gift is bound to vest, if it vests at all, within the specified period and so the gift is valid. In a gift by will,

> 'to all my grandsons alive 100 years from my death. I hereby state that the perpetuity period for the purpose of this gift is to be 80 years from my death',

it is clear at the outset that the gift cannot vest within the fixed period and this is void.

When used in this way the fixed period permitted by the Act in effect replaces the common law perpetuity period: in order to judge whether the gift is void or valid at the outset, the common law period is replaced by the fixed period permitted by the Act.

In another situation the fixed period permitted by the Act serves an additional role. Not merely does it replace the common law perpetuity period for the purpose of deciding at the outset whether the gift is valid or whether it is void, or whether since the Act of 1964 we can 'wait and see'; in addition, it constitutes the period during which we may 'wait and see'. For example, in a gift by will,

> 'to A's first grandson to marry, I hereby state that the perpetuity period for the purpose of this gift is to be 80 years from my death',

we have first to decide whether at the outset the gift is valid or void or whether we can wait and see. Since the gift is not bound to vest within the perpetuity period fixed it is not valid at the outset. It is not bound to vest outside the period fixed so it is not void. It may vest within the perpetuity period fixed in the instrument, so the Act permits us to wait and see. For how long may we wait and see? The answer is, for the duration of the period fixed.[9] Thus where the grantor specifies a fixed period as the perpetuity period and where we are permitted to wait and see, the period during which we may 'wait and see' is not governed by the statutory lives but by the fixed period. (In the last example, if no grandson of A has married by the end of the 80-year period, then the gift fails.)

Position since the 1964 Act if no lives are available

Consider the example at 10 above, on p 218 a gift by will

> 'to the first man to swim the North Sea'.

We saw that this gift was void at common law as there was no certainty that the gift would vest within 21 years of the death of any person alive at the testator's death. Since, however, it is possible that the gift would vest within this period,

---

9   Section 3(4). See M & W, p 221. (Contra, Maudsley, p 114, where it is stated that the wait and see period here is the statutory lives plus 21 years.)

the 1964 Act allows us to wait and see whether the gift does vest within the statutory period. But what is the statutory period? None of the statutory lives is available. In this situation the Act provides[10] that the period during which one may wait and see shall be 21 years. Thus, in the case of the above gift, if no one has swum the North Sea by the expiry of 21years, the gift fails.

Presumption as to age of child-bearing under the 1964 Act

We have now completed our examination of the common law perpetuity rule and the two principal modifications made by the 1964 Act, namely the introduction of the 'wait and see' principle and the alternative fixed perpetuity period with a maximum of 80 years.

These two modifications reduce the likelihood of gifts being made void because of infringements of the common law rule, but they do not eradicate completely the possibility of an irrational position arising. Consider the gift used as an illustration earlier:[11] a gift by will,

'to A's first son to be called to the Bar', A being alive and having two sons, B and C, at the testator's death.

Even if A is a woman of 70, or is a man whose reproductive organs have been removed, the gift, as we saw, is void at common law.[12]

The 'wait and see' provisions of the 1964 Act would permit us to wait and see whether a son of A is called to the Bar within the statutory perpetuity period. If one is so called, the gift is valid; if not, it fails. But it is absurd that there should be any uncertainty as to the validity of the gift. The only way in which the gift could vest outside the common law perpetuity period would be for A to have another son. Since in either of the circumstances posed it is plain that A cannot have another child, the gift must in practice vest, if it vests at all, within the lives of B and C, and so ought in all reason to be treated as valid at the outset.

To remove the absurdity, the 1964 Act provides[13] that certain presumptions with regard to child-bearing are to operate.[14] These are that a male under the age of 14 cannot have a child, and that a female under the age of 12 and over the age of 55 cannot have a child. The Act further provides[15] that evidence may be given to show that a person will or will not be able to have a child (eg that a woman between the ages of 12 and 54 or that a man of any age over 13 will not be able to have a child). Thus, to return to our example, if A is a woman of 70 she is presumed not to be capable of having a child, and so the gift will be valid. If A is a man who has had his reproductive organs removed, then medical evidence of this may be produced and, if accepted, the gift will be valid at the outset.

---

10   Section 3(4)(b).
11   See p 220.
12   *Jee v Audley* (1787) 1 Cox Eq Cas 324; (M & B).
13   Section 2(1)(a).
14   Ie with reference to the determination of a question arising on the application of the rule against perpetuities; not for any other purpose, section 2(1).
15   Section 2(1)(b).

What, it may be asked, if a gift is to be valid as a result of the statutory presumption as to age of child bearing, and the property is distributed on the basis that there can be no more children, and subsequently a child is in fact born, or a child is adopted? The Act provides[16] that 'Where any such question is decided by treating a person as unable to have a child at a particular time, and he or she does so, the High Court may make such order as it thinks fit for placing the persons interested in the property comprised in the disposition, so far as may be just, in the position they would have held if the question had not been so decided.'

It should be noted that the statutory presumptions as to child bearing apply only with regard to determining the validity of a gift under the perpetuity rule; and, further, that they have no application where a gift is valid at common law. In this latter connection consider a gift 'to the first son of Mrs A to attain 21 for life, with remainder to B', where Mrs A is 76 and has no children. The gift is valid at common law. If Mrs A dies without having children, the property passes to B. But the property cannot[17] be passed to B on the testator's death, as the contingent gift is valid, and continues in existence until Mrs A's death. The statutory presumption in the 1964 Act that Mrs A can have no child is irrelevant.

The unborn spouse

Consider a gift by a testator to,

'my son A (a bachelor) for life, with remainder to any wife of A who may survive him for life, with remainder to their children living at the death of the survivor'.

The gifts to A and to the wife are valid, but the gift to the children at common law is void.[18] The reason is that A may marry someone who has not yet been born at the testator's death. So any wife of A cannot be treated as a life in being. The children may become entitled (on the wife's death) more than 21 years from the death of A (or any other person alive at the testator's death).

The Act provides[19] that in the case of a gift such as this (ie 'where a disposition is limited by reference to the time of death of the survivor of a person in being ... and any spouse of that person') one must 'wait and see' whether the gift vests (ie whether any surviving wife of A dies) within the statutory perpetuity period (in our example, within 21 years from A's death).

---

16   Section 2(2).
17   Unless, that is, there is an application to the court for an order, made under its inherent jurisdiction, authorising distribution on the basis that Mrs A can have no children. See *Re White* [1901] 1 Ch 570.
18   *Re Frost* (1889) 43 Ch D 246; (M & B). Cf *Re Garnham* [1916] 2 Ch 413, (gift in the form 'to A for life with remainder to any wife he may marry for life, with remainder to the children of the marriage.' Held, valid, (gift to children cannot vest later than death of A and A is a life in being.))
19   Section 5.

If it does so vest, the gift takes effect as the testator directed. If it does not (ie if A's widow survives him for more than 21 years) then at the end of the period those children living at that time acquire vested interests (in remainder) in the property and they (or if they die between the end of the statutory period and the widow's death, their estates) will take on the widow's death.

Age reduction

AGE REDUCTION UNDER THE LAW OF PROPERTY ACT 1925

We have seen that the rigidity of the perpetuity rule as it existed at common law rendered many dispositions void. We have seen that the 1964 Act relaxed the rule in a number of ways, but the 1964 Act was not the first to intervene in order to save a gift that would otherwise be void under the common law rule.

The Law of Property Act 1925 took the first step in this direction. The assistance given by the 1925 Act can best be understood by looking at the example of a gift by a testator who died in 1920,

'to the first son of A to attain the age of thirty', A being alive at the time of the testator's death, and having one son, B, aged 18.

At common law the gift was void, but if the gift had been,

'to the first son of A to attain the age of 20'

it would have been valid. The gift would have been bound to vest, if it vested at all, within a life in being (that of A) plus 21 years. The Law of Property Act 1925, s 163 enacted that where:

(a) the gift would be void under the common law rule, and
(b) the invalidity was due to the fact that the vesting of the gift had been made to depend on a beneficiary attaining an age greater than 21,

then, in the case of dispositions coming into operation after 1925, the disposition was to be read as if the age that had caused the gift to infringe the rule was deleted and in its place the age of 21 substituted.

So, if the testator who made the gift,

'to the first son of A to attain the age of 30',

(which we considered above) had died in 1926, '21' would be substituted for '30' and so the gift would be valid. If A had a son aged 22 at the time of the testator's death, then the effect of the substitution of 21 for 30 would be to vest the gift in the son immediately. If the son had been 19 at the testator's death, he would have two years to wait until the gift vested. This pushing forward to the time of entitlement is known as '*accelerating*' a gift.

It must be noticed that in order for a gift to benefit from the saving effect of the Act, it had to be void under the common law rule. If it was valid without the assistance of the section, then no substitution of 21 for an age greater than 21 was permitted.

AGE REDUCTION UNDER THE 1964 ACT

The 1964 Act also contains age reduction provisions.[20] These apply to all dispositions which come into operation after 15 July 1964. Section 163 of the 1925 Act was replaced by s 4(6) of the 1964 Act, but the section still applies to instruments which came into operation before 16 July 1964 (and after 1925). The provisions of the 1964 Act are similar in principle to those in the 1925 Act, but differ in two important respects.

The first difference stems from the 'wait and see' principle introduced by the 1964 Act. The effect of this principle is, as we have seen, that certain gifts which would otherwise be void will be valid if they vest within the prescribed period. This principle would, without any substitution of 21 in place of a greater age, save some gifts. For example, in the gift which we have considered,

> 'to the first son of A to attain the age of 30', A being alive at the testator's death and having one son, B, aged 18,

the gift is void at common law, but since it is possible that the gift may vest within the perpetuity period, the Act of 1964 requires us to wait and see whether a son of A does attain the age of 30 within the statutory period. If he does, the gift is valid. In this case the gift will be valid without any substitution of one age for another. But if it later becomes apparent that the gift cannot vest within the statutory period, and so, without some further assistance, would be void, at that point the 1964 Act allows a lesser age to be substituted for the age in the disposition. For example, in the above example, if B died in 1966, one year after the gift came into operation, if A had another son C in 1967, and if A died two years later in 1969, then since the gift could not vest until 1997, and since this would be outside the statutory period (which would end in 1990, ie at the end of the life in being, A, plus 21 years) the gift would be void. The 1964 Act would at this point[1] allow a lesser age to be substituted for 30 in order that the gift should be saved.

If it is apparent at the time that the grant comes into operation that the gift cannot vest within the 'wait and see' period, then the Act permits the substitution to be made at the time the grant comes into operation.

We have said that in the circumstances we have been considering the 1964 Act permits a lesser age to be substituted for an excessive age. What is the lesser age that may be substituted? Where the Law of Property Act 1925 applied, 21 was the age that was substituted for an excessive age. The 1964 Act departs from this practice and this departure marks the second difference between the age reduction provision of the 1925 and the 1964 Acts.

The Act of 1964 provides that where a lesser age may be substituted in order to save a gift from being void, the age to be substituted is the nearest age that would prevent the gift from being void. We can illustrate the effect of this by the example which we considered above in a gift by a testator,

> 'to the first son of A to attain 30, A being alive at the testator's death and having one son, B, aged 18.

---

20   Section 4.
1   Ie at A's death in 1969.

We saw that in these circumstances the 'wait and see' principle was applicable, and so had to be applied. We saw too that it might later become apparent that the gift could not vest within the prescribed period. In our example we found that the statutory perpetuity period ended in 1990, but the gift would not vest until C attained 30 in 1997. If, however, the age that C had to attain in order for the gift to vest had been not 30, but 23, then the gift would have been vested in 1990, and so been valid. It is this age, 23, the nearest age which prevents the gift from being void, that the 1964 Act provides shall be substituted.

So from A's death, the gift is to be read as if it were 'to the first son of A to attain 23'. At A's death in 1969, A's son, C, is two years old. We can say from this time that the gift cannot be void for perpetuity, but we cannot say whether it will vest in C until 21 more years have passed and C has attained the age of 23. During this time we must, in one sense, 'wait and see'. But note that we are not waiting to see if the gift will be void for perpetuity. We are merely waiting to see whether it does in fact vest in C.

Finally, it should be noted that the age reduction provisions of the 1964 Act are not affected by the reduction in the age of legal majority to 18 by section 1 of the Family Law Reform Act 1969.

GIFTS TO A CLASS

So far in this chapter we have been concerned principally with gifts to an individual – 'to the first son of A to attain 21'. We must now consider gifts to a class – 'to all the sons of A who attain 21'. In the main, the principles relating to gifts to individuals apply equally to gifts to a class. Thus the common law rule is first applied. If the gift would fail at common law, then, if the necessary conditions are satisfied, resort may be had to the Act of 1964. (Between 1925 and the Act of 1964, s 163 of the Law of Property Act 1925, concerning age reduction, was available.)

Class gifts under the perpetuity rule at common law

The common law rule is that if the interest of any one member of the class of donees might vest outside the perpetuity period, the gift to the whole class is void. So unless it is certain at the time the instrument comes into operation that the interest of *every* member will cease to be contingent before the end of the perpetuity period, the gift to the *whole* class is void.

It will be recalled that in the context of the rule against perpetuities for the interest of a beneficiary to cease to be contingent, not only must the identity of the beneficiary be known, and not only must he have satisfied any condition specified in the disposition but, in addition, the size of share that he is entitled to must be known. So, even if some members of the class have satisfied the condition specified in a gift, their interest does not cease to be contingent until the size of their share is known, and this will not be known until it is known how many persons will qualify for a share. It is therefore incorrect to say that a gift to a class will be void 'if the interests of some members are bound to vest within the perpetuity period, and the interests of others are not'; because in the case of a gift to a class, the interest of *no* member vests until the interest of *every* member vests. In the context of perpetuities, vesting does not take place by stages as each member satisfied a condition specified. There is only one time of vesting, and that is when the number of members in the class qualified to participate becomes fixed.

We can illustrate the common law rule by the example of a gift by will,

> 'to all A's grandchildren', A being alive and having one child, B, but no grandchildren at the testator's death.

It will not be known how many grandchildren of A there will be, and so what share each beneficiary will be entitled to take, until it is no longer possible for any more grandchildren of A to be born. This will not be until A himself and all his children have died, and since this may not be until after the end of the perpetuity period at common law the gift to the whole class is void.

The rule in *Andrews v Partington*[2]

The rule in *Andrews v Partington*[3] is a rule of construction adopted by the common law to give effect to the presumed intention of one who makes a gift to a class of persons. The rule is therefore excluded by the direction of the settlor, either express or implied.[4] To exclude the rule, the words used must be specific and emphatic,[5] and inescapably incompatible with the application of the rule.[6]

It is an effect of the rule to save some gifts to a class from infringing the rule against perpetuities. Consider a gift by will by a testator (T),

> 'to all A's sons who attain 21', A being alive at the testator's death and having two sons who have reached the age of 21.

The interest of these two sons is still contingent for the purpose of the perpetuity rule, as the third condition of vesting is not yet satisfied (the size of their share is not yet certain). A may have more sons, and these may attain 21 and so become entitled to a share. So it is not until A is dead (and so can have no more children) and all his sons have attained 21 or died under that age, that we know how many beneficiaries are entitled and thus what the share of each is to be. It is not until this point is reached that the gift ceases to be contingent. This might not be for many years after T's death. For example, if at T's death

---

2 (1970) 34 Conv (NS) 393 (J. G. Riddall).
3 (1791) 3 Bro CC 401.
4 *Re Wernher's Settlement Trusts* [1961] 1 WLR 136 at 140; *Scott v Earl Scarborough* (1838) 1 Beav 154; *Re Courtenay* (1905) 74 LJ Ch 654; *Re Henderson's Trusts* [1969] 3 All ER 769, [1969] 1 WLR 651; *Re Edmondson's Will Trust* [1972] 1 All ER 444, [1972] 1 WLR 183; *Pearks v Moseley* (1880) 5 App Cas 714 at 725; *Hale v Hale* (1876) 3 Ch D 643 at 646.
5 *Re Chapman's Settlement Trusts* [1978] 1 All ER 1122, [1977] 1 WLR 1163, CA.
6 *Re Clifford's Settlement Trusts* [1981] Ch 63, [1980] 1 All ER 1013; *Re Tom's Settlement* [1987] 1 All ER 1081, [1987] 1 WLR 1021.

A was aged 42, and if A died at the age of 70, his youngest son being aged five at his death, then the gift to the class would not cease to be contingent until that son died or attained 21, 54 years after T's death.

Is this gift void for perpetuity? No. The gift is bound to vest within the life in being of A plus 21 years. Does this mean that T's executors are bound to retain the money for the whole 54 years before they can distribute it? If this were so, it is quite possible that A's elder sons would by then have died. Admittedly, if they died their share would go to their estates,[7] but the knowledge that this would happen might provide little consolation to the elder sons as they waited impatiently for the gift to vest, seeing old age creep up on them and their capacity to enjoy the money diminish. 'Is this', they might think, 'what T intended to happen? Did T really intend that the money should not be shared out until it became impossible for any more of our brothers to become entitled? Surely', they might think, 'what ought to happen is that after a certain point the number of us brothers who can become entitled ought to be fixed and if our father, A, has any more sons after that time then they ought to be regarded as being born too late to be entitled to a share, regardless of whether they reach 21 or not. If this was done,' they think, 'there would be no need for us to wait so long before we get a share of the money.' What ought to happen, they may decide, is that there ought to be a rule that after a certain point the group of people who can stand a chance of qualifying for a share (by satisfying the prescribed condition or conditions) ought to be fixed. At some point the door to the class ought to be closed. Anyone born before the door to the class is closed should be entitled to a share provided he has already satisfied or later satisfies the conditions attached to the gift. Anyone born after the door to the class is closed should be incapable of qualifying, and so get nothing. This was, in fact, the line of thinking adopted by the common law, and rules were laid down for determining at what point the door to a class was to close. These rules are called the 'class closing rules'.

The rules consist of a general rule and an exception to it. The general rule (the rule in *Andrews v Partington*) is that in the case of a gift to a class of persons, the class closes when the first member becomes *entitled* (by satisfying the stipulated condition) *in possession*,[8] ie not merely in remainder. So in the case of a gift,

'to A for life with remainder to all the sons of B who attain 21',

if one son of B attains 21 before A dies, the class does not close at that point, as the gift to the class is still in remainder. It will not become in possession until A dies.[9] But when A does die, then both requirements of the rule will have been satisfied and the class will close at this point. In the case of a gift by will,

---

7 Since their interests are vested for the purposes of succession. See Chapter 13.
8 See *Re Emmet's Estate* (1880) 13 Ch D 484.
9 This remains the position if A releases his life interest with the intention of accelerating the interests of the remainderman. Re *Kebty-Fletcher's Will Trusts* [1969] 1 Ch 339, [1967] 3 All ER 1076 (reversing *Re Davies* [1957] 3 All ER 52, [1957] 1 WLR 922); *Re Harker's Will Trusts* [1969] 3 All ER 1, [1969] 1 WLR 1124; (1970) 34 Conv (NS) 393 (J. G. Riddall).

'to all X's grandchildren who attain 21',

where X has one grandchild of 10, one of 17 and one of 23 at the testator's death, since one member of the class has attained 21 at the testator's death, and since the property is available in possession from the testator's death, the class closes at that time. The three grandchildren constitute the class. The grandchild of 23 is entitled to his one-third share immediately; the other two are entitled to a one-third share when they attain 21. If one of these two, say the one of 17, dies before reaching the age of 21, then his one-third share accrues to the other two. (The son aged 23 receives half of the one-third share immediately, and the son aged ten will receive the other half of the one-third share (along with his own one-third share) when he attains 21.) No grandchild born after X's death is entitled to any share.

The exception to the rule in *Andrews v Partington* is that where the only condition for entitlement is birth (and not, eg, attaining 21) and no member of the class is born before the gift to the class falls into possession, then no class closing rule applies, and so the class remains open indefinitely, ie until it is no longer possible for any further person to become a member of it.[10] Thus in a gift by will,

'to A for life, with remainder to all B's sons',

and no son has been born to B before A dies, the class remains open until no further sons can become members of the class.[11] This point will not be reached until B dies. So it is on B's death that the class closes, and it is not until then that the property can be distributed. (The gift does not infringe the perpetuity rule: it vests immediately on the death of a life in being, B.)

When the rule in *Andrews v Partington* applies, it brings forward the time when a class closes. This may have the effect of ensuring that the time of vesting is bound to occur within the perpetuity period, with the consequence that the gift may thus be saved from infringing the perpetuity rule. The following three dispositions provide examples of gifts saved by the operation of the rule. A gift by will,

'to all A's children who shall attain 25' where A is alive and has three children, B, aged 27, C, aged 14, and D, aged 10.

Since a member of the class, B, has fulfilled the condition specified, the class closes at the testator's death. The class consists of B, C and D. The gift will vest when C and D have attained 25 or died under that age. C and D are lives in being. The gift cannot vest outside their life times and so is valid.[12] Without the closing of the class, the gift would have been void. As a result of the class closing rule it is valid: it is valid *at common law*.

A gift by will,

'to all A's grandsons', where A is alive and has one grandson, B.

---

10   *Shepherd v Ingram* (1764) Amb 448.
11   *Re Bleckly* [1951] Ch 740 at 749 and 755.
12   *Picken v Matthews* (1878) 10 Ch D 264; (M & B).

Since a beneficiary has fulfilled the condition specified (birth as a grandson of A), the class closes at the testator's death. The gift also vests at this point. Here also the rule saves the gift.

A gift by will,

> 'to A for life with remainder to all B's grandsons who attain 21', where B has two grandsons, C, aged 24, and D, aged 7, at the testator's death.

The class will close at A's death, since at this point a beneficiary (C) becomes entitled in possession. (It is immaterial that C might die during A's lifetime, since if he does so, his interest, being vested for the purposes of *succession*,[13] will pass under his will or intestacy to a person who on A's death will be entitled to take in C's place.) The only persons within the class will, therefore, be B's grandsons born before A's death. (They will only be entitled to *take* under the gift if they attain 21.) Every grandson of B alive at A's death will attain 21 (if he attains 21) within 21 years of the death of A (a life in being). Thus the gift in remainder is valid. Here too the gift is saved by the rule.

The rule will, however, by no means always save a class gift.[14] For example, in a gift by will,

> 'to all the children of A who shall attain 25', where A is alive and has two children, B, aged 24, and C, aged 10,

the class will close when a child of A attains 25. This is not bound to occur within the perpetuity period: B and C may die; A may have another child, D, and then die; D will attain 25 more than 21 years from A's death. The gift is void at common law.

Class gifts under the Act of 1964

'Wait and see'

The 'wait and see' provisions apply in the case of class gifts as they do in the case of individuals: if the gift is void at common law, but may vest with the statutory 'wait and see' period, then it is necessary to wait and see whether the gift does vest within this period.

Age reduction

In the case of dispositions coming into operation after 15 July 1964,[15] the age reduction provisions of the 1964 Act apply to class gifts in the same manner that they apply to a gift to an individual.[16] For example, a gift by will,

---

13 See Chapter 13.
14 See, eg *Re Dawson* (1888) 39 Ch D 155; Cf *Re Drummond's Settlement* [1988] 1 All ER 449; [1986] Conv 427 (P. Luxton).
15 Between the end of 1925 and the 1964 Act, the age reduction provision of s 136 of the Law of Property Act 1925 operated in relation to class gifts as it did to gifts to individuals. See p 233.
16 Section 4(1).

'to all X's children who reach the age of 30', where X is alive but childless at the testator's death,

is void under the common law rule. (The class closing rule does not save it.)

However, since the gift may vest within the perpetuity period, the Act makes it permissible to wait and see whether it does, in fact, vest within the statutory 'wait and see' period. If X later dies, leaving three sons aged six, four and two, then at that point it becomes apparent that the gift cannot vest (ie all the members of the class attain 30) within the statutory wait and see period, namely X's life plus 21 years. (The youngest child would not attain 30 until 28 years after X's death.) In order for the gift to be sure of vesting within the 'wait and see' period, the age specified in the gift would have to be 23. If this had been the age specified, the youngest child (aged two at X's death) would be certain to have attained this age within 21 years of X's death. This being so, the 1964 Act results in 23 being substituted for that specified in the gift.[17]

CLASS REDUCTION[18]

If a gift to a class is void at common law because the gift would vest outside the common law period, but the gift could vest inside the period, then, as we have seen, one may wait and see for the statutory period whether the gift does, in fact, vest inside the period. If, at the end of the period, it transpires that the gift to the class has not vested, because one or more members have not satisfied the condition precedent (eg been called to the Bar) with the result that, without more, the whole gift would fail, then the gift takes effect as a gift to those members of the class who have satisfied the condition; those who have not are excluded. For example, in a gift by will,

'to all A's sons who are ordained', where A is alive at the time the grant comes into operation and has one son, B, who is not ordained,

since A may have more sons, and then A may die, and more than 21 years may then elapse before all A's sons either become ordained or die, the gift is void at common law.[19] But as the gift may vest within the common law perpetuity period, under the 1964 Act we wait and see whether it does in fact vest within the 'wait and see' period.[20] If, before the end of this period, all A's sons are ordained, then the gift vests when the last son becomes ordained. But if, by the end of the period, some of the sons have been ordained, and others have not, then at this point it becomes apparent that the inclusion of the unordained sons in the class would cause the gift to be void.[1] The disposition is read as if the unordained sons were excluded from the class, and the gift takes effect for the benefit of those sons who have been ordained.

---

17   Ibid.
18   *Class closing and the wait and see rule*, P. Sparkes and R. Snape [1988] Conv 339.
19   The gift is not assisted by the rule in *Andrews v Partington*.
20   Section 4(4).
 1   This is because, as will be remembered, a class gift cannot be partially good and partially bad. To be valid the contingent interests of all the members of the class must vest within the relevant period.

If neither the age reduction nor the class reduction provisions of the 1964 Act would by themselves be sufficient to save a class gift which it became apparent would otherwise be void, the 1964 Act[2] permits the age reduction provisions to be combined with class reduction provisions, if the combined effect will save the gift.

MISCELLANEOUS MATTERS

1. Why have statutory lives?

Under the 1964 Act the wait and see period consists of the statutory lives plus 21 years. But why have a statutory list? Why not merely wait and see for the common law perpetuity period? This is a question that has been the subject of debate.[3] In at least one jurisdiction[4] where reform of perpetuity law has been undertaken,[5] it is in fact the common law period that has been made the wait and see period. In this country, the view has prevailed that the common law period cannot serve for this purpose, and that it is therefore necessary to have a statutory list. What is wrong with making the common law period the wait and see period? The answer will be seen by asking, if the common law period of lives in being plus 21 years is proposed for the wait and see period, which sense[6] of the term 'lives in being' is intended? Lives in being in the first sense – everyone in the world at the time when the grant comes into operation, plainly will not do, since it would not be possible to know when the wait and see period ended, as it would not be possible to ascertain the date of the death of the last person alive at the testator's death. Nor will lives in being in the second sense be of any more use. The reason is that these lives are the lives within 21 years from the expiry of which it can be shown (if it *can* be shown) that the gift must vest, if it vests at all. But if there are lives in being in the second sense the gift is valid at common law, and so there is no need to wait and see for any period whatsoever. Thus since lives in being in the second sense only exist if the gift is valid at common law, and the need for a wait and see period arises only if the gift is void at common law, lives in being in the second sense cannot provide us with a wait and see period.[7] But if we are going to wait and see, we have got to know for how long it is permissible to wait and see. So if the wait and see period is to be measured by reference to the lifetimes of certain persons plus 21 years it is necessary for the identity of these persons to be ascertained.[8] This the 1964 Act achieves by providing a list.[9]

---

2   Section 4(3).
3   See in particular, R. H. Maudsley, *The Modern Law of Perpetuities*; and the reply by R. L., Deech (1981) 97 LQB 593 at 605-607.
4   Western Australia.
5   For a survey of methods adopted in various jurisdictions for reform of the law of perpetuities, see Maudsley, op cit, App V.
6   See p 222.
7   (1965) 81 LQR 106 (D. E. Allen).
8   See Maudsley, pp 87-106.
9   Section 3(5).

2. Gifts that follow a void disposition

In a gift such as that,

> 'to my eldest son for life, with remainder to his widow for life, with remainder to A in fee simple,'

there are three distinct dispositions within the one grant. As we saw earlier, each separate disposition must comply with the perpetuity rule. The question we consider now is whether the invalidity of one part of a gift affects the other part or parts. For example, in a gift consisting of two parts, A and B;

1. If Part A is good and Part B is bad, is the validity of Part A affected by Part B being bad? The answer here is, no. The fact that a valid disposition is followed by an invalid one never affects the validity of the first.[10]

2. If Part A is bad and Part B is good, is the validity of part B affected by Part A being bad? The answer to this question is that at common law, if the second (valid) disposition is dependent on the first (void) disposition, the second disposition, although it does itself not infringe the perpetuity rule, is void.[11] 'Dependent' here means dependent on the prior gift not taking effect. For example, in a gift by will,

> 'to A's first grandson to be called to the Bar, but if he has no such grandson, then to B for life',

as the gift to B is a gift to a living person, the gift to B in itself does not infringe the rule. But since it only takes effect if no grandson of A is called to the Bar, it is dependent on the prior gift, and since the prior gift is void, the gift to B is void also.

If the second disposition is not dependent on the first, then at common law its validity is not affected by the fact that the prior gift is void.[12] For example, in a gift by will,

> 'to A's first grandson to be ordained for life, with remainder to B in fee simple',

at common law the prior disposition fails and the gift to B takes effect forthwith.

The 1964 Act abolishes the common law rule relating to dependent gifts and provides[13] that a gift is not to be void merely because it is dependent on another, void, gift.

---

10 *Re Brown and Sibly's Contract* (1876) 3 Ch D 156.
11 *Re Hubbard's Will Trusts* [1963] Ch 275, [1962] 2 All ER 917; *Re Buckton's Settlement Trusts* [1964] Ch 497, [1964] 2 All ER 487; *Re White Rose Cottage* [1964] Ch 483, [1964] 1 All ER 169. The position is no different where the second disposition is to a charity; *Re Mill's Declaration of Trust* [1950] 2 All ER 292.
12 *Re Abbot* [1893] 1 Ch 54.
13 Section 6.

3. Conditional and determinable interests

In Chapter 3 we saw that if G grants land 'to A in fee simple on condition that the land shall not be used for any purpose other than agriculture', then A acquires a conditional fee simple (a fee simple subject to a condition subsequent) and G retains a right of re-entry. G's right of re-entry is a contingent interest, since a condition must be fulfilled before G becomes entitled to exercise it. A right of re-entry is thus subject to the rule against perpetuities. So, if a right of re-entry might become exercisable after the end of the perpetuity period, at common law it is void.[14] In the above example, since the right of re-entry might become exercisable (in the hands of G's successors in title) after the expiry of the perpetuity period, the right of re-entry is void at common law. Since the right of re-entry is void, A's fee simple is absolute. The position would be the same if G had made a gift over after the grant of the conditional interest (eg ' ... and in the event of the land being used other than for agriculture, to B'). Here, too, unless the period during which the condition might occur is limited to the perpetuity period, the gift over is void, and the fee simple absolute.[15] Thus for a condition subsequent to be valid, and for a right of re-entry retained by the grantor (or a gift over) to be valid, at common law it was necessary to restrict the period during which the condition was to operate to the perpetuity period (eg in the above example by adding 'for a period of 21 years from the date of this grant').

The Act of 1964 applies to rights of re-entry in the same way as to other contingent interests. Thus the wait and see provision applies. (In the example above the fee simple would remain conditional until the expiry of the statutory lives plus a further 21 years. If the condition had not by then been fulfilled, the fee simple would become absolute.) It would seem that the 80-year period could be employed as a perpetuity period in relation to the grant.

The application of the rule against perpetuities to determinable interests differs from its application to conditional interests in two ways. It will be recalled that if G grants land 'to A in fee simple until the land ceases to be used for ecclesiastical purposes' then A acquires a determinable fee simple and G retains a possibility of reverter. The first of the differences we have referred to relates to the determining event. In the case of a conditional fee simple, if the condition might occur after the end of the perpetuity period, at common law the condition is void, with the result that the fee simple is absolute. But in the case of a determinable fee simple, there is no requirement that the determining event must be bound to occur, if it occurs at all, within the perpetuity period. So if A granted land to B in 1700 'until the land ceases to be used for ecclesiastical purposes', and the land ceases to be used for ecclesiastical purposes in, say, 2125, then (unless statute in the meantime changes the position) at that time the fee simple will come to an end.

---

14 *Imperial Tobacco Co v Wilmott* [1964] 2 All ER 510, [1964] 1 WLR 902; *Re Pratt's Settlement Trusts* [1943] Ch 356, [1943] 2 All ER 458.

The second difference between conditional and determinable fees in the sphere of perpetuities is that whereas at common law a right of re-entry (or a gift over) is subject to the rule (ie it is void unless it is bound to become exercisable, if it becomes exercisable at all, within the perpetuity period), a possibility of reverter is (notwithstanding that it is a contingent interest) not subject to the rule.[16] Thus, in the example above, if the fee simple granted to B ended in 2125, then at that point the fee simple would become vested in G's successor in title. A point of similarity between conditional and determinable fees is, however, that a gift over following a determinable fee simple is (like a gift over following a conditional fee simple) subject to the rule.[17] Thus if A grants land to B in the terms above, with a gift over on the land ceasing to be used for ecclesiastical purposes to C, then the gift over to C, since it is not bound to vest, if it vests at all, within the perpetuity period, is void.[18] The result here, however, is not that the fee simple is absolute. The limitation determining the fee, not being subject to the rule, remains valid; the possibility of reverter takes effect and the fee simple vests in G's successors in title.

The 1964 Act[19] provides that in the case of a grant of determinable interest made after the commencement of the Act the common law rule against perpetuities is to apply to the determinable interest (ie with regard to the determining event and the possibility of reverter) in the same way that the rule applies to a grant of a conditional interest. Thus in the case of the grant of a determinable interest made after the Act, if the interest might determine after the end of the common law period it is necessary to wait and see for the statutory period whether the determining event occurs before the expiry of this period. If it does, the revertee, (or, if there is a gift over, the person entitled under the gift over) becomes entitled. If it does not, the fee simple becomes absolute.[20]

Thus in the case of grants taking effect after 15 July 1964, determinable interests and conditional interests are, with regard to perpetuities, placed on the same footing, but it should be noted that in the case of the many grants of determinable interests made before the 1964 Act, the old law continues to apply. The table below summarises the position.[1]

---

15   *Re Bowen* [1893] 2 Ch 491; *Re Peel's Release* [1921] 2 Ch 218.
16   *Re Tilbury West Public School Board and Hastie* [1966] 2 OR 20, 55 DLR (2d) 407. The decision in *Hopper v Liverpool Corpn* (1943) 88 Sol Jo 213, that a possibility of reverter is subject to the rule is generally, regarded as not representing the law. See M & W, p 245.
17   *Re Wightwick's Will Trusts* [1950] Ch 260, [1950] 1 All ER 689. The position is no different where the gift over is to a charity; *Re Chambers Will Trusts* [1950] Ch 267; *Re Bowen* [1893] 2 Ch 491.
18   If A directed that on the occurrence of the determining event there should be a gift over to the person entitled to his residuary estate then, since this would be the person entitled by operation of law to the reverter, the gift takes effect; *Re Randell* (1888) 38 Ch D 213; *Re Blunt's Trust* [1904] 2 Ch 767.
19   Section 12(1).
20   Section 12(1).
 1   For the effect of the Reverter of Sites Act 1987, see p 72.

		Disposition made before 16 July 1964	Disposition made on or after 16 July 1964
Conditional fee simple	Condition	Subject to the rule	(Still) subject to the rule, but 'wait and see' under the 1964 Act.[2]
	Right of re-entry	Subject to the rule	(Still) subject, but wait and see'.[3]
	Gift over	Subject to the rule	(Still) subject, but 'wait and see'.[3]
Determinable fee simple	Determining event	Not subject to the rule	Subject, but 'wait and see'.[3]
	Possibility of reverter	Not subject to the rule	Subject, but 'wait and see'.[3]
	Gift over	Subject to the rule	(Still) subject, but 'wait and see'.[3]

4. Kindred rules

The rule against perpetuities is concerned with the time of the initial vesting of a gift. The rule is to be distinguished from the rule against, sometimes termed the rule against perpetual trusts (which is concerned with the duration of a trust once it is established), and from the rule against accumulations (which is concerned with the duration of the period for which income may validly be directed to be accumulated). These two rules share certain features with the rule against perpetuities, but their proper place for study lies, it is suggested, within the law of trusts.[4]

5. Perpetuities and 'test tube babies'[5]

The effect of the introduction of sperm storage is to render void certain gifts that would otherwise be valid at common law. For example, in a gift 'to the first son of A to attain 21' (a gift that hitherto has been valid), A may provide sperm that is stored and not used to fertilise a woman until 100 years after his

---

2 If the rule is infringed, on occurrence of the terminating event the property passes to the person entitled to the reverter.
3 If not saved, the fee simple becomes absolute.
4 See Riddall *The Law of Trusts* (5th edn) p 55.
5 In 1982 the government established a Committee of Inquiry into Human Fertilisation and Embryology. The committee's terms of reference included legal implications in this sphere.

death. Thus the gift is not bound to vest, if it vests at all, within the common law perpetuity period. Clarification could be obtained by a statute that provided that in applying the common law rule against perpetuities no account was to be taken of the possibility of a gift vesting outside the perpetuity period by reason of the use of artificial insemination.

6. Interests not subject to the rule against perpetuities

The following interests are at common law not invalid by reason of the fact that they may vest (or become exercisable, as the case may be) outside the perpetuity period.

(i)   A remainder following a fee tail, provided that the remainder must vest either during the existence of the fee tail or at the moment of its termination.[6]

(ii)   A landlord's right to re-enter leased property in the event of a breach by the tenant of a condition in the lease.[7]

(iii) A mortgagor's right under a mortgage to pay off the mortgage debt.[8]

(iv)   A rentcharge holder's right[9] to re-enter property subject to the rentcharge in order to enforce payment of the rentcharge.[10]

(v)   A contract other than one giving rise to an interest in land, eg a contract by A to pay money to B on the occurrence of a specified future event.[11]

(vi)   A contract giving rise to an interest in land (including an option eg to purchase land) as between the original parties (and their estates); and an option to renew a lease, as between the original parties or their successors in title (ie including assignees[12]).[13]

(vii) The Social Security Act 1973[14] provides that occupational pension schemes that satisfy certain conditions are to be 'exempt from the operation of any rules of law relating to perpetuities which would otherwise invalidate, or might be taken to invalidate, any of the trusts of the scheme or any disposition made under it ... '

7. The debate

The rule against perpetuities has been the subject of much debate. The main issues have been: who are lives in being at common law? Should the common law rule be modified by statute? If the rule ought to be modified, in what way? And, if 'wait and see' is to be introduced, how should the wait and see period

---

6   *Heasman v Pearse* (1871) 7 Ch App 275; *Re Mountgarret* [1919] Ch 294. See Chapter 22.

9   Under LPA 1925, s 121(3).

10   LPA 1925, s 121(6) and Perpetuities and Accumulations Act 1964, s 11.

11   *Walsh v Secretary of State for India* (1863) 10 HL Cas 367.

12   *London and South Western Rly Co v Gomm* (1881) 20 Ch D 562; (M & B).

13   For changes made by the Act of 1964, see ss 3(3) and 9(1) and (2).

14   Section 1, repealing and replacing s 1 of the Superannuation and other Trust Funds (Validation) Act 1927.

be measured?[15] In 1993 the Law Commission published[16] a Consultation Paper that listed what it regarded as defects in the current law and invited comments on certain options for reform.

SUMMARY

At common law, the grant of a contingent interest is void ab initio unless it is certain that the interest will vest, if it vests at all, within a life or lives in being when the grant comes into operation, plus a further period of 21 years from the expiry of the last life in being, plus any relevant gestation periods.

A life in being is the life of any person alive when the gift comes into operation.

A 'royal lives clause' is one by which the settlor limits the time of vesting by reference to the life (or lives) of a person (or persons) specified in the gift.

At common law it is not permissible to 'wait and see' whether the gift vests within the perpetuity period.

The Perpetuities and Accumulations Act 1964 makes it permissible, where a gift is void at common law, to wait and see whether the gift vests within a statutory perpetuity period consisting of the lives of persons specified in the Act.

The 1964 Act entitles a settlor to fix his own perpetuity period of not exceeding 80 years.

The 1964 Act introduced presumptions with regard to the ages at which children could be born.

The Law of Property Act 1925 and the 1964 Act introduced provisions that enabled an age specified in a gift to be reduced in order that a gift should not be void under the rule.

At common law, a gift to a class was void if the interest of any member could vest outside the perpetuity period.

The application of the rule in *Andrews v Partington* could save a class gift from infringing the perpetuity period.

The 1964 Act contained provisions that enabled a class to be reduced in order to save a gift from infinging the rule.

---

15 The debate on these topics can be traced through the literature, the main constituents of which, in chronological order, have been (1938) 51 Harvard LR 638, W. B. Leach (1938) *Perpetuities in a Nutshell*; J. C. Gray (1952) 68 LQR 35, *The Rule against Perpetuities* (4th edn); W. B. Leach *Perpetuities – Staying the Slaughter of the Innocents* (1953) 52 Mich LR 179; L. M. Simes 1955 *Is the Rule Against Perpetuities Doomed?*; L. M. Simes 1957 *Public Policy and the Dead Hand*; R. E. Megarry and H. W. R. Wade 1957 *The Law of Real Property* (1st edn) (5th edn, (1984); W. B. Leach and O. Tudor 1962 *The Rule Against Perpetuities*; J. H. C. Morris and W. B. Leach (1963) 6 UWALR 27 *The Rule Against Perpetuities* (2nd edn); D. E. Allen 1964) 80 LQR 486 *The Rule Against Perpetuities Restated*; J. H. C. Morris and H. W. R. Wade (1965) 81 LQR 106 *Perpetuities Reform at Last*; D. E. Allen 1966 *Who are the Lives in Being?*; L. M. Simes (1970) 86 LQR 357, *Handbook of the Law of Future Interests* (2nd edn); R. H. Maudsley (1975) 60 Cornell LR 355 *Measuring Lives Under a System of Wait and See*; R. H. Maudsley (1975) 60 Cornell LR 380, *Perpetuities: Reforming the Common Law Rule – How to Wait and See*; S. Fetters 1979, *Perpetuities – The Wait and See Disasert*; R. H. Maudsley (1981) 79 LQR 593 *The Modern Law of Perpetuities*; R. L. Deach *Lives in Being Revivied*; R. L. Deach (1984) 4 OJLS 454 *The Rule Against Perpetuities Abolished*.

16 *The Law of Trusts: The Rules against Perpetuities and Excessive Accumulations* Consultation Paper No 133 [1995] Conv 212 (P. Sparkes).

CHAPTER 15

Formalities

Introduction

The meaning of the term 'formality' can be explained by an illustration. T^1 and T^2 hold Blackacre on trust for A for life with remainder to B in fee simple. A transfers his interest under the trust to C. T^1 and T^2 then hold Blackacre on trust for C for as long as A lives. (C will hold a life estate *pur autre vie*). In assigning his interest to C, A was assigning an equitable life interest in the land. The Law of Property Act 1925 provides that an assignment of any equitable interest in any form of property (realty or personalty) must be in writing. So if A merely says to C 'I hereby assign to you, C, my life interest in Blackacre,' then even if there were witnesses present, A's words have no effect. The equitable interest remains in A. But if A writes on the back of an envelope 'I assign my interest in Blackacre to C. (Signed) A', then A's life interest in the land becomes vested in C.

The requirement that certain transactions affecting dispositions of property must comply with a prescribed written formality was first introduced by the Statute of Frauds (1677).[1] The requirement, referred to above, that an assignment of an equitable interest must be in writing is now contained in s 53(1)(c) of the Law of Property Act 1925. This states:

> 'a disposition of an equitable interest ... must be in writing signed by the person disposing of the same, or by his agent thereunto lawfully authorised in writing ...'

From this we learn that the assignment, in order to be valid, must be signed either by A himself (the 'person disposing of the same') or by his agent authorised for that purpose in writing.

In considering what formalities may be required for a particular transaction, it is necessary to ascertain not only whether the transaction must be in writing or whether, as we shall see applies in the case of some transactions, it can be by word of mouth (ie orally, or by '*parol*'), but also, if the transaction must be in writing, whether there are special requirements as to the execution of the document, in particular whether it must be in the form of a deed.[2]

Deeds

From early times a deed has been regarded as being at the highest level of formality that can be required, the more important forms of transaction

---

1   For the history of the statute, see Holdsworth, Vol VI, 379-397.
2   For the purposes served by requiring particular formalities, see (1984) 100 LQR 376 (S. Moriarty).

therefore being required to be by deed. The gravity with which deeds were regarded we reflected by the requirement that a document, in order to take the form of a deed, had not only to be signed but also sealed. Originally sealing was done by the originator making a mark as with the embossment of a signet ring on the surface of hot wax (by convention red wax) on the document. In later times the existence of a seal was accepted as being indicated by the presence of a circle of red paper being affixed to the document or, later, by the document having printed on it a circle containing the letters 'LS' (locus sigilli).

The requirement that for a document to be a deed it must be sealed was abolished[3] by section 1 of the Law of Property (Miscellaneous Provisions) Act 1989.[4] This provides that for a document to be a deed—

1. The instrument must make 'it clear on its face that it is intended to be a deed' eg by describing itself as a deed or expressing itself to be signed or executed as a deed or by, as previously, having printed on it a circle carrying the letters 'LS', or having affixed to it a circle of red paper. ('The client likes to see a red seal. It gives him the feeling that due solemnity had been accorded to the transaction'[5].)
2. The instrument must be executed by,
    (a) being signed by the originator in the presence of a witness who attests the signature; or,
    (b) being signed by some other person at the direction of the originator, in his presence, and in the presence of two witnesses who each attest the signature.
3. The instrument must (continuing the pre-existing rule) be 'delivered' by the originator or a person authorised to do so on his behalf.[6]

The Act confirmed the common law principle that 'sign' includes making one's mark (eg by a cross) on the document.

The provisions of the Act relating to deeds altered the requirements for validity in all cases where a deed is required to be used. But the Act did not alter the position with regard to the *types* of transaction that must, to be effective, be by deed.

A deed becomes 'delivered' if the originator does some act showing that he intends to be bound by it, as by saying such words as 'I deliver this my act and deed' or by doing some act which shows that the deed is intended to be operative, as by handing the deed to the other party. Actual delivery to the other party may thus constitute 'delivery', but actual delivery will not constitute delivery unless the intention is present that 'delivery' should be made. (Conversely, 'delivery' may be made without the document being actually delivered to the other party.) A document that has been executed but not

---

3 Implementing the recommendations of the Law Commission, *Deeds and Escrows* (1987) (Law Com No 163).
4 With one exception. A corporation aggregate continues to be required to affix its corporate seal.
5 [1990] Conv 1.
6 [1989] 105 LQR 553 [1990] Conv 85 (D. N. Clarke).

delivered is termed an '*escrow*' or a document '*in escrow*'.[7] For example, if a vendor (V) is selling land to a purchaser (P), V may execute the conveyance some days before the date when the conveyance is to take effect. The conveyance remains in escrow until the conveyance is completed on P paying the purchase price and V handing over the conveyance, which thereupon becomes 'delivered', and thus a deed. Or L may execute a lease and deliver it to T in escrow on condition that it is not to be 'delivered' until T has performed some act (eg until T has assigned the counterpart of the lease and delivered it to L[8]). Where a deed is delivered in escrow it is not recallable, and on the performance of the condition on which it is delivered, it becomes binding.[9] (We may note here the difference between a deed *inter partes* and a deed *poll*. The former is executed by both parties to the deed (or by both parties, and others); a deed poll is executed unilaterally (eg as in a deed of gift).)

We have mentioned three 'levels' of formality: by deed, in writing (but not by deed) and by parole. One further type of formality remains to be mentioned, the requirement that a transaction should be *evidenced* in writing – not that the transaction should be *in* writing but that some written evidence exists (and can be produced) that the transactions took place. The four 'levels' of formality thus are:

1. By deed.
2. In writing.
3. Evidenced in writing.
4. By parole.

We are now in a position to set out the kinds of transactions that, to be valid, are required to comply with one or other of the formalities set out above.

Formalities required in various transaction

Formality required	Transaction
1. Deed	Conveyance of a legal estate or legal interest in land including the granting of certain forms of legal lease. LPA 1925, s 52(1).
2. In writing: (a) signed by the person disposing of the same, or by his agent authorised in writing;	Disposition of an equitable interest (in any form of property). LPA 1925, s 53(1)(c).
(b) signed by the testator (or by some other person in his presence and by his direction), in the presence of two or more witnesses present at the same time, who sign the will in the presence of the testator.	Will. Wills Act 1837, s 9.

---

7   For examples see *Glessing v Green* [1975] 2 All ER 696, [1975] 1 WLR 863; *Vincent v Premo Enterprises (Voucher Sales) Ltd* [1969] 2 QB 609, [1969] 2 All ER 941, *Longman v Viscount Chelsea* (1989) 58 P & CR 189, CA, [1990] Conv 1.
8   As in *Beesly v Hallwood Estates Ltd* [1961] Ch 105, [1961] 1 All ER 90.
9   *Beesly v Hallwood Estates Ltd*, supra.

Formality required	Transaction
(c) signed by both parties.	Contracts for the sale or other disposition of land. Law of Property (Miscellaneous Provisions) Act 1989.
3. Evidenced in writing: signed by the person declaring a trust:	Declaration of trust respecting land or any interest in land. LPA 1925, s 53(1)(b).
4. By parole only.[10]	Transactions other than those listed above.

It will be noted that prior to the 1989 Act it was only in the case of the execution of a will that the signatur of a witnesses was required.[11] After the Act the signature of a person executing a deed is required to be witnessed. Before the Act deeds were in practice usually witnessed, but this was done as a matter of convenience (in case any dispute later arose regarding the genuineness of the signature of the person executing the deed) not as legal necessity. Thus the absence of the signatures of a witness did not then invalidate a deed.

The following points in the table above call for attention.

REGARDING 1: CONVEYANCE OF A LEGAL ESTATE

The formalities for the creation of leases are subject to special rules. These are considered in Chapter 17. Certain legal leases must, as the table states, be by deed.

REGARDING 2(A): DDISPOSITION OF AN EQUITABLE INTEREST

Section 53(1)(c) applies to any equitable interest in any form of property. Thus it applies to an equitable interest in personalty as well as an equitable interest in realty.[12]

REGARDING (2C): CONTRACTS FOR THE SALE OR OTHER DISPOSITION OF LAND

The requirement that a contract for the sale or other disposition of land must be in writing and signed by both parties was introduced by section 2 of the Law of Property (Miscellaneous Provisions) Act 1989.[13] Prior to the Act, for such a contract to be enforceable the agreement was required, by section 40 of the Law of Property Act 1925, to be either (a) *in* writing, or (b) *evidenced* by 'some note or memorandum' signed (in either case) by the party to be charged or by some other person authorised by him to do so, or (c) evidence by an act of part performance. (Part performance is explained later.) Section 40 of the 1925 Act was repealed by the Act of 1989.

Section 2 of the 1989 Act provides:

---

10 Unless subject to special requirements not considered in this chapter.
11 Witnesses are required in certain other instances, eg where a power of attorney is executed by the direction and in the presence of the donor; Powers of Attorney Act 1971, s 1.
12 (1979) 43 Conv (NS) 17 (G. Battersby).
13 [1989] Conv 431 (P. H. Pettitt); (1989) 105 LQR 553 (R. E. Annand).

'(1) A contract for the sale or other disposition of an interest in land can only be made in writing and only by incorporating all the terms which the parties have expressly agreed in one document or, where contracts are exchanged, in each.

(2) The terms may be incorporated in a document either by being set out in it or by reference to some other document.

(3) The document incorporating the terms or, where contracts are exchanged, one of the documents incorporating them (but not necessarily the same one) must be signed by or on behalf of each party to the contract.

(4) Where a contract for the sale or other disposition of an interest in land satisfies the conditions of this section by reason only of the rectification of one or more documents in pursuance of an order of a court, the contract shall come into being, or be deemed to have come into being, at such time as may be specified in the order.'[14]

The following points call for attention:

1.   It is important in this field to distinguish between, on the one hand, a *contract*, eg by which V promises that he will sell Blackacre to P, in return for P's promise that he will pay £5,000 for the land (the contract passing no legal title in the land whatsoever); and, on the other hand, a *conveyance* – the actual transfer of the legal fee simple by V to P. V and P may make the contract in January, the conveyance may not be executed until June. It is with the contract, not the conveyance, that s 2 is concerned.

2.   Section 2 of the 1989 Act applies to a contract for the *sale or other disposition of land*. So the section applies to other dispositions of land, besides sale. Thus if A contracts that he will mortgage the land to B, the contract must comply with s 2. But the section does not[15] apply to a contract to grant a lease that is for a period not exceeding three years, and takes effect in possession and is for the best rent reasonably obtainable without taking a fine, the reason being that the grant of such a lease can be made orally,[16] and it would be anomalous to require a higher level of formality for a contract to grant such a lease than for the grant itself.

3.   Section 2 applies to a contract for the sale or other disposition of land or *an interest in land*. So the section applies to contracts for the disposition of equitable as well as legal interests in land. The section does not apply to contracts for the grant of a licence,[17] a licence not being an interest in land.[18] Where V grants P an option to purchase land, the grant constitutes a contract conditional on P's acceptance. The grant must, but the acceptance need not, comply with section 2.[19]

4.   Section 2 of the 1989 Act requires the contract to be *in* writing. It is no longer sufficient, as it was under section 40 of the 1925 Act, for the contract to

---

14   *Wright v Robert Leonard (Developments) Ltd* [1994] NPC 49; *Commission for the New Towns v Cooper (Great Britain) Ltd* [1995] Ch 259, [1995] 2 All ER 929.

15   Section 2(5).

16   See Chapter 17.

17   See Chapter 20.

18   *Ashburn Anstalt v Arnold* [1989] Ch 1, [1988] 2 All ER 147; M & R.

19   *Spiro v Glencrown Properties Ltd* [1991] Ch 537, [1991] 1 All ER 600 [1991], (M & B); *Armstrong & Holmes Ltd v Holmes* [1994] 1 All ER 826, [1993] 1 WLR 1482; [1994] Conv 483 (N. P. Gravells).

be *evidenced* by some writing,[20] for example by an exchange of letters between the parties (or by a letter from the party against whom the contract was sought to be enforced) that shows that an oral agreement had been made.

5.   The written document that constitutes the contract must incorporate[1] all the terms of the contract, either by setting out the terms or by referring to another document (eg one setting out standard conditions for parties to a particular type of transaction). But where a contract contains all the terms necessary for the sale or other disposition of land (and otherwise complies with section 2), but omits to state some other matter that had been agreed by the parties, it may be held that the contract is nevertheless valid because all the necessary terms for the disposition of an interest in land had been included, and that the agreement on the other matter formed an agreement that, not constituting a 'land contract', did not have to comply with section 2 and so was enforceable as a valid (collateral) contract under the general law of contract.

6.   The document must be signed[2] on behalf of each party to the contract. (Under section 40, the written contract, or the note or memorandum that provided evidence of the contract, did not have to be signed by both parties, only by the party against whom the contract was sought to be enforced, ie by the defendant in an action in which a decree of specific performance was sought.)

7.   The section applies not only to the making of a contract at the outset, but also to the variation of any material term.[3]

8.   The section applies only to contracts made after the date on which the section was brought into force, 27 September 1989.[4]

9.   The section does not apply to a contract made in the course of a public auction (when the contract is made at the fall of the auctioneer's hammer), nor to a contract regulated under the Financial Services Act 1986.[5]

10.   The section does not, it has been held,[6] apply to a 'lock-out' agreement. A lock-out agreement is one in which a seller agrees with an intending buyer that for a specified period (commonly two weeks) he will not accept an offer from another person. Where a seller is willing to make a lock-out agreement the buyer receives protection against being 'gazumped', ie, being told by the seller, in the period between the offer and the contract being signed, that he has received a higher offer and that if the buyer wishes to buy the property he must match the higher price of lose the property. A lock-out agreement does not ensure that a buyer who has made an offer will get the property. But if the seller breaks the agreement (by selling to a higher bidder) the buyer has an action for damages for breach of contract – damages at a level the prospect of

---

20   *Long v Tower Hamlets London Borough Council* [1996] 2 All ER 683, [1996] 3 WLR 317.
1   *Record v Bell* [1991] 4 All ER 471, [1991] 1 WLR 853; [1991] Conv 471 (M. Harwood); [1991] CLJ 999 (C. Harpum); *Tootal Clothing Ltd v Guinea Properties Management Ltd* [1992] 41 EG 117, [1993] Conv 89 (P. Luther); *Wright v Robert Leonard (Developments) Ltd* [1994] NPC 49, (1996) 140 Sol Jo 564.
2   Section 2(3). *First Post Homes Ltd v Johnson* [1995] 1 WLR 1567; [1995] Conv 484 (M. P. Thompson).
3   *McCausland v Duncan Laurie Ltd* [1992] 1 WLR 38, CA.
4   Section 2(7).
5   Section 2(5).
6   *Pitt v PHH Asset Management Ltd* [1993] 4 All ER 961, [1994] 1 WLR 327, CA.

which may dissuade the seller from gazumping. A lock-out agreement is not subject to section 2 by reason of its being held to be a collateral agreement and as such outside the section, as noted above.

11.   Prior to the repeal of section 40 of the 1925 Act, a contract for the sale or other disposition of land was enforceable not only if it complied with the requirements of the section, but also (as noted above) if the requirements of an equitable doctrine, the doctrine of part performance, were complied with. This doctrine was developed by equity during the previous two centuries to remedy injustices that could arise from fraudulent reliance on section 4 of the Statute of Frauds (1677) (the provision from which section 40 of the Law of Property Act 1925 was derived). The doctrine, the continued validity of which had been confirmed by section 40(2) of the 1925 Act, was effectively (though not specifically) abolished by section 2 of the 1989 Act. Although dead, the shadow of the doctrine is likely to haunt the law for decades to come. For this reason, and because a host of earlier cases are intelligible only if the nature of the doctrine is understood, a brief note on the doctrine follows.

The doctrine of part performance[7]

The Statute of Frauds 1677 provided that a contract for the sale or other disposition of land must, to be enforceable, be in writing or be evidenced by some writing. The section (like its successor, section 40(1) of the 1925 Act) did not make the contract that failed to comply with the statute void, it merely made it unenforceable.

With time, equity came to accept that, notwithstanding the absence of any writing, if one party did some act in relation to the contract that would, on the balance of probabilities, not have been done if no contract had been entered into, the act performed would be treated as evidence of the existence of a contract and entitle the party who had performed the act to enforce it. (The doctrine was not, incidentally, that if one party did his part of the contract, he was entitled to compel the other party to perform his. The act of part performance that brought the doctrine into play might or might not be one that the contract required to be performed.)

For example, suppose that V contracted to sell his house to P. The contract was oral. Before conveying the title to P, V allowed P into the house to make certain alterations to the bedrooms. P later declined to complete, relying on the fact that section 2 of the 1677 Act (or, after 1925, section 40 of the 1925 Act) had not been complied with. Here Equity would be prepared, at its discretion, to treat V's willingness to allow P into the house to alter the bedrooms as sufficient evidence of the existence of a contract to enable V to enforce the contract against P (by means of a decree of specific performance). A multitude of cases came before the courts on the question as to whether a particular act was or was not a sufficient act by one party to enable him, by virtue of the doctrine, to enforce a contract.

---

7   For a fuller treatment see pp 235-244 of the 4th edn of this book.

The factor that enabled equity to apply the doctrine was that neither the Statute of Frauds (1677) nor the Act of 1925 made a contract without writing void, but merely unenforceable. Equity's contribution was to evolve a form of evidence that it treated as an acceptable alternative to that required by statute.

Under the Act of 1989 a contract that does not comply with the requirements of section 2 is not merely unenforceable, it is a nullity. Thus the doctrine of part performance was left with no role to play: it was left by the 1989 Act as a prop with nothing to prop up.[8]

It may be helpful here to recapitulate.

1. Before the Law of Property (Miscellaneous Provisions) Act 1989, for a contract for the sale or other disposition of land to be enforceable it had to be,
    (a) in writing; or
    (b) evidenced by some writing; or,
    (c) evidenced by a sufficient act of part performance.
2. After the 1989 Act for such a contract to be valid it must:
    (a) be in writing; and,
    (b) be signed by both parties; and,
    (c) incorporate (directly or by reference to another document) all the contract's terms.

What if, after the 1989 Act, V and P agree that P should purchase V's house, the contract is not put into writing (or is not signed by both parties), P pays V a deposit of £1,000 and later V declines to complete? Or if, at P's request, V undertakes certain work on the property, and then P declines to complete? The Law Commission, in its recommendations that led to the passage of the 1989 Act, envisaged that in such circumstances a remedy would lie in quasi-contract, in the first case by P for the return of the money (on the grounds of total failure of consideration), in the second case by V for the value of the work done (based on *quantum meruit*).

As a further remedy in the event of injustice, the Commission cited the possibility of action in equity for rectification, or one based on proprietary estoppel. The Commission therefore saw 'no cause to fear that the recommended repeal and replacement of the present section [section 40] as to the formalities for contracts for the sale or other disposition of land will inhibit the court in the exercise of the equitable discretion to do justice between parties in individual otherwise hard cases.'[9] An examination of the circumstances in which proprietary estoppel might provide an adequate remedy where injustice followed from a failure to comply with the requirements of section 2, concluded that, 'The Law Commission declined to provide a substitute for the doctrine of part performance on the basis that there were sufficient remedies available in the existing law to deal with hard cases and these doctrines had the advantage over part performance of being more flexible. [But] there is no certainty that

8   For the possible continued influence of the doctrine see *Morritt v Wonham* [1993] NPC 2. For a comment on the bizarre nature of the decision, see M. P. Thompson, [1994] Conv 233.

there will be remedies available or that their availability will be adequate. It seems that the relevant law is even less clear than the doctrine of part performance.

'It can only be concluded that there should have been a detailed consideration of the availability of remedies before the law was changed. In view of the potential imbalance between the parties and the various issues to be determined in relation to each relevant doctrine, it is not an area that it is desirable to have developed on a case by case basis. There are a number of issues of principle that need to be considered. It would have been better had the Law Commission considered these so that they could have been elucidated and, if necessary, set out in legislation.'[10]

Regarding 3(a): Declarations of trust

(i)   A declaration of trust can arise in two ways:
(A)   A holds Blackacre in fee simple. He transfers the land to T^1 and T^2 on trust for B. The transaction comprises two elements:
   (a)   the transfer of the legal fee simple from A to T^1 and T^2;
   (b)   the creation of the trust. The trust is created by A's *declaration* that T^1 and T^2 are to hold the land, not beneficially, but as trustees on trust for B.

In considering what formalities must be observed for A to vest the land in T^1 and T^2 on trust for B it is necessary to consider (a) and (b) above separately.
   (a)   In order to convey the legal fee simple to T^1 and T^2, A must execute a deed.
   (b)   In order to create the trust, A's declaration that T^1 and T^2 are to hold the land on trust for B must comply with s 53(1)(b) and thus be evidenced by some writing signed by A. If A conveys the legal fee simple to T^1 and T^2 by deed, and (as may in some instances be done) in that deed declares that T^1 and T^2 are to hold the land on trust for B, then s 53(1)(b) is satisfied.

(B)   Suppose that A holds the legal fee simple absolute. He wishes to constitute himself trustee of the land for B, ie he wishes to give to B the beneficial interest in the land. A therefore declares that henceforth he holds Blackacre on trust for B. There is no need to transfer the legal estate to a trustee or trustees: the legal estate is already vested in the person, A, who is henceforth to hold the land as trustee. So here we are concerned solely with the declaration of trust and, under s 53(1)(b), this declaration must be evidenced in writing signed by A. Thus there is no need for the declaration itself to be *in* writing; it is

9   Working Paper No 92 (1985), para 5.4.
10   *Estoppel: An Adequate Substitution for Part Performance?* C. Davis, (1993) 13 OJLS 99.

sufficient if B can produce evidence, in writing, of the declaration, signed by A: if the declaration is 'manifested and proved by some writing'. Thus if B can produce a letter signed by A saying 'You remember that last Saturday I told you that from then on I was holding Blackacre on trust for you? Well, I've changed my mind', then notwithstanding that the declaration itself was oral (and notwithstanding A's attempt to change his mind), the letter will satisfy s 53(1)(b) and B can enforce the trust against A.

We can illustrate, and contrast (A) and (B) above thus:

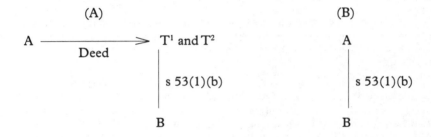

(ii) Section 53(1)(b) relates only to a declaration of trust respecting land (or any interest in land). Thus a declaration of trust in which the trust property is personalty need not comply with s 53(1)(b) and can be made orally. So if A transfers certain shares to T^1 and T^2 and declares (eg he tells them over the telephone) that they are to hold the shares on trust for B, a valid trust is created. If B is to enforce the trust against T^1 and T^2 he will, of course, have to produce evidence, for example that of witnesses to the telephone call, sufficient to satisfy the court that the declaration by A was made. But the mere fact that the declaration of trust was oral does not invalidate the creation of the trust.

Similarly if A holds certain shares, and he declares that he holds them henceforth on trust for B, this oral declaration creates a valid trust. Again, the question of proof is a separate matter.

(iii) It must further be noted that s 53(1)(b) applies to a declaration of trust respecting *any* interest in land. Thus it applies to a declaration of trust respecting a legal or an equitable interest in land. In (A) and (B) in para (i) above, the property in respect of which a trust was declared was a legal interest in land. Now consider an example of a declaration of trust respecting an equitable interest in land. Suppose that a settlor (S) settles Blackacre on trust for A for life with remainder to B in fee simple. B now holds an equitable interest in remainder. He wishes this interest to be held on trust for C. B can therefore either assign his equitable interest to t^1 and t^2 on trust for C, or he can declare himself trustee of the interest for C; thus:

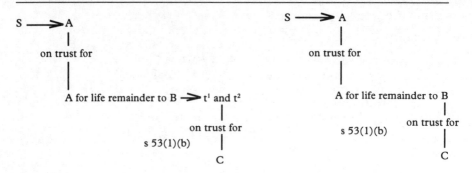

In each case the declaration by B (either that t[1] and t[2] hold the interest on trust for C, or that he himself holds the interest on trust for C) is a declaration of trust respecting an interest in land. It must therefore comply with s 53(1)(b) and thus be evidenced in writing, signed by B.

The transfer by B of his equitable interest to t[1] and t[2] is a disposition of an equitable interest in property. It must therefore comply with s 53(1)(c) and so must be in writing. If B makes a written (and signed) assignment of his interest to t[1] and t[2] on trust for C, this will not only comply with s 53(1)(c) (as regards the disposition) but will also be (more than) sufficient to satisfy s 53(1)(b) (as regards the declaration of trust).

It should be noted that if the law prescribed a certain level of formality for a certain transaction, that requirement is met if that level of formality, or any higher level of formality, is used. Thus if a disposition of an equitable interest is made by deed, this is sufficient – more than sufficient – to satisfy s 53(1)(c). Again, if the declaration of trust in land is made by the person able to declare the trust in writing, this is sufficient – more than sufficient – to satisfy s 53(1)(b).

However, the requirements as to whether the transaction must be signed by the originator, or whether it can be signed by an agent, and as to how the agent may be authorised, must also be satisfied. Thus, although s 53(1)(b) is more than satisfied if a declaration is in writing (and not merely evidenced in writing), the provision that the signature must be that of the person able to declare the trust must also be observed.

In Chapter 5 we saw that a trust may be either express, or implied (including resulting) or constructive. Section 53(2) provides that the requirements of s 53(1)(b) (declaration of trust) and s 53(1)(c)[11] (assignment of equitable interests) do not apply to implied (including resulting) or constructive trusts. The formalities prescribed by s 53(1)(b) thus apply only where a trust is created expressly, and those by s 53(1)(c) only apply where there is an express assignment, and not, eg, where an equitable interest arises from a finding that a constructive trust exists.[11]

---

11   *Neville v Wilson* [1997] Ch 144, [1996] 3 All ER 171, CA; [1996] Conv 368 (M. P. Thompson), [1996] CLJ 436; (1997) 113 LQR 213 (P. Milne).

'Formality' and 'Form'

In this chapter we have been concerned with formalities, not with 'form'. ie with a particular form of wording. In the case of many transactions, for example in the case of a conveyance of a legal fee simple, certain forms of wording have become customary. But there are few instances where a certain specified form of wording is required, for example in connection with the creation of mortgages.[12]

Whilst the use of a particular form of wording is required only in a few, and exceptional instances, the observance of the correct formality is frequently of critical importance.

SUMMARY

A conveyance of a legal fee simple must be by deed.

The grant of any other lease that takes effect in possession and is for a period not exceeding three years and is for the best rent reasonably obtainable may be made orally.

The grant of any other lease must be by deed.

The grant of any other legal interest, eg an easement, must be by deed.

The assignment of an equitable interest in any form of property must be in writing.

A declaration of a trust of land must be evidenced in writing.

Prior to the Law Reform (Miscellaneous Provisions) Act 1989, a document was a deed if it was signed, sealed and delivered. After the Act a deed is required to be signed and witnessed, and delivered.

Prior to the Law Reform (Miscellaneous Provisions) Act 1989, a contract for a disposition of an interest in land was required to be either in writing, or evidenced in writing or by an act of part performance. After the Act a contract for the disposition of an interest in land must be in writing and signed by both parties.

The effect of the Law Reform (Miscellaneous Provisions) Act 1989 is to render the doctrine of part performance purposeless.

---

12   See Chapter 23.

CHAPTER 16

The Doctrine in Walsh v Lonsdale[1]

Creation of an equitable fee simple

IMPERFECT CONVEYANCE

We have learned that a transfer of a legal fee simple must be by deed. Thus if a vendor (V) purports to convey the legal estate to a purchaser (P) by a document which is not a deed (because before the Law of Property (Miscellaneous Provisions) Act 1989 it was not under seal; or after the Act, because it was not witnessed), the document is ineffective to transfer the legal fee simple, which therefore remains in V. The conveyance is 'imperfect' (or 'informal'). But let us suppose that P has paid V the purchase price of £5,000. Does the document executed by V give P no interest in the land? The answer is that the document may give P an equitable fee simple in the land. How is this result obtained? We can set out the steps in the chain of reasoning in the following way. The matter is best explained in the context of the law as it stood before the Law of Property (Miscellaneous Provisions) Act 1989 abolished the requirement that a deed must be under seal, and required a contract to be signed by both parties.

1. The document (which, let us suppose, was dated 1 June) was insufficient to convey the legal fee simple to P. Thus P would have paid his money, yet received no legal interest in the land.

2. If the document had been intended to be a contract for the sale of the land, then, being in writing, it would (being in compliance with s 40(1) of the Law of Property Act 1925 and, before that, s 4 of the Statute of Frauds (1677)) have constituted a contract enforceable by P against V.

3. It became established that if P sought a remedy against V in the Court of Chancery, equity would treat the imperfect conveyance as a contract for the sale of the land by V to P (ie a contract by V that he would transfer the legal estate to P on 1 June).

4. Further, equity would grant P a decree of specific performance against V requiring him to carry out the contract by executing a deed transferring the legal fee simple to P.

5. Since equity treated the imperfect conveyance as a contract by V to convey the legal estate to P on 1 June, equity was prepared to grant a decree of specific performance against V on any day from 1 June onwards.

6. Thus if P sought a decree against V on, say, 1 July, then (provided there was no reason for equity to decline to exercise its discretion in his favour) P could obtain the decree on that day.

---

1 (1882) 21 Ch D 9; (M & B); [1987] 7 OJLS, No 1, 60 (S. Gardner).

7. Since V ought to have executed the deed immediately on the grant of the decree on 1 July, and since equity looked on that as done which ought to be done, it became established that equity would regard P as holding an (equitable) fee simple from the date of the decree. (The legal fee simple remained with V, because no deed had been executed.)

8. Finally, it became established that since the imperfect conveyance (being treated by equity as a contract) imposed an obligation on V to convey the legal estate to P on 1 June, and since equity looked on that as done which ought to be done, equity would regard the parties as being in the same position as if V had conveyed the fee simple to P on 1 June. Thus, in the eyes of equity, from 1 June, from the date of the imperfect conveyance, P held an equitable fee simple in the land. The legal fee simple continued in the hands of V, but since from 1 June it was subject to P's equitable interest, from that date V held the legal fee simple, no longer as beneficial owner, but as a trustee, on trust for P. Since the trust was imposed by equity, it was a constructive trust: V held as a constructive trustee.

In the above example, which related to the position before the Law of Property (Miscellaneous Provisions) Act 1989 (hereinafter in this Chapter, 'the 1989 Act'), V should have used a deed to convey the legal fee simple to P, but the conveyance was merely in writing (and not, as then required, under seal). If the conveyance was not even in writing, the same principles might nonetheless have applied. We know, from the previous chapter, that in order to be enforceable, a contract for a disposition of an interest in land had (before the 1989 Act) to be either in writing, or evidenced in writing, or evidenced by an act of part performance. Thus, if V's conveyance to P was merely oral, then provided that P could either (a) produce evidence, in writing signed by V, of V's intention to convey the legal estate to him, or (b) show a sufficient act of part performance by himself, P would have obtained an equitable fee simple from the moment of the oral conveyance. He obtained an equitable fee simple for the same reasons that we have already considered – the oral transactions together with either the evidence in writing or the act of part performance would have been sufficient to create a contract enforceable against V; V should have carried out the contract; equity would have granted specific performance of the contract; and equity looked on that as done which ought to have been done.

The kinds of act of part performance by P that would have been sufficient in this context were the same as those that would have been sufficient in the context of a contract. Thus if V made an oral disposition of the land to P, and P entered into possession of the land with V's consent, then, since that constituted a sufficient act of part performance by P, P obtained an equitable fee simple, from the date of the oral disposition. (Acceptance by the court of P's act as a sufficient act of part performance opened the gate to evidence of all the terms of the transaction, including the date on which it took effect.)

IMPERFECT CONVEYANCES AFTER THE 1989 ACT

The 1989 Act affects the position in two ways:

1. A conveyance will be imperfect after the Act if (in our example) V's signature is not witnessed.

2. A contract for the sale or other disposition of land is valid only if it is signed by both parties.

Thus where V purports to convey land to P after the 1989 Act in a document that is not a deed (eg because it is not witnessed), but the purported conveyance is in writing signed by V and P (and so complies with the requirements of the 1989 Act for contracts for the sale of land), the chain of reasoning set out above holds good and P will obtain an equitable fee simple. After the 1989 Act P will not, however, as before the Act, obtain an equitable fee simple based merely on the existence of evidence in writing, or on an act of part performance.[2] The effect of the 1989 Act is thus markedly to restrict the circumstances in which an imperfect conveyance gives rise to the creation of an equitable fee simple. By the Act equity's hands are substantially tied. Whether equity will wrestle free, so as to be able to continue to provide a remedy where it considers that injustice has been done remains to be seen.

EXPRESS CONTRACT

If equity is prepared to regard an imperfect conveyance as a contract (and from this starting point give P an equitable fee simple), does the same consequence (ie P obtaining an equitable fee simple) follow from a transaction which is not merely a transaction which equity is prepared as it were to 'pretend' is a contract, but which in fact *is* a contract for the disposition of the land? The answer is, yes. Thus if V makes a contract with P for the sale of Applecroft to P, from the time the contract comes into existence, P acquires an equitable fee simple in the land. (After the 1989 Act P will acquire an equitable fee simple only if the contract complies with section 2 of the Act.)

CONSIDERATION

The doctrine with which this chapter is concerned thus rests either (A) on an actual contract, or (B) on a conveyance which equity is prepared to treat as if it had been a contract. In the case of (A), in order for a contract to exist, all the elements of a valid contract must necessarily be present, including consideration, ie the price agreed between V and P. In the case of (B) the circumstances must be such that equity is willing to treat the conveyance as if it had been an enforceable contract. Thus in (B) if a necessary element of a valid contract is lacking, the chain of reasoning which leads to P obtaining an equitable fee simple is broken. Thus it is necessary for P to give consideration for the imperfect conveyance. Without consideration P obtains nothing. Thus if V purports to convey the legal fee simple to P and the purported conveyance is by way of gift, P obtains neither a legal nor an equitable interest in the land. As P gives no consideration, equity regards him as deserving no assistance. If V had intended to make a gift of Blackacre to P, and had failed to do so because the incorrect formality was used, equity considers that it is up to V to put the matter right, if he so wishes. If he decided not to perfect the imperfect gift (by executing a deed) equity will not compel him to do so. In refusing to intervene

2   [1990] Conv 441 (J. Howell).

equity acts in accordance with its maxim, 'There is no equity to perfect an imperfect gift' and with the maxim 'Equity will not assist a volunteer'. These two maxims are met in various branches of the law of property, but often, as in the matter under discussion, they complement each other and lead to the same result.

EFFECT OF ACQUISITION OF AN EQUITABLE INTEREST

In the instances we have discussed, P acquires an equitable fee simple in the land. But the effect of his acquiring an equitable fee simple is not in all respects the same in the case of an enforceable contract as it is in the case of an imperfect conveyance. For example, let us suppose that V makes a conveyance of the fee simple in Blackacre to P on 1 June in a document that is signed by V and P but V's signature is not witnessed (and so the document is not a deed), and let us suppose that Blackacre had previously been leased to T for seven years at a rent of £100 a month. From 1 June P holds the equitable fee simple in the land. Therefore rent which accrues after that date must be held by V on trust for P.

Contrast this with the situation in which V makes an enforceable contract with P on 1 June that he will convey the legal fee simple to him on 1 July. In this case P acquires an equitable fee simple in the land on 1 June and from then on V holds the legal fee simple on trust for him. But rent paid by T for June belongs to V beneficially. It is not until after the date fixed for completion has passed that if T pays rent to V, he holds this on trust for P. Similarly, if the land had not been leased to T, V would have been able to retain possession of the land until the date for completion.

If V can retain possession of the land until completion or, if it is leased, he can keep the rent payable before completion, does the fact that, from the date of the contract, he holds the legal fee simple on trust for P have any practical consequence? The answer is that it does. From the date of the contract he holds the legal estate as trustee for P and commits a breach of trust if he does anything inconsistent with the fiduciary duty that he owes to P. It is not inconsistent with this duty for him to retain possession until completion, or, if the land is leased, to retain the rent paid by T before the date of completion; but, as regards the property itself, this must be protected and managed with the same care that a trustee is obliged to take of any property that he holds as a trustee. Further, and this is a matter of crucial importance, since a trustee is not under a duty to insure trust property, if the property is destroyed, the loss falls on P.[3] So it is important that before signing a contract for the purchase of land, P should arrange for the property to be insured from the date of the contract unless the contract provides that the seller should be responsible for insuring the property, or otherwise protects the buyer in the event of damage to the property, between the date of the contract and completion.[4]

However, whilst a trust comes into existence at the time of the contract, it must be conceded that the fiduciary relationship between vendor and purchaser

3 See *Rayner v Preston* (1881) 18 Ch D 1.
4 As, for example, in Condition 5 of the Standard Conditions of Sale. See Law Commission Report *Transfer of Land: Risk of Damage after Contract for Sale*, (Law Com No 191, 1990).

is not identical with that which exists between a trustee and a beneficiary under other forms of trust. As Maitland says, 'the trusteeship of the unpaid vendor is a very peculiar trusteeship ... He (the vendor) can say I will not part with this land until I am paid. Then if the purchaser will not pay he ... can go to the Court; the Court will order the purchaser to pay within a reasonable time, and in default of payment the purchaser will lose his right to the land under the contract, and the vendor will then be in the same position as that in which he was before the contract was made, he will be owner at law and in equity'.[5]

P's EQUITABLE INTEREST: THIRD PARTIES

If V makes a contract with P on 1 June that he will convey Blackacre to P on 1 July for £5,000, the result is, as we have seen, that from 1 June P acquires an equitable fee simple in the land. Suppose that on 2 June, V meets Q, who says, 'I will give you £7,500 for Blackacre.' V agrees, and executes a deed conveying the legal fee simple in Blackacre to Q. Q now holds the legal fee simple in Blackacre. The question then arises, does he hold the land subject to, or free from, P's equitable interest? If he holds it subject to P's equitable interest, he holds the land, as did V, as trustee for P, and, under the rule in *Saunders v Vautier*[6] P can require Q to convey the legal estate to him. If Q takes the land free from P's equitable interest, P's only remedy lies against V for breach of trust.

Before 1926 the question whether Q took free from, or subject to, P's equitable interest was determined in accordance with rules relating to the bona fide purchaser. Thus if Q could show that he was a bona fide purchaser without notice, actual or constructive, of P's equitable interest (he is, we know, a purchaser for value of the legal estate), then he would take free from P's equitable interest. If he was not able to show that he took without notice of V's contract with P, then he took subject to P's equitable interest.

The Land Charges Act 1925[7] provided that after 1925 an interest of the kind held by P was to be registrable in the Land Charges Register under the heading of what the Act terms 'Estate contracts'. Thus after 1925, whether P's interest binds Q now depends, not on whether or not Q had notice of P's interest, but on whether P registered his interest in the Land Charges Registry. If he did so before V's conveyance to Q, Q would take the legal estate subject to P's interest. If he failed to do so, Q would take free of P's interest, irrespective of whether or not he had notice, actual or constructive, of P's interest.[8]

We have said that the interest that P acquired as a result of the contract between V and himself is registrable as an estate contract. If P acquires an equitable interest as a result of an imperfect conveyance of Blackacre from V to himself, the equitable interest that P thereby acquires is similarly registrable. Although a conveyance (albeit an imperfect one) and not a contract is concerned, the interest that P acquires is registrable as an estate contract.

---

5   Maitland, *Equity*, p 315.
6   (1841) 4 Beav 115. See Chapter 5.
7   Section 10(1) (now s 2(4) of the LCA 1972.)
8   Subject to what is said in Chapter 25.

Creation of an equitable lease

We began by considering the position where V makes an imperfect conveyance of a legal fee simple to P. We saw that the starting point was that V should have used a deed to convey the fee simple to P but failed to do so.

A conveyance of a legal fee simple is, however, not the only transaction for which a deed is required. A deed is also required for the creation of a lease for a period not exceeding three years. So if a landlord (L) wishes to grant a tenant (T) a lease of Whiteacre for seven years at a rent of, say, £500 a year, in order to give T a legal lease, the grant of the lease must be by deed. If the grant of the lease is not by deed, but is in a document signed by L and T (thus complying with s 2 of the 1989 Act), T acquires an equitable lease of the land (for seven years at a rent of £500 a year). The reason is the same as that which applied in the case of the imperfect grant of the fee simple. (Before the 1989 Act, T acquired an equitable lease if the grant was not by deed and was either in writing or evidenced in writing (under s 40) or was evidenced by an act of part performance, eg by allowing T to go into possession of the property.)

Similarly, if L enters into a valid contract (before the 1989 Act, under s 40, after the 1989 Act, under s 2 of the Act) with T on, say, 1 June that he will grant him a lease of the land for seven years at £500 a year payable in advance, the lease to commence on 1 July, then T acquires an equitable lease from the moment of the contract. He does not acquire a right to occupy the land until 1 July, but from 1 June the existence of T's equitable lease imposes on L a duty not to deal with the land inconsistently with T's interest.

DIFFERENCES BETWEEN AN EQUITABLE AND A LEGAL LEASE

If T acquires an equitable lease that he can enforce against L, since this entitles him to possession of the land, what difference does it make to T that his lease is an equitable one and not a legal one? The answer is that it may make no difference. T may occupy the land for the full period of the lease paying whatever rent is due and his enjoyment of the land may be no different from that which he would have had if the lease had been legal. On the other hand, the fact that the lease is equitable and not legal may in some circumstances be of consequence. For example:

1. If L conveys the legal fee simple to X, then, before 1926, if X was a bona fide purchaser without notice of T's equitable lease, X took free of T's interest. (If T had taken possession, his interest would normally bind X, since his possession would constitute notice to X.[9])

After 1925, T's equitable lease is registrable as an estate contract.[10] Thus if T registered his interest, X will take the land subject to T's lease irrespective of whether he had notice of the lease. If T failed to register his interest, X would take the land free of T's equitable lease notwithstanding that X has notice of the lease, eg because T is in possession.[11]

---

9   *Hunt v Luck* [1902] 1 Ch 428 at 432.
10   Land Charges Act 1972, s 2(4). See Chapter 23.
11   *Hollington Bros Ltd v Rhodes* [1951] 2 All ER 578n; (M & B).

If L had granted a *legal* lease to T, and had then transferred the legal estate to X, since legal interests (ie T's legal lease) bind all the world, X would have taken the legal fee simple subject to T's legal lease, irrespective of any question of notice or registration.

2. Further, if T holds a legal lease, he can claim to be a bona fide purchaser of the legal estate in the event of his seeking to show that he is entitled to take the lease free of some prior equitable interest that is subject to the bona fide purchaser rule. This is because, as we have seen,[12] a lessee is a purchaser *pro tanto*.

3. Differences between legal and equitable leases exist with regard to the creation of easements under s 62 of the Law of Property Act 1925. This matter is explained in Chapter 18.

4. Like all equitable interests, the interest of a tenant under an equitable lease can only be enforced at the discretion of the court. If T bases his claim to an equitable lease on a contract by L to grant him a lease, then if for any reason (eg due to T's conduct since the contract was made) the circumstances are such that the court would decline to grant a decree of specific performance, the claim to hold an equitable lease fails. Thus where L granted a legal lease to T containing a covenant against subletting, and T (in breach of the covenant) entered into a contract to sublet the property to ST, ST failed in his attempt to enforce rights as a tenant under an equitable sublease against T.[13]

CONSIDERATION

In dealing with the creation of an equitable fee simple we saw that consideration must be present if an equitable fee simple is to come into existence. The same principle applies in relation to leases. Thus if L makes an imperfect grant for a lease of seven years to T, and no rent is payable by T, nor any other consideration from T exists, then no equitable lease is created and T acquires nothing. L's grant was by way of gift and, as we have seen, equity will not assist a volunteer.

Other transactions

Section 52 of the Law of Property Act 1925 provides that 'all conveyances of land or of any interest therein are void for the purpose of conveying or creating a legal estate unless made by deed'. Thus if V wishes to grant P a legal easement, then (since an easement is an 'interest' in land) the grant must be by deed. By analogy with the principles explained in this chapter, if V contracts with P that he will grant him the easement concerned, P acquires an equitable easement. Similarly, if V purports to grant the easement but does not use a deed, then provided that the grant of the easement is in a form that is sufficient to satisfy the requirements for the existence of, before the 1989 Act, an

---

12   See Chapter 5.
13   *Warmington v Miller* [1973] QB 877, [1973] 2 All ER 372. See also *Cornish v Brook Green Laundry Ltd* [1959] 1 QB 394, [1959] 1 All ER 373; *Coatsworth v Johnson* (1886) 54 LT 520; (M & B).

enforceable[14] or, after the Act, a valid contract and provided that P gives consideration for the grant, P acquires an equitable easement.

The same principles apply in the case of other transactions for which a deed is required; for example, the creation of a legal mortgage.[15] Thus a mortgage which is (after the 1989 Act) in writing and signed by both parties creates an equitable mortgage.

Walsh v Lonsdale[16]

This chapter is headed 'The doctrine in *Walsh v Lonsdale*'. Which of the principles discussed in this chapter constitute that doctrine? The answer is that the principles relating to a conveyance of the fee simple are commonly attributed to the case of *Lysaght v Edwards*;[17] the principles relating to leases, to *Walsh v Lonsdale*; the principles relating to other transactions, such as the grant of mortgages or easements, are usually referred to as arising by analogy with the doctrine of *Walsh v Lonsdale*. Sometimes, however, for convenience, the authority for the principles we have discussed relating to all these forms of transaction is cited as being the case of *Walsh v Lonsdale*. Yet the fact is that all the principles that form the subject matter of this chapter had been settled before the case of *Walsh v Lonsdale* was decided. For example, by the time of *Parker v Taswell*,[18] in 1858, it had been established that equity would treat an imperfect case (a lease in writing) as a contract to grant a lease, and it had already by then been accepted that a contract to grant a lease created an equitable lease giving the lessor and lessee the rights and obligations contained in the contract.

What then, it may be asked, did *Walsh v Lonsdale* add? In order to answer that question, one matter relating to the creation of legal leases must be explained. We have seen that a deed must be used to create a lease for a period no exceeding three years. The creation of a (legal) lease from a lesser period, including a yearly, monthly, weekly, or other 'periodic' lease, may be merely oral. Further, if a person goes into possession of land and pays rent at so much, eg a month, and this rent is accepted by the landlord then at common law he becomes a monthly tenant (and similarly if he pays by the week, or the quarter, etc). Such a tenant is at common law obliged to pay the rent at the end of the relevant period; in our example, at the end of each month. At common law he is thus under no obligation to pay the rent in advance.

In *Walsh v Lonsdale*, Walsh (W) and Lonsdale (L) entered into a contract that L would grant W a seven-year lease of a weaving mill at Darwen in Lancashire. The contract stated that the lease should provide that rent should be payable on L's demand, one year in advance. L did not execute a deed granting the lease to W, but he allowed W to go into possession of the mill. A

---

14   *McManus v Cooke* (1887) 35 Ch D 681; (M & B).
15   See *Dance v Welwyn Hatfield District Council* [1990] 1 WLR 1097.
16   (1882) 21 Ch D 9; (M & B).
17   (1876) 2 Ch D 499; (M & B).
18   (1858) 2 De G & J 559.

year later W paid a year's rent (ie in arrears) to L. Six months later L demanded a year's rent in advance. W refused to pay the rent in advance claimed by L. L, exercising the ancient remedy of a lessor, distrained for the rent he had claimed (ie he went on to the land and removed some of W's chattels). W claimed that, since L had had no right to require payment of the rent in advance, L's action in distraining on the land had been wrongful, and he sued L accordingly. The case thus turned on whether L had, or had not, been entitled to claim the rent in advance. If he had, his distress had been lawful; if he had not, it had been wrongful.

At common law (as we have explained) since W had paid, and L accepted, one year's rent, this made W a yearly tenant. As a yearly tenant W, at common law, was under no obligation to pay rent in advance. Thus, at common law, W was under no obligation to pay the next rent until the end of the second year. However, in equity, since L had contracted with W for the grant of a seven-year lease, W held a seven-year (equitable) lease. Further, that equitable lease was held under the same terms as those contained in the contract to grant the lease. Thus, under the equitable lease W was obliged to pay a year's rent in advance if L demanded it. L had demanded it, so in equity W was under an obligation to pay in advance. The position was, therefore, that at common law W was under no obligation to pay the rent demanded by L (and so L's distress was wrongful); in equity, W was under an obligation to pay in advance (and so L's distress was lawful).

The court held that the position in equity prevailed over that at common law. Thus W had been under an obligation to pay the rent in advance demanded by L; his refusal to do so had been wrongful, and thus L's distress lawful. W therefore failed in his action. In making this judgment the court was applying the provision of s 25(11) of the Judicature Act 1873 that 'in matters ... in which there is any conflict, or variance between the Rules of Equity and the Rules of Common Law with reference to the same matter, the Rules of Equity shall prevail'. The case therefore did not decide anything new. It merely provided an illustration of s 25(11) of the 1873 Act in operation. For this reason it might be more accurate to refer to the principles discussed in this chapter as the doctrine of *Parker v Taswell*, but it is too late to change now. *Walsh v Lonsdale* has collected the credit, and there the matter will stand. Perhaps one compromise would be to speak not of 'the doctrine of *Walsh v Lonsdale*' but of 'the doctrine in *Walsh v Lonsdale*' meaning the doctrine, settled in a series of earlier cases (culminating in *Parker v Taswell*), which was applied together with s 25(11) of the 1873 Act, in arriving at the decision in *Walsh v Lonsdale*.

HOW EQUITABLE INTERESTS ARISE

Having explained the operation of the rule in *Walsh v Lonsdale* we are now in a position by way of postscript to this chapter to set out all the circumstances in which an interest must be equitable. These are as follows:

1. Where, as seen in this chapter, an interest arises under the rule in *Walsh v Lonsdale* (the correct formality not having been observed by the grantor for the creation of a legal interest).

2. Where land is granted, for any interest, to an infant.[19]
3. Where an interest in land is granted which is not an interest listed in s 1(1) and (2) of the Law of Property Act 1925.[20]
4. Where an interest is granted out of an interest that is itself equitable. For example, if A holds an equitable fee simple and he grants a lease to B, the lease is equitable.
5. Where property is conveyed to trustees expressly on trust for a beneficiary.
6. Where the holder of a legal estate declares that he holds the property on trust for a specified beneficiary.
7. Where a trust arises from an implied intention to create a trust (thus resulting in the creation of an implied trust).[1]
8. Where a trust is imposed by equity irrespective of the intention of any person (thus creating a constructive trust).

SUMMARY

An imperfect conveyance of the legal fee simple (or other interest) in land (one that is not by deed) that satisfies the requirements of an enforceable contract and is for consideration creates an equitable fee simple (or other interest).

An express enforceable contract to convey the legal fee simple (or other interest) in land for consideration creates an equitable fee simple (or other interest).

Where an equitable interest comes into existence under 1 above the legal fee simple is held by the vendor on trust for the purchaser who can require the vendor to execute a deed transferring the legal estate to him.

Where an equitable interest comes into being under 2 above the legal estate is held by the vendor on trust for the purchaser; the purchaser is not entitled to possession until the contractual date for him to take possession; in the intervening period the purchaser is responsible for insuring the property.

In order for an equitable interest that arises under 1 or 2 above to bind the purchaser of the legal estate, it must be registered as an estate contract in the Land Charges Register.

Differences in their effect exist between legal leases and equitable leases.

---

19   LPA 1925, s 1(6).
20   See Chapter 6.
 1   See Chapter 5.

CHAPTER 17

Leases[1]

Introduction

Leases and licences

L (which in this chapter represents 'lessor', or 'landlord') holds the fee simple in Redacre. Since he does not wish to occupy the land himself, he grants T (which in this chapter represents 'tenant') the right to occupy the land in return for an agreed sum of money. Provided that certain conditions are satisfied, the right which L has granted T is a lease. If the necessary conditions are not satisfied, the right is not a lease, but a licence.

There are several reasons why it may matter whether the right which a person holds is a lease or a licence. Thus:

1. If T holds a lease, and L transfers the land to X, T's lease will bind X.[2] If the right granted is a licence, it will not bind C, and the grantee's only remedy, if any, will be against L (for damages for breach of contract). The difference in outcome is due to the fact that a lease is an *interest* in land, a proprietary interest. A licence is not an interest in land;[3] it exists as a *contract* between the lessor and lessee.

2. It follows from what we have said about the nature of the two matters that if L grants a lease for, say, seven years and T dies, the lease, being T's property, does not come to an end. The unexpired portion of the lease forms part of T's estate and so passes under his will or intestacy. But if L had granted a licence, then the death of the licensee brings the licence to an end.

3. If T holds a lease and L enters the property without T's consent, L is a trespasser and liable to T as such. If T held merely a licence, L might be liable to T for breach of contract, but he would not be a trespasser.

---

1   Woodfall, *Landlord and Tenant*; D. Yates and A. J. Hawkins, *Landlord and Tenant Law*; D. L. Evans, *The Law of Landlord and Tenant*; Hill and Redman, *Law of Landlord and Tenant*. On the need for an 'energetic and systematic' reform of the law of leases, and a rationalisation of the fragmented legislation that protects tenants, see Law Commission *Landlord and Tenant: Reform of the Law* (Law Com No 162, 1987).
2   At least, if it is a legal lease. For the present position regarding equitable leases, see Chapter 25.
3   A licensee may, however, qualify as a person 'interested in land' in order to qualify for compensation under s 107 of the Town and Country Planning Act 1990: *Pennine Raceway Ltd v Kirklees Metropolitan Council* [1983] QB 382, [1982] 3 All ER 628, CA; [1983] Conv 317 (JEM).

4. If T holds a lease, the law implies certain covenants by T and by L with regard to matters affecting the tenure of the land. These are considered later.[4] These covenants are not implied in the case of a licence.[5]

5. Enfranchisement, and extension of leases[6]

(a) If T holds a lease he may be able to take advantage of the provisions of the Leasehold Reform Act 1967.[7] In order to come within the terms of the Act a tenant must have occupied a '*house*'[8] as his residence for a period of three years, the original tenancy having been granted for a fixed period exceeding 21 years at a low rent.[9] A tenant who can satisfy these conditions can require his landlord either (a) to transfer to him the fee simple in land, in return for a price calculated according to formulae prescribed by the Act (as amended[10]); or (b) to grant him a new lease in substitution for the existing lease for a period ending 50 years after the expiry of the existing lease, at a rent equivalent to the current letting value of the land (ie without buildings on it). One or other claim, or both, may be rejected or modified by the landlord in certain situations set out in the Act.[11] For example, either form of claim may be defeated by a landlord who can show that he reasonably requires the house as a residence for himself or a member of his family.[12]

(b) The right to secure an extension to a lease was conferred on the tenants of *flats* by the Leasehold Reform, Housing and Urban Development Act 1993. Under the Act, a qualifying tenant (one who holds for a lease originally granted for a period of more than 21 years at a low rent, as defined in the Act, and who satisfies prescribed residency conditions) can require the landlord, subject to terms being agreed (or settled by a local leasehold valuation tribunal), to accept surrender of the existing lease and grant a new lease for a period equivalent to the unexpired period of the old lease plus ninety years.

(c) A tenant of a flat (which is one of at least two other flats in the same building) under a lease for a low rent for a term exceeding 21 years and who occupies the flat as his principal home is given a right by the Leasehold Reform, Housing and Urban Development Act 1993,[13] to acquire, together with other

---

4   See p 293.
5   Though in particular instances the court may hold that a licence contains an implied undertaking where this is necessary to give business efficacy to the agreement. See *Western Electric Ltd v Welsh Development Agency* [1983] QB 796, [1983] 2 All ER 629.
6   [1994] Conv 211 (S. Bright); D.N. Clarke *Leasehold Enfranchisement - the New Law* [1994] Conv 223.
7   As amended by: Housing Act 1974; Housing Act 1980; Housing and Planning Act 1986; Leasehold Reform, Housing and Urban Development Act 1993; Housing Act 1996.
8   Section 2(1). See *Tandon v Trustees of Spurgeous Homes* [1982] AC 755, [1982] 1 All ER 1086 (shop with living accommodation above a 'house' within the meaning of the Act); and *Poland v Earl Cadogan* [1980] 3 All ER 544.
9   Under the 1967 Act a low rent was one less than two-thirds of the rateable value of the premises. Eligibility has been extended by later legislation, most recently the Leasehold Reform, Housing and Urban Development Act 1993, ss 63-66, and the Housing Act 1996, Part III.
10 Leasehold Reform, Housing and Urban Development Act 1993, s 66, Sch 15.
11 Sections 17, 18, 19, 20, 33.
12 Section 18.
13 As amended by the Housing Act 1996.

tenants in the same building (provided that they hold at least two-thirds of the flats in the building), the landlord's interest in the reversion.[14] Thus if A, B, C, D, E and F are tenants in a block of flats, and A, B, C, and D wish to exercise their right under the Act, and hold qualifying leases, together they can require the landlord to transfer the fee simple in land to them, perhaps forming themselves into a company, X plc, for the purpose. In such a case X plc, in which the shares are owned by A, B, C and D owns the fee simple in the land subject to the leases to all the tenants in the block, including A, B, C and D, the advantage of the arrangement intended by the legislation being that management of the block will be vested in those (or the majority of those) who live there.

The acquisition by a tenant (alone or together with other tenants, as the case may be) of the freehold (of a house or a building containing flats) under any of the above legislation is termed 'enfranchisement'. (Enfranchisement is to be distinguished from the securing of an extension of a lease (eg under (b) above).)

6. A tenant under a lease is capable of coming under the protection of those statutes, known collectively as the Rent Acts, that provide a measure of security of tenure, and place restrictions on a landlord's ability to increase rent. The present law relating to security of tenure and control of rents is principally contained (a) for tenants of residential properties in the Rent Act 1977 (as amended) (tenancies within the protection of which are termed 'protected tenancies' or, after the expiry of a protected tenancy, a 'statutory tenancy', the two collectively termed 'regulated tenancies'); the Housing Act 1988, which stopped the creation of protected tenancies after 15 January 1989 and introduced two new forms of tenancy ('assured tenancies' and 'assured shorthold tenancies') with reduced security of tenure and entitlement to rent control; and the Housing Act 1996;[15] (b) for tenants of publicly owned (eg by a local authority) residential property, in the Housing Act 1985, tenancies within the protection of which are termed 'secure tenancies'; (c) for business premises, in Part II of the Landlord and Tenant Act 1954; (c) for agricultural premises, in the Agricultural Holdings Act 1986 and, for agricultural tenancies created after 31 August 1995, the Agricultural Tenancies Act 1995.[16]

The legislation has generally[17] no application to land occupied under a licence.

7. Under the Housing Act 1996, a tenant under a lease has a right, subject to conditions in the Act, to obtain confirmation of the court that a service charge demanded by a landlord is reasonable.

---

14 Section 1. The Act supplements a right conferred by the Landlord and Tenant Act 1987, s 1 on tenants of flats, to require a landlord who wishes to sell the reversion to grant them a right of first refusal (thus assisting them in forming a collective for the purchase of the block). Failure to serve a notice offering the property to the tenants is an offence, Housing Act 1996 (Housing Act 1996 (Commencement No 2 and Savings) Order 1996.

15 Under which all new tenancies created on or after 28 February 1996 are to be assured shorthold tenancies unless notice to the contrary is given by the landlord.

16 *Farm Business Tenancies - The Agricultural Tenancies Act 1995* A. Sydenham and N. Mainwaring; [1996] Conv 243 (J. M. Bishop).

17 The exceptions are limited, eg Housing Act 1985, s 79(3).

8. A lease is capable of being an overriding interest under the Land Registration Act 1925, s 70(1)(g) (treated in Chapter 26), a licence is not.

Nature

As an agreement between two parties, a lease is a contract and, as such, is subject (to the extent that these are relevant, and not excluded by statute[18]) to the law relating to contracts.[19] But a lease is more than a contract between two parties in that, as an *interest* in land, it is capable of binding a third party, ie a purchaser of the freehold from the lessor. A lease is thus a contract and it is also an interest in land. A lease, like a coin, has two sides; which side you see depends on which side you look at.

Essentials of a lease

For a right to be capable of being a lease two conditions must be fulfilled:

(1) The duration of the lease must be certain.
(2) The tenant must have exclusive possession.

Certainty of duration

To comply with this requirement:

(a) The date of the commencement of the lease must, before the lease takes effect, be either fixed or ascertainable.
(b) The maximum duration must, before the lease takes effect, be either fixed or ascertainable.[20]

If no date for the commencement of the lease is stated, the lease is usually deemed to be intended to commence from the date of the grant of the lease.

Here are some examples of the application of the above principles.

(i) A grant to A commencing on a fixed date and lasting, eg for the duration of a partnership, or for 'the duration of the war'[1] complies with (a) above, but infringes (b) and so cannot create a lease.

---

18 Eg Unfair Contract Terms Act 1977, s 3(1). *Electricity Supply Nominees Ltd v I A F Group Ltd* [1993] 3 All ER 372, [1993] 1 WLR 1059.
19 Eg frustration. *National Carriers Ltd v Panalpina (Northern) Ltd* [1981] AC 675, [1981] 1 All ER 161; repudiation; *Hussein v Mehlman* [1992] 32 EG 59, 1993 Conv 71 (S. Bright); [1995] Conv 379 (M. Pawlowski). On the contractualisation of leases, see [1996] Conv 460 (M. Pawlowski).
20 2 Bl Com (1st edn, 1766) 143; *Harvey v Pratt* [1965] 2 All ER 786, [1965] 1 WLR 1025.
1   *Lace v Chantler* [1944] KB 368, [1944] 1 All ER 305; (M & B). Leases in such terms granted during the 1939-45 war were converted into terms of ten years (determinable after the end of the war on the giving of notice) by the Validation of War-Time Leases Act 1944.

(ii)   Similarly the grant of a tenancy limited to terminate on the land being required by the landlord 'for road widening purposes' infringes (b) and creates no lease.[2]

(iii)   A grant to B to determine on his death or the expiry of 20 years, whichever period is the longer, has no fixed maximum duration and therefore infringes (b) and so cannot create a lease.

(iv)   A lease to C to determine on his death or the expiry of 20 years, whichever period is the shorter, complies with (b) since a maximum duration is fixed. (It is immaterial that the lease may be cut short before the maximum period is reached.) The grant is thus capable of creating a lease. The effect of the Law of Property Act 1925[3] on such a grant is considered later.[4]

(v)   A contract by E to grant F a lease for seven years commencing when E vacates the premises cannot create any lease since the commencement of the lease is neither fixed nor ascertainable before the lease commences.

(vi)   If G grants H a lease commencing on 1 January next, without specifying the duration of the lease, but G states the duration of the lease before 1 January, condition (b) is satisfied; if he does not do so, it is not.

(vii)   A lease terminable by the landlord or tenant giving specified notice to the other party except in certain specified circumstances (eg the land being required for the purposes of the lessor's business[5]) has been held not to conflict with the principle at (b) above and thus is valid. (But we may note here that a restriction on termination which takes the form of a provision that the lease may be terminated only by one party (eg by the tenant[6]) is void, since such a restriction is repugnant to the very nature of a lease. The restriction is struck out, leaving the lease standing as agreed in all other respects.)

(viii)   An arrangement under which A Ltd was entitled to remain in possession until a specified date after which the company could be required to give up possession on not less than one quarter's notice was held by the Court of Appeal in *Ashburn Anstalt v Arnold*[7] to comply with requirement (b). Speaking of the arrangement Fox LJ said,[8] '[It] could be brought to an end by both parties in circumstances which are free from uncertainty in the sense that there would be no doubt whether the determining event had occurred. The vice of uncertainty, in relation to the duration of a term is that the parties do not know where they stand. Put another way, the court does not know what to enforce. That is not the position here.'

It will be convenient at this point to mention that whilst originally there was no restriction on the length of time which might exist between the execution of the lease and the time when the right to take possession arose, the Law of

2   *Prudential Assurance Co Ltd v London Residuary Body* [1992] 2 AC 386, [1992] 3 All ER 504, HL [1993] Conv 461 (P. F. Smith); [1993] CLJ 26 (S. Bridge); [1994] 57 MLR 117 (D. Wilde).
3   Section 149(6).
4   See p 288.
5   *Re Midland Rly Co's Agreement* [1971] Ch 725, [1971] 1 All ER 1007; (M & B).
6   *Centaploy Ltd v Matlodge Ltd* [1974] Ch 1, [1973] 2 All ER 720; (M & B).
7   [1989] Ch 1, [1988] 2 All ER 147, [1988] 2 WLR 706; (M & B); Applied in *Canadian Imperial Bank of Commerce v Bello* (1991) 136 Sol Jo LB 9, CA.
8   At 716.

Property Act 1925 provides[9] that any lease executed after 1925, granted for a rent or fine, in which the right to take possession arises more than 21 years from the date of the execution of the lease, is void. Further, any contract to grant such a lease is also void. Thus, if L contracts with his employee, T, that if T will, eg accept a transfer to a post in Durham, L will execute a 50-year lease of a certain house in Cornwall at a certain rent, giving T the right to possession on his retirement in 30 years' time, the contract is void. However it should be noted that if L contracts with T that if, eg T remains in L's employment until his retirement in 30 years' time, he will then execute a 50-year lease of the house in Cornwall (taking effect immediately on T's retirement), the contract would not infringe the Act. Similarly, if L grants T a lease for, say, 30 years, and the lease contains a provision that if at the end of that period T so elects, L will grant him a fresh lease for a specified period (if the lease contains 'an option of for renewal'), the contract that the option constitutes does not infringe the Act.[10] Thus a restriction is placed on the length of time that may exist between the grant of a lease and the time when the tenant may take possession, but not between a contract to grant a lease and the grant.

A lease which gives a right to possession, not immediately, but at some date after the date of the execution of the lease (eg on the expiry of an existing lease to another tenant), is termed a 'reversionary' lease. (A 'reversionary interest' is an interest that arises (or, as in the case of a reversionary lease, gives a right to possession) at some point of time in the future.)

Exclusive possession

The lease must give T an interest in land that entitles him to exclude all other persons, including L, from the premises. Thus if L retains the right to enter the premises at will, or if he remains in general control of the property or if he retains the right to occupy the property with T,[11] then T is not a tenant, but a licensee.[12] (Whether or not exclusive possession exists is a question of fact to be decided by the court by reviewing all the evidence in each case.[13])

Applying the above principle, the following have been held to be no more than licensees: a lodger at an inn or a boarding house or in a room or rooms of a house;[14] a person holding the right to use the refreshment room of a theatre for the purpose of selling refreshments;[15] a person who hired a stall at an exhibition for certain hours in a day;[16] a person who had the right to use a graving dock, certain aspects of control over which (eg responsibility for cleaning

 9 Section 149(3).
10 See *Re Strand and Savoy Properties Ltd* [1960] Ch 582, [1960] 2 All ER 327; (M & B); *Weg Motors Ltd v Hales* [1962] Ch 49, [1961] 3 All ER 181; (M & B).
11 *Somma v Hazelhurst* [1978] 2 All ER 1011, [1978] 1 WLR 1014; (M & B); cf *Gray v Brown* (1992) 25 HLR 144, CA.
12 And thus is deprived of the protection of the Rent Acts. See *Somma v Hazelhurst*, ante.
13 *Brooker Settled Estates Ltd v Ayers* (1987) 54 P & CR 165, CA.
13 *Allan v Liverpool Overseers* (1874) LR 9 QB 180; *Appah v Parncliffe Investments Ltd* [1964] 1 All ER 838, [1964] 1 WLR 1064.
15 *Clore v Theatrical Properties Ltd* [1936] 3 All ER 483.
16 *Rendell v Roman* (1893) 9 TLR 192.

the dock daily and opening and closing the dock gates) were retained by the corporation which owned the docks;[17] a person who occupied a furnished bed-sitting room in a house let off as bachelor service apartments, with a housekeeper to clean the rooms daily and provide clean linen each week.[18]

The dividing line between a tenant and a lodger is not always easy to draw,[19] since a person may have exclusive possession but, because of the degree of control retained by the landlord, nevertheless be a lodger, and thus merely a licensee.[20] In *Street v Mountford*,[1] Lord Templeman explained the matter thus: 'The occupier is a lodger if the landlord provides attendance or services which require the landlord or his servants to exercise unrestricted access to and use of the premises. A lodger is entitled to live in the premises but he cannot call the place his own.'[2]

There is another instance in which a person may have exclusive possession and yet not be a tenant: it has long been accepted that land is held by a licence when it is held under a 'service occupancy', ie where it is necessary for a person to occupy property in order properly to perform his contract of employment[3], as where a caretaker is required to occupy a flat in the premises for which he is responsible, or a warden of an old people's home is required to live in accommodation in the house.

Rent not an essential characteristic

In 1987 *Ashburn Anstalt v Arnold*[4] took the matter a step further. In 1973 A assigned the lease of certain premises to M. As a term of the arrangement it was agreed that A should be allowed to remain at the property as a licensee, without rent, until 29 September 1973, after which date, A could be required to give up possession on not less than one month's notice. The lease subsequently passed into the hands of the holder of the freehold reversioner, the lease thus merging with the freehold. The freehold later passed into the hands of the plaintiff who sought an order for possession against A. If the arrangement of February 1973 created no more than a licence, the plaintiff was entitled to succeed. If it created a lease, he was not (A being protected from eviction by the Landlord and Tenant Act of 1954). The arrangement had given A exclusive possession and, the court held, after reviewing the question of certainty of duration (considered earlier), a term. But it imposed no rent. Did this mean that the arrangement, lacking one of the hallmarks cited by

---

17   *Wells v Kingston-upon-Hull Corpn* (1875) LR 10 CP 402.
18   *Marchant v Charters* [1977] 3 All ER 918, [1977] 1 WLR 1181; (M & B).
19   See (1985) 48 MLR 712 (S. Anderson).
20   As in *Marchant v Charters* [1977] 3 All ER 918, [1977] 1 WLR 1181; (M & B).
1   [1985] AC 809, [1985] 2 All ER 289; (M & B).
2   At 293.
3   *Hughes v Chatham Overseers* (1843) 5 Man & G 54, 77; *Thompsons (Funeral Furnishers) Ltd v Phillips* [1945] 2 All ER 49; cf *Royal Philanthropic Society v County* (1985) 18 HLR 83; [1986] Conv 215 (P. F. Smith).
4   [1989] Ch 1, [1988] 2 All ER 147, CA; [1988] LQR 175 (P. Sparkes), (1988) 51 MLR 226 (J. Hill), [1988] Conv 201 (M. P.Thompson).

Lord Templeman in *Street v Mountford*,[5] could not be a lease? The Court of Appeal held that this result did not follow. If the three hallmarks were present a lease certainly existed. Since, both at common law and according to the definition of a lease in the Law of Property Act 1925, a lease could be for rent or for no rent, the absence of a requirement for rent in the 1973 agreement did not preclude the arrangement constituting a lease. Because exclusive possession had been conferred and no uncertainty existed with regard to duration, and since what mattered, as had been held in *Street v Mountford*, was substance not form, the arrangement constituted, the court held, a lease, not a licence.

LEASE OR LICENCE?

Of the reasons why it may matter whether an agreement constitutes a lease or a licence mentioned at the beginning of this chapter, the most important has concerned the application of the Rent Acts (the most important, that is, until the reduction in the scope and impact of these Acts in recent times, in particular by the Housing Acts of 1985 and 1988[6]): if a person occupies land as a tenant, then, subject to certain statutory exceptions,[7] he is entitled to the protection of the Acts. If he occupies land as a licensee, then generally[8] he is not.

So it has happened that from time to time those allowing others to occupy their property have sought to ensure that the occupier held as a licensee not as a tenant. There have been three ways in which this has been sought to be achieved. We must consider what these are and, in each case, the attitude of the courts to the methods adopted.

1. The label

In the grant the landowner (whom in this section we shall, for convenience, call a 'landlord', whether what is granted, or purported to be granted, is a lease (or sub-lease) or a licence) may refer to the arrangement that is to exist as a licence and the terminology may be couched accordingly, eg money due may be termed a 'licence fee'. In such a case the wording indicates an intention by the landlord (and, from his acceptance of the terms, the occupier) that the land should be held under a licence. But should the intention of the parties be conclusive as to what exists? Generally, at common law, the court, in accordance with the principle of freedom of contract, will seek to give effect to the intentions of the parties as expressed in an agreement. But where an arrangement exists that has the characteristics to satisfy the requirements of a lease (ie exclusive

5 [1985] AC 809, [1985] 2 All ER 289, HL; (M & B).
6 Since the beginning of 1989 only a minority of tenants renting from private landlords have the benefit of controlled rent and security of tenure.
7 A tenancy is not protected if the dwelling is bona fide let at a rent which includes payments in respect of board or attendance (Rent Act 1977, s 7), nor if it is held for a shorthold tenancy under the Housing Act 1980, s 52. See also, for business tenancies, s 38(4) Landlord and Tenant Act 1954.
8 See p 272.

possession and possession for a fixed term), can the arrangement be a licence on the ground that it is so termed in the contract under which the arrangement is brought into existence? This was the question which (after a period of uncertainty[9]) fell to be determined by the court in *Street v Mountford*.[10] In this case, S granted M the right to occupy two rooms in a house for £37 per week. The agreement was entitled 'licence agreement' and contained a declaration by M that she understood that the agreement did not give her a tenancy protected by the Rent Acts. The Court of Appeal declared that M held the rooms as a licensee. On appeal to the House of Lords, Lord Templeman (with whom the House agreed) held[11] that if an agreement had the three hallmarks of a tenancy, namely exclusive possession, a term and a rent, then (save in 'exceptional circumstances'[12]) the agreement produces a tenancy and 'the parties cannot alter the effect of the agreement by insisting that they only created a licence. The manufacturer of a five-pronged implement for manual digging results in a fork even if the manufacturer, unfamiliar with the English language, insists that he intended to make and has made a spade.'[13] M, having exclusive possession and holding for a fixed term, therefore held as a tenant, not a licensee, and was thus entitled to the protection of the Rent Acts. In deciding whether a grant creates a lease or licence, the test is therefore one of substance not of form.[14]

2.   Non-exclusive possession

In the grant the landlord may seek to prevent exclusive possession being obtained by providing that the premises are to be occupied by the grantee and the landlord, or the grantee and another person, or by the grantee, the landlord and another person. In two cases[15] in 1978 the court concluded that a grant that purported to prevent exclusive possession created a lease, on the ground that the grant had been preceded by an oral agreement that there would be

---

9   Cf *Facchini v Bryson* [1952] 1 TLR 1386; *Cobb v Lane* [1952] 1 All ER 1199; *Murray, Bull & Co Ltd v Murray* [1953] 1 QB 211, [1952] 2 All ER 1079.

10   [1985] AC 809, [1985] 2 All ER 289; (M & B); (1985) 48 MLR 712 (S. Anderson); [1985] CLJ 351 (S. Tromans); [1985] Conv 328 (R. Street); [1986] Conv 39 (D. N. Clarke); [1986] Conv 344 (S. Bridge); followed in *Bretherton v Paton* (1986) 278 Estates Gazette 615; *University of Reading v Johnson-Houghton* (1985) 276 Estates Gazette 1353; [1986] Conv 275 (C. P. Rogers); [1986] Conv 39 (D. N. Clarke).

11   Approving *Addiscombe Garden Estates Ltd v Crabbe* [1958] 1 QB 513, [1957] 3 All ER 563 and adopting the language of Windeyer J in *Radaich v Smith* (1959) 101 CLR 209 at 222.

12   Eg where there is no intention to create legal relations, (see p 282, infra) where there is occupancy pursuant to a contract of employment (see p 276, ante), *Davies v Brenner* [1987] CLY 163; or where a local authority, in performance of its duty to the homeless under the Housing Act 1985, permitted a family to occupy premises for a 13-week period under a 'Licence to Occupy', which conferred exclusive possession; *Ogwr Borough Council v Dykes* [1989] 2 All ER 880, [1989] 1 WLR 295; CA; [1989] Conv 192 (JEM); cf *Eastleigh Borough Council v Walsh* [1985] 2 All ER 112, [1985] 1 WLR 525, HL.

13   At 819.

14   On the decision and its implications, see K. Lewison, *Lease or Licence?* (1985).

15   *Demuren v Seal Estates* (1978) 249 Estates Gazette 440; *O'Malley v Seymour* (1978) 250 Estates Gazette 1083.

exclusive possession, with the consequence that the subsequent grant was no more than a sham, a sham that the court would disregard.

In instances where there was no such reason for looking behind the terms of an arrangement, the court accepted agreements at their face value and if exclusive possession was excluded, then a licence was found to exist,[16] however improbable in practice it might be that the arrangement would be implemented as set out in the agreement. For example, in *Somma v Hazlehurst*[17] parties who wished to live together each signed separate agreements under which they agreed to share the property with each other and with the landlady. The Court of Appeal held that the arrangement created a licence.

In *Street v Mountford*,[18] however, in the House of Lords (1985) this literal approach to the construction of occupation agreements was rejected.[19] What mattered, Lord Templeman indicated, was whether there was an *intention* that there should be exclusive possession. In *Somma v Hazlehurst* there had been an intention that the room should be held by the two occupants with exclusive possession (so that they 'might live together in undisturbed quasi-connubial bliss making weekly payments'[20]). The occupants thus should have been held to be tenants:[1] the agreement itself had been a sham, and 'the court should ... be astute to detect and frustrate sham devices and artificial transactions whose only object is to disguise the grant of a tenancy and to evade the Rent Acts'.[2] The decision in *Street v Mountford* concerned the occupation of residential property. There were indications in the speech by Lord Templeman that he considered that the same principles applied in the case of both residential and non-residential property[3] and it has since been held that this is the case.[4]

The line adopted by the House of Lords in *Street v Mountford* was followed by the same court in *Antoniades v Villiers*.[5] A landlord granted a man the right to occupy a top floor flat. In a separate but identical agreement the landlord granted the man's girlfriend the like right. The agreements were made

16 *Aldrington Garages Ltd v Fielder* (1978) 37 P & CR 461; *Sturolsen & Co v Weniz* (1948) 272 Estaes Gazette 326.
17 [1978] 2 All ER 1011, [1978] 1 WLR 1014.
18 [1985] AC 809, [1985] 2 All ER 289, HL; applied in *Skipton Building Society v Clayton* (1993) 66 P & CR 223.
19 The decision was foreshadowed by the decision of the House of Lords in *Eastleigh Borough Council v Walsh* [1985] 2 All ER 112, [1985] 1 WLR 525.
20 At 825.
 1 As held in *Caplan v Mardon* [1986] CLY 1873. See also *Hadjiloucas v Crean* [1987] 3 All ER 1008, [1988] 1 WLR 1006, CA.
 2 At 825. Explained in *Hadjiloucas v Crean*, supra.
 3 See references at 816, 822, 824 to cases concerning non-residential property: *Glenwood Lumber Co Ltd v Phillips* [1904] AC 405; *Addiscombe Garden Estates Ltd v Crabbe* [1958] 1 QB 513, [1957] 3 All ER 563; *Shell Mex & BP Ltd v Manchester Garages Ltd* [1971] 1 All ER 841, [1971] 1 WLR 612.
 4 *London and Associated Investment Trust plc v Calow* (1986) 280 Estates Gazette 1252 (Paul Baker QC sitting as a Deputy High Court Judge of the Chancery Division), [1987] Conv 137 (S. Bridge); *Dresden Estates Ltd v Collinson* (1987) 281 Estates Gazette 1321, CA (arrangement described as licence enabled owner to require 'licensees' to transfer their occupation to other premises within the property; held, since exclusive possession not conferred for whole period, arrangement created a licence). See also *Dellneed Ltd v Chin* (1987) 281 Estates Gazette 531.

contemporaneously. Each was expressed to be made as a licence, the parties being referred to as 'licensor' and 'licensee'. Each stated that the Rent Acts were not to apply, that the licensor was 'not willing ... to grant exclusive possession', and that the use of the flat was 'in common with the licensor and such other licensees or invitees as [he] may permit from time to time ... ' The Lords held that the two agreements were interdependent and constituted a single agreement. The real intention had been to confer exclusive possession, the purported right to introduce further occupiers being a pretence to avoid the Rent Acts (the word 'pretence', Lord Templeman said, being a more accurate description of what was involved than the phrases 'sham devices' and 'artificial transactions' used in *Street v Mountford*).

The outcome was different, however, in *AG Securities v Vaughan*[5] (an appeal heard by the House of Lords together with *Antoniades v Villiers*). A landlord granted four persons, by separate agreements, made on separate dates and for different payments, the right to the exclusive use of a four-bedroom flat for six month (renewable) terms, in common with three other occupants who had or might from time to time be granted the like right. The four agreements, the Lords held, were independent of each other and did not confer on any one occupant a right to exclusive possession. The agreements thus constituted licences, not leases.

That a licence, not a lease, existed was the outcome also in *Mikeover Ltd v Brady*,[6] the deciding factor here being held to be the absence of a joint obligation on the occupants to pay the monthly sum due ($£173.32$) and, instead, the imposition on each of them of individual and separate obligations to pay $£86.66$, half the total due. (The authority of the decision is weakened by the failure of the court to appreciate that the term 'joint tenancy' in the context of a lease does not carry, as the court assumed, the same meaning as the term when used in the context of co-ownership.) In *Stribling v Wickham*,[7] in which case also a licence, not a lease, was found to exist, each of three occupants was responsible for payment of a proportion of the total sum due, a further factor militating against the creation of a jointly held lease being that each individual occupant's occupation was terminable on 28 days' notice on either side, by the landlord or by any one occupant.

3.   The pseudo-lodger

An attempt may be made to make an occupier a licensee by providing that the landlord should provide services that would make the occupier a lodger. In *Crancour v Da Silvaesa*[8] A and B were permitted to occupy rooms in a house except between 10.30 am and midday for 26 weeks. L retained 'an absolute

5   [1990] 1 AC 417; (M & B). Followed in *Aslan v Murphy* [1989] 3 All ER 130, [1990] 1 WLR 766, CA, (M & B); (arrangements purporting to prevent exclusive possession held to be pretences).
6   [1989] 3 All ER 618, CA (M & B). See also *Smith v Northside Developments Ltd* (1987) 55 P & CR 164, CA; [1989] Conv 55.
7   (1989) 21 HLR 381, CA; [1989] Conv 192 (JEM); (M & B).
8   (1986) 278 Estates Gazette 618, CA; (1987) 50 MLR 226 (A. J. Waite).

right of entry ... for the purposes of exercising ... management and control ..., cleaning ... , providing ... attendance'. A claimed that no cleaning had been carried out. It was held that there were sufficient doubts as to whether the arrangement was a sham to make it inappropriate for the court to make an order (under RSC Order 113) that A and B should give up possession. In the case of a purported lodging agreement, it is thus clear that the court will look behind the wording of agreement to find the reality of the arrangement that has been entered into. For example, in *Luganda v Service Hotels Ltd*[9] a bed-sitting room in premises described as a 'hotel' and consisting of rooms separately occupied, was held to be occupied under a lease and so protected under the Rent Acts. On the other hand, in *Westminster City Council v Clarke*[10] it was held that single rooms, each with a bed and limited cooking facilities, in a hostel for single men, occupied under a 'licence to occupy' which gave no right to exclusive occupation to any one particular room, were held under a licence, not a lease.

The relevant intention

From what has been said it will be clear that whether a lease or a licence is created depends on the intention of the parties. But the intention that is relevant is concerned not with the label that parties attach to the agreement nor with the arrangement that the agreement purports to establish, but with characteristics that the parties intend the arrangement should have: ' ... the only intention that is relevant is the intention demonstrated by the agreement to grant exclusive occupation for a term at a rent'.[11] If the characteristics of the arrangement are those of a lease, then it is a lease that is created: if the thing has three prongs, it is a fork (regardless of the fact that it carries a label saying 'Spade').

This was the message of *Street v Mountford*, and its simplicity was as manifest as it was welcome. The position, as will have been realised, has not proved as straightforward as the decision suggested. Thus, (1) cases have shown that for a variety of reasons (for example, separate agreements for separately payable payments) there may be no exclusive possession. (2) In *Street v Mountford* itself, Lord Templeman accepted that there could be exceptional circumstances in which, notwithstanding that there was exclusive possession for a rent, a licence, not a lease existed. These, he said, included, (a) where the circumstances showed that there was no intention to create a legal relationship (a matter dealt with below); (b) where the occupancy was within one of a limited number of special categories, for example under a contract for the sale of land, or pursuant to a contract of employment,[12] or referable to the holding of an office; (c) where the grantor had no legal power to create a tenancy.[13]

---

9 [1969] 2 Ch 209, [1969] 2 All ER 692.
10 [1992] 2 AC 288, [1992] 1 All ER 695, HL, [1992] Conv 285 (D. S. Cowan).
11 Per Lord Templeman, *Street v Mountford*, supra at 826.
12 At any rate where an employee is required to occupy premises for the better performance of his duties, as in *Norris v Checksfield* [1991] 4 All ER 327, [1991] 1 WLR 1241, CA.
13 As in *Camden Borough Council v Shortlife Community Housing Ltd* (1992) 90 LGR 358.

Ogwr Borough Council v Dykes concerned a woman whose tenancy of a council house was terminated for non-payment of rent. In pursuance of its duty to homeless persons imposed by the Housing Act 1985, the Council allowed the woman and her young children to remain in possession of the same house for a period of 13 weeks under an agreement headed 'Licence to occupy temporary accommodation'. Did the agreement constitute a lease or a licence? The Court of Appeal held that the agreement created a licence. The right to exclusive possession had been granted by the Council in discharge of its statutory duties, in terms, acknowledged by the occupant, that specifically negatived the intention to create a tenancy. Notwithstanding that exclusive possession had been granted for a term (and for a rent) the agreement constituted a licence. The decision suggested that the Court of Appeal had begun to wobble: that a three-pronged instrument might, after all, be a spade.

The rationale for the decision was, perhaps, that occupation permitted by a local authority under its statutory duty to homeless persons should be regarded as a circumstance of the kind that Lord Templeman indicated could exist by way of exception to the general rule. However that may be, a return to the pure doctrine of *Street v Mountford* was not long afterwards demonstrated. In *Family Housing Association v Jones*[15] a homeless woman was housed in a self-contained flat by a housing association which managed certain local authority-owned properties as temporary accommodation for homeless families, under an agreement that was described as a 'licence' and expressed to be granted on the basis that the woman did not have exclusive possession as against the association. The Court of Appeal held that the totality of the circumstances showed that the woman did have exclusive possession and that the agreement contained all the requirements for the creation of a weekly tenancy.

Intention to create legal relations

Whether it is a lease or a licence (ie a contractual licence) that is created, the parties must have intended that a legally binding relationship should have been created.[16] Where one person allows another to occupy premises, albeit with exclusive possession, but there is no intention to create legal relations, then the occupier holds merely as a bare licensee – one whose entitlement can be ended at any time. In a number of cases the courts have held that no lease or licence existed because an intention to create legal relations was lacking.[17] This may be the outcome when one person allows another to occupy his property as a result, for example, of a 'family arrangement, an act of friendship

---

14   [1989] 2 All ER 880, [1989] 1 WLR 295.
15   [1990] 1 All ER 385, [1990] 1 WLR 779. The decision in *Ogwr Borough Council v Dykes* was distinguished and its correctness doubted. The matter was remitted to the county court for decision in the light of the Court of Appeal's ruling.
16   [1987] Conv 56 (G. McCormack).
17   *Booker v Palmer* [1942] 2 All ER 674; *Marcroft Wagons Ltd v Smith* [1951] 2 KB 496, [1951] 2 All ER 271; *Errington v Errington and Woods* [1952] 1 KB 290, [1952] 1 All ER 149; *Cobb v Lane* [1952] 1 All ER 1199; *Isaac v Hotel de Paris Ltd* [1960] 1 All ER 348, [1960] 1 WLR 239; *Heslop v Burns* [1974] 3 All ER 406, [1974] 1 WLR 1241.

or generosity or such like',[18] as where an employer allowed the daughter of a deceased employee to remain in the cottage which her father had occupied.[19]

Rationale rests on public policy

By way of background we may note that in seeking the true intentions of a landlord and an occupier (or occupiers) of premises, the courts have applied a principle of general application in English law, namely that, whatever the nature of a transaction, the court will override[20] sham devices[1] and give effect to what was the real intention of the parties. Such shams have been described[2] as acts done, or documents executed, with the intention of giving the appearance of creating between the parties legal rights and obligations different from the actual legal rights and obligations (if any) which the parties intend to create.

Types of lease

Leases for a fixed period

Leases for three months, for seven years, or for 99 years are examples of such a lease.[3]

There is no restriction on the length of the time for which a lease may be granted. A restriction does exist, however, in the case of a contract by a landlord to grant a new lease to a tenant on the expiry of an existing lease. Under the Law of Property Act 1922,[4] a contract for the renewal of a lease[5] at the end of an existing lease is void if the period of the new lease is more than 60 years.

A lease for a fixed period ends automatically when the period expires. There is thus no need for the landlord to give the tenant notice to quit in order to terminate the lease.[6] The landlord cannot terminate the lease before the end of the period (unless, and in certain circumstances explained later, the tenant is in breach of his undertaking; eg he fails to pay the rent due). Nor can the tenant terminate the lease before the end of the period (though he can ask

---

18 Denning LJ, *Facchini v Bryson* [1952] 1 TLR 1386 at 1389.
19 *Marcroft Wagons Ltd v Smith*, supra.
20 As in *Gisborne v Burton* [1989] QB 390, [1988] 3 All ER 760, CA; cf *Hilton v Plustitle* [1988] 3 All ER 1051, [1989] 1 WLR 149, CA; [1989] Conv 196 (C. Rodgers).
1 Or 'pretences' as Lord Templeman preferred, in *Street v Mountford*, supra.
2 Per Diplock LJ, *Snook v London and West Riding Investments Ltd* [1967] 2 QB 786, 802, CA.
3 A holiday cottage let on a time share basis for a period of one week in every year for 80 years is held for 80 separate periods of one week (not for a period of 80 years) and thus, not being a lease for a period exceeding 21 years, is not zero rated for value added tax under Sch 4 of the Finance Act 1972; *Cottage Holiday Associates Ltd v Customs and Excise Comrs* [1983] QB 735.
4 Sch 15, para 7.
5 Or a sub-lease.
6 This rule is subject to certain statutory exceptions, eg in the case of agricultural holdings.

the landlord to accept his surrender of the lease).

A lease for any period is a 'term of years' within the definition of the latter in the Law of Property Act 1925[7] and is thus capable of being a legal estate under s 1 of the Act.

Periodic leases

Weekly, monthly, quarterly, and yearly leases are examples of periodic leases.

CHARACTERISTICS

A periodic tenancy is one that continues indefinitely until ended by proper notice by either party. The length of the notice required to terminate such a lease depends (subject to agreement to the contrary and subject to what is said below) on the form that the periodic lease takes: a weekly lease can be terminated by giving a week's notice, a monthly lease by giving a month's notice, and so on, the notice expiring in each case at the end of a completed period.[8]

If neither party gives notice, the lease continues for ever. If the landlord dies, the reversion passes under his will or intestacy; if the tenant dies, the lease passes under his will or intestacy. This might suggest that the lease is of indefinite duration, and thus run counter to the rule that a lease must be of fixed duration. However, this is not so, since the law regards the lease at the outset as being for a fixed period of, eg in the case of a yearly lease, one year. If no notice to terminate is given, with the result that the lease continues, the law regards the lease as being for another fixed period of one year, and so on.

A periodic lease is a 'term of years' within the definition of the Law of Property Act 1925[9] and is thus capable of being a legal estate under s 1 of the Act.

CREATION

A periodic lease may be created expressly where some term such as 'yearly lease', 'yearly tenant', 'yearly tenancy', is used; or where more informal words such as 'from year to year' are used. Further, a periodic tenancy is created where (in the absence of any other indication[10] as to the type of lease granted) there is express reference to the period of notice required to terminate the lease. Thus a lease to A determinable on the giving of six months' notice creates a six-monthly lease.

If there are no express words creating a particular form of lease nor any

---

7   Law of Property Act 1925, s 205(1)(xxvii).
8   [1992] Conv 263 (E. Cooke).
9   Section 205(1)(xxvii).
10   As in *Javad v Aqil* [1991] 1 All ER 243, 1 WLR 1007, CA (M & B) (tenancy at will held to have been created).

other circumstances from which an intention to create a certain form of lease may be inferred, then, by implication of law, a periodic lease arises. The form which the periodic lease thus created will take will depend on the period with reference to which the rent is measured. Thus if the lease is to A at '£250 a year', or at '£250 per annum', a yearly lease arises; if it is to B at '£15 a week', or at '£15 weekly', a weekly lease arises; and so on. What matters is the period by which the rent is measured; it is immaterial that the rent may be payable at some other interval. Thus a lease to A at '£90 a quarter, payable monthly', creates a quarterly not a monthly lease.[11]

A periodic lease may arise at the expiry of an existing lease. For example, suppose that L leases land to T for seven years at a rent of £520 a year, payable quarterly. T thus holds a lease for a fixed period of seven years. At the end of that time he remains in possession of the land (he 'holds over'), and pays a month's rent, which T accepts. The result is that, provided there are no circumstances indicating some other intention, T holds by implication of law as a monthly tenant under a periodic lease. If he had paid a quarter's rent, and T had accepted this, he would have held under a quarterly tenancy; and so on. The terms of the expired lease will continue to apply to the new periodic tenancy except in so far as any term is inconsistent with the new periodic tenancy created.[12]

NOTICE

Although in general the length of notice required to terminate a periodic lease depends on the form of the lease, the following exceptions exist.

Yearly leases

At common law, in the absence of a contrary intention,[13] a yearly tenancy can be determined only on the anniversary of its commencement, and to achieve this either party must give at least half a year's prior notice. If the lease began on one of the customary quarter days (Lady Day, Midsummer, Michaelmas or Christmas) 'half a year' means 182 days.

Quarterly, monthly and weekly leases

The common law rules are now subject to certain statutory exceptions. For example, under the Protection from Eviction Act 1977,[14] in the case of premises let as a dwelling a minimum of four weeks' notice is required.

---

11 See *Adler v Blackman* [1953] 1 QB 146, [1952] 2 All ER 945; (M & B); [1991] CLJ 323 (S. Bridge).
12 Eg a covenant to repair is not inconsistent with a yearly tenancy and so will apply to a newly created periodic tenancy; *Wyatt v Cole* (1877) 36 LT 613. Similarly in the case of a covenant to carry on a specified trade. *Sanders v Karnell* (1858) 1 F & F 356. But a covenant to paint every three years is not consistent with a yearly tenancy and so ceases to apply; *Pinero v Judson* (1829) 6 Bing 206.
13 And statutory exception, eg in the case of agricultural holdings.
14 Section 5, replacing the Rent Act 1957, s 16.

Tenancies at will

If L permits T to occupy land as a tenant and the arrangement is such that the tenancy may be determined by L or T at any time, T occupies the land as a tenant at will. For example, where T, after the expiry of a lease, remains in possession of the property with the permission of L, then T holds as a tenant at will. If T subsequently pays rent at, eg £50 a month, which L accepts, thereafter T holds, by implication of law, under a periodic, monthly lease.[15]

As regards rent, unless it is agreed that the occupation is to be rent-free, as a tenant at will T must pay L compensation for the period of his occupation. If either T or L dies the tenancy comes to an end. It also comes to an end if L assigns his interest in the land, or if T purports to assign such interest as he has, or if L or T do any act inconsistent with the continuance of the tenancy.[16]

Whether or not a tenancy at will is within the definition of a 'term of years' in the Law of Property Act 1925[17] (and thus capable of being a legal estate) is uncertain. It has been suggested that a tenancy at will is 'not a species of estate but a mere relationship of tenure unaccompanied by any estate'.[18] Viewed in this light the relationship has affinities with that which existed between a feudal tenant and his lord before the notion of estates was introduced into the framework of tenures. Since the duration of the tenancy is not fixed, a tenancy at will is perhaps not really a lease at all. It is, however, more than a licence, since the relationship is more than a purely contractual one, as L and T agreed that T should hold the land as L's tenant.

Tenancies at suffrance

If L grants T a lease of land and the lease expires, and T remains in possession of the land without L's permission, then he is said to hold as a tenant at suffrance. L may claim possession at any time. L has a claim[19] against T for 'use and occupation' of the property during his period of possession.[20]

If T pays rent which L accepts, T becomes a tenant under a periodic lease; if L consents to T remaining but no rent is agreed, he becomes a tenant at will; if L dissents from T's possession, T becomes a trespasser. (It will be noted that T is not a trespasser at the outset because his original entry was not unlawful, being by virtue of his lease.)

A tenant at suffrance thus does not hold under a true tenancy. He does not even hold of his lord, as does a tenant at will. The arrangement has acquired

---

15   *Martin v Smith* (1874) LR 9 Exch 50.
16   Eg if L enters the land and carries away stone or cuts timber; *Turner v Doe d Bennett* (1842) 9 M & W 643; or if T commits waste; *Countess Shrewsbury's Case* (1600) 5 Co Rep 13b.
17   Section 205(1)(xxvii).
18   M & W, p 655.
19   *Leigh v Dickeson* (1884) 15 QBD 60.
20   There is no presumtpion that the amount payable should continue to be that paid under the lease. The appropriate payment is the rent obtainable on the open market; *Dean and Chapter of the Cathedral and Metropolitan Church of Christ Canterbury v Whitbread plc* (1995) 72 P & CR 9.

the name tenancy because the parties were originally landlord and tenant, but it is a misnomer. It has been suggested[1] that a tenant at suffrance is no more than a squatter. The position of the squatter is considered later.[2]

Tenancy by estoppel[3]

Suppose that L builds a house on a piece of waste land which belongs to O. Later L purports to grant a lease of the house to T. Since L has no estate in the land, T can acquire no estate either. Nevertheless, the purported grant is not without effect. For example, suppose that later, before the expiry of the purported lease, L attempted to put T out of the house, saying 'You have no lease because I could not have granted you one. You have no interest in the land. I built the house and you must go.' Notwithstanding that T has no interest in the land, L is estopped from denying that T has the right he purported to grant him. And, conversely, T is estopped from denying his obligation under the purported lease, eg to pay L the rent agreed[4] or to keep the premises in good repair.[5]

The arrangement which has come into existence is termed a tenancy by estoppel.[6] Such a tenancy has most of the characteristics of a true lease. For example, the tenancy may be for a fixed period, or may be periodic, according to the terms of the grant or the circumstances in which it came into existence. Further, not only is the tenancy enforceable between the parties but the tenancy can be assigned by L or can pass under his will or intestacy. If L later acquires the fee simple in the land, T acquires a legal lease subject to the same terms as the original one purported.[7] When L acquires the fee simple this is said to 'feed the estoppel'; ie the legality is 'fed through' to T.[8]

While dealing with the principle of acquisition of title by estoppel (and the notion of a legal title being 'fed through'), it will be convenient to mention here that the principle described applies also in the case of the grant of a mortgage. Thus if R wishes to borrow money on the security of land, and in order to secure the loan he purports to mortgage to E land the title to which he does not in fact hold, then if R later acquires the legal title to the land, the legality is fed through to E who thereupon holds a legal mortgage.[9]

---

1   M & W, p 656.
2   See Chapter 24.
3   See J. Martin (1978) 42 Conv (NS) 137.
4   *Pargeter v Harris* (1845) 7 QB 708 at 745.
5   If T surrenders the lease to L he remains liable for breaches of covenant that occurred before the surrender (unless the reason for the surrender was that T was ousted by someone with a better title than L); *Industrial Properties (Barton Hill) Ltd v Associated Electrical Industries Ltd* [1977] QB 580, [1977] 2 All ER 293; (M & B), not following *Harrison v Wells* [1967] 1 QB 263, [1966] 3 All ER 524.
6   A tenancy by estoppel may arise also where L is merely a licensee (and so has no power to grant a lease).
7   *Woolwich Equitable Building Society v Marshall* [1952] Ch 1, [1951] 2 All ER 769.
8   See *Grace Rymer Investments Ltd v Waite* [1958] Ch 831, [1958] 2 All ER 777.
9   *First National Bank v Thompson* [1996] Ch 231, [1996] 1 All ER 140.

Leases for life: leases determinable on death, and leases determinable on marriage

Before 1926, if L granted T a lease for his (T's) life, this conferred on T a life estate[10] in the land (ie a freehold estate). If L granted T a lease for, say, 21 years, terminable during that period by T's marriage or by T's death, then T held a lease for this period, but which terminated if T married or died before the expiry of the lease. (The grant did not infringe the rule that a lease must be for a fixed period, since the maximum duration was fixed.)

By s 149(6) of the Law of Property Act 1925, if L grants T,

(a) a lease for life (whether that of T or someone else); or
(b) a lease for a fixed period determinable during that period on a person's death (whether that of T or someone else); or
(c) a lease for a fixed period determinable during that period on T's marriage,

and the lease is granted at a rent or for a fine[11] the interest which T receives is converted into a lease for 90 years. This provision applies whether the grant was made before 1926 or after 1925. Under the section, if the death or marriage referred to in the grant occurs, the lease does not end but either party[12] may determine it by serving on the other at least one month's written notice.[13]

Renewable leases

If L grants T a lease for (say) ten years and the lease provides that (say) one month before the expiry of the ten years T shall have a right[14] on paying L £100 to call on L to grant him a fresh lease for the same period and at the same rent as the first one, then such a lease is termed a renewable lease. If T exercises the option L must grant him a fresh lease. When the second ten-year period expires, unless L chooses to grant him another lease, T's interest in the land ends. However, if the first lease provides that at the end of the first lease T shall have a right to call on L to grant him a fresh lease on the same terms as the first one, ie, including the term giving T the right to call on L for further renewal, then, provided that T exercises the option at the end of each successive ten-year period, his interest can last indefinitely (each link that is added to the chain giving T the right, when the time comes, to add another link). Only if T omits to exercise the option will his interest come to an end. A lease in this form is termed a perpetually renewable lease.[15]

10   If the grant was for the life of any other person, T received a life estate *pur autre vie*.
11   If L granted T a lease for life without a rent, then the land became settled land under the Settled Land Act 1925 and T had all the powers of a Tenant for Life and was entitled to have the legal estate vested in him; SLA 1925, s 20(1)(iv).
12   Eg on T's death, L or T's estate.
13   The notice expiring on one of the special quarter days, if any, applicable to the lease; otherwise, on one of the customary quarter days.
14   For registration of the right (an *option*), see Chapter 25.
15   For an example, see *Re Hopkin's Lease* [1972] 1 All ER 248, [1972] 1 WLR 372. Cf *Marjorie Burnett Ltd v Barclay* (1980) 258 Estates Gazette 642; (M & B). See also *Parkus v Greenwood* [1950] Ch 644, [1950] 1 All ER 436.

By the Law of Property Act 1922[16] all perpetually renewable leases existing at the end of 1925 or created after 1925 are converted into leases for 2,000 years calculated from when the lease was granted. The new lease is subject to the same terms as the one it replaces except that the following changes are imposed:

1. T may end the new lease on any date that the original lease would have ended if it had not been renewed, provided that T gives L notice in writing at least ten days before the date of termination. If T does not do so, the lease continues.
2. Every assignment of the lease and every devolution of the lease (eg to T's next of kin on T's intestacy) must be registered with L within six months of the assignment or devolution; and T must pay L a fee of one guinea.
3. If T assigns the leases he ceases to be liable to L for any breaches of covenant in the original lease committed after the assignment.
4. If the original lease required T to make a payment to L on exercising the option to renew, and if the original lease was granted before 1925, the payment is converted into additional rent; if it was granted after 1925, the requirement for the payment is void.

It will be seen that the Act does not alter the position that it is T, not L, who decides whether the lease shall continue, but whereas before 1926 the lease ended if T did nothing, after 1925 the lease continues unless T does something.

'Protected shorthold tenancies', and other tenancies under the Rent Acts and Housing Acts

A 'protected shorthold tenancy' is not a type of lease, but the name given to a lease for a fixed period that is exempted,[17] if it complies with certain conditions,[18] from the full effect of the Rent Acts.[19] Similarly, 'regulated tenancies', 'protected tenancies', 'protected shorthold tenancies', 'regulated tenancies', 'statutory tenancies' (and, formerly, 'controlled tenancies') are not types of lease, but terms attached to tenancies having certain characteristics (and certain forms of protection) under the Rent Acts. ('Assured tenancies' and 'Secure tenancies' arise under the Housing Acts of 1980 and 1985 respectively.)

Formalities

If (1) L grants a lease to T for seven years; (2) T sublets part of the land to ST for one year; (3) T assigns his lease (ie the unexpired part) to A; (4) L assigns

---

16 Section 14 and Sch 15, paras 1, 5.
17 Housing Act 1980, s 52.
18 The letting must initially be for a fixed term of between one and five years. Notice in the statutory form must be given to the tenant that the lease is to be a shorthold tenancy.
19 The principal effect is that at the end of the period the landlord can, after giving notice to the tenant and applying to the court, recover the land.

the reversion to P; (5) ST assigns his sub-lease (ie the unexpired term) to B, this series of transactions can be represented thus:

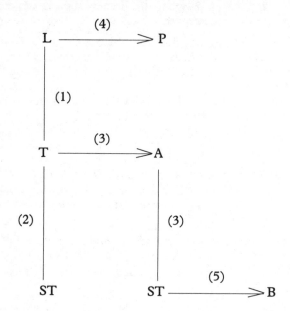

It will be noted that:

(1) when T assigns his lease to A, ST's landlord ceases to be T, and becomes A;

(2) when T assigns his lease to A, as regards that part of the land let to ST, T is assigning a reversion, ie the reversion on ST's lease;

(3) the final result is that P holds the fee simple; the land is leased to A; (A occupies part of the land; the remainder is occupied by B);

(4) when B's sub-lease expires, A will be entitled to possession of all the land; when A's lease expires, P will be entitled to possession of all the land. T's lease (and A's lease after the assignment) is sometimes referred to as the *head lease* in order to distinguish it from the sub-lease.

When considering what formality is required for a transaction relating to a lease it is necessary to consider:

(1) whether the transaction concerned is (a) the creation (ie the granting) of a lease or a sub-lease; or (b) the assignment of a lease or a sub-lease;

(2) in the case of the creation of a lease or a sub-lease whether one is speaking of (a) the formalities required for the creation of a legal lease or sub-lease; or (b) the conditions to be satisfied for the creation of an equitable lease or sub-lease;

(3) in the case of an assignment of a lease or sub-lease, whether the lease or sub-lease to be assigned is (a) a legal lease or sub-lease; or (b) an equitable lease or sub-lease;

(4) in the case of an assignment of a lease or a sub-lease, whether one is speaking of (a) the formalities required for the lease or sub-lease to be assigned legally; or (b) the conditions to be satisfied for an equitable assignment of the lease or sub-lease;

(5) whether one is speaking of (a) the transaction itself (ie the granting of the lease or the sub-lease or the assignment of the lease or sub-lease); or (b) a contract to carry out the transaction (eg a contract between T and A that T will assign the lease to him).

CREATION OF LEASES

Creation of a legal lease

For L to grant a legal lease to T, L must hold a legal estate in the land. If L holds merely an equitable fee simple, any lease he grants will necessarily be equitable.

Assuming that L holds a legal estate in the land, if the lease which L grants to T,

(a) takes effect in possession; and
(b) is for a period not exceeding three years; and
(c) is for the best rent reasonably obtainable without taking a fine,

no special formality need be complied with in order to create a legal lease.[20] Thus such a lease may be created in writing (not by deed) or even orally.

However, if the lease,

(a) does not take effect in possession; or
(b) is for a period exceeding three years; or
(c) is not for the best rent reasonably obtainable without taking a fine,

in order to create a legal lease, the grant must be by deed.[1]

A lease takes effect 'in possession' if it gives a right to possession immediately, and not at some time in the future. The phrase 'three years' includes a periodic lease (weekly, monthly, quarterly, etc) for any period of three years or less.

The rules governing the creation of a sub-lease are the same as those relating to the creation of a head lease.

Creation of an equitable lease

How an equitable lease may arise under the doctrine in *Walsh v Lonsdale* has been explained in Chapter 16. It may be added that a lease will necessarily be

---

20 LPA 1925, s 54(2); [1992] Conv 252 (P. Sparkes).
1 LPA 1925, s 52(1), under which any conveyance creating a legal estate (eg a legal lease) is void unless by deed.

equitable if the interest held by the lessor is equitable. For example if V contracts to sell Blackacre to P, and P thereupon leases the land to T, since at the date of the lease P held an equitable fee simple, T obtains an equitable lease.[2] (The differences between legal leases and equitable leases were noted in Chapter 16.)

ASSIGNMENT OF LEASES

Assignment of legal leases

LEGAL ASSIGNMENT OF A LEGAL LEASE

If L holds a legal fee simple in Blackacre, and he grants a legal lease of the land to T, T holds a legal estate in the land. He holds a legal estate in the land irrespective of whether his lease is a periodic lease, or a lease for a fixed period of eg seven days or 9,999 years. As seen in Chapter 15, in order to convey a legal estate in land a deed must be used. A deed must thus be used for the assignment of *any* legal lease, irrespective of its length. It will therefore be seen that if L *grants* T a legal lease for six months this may be done orally; but for T to make a legal *assignment* of the lease to A, this must be by deed.[3]

EQUITABLE ASSIGNMENT OF A LEGAL LEASE

If T holds a legal lease of Blackacre, and he assigns the lease to A, and he fails to use a deed, but the assignment is in writing and complies in other respects with s 2 of the Law Reform (Miscellaneous) Provisions Act 1989, and A gives consideration, then, under the doctrine in *Walsh v Lonsdale*, there is a valid equitable assignment to A. Since the assignment is equitable, the lease which A holds is equitable, the legal lease remaining with T, who now holds on trust for A.

ASSIGNMENT OF EQUITABLE LEASES

If T holds an equitable lease (eg because the grant by L failed to comply with the legal requirement, and took effect under the doctrine in *Walsh v Lonsdale*) then, since the interest that T holds is equitable, in order to assign the lease to A, the assignment must, under s 53(1)(c) of the Law of Property Act 1925 be in writing signed by T (or by his agent authorised in writing).[4]

---

2   See *Industrial Properties (Barton Hill) Ltd v Associated Electrical Industries Ltd* [1977] 2 WLR 726 at 747-748.

3   *Crago v Julian* [1992] 1 All ER 744, [1992] 1 WLR 372, CA (undertaking in divorce proceedings to assign the lease failed to do so as not by deed). Cf *Thomas Pocklington's Gift Trustees v Hill and Sullivan* (1989) 21 HLR 391, CA; see [1989] Conv 289 (JEM).

4   See Chapter 15.

It will be convenient to mention here that if L leases land to T for, say, seven years, and later T sub-leases the land to X for the whole of the unexpired portion of his,[5] T's, lease, then irrespective of the intention of T and X, the sub-lease to X operates as an *assignment* by T to X of the lease.[6] Thus T ceases to be L's tenant and X becomes L's tenant in T's place. Any covenants made by T (eg to pay rent, to undertake repairs) become binding on X.

CONTRACTS

Under section 2 of the Law of Property (Miscellaneous Provisions) Act 1989[7] a contract for the sale or other disposition of an interest in land must be made in writing, incorporating all the terms expressly agreed, signed by or on behalf of each party. The granting of a lease, legal or equitable, is a disposition of land. The assignment of a lease, legal or equitable, is also a disposition of an interest in land. Thus a contract for the granting or assignment of any lease, legal or equitable, must comply with section 2 of the 1989 Act.

To this rule there are certain exceptions, the principal exception being that, a contract for the grant of a lease taking effect in possession for a term not exceeding three years at the best rent reasonably obtained (the grant of which may be made orally) is not subject to the requirements of section 2 (and so, like the grant, may be made orally).[8]

Obligations of a landlord and a tenant

Introduction

Consider these questions. L leases 17 Blackacre Terrace to T for three years. When T goes into the house he finds that the kitchen floor is flooded and the ceiling of a bedroom has fallen in. Is L under any obligation to put matters right? Later, a chimney collapses. Is it T or L who is responsible for the repair? L writes to T requesting T to pay rent in advance. Is T under any obligation to do so? T receives a bill for council tax. Is it T or L who is liable for paying this? T finds that L has cut off his electricity supply. What right does T have

---

5   Or for a longer period than the unexpired portion.
6   *Milmo v Carreras* [1946] KB 306, [1946] 1 All ER 288; (M & B).
7   See Chapter 15.
8   Section 2(5). The other exceptions are contracts made in the course of a public auction and contracts regulated under the Financial Services Act 1986.

against L?T decides that he wants to sublet the attic to ST. Can he do so?T later wishes to assign his lease to A. Can he do so?The questions raised here (fitness of the premises at the outset, repairs, council tax, freedom from interference by the landlord, subletting and assignment) represent the matters with which we shall be concerned in considering the obligations of a landlord and of a tenant.

In seeking an answer to such questions as these it is necessary:

1. To look at the terms of the lease. For example:
    (a) the lease may contain express covenants, for example regarding liability for repairs; or,
    (b) the lease may be silent on the point at issue. In this case it is necessary to consider what conditions, if any, are implied at common law; or,
    (c) the lease (or contract for the lease) may state that the 'usual covenants' are to apply. Certain covenants have become accepted by the law as being 'usual' covenants.[9] What these are will be seen shortly.
2. To consider whether the terms of the lease are subject to any statute and, if so, to consider whether the statutory provision (i) applies only if there is no provision to the contrary in the lease; or (ii) applies irrespective of any provision to the contrary in the lease.

The distinction should be noted between:

(a) the duty, if any, imposed by common law or the terms of a lease, to repair – a duty the breach of which entitles a tenant to compel (by injunction) a landlord to undertake repairs, or claim damages arising from his failure to do so (or to seek both remedies); and,
(b) a duty that may exist at common law in negligence (or under statute, eg under the Defective Premises Act 1972) – a duty the breach of which entitles a tenant (or some other person, eg a visitor) to seek damages for injuries or other loss suffered.

The duty under (a) above is a matter of land law and contract; that under (b) is a matter of tort. The two issues may, though, be interdependent, as where a claim in negligence rests on the existence of a duty by a landlord to repair. Where a landlord is under no duty (common law, statutory or contractual) to repair, a claim may lie that rests solely in tort for breach of the general common law duty of care. Where such a claim succeeds the effect of the decision is not to impose a *duty* (ie enforceable by injunction) to repair, merely to confer damages that have resulted from non-repair. (In a recent case[10] the court, it is submitted, misdirected itself by failing to keep the two aspects of the matter distinct, finding that as liability existed in tort, a term was to be implied imposing a duty to repair.)

---

9   See *Chester v Buckingham Travel Ltd* [1981] 1 All ER 386, [1981] 1 WLR 96; *Flexman v Corbett* [1930] 1 Ch 672.
10 *McAuley v Bristol City Council* [1992] 1 QB 134, [1992] 1 All ER 749, CA.

Fitness for purpose at the outset of the tenancy

THE LEASE IS SILENT

At common law, if a house is let furnished there is an implied condition that the premises shall at the outset of the tenancy be fit for human habitation.[11] If let unfurnished no such condition exists.[12]

THE LEASE PROVIDES THAT THE 'USUAL COVENANTS' ARE TO APPLY

The 'usual covenants' do not include a covenant that the premises are fit for habitation or for any other purpose.

STATUTORY PROVISIONS

If a house is let[13] at a low rent, under the Landlord and Tenant Act 1985[14] there is an implied condition[15] that the house is fit for human habitation at the beginning of the tenancy.[16]

Liability for repairs and maintenance during the existence of the tenancy[17]

THE LEASE IS SILENT

The liability of the tenant varies according to the type of lease.[18]

Leases for a fixed period

A tenant under such a lease is liable for repairs and must maintain the premises in the same condition that he found them. This is because statute[19]

---

11   *Smith v Marrable* (1843) 11 M & W 5.
12   *Cavalier v Pope* [1906] AC 428, HL: *McNerny v Lambeth Borough Council* (1988) 21 HLR 188, CA; [1988] Conv 216 (P. F. Smith).
13   The provision does not apply if the lease is for three years or more (and is not determinable before three years have expired) and the lease provides that the tenant is to put the house into a condition reasonably fit for habitation.
14   Section 8(2). See D. Morgan, 'Unfit housing: the issue of "reasonable cost"' (1979) 43 Conv (NS) 414.
15   The condition cannot be excluded by any term in the lease to the contrary; s 6(2).
16   The provision was formerly contained in the Housing Act 1957, s 6.
17   For the problems that can arise for landlords and tenants over the management of privately owned blocks of flats, and recommendations on how these might be resolved, see the Report of the Committee under the Chairmanship of E. G. Nugee QC (1985); [1986] Conv 12 (A. J. Hawkins). The main findings of the Report were implemented in the Landlord and Tenant Act 1987. Protection to tenants against, inter alia, unreasonable service charges was given by the Housing Act 1996. For proposals for reform see *Landlord and Tenant: Responsibility for State and Condition of Property*, (item 5 of Sixth Programme of Law Reform: Landlord and Tenant), Law Com No 238 (1995).
18   *Cavalier v Pope* [1906] AC 428, HL.
19   Statute of Marlbridge 1267.

has made a tenant for a fixed term of years liable[20] for voluntary and permissive waste.

Yearly leases

At common law a tenant under such a lease is liable to keep the premises wind- and water-tight, 'fair wear and tear' excepted. The effect of the exception is that the tenant is not liable for damage which results from the ordinary operation of natural forces or from reasonable use of the premises. But the exception does not remove liability from the tenant for consequential damage, eg damage caused by rain dripping through places where roof tiles have slipped.

Weekly tenancies

A weekly tenant is not responsible for repairs and maintenance,[1] but he is nonetheless liable if he fails to 'take proper care of the place',[2] eg by failing to clean the chimney when necessary, or to unstop the sink when it gets blocked, or to turn off the water if he is leaving the premises during weather when water is likely to freeze in pipes.

Other period tenancies

The position of the tenant is uncertain but is probably similar to that in a weekly tenancy. A landlord is at common law under no obligation to carry out repairs or maintenance.[3] This rule does not, however, preclude a finding by the court of an implied term that the landlord should be responsible for repairs (or for certain kinds of repair[4]).

THE LEASE PROVIDES THAT THE 'USUAL COVENANTS' ARE TO APPLY[5]

The 'usual covenants' include a covenant by the tenant to keep the premises in repair and to deliver them up in repair at the end of the lease. If the landlord has expressly undertaken any obligation to repair (eg to maintain the plumbing) the 'usual covenants' include a covenant by the tenant to permit the landlord to enter and view the state of repair.

---

20   See *Mancetter Development Ltd v Garmanson Ltd* [1986] QB 1212, [1986] 1 All ER 449.
1   *Mint v Good* [1951] 1 KB 517, [1950] 2 All ER 1159.
2   *Warren v Keen* [1954] 1 QB 15; Lord Denning at 20.
3   *Cavalier v Pope*, supra.
4   *Barrett v Lounova (1982) Ltd* [1990] 1 QB 348, [1989] 1 All ER 351, CA (tenant of dwelling house covenanted to do all inside repairs; lease silent as to external repairs; held that since tenant's covenant would eventually become impossible to perform without repair of exterior, in order to give business efficacy to the agreement, an obligation to repair the exterior was to be imposed on the landlord); [1988] Conv 448, (P. F.Smith); *King v South Northamptonshire District Council* (1991) 90 LGR 121 (implied obligation to maintain path leading to a council house).
5   [1992] Conv 18 (L. Crabb).

THE LEASE CONTAINS AN EXPRESS PROVISION AS TO LIABILITY FOR REPAIRS

An obligation to 'repair'[6] (whether imposed on the landlord or tenant) normally includes liability for replacing the whole building in the event of its destruction, eg by fire. It also includes the replacing of subsidiary parts of a building that can no longer be repaired (eg a cracked wash basin).[7]

The meaning of the words 'fair wear and tear excepted' when used expressly in a lease is the same as that explained above.

STATUTORY PROVISIONS

(A) If a house is let[8] at a low rent, under the Landlord and Tenant Act 1985[9] there is an implied condition[10] not only, as we have seen, that the house shall be fit for human habitation at the beginning of the tenancy, but also that the landlord will maintain it in this condition[11] during the tenancy.[12]

(B) If a dwelling house is leased for a period of less than seven years, the Landlord and Tenant Act 1985[13] provides that there shall be an implied covenant[14] by the landlord that he will:

(a) keep the exterior and structure of the premises[15] in repair[16] (including drains, gutters and external pipes), and,

(b) repair and keep in working order installations in the house for:

(i) the supply of water, gas and electricity and for sanitation including basins, sinks, baths and sanitary conveniences; but not fixtures or appliances for making use of the supply of water, gas or electricity, (eg ovens);

(ii) space heating or water heating.

6　For the obligation on a tenant to keep in 'good tenantable repair', see *Proudfoot v Hart* (1889) 25 QBD 42. Where a defect occurs within the leased premises, the breach of the landlord's obligation occurs only when he has notice of the defect and fails to effect repairs; *British Telecommunications plc v Sun Life Assurance Society plc* [1996] Ch 69, [1995] 4 All ER 44.

7　See *Ravenseft Properties Ltd v Davstone (Holdings) Ltd* [1980] QB 12, [1979] 1 All ER 929; (1979) 43 Conv (NS) 429 (P. F. Smith); [1987] Conv 224 (P. F. Smith).

8　With the exception noted above, see footnote 13, p 295.

9　Section 8(1).

10　The condition cannot be excluded by any term in the lease to the contrary.

11　See *Summers v Salford Corpn* [1943] AC 283, [1943] 1 All ER 68 (jammed window); *Fraser v Hopewood Properties* [1986] CLY 1843 (leaking roof caused flat to smell like crypt of a church).

12　The provision was formerly in the Housing Act 1926, s 2.

13　Section 11, replacing the Housing Act 1961, ss 32, 33.

14　The covenant may not be excluded unless the county court authorises exclusion as being reasonable.

15　For the application of the section to flats, see *Campden Hill Towers Ltd v Gardner* [1977] QB 823, [1977] 1 All ER 739; *Liverpool City Council v Irwin* [1977] AC 239, [1976] 2 All ER 39; *Douglas-Scott v Scorgie* [1984] 1 All ER 1086, [1984] 1 WLR 716.

16　See *Quick v Taff-Ely Borough Council* [1986] QB 809, [1985] 3 All ER 321 (condensation not due to lack of repair); *Trustees of the Dame Margaret Hungerford Charity v Beazeley* (1993) 26 HLR 269 (stage may be reached when only practical means of keeping a roof in repair is to replace it); [1994] Conv 415 (J. Morgan).

In determining the standard of repair required by the covenant, the Act[17] requires regard to be had to the age, character and prospective life of the dwelling house and the location[18] in which it is situated.

(c) If a landlord sues a tenant for damages for breach of a covenant to repair, then under the Landlord and Tenant Act 1927,[19] the damages awarded may not exceed the diminution in the value of the reversion resulting from the failure to do the repairs.[20] If the premises are to be demolished, no damages at all are recoverable.

(d) The Housing Act 1996 imposes on landlords of houses in multiple occupation a duty to ensure that their premises are safe. Failure to observe the duty is an offence.

ENFORCEMENT OF A LANDLORD'S OBLIGATION TO REPAIR

Where a landlord is responsible for repairs and he fails to discharge this responsibility, it has been held that a tenant is entitled, having carried out the repairs, to recoup himself by making deductions as appropriate from future payments of rent:[1] that he is entitled in equity to set off[2] the cost of repair against rent due.

Further, it has been held that where a landlord has consistently failed to comply with the requirement of section 11 of the Landlord and Tenant Act 1985, the tenant is entitled to treat the lease as repudiated (and eg vacate the premises, return the keys and pay no more rent, these actions thereby constituting acceptance of the repudiation[3]).

LIABILITY FOR DAMAGE DUE TO FAILURE TO REPAIR

It will be appreciated that the question whether a landlord is under an obligation to repair leased premises is distinct from the question whether he is liable for loss or injury due to his failure to fulfil the obligation.

A landlord may be in breach of the obligation to repair yet not liable for loss suffered as a result, eg if he had taken all steps reasonable in the circumstances. The former question lies with contract, the latter in tort.

---

17   Section 11(3).
18   The words 'age, character' and 'locality' are derived from *Proudfoot v Hart* (1890) 25 QBD 42.
19   Section 18. See *Mather v Barclays Bank* [1987] 2 EGLR 254 (guidance on application to a modern commmercial lease), (1988) 104 LQR 372.
20   *Shortlands Investments Ltd v Cargill plc* [1995] 1 EGLR 51.
1   For the principle, see *Rawson v Samuel* (1841) Cr & Ph 161, at 178 (Lord Cottenham LC).
2   *Melville v Grapelodge Developments Ltd* (1978) 39 P & CR 179; *Lee-Parker v Izzet* [1971] 3 All ER 1099, [1971] 1 WLR 1688; (1976) 40 Conv (NS) 196 (P. M. Rank). See also *British Anzani (Felixstowe) Ltd v International Marine Management (UK) Ltd* [1980] QB 137, [1979] 2 All ER 1063; [1981] Conv 199 (A. Waite); [1983] Conv 373; *Connaught Restaurants Ltd v Indoor Leisure Ltd* [1994] 4 All ER 834, [1994] 1 WLR 501, (clear words in lease needed to exclude equitable right to set off); *Eller v Grovecrest Investments Ltd* [1994] 4 All ER 845, [1995] 2 WLR 278 (right of set-off available also against landlord's distraint on tenant's goods and chattels).
3   *Hussein v Mehlman* [1992] 32 EG 59 (leaking roof, collapsed bedroom ceiling, burst water pipes and no heating); [1993] Conv 71 (S. Bright); [1993] CLJ 212 (C. Harpum).

Rent

THE LEASE SILENT

In the absence of an express provision as to the rent payable, at common law[4] there is an implied condition that the tenant shall pay a reasonable sum. Subject to agreement to the contrary, rent is payable in arrears.

THE LEASE PROVIDES THAT THE 'USUAL COVENANTS' ARE TO APPLY

The 'usual covenants' include a covenant by the tenant to pay rent; and also a condition that the landlord shall have a right of re-entry for non-payment of rent.

THE LEASE CONTAINS EXPRESS PROVISION AS TO RENT

Normally a lease will include a provision. Today rent usually takes the form of payment of a specified sum of money but there is nothing to prevent rent from being in kind or by the provision of services (eg agricultural work).

Where there is express agreement that rent is to be paid, but it is stated that the sum due is 'to be agreed' then the lease (and also a contract for a lease in these terms) is void for uncertainty.[5] On the other hand there is no uncertainty where it is provided that the rent is to be determined 'having regard to the market value' (and this is so even if no provision is made as to the means by which the rent is to be fixed[6]).

STATUTORY PROVISIONS

In certain circumstances the rent which a landlord is entitled to charge is subject to a maximum fixed according to means laid down by statute.[7] The control of rents constitutes one of the two principal ways in which the state intervenes in the relationship between landlord and tenant in order to protect the tenant against exploitation by the landlord of a situation in which, because of the shortage of building, he could, if market forces were allowed free play, charge higher rents than the state considers reasonable. (The other principal way in which the state intervenes in order to protect a tenant is by providing a measure of security against eviction.)

Council tax

THE LEASE SILENT

Liability to pay council tax rests with the tenant. Council tax was introduced by the Local Government Finance Act 1992. The tax replaces Community Charge, which had replaced the system of local taxation termed 'rates'.

---

4   Reinforced by statute: Distress for Rent Act 1737, s 4.
5   *King's Motors (Oxford) Ltd v Lax* [1969] 3 All ER 665, [1970] 1 WLR 426; (M & B).
6   *Brown v Gould* [1971] 2 All ER 1505; (M & B).
7   Eg under the Rent Acts and related legislation; see p 272, supra.

THE LEASE PROVIDES THAT THE 'USUAL COVENANTS' ARE TO APPLY

The 'usual covenants' include a covenant by the tenant to pay rates.

Freedom from interference by the landlord

THE LEASE IS SILENT

At common law there is an implied covenant by the landlord[8] that the tenant will have 'quiet enjoyment'. The phrase 'quiet enjoyment' connotes freedom from physical interference with the tenant's enjoyment of the land.[9] 'Quiet' here does not refer to freedom from noise but rather 'peaceable', though it is possible that noise might constitute a breach of the covenant (as well as being grounds for an action in tort for nuisance[10]).

THE LEASE PROVIDES THAT THE 'USUAL COVENANTS' ARE TO APPLY

The usual covenants include a covenant by the landlord that the tenant will have 'quite enjoyment'. This confirms but does not add to the position at common law.

EXPRESS PROVISION

It is common for a covenant for quiet enjoyment to be expressly included, conferring protection appropriate to the circumstances of the lease.[11]

DEROGATION FROM GRANT

A landlord may also be constrained from acting to the detriment of the tenant by the application of the principle that a grantor may not derogate from his grant. The principle is illustrated by a case[12] in which M leased land to A, a timber merchant. In order for the timber to dry, there needed to be a free flow of air to the sheds where the timber was stacked. A retained adjoining land. After M's death this passed to L. L proposed to build on the land in such a way that the free flow of air to the sheds on the land leased to A would be interrupted. It was held that this would constitute a derogation from grant and that L was therefore not entitled to build so as to interrupt the access of air to A's sheds. It will be noted that the interruption of the air would not have constituted either a tort or a breach of the covenant for quiet enjoyment, and T would thus have had no action under either of these heads. The principle of derogation

---

8   See *Queensway Marketing Ltd v Associated Restaurants Ltd* (1984) 271 Estates Gazette 1106.
9   *Perera v Vandiyar* [1953] 1 All ER 1109, [1953] 1 WLR 672, CA (cutting off electricty and gas in order to induce tenant to leave).
10 *Sampson v Hodson-Pressinger* [1981] 3 All ER 710.
11 Such a covenant is not enforceable against a predecessor of the covenantor; *Celsteel v Alton House Holdings Ltd* [1986] 1 All ER 608, [1986] 1 WLR 512; (M & B).
12 *Aldin v Latimer Clark, Muirhead & Co* [1894] 2 Ch 437.

from grant thus confers on a tenant a wider range of protection than the covenant for quiet enjoyment; but in many instances a matter may fall within both spheres.

Assignment, subletting, parting with possession[13]

THE LEASE IS SILENT

In the absence of any stipulation to the contrary, at common law a tenant is entitled to assign the lease, or sublet, or part with possession of the premises (eg let someone else live in the house).

THE LEASE PROVIDES THAT THE 'USUAL COVENANTS' ARE TO APPLY

The 'usual covenants' include no covenant that alters the position at common law.

THE LEASE CONTAINS AN EXPRESS COVENANT AGAINST ASSIGNMENT, SUBLETTING OR PARTING WITH POSSESSION[14]

If the covenant is against assignment, subletting or parting with possession 'without licence or consent', then, by the Landlord and Tenant Act 1927,[15] the covenant is deemed to be subject to a proviso that the licence or consent should not unreasonably be withheld. The onus is on the tenant to show that the refusal of consent was unreasonable.[16]

The courts have held that consent was reasonably withheld when the person to whom the tenant proposed to assign the property would use the property to compete for trade with other property belonging to the landlord;[17] when the references provided for the proposed assignee were unsatisfactory;[18] when the reason for the proposed assignment was to bring the tenancy within the protection of the Rent Acts;[19] and when the assignment would enable the proposed assignee to claim advantage of the Leasehold Reform Act 1967.[20]

---

13 For proposals for reform, see Law Commission, *Codification of the Law of Landlord and Tenant – Covenants restricting dispositions, alterations and change of user* (Law Com No 141); [1986] Conv 240 (A. J. Waite); *Leasehold Conveyancing* (Law Com No 161).

14 [1988] Conv 45 (G. Kodilinye). For recommendations for reform, see Law Com No 161.

15 Section 19(1). The Landlord and Tenant (Covenants) Act 1995 added sections 1(A) to (E). Under these new provisions, in the case of a lease granted after 1995 (except for residential, and agricultural (s 19(4)) leases), where a landlord and tenant agree the circumstances in which the landlord may refuse consent to an assignment, if one of those circumstances exists, the landlord's refusal of consent will not be unreasonable.

16 *Pimms Ltd v Tallow Chandlers in the City of London* [1964] 2 QB 547, 564.

17 *Shanly v Ward* (1913) 29 TLR 714.

18 *Premier Confectionery (London) Co Ltd v London Commercial Sale Rooms Ltd* [1933] Ch 904.

19 *Lee v K Carter Ltd* [1949] 1 KB 85, [1948] 2 All ER 690; *West Layton Ltd v Ford* [1979] QB 593, [1979] 2 All ER 657.

20 *Norfolk Capital Group Ltd v Kitway Ltd* [1977] QB 506, [1976] 3 All ER 787; *Bickel v Duke of Westminster* [1977] QB 517, [1976] 3 All ER 801. See also *Rossi v Hestdrive Ltd* (1985) 274 Estates Gazette 928.

On the other hand, the courts have held that consent was unreasonably withheld when the proposed assignee was already a tenant of the landlord concerned who would vacate other property which the landlord would then have difficulty in re-letting;[1] when the landlord's reason for the withholding of consent was that he wished to recover the property for himself;[2] when the ground for the refusal was that the assignee (of a long lease of a flat) intended to sublet the property for some years;[3] when the reason was the landlord's objection to the proposed assignee's intention to use the premises, the usage of which was limited to the trade of printing, as offices;[4] and when the refusal of consent was designed to achieve a collateral purpose wholly unconnected with the terms of the lease and extraneous to the intention of the parties when the lease was granted (notwithstanding that the purpose was in accordance with good estate management).[5]

If the covenant against assigning, subletting or parting with possession is absolute then, although the landlord can waive the covenant if he so wishes, he cannot be compelled to do so, regardless of how unreasonable his attitude may be.[6] (Further, if a tenant covenants that before assigning or subletting he will first offer to surrender the lease, the Landlord and Tenant Act 1927 does not affect the validity of this covenant.[7])

If a tenant assigns the lease or sublets the property in breach of a covenant against assignment or subletting (ie in breach of an absolute covenant or, where the landlord is not entitled to withhold consent unreasonably, without seeking the landlord's consent) then the assignment is valid as between the tenant and the assignee;[8] and the sub-lease is valid as between the tenant and the sub-tenant. But the tenant is liable for damages for breach of covenant, and if the lease contained a clause entitling the landlord to forfeit the lease in the event of breach of the covenant against assignment or subletting, the sub-lease may be determined thereunder (by the grant of an injunction requiring the assignee (or the sub-tenant) to surrender the lease (or sub-lease)).[9]

Further, where a tenant, in breach of covenant, sub-lets the property, and the landlord serves a notice to quit on the tenant on the ground that his interest has been materially prejudiced by a breach that is not capable of being remedied

1   *Re Gibbs and Houlder Bros & Co Ltd's Lease* [1925] Ch 575.
2   *Bates v Donaldson* [1896] 2 QB 241. See also *Greene v Church Comrs for England* [1974] Ch 467, [1974] 3 All ER 609.
3   *Rayburn v Wolf* (1985) 50 P & CR 463, CA.
4   *Killick v Second Covent Garden Property Co Ltd* [1973] 2 All ER 337, [1973] 1 WLR 658, CA.
5   *Bromley Park Garden Estates v Moss* [1982] 2 All ER 890, [1982] 1 WLR 1019; [1983] Conv 140 (L. Crabb); see also *International Drilling Fluids Ltd v Louisville Investments (Uxbridge) Ltd* [1986] Ch 513, [1986] 1 All ER 321, CA; [1986] Conv 287 (L. Crabb).
6   See *Bocardo SA v S & M Hotels Ltd* [1979] 3 All ER 737, [1980] 1 WLR 17; R. Sheldon and M. Friend (1982) 98 LQR 14.
7   *Alder v Upper Grosvenor Street Investment Ltd* [1957] 1 All ER 229, [1957] 1 WLR 227; *Bocardo SA v S & M Hotels Ltd* [1979] 3 All ER 737, [1980] 1 WLR 17. See C. G. Blake [1980] Conv 418.
8   *Peabody Donation Fund Governors v Higgins* [1983] 3 All ER 122, [1983] 1 WLR 1091, CA.
9   *Hemingway Securities Ltd v Dunraven Ltd* [1995] 1 EGLR 61; [1995] Conv 416 (P. Luxton and M. Wilkie).

(eg by an award of damages), the landlord is entitled to an order for possession against the sub-tenant (thereby ending the sub-lease).[10]

In addition to the Landlord and Tenant Act 1927, certain other statutes affect the ability of a tenant to assign or sublet the property demised. Thus, the Race Relations Act 1976[11] makes it unlawful to withhold consent in such a way as to discriminate against a would-be assignee or sub-tenant on grounds of race or colour.[12] Under the Landlord and Tenant Act 1988 where a lease contains a covenant by the tenant not to assign or sublet (or charge or part with possession) without the consent of the landlord, consent that is not unreasonably to be withheld, and the landlord receives an application for consent, the Act imposes on the landlord a duty[13] to the tenant within a reasonable time either (a) to give consent and serve notice on the tenant of his decision; or, (b) if it is reasonable to refuse consent (or to give consent subject to certain conditions), to serve notice on the tenant of the decision, with the reasons for the refusal (or for the imposition of the conditions). By the Act[14] the onus is placed on the landlord to show that refusal of consent is reasonable (ie not on the tenant to show that refusal is unreasonable).

Termination of lease

Here we consider the ways in which a lease may be determined, otherwise than by expiry (ie at the end of a fixed term) or by the giving of notice[15] (ie in the case of a periodic lease[16]).

1.   Surrender

If T surrenders his lease to L, and L is his immediate landlord, and L accepts the surrender, T's lease is merged in L's reversion and thus comes to an end.[17]

---

10   *Pennell v Payne* [1995] QB 192, [1995] 2 All ER 592, CA; *Brown v Wilson* (1949) 208 LT 144, overruled.
11   Section 24.
12   See also Law of Property Act 1925, s 144; Sex Discrimination Act 1975, s 31; Rent Act 1977, s 98, Sch 15, Case 6; Housing Act 1957, s 104; Housing Act 1980, ss 17, 19, 35 and 36 also affect the ability to assign or sublet.
13   For breach of which an action in tort lies for breach of statutory duty, s 4.
14   Section 1(6).
15   Where a lease is held jointly by two or more persons, in the absence of a term to the contrary, a periodic tenancy is terminable by a notice to quit given by any one tenant without the concurrence of the others; *Hammersmith and Fulham London Borough Council v Monk* [1992] 1 AC 478, [1992] 1 All ER 1, HL; (1992) 108 LQR 375 (J. Dewar); [1992] Conv 279 (S. Goulding); *Crawley Borough Bouncil v Ure* [1996] 1 All ER 724, CA.
16   Or a lease for a fixed term that contains a term enabling the lease to be terminated by notice.
17   See [1996] Conv 284 (N. Hopkins).

IfT expressly surrenders the lease, the Law of Property Act 1925[18] requires a deed to be used, irrespective of the length of the unexpired lease surrendered and irrespective of the manner in which the lease was created.

IfT or L (or both of them) do some act that shows an intention to end the lease, and the circumstances are such that it would be inequitable for them to rely on the fact that there had been no express surrender by deed accepted by L, then they may be estopped from denying that a surrender has occurred, and a surrender by operation of law takes effect.[19] For example, if T gives up possession of the property and L accepts this as a surrender, a surrender by operation of law occurs.

2.   Merger

Merger may occur in two situations:

(1) If L leases land to T, and subsequentlyT's lease and L's reversion pass into the hands of a third party, the lease, being merged with the reversion, comes to an end.
(2) If L leases land to T, and T subsequently acquires L's reversion, the lease is merged with the reversion and comes to an end. It will be noted that in this situation, merger is the converse of surrender.

3.   Disclaimer

The Insolvency Act 1986 gives a trustee in bankruptcy power to disclaim onerous property which has become vested in him. IfT's lease is near to expiry and imposes liabilities on T, eg to repair, the lease may constitute more of a liability than an asset. In such a situation the trustee may, with the leave of the court, disclaim the lease. The effect of the disclaimer as between L andT is to determine the lease.[20] Disclaimer does not, however, affect the rights of third parties. For example, ifT had mortgaged the lease to E, the court may make an order vesting the lease in E.

Certain other statutes have given rights of disclaimer; for example, if leasehold property was rendered unfit by war damage, the tenant was given power to disclaim the lease.[1]

---

18   Section 52.
19   As in *Foster v Robinson* [1951] 1 KB 149, [1950] 2 All ER 342. See also *Collins v Claughton* [1959] 1 All ER 95, [1959] 1 WLR 145.
20   *Re Park Air Services plc* [1996] 1 WLR 649. On calculation of a landlord's loss, see *Re Park Air Services plc* (1996) 141 Sol Jo LB 112.
 1   Landlord and Tenant (War Damage) Acts 1939 and 1941.

4.   Forfeiture[2]

THE RIGHT TO FORFEIT A LEASE

Although under a lease certain obligations may be imposed on the landlord and on the tenant (some arising at common law, some arising expressly) a breach by the tenant of any of these obligations does not of itself give the landlord the right to forfeit the lease. He may have remedies (eg an action for damages or for an injunction) but he has no right to forfeit the lease unless, either (1) the lease expressly provides that the landlord shall have a power of forfeiture, ie by the inclusion of a forfeiture clause such as, 'Provided always that if the tenant commits a breach of covenant or becomes bankrupt it shall be lawful for the lessor to re-enter upon the premises and immediately thereupon the term shall absolutely determine; or (2) the lease is granted expressly 'on condition that', or 'provided that' the tenant fulfils specified undertakings (whether worded as covenants or not). If the lease is in this form the landlord has a right of forfeiture notwithstanding that no forfeiture clause is included in the lease.

A landlord exercises a power of forfeiture by re-entering the land. A right to forfeit a lease is for this reason sometimes referred to as a 'right to re-enter' or a 'right of re-entry'.

ENFORCEMENT OF A RIGHT OF RE-ENTRY

A landlord who has a right to re-enter may enforce the right in two ways:

1. By physically entering the land. However, if a landlord uses force in re-entering he may commit a criminal offence under the Criminal Law Act 1977.[3] Furthermore, if the property is let as a dwelling house, under the Housing Act 1988 it is an offence to enforce a forfeiture otherwise than by proceedings in court while any person is lawfully residing on any part of the premises.
2. By issuing a writ for possession of the property. If the court[4] makes an order for possession the effect of the order is to determine the lease. If the tenant refuses to leave the property he can be evicted by a bailiff of the court.

PROTECTION OF A TENANT AGAINST FORFEITURE

Since the law 'leans against forfeiture', not only is there a heavy burden of proof on the landlord but, further, equity and statute have intervened so as to

---

2   *The Forfeiture of Leases*, M. Pawlowski. For proposals for reform and simplification of the law, including the abolition of re-entry and forfeiture and their replacement by the making, on the occurrence of a 'termination order event', of a 'termination order' by the court, see [1994] Law Com 221 (revising proposals made in [1985] Law Com 142), [1994] Conv 177 (H. W. Wilkinson); (1995) 58 MLR 547 (N. Hopkins).
3   Sections 6 and 7. The Act replaces and repeals (s 65 and Sch 13) the Forcible Entry Acts of 1381, 1391, 1429, 1588 and 1623.
4   The jurisdiction is affected by statute, in particular the Housing Act 1996.

provide a measure of protection to tenants in certain cases. What these cases are we must now consider. Special rules apply to forfeiture for non-payment of rent, and these will be considered first.

NON-PAYMENT OF RENT

At common law a landlord who had a right of re-entry was required before exercising the right to make (unless exempted by the terms of the lease) a 'formal demand' for the rent. A formal demand was made by the landlord or his agent demanding the exact sum due on the day when it was payable, at the premises leased, at such a time before sunset as would give time for the money to be counted out, the demand continuing until sunset.

As a result of the changes made by the Common Law Procedure Act 1852[5] the position today is as follows:

1. If (a) half a year's rent is in arrears; and (b) there are not sufficient chattels to be found on the premises to enable the landlord to recover the arrears due by levying distress, a landlord is exempted by the Act of 1852 from making a formal demand.
2. If the lease exempts the landlord, no formal demand need be made.
3. In all other cases (which are likely to be rare because express exemption is normal practice) formal demand must still be made.

At common law, therefore, the position was that if, for example, L granted T a lease for 99 years at a premium of £1,000 and a rent of £10 a year, and the lease gave L a right of re-entry, and T failed to make the first payment of rent on the day due, L could, if necessary after making formal demand, forfeit the lease.

RELIEF

However, because the loss to the tenant might (as in the above example) be out of all proportion to his fault, equity intervened in order to give tenants the chance of saving themselves from the consequences of their default. Equity does not deny the landlord's right to forfeit the lease, but if the tenant pays the rent due and any expenses which the landlord has incurred, equity may restore the tenant to his former position. This remedy is termed 'relief'. The ancient jurisdiction to grant relief is confirmed by the Supreme Court Act 1981.[6]

A tenant can apply for relief either at the time when the landlord brings an action for possession, or after the landlord has re-entered.[7] The Common Law Procedure Act 1852 provided that a claim for relief must be brought within six months of actual re-entry by the landlord. If relief is granted the effect is that

---

5   Section 210.
6   Section 38.
7   *Lovelock v Margo* [1963] 2 QB 786, [1963] 3 All ER 13; *Thatcher v CH Pearce & Sons (Contractors) Ltd* [1968] 1 WLR 748 (since relief is an equitable remedy, no statutory rule of limitation applies).

the tenant continues to hold under the terms of the original lease.[8] (No new document need be executed.)

Like other equitable remedies, relief is granted at the discretion of the court.[9] For example, relief was refused when a tenancy had been treated as being at an end and no rent had been paid for 22 years before the landlord forfeited the lease.[10]

OTHER BREACHES

Where forfeiture is for breach of a covenant or condition other than for payment of rent, statute provides certain forms of protection to the tenant. (The anomaly that the statutory protection does not[11] apply to forfeiture for non-payment of rent has been addressed by the Law Commission.[12])

Law of Property Act 1925, section 146

(A) THE STATUTORY NOTICE

Section 146(1) of the Law of Property Act 1925 provides that before a landlord proceeds to enforce a forfeiture (whether by re-entering or seeking an order for possession) he must serve on the tenant a notice[13] which:

(a) specifies the breach complained of; and
(b) requires the breach to be remedied, if this is possible;[14] and
(c) requires the tenant to pay compensation in money if the landlord so requires.

---

8   *Hynes v Twinsectra Ltd* [1995] 2 EGLR 69.
9   The jurisdiction to grant relief will not be extended to include relief against forfeiture of a contracutal licence; *Sport International Bussum BV v Inter-Footwear Ltd* [1984] 1 All ER 376, [1984] 1 WLR 776, HL. The High Court is barred by s 138(7) of the County Courts Act 1984 from granting relief where a lessee is sued in the county court to enforce a right of re-entry for non-payment of rent and the lessee fails to comply with the requirements (relating to the period within which application must be made) of s 138 of the 1984 Act; *Di Palma v Victoria Square Property* [1986] Ch 150, [1985] 2 All ER 676, CA. In s 138 of the 1984 Act, since 'lessee' includes a sublessee, the term includes also a mortgagee; *United Dominions Trust v Shellpoint Trustees Ltd* [1993] 4 All ER 310, CA; *Escalus Properties Ltd v Robinson* [1996] QB 231, [1995] 4 All ER 852, CA.
10   *Public Trustee v Westbrook* [1965] 3 All ER 398, [1965] 1 WLR 1160.
11   LPA 1925, s 146(11).
12   See p 305, n 2.
13   As to whether a fresh notice must be served after a waiver of a breach, see *Greenwich London Borough Council v Discreet Selling Estates Ltd* [1990] 2 EGLR 65; [1991] Conv 222 (J. E. Martin).
14   *Rugby School (Governors) v Tannahill* [1935] 1 KB 87; (M & B) (breach of covenant against use of premises for immoral purposes not capable of remedy); *Dunraven Securities v Holloway* (1982) 264 Estates Gazette 709; cf *Glass v Kencakes Ltd* [1966] 1 QB 611, [1964] 3 All ER 807; *Expert Clothing Service and Sales Ltd v Hillgate House Ltd* [1986] Ch 340, [1985] 2 All ER 998, CA; (M & B) (breach of covenant to reconstruct premises within specified time capable of being remedied by work being carried out within a reasonable time); *Savva v Houssein* (1996) 73 P & CR 150, CA.

The purpose of the notice is thus to warn the tenant of impending forfeiture and thus give him a chance, if this is possible, to put matters right.[15]

(B)   TIME TO COMPLY WITH THE NOTICE

Further, s 146(1) requires the landlord to give the tenant a reasonable time to comply with the notice. 'Reasonable time' is not defined, but in normal circumstances three months is usually considered sufficient. If a breach cannot be remedied[16] the landlord must nevertheless allow a reasonable time to elapse after serving the notice in order to give the tenant a chance to consider his position. Fourteen days has been held to be sufficient.[17]

(C)   RELIEF

If the tenant fails to comply with the notice within a reasonable time the landlord may proceed to enforce the forfeiture by the means explained above (ie re-entry or action). However, s 146(2) provides that where a landlord 'is proceeding, by action or otherwise, to enforce ... a right of re-entry or forfeiture,') the tenant[18] may apply to the court for relief.[19]

The right of a tenant to seek relief endures up until such time as the landlord obtains from the court an order for possession. Thus a landlord is not able to defeat a tenant's entitlement to seek relief by taking physical possession of the premises, prior to obtaining an order from the court empowering him so to do.[20]

The court has discretion to grant relief, having regard to 'the proceedings and conduct of the parties ... and to all other circumstances'.[1]

These are the general rules, but there are the following exceptions,

---

15   The section has no application where the landlord carries out repairs and then claims compensation from the tenant for breach of the tenant's covenant to repair. *SEDAC Investments Ltd v Tanner* [1982] 3 All ER 646, [1982] 1 WLR 1342.

16   Eg where T sublets in breach of a covenant against subletting (the breach is not remedied even by T securing a surrender of the sub-lease.) *Scala House and District Property Co Ltd v Forbes* [1974] QB 575, [1973] 3 All ER 308; (M & B).

17   *Civil Service Co-operative Society Ltd v McGrigor's Trustee* [1923] 2 Ch 347.

18   Relief may be granted notwithstanding that the forfeiture is prompted by disclaimer by the tenant of the landlord's title; *W G Clark Ltd v Dupre Ltd* [1992] 1 All ER 596.

19   Where s 146 applies the ancient equitable jurisdiction of the court to grant relief (which still exists with regard to non-payment of rent, see supra) is no longer exercisable. *Official Custodian for Charities v Parway Estates Development Ltd* [1985] Ch 151, [1984] 3 All ER 679, CA; *Smith v Metropolitan City Properties Ltd* (1985) 277 Estates Gazette 753; not following *Abbey National Building Society v Maybeech Ltd* [1985] Ch 190, [1984] 3 All ER 262. (Cf *Ladup Ltd v Williams and Glyn's Bank plc* [1985] 2 All ER 577.) See S. Tromans [1986] Conv 187 at 192.

20   *Billson v Residential Apartments Ltd* [1992] 1 AC 494, [1992] 1 All ER 141, HL; [1992] Conv 273 (P. F. Smith).

1   For an example of the exercise of this discretion, when the tenant's health and age were held to be relevant circumstances, see *Central Estates (Belgravia) Ltd v Woolgar (No 2)* [1972] 3 All ER 610, [1972] 1 WLR 1048. See also *GMS Syndicate Ltd v Gary Elliott Ltd* [1982] Ch 1, [1981] 1 All ER 619 (relief granted in respect of part only of the demised premises).

(A)   'NO NOTICE, NO RELIEF'

In some instances s 146 does not apply and so no notice need be given and, further, the remedy of relief is not available. (The rule is 'no notice, no relief'.)

(1) Breach of covenant for inspection in a mining lease. If L grants a mining lease to T, the rent may take the form of a royalty that varies with the quantity of mineral extracted. L will therefore want to know how much mineral T has mined. The lease is thus likely to contain a covenant requiring T to keep a weighing machine and proper records, and entitling L to inspect these. If T is in breach of such a covenant the statute provides[2] that the rule is to be no notice, no relief.

(2) If:
   (a) the lease provides that the landlord shall be entitled to re-enter in the event of the tenant becoming bankrupt,[3] and the tenant does become bankrupt;[4] and
   (b) the land leased consists of (i) agricultural or pastoral land; or (ii) mines or minerals; or (iii) a public house; or (iv) a furnished house; or (v) property with respect to which the personal qualifications of the tenant are of importance for the preservation of the value or the character of the property,[5]

then the Act provides[6] that the rule is to be no notice, no relief.

(B)   NO PROTECTION AFTER ONE YEAR

If (a) there is a provision for re-entry on the bankruptcy of the tenant and the tenant becomes bankrupt (as in (2)(a) above) and
   (b) the land is land other than that listed in (2)(b) above,

then if the landlord wishes to enforce the forfeiture during the year following the bankruptcy, he must comply with s 146 and serve the statutory notice, and the tenant can apply for relief. But after one year has elapsed the landlord is no longer required to serve the statutory notice before enforcing the forfeiture and the court has no power to grant relief.

Housing Act 1996

The Act imposes restrictions on the entitlement of a landlord to forfeit a lease for non-payment of a service charge.[7]

---

2   LPA 1925, s 146(8), (11).
3   Or the lease is taken in execution, ie sold by a creditor in pursuance of a writ of execution.
4   Or in the event of a creditor of the tenant obtaining a writ of execution empowering him to sell the tenant's interest in the lease.
5   See *Earl Bathurst v Fine* [1974] 2 All ER 1160, [1974] 1 WLR 905.
6   LPA 1925, s 146(9).
7   The Act entitles the tenant to challenge unreasonable service charges and bad management through a leasehold valuation tribunal (instead of taking proceedings in court).

SUBTENANTS[8]

If L leases land to T, and T subleases the land to ST, and L forfeit's T's lease, ST's lease automatically comes to an end.[9] Under the Law of Property Act 1925[10] (as amended[11]) ST may apply for relief against the forfeiture of T's lease irrespective of the ground on which it is forfeited. Thus even if T is not entitled to seek relief (eg because he is in breach of an inspection covenant in a mining lease) ST may nevertheless do so.

The court may make an order under which ST acquires a lease from L for a period not exceeding the unexpired period of his former lease from T.[12] The court may impose conditions in the new lease requiring ST, eg to pay a higher rent to L than he had to T, or to covenant to perform the covenants that had been entered into by T.

Similarly, if L leases land to T, and T mortgages the lease to E, and L forfeits T's lease (thus removing E's security), E can apply to the court for relief against the forfeiture and the court may make the same order in favour of E that it can in favour of ST.[13]

WAIVER

It may happen that a landlord who becomes entitled to re-enter acts in such a way as to indicate that he has elected to treat the lease as still continuing.[14] In this case he is treated as having waived his right to re-enter and he loses the right to re-enter in respect of the breach concerned (though not in respect of a subsequent breach).

A landlord may waive his right to re-enter expressly or impliedly. He does so impliedly if, being aware of the circumstances that have entitled him to forfeit the lease, he does some act that recognises the lease as still being in existence, eg by suing for, or accepting, rent from T which has fallen due since the breach. In the case of a continuing breach, one act of waiver does not have permanent effect: if the breach continues after the act of waiver, the right to forfeit the lease re-arises.[15]

SUMMARY

See Appendix II, p 568.

---

8   [1986] Conv 187 (S. Tromans).
9   See *Official Custodian for Charities v Mackey* [1985] Ch 168, [1984] 3 All ER 689.
10 LPA 1925, s 146(4). See *Hammersmith and Fulham London Borough Council v Top Shops Centres Ltd* [1990] Ch 237, [1989] 2 All ER 655; [1992] CLJ 219 (L. Tee).
11 LP(Am)A 1929, s 1.
12 See *Cadogan v Dimovic* [1984] 2 All ER 168, [1984] 1 WLR 609.
13 LPA 1925, s 146(5)(b).
14 *Matthews v Smallwood* [1910] 1 Ch 777; (M & B); *Expert Clothing Service and Sales Ltd v Hillgate House Ltd* [1986] Ch 340, [1985] 2 All ER 998, CA (no waiver); *Re a debtor (No 13A10/95)* [1996] 1 All ER 691.
15 *Doe d Ambler v Woodbridge* (1829) 9 B & C 376; *Cooper v Henderson* (1982) 263 Estates Gazette 592, CA.

CHAPTER 18

Easements[1]

EASEMENTS AND LICENCES

D (which in this chapter represents the term 'dominant owner') owns Redacre, on which stands his house, Redacre Lodge. Adjoining Redacre is Greenacre, owned by S (which in this chapter represents the term 'servient owner'). In order that D may have access to a road on the far side of Greenacre, D requests and S grants for a sum of £100 the right to cross Greenacre by a track. Provided that certain conditions are fulfilled, the right which S has granted to D is an *easement*. If the necessary conditions are not satisfied, then D's right is not an easement but merely a licence. Why does it matter whether D's right is an easement or a licence? It is true that whether D holds an easement or a licence, if S later attempts to stop him crossing Greenacre, D can sue him (provided that if the right is a licence, it constitutes an enforceable contract between S and D). But if S sold Greenacre to T, could T say to D, 'You were granted that right by S, not by me. You're not crossing my field'? Alternatively, if E bought Redacre from D, could S say to E 'I granted that right to D, not to you. You're not crossing my field'?

The question posed is thus whether the benefit of the original grant will run with the land (ie Redacre) into the hands of E, and whether the burden of the grant will run with the land (ie Greenacre) into the hands of T. The answer is that if the grant by S creates an easement, the benefit and burden run with the respective pieces of land.[2] If the grant is not an easement, but merely a licence, the basic rule[3] is that benefit and burden do not so run.

Further, if D holds an easement across Greenacre, and a stranger X, obstructs D's right of way, D can himself sue X. If D's right is merely a licence, D can bring no action against X: only S can sue X.[4]

To interfere with an easement (whether the interference is, in our example, by S or X) is to commit the tort of nuisance.[5] The dominant owner thus has an action for damages at common law for the loss he has suffered. In addition, or in the alternative, he can seek an injunction to restrain the continuance of the infringement. The grant of the injunction is at the discretion of the court. The

---

1 See Gale *Easements*; P. Jackson *The Law of Easements and Profits*; C. Sara *Boundaries and Easements*.
2 *Godwin v Schweppes Ltd* [1902] 1 Ch 926.
3 Which is subject to certain exceptions. See p 347.
4 *Hill v Tupper* (1863) 2 H & C 121 (M & B).
5 For the relationship between land law and tort in the sphere of easements, see A. J. Waite [1987] Conv 47.

general rule has been that an injunction will not be granted where damages will provide an adequate remedy.[6]

THE CONDITIONS TO BE FULFILLED FOR A RIGHT TO BE CAPABLE OF BEING AN EASEMENT[7]

In order that a right may be capable of being an easement the following conditions must be satisfied:

1.   There must be a dominant and a servient tenement[8]

A 'tenement' is any land held for a freehold or leasehold estate. It is the term used by convention in the context of easements to refer to a piece of land (or portion of land, eg a flat). In the example we have used, Redacre is the dominant tenement and Greenacre the servient tenement. This condition in our example is therefore satisfied. But if D, the person to whom S granted the right to cross Greenacre, had owned no land, then, since there would be no dominant tenement, this first condition would not be satisfied. D's right would be no more than a licence.[9]

An alternative way of expressing this principle is to say that easements cannot exist 'in gross', ie not appurtenant to any land.[10]

2.   The right must accommodate the dominant tenement

The right must be connected with the use,[11] and must improve the usefulness or amenity, of the dominant tenement. In our example, the right to cross Greenacre would improve the amenity of Redacre and this condition is therefore satisfied.

On the other hand, if the right had been merely for the personal advantage of D, then this condition would not be satisfied.[12]

Although the right must be connected with the use of the dominant tenement, this does not mean that the dominant and servient tenements must necessarily be contiguous.[13] For example, if a farmer grants to a water company the right to put pipes under his land, this right, since it accommodates the

6   *Lyme Valley Squash Club Ltd v Newcastle under Lyme Borough Council* [1985] 2 All ER 405; *Pugh v Howells* (1984) 48 P & CR 298, CA.
7   Peel (1964) 28 Conv (NS) 430.
8   *London and Blenheim Estates Ltd v Ladbroke Retail Parks Ltd* [1994] 1 WLR 31, CA.
9   Another illustration is provided by *Quicke v Chapman* [1903] 1 Ch 659.
10 For an argument that to meet modern needs easements in gross should be accepted by the law, see N. F., Sturley, 'Easements in Gross' (1980) 96 LQR 557.
11 *Ackroyd v Smith* (1850) 10 CB 164; *Moody v Steggles* (1879) 12 Ch D 261; *Hamble Parish Council v Haggard* [1992] 4 All ER 147, [1992] 1 WLR 122.
12 *Hill v Tupper* p 266 ante; (M & B).
13 *Pugh v Savage* [1970] 2 QB 373, [1970] 2 All ER 353.

land on which the company's reservoir stands, complies with this condition. But the Board's land, the dominant tenement, and the farmer's land, the servient tenement, may be many miles apart. An easement in the form of a right of way must be contiguous to the dominant land in that it gives direct access to that land (ie without any 'missing link' before the dominant tenement is reached).[14]

3. The dominant and servient tenements must not be both owned and occupied by the same person[15]

This, at first sight, seems no more than a statement of the obvious: in our example, if both Redacre and Greenacre had been owned by D, he would have no need of an easement (or any other right) in order to cross Greenacre, his own land. The condition does, however, raise the question as to the position when the dominant or servient tenements, or both, are held under a lease. Consider the following situations:

(i) D owns Redacre and Greenacre. He leases Greenacre to S for 99 years. Later, when D finds he needs access across Greenacre, S can grant him an easement to cross Greenacre. Here the dominant and servient tenements are owned by the same person (D), but not occupied by the same person. So the third condition is not infringed.

(ii) S owns Greenacre. L owns Redacre and leases it to D for 99 years. S can grant D an easement to cross Greenacre. The third condition is not infringed.

(iii) L owns Redacre and Greenacre. He leases Redacre to D and Greenacre to S. S can grant an easement to D to cross Greenacre. The third condition is not infringed. (The easement can last no longer than the unexpired portion of S's lease.)

It will thus be noted that a landlord may grant[16] an easement to a tenant over land retained by the landlord; and a tenant may grant[17] an easement to his landlord over the land leased to him.

4. The right must 'lie in grant'

The meaning of the dictum 'all easements lie in grant' is that all easements must be capable of being granted by a grantor to a grantee. The consequences which follow from this are as follows:

---

14 *Todrick v Western National Omnibus Co Ltd* [1934] Ch 190.

15 Holding each in the same capacity. If X held Redacre as a trustee and Greenacre beneficially, this condition would not be infringed.

16 By express, or by implied grant (as in *Borman v Griffith* [1930] 1 Ch 493); (M & B). There can be no acquisition of an easement by prescription by a tenant against his landlord. See post.

17 By express, or by implied grant. There can be no acquisition of an easement by prescription by a landlord against his tenant. See post.

(A)   THE RIGHT MUST BE SUFFICIENTLY DEFINITE TO BE CAPABLE OF FORMING
THE SUBJECT-MATTER OF A GRANT

It is a *sine qua non* of property that it is assignable. For something to be capable
of being granted to another, it must be known what it is that is being granted.
The matter granted must therefore be sufficiently definite. An easement, being
a right of property, must therefore be sufficiently definite to be capable of
forming the subject-matter of a grant.

The following matters have been held to satisfy this requirement:

1. A right to receive light through a defined aperture in a building (eg a
window or a skylight).[18]

2. A right to the passage of air through a defined channel (eg through a
ventilation shaft).[19]

3. A right to have a building supported, eg by the wall of another building.[20]

4. A right to project a building over another's land.[1]

5. A right to have rainwater drop from the eves of one's premises onto the
land of another.[2]

6. A right to project the bowsprit of ships using a dock over a wharf
belonging to another.[3]

7. A right to discharge water onto the land of another.[4]

8. A right to enter the land of another to open sluice gates.[5]

9. A right to pollute the water of a stream or river[6] (ie an easement to
infringe the natural right of lower riparian owners to receive water unpolluted).

10. A right to fix a sign board on a neighbouring house.[7]

11. A right to let down the surface of land by mining under it[8] (ie an
easement to infringe the natural right of another to have his land supported).

12. A right to use a lavatory on another's land.[9]

13. A right to require a servient owner to maintain a cattle-proof fence or
wall on his own land for the advantage of the dominant owner.[10] (If an owner
fences his land merely for his own convenience, this is not capable of creating
an easement.)

14. A right to hang clothes on a line passing over another's land.[11]

15. A right to store coal in another's shed.[12]

18   *Easton v Isted* [1903] 1 Ch 405.
19   *Bass v Gregory* (1890) 25 QBD 481; *Cable v Bryant* [1908] 1 Ch 259.
20   *Dalton v Angus & Co* (1881) 6 App Cas 740; *Brace v South Eastern Regional Housing Association
     Ltd* (1984) 270 Estates Gazette 1286, CA.
1   *Suffield v Brown* (1864) 4 De GJ & Sm 185.
2   *Thomas v Thomas* (1835) 2 Cr M & R 34.
3   *Suffield v Brown*, ante.
4   *Mason v Shrewsbury and Hereford Rly Co* (1871) LR 6 QB 578 at 587.
5   *Simpson v Godmanchester Corpn* [1897] AC 696.
6   *Baxendale v McMurray* (1867) 2 Ch App 790.
7   *Moody v Steggles* (1879) 12 Ch D 261.
8   *Rowbothom v Wilson* (1860) 8 HL Cas 348 at 362.
9   *Miller v Emcer Products Ltd* [1956] Ch 304, [1956] 1 All ER 237.
10   *Jones v Price* [1965] 2 QB 618, [1965] 2 All ER 625; *Crow v Wood* [1971] 1 QB 77, [1970]
     3 All ER 425; *Egerton v Harding* [1975] QB 62, [1974] 3 All ER 689.
11   *Drewell v Towler* (1932) 3 B & Ad 735.
12   *Wright v Macadam* [1949] 2 KB 744, [1949] 2 All ER 565; (M & B).

16. A right to lay and maintain drains, sewers, pipes and cables under, on, or over another's land; and to enter the land to maintain these.[13]

17. A right to use a private car park.[14]

18. A right to cross land between two specified termini, over every part of the land and not merely between the termini.[15]

19. A right to abstract water from a mill pond.[16]

20. A right to park cars on another's land (provided that space remains after cars of the dominant owner have been parked[17]).

The following matters have been held to be too indefinite to be capable of forming an easement.

(a) A right to a view[18], sometimes termed a right of 'prospect'. (It may be possible, however, to protect a view by means of a covenant against building on other land in a way that would interrupt the view.[19])

(b) A right to privacy.[20] (It may be possible to guard against an invasion of privacy, eg by noise, by an action in tort for nuisance.[1])

(c) A right to a general flow of air over land (eg to a windmill[2] or a chimney.[3]) (Cf 2 above.)

(d) A right to have the wall of a building protected from the weather by an adjoining building.[4] (Cf 3 above.)

(e) A right for branches of a tree to overhang another's land.[5] (Cf 4 above.)

In this chapter illustrations are based on a right of way. The above list serves as a reminder that easements take many forms, of which a right of way is only one.

A right of way may itself take various forms. It may, for example, be a right to go on foot, to go on horse back, to drive cattle, or to drive vehicles.[6] What right exists will depend on the terms of the grant[7] and the interpretation of these by the court, for example, that a right to 'a full and free right of way ... on foot only along the pedestrian walkways' between a supermarket and a car

---

13 *Simmons v Midford* [1969] 2 Ch 415, [1969] 2 All ER 1269; *William Sindall plc v Cambridgeshire County Council* [1994] 3 All ER 932 (severage down a pipe).

14 *Re Ellenborough Park* [1956] Ch 131, [1955] 3 All ER 667; (M & B).

15 *Duncan v Louch* (1845) 6 QB 904.

16 *Cargill v Gotts* [1981] 1 All ER 682, [1981] 1 WLR 441.

17 *London and Blenheim Estates Ltd v Ladbroke Retail Parks Ltd* [1992] 1 WLR 1278, 1288, [1993] 1 All ER 307, 317.

18 *Aldred's Case* (1610) 9 Co Rep 57b at 58b.

19 See Chapter 21.

20 *Browne v Flower* [1911] 1 Ch 219 at 225.

1 See *Kennaway v Thompson* [1981] QB 88, [1980] 3 All ER 329; [1984] Conv 429 (P. Polden).

2 *Webb v Bird* (1862) 13 CBNS 841.

3 *Bryant v Lefever* (1879) 4 CPD 172; (M & B).

4 *Phipps v Pears* [1965] 1 QB 76, [1964] 2 All ER 35; (M & B); (1964) 28 Conv (NS) 450 (M.A. Peel). Cf *Bradburn v Lindsay* [1983] 2 All ER 408.

5 *Lemmon v Webb* [1895] AC 1.

6 *Kain v Norfolk* [1949] Ch 163 (grant in 1919 of right to drive 'carts' held to cover vehicles propelled by any means and so included motor lorries).

7 See *Scott v Martin* [1987] 2 All ER 813, [1987] 1 WLR 841 (right of way over 'private road' included right of way over verges on either side of metalled carriageway).

park extended to a right to push trolleys along the walkways.[8] In the case of a grant in general terms (eg a 'right of way'), the right conferred will depend on the surrounding circumstances,[9] eg the nature of the way (eg whether a footpath or road); the use of the dominant land; and the quantum of user at the time of the grant.[10] Where S grants D a right of way across his land Greenacre to reach D's land Redacre, the right is confined to enabling D to have access to Redacre; it does not extend to giving D a right to use the way across Greenacre as a means of access to other land adjoining Redacre, which D subsequently acquires.[11] The existence of a right of way entitles the dominant owner to repair the way but not to improve it.[12]

Where there is a strip of land between two houses, wide enough to allow the passage of only one vehicle, giving access to two garages, one belonging to each house, it may be that (a) each owner owns the land up to the middle line, and has an easement to use the other half; or (b) one party owns the strip and the other has an easement over it; or, (c) the strip is owned by both parties who use the strip in their capacity as co-owners of the land.[13]

We may note here that where D holds an easement of light, he is entitled to receive enough light to render the occupation of a house comfortable according to the ordinary notions of mankind, or, in the case of business premises, to enable him to carry on his business as effectively as before S created any obstruction.[14]

(B)   THERE MUST BE A CAPABLE GRANTOR AND A CAPABLE GRANTEE

Thus if S is a statutory corporation which has no power to grant easements[15] then, since there is no capable grantor, any purported grant for an easement is void.

Further, if a grant is made to a corporation which has no power to acquire easements, since there is no capable grantee, the grant is void. Similarly there

---

8   *Soames-Forsythe Properties Ltd v Tesco Stores Ltd* [1991] EGCS 22.
9   See *St Edmundsbury and Ipswich Diocesan Board of Finance v Clark (No 2)* [1975] 1 All ER 772, [1975] 1 WLR 468; *Bracewell v Appleby* [1975] Ch 408, [1975] 1 All ER 993; *Keefe v Amor* [1965] 1 QB 334, [1964] 2 All ER 517; (M & B); *British Railways Board v Glass* [1965] Ch 538, [1964] 3 All ER 418; (M & B); *Woodhouse & Co Ltd v Kirkland (Derby) Ltd* [1970] 2 All ER 587, [1970] 1 WLR 1185.
10   *Jelbert v Davis* [1968] 1 All ER 1182, [1968] 1 WLR 589.
11   *Harris v Flower* (1904) 74 LJ Ch 127; but see *Graham v Philcox* [1984] QB 747, [1984] 2 All ER 643 CA; (M & B); (easement giving access to first floor of a coach house gave access to both floors after purchase of whole building by dominant owner); [1986] Conv 60 (P. Todd); (1985) 82 LSG 341 (P. Kenny); and *National Trust Places of Historic Interest or Natural Beauty v White* [1987] 1 WLR 907; [1987] Conv 365 (JEM).
12   See *Mills v Silver* [1991] Ch 271, [1991] 1 All ER 449; (M & B) (grantee of prescriptive (see infra) right of way not entitled to improve way by laying down a stone road along its course); [1992] CLJ 220 (C. Harpum).
13   See *Williams v Usherwood* (1981) 45 P & CR 235, CA; [1983] Conv 398 (M. Dockray).
14   *Colls v Home and Colonial Stores Ltd* [1904] AC 179; (M & B). See also *Sheffield Masonic Hall Co Ltd v Sheffield Corpn* [1932] 2 Ch 17; *Allen v Greenwood* [1980] Ch 119, [1979] 1 All ER 819; [1984] Conv 408 (A. H. Hudson).
15   Or if S has power to grant an easement only if certain permission has been obtained and there is no evidence that this has been given expressly or impliedly; *Oakley v Boston* [1976] QB 270, [1975] 3 All ER 405.

can be no grant of an easement to a fluctuating body (such as the inhabitants of a named village) which has no corporate status. (How such a body may acquire the benefit of a right comparable with an easement is explained in Appendix II.)

5.   The right must not entail expenditure by the servient owner

The general rule[16] is that a right is unlikely to be accepted as capable of being an easement if it involves the servient owner in expenditure of money[17] (and this is so notwithstanding that the would-be dominant owner is willing to reimburse the potential servient owner for any expenditure incurred[18]). An easement of fencing is an exception to this rule.[19] An easement of support might seem to be another exception, but such an easement does not impose on the servient owner any obligation to maintain a supporting building in repair.[20]

6.   The right must be against other land

An easement is a right *against* other land. It is not a right to possession of other land. It was on this ground that a claim to stand an unlimited number of vehicles on another's land, since this was held to amount to a claim of joint possession of the land, was held not to be capable of being an easement.[1] A right to park cars on another's land is capable of being an easement only if the terms of the grant are such as to leave the servient owner reasonable use of his land.[2]

7.   New forms of easement

We can say with certainty that some rights (eg those listed above) are capable of being easements, since the courts have accepted them as capable of being such. We cannot say with certainty whether other rights will be accepted as easements, but the courts have accepted that 'The category of ... easements must alter and expand with the changes that take place in the circumstances of mankind'.[3] Thus the list of easements is not closed. New rights will be accepted as being capable of being easements if they conform to the principles relating to the nature of an easement that we have considered.

---

16   [1985] CLJ 458 (A. J. Waite).
17   See *Regis Property Co Ltd v Redman* [1956] 2 QB 612, [1956] 2 All ER 335.
18   *Rance v Elvin* (1983) 127 Sol Jo 732.
19   *Jones v Price* [1965] 2 QB 618, [1965] 2 All ER 625; *Crow v Wood* [1971] 1 QB 77, [1970] 3 All ER 425; (M & B).
20   *Jones v Pritchard* [1908] 1 Ch 630 at 637; *Bond v Nottingham Corpn* [1940] Ch 429 at 438-439.
 1   *Copland v Greenhalf* [1952] Ch 488, [1952] 1 All ER 809 (M & B); but see *Pye v Mumford* (1848) 11 QB 666.
 2   See *London and Blenheim Estates v Ladbroke Retail Parks Ltd* [1992] 1 WLR 1278, *per* Judge Paul Baker; affirmed [1994] 1 WLR 31, CA.
 3   *Dyce v Lady Hay* (1852) 1 Macq 305 at 312, per Lord St Leonards.

Acquisition of easements

An easement may be acquired in the following ways:

1. By statute.
2. By grant or a reservation, which may be:
   A. express grant or reservation,
   B. implied grant or reservation,
   C. presumed grant (otherwise termed 'prescription').

1.   BY STATUTE

A private (including a local) Act of Parliament sometimes creates an easement. For example, a private Act of 1754 allowed certain persons to convert a brook into a canal. It was later held[4] that the Act conferred a right of support for the canal.

Certain public Acts confer on local authorities or utility companies powers to lay sewers or gas or electricity or water mains. The exercise of such a power creates a right against another's land which has some, but not necessarily all, the characteristics of an easement; for example there need not be a dominant tenement.[5]

EXPRESS GRANT OR RESERVATION

Express grant

If S owns Greenacre and D owns Redacre, S may make an express grant to D of an easement across Greenacre.

After 1925 an easement for an interest equivalent in length to a fee simple absolute in possession or equivalent to a term of years absolute is as seen in Chapter 6, one of the estates in land that is capable of existing as a legal interest. We saw, too, in that chapter, that such an easement could exist also as an equitable easement, and we saw that an easement such as an easement for life, since it cannot exist as a legal easement, can exist only as an equitable easement.

Further, as seen in Chapter 15, a disposition of a legal interest in land must be by deed. If the grant of an easement is not by deed, but complies with s 2 of the Law of Property (Miscellaneous Provisions) Act 1989, and D gives consideration to S, then D acquires an equitable easement. If the transaction takes the form, not of a grant of an easement, but of a *contract* to grant an easement, then if the contract is for consideration and complies with section 2

---

4   *London and North Western Rly Co v Evan* [1893] 1 Ch 16.
5   The nature of such statutory rights is examined by J. F. Garner (1956) 20 Conv (NS) 208.

of the Law of Property (Miscellaneous Provisions) Act 1989, in this circumstance also an equitable easement is created.[6]

Regarding the difference it makes to D whether his easement is legal or equitable, before 1926, if D held an equitable easement, and S sold Greenacre to P, and P could show that he was a bona fide purchaser for value without notice, then P took free of D's equitable easement. If D held a legal easement, then it bound P (and any one else who acquired Greenacre) irrespective of whether he had notice. Equitable easements created after 1925 were made registrable by the Land Charges Act 1925.[7] If such an easement is registered it binds P; if not, it does not. A legal easement is not registrable and, as before 1926, binds P irrespective of whether or not he has notice of it.

Express reservation

If D owns Redacre and Greenacre, and he proposes to sell Greenacre to S, but to retain the right to cross Greenacre, then, in the conveyance to S, he may reserve the right to cross Greenacre as an easement. Before 1926, if D was to obtain a legal easement, S (as well as D) had to execute the conveyance. This was necessary for the following reason. An easement lay in grant. We have already considered some aspects of the meaning of this phrase. Another was the principle that an easement could only be granted by one person to another. Thus for D to acquire an easement over Greenacre there had to be a conveyance of the fee simple to S (signed by D) and then a notional grant by S of the easement to D. Hence the need for S to execute the conveyance.

After 1925, by s 65 of the Law of Property Act, D may reserve a legal easement[8] without any execution of the conveyance by S.

IMPLIED GRANT OR RESERVATION

When dealing with implied grants and reservations we are concerned with the situation where a landowner disposes of part of his land, and retains the remainder.

In the case of an implied grant of an easement, S owns Redacre and Greenacre, he grants Redacre to D and impliedly grants to D certain easements over Greenacre, the land which he retains.

In the case of an implied reservation of an easement D owns Redacre and Greenacre. He grants Greenacre to S and impliedly reserves to himself certain easements over Greenacre, in favour of Redacre, the land he retains.

---

6 Provided that at the date of the contract the dominant tenement has been specifically identified. *London and Blenheim Estates Ltd v Ladbrook Retail Parks Ltd* [1994] 1 WLR 31, CA.
7 Section 10(1); now Land Charges Act 1972, s 2.
8 Or any other legal estate or interest.

Implied grant

S owns Redacre and Greenacre. He grants Redacre to D. What easements does S thereby impliedly grant to D over Greenacre, the land he retains? Such implied grants fall to be considered under the following heads.

1.   EASEMENTS OF NECESSITY[9]

If, at the time D acquires Redacre, his only[10] means of access to Redacre is over Greenacre (eg if Redacre is surrounded by Greenacre, or if it is surrounded by Greenacre and land belonging to one or more[11] other persons) then S impliedly grants to D, along with the land, an easement of way[12] sometimes termed a 'way of necessity' across Greenacre, so as to reach Redacre. The decision as to the route to be used rests with S:[13] it will lie where 'he can spare it best',[14] but it must be one which is convenient for D,[15] and once selected, it cannot be changed.[16] In the case of a way of necessity, necessity refers to something that is necessary in order to be able to use the land (ie to use it for at least *something*), it does not refer to something that is necessary in order to have reasonable enjoyment of the property. Thus where certain land could be reached from an adjoining public footpath, it was held that no easement of necessity existed for the passage of vehicles.[17]

S similarly impliedly grants to D any other form of easement (eg a right to construct a ventilation shaft[18]) without which D would not be able to derive any benefit from the land granted to him.[19]

In *Nickerson v Barraclough*[20] Megarry J indicated that a way of necessity (ie as a means of access to land-locked land) had its basis in a rule of public policy that no transaction should without good reason be treated as being effectual to deprive any land of a suitable means of access. On appeal,[1] however, in obiter in the Court of Appeal, this notion was rejected and the traditional view that ways of necessity were founded on the implied intention of the parties was re-asserted: they were based 'upon the implication to be drawn from the fact that unless some way is implied, a parcel of land will be inaccessible. From that fact the implication arises that the parties must have intended that

---

9   (1981) 34 CLP 133 (P. Jackson).
10   Or only way other than one that is precarious (ie exercisable merely under a revocable licence) (1880) 13 Ch D 798; (M & B).
11   *Barry v Hasseldine*, ante.
12   Limited to purposes for which Redacre was used at the time of the grant; *London Corpn v Riggs* (1880) 13 Ch D 798; (M & B).
13   *Bolton v Bolton* (1879) 11 Ch D 968 at 972.
14   Cruise, Vol 3, 87.
15   *Pearson v Spencer* (1861) 1 B & S 571.
16   *Deacon v South Eastern Rly Co* (1889) 61 LT 377.
17   *MRA Engineering Ltd v Trimster Co Ltd* (1987) 56 P & CR 1. See also *Manjang Drammeh* (1991) 61 PCR 194 (no easement of necessity where access available from publicly navigable river).
18   *Wong v Beaumont Property Trust Ltd* [1965] 1 QB 173, [1964] 2 All ER 119; (M & B).
19   *Pwllbach Colliery Ltd v Woodman* [1915] AC 634; *Stafford v Lee* [1992] 45 LS Gaz R 27.
20   [1980] Ch 325, [1979] 3 All ER 312.
1   [1981] Ch 426, [1981] 2 All ER 369.

some way giving access to the land should have been granted'. The basis of a way of necessity is of significance. If such a way is based on public policy, then it cannot be excluded. If it is based on implied intention, it can be excluded by evidence that the parties had no intention that an easement should arise (eg by a clause in the conveyance expressly excluding any right of way).[2]

2. INTENDED EASEMENTS

S also impliedly grants to D such easements over Greenacre as are necessary to carry out what must be the common intention of S and D as to the particular use to which Redacre would be put.[3]

An example is the implied grant of an intended easement of support.[4] Further, every grant of an easement carries with it a grant of such ancillary rights as are reasonably necessary for the exercise or enjoyment of the easement. Thus an easement of drainage carries with it a right to enter the servient land to clear a blockage or carry out repairs.[5]

3. EASEMENTS IMPLIEDLY GRANTED UNDER THE RULE IN *WHEELDON V BURROWS*

'Quasi-easements'

S owns Redacre and Greenacre. Suppose:

(i)   that a drive leading to Redacre crosses Greenacre;
(ii) that an overhead wire carrying electricity to Redacre crosses Greenacre;
(iii) that a sewer from Redacre runs beneath Greenacre;
(iv) that S has been in the practice of collecting water from a pump on Greenacre to water his kitchen garden on Redacre.

S has a right to use the drive, to have the electricity wire over Greenacre, etc by virtue of his ownership of Greenacre. If he ceased to own Greenacre, he would in each case have needed an easement in order to be able to use the drive, etc. Rights such as these are termed quasi-easements. A quasi-easement is thus a right which a person has over his own land which, if the land was not his own, could not be exercised without the existence of an easement.

If S transfers Redacre to D, does D acquire as easements those rights which were exercised as quasi-easements by S? The answer is that under the rule in *Wheeldon v Burrows*[6] S impliedly grants to D, as legal easements, all those quasi-easements that had been exercised over Greenacre which:

---

2   See [1981] Conv 442 (L. Crabb); (1982) 98 LQR 11 (P. Jackson).
3   *Jones v Pritchard* [1908] 1 Ch 630.
4   *Richards v Rose* (1853) 9 Exch 218 at 221.
5   *Jones v Pritchard*, supra. Cf *Duke of Westminster v Guild* [1985] QB 688, [1984] 3 All ER 144; [1985] Conv 66 (P. Jackson).
6   (1879) 12 Ch D 31; (M & B).

(1) at the time of the transfer to D were in fact used by S for the benefit of Redacre;[7] and

(2) either (a) were necessary to the reasonable enjoyment of Redacre;[8] or[9] (b) were continuous and apparent.

Thus D acquires Redacre together with the easements over Greenacre that arise under the rule.

'necessary to the reasonable enjoyment of the land granted'

To comply with this condition the quasi-easement does not have to be one without which the property could not be used at all; it must be one that is necessary for there to be reasonable enjoyment of the land; ie if there can be reasonable enjoyment without exercise of the quasi-easement, the rule does not apply.[10]

'apparent'

This means that the existence of the quasi-easement must be discoverable on 'a careful inspection by a person ordinarily conversant with the subject'.[11] For example, where A claimed an implied grant of an easement entitling him to go on to B's land in order to clear the gutters of his, A's, cottage, which could only be reached from B's land, the claim under the rule in *Wheeldon v Burrows* failed as there was nothing 'apparent' to indicate the existence of the easement claimed.[12]

'continuous'

It has been held that this means that the use must have been constant and uninterrupted.[13] The fact that use of a made-up road and use of a worn track[14] have been accepted as being 'continuous', suggests, however, that the true test is whether the use has been permanent and uninterrupted, rather than constant and uninterrupted.[15]

Let us apply these principles to the examples above:

(i) The drive. This would comply with condition 1 and with both 2(a) and (b).[16]

(ii) The electric wire. This would comply with condition 1 and 2(b).[17]

---

7   *Sovmots Investments Ltd v Secretary of State for the Environment* [1979] AC 144, [1977] 2 All ER 385; (M & B); *Re St Clement's, Leigh-on-Sea* [1988] 1 WLR 720.
8   As in *Borman v Griffith* [1930] 1 Ch 493; (M & B).
9   'Or' not 'and'.
10   *Wheeler v J J Saunders Ltd* [1996] Ch 19, [1995] 2 All ER 697, CA.
11   *Pyer v Carter* (1857) 1 H & N 916 at 922, per Watson B.
12   *Ward v Kirkland* [1967] Ch 194, [1966] 1 All ER 609.
13   *Suffield v Brown* (1864) 4 De GJ & Sm 185 at 199.
14   *Brown v Alabaster* (1887) 37 Ch D 490; *Hansford v Jago* [1921] 1 Ch 322.
15   M & W, p 835.
16   *Borman v Griffith*, ante. *Brown v Alabaster* (1887) 37 Ch D 490; (M & B).
17   *Watts v Kelson* (1870) 6 Ch App 166 (visible pipes carrying water supply).

(iii) The underground sewer. This would comply with condition 1 and probably with 2(a). If for some reason it was shown not to comply with 2(a), it might, nevertheless, depending on the facts, be shown to comply with 2(b), for example, there might be one or more inspection covers which would make the existence of the sewer 'apparent'.

(iv) Water from the pump. This would comply with condition 1 but would probably fail to comply with conditions 2(a) and (b).[18]

Grants to two (or more) persons

If S owns Redacre and Greenacre, and when he granted Redacre to D, he at the same time granted Greenacre to X, under the rule in *Wheeldon v Burrows*, D would acquire the same easements over Greenacre as he would if S had retained Greenacre. S impliedly grants the *Wheeldon v Burrows* easements to D; and he grants Greenacre to X impliedly subject to these easements.[19]

Devises to two (or more) persons

If in his will S left Redacre to D and Greenacre to X, the same principles apply as in the case of inter vivos grants to D and to X. D acquires the *Wheeldon v Burrows* easements over Greenacre.[20]

Derogation of grant

Consider the example at the beginning of the treatment of the rule. S did not expressly convey to D easements relating to the drive, the electric wire or the sewer. But what would have been the effect of the transaction if the easements implied under the rule had not passed? S would have granted the land to D, but by declining to allow D the use of the three easements he would have prevented D from using the land in a way it was reasonable for D to have expected to be able to use the land. S would have granted with one hand and withheld with the other: he would have derogated from what it was reasonable for D to assume had been granted to him. It is a principle of law – a principle 'as well established by authority as it is consonant to reason and good sense'[1] – that a grantor may not derogate from his grant.[2] It is this principle, therefore, that underlies the implied grant of an easement, whether an easement of necessity, an intended easement, or an easement arising under the doctrine in *Wheeldon v Burrows*.

4.   EASEMENTS ARISING UNDER S 62 OF THE LAW OF PROPERTY ACT 1925

'General words'

When A conveys land to B it is generally the intention that B shall acquire the same rights in connection with the land as had been enjoyed by A. In order to

---

18   *Polden v Bastard* (1865) LR 1 QB 156.
19   *Swansborough v Coventry* (1832) 2 Moo & S 362.
20   *Phillips v Low* [1892] 1 Ch 47.
 1   Per Thesiger LJ, *Wheeldon v Burrows* (1879) 12 Ch D 31 at 49.

give effect to this intention it was originally the practice in conveyances to insert, at the end of the description of the property (the 'parcels'), a number of 'general words' setting out all those rights[3] relating to the land which had been enjoyed in connection with it.

Section 62

Today it is no longer necessary to include the 'general words', since s 62 of the Law of Property Act 1925 (which replaced a similar provision in the Conveyancing Act 1881[4]) provides that, if no contrary intention[5] is expressed,[6] every 'conveyance of land shall be deemed to include and shall ... operate to convey, with the land ... all easements, rights and advantages whatsoever appertaining or reputed to appertain to the land ... or, at the time of the conveyance .. enjoyed with the land or any part thereof ...'[7]

The section does not apply unless the transferor of the land had power (eg legal capacity) to make a grant expressly of the rights concerned.[8]

Diversity of occupation

After some uncertainty[9] it has now been established[10] that s 62 operates only where, before the conveyance, the two tenements were not owned and occupied by the same person. 'There must be some diversity of ownership or occupation'[11] of the two tenements prior to the conveyance relied on. (It seems that the requirement that there must be diversity of occupation does not apply where the claim is for an easement of light.[12]) Thus if S owns Redacre and Greenacre, and he exercises quasi-easements over Greenacre, and then conveys or leases Redacre to D, D does not (under s 62) acquire as easements the rights exercised as quasi-easements by S before the conveyance, since before the conveyance the two tenements were owned and occupied by the same person, S. (D may, however, acquire as easements the quasi-easements exercised by S if the conditions for the rule in *Wheeldon v Burrows* to apply are satisfied.)

---

2   See *Lyme Valley Squash Club Ltd v Newcastle under Lyme Borough Council* [1985] 2 All ER 405; [1985] Conv 243 (HWW).
3   In addition to existing easements, the benefit of which pass automatically with the land; *Godwins v Schweppes Ltd* [1902] 1 Ch 926.
4   Section 6.
5   As in *Bridle v Ruby* [1989] QB 169, [1988] 3 All ER 64; [1989] Conv 261. *Pretoria Warehousing Co Ltd v Shelton* [1993] EGCS 120, CA (no sufficient contrary intention to exclude section); [1994] Conv 238 (A. Dowling).
6   LPA 1925, s 62(1).
7   See *Graham v Philcox* [1984] QB 747, [1984] 2 All ER 643, CA; (M & B); [1985] Conv 60 (P. Todd); [1985] CLJ 15 (S. Tromans).
8   Section 62(5); *Re St Clements, Leigh-on-Sea* [1988] 1 WLR 720.
9   Compare *Long v Gowlett* [1923] 2 Ch 177 at 200-203 with *Wright v Macadam* [1949] 2 KB 744 at 748.
10 *Sovmots Investments Ltd v Secretary of State of the Environment* [1979] AC 144, [1977] 2 All ER 385; (M & B); (1979) 43 Conv (NS) 113 (C. Harpum).
11 Per Sargant J, *Long v Gowlett* [1923] 2 Ch 177 at 201.
12 *Broomfield v Williams* [1897] 1 Ch 602.

Thus if S owns plots of land, and he disposes of one of them to D, he must always beware of impliedly granting to D easements under the doctrine in *Wheeldon v Burrows*;[13] but he need have no fear of s 62 operating to convey an easement to D unless D or some other person had been in occupation prior to the conveyance. (S may always protect himself against granting more than he intends by ensuring that the conveyance to D expressly excludes the operation of both the doctrine in *Wheeldon v Burrows* and s 62.)

Illustrations

The operation of the restriction which has just been explained, and of the section generally, can be illustrated by some examples.

1. S owns Redacre and Greenacre. S leases Redacre to C. S permits C to take wheeled vehicles across Greenacre to reach Redacre. On the expiry of C's lease S sells Redacre to D. The conveyance expressly grants D a right of way across Greenacre on foot. Since the right to cross Greenacre with wheeled vehicles was a 'right' which was 'appertaining' to Redacre, s 62 will operate to grant to D the right of way for wheeled vehicles which had been enjoyed previously by C.[14] And this result ensues notwithstanding that the permission granted by S to C was precarious, ie revocable at any time by S.[15] Thus although the right exercised by C before the conveyance was merely a revocable licence, after the conveyance it becomes an easement of which Redacre is the dominant tenement and Greenacre the servient tenement.

2. S owns Redacre and Greenacre. On Redacre is a house, the north wall of which immediately adjoins the boundary with Greenacre. S allows D to occupy Redacre, and permits him to go on to Greenacre whenever necessary to carry out repairs and clear the gutters on the north side of the house. Later, S conveys the freehold of Redacre to D. Section 62 will operate to convey to D the right to go on to Greenacre for the purposes mentioned. Thus whilst what D had done before the grant was by authority of a revocable licence, after the grant, he can do by virtue of an easement. So, as in the previous example, s 62 results in the creation of an easement where none had existed before.[16]

The effect of the section may sometimes operate to the advantage of a tenant who has been permitted by his landlord to enjoy certain additional rights not mentioned in the lease. The next three examples illustrate instances of this.

3. S intends to grant D a lease of Redacre. He lets D into possession of Redacre and gives him permission to cross Greenacre. D at this stage has no more than a licence, revocable by S, to cross Greenacre. S then executes a lease of Redacre to D. The grant of a lease is a 'conveyance' within s 62. The permission to cross Greenacre was a right appertaining to Redacre. The grant of the lease therefore carries with it, by virtue of s 62, the right to cross Greenacre, which thereupon becomes an easement.[17]

---

13 Supra.
14 *Gregg v Richards* [1926] Ch 521.
15 *Wright v Macadam* [1949] 2 KB 744 at 750; (M & B).
16 *Ward v Kirkland* [1967] Ch 194, [1966] 1 All ER 609.
17 *Goldberg v Edwards* [1950] Ch 247; (M & B).

4. S leases Redacre to D. S then gives D permission to store coal in a shed on Greenacre. On the expiry of the lease S grants a fresh lease to D. The grant of the new lease is a conveyance within s 62. D therefore acquires an easement to store coal in the shed on Greenacre.[18]

5. S leases Redacre to D. S then gives D permission to cross Greenacre. Later S sells the fee simple in Redacre to D. The conveyance carries with it the right to cross Greenacre which thereupon becomes an easement in favour of Redacre.[19]

It will be noted that in all the above five examples, the section was able to operate as in no case had the two tenements been both owned and occupied by S prior to the relevant conveyance.

6. X owns two plots of land, Redacre and Greenacre. A river flows through the two plots. On the lower plot, Redacre, X has a water mill. X is in the practice of clearing reeds from the banks and the bed of the river where it passes through the upper plot, Greenacre. X sells Redacre to D and Greenacre to S. In order to maintain a clear flow of water to the mill D claims that he has an easement (under s 62) to go on to Greenacre to clear the reeds from the river. His claim fails as prior to the conveyance to him the two plots of land were both owned and occupied by the same person, X.[20]

Comparison between the doctrine in Wheeldon v Burrows and s 62

1. The doctrine in *Wheeldon v Burrows* relates only to quasi-easements which were either continuous and apparent, or were necessary for the reasonable enjoyment of the land. Under s 62 easements can be created which comply with neither of these two requirements.[1]

2. Section 62 operates where there is a 'conveyance' of land. This includes[2] a conveyance of the legal fee simple or the grant of a legal lease, but it does not include a transfer of an equitable fee simple (eg by a contract for the sale of the land) or the creation of an equitable lease (eg by a contract to grant the lease[3]). The doctrine in *Wheeldon v Burrows* applies not only in cases where there is a 'conveyance' as defined in relation to s 62 but also on the creation of an equitable fee simple (by a contract for the sale of the land), on the creation of an equitable lease (by an enforceable contract to grant a lease[4]) and on a devise (ie to two or more persons).

3. Section 62 operates only where there has been diversity of ownership or occupation of the two tenements prior to the conveyance. The rule in *Wheeldon v Burrows* imposes no such requirement.

---

18   *Wright v Macadam* [1949] 2 KB 744, [1949] 2 All ER 565; (M & B).
19   *International Tea Stores v Hobbs* [1903] 2 Ch 165.
20   *Long v Gowlett* [1923] 2 Ch 177; (M & B) (an additional ground for the decision in this case was that the right claimed was not one which 'appertained' to Greenacre); *Sovmots Investments Ltd v Secretary of State for the Environment* [1979] AC 144, [1977] 2 All ER 385; (M & B).
1   *Goldberg v Edwards* [1950] Ch 247; (M & B).
2   LPA 1925, s 205(1)(i), (ii).
3   *Borman v Griffith* [1930] 1 Ch 493; (M & B).
4   Ibid.

4. Although both the rule in *Wheeldon v Burrows* and s 62 may result in the creation of an easement where none existed before, neither can convert into an easement a right which by its nature is not capable of existing as an easement.[5] It was for this reason that a right to receive hot water through pipes in a flat was held not to be converted into an easement by s 62 in a lease of the flat.[6]

5. Under both, the subject matter of the right must be one which appertains to the would-be dominant tenement. For example, suppose that S owned Redacre and Greenacre. He leased Redacre to D, and later allowed him to graze cattle on Greenacre. If S later sold Redacre to D, the right to graze cattle would not pass to D under the rule in *Wheeldon v Burrows* or under s 62 as the right does not appertain to Redacre: it does not 'accommodate' Redacre. The right to graze cattle on Greenacre would remain on the same basis (eg as a revocable licence granted to D) as before the conveyance of Redacre to him.[7]

6. Under both, the right to be obtained by D must be one that S would be capable of being granted by express grant. For example, in *Green v Ashco Horticulturalist Ltd*,[8] in 1931 L leased premises to T for use as a greengrocer's shop. The shop backed onto a yard, from which there was access through wooden doors to a passageway. The doors were often kept closed out of business hours and, to go through at such times, T had to ask an employee of L to open them. T made considerable use of the passageway and yard for getting goods to his shop. In 1959 the lease to T was renewed. Later L sold the freehold of the shop premises to D. D claimed a right of way across the yard under s 62. It was held that the form of use – intermittent and consensual – was not of a kind that could have been granted as an easement. D's claim therefore failed.

7. Another characteristic shared by the rule in *Wheeldon v Burrows* and s 62 is that neither can confer a benefit on a third party. For example, if A owns Redacre and he has been in the practice of walking, with C's permission, over C's land Blueacre, and A conveys Redacre to B, neither the rule in *Wheeldon v Burrows*[9] nor s 62[10] confers on B any right to walk across Blueacre.

Operation by express grant

The effect of s 62 is not that S impliedly grants D the rights referred to in the section. The section states that 'A conveyance of land shall be deemed to include, and by virtue of this Act operate to convey, with the land, all ... easements, rights', etc. Thus, since a conveyance of land is deemed to include a grant of easements concerned, the effect of the section is that in executing the conveyance (without expressing an intention that s 62 is not to apply) S makes an express grant of the easements concerned to D.

5   See *Pinemain Ltd v Welbeck International Ltd* (1984) 272 Estates Gazette 1166; [1986] Conv 50 (S. Murdoch).
6   *Regis Property Co Ltd v Redman* [1956] 2 QB 612, [1956] 2 All ER 335; *Phipps v Pears* [1965] 1 QB 76, [1964] 2 All ER 35.
7   *White v Williams* [1922] 1 KB 727. See also *Bartlett v Tottenham* [1932] 1 Ch 114.
8   [1966] 2 All ER 232, [1966] 1 WLR 889.
9   (1879) 12 Ch D 31.
10 *Quicke v Chapman* [1903] 1 Ch 659.

However, because of the similarities between the effect of the rule in *Wheeldon v Burrows* and s 62 it is convenient, and customary, to deal with s 62, which strictly relates to express grants, after dealing with implied grants, as we have done here.

Anomalous nature of s 62

Consider the fourth example on p 326. Here S leased Redacre to D. S then gave D permission to store coal in a shed on Greenacre. On the expiry of the lease S granted a fresh lease to D. As a result of the operation of s 62, the conveyance (ie the grant of the lease) operated to convert what had hitherto been a bare licence, revocable by S at any time, into an easement which was binding on the owners of Greenacre, and the benefit of which ran with the lease of Redacre (ie for the benefit of any assignees of the lease). This effect is produced, as we have seen, because s 62 provides that the grant of the new lease is to be 'deemed to ... convey with the land ... all ... advantages' (and the right to use the coal shed is no more than an 'advantage') ' ... enjoyed with the land ... '

It can be argued that the effect of the section is anomalous. Why should a revocable licence be converted into an irrevocable easement? It would be more logical, it might be argued, if the section operated to convey to D no more than what he had enjoyed under the former lease, namely the right to keep coal in the shed until S told him to stop doing so. Indeed, it is arguable that this is how the section ought properly to be interpreted: that the 'easements, rights and advantages' conveyed with the land should have the same nature, no more and no less, as they did before the conveyance. But this is not how the section has been construed, and the weight of authority against any such view is at present so great as to be unassailable. Only statute could change the position.

Although the section might seem to be capable of producing unexpected results, its operation can be defended on the ground that the section can prevent what could, without it, be an injustice: when D agreed to take a fresh lease of Redacre from S it is reasonable to suppose that he did so on the assumption that he would be allowed to continue to use the coal shed. For S to grant D a fresh lease and the next day tell him that he could no longer use the shed could be regarded as amounting, if not to misrepresentation, at least to a derogation from what it was reasonable for D to believe had been granted to him. So the section, although at first sight being capable of causing an anomalous effect, may assist in producing a just result by preventing a derogation from grant (and seen in this light the rationale of the section thus has, as noted earlier, the same basis as the rule in *Wheeldon v Burrows*).

Implied reservation

D owns Redacre and Greenacre. He grants Greenacre to S. What easements does D impliedly reserve to himself over Greenacre, the land he has granted away? He impliedly reserves the following.

1. EASEMENTS OF NECESSITY

The same principles apply as in the case of an implied grant. Thus, if at the time he grants Greenacre to S, D's only means of access to Redacre is over Greenacre, D impliedly reserves an easement of way over Greenacre.

2. INTENDED EASEMENTS

The same principles apply as in the case of an implied grant. D impliedly reserves such easements over Greenacre as are necessary to carry out what must have been the common intention of S and D as to the use to which Redacre would be put.[11]

C PRESUMED GRANT ('PRESCRIPTION')[12]

In some circumstances the court will presume that the owner of Greenacre had granted the owner of Redacre an easement over Greenacre. For example, if successive owners of Redacre had been in the practice of using a path across Greenacre for, say, 30 years, without the owners of Greenacre at any time raising an objection, then it would seem unjust if an owner of Greenacre later sought to terminate something which, by then, had become so well established.

It is in such a circumstance as this that the court, in seeking to uphold the right, may presume that at some time in the past an owner of Greenacre had granted an easement to the owner of Redacre. By this means a lawful basis for the right will be provided.[13] And this step the court may take notwithstanding that there is no evidence of a grant ever having actually been made.[14] This presumption of a grant is termed 'prescription' (but, we may for convenience note here, no presumption of grant will be made if the user on which the claim rests is contrary to statute[15]).

Certain conditions which had to be fulfilled before a grant would be presumed were developed by the courts of common law. The Prescription Act 1832 left the common law principles in all essentials intact[16] but supplemented them in various ways and, in some respects, improved a claimant's position. A person claiming an easement by prescription may do so either under the 1832 Act or under the principles of common law, or under both. Thus a claim may fail at common law but succeed under the Act.[17]

---

11 *Re Webb's Lease* [1951] Ch 808, [1951] 2 All ER 131; (M & B).
12 For proposals for reform, see Law Reform Committee, 14th Report (Cmnd 3100, 1966) recommending, in particular, that the prescription period of 20 years under the Act of 1832 should be reduced to the limitation period (viz 12 years); see Chapter 24.
13 Regarding the basis of prescription, see Fry J, *Dalton v Angus* (1881) 6 App Cas 740 at 773-774. See p 334, infra.
14 ' ... neither judge nor any one else [having] the shadow of a belief that any such instrument ... ever existed', per Cockburn CJ, *Bryant v Foot* (1867) LR 2 QB 161 at 181; (M & B).
15 *Cargill v Gotts* [1981] 1 All ER 682, [1981] 1 WLR 441.
16 *Healey v Hawkins* [1968] 3 All ER 836, [1968] 1 WLR 1967; (M & B).
17 And vice versa; *Hulbert v Dale* [1909] 2 Ch 570; (M & B).

Where an easement arises by prescription, the presumption is always that an easement *in fee*, equivalent to a fee simple absolute in possession (ie a permanent right), has been granted.

There are two forms of prescription at common law, both of which may still be called in aid today:

1. The original, earlier, form of prescription at common law, which is now referred to as 'prescription at common law'.
2. A later development of the common law termed the doctrine of the 'lost modern grant'.

PRESCRIPTION AT COMMON LAW

Certain conditions must be satisfied for a claim by prescription under this head to succeed. They are as follows:

1.   THERE MUST BE USER FOR THE REQUISITE PERIOD

To establish a claim use (*'user'*) of the easement had originally to be shown since 1189.[18] It became accepted,[19] however, that user for 20 years raised a rebuttable presumption that there had been user since 1189. Thus if D claims an easement over S's land and D can prove user for 20 years, this raises the presumption that there has been user since 1189. But this is only a presumption. If S can rebut the presumption by showing that there could not have been user since 1189, or that there had in fact not been user since that time, the presumption is rebutted and the claim fails.

For example, if D claims an easement of light for a window of a building on his land, and he can show that there had been an uninterrupted flow of light to the window for 20 years, the presumption arises that there has been such a flow of light since 1189. But if S points to the date '1800' carved on the end of the building, the presumption is rebutted.[20] There could not have been user since 1189, as the building had only been standing since 1800. So D's claim fails. (It was for this reason that it was difficult to establish a claim to an easement of light under the original common law doctrine.)

2.   THERE MUST BE SUFFICIENT CONTINUITY OF USER

Use during the requisite period must have been sufficiently continuous.[1] This does not mean that user must have never ceased. What is required is

---

18   The Statute of Westminster the First (1275), fixed the year 1189 as the limit of legal memory. A right enjoyed at that date could not be challenged. The date came to be adopted as a basis for a claim by prescription.
19   For an account of how this came about, see *Byrant v Foot, ante*, per Cockburn CJ at pp 179-182.
20   *Duke of Norfolk v Arbuthnot* (1880) 5 CPD 390 (evidence that church built about 1380 defeated claim).
1   *Dare v Heathcote* (1856) 25 LJ Ex 245.

that the user must have been of such a frequency as to indicate an assertion of continuous user.[2] Provided that the intervals between user are not excessive, it is normally sufficient for the claimant to show that there was user whenever circumstances required it.[3] Further, user is not prevented from being continuous if there is a minor alteration in the user itself (eg a minor change in the route of a footpath) during the period of user on which the claim is based.[4] Nor is user prevented from being continuous by an increase in the quantum of use (eg an increase in the amount of water drawn from a mill-pond on the servient tenement) provided that the increase it not attributable to a change in the purpose of the user and that the increase is not so great that the practical burden on the servient tenement is drastically increased.[5]

3(A)   THERE MUST BE USER AGAINST A FEE SIMPLE OWNER OF THE SERVIENT TENEMENT

As we have said, where an easement arises by prescription, the court presumes that an easement in fee was granted. The only person capable of making such a grant would be a fee simple owner. Thus if D claims an easement by prescription against S and S is able to show that at the commencement of the period of user the land was occupied by someone other than a fee simple owner (eg that it was at that time occupied by a lessee), then since this demonstrates that an easement in fee (the only form of easement capable of being created by prescription) could not have been granted by the occupier, D's claim will fail. It might be thought that if S leased Greenacre to T for, say, 99 years and later D began to cross Greenacre to reach his own land Redacre, and did so for 20 years, D would acquire an easement which, whilst not binding on S, was binding against T for the remainder of the lease. But this is not so: D acquires no easement.[6]

If D had crossed Greenacre for 20 years and at the beginning of that time the land had been occupied by S, the owner of the fee simple, and later S had leased the field to T this would not affect D's claim since a fee simple owner had been in occupation at the beginning of the period, and this suffices.[7]

---

2   *White v Taylor (No 2)* [1969] 1 Ch 160, [1968] 1 All ER 1015, a case relating to rights of common (see post) but the principle is the same in the case of easements; *Dare v Heathcote* (1856) 25 LJ Ex 245.
3   Eg as where D crossed S's field six to ten times a year in order to take gear for trimming the hedges and repairing the fences of a field belonging to D on the far side of S's land; *Diment v NH Foot Ltd* [1974] 1 WLR 1427 at 1430; (M & B).
4   *Davis v Whitby* [1974] Ch 186, [1974] 1 All ER 806; (M & B).
5   *Cargill v Gotts* [1981] 1 All ER 682, [1981] 1 WLR 441, CA.
6   Nor is a claim available to D under the doctrine of lost modern grant (see p 336. *Simmons v Dobson* [1991] 4 All ER 25, [1991] 1 WLR 720.
7   Further, if a claim is based on the 20-year period under the Prescription Act 1832 (see post), it is immaterial that S is not in occupation at the beginning of the 20-year period, if S (or his predecessor in title) was in occupation at the time when the *total* period of user relied on by D started; *Pugh v Savage* [1970] 2 QB 373, [1970] 2 All ER 353.

3(B)   THERE MUST BE USER BY OR ON BEHALF OF A FEE SIMPLE OWNER OF THE DOMINANT TENEMENT

The claim can be made either by the fee simple owner of the dominant tenement, or on behalf of this owner, eg by a tenant on behalf of this landlord. Thus, suppose that the occupiers of Redacre have been in the practice of using a path across Greenacre for more than 20 years, and that the succession of events has been this:

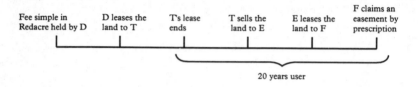

At the beginning of the user the land is let to T. This does not infringe the rule we are considering since here the user (by T) is regarded as being on behalf of the fee simple owner (D). At the end of the 20 years, when F claims an easement by prescription, he does so on behalf of the fee simple owner, E. Thus if F's claim succeeds, an easement in fee arises, and the benefit of this is annexed to the dominant tenement and so accrues to E on the expiry of F's lease (and to all subsequent holders of the land). What F cannot do is claim an easement on his own behalf (ie for the unexpired portion of his lease); though if the claim on behalf of E succeeds he will enjoy the benefit of the easement during the remainder of his tenancy.

3(C)   THERE MUST BE USER BY OR ON BEHALF OF ONE FEE SIMPLE OWNER AGAINST A DIFFERENT FEE SIMPLE OWNER

(i) Suppose that S owns Redacre and Greenacre. He leases Redacre to D for 999 years. D crosses Greenacre for 20 years. D claims an easement against S. The claim must fail, since there has been user on behalf of a fee simple owner against the same fee simple owner. Thus a tenant cannot acquire an easement by prescription against and held by his landlord.[8]

(ii) Suppose that D owns Redacre and Greenacre. He leases Greenacre to S. D crosses Greenacre for 20 years. D claims an easement against Greenacre. If a grant was to be presumed, it could only be an easement in fee. But such an easement would bind not only S, during the continuance of his lease, but also D (the owner of the reversion) on the expiry of the lease. The result would be that D had an easement against himself. This is not possible. Therefore D's claim fails. Thus a landlord cannot acquire an easement by prescription against land held by his tenant.

---

8   *Kilgour v Gaddes* [1904] 1 KB 457; (M & B).

(iii) Suppose that X owns Redacre and Greenacre; he leases Redacre to D and Greenacre to S. D crossed Greenacre for 20 years. D claims an easement against S. Here also the claim must fail, since if it succeeded, the result would be that an easement had been acquired on behalf of X, against himself. Thus a tenant cannot acquire an easement by presecription[9] against another tenant of the same landlord.

(With regard to the illustrations above it should be noted that as between landlord and tenant, and between tenants of the same landlord, easements may come into existence as a result of express or implied grants (or reservations).)

4. THE USER MUST BE AS OF RIGHT

We have seen that the basis of prescription is that the court presumes the existence of the grant of an easement. The fact that D has crossed S's land is treated as evidence that a grant of an easement must have been made. But let us suppose that S had protested at D crossing his land, and had locked the gate to Greenacre; and that D had broken the lock. This does not support the theory of a grant by S. On the contrary, it shows that D is crossing the land despite S's objection, not by virtue of some grant by S.

Further, if the theory of a grant is not to be undermined, D must show that D knew, or could have known, of D's user and yet made no objection. For if S did not know, and was not in a position to know, of D's user, he would not have been in a position to object; and it is the lack of objection which is a foundation of the theory.

The theory of a grant would be undermined also if S could show that there was no need to presume a grant to account for D's user. For example, if S had given D permission to cross Greenacre, it would be to this consent that D's user would be attributable.

Thus, in order to establish a claim by prescription, the user must be in accordance with, and not serve to rebut, the presumption that user was attributable to the grant of an easement. This is the principle expressed in the statement – 'user must have been *as of right*', by which is meant, 'the user must be exercised *as if it* had been exercised *as of right* by virtue of an easement having been granted'.

In defining user as of right English law has adopted[10] the definition of Roman law as to the nature of user that will support a claim by prescription. According to this definition such user must be *nec vi* (without force), *nec clam* (without secrecy) and *nec precario* (without permission).

nec vi (without force)

Force here includes: (a) physical violence (as where D broke the lock to the gate); and (b) protests, either in the form of lodging a protest with D,[11] or by taking legal proceedings against D, eg by bringing an action for trespass.[12]

---

9   Or under the doctrine of lost modern grant (see p 310); *Simmons v Dobson* [1991] 4 All ER 25, [1991] 1 WLR 720; (M & B); [1992] Conv 167 (P. Sparkes).

10   *Sturges v Bridgman* (1879) 11 Ch D 852; *Gardner v Hodgson's Kingston Brewery Co* [1903] AC 229, 239.

11   *Gardner v Hodgson's Kingston Brewery Co Ltd* [1903] AC 229; (M & B).

12   *Eaton v Swansea Waterworks Co* (1851) 17 QB 267.

nec clam (without secrecy)

'Secrecy' includes any situation where D's user is not apparent to S, and would not have become apparent to him even if he had exercised diligence in the protection of his interests.[13] Thus where the sides of X's dock were attached by underground rods to adjoining land belonging to Y, since Y could not have known of the existence of the rods, X's user was not *nec clam* and so a claim by prescription by X (to retain the rods in Y's ground) failed.[14]

To say that the user must have been merely without 'secrecy' does not, however, go far enough. The Roman adage is not sufficiently positive to represent the position in English law. The requirement we are describing is not so much a negative requirement relating to the form of user by D, as a positive requirement relating to the state of mind of S. The reason is that the foundation on which the courts built the presumption of the grant of an easement is the acquiescence by S in D's user.

ACQUIESCENCE THE KEY

The importance of acquiescence was expressed by Fry J in *Dalton v Angus*[15] when he said: '...the whole law of prescription and the whole law which governs the presumption or inference of a grant or covenant rests upon acquiescence ... it becomes then of the highest importance to consider of what ingredients acquiescence consists. In many cases, as, for instance, in the case of that acquiescence which creates a right of way, it will be found to involve, first, the doing of some act by one man upon the land of another; secondly, the absence of right to do that act in the person doing it; thirdly, the knowledge of the person affected by it that the act is done; fourthly, the power of the person affected by the act to prevent such act either by action on his part or by action in the courts; and lastly, the abstinence by him from any such interference for such a length of time as renders it reasonable for the courts to say that he shall not afterwards interfere to stop the act being done.' Thus S can only be regarded as having acquiesced in D's user if S had knowledge of the user; or, at least, if he 'must be taken to have (had) a reasonable opportunity of becoming aware of that enjoyment'[16] and had taken no action to stop it.[17]

nec precario (without permission)

The user must be without permission. If no permission has been given it will be immaterial that D's user had been in the belief that permission had been given[18]

---

13   *Union Lighterage Co v London Graving Dock Co* [1902] 2 Ch 557; see also *Liverpool Corpn v H Coghill & Son Ltd* [1918] 1 Ch 307.
14   *Union Lighterage Co v London Graving Dock Co*, ante.
15   (1881) 6 App Cas 740 at 773-774; (M & B).
16   *Union Lighterage Co v London Graving Dock Co*, ante, per Romer LJ at 571.
17   A good example is provided by *Diment v N. H. Foot Ltd* [1974] 2 All ER 785, [1974] 1 WLR 1427; (M & B).
18   And this is so where the belief is also held by S; *Bridle v Ruby*, infra (the case concerned a claim under the doctrine of the lost modern grant, see infra, but the decision would seem to apply also to other forms of prescription).

(eg by a previous holder of the servient land to a previous hold of the dominant land).[19]

Any form of permission by S to D, irrespective of whether D gives consideration for S's consent,[20] and irrespective of whether the consent is given once, or is renewed periodically, defeats a claim that the user was as of right.[1]

However, it may be that after S has given permission to D to cross Greenacre, D's user continues for such a period that he would be able to satisfy the court that his user had ceased to be in reliance on S's consent, and had become user *nec precario*, and thus sufficient to support a claim by prescription.[2]

S can prevent the possibility of such a claim arising if, when he initially gives permission to D, he does so subject to D making, for example, an annual payment to him. Each payment by D indicates the giving of consent by S. Only if S allowed D's payments to lapse would it be possible that D's user might become *nec precario*.

Since the basis of the presumption of a grant is S's acquiescence in D's user, it follows that for S to have acquiesced in D's user, D's user must have been of a kind to which S could have objected if he had wanted to. For example, in *Sturges v Bridgman*[3] a confectioner used a pestle and mortar in a workshop that abutted on the garden of a physician. The noise was no nuisance to the physician until, more than 20 years later, the physician built a consulting room at the end of the garden. The physician then sought an injunction to restrain the confectioner from making the noise. The confectioner claimed that he had acquired an easement by prescription to make the noise. It was held that he had acquired no easement: until the consulting room had been built the noise had not constituted a nuisance; until then the physician could not have objected; therefore the physician could not be said to have acquiesced in the noise. Thus the user had not been *nec precario*, and so could not support a claim to an easement by prescription.

Attempts to defeat a claim based on prescription by the argument that acquiescence by S, – tolerance by S of D's user, was to be construed as user with the implied permission of S, with the result that the user was not *nec precario* and so not as of right, have failed.[4] Indeed, '[i]t is difficult to see how, if there is such a principle, there could ever be a prescriptive right ...'[5]

User not contrary to statute

Since S has no power to legitimise a criminal act, it follows that S has no power to authorise use of a way in a manner prohibited by criminal law. So an

19 *Bridle v Ruby* [1989] QB 169, [1988] 3 All ER 64; (M & B).
20 *Gardner v Hodgson's Kingston Brewery Co Ltd* [1903] AC 229; (M & B).
 1 It has been held that if S and D agree about a minor alteration in the *form* of user (eg a minor change in the route of a path used by D over S's land) this does not entitle S to claim that D's user after the alteration has become user by his consent; *Davis v Whitby* [1974] Ch 186, [1974] 1 All ER 806; (M & B).
 2 *Healey v Hawkins* [1968] 3 All ER 836, [1968] 1 WLR 1967; (M & B).
 3 (1879) 11 Ch D 852.
 4 *Mills v Silver* [1991] Ch 271 at 324; (M & B).
 5 Per Dillon J, *Mills v Silver*, supra, at 330.

easement cannot be acquired by prescription where the use sought to be relied on is illegal under statute. In *Hanning v Top Deck Travel Group Ltd*,[6] for a period of some 27 years D's buses used a track across a common, the fee simple in which was held by trustees (S), to reach a farm where the buses were maintained. Section 193(4) of the Law of Property Act 1925 makes it an offence to drive a vehicle on a common. This, the court held, precluded the acquisition of D of an easement to use the track with his vehicles. (The same rule applies where a claim is made[7] that a public right of way has been, ie after long usage, created by presumed dedication.[8])

The principle explained constitutes in effect a fourth 'nec ... ': *nec contra legem*.

User as an easement

We have said that the user must be exercised as if it had been exercised of right by virtue of an easement. Now suppose that D, the owner of Redacre, crosses S's land, Greenacre, for ten years. D then buys Greenacre from S. He retains Greenacre for two years, and continues to cross the land during that time. D then sells Greenacre to X. D continues to cross Greenacre for a further eight years. D then claims an easement. D can show 20 years' user, but his claim will fail since he cannot show 20 years' use as *of right*, since for two years his user was by virtue of his ownership of the land he crossed. Thus during any time when the dominant and servient tenements are in the same hands (when there is 'unity of possession'), the user is not as of right and therefore cannot count towards the requisite period. Further, the period of unity of possession breaks the continuity of the user and thus, in accumulating user for the requisite period, the user must be started afresh once the period of unity of possession has ended.[9]

These, then, were the requirements for a claim by prescription in the earlier form at common law, and as we have said, a claim in this form may be made today. We now turn to the other form of prescription at common law.

THE COMMON LAW DOCTRINE OF THE LOST MODERN GRANT[10]

We have seen that if D claims an easement of way across Greenacre based on 20 years' user, and S can show that there could not have been user since 1189, then D's claim fails. It was on this rock that, despite uncontested evidence of user stretching over a long period, many claims foundered. The courts, however, wished to be able to uphold claims where user as of right for a sufficient period

6   (1994) 68 P & CR 14.
7   At common law or under Highways Act 1980, s 31.
8   *Robinson v Adair* (1995) Times, 2 March.
9   *Hulbert v Dale* [1909] 2 Ch 570; (M & B).
10   The doctrine was confirmed and explained in *Dalton v Angus & Co* (1881) 6 App Cas 740; see also *Phillips v Halliday* [1891] AC 228, 231.

had been shown. It was in pursuance of this aim that the common law doctrine of the lost modern grant was evolved.[11]

Under this doctrine, if something prevents a claim under the earlier common law form of prescription[12] from succeeding, and if user as of right for a sufficient period can be shown,[13] the court may presume that an actual grant of the easement had been made some time after 1189, but before the commencement of the period of user relied on, and that the deed making the grant had subsequently been lost. Thus if D claims an easement against S, and S can show that there was a period of unity of possession during the period of user, this, as we have seen, will defeat a claim under the original doctrine; but it may not defeat a claim under the doctrine of the lost modern grant.[14]

The doctrine, being a form of common prescription, is not totally outside the principles that regulate prescription at common law, considered above. Thus the doctrine will not be permitted to entitle a tenant to claim an easement by prescription against another tenant of the same landlord.[15]

The doctrine of the lost modern grant removed some of the pitfalls which lay in front of a person who claimed an easement by prescription, but uncertainties and difficulties remained. It was in an attempt to remove these that the Prescription Act 1832 was passed.

THE PRESCRIPTION ACT 1832

The Act does not supersede the common law forms of prescription, under which claims can still be made, but gave an additional, statutory basis for a claim.[16] The Act treats easements of light differently from other easements.

Easements other than easements of light

The Act, as it relates to the acquisition of easements other than easements of light, provides for two periods of user, namely 20 years and 40 years. The effect of the Act, broadly, is that user for 20 years gives rise to a claim by prescription, but the claim can be defeated on a number of grounds. If the user is for 40 years the number of grounds on which the claim can be defeated is reduced.

20 YEARS' USER

Section 2 of the 1832 Act

Section 2 of the Act begins by providing that 'no claim which may be lawfully made at common law ... when such matter ... shall have been actually enjoyed

---

11 Development dates from the eighteenth century.
12 Or under the Prescription Act 1832; eg because the user is not 'next before some suit or action' (see p 338, infra); *Mills v Silver* [1991] Ch 271 at 324, 328. See also *Bridle v Ruby* [1989] QB 169, [1988] 3 All ER 64.
13 There is no fixed period. User for 20 years or more is usually sufficient.
14 *Hulbert v Dale* [1909] 2 Ch 570; (M & B).
15 See p 332, supra; *Simmons v Dobson* [1991] 4 All ER 25, [1991] 1 WLR 720.

... without interruption for the full period of 20 years, shall be defeated ... by showing only that such ... matter was first enjoyed at any time prior to such period of 20 years, but nevertheless such claim may be defeated in any other way by which the same is now liable to be defeated'.

Effect of 20 years' user under s 2

We saw that under the original form of prescription at common law, if D can show 20 years' user as of right this raises a presumption of user since 1189, but that this was rebuttable by evidence that there could not, in fact, have been user as of right since that time. The effect of s 2 of the Act is to remove this ground for defeating a claim based on user for 20 years.

Other common law conditions applicable

As regards the period of user, the Act thus acts negatively, in that it removes what had hitherto been an obstacle to a successful claim. But s 2 expressly provides that a claim under the Act based on 20 years' user can be defeated in any other way that a claim at common law is liable to be defeated. Thus if any of the other conditions necessary for a claim at common law to succeed are not fulfilled, a claim based on 20 years user fails.[17]

Section 4: 'next before some suit or action'

Section 4 provides that the period of 20 years is to be ' ... taken to be the period next before some suit or action wherein the claim or matter ... shall have been ... brought into question ... '

If the occupiers of Redacre habitually cross Greenacre for 20 years this does not in itself lead to the acquisition of an easement under the Act. The period of user required is 20 years 'next before', ie immediately preceding, the bringing of an action. If no action is brought, no period of user, for the purpose of a claim under the Act, exists.[18] The action can be brought by S or D; eg S may bring an action against D for trespass or D may bring an action in nuisance against S for interfering with what he claims is an easement, or D may seek a declaration that he is entitled to an easement.

'Without interruption'

Section 2 states that the user ' ... shall have been actually enjoyed ... without interruption ... for the full period ... '

---

16 A claim can thus be made in reliance on each of the three forms of prescription; *Pugh v Savage* [1970] 2 QB 373, [1970] 2 All ER 353; *Healey v Hawkins* [1968] 3 All ER 836, [1968] 1 WLR 1967. And is generally so made; *Mills v Silver* [1991] Ch 271 at 324, 328.
17 Eg that the user had been by consent; *Reilly v Orange* [1955] 2 QB 112, [1955] 2 All ER 369; (M & B); see also *Davies v Du Paver* [1953] 1 QB 184, [1952] 2 All ER 991; (M & B); or that the user had not been sufficiently continuous; *Hollins v Verney* (1884) 13 QBD 304 at 314, 315.
18 *Hyman v Van den Bergh* [1908] 1 Ch 167; (M & B).

Interruption' here refers not to interruption of user by D[19] but to interruption by S, or by some third party.[20] Interruption thus consists of some hostile interruption, or prevention, of enjoyment of user by any person.

Under s 4, in order that a matter should rank as an 'interruption', there must be not only be interruption of user, but also acquiescence by D for at least one year after he has notice of it. Acquiescence is a state of mind, evidenced by conduct.[1] Non-acquiescence is best proved by the commencement of proceedings. It is proved also by evidence of protests.[2] The onus is on the person claiming an easement to show that he had effectively communicated his objection to the defendant, and had maintained that objection.[3]

Suppose that D crosses Greenacre for 19 years and a day. S padlocks the gate and keeps it locked for 364 days. On the first day of the 21st year D issues a writ against S. His action will succeed. The interruption by S has not been acquiesced in by D for a full year and so does not rank as an 'interruption' under the Act. Thus D can show 20 years' user without interruption next before his action. This is the reason for the dictum 'user for 19 years and a day is as good as user for 20 years' but, as will have been seen, this is only so provided that D issues his writ on the first day of the 21st year.

Section 7: deductions

Section 7 provides that 'the time during which any person otherwise capable of resisting any claim ... shall be an infant, idiot, *non compos mentis*, or tenant for life or during which any action or suit shall have been pending ... shall be excluded in the computation of the 20-year period'.

Any such times as those specified must, then, be deducted from the period of D's user. The purpose of this provision is to exclude periods when the fee simple owner of the servient land (Greenacre) is not in a position to object to D's user. But a period so deducted does not break the continuity of the user; ie a period of user before the period deducted may be added to the period of user after it.[4]

40 YEARS' USER

Section 2 of the 1832 Act

Section 2, after making the provision relating to 20 years user which we have examined, continues ' ... where any such way or other matter as herein last before mentioned shall have been so enjoyed as aforesaid' (ie without interruption) 'for the full period of 40 years, the right thereto shall be deemed absolute and

---

19 *Carr v Foster* (1842) 3 QB 581.
20 *Davies v Williams* (1851) 16 QB 546.
 1 *Davies v Du Paver* [1953] 1 QB 184, [1952] 2 All ER 991.
 2 *Glover v Coleman* (1874) LR 10 CP 108. See also *Newnham v Willison* (1987) 56 P & CR 8, but see [1989] Conv 355 (JEM), *dubitante*.
 3 *Presland v Bingham* (1889) 41 Ch D 268.
 4 *Pugh v Savage* [1970] 2 QB 373, [1970] 2 All ER 353.

indefeasible, unless it shall appear that the same was enjoyed by some consent or agreement expressly given or made for that purpose by deed or writing'.

Consent

We have seen that in the case of the shorter period, the position is the same as at common law, namely, that if the user is with permission (ie is not *nec precario*) the user is not as of right, and so the claim fails. This is so regardless of whether the consent is oral or in writing, and whether the consent is given at the beginning and extending throughout, or given from time to time during the period of user, and whether the consent is express or is inferred, eg from D having made S an annual payment.[5]

As regards the 40-year period, the effect of s 2 is that if consent to the user is given at the beginning of the period, and the consent is given merely orally, then (notwithstanding that the user is not *nec precario*) the fact that this consent has been given will not defeat the claim. But if the claim is of any other kind, eg if it is at the beginning of the period but is in writing, or if it is given periodically (eg renewed each year, either orally or in writing), the claim is defeated.

The effect of the provision in s 2 that the claim is to be deemed 'absolute and indefeasible' is thus, as regards consent, to modify a requirement of the common law.

User against a fee simple owner

There is another respect in which, so it appears, user for 40 years modifies the common law position. We have seen that, at common law, if the servient land was occupied at the beginning of the period by a tenant for life or a tenant under a lease, then the rule that user must be against the fee simple owner of the servient tenement was infringed and the claim failed. It has been held that in the case of a claim based on 40 years, a claim would not be defeated by these circumstances.[6]

Section 4: 'next before some suit or action'

The requirement applies to the 40-year period in the same manner as to the shorter period.

'without interruption'

Here also, the principles are the same in the case of the longer and shorter periods.

Section 8: deductions

Section 8 provides that 'when any land ... over which any ... way, or other convenient watercourse or use of water shall have been enjoyed hath been ...

---

5   *Gardner v Hodgson's Kingston Brewery Co Ltd* [1903] AC 229; (M & B).
6   *Wright v Williams* (1836) 1 M & W 77; contrary held in *Davies v Du Paver* [1953] 1 QB 184, [1953] 2 All ER 991; (M & B).

held under ... any term of life, or any term of years exceeding three years ... the time of enjoyment of such way or other matter ... shall be excluded in the computation of the said period of 40 years ... [provided that] the claim shall within three years next after the end of ... such term be resisted by any person entitled to the reversion ... '

It has been suggested that the word 'convenient' here is a misprint for 'easement'. If so, s 8 (like s 7), which we considered above, applies to all forms of easement.[7]

It will be seen that s 8 is similar to s 7, considered above, in that it provides for certain periods to be deducted from the period of user on which the claim is based. In the case of s 8, deduction may be made in respect of any period of user when the servient land was occupied by a tenant for life (as in s 7) or (unlike s 7) by a tenant under a lease exceeding three years.

The nature of the deduction is the same as that made under s 7: a deduction reduces the period of user but does not break it, user before the deduction being added to user after it.

If D claims an easement under the Act against S, and S resists the claim, it is S who will wish to avail himself of s 8 (or s 7) in order to reduce the period of user relied on by D, with the aim of showing that the user by D did not amount to the period of 40 (or 20) years required. But s 8 adds the condition that S may only make the deduction if the claim is resisted by any person entitled to the reversion within three years after the end of the lease or life interest. For example, suppose that (i) S owns the fee simple in Greenacre; (ii) he leases it to T; (iii) D commences user of a path across Greenacre; (iv) D's user continues for 36 years; (v) T's lease ends; (vi) D's user continues for a further four years; (vii) D seeks a declaration that he is entitled to an easement under the 1832 Act. S resists the claim. D's claim will succeed. S cannot deduct the period of the lease because the claim was not resisted within three years of the lease ending.

Easements of light

Section 3 provides 'when ... the ... use of light to ... any dwelling house, workshop of other building[9] shall have been actually enjoyed ... for the full period of 20 years without interruption,[10] the right thereto shall be deemed absolute and indefeasible ... unless ... the same was enjoyed by some consent ... given for that purpose by deed or writing.'

---

7 *Laird v Briggs* (1880) 50 LJ Ch 260 at 261, per Fry J.
8 The amount of light which may be acquired as an easement under s 3 is the amount required for the use of a building for any ordinary purpose for which the building has been constructed or adapted. *Allen v Greenwood* [1980] Ch 119; (M & B) (acquisition under s 3 of easement of light to a greenhouse sufficient for cultivation of plants).
9 The right that arises if s 3 is satisfied is a right to light to a building, not merely to a particular room (or rooms) within it;; *Carr-Saunders v Dick McNeil Associates Ltd* [1986] 2 All ER 888, [1986] 1 WLR 922; [1987] Conv 366.
10 Continuity of use is not broken by the building to which a right of light is appurtenant being rebuilt; *Smith v Baxter* [1900] 2 Ch 138.

The following points call for attention.

1. The section does not begin (as does s 2, relating to the acquisition of other easements by user for the 20- and 40- year periods) 'no claim which may be lawfully made at common law ... ' Thus, in the case of a claim under the Act to an easement of light, there is no need for the common law conditions to be fulfilled. Important consequences follow from this:

(a) The user need not be against a fee simple owner of the servient tenement.

(b) The user need not be by or on behalf of one fee simple owner against another fee simple owner. Thus:

   (i)   A tenant can acquire an easement of light under the Act against land held by his landlord.

   (ii) A landlord can acquire an easement of light under the Act against land held by his tenant.

   (iii) A tenant can acquire an easement of light under the Act against another tenant of the same landlord.[11]

(c) The user need not be as of right. Thus:

   (i)   The user need not be user as an easement. For this reason a period of unity of possession during the period of user will not defeat a claim to an easement of light under the Act, but merely causes a suspension in the running of the period; the period of unity of possession thus, in effect, merely having to be deducted from the period of user. If what remains amounts to 20 years, the claim succeeds.

   (ii) The user need not be:

   nec vi: thus if, in order to obtain unobstructed light, D knocked down a wall on Greenacre, this would probably not defeat D's claim;

   nor *nec clam*: thus if it was not apparent from Greenacre that D was enjoying user of light, this would not defeat the claim;

   nor *nec precario*: thus if S gave D oral consent for the user from year to year on D making an annual payment, this would not defeat the claim. However, the Act does specifically provide that one form of consent will defeat a claim, namely, consent in writing.

2.   *'without interruption'*

The same principles apply as in the case of other easements; ie interruption refers to adverse obstruction by S, not discontinuance of use by D.[12]

3.   *'next before some suit or action'*

These words do not appear in s 3, but it has been held[13] that the period of user must be that immediately preceding an action, as in the case of a claim to other forms of easement under the Act.

---

11 *Fear v Morgan* [1906] 2 Ch 406; on appeal sub nom *Morgan v Fear* [1907] AC 425.
12 *Smith v Baxter* [1900] 2 Ch 138.
13 *Hyman v Van den Bergh* [1908] 1 Ch 167; (M & B). See also *Dance v Triplow* [1992] 17 EG 103; [1992] Conv 197 (J. Martin).

4. Deductions

Sections 7 and 8 do not apply to a claim under the Act to an easement of light, and thus no deductions under these sections can be made. So if S is a lunatic throughout D's user, or if the land is leased throughout that time, this does not defeat D's claim.

The absence of deductions, and the fact that the user need not be as of right, thus considerably improve D's chances of acquiring an easement of light.

RIGHTS OF LIGHT ACT 1959

Suppose that D and S each own a shop, next door to each other, in a row of shops. During the 1939-45 war, a bomb destroys S's shop, leaving an empty space. D constructs a window in what had previously been the party wall with S's building. D thus receives light across S's land. 15 years later S's land is still empty. S realises that if he does not interrupt D's user of light, in another five years D will acquire an easement of light under the 1832 Act. So S constructs a large wooden hoarding on his land, blocking the light to D's window. The hoarding constitutes an interruption to D's user light and prevents D acquiring an easement.

If it had been necessary for S to take this action, the result would have been that thousands of hoardings would have been constructed for this purpose on bombed sites in London and elsewhere after the war. It was, inter alia, in order to enable servient owners to prevent neighbouring owners from acquiring an easement of light under the Act without having to construct such hoardings, that the Rights of Light Act 1959 was passed. This was achieved by enabling S to register a notice (which in effect then constitutes a notional obstruction) in the local land charges register. The notice must identify S's land and D's land, and specify the size and position of the obstruction to which the notice is intended to be equivalent. (The Act is of general application and is not limited to the sites of buildings destroyed by enemy action.)

Before the notice can be entered in the register S must obtain a certificate from the Lands Tribunal certifying that notice has been given to those likely to be affected (eg D), or that a temporary notice should be registered on the grounds of exceptional urgency.

Use of machinery provided by the Act avoids the difficulty that planning permission for the erection of a hoarding to obstruct light might be refused.

When registered, the notice takes effect as if an obstruction had in fact been erected, and had been known to, and acquiesced in by, those concerned. If D objects he can claim cancellation of the notice. Whether or not he will succeed will depend on whether or not he can show that by that date he has acquired an easement of light.

'ANCIENT LIGHTS'

In the phrase 'ancient lights', the word 'light' refers to apertures that admit light. 'Ancient lights' are windows (or, eg skylights) that have been in position for a considerable period and to which an easement of light is therefore likely to have been acquired by prescription.[14]

'ACQUIESCENCE'

It may be of assistance to mention that acquiescence occurs in two contexts in the law of prescription:
1. With reference to D's user: for D's user to be as of right S must acquiesce in the user.
2. With reference to an objection by S to D's user: in order that S's interruption in D's user should rank as an interruption in the prescription period D must acquiesce (ie submit without protest) in the interruption for one year.

CHANGES IN EXTENT OF USER

It may happen that after an easement over S's land has come into existence, the amount of user by D increases. Such an increase may be in the level of use or in the kind of use exercised. Can S successfully object to such changes in the extent of D's user?

Formerly an express grant (or reservation) in unequivocal terms (for example, a grant of a right of way for all purposes with or without vehicles) was held to confer unrestricted access notwithstanding damage or loss of value to the servient tenement caused by an increase in the volume or nature of the user.[15] More recently it has been held that whether an increase in user is permissible is to be determined by looking to the intention of the parties as ascertained from the words of the grant as interpreted by the court and from the surrounding circumstances; as, for example, where a grant of a right of passage along a track to 'pass and repass on foot and with or without motor vehicles' was held, in the light of the nature of the track, not to extend to use of the track by heavy lorries.[16]

Where an easement arises from an implied grant (or reservation) the answer will depend on what the court decides was the nature of the right impliedly granted, as for example where it was held that an implied right of way for domestic, warehouse or manufacturing purposes did not extend to a right of way for access to a railway station.[17]

Where the easement arises by prescription, the outcome will depend on what the courts find to have been the nature of the user during the period that provided the basis of the prescriptive claim: the easement will confer a right to continue to do what had been done during that period, but no more;[18] as, for example, where it was held that a prescriptive right of way to a field was for

14   See *Jackson v Duke of Newcastle* (1864) 3 De GJ & Sm 275 at 291.
15   *White v Grand Hotel Eastbourne Ltd* [1913] 1 Ch 113.
16   *White v Richards* (1993) 68 P & CR 105, [1993] RTR 318,. See also *Bulstrode v Lambert* [1953] 2 All ER 728, [1953] 1 WLR 1064; *Baxendale v North Lambeth Liberal and Radical Club Ltd* [1902] 2 Ch 427.
17   *Milner's Safe Co Ltd v Great Northern and City Rly Co* [1907] 1 Ch 208.
18   *Devlin v Dewry* [1953] CPL 482.

agricultural purposes only and therefore did not extend to a right of passage for caravans or for people to reach the field as a camping ground.[19]

In deciding whether, in any case, an injunction should be granted to restrain an increase in user, the court will take into account the degree to which the change casts a burden on the servient land.[20] Changes that are *de minimis* will be disregarded.[1]

Extinguishment of easements

1.   By release

EXPRESS RELEASE

If D is to extinguish the easement across Greenacre he must, at common law, do so by deed.

If D made the release merely in writing and S gave him consideration for releasing the easement, it would seem that the release would be binding in equity under the doctrine in *Walsh v Lonsdale*.

If this doctrine was not applicable (eg because S gave no consideration) then the release may nevertheless be binding in equity if it would be inequitable for D to claim that the easement still existed; eg where D had orally agreed to release an easement of light, and S had spent money on a building which obstructed D's light.[2]

IMPLIED RELEASE

If S, on whom the burden rests,[3] can show that by his conduct D intended[4] to abandon the right to the easement over Greenacre, the easement is extinguished by implied release.

Whether there is an intention to abandon an easement is a question of fact to be decided in each case.[5]

Conduct showing such an intention may consist of:

(a)   a particular act, as where D has an easement of light to a building on Redacre and he demolishes the building without any intention of replacing it;

---

19   *RPC Holdings Ltd v Rogers* [1953] 1 All ER 1029.
20   *Thomas v Thomas* (1835) Cr M & R 34; *Todrick v Western National Omnibus Co Ltd* [1934] Ch 190.
1   *Harvey v Walters* (1873) LR 8 CP 162.
2   *Waterlow v Bacon* (1886) LR 2 EQ 514.
3   The burden is a heavy one. See *Re Yateley Common, Hampshire* [1977] 1 All ER 505, [1977] 1 WLR 840 (a case concerning a profit, but the principle is the same. See Chapter 19).
4   See [1995] Conv 291 (C. J. Davis) (intention not enough. Extinguishment should occur only if S has acted in reliance of the easement being abandoned, D thereby being estopped from asserting easement's continued existence).
5   *Huckvale v Aegean Hotels Ltd* (1989) 58 P & CR 163; [1990] Conv 283 (G. Kodilinye).

(b) non-user for a period sufficiently long to raise a presumption of abandonment. Twenty years' non-user is usually sufficient to raise this presumption, but non-user, however long, is not necessarily conclusive, and if D can give a satisfactory explanation for the non-user (eg that he has not needed to use the easement or that he has for some reason been prevented from using it[6]), the presumption is rebutted and the easement not extinguished;

(c) a particular act followed by a period of non-user, as where D has an easement of light to windows in a wall in a building on Redacre, and he replaces the wall by one which has no windows in it and takes no steps to assert the easement of light for 17 years.[7] (It will be noted that the act and the non-user might, separately, not have been sufficient to constitute conduct showing an intention to abandon the easement.)

2. By unity of ownership and possession of the dominant and servient tenements[8]

If it comes about that the fee simples absolute in Redacre and Greenacre become vested in one person, and that person is in actual possession of both pieces of land (eg where D sells Redacre to X and S leaves Greenacre to X in his will, and X occupies both plots), the easement across Greenacre is extinguished. If X later sold the pieces of land to two different owners the easement would not be revived.[9]

If D, the owner of Redacre, acquires an easement across S's land, Greenacre, D leases Redacre to T, and subsequently sells the fee simple reversion in Redacre to S, the easement in favour of Redacre continues in existence (for the benefit of T) until the expiry of the lease. At that point the easement is extinguished.[10]

Suppose that D, the owner of Redacre, has an easement across S's land Greenacre. D then leases Redacre to S. The dominant and servient tenements would not be both owned and occupied by the same person, so the easement would not be extinguished. But S, as owner of Greenacre, would not need the easement across Greenacre. In this situation the easement is suspended. When S's lease ends the right revives. Thus if D sold the fee simple reversion in Redacre to E, when S's lease of Redacre came to an end and E became entitled to possession of the land, the easement would be revived and, by virtue of the easement, E would have a right of way across Greenacre.

3. By statute

An easement may be extinguished expressly or by implication by the provisions of a statute. As an example of the latter, an easement may be extinguished by

---

6 See *Re Yateley Common, Hampshire*, ante.
7 *Moore v Rawson* (1824) 3 B & C 332; (M & B).
8 See (1977) 41 Conv (NS) 107.
9 Although a fresh easement might arise by way of a (fresh) implied grant.
10 *Richardson v Graham* [1908] 1 KB 39.

the construction of a building erected under a power conferred on a railway to purchase land compulsorily and erect certain buildings on it.[11]

LEGAL AND EQUITABLE EASEMENTS

In order to grant a legal easement, the grant must, as noted in Chapter 15, be by deed. An equitable easement will arise (a) where the grant is not by deed but an equitable easement arises under the doctrine in *Walsh v Lonsdale* (see Chapter 16); or, (b) where (irrespective of whether or not a deed is used) the grantor holds merely an equitable fee simple in the servient land. An easement which arises by prescription is legal. An easement arising by way of implied grant (or reservation) may be legal or equitable, according to the circumstances.[12]

EASEMENTS ARISING BY ESTOPPEL[13]

In addition to arising by grant (ie whether express, implied or presumed) an easement (or, at least, a right in the nature of an easement) may be held by the court to have arisen as a result of the application of the equitable doctrine of estoppel, the doctrine by which, in certain circumstances, one party may, because of his conduct, be estopped from denying the entitlement of another to exercise a certain right. In the sphere of easements estoppel may for convenience be considered under two heads.

1. Mutual burden and benefit

The principle here is that 'when adjoining owners of land make an agreement to secure continuing rights and benefits for each of them in or over the land of the other, neither of them can take the benefit of the agreement and throw over the burden of it.[14] Thus in *Hopgood v Brown*,[15] B built a manhole on C's land to serve as a junction for the collection of water along pipes from B's land and from adjacent land belonging to C, and from which the water flowed by a single pipe under B's land to a main drain under a road. C's land was later conveyed to H. H claimed the manhole to be a nuisance. It was held that the drainage system conferred on H and B's rights in the nature of reciprocal licences so that H could not revoke B's licence to discharge water beneath the manhole on his land while he, H, continued to enjoy the benefit of being able to discharge water through the drain beneath B's land.

---

11 *Duke of Bedford v Dawson* (1875) LR 20 Eq 353.
12 Eg an easement arising under s 62 will be legal; an easement arising under the rule in *Wheeldon v Burrows* may possibly be equitable (eg if the dominant owner holds only an equitable interest in the land).
13 [1992] Conv 239 (M. Lunney).
14 Per Lord Denning MR, *ER Ives Investments Ltd v High* [1967] 2 WLR 789 at 795.
15 [1955] 1 All ER 550, [1955] 1 WLR 213; (M & B).

2.   Estoppel by conduct

The principle here is that if the owner of land, A, allows B to act to his detriment (eg by expending money,[16] or by selling off part of his, B's, land[17]) in the expectation, created or encouraged by A, that B will be allowed to exercise certain user over A's land, then B is estopped from denying A right to the user concerned. For example, in *Ward v Kirkland*,[18] W, the owner of a cottage, asked R, the owner of adjoining land, for permission to construct a drain under his land to carry away water from a bath which W wished to install in his cottage. R gave permission and W built the drain. Later R sold his land to K. K demanded that the drain should be removed. It was held that as the drain had been laid at W's expense and in reliance on the permission given by R without stipulation as to the period for which permission was given, W acquired an equitable right to retain the drain in position permanently.[19] In *Rochdale Canal Co v King*,[20] K, in 1829, being about to erect a mill by the Company's canal, applied to the Company for permission to take water from the canal for the purpose of generating steam. The Company did not seem to refuse the application and the pipes were laid down in the presence of the Company's engineers. Twenty-four years later the Company sought an injunction to restrain K from taking water to generate steam. It was held that the Company was bound by its acquiescence and an injunction was refused.

Sometimes the same conclusion may be reached by the application of more than one of the principles we have been considering. For example, in *ER Ives Investments Ltd v High*,[1] in 1949, H bought the site of a bombed building in Norwich and started to build a house on it. At about the same time A bought a site adjoining H's land and started to build a block of flats on that. The foundations of A's flats encroached beneath H's land, extending a foot over the boundary some feet below ground level. After H had objected to A's trespass, an agreement, which was subsequently evidenced in letters, was made under which A was to be allowed to retain the foundations of his flats on H's land, and H was to have a right of way from his land across the yard of A's flats so as to give him access to a road. In 1950, A sold the site to B, who knew of the agreement. H continued to use the right of way. In 1959 H built a garage which was so constructed that access to it could only be gained by crossing the yard of the flats. B raised no objection to the building of the garage or H's use of the yard to gain access to it. In 1962 the flats were put up for auction and sold to I. The particulars of sale referred to H's right of way across the yard, and the conveyance of the flats from B to I stated that the property was conveyed subject to the right of way. Later, I sought an injunction restraining H from using the yard. It was held that both by reason of the mutual benefit and

---

16   *Ward v Kirkland* [1967] Ch 194, [1966] 1 All ER 609.
17   *Crabb v Arun District Council* [1976] Ch 179, [1975] 3 All ER 865; (M & B).
18   [1967] Ch 194, [1966] 1 All ER 609.
19   Another illustration is provided by *Crabb v Arun District Council* [1976] Ch 179, [1975] 3 All ER 865; (M & B).
20   (1853) 16 Beav 630.
1   [1967] 2 QB 379, [1967] 1 All ER 504; (M & B). See also *Soames-Forsythe Properties Ltd v Tesco Stores Ltd* [1991] EGCS 22 (equitable easement to stack supermarket trolleys).

burden under the agreement of 1949, and also by reason of the acquiescence of I's predecessor in H's rights under the agreement H had in equity a right of way across the yard.

We have referred to these rights arising by estoppel as being 'in the nature of easements'. They have the characteristic of an easement in that they are rights exercisable by one landowner against land owned by another. If a right of this kind is not an easement it is a licence. The difference between an easement and licence is, as noted previously, that an easement is proprietary (and so is capable of binding a purchaser); a licence is not. Since the indications are that rights of the kind described bind a transferee, it seems that these rights partake of the nature of an easement rather than that of a licence.

As these rights arise by application of the equitable doctrine of estoppel, they are necessarily equitable. This raises the question – since the rights are equitable must they, in order to bind a purchaser, be registered under the Land Charges Act 1972? The Act provides for the registration in Class D (iii) of 'equitable easements' which are defined as 'any easement right or privilege over or affecting land ... and being merely an equitable interest'. In *ER Ives Investments Ltd v High*,[2] H claimed that even if I had acquired an equitable right – whether licence or easement – to reach his garage, this was not binding on him, a purchaser, owing to the fact that it had not been registered under the Land Charges Act 1925. Lord Denning held that an equitable easement within the meaning of Class D (iii) referred to those proprietary interests in land which before 1926 would have been recognised as being capable of being conveyed or created at common law, but which since 1926 can only take effect (because of s 1 of the Law of Property Act 1925) as an equitable interest. An example of such an interest, he said, would be a *profit a prendre* for life. H's right was of a kind that had never been capable of existing as a legal interest, before 1926 or after 1925. It therefore fell outside Class D (iii). Danckwerts LJ agreed that H's right was not registrable. The failure to register therefore did not defeat H's claim.

ACCESS TO NEIGHBOURING LAND ACT 1992[3]

If D needs to go onto S's land in order to effect repairs or other works on premises on his land (as where one side of his house abuts directly onto S's land), it may be that D has the benefit of an easement that entitles him to go onto S's land in order to carry out the work concerned (an easement sometimes termed a right of 'ladderstead', ie a right, inter alia, to place ladders on S's land to reach some part of D's building). Where D has no such right, neither by express, implied nor presumed grant, nor under any equitable principle, then, until the intervention of statute, D was effectively prevented from carrying out the work needing to be done except on such terms as S might dictate.

---

2   Supra.
3   See M. Aldridge, *Boundaries, Walls and Fences.*

Under the Access to Neighbouring Land Act 1992,[4] where a person (D), wishes, but has no right, to go on to land adjoining his own belonging to another person, (S), in order to carry out repairs or maintenance to buildings or certain other specified[5] works, and S declines to consent to D so doing, D may apply to the court for an 'access order' entitling him to go onto the adjoining land for the purpose for which the application is made. If the court is satisfied that the works are reasonably necessary for the 'preservation' of D's land, and that they cannot be carried out, or would be substantially more difficult to carry out, without the making of an order, and provided that the making of an order will not impose on S an unreasonable degree of disturbance or hardship, the court is required[6] to make the order,[7] subject to such terms and conditions[8] as appear to the court to be necessary for the purpose of avoiding loss, damage, injury, or inconvenience to S.

SUMMARY

For a right to be an easement six conditions must be satisfied.

Easements may be acquired by statute, by express grant or reservation, by implied grant or reservation, by prescription, or by estoppel.

Prescription arises at common law, under the doctrine of the lost modern grant, or under statute, principally the Prescription Act 1832.

Easements may be extinguished by release, by unity of ownership and possession, or by statute.

---

4   [1992] Conv 225.
5   Section 1(4).
6   Section 1(2).
7   The order is registrable under the Land Charges Act 1972 or under the Land Registration Act 1925. See Chapters 25 and 26. Subject to protection by registration, an access order is binding on successors in title to the land subject to the order; s 4.
8   Section 2.

CHAPTER 19

Profits à prendre

Introduction

D (which in this chapter, as in the last, represents the term 'dominant owner') owns Redacre. Adjoining Redacre is Greenacre, owned by S (which in this chapter, as in the last, represents the term 'servient owner'). S grants D the right to cut and take away the grass growing on Greenacre. Provided that certain conditions are fulfilled the right which S has granted D is a *profit à prendre'* (or a 'profit' for short). If the necessary conditions are not fulfilled then D's right is not a profit but may be a licence.

A profit bears many resemblances to an easement. One difference between an easement and a profit, already apparent, is that whereas an easement is a right over or against another's land, a profit is a right to take something from another's land.

PROFITS APPURTENANT AND PROFITS IN GROSS

Another difference must be now explained. In the case of an easement there must, as we have seen, always be a dominant and a servient tenement. In the case of a profit, whilst there must always be a servient tenement (the land from which the thing is taken), there need not necessarily be a dominant tenement.

Thus if S makes the grant to D as owner of Redacre, Redacre becomes the dominant tenement.

If D owns no adjoining land, S may grant the profit to D personally.

In this case, whoever becomes entitled to possession of Redacre, including a tenant under a lease, enjoys the benefit of the profit. The benefit of the profit thus runs with the land of the grantee of the profit.

In this case the right is D's own private property. He can, eg sell the right to X, or give it to Y, or leave it in his will to Z.

Therefore, if D parts with Redacre, he ceases to be entitled to the profit.

If D owns the adjoining land, Redacre, but if the profit is granted to D personally, he will continue to enjoy the benefit of the profit irrespective of whether he retains or parts with Redacre.

A profit, the benefit of which is annexed by the act of the parties to a dominant tenement, is termed a *profit appurtenant*.

A profit which is granted to someone personally is termed a profit *in gross*.

PROFITS AND LICENCES

As in the case of easements, if D's right is a profit and a stranger (X) interferes with his enjoyment of the right, D can sue X. If D's right is merely a licence, he cannot himself sue X but would have to rely on S doing so.

SEVERAL PROFITS AND PROFITS IN COMMON

Suppose that S grants D a profit to pasture cattle on Greenacre. If D has been granted the exclusive right (ie to the exclusion of all others including the grantor, S) the profit is termed a several profit (the word 'several' being derived from the Latin 'separ', separate). If S has granted the right not only to D but also to one or more other persons, (or if S has granted the right to D but not excluded himself from continuing to be entitled to pasture cattle, so that the entitlement is shared by S and D) the profit is termed a profit in common. An alternative name for a profit in common is a right of common.

RIGHTS OF COMMON AS INCIDENT OF TENURE

It will be recalled that a right of common might be an incident of tenure of a villein tenant or of a tenant holding by the free tenure of common socage.[1] It will also be recalled that when copyhold tenure was enfranchised (ie converted into common socage) any rights of common were preserved; ie they continue indefinitely.[2]

QUANTUM

In the case of a profit appurtenant, the amount taken from the servient tenement must be restricted[3] either to a particular figure, eg the right to pasture fifty cattle, or to a number ascertained by reference to a particular test which determines the upper limit.[4] The forms which the test can take vary according to different forms of profit; for example a profit appurtenant to take fish (without any quantum being fixed) gives a right to take fish sufficient for the needs of the dominant tenement (ie not, eg to take fish for sale[5]).

In the case of a profit in gross, on the other hand, the quantum can be either restricted or unrestricted. If the quantum is unrestricted, the profit is termed a profit 'without stint'.

Conditions for a right to be a profit

For a right to exist as a profit, the thing taken must comply with two requirements.

---

1 See Chapter 2.
2 Ibid.
3 *Anderson v Bostock* [1976] Ch 312, [1976] 1 All ER 560.
4 If D holds a *profit à prendre* to pasture cattle on certain land, then D may license X, a stranger, to put his (X's) cattle on the common, provided that the total number of D's cattle and X's cattle on the common do not exceed the number of cattle which D is entitled to pasture; *Davies v Davies* [1975] QB 172, [1974] 3 All ER 817.
5 *Harris v Earl of Chesterfield* [1911] AC 623.

1. It must be either part of the land itself (eg sand from a quarry); or crops grown on the land; or wild animals living on it.
2. It must be susceptible of ownership before it was taken. Since water in a river is not owned by anyone, there can be no profit to take water from a river. Nor can there be a profit to take water from a spring or a pump, or to water cattle at a pond (though such rights can exist as easements).

As in the case of easements, a profit is a right against the land of another, not a right *to* land.[6]

Types of profit

Profits take, inter alia, the following forms:

A right to pasture cattle (a profit of pasture). (Where commoners of one common (A) have rights over an adjoining common (B), and the commoners of common B have corresponding rights over common A, then the right of common of each group is termed a right of common pur vicinage.[7])
A right to take wood as hay-bote, house-bote or plough-bote (a profit of estovers).
A right to take fish (a profit of piscary).
A right to take part of the land itself, eg stone, sand, gravel, coal (profits in the soil).
A right to take peat or turf (a profit of turbary).

Acquisition of profits

The ways in which a profit may be acquired are similar to those in which an easement is acquired.[8] The following matters call for attention.

1. EXPRESS GRANT OR RESERVATION

The principles are the same as in the case of easements. It is only by express grant or reservation that a profit without stint can be acquired.

2. IMPLIED GRANT OR RESERVATION

(a) There is no form of profit which corresponds to an easement of necessity. (It is uncertain whether there can be an intended profit.)
(b) The doctrine of *Wheeldon v Burrows* does not apply to profits, but s 62 of the Law of Property Act 1925 does apply.[9]

---

6 See *Brackenbank Lodge v Peart* (1996) Times, 26 July.
7 For an example, see *Newman v Bennett* [1981] QB 726, [1980] 3 All ER 449.
8 See p 324.
9 *White v Williams* [1922] 1 KB 727.

3.   PRESUMED GRANT (PRESCRIPTION)

(A)   PRESCRIPTION AT COMMON LAW (AND UNDER THE DOCTRINE OF THE LOST MODERN GRANT)

The same principles apply as in the case of easements.[10] Profits appurtenant or in gross can be acquired by this means.

(B)   THE PRESCRIPTION ACT 1832[11]

(a) Only a profit appurtenant can be acquired under the Act.
(b) The periods of user are 30 years and 60 years (instead of the 20-year and 40-year periods for easements).
(c) Section 8 does not apply to profits and the deductions referred to in this section therefore need not be made (thus improving the chances of the person claiming the profit).
(d) Under the Commons Registration Act 1965,[12] in the case of a claim by prescription to a profit in common, any period when:
  (i) a right to graze was not exercised and the servient tenement was requisitioned; or
  (ii) a right to graze could not be, or was not, exercised for reasons of animal health (eg to prevent the spread of foot and mouth disease),
  is excluded from the computation of the 30- or 60- year period (but does not count as an interruption).[13]

4.   ANNEXATION BY OPERATION OF LAW: PROFITS APPENDANT

In dealing with the tenure of common socage, we saw[14] that certain of the incidents of this tenure might be of a manorial character; for example, the custom of the manor might give tenants by common socage a right to let their pigs feed in the woods of the waste. (We now know that such a right is a *profit à prendre*.)

Before the Statute Quia Emptores (1290), if the lord of the manor granted land by way of subinfeudation[15] to a tenant holding by a free tenure (eg common socage), and if the land granted consisted of arable land, the tenant acquired (together with the land granted) a right to pasture certain animals on the waste land of the manor.

The animals to which the right extended were those needed to plough the land granted (namely horses and oxen), and to manure it (namely cows and sheep). The right extended to no more animals (of the kinds mentioned) than

---

10 For example, see *Tehidy Minerals Ltd v Norman* [1971] 2 QB 528, [1971] 2 All ER 475; (M & B); *Lord Dynevor v Richardson* [1995] Ch 173, [1995] 1 All ER 109 (rejection of registration of grazing right held to constitute interruption of acquiescence in the exercise of the claimed right).
11 For illustrations, see *Davies v Williams* (1851) 16 QB 546; *Davies v Du Paver* [1953] 1 QB 184, [1952] 2 All ER 991; (M & B).
12 Section 16.
13 See Chapter 18.
14 See Chapter 2.
15 See Chapter 3.

could be maintained during the winter by the land granted (the number *'levant and couchant'*[16] on the land granted).

The land granted thus became a dominant tenement and the manorial waste a servient tenement. The profit was not a profit appurtenant, since a profit appurtenant is one created by the act of the parties and the profit of which we speak was annexed to the dominant land by operation of law. It is for this reason classified separately, as a *'profit appendant'*.

After the Statute of 1290 no further subinfeudation of land held by a free tenure was possible. Thus no further commons appendant could arise. However, a profit appendant created before the statute continued in existence and may still exist today.

In Chapter 2, in illustrating the incidents of tenure that can exist at the present day, we said 'Simon Galton holds Quebec Farm. It is an incident of his tenure that he has a right of common to pasture 60 sheep on the hills above Dale'. It may be that this right is a common appendant, the right having come into existence before 1290 when the lord of the manor of Dale first granted the land now represented by Quebec Farm, to a tenant holding by common socage, the figure of 60 having come to be accepted as the number of sheep levant and couchant on the land.

At the present day it is unlikely that any distinction will exist between the rights of a holder of a profit appurtenant and those of the holder of a profit appendant.[17]

Classification of profits

Profits can be classified as follows:

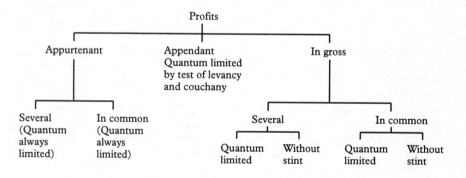

16   For the test of levancy and couchancy, see *Re Ilkley and Burley Moors* (1983) 47 P & CR 324.
17   *Davies v Davies* [1974] 3 WLR 607 at 610.

Extinguishment of profits

Profits may be extinguished by the same means as easements[18] and broadly the same principles apply in the case of each. The following matters call for attention.

1. Extinguishment by unity of ownership and possession of the dominant and servient tenements[19] can occur only in the case of profits appurtenant or appendant.

2. Profits taking the form of rights of common may be extinguished (in addition to the ways in which an easement may be extinguished[20]) in the following ways:

(A) APPROVEMENT

A lord of the manor had a right at common law to take for his separate use part of the waste over which his tenants had rights of pasture. This was termed 'approvement' of the waste and resulted in the extinguishment of rights of common over the land taken. Approvement is now regulated by the Commons Act 1876 and the Law of Commons Amendment Act 1893.

(B) ENCLOSURE

The period lasting from the end of the Middle Ages until the last century witnessed a process, which reached its height in the eighteenth century, in which, in one manor after another, the open fields and waste land of the manor were divided up into separate fields. Those who had held land in the manor before the enclosure were entitled to be allocated land in the form of the new, separate, fields.

Where some or all of the waste was left unenclosed, entitlement to a right of common might be transferred to parcels of land held in place of the strips in the open fields. For example, a copyholder holding seven strips in each of the three open fields before enclosure, with certain rights of grazing on the manorial waste on the moors above the village, might, after enclosure, hold five enclosed fields to which were annexed specified rights of grazing on the waste. However, where all the waste was enclosed then any rights of common were necessarily extinguished.

Enclosure might be undertaken by agreement between all the land holders in the manor or, if this was not forthcoming, by authority of a private Act. The procedure governing enclosure is now governed by the Commons Act 1876 under which approval by the Minister of Agriculture and confirmation by Parliament must be obtained.

---

18 Eg by implied release (as was unsuccessfully claimed in *Re Yateley Common, Hampshire* [1977] 1 All ER 505, [1977] 1 WLR 840).
19 See Chapter 18.
20 *Ward v Ward* (1852) 7 Exch 838.

(C) UNDER THE COMMONS REGISTRATION ACT 1965

The extinguishment of certain profits forms one aspect of this Act. The Act is considered separately below.

Common land[1] and the Commons Registration Act 1965

Land over which two or more persons have a right of common is termed common land. Thus if A, B and C have a right (whether appurtenant, appendant or in gross) to pasture cattle on the waste land of the manor of Dale, then that land is common land and A, B and C are termed commoners. The land, it will be noted, belongs to the lord of the manor of Dale, or to the person to whom it has from him subsequently passed.[2] (To think that common land belongs to no-one, or to the general public, or to the inhabitants of a village, or to those who exercise rights of common over it, are familiar, but erroneous, impressions.)

The Commons Registration Act 1965 was passed to remove uncertainties relating to rights of common and common land. For example, to return to a previous example,[3] annexed to Quebec Farm, Simon Galton had the right to graze 60 sheep on the moors above the village. Suppose that he ceases to exercise this right. Many years later he sells the farm to P. P puts 100 sheep on the moors. Other commoners object. Some say P has no right of pasture. Others say he has no right to pasture as many sheep as he has done. Evidence of the old rights may be lost. How is the dispute to be resolved? To take another example, a farmer owning land bordering the moors, walls off land to form for himself an additional field, claiming that he is rebuilding an old boundary wall. Those having rights of common over the moors object, but they find that evidence of the old boundaries has been lost. How can this dispute be settled? Again, a gliding club occupies moorland on the edge of an escarpment. The commoners, whose sheep are disturbed, object. But who owns the moor? The last traceable lord of the manor died in 1840. Who has become entitled to his estate?

In order to remove such uncertainties as these the Commons Registration Act 1965 provided that two matters should be registrable with the appropriate local authority. These are:

(1) common land,[4] including its territory and its owner;

---

1 G. D. Gadsden *The Law of Commons* (1988); P. Clayden *Our common land: the law and history of commons and village greens* (1985).
2 Who is likely to be entitled, by virtue of his ownership of the land, to pasture cattle on the land along with those of the commoners.
3 See Chapter 2.
4 By s 22(1) 'common land' includes not only land subject to rights of common but also any 'waste land of a manor not subject to rights of common'. See Chapter 1 and *Re Box Hill Common* [1980] Ch 109, [1979] 1 All ER 113, CA, disapproving *Re Chewton Common, Christchurch* [1977] 3 All ER 509, [1977] 1 WLR 1242.

(2) rights of common[5] over the land, including the nature and extent of the right, the holder of the right; and the land, if any, to which the right is appurtenant or appendant.

Persons claiming ownership of common land or of rights of common were given until 31 July 1972 to lodge their claims. Responsibility for deciding disputed claims[6] was laid on Commons Commissioners.[7]

If the holder of a right of common failed to submit his claim in time, his right was lost and the profit extinguished. Registration is, the Act provides,[8] conclusive evidence of the matters registered.

The Act contains provisions relating to the amendment[9] and the rectification[10] of the register and also, in the event of land ceasing to be common land (eg by the owner of the land purchasing the commoners' rights) for de-registration.[11]

The Act of 1965 provides[12] also for the registration of town and village greens (as defined by the Act[13]) and confers certain protection on greens so registered.

Proposals for reform of the law, which would remove anomalies and uncertainties, and, subject to certain conditions, give the public a right of access to common land, were made in 1985 by the Common Land Forum, a working party set up by the Countryside Commission and comprised of representatives of bodies[14] having a concern with common land.

---

5   Including a right of common created under an inclosure award; *Re Turnworth Down, Dorset* [1978] Ch 251.
6   Ie in the event of objections to claims made; section 5. See *Re Sutton Common, Wimbourne* [1982] 2 All ER 376, [1982] 1 WLR 647.
7   Subject to appeal on points of law to the High Court. See *Wiles v Gee* [1973] 2 All ER 1214, [1973] 1 WLR 742.
8   Section 10.
9   Section 13. See *President and Scholars of Corpus Christi College, Oxford v Gloucestershire County Council* [1983] QB 360, [1982] 3 All ER 995.
10   Section 14. See G. Gadsden (1982) 126 SJ 815.
11   The Common Land (Rectification of Registers) Act 1989 provided for the removal from the register of land on which there was, and had been since 5 August 1945, a dwelling house (or land which was, and had been since the same date, ancillary to a dwelling house). The period within which an application for removal from the register might be made expired on 21 July 1992.
12   Section 1(1).
13   Section 22(1)(b).
14   Eg the Open Spaces Society (founded in 1865), 25A Bell Street, Henley-on-Thames, Oxon RG9 2BA.

CHAPTER 20

Licences, and Equitable Rights to Occupy Land[1]

'The function of the lawyer is to give precise answers to questions based upon a law which is certain.' Peter Pain J (1981) 10 ILK 138.

INTRODUCTION

In Chapter 17 it was seen that if A permits B to occupy land, and the circumstances are such that B does not hold a lease (either because the conditions necessary for a lease to exist are not satisfied, or because it is the intention that no tenancy should exist), then B holds under a licence, as licensee.

In terms of every day life it commonly happens that the important difference between a tenant and a licensee is that the former enjoys the benefit of the legislation relating to leasehold enfranchisement (and security of tenure and rent control), and the latter does not.[2] But in terms of property law the crucial difference between the two is that a lease constitutes an interest in land; it is *proprietary* in its nature; it is an interest *in rem*, and in consequence it is capable[3] of binding a purchaser. A licence, on the other hand, constitutes a relationship solely between the licensor and the licensee: it is not proprietary: it is not an interest *in rem*, with the result that a licence is not binding on a purchaser.[4] Thus if a licensor disposes of the land the licensee has no remedy against the purchaser if the latter puts him off the land, and this is so irrespective of whether the transfer is for value or by way of gift, and irrespective of whether the transferee does or does not have notice of the licence. To the extent that the licensee has any remedy, it is against the licensor.[5]

---

1   I. J. Dawson and R. A. Pearce *Licences Relating to Occupation and Use of Land* (1979); Spencer Bower *The Law Relating to Estoppel by Representation* (3rd edn, 1977).
2   For the way in which licences have been employed in attempts to avoid the Rent Acts, see P. Robson and P. Watchman [1980] Conv 27.
3   A legal lease binds all the world; an equitable lease (since 1925) binds a purchaser if it is registered under the Land Charges Act 1972; see Chapter 25.
4   *Clore v Theatrical Properties Ltd and Westby & Co Ltd* [1936] 3 All ER 483.
5   *King v David Allen & Sons Billposting Ltd* [1916] 2 AC 54; (M & B).

Forms of licence at common law

At common law licences are of three kinds.

A. Bare licences

If R (which in this chapter represents 'licensor') confers a licence on E (which in this chapter represents 'licensee'), and E gives no consideration to R, then the licence is a bare licence. For example, if R invites E to use his flat, or he permits E to park a caravan on his field, he confers on E a bare licence. A bare licence is revocable at any time.[6] If the licence is revoked and E declines to leave, he becomes a trespasser and is liable as such to R.[7]

B. Contractual licences

If E gives consideration to R for the grant of the licence, the grant of the licence thus forming the subject matter of a contract between them, the licence is a contractual licence. Thus a ticket-holder at a cricket match is a contractual licensee. The duration of a contractual licence, and whether such a licence may be revoked, depends on[8] the terms, express or implied, of the contract.[9] For example, if E buys a ticket for a theatre, the contract (in the absence of express terms incorporated into the contract) contains an implied term that the licence is to exist for the duration of the play and is not revocable (except on grounds of E's conduct) during that time.[10] In the absence of any term as to duration or revocation there is an implied term that the licence may be revoked by the licensor on the giving of reasonable notice.[11] If a contractual licence is revoked otherwise than according to the terms, express or implied, of the contract then the licensee can obtain a decree of specific performance

---

6   *Booker v Palmer* [1942] 2 All ER 674.
7   *Thomas v Sorrell* (1673) Vaugh 330 at 351.
8   Except where the licensee is a body conducting a public function, in which case the licensor cannot terminate the licence without giving reasonable notice, this being sufficient time for practical arrangements to be made to safeguard the public service according to the statutory scheme in respect of which the licensee (eg the governing body of a school) operates. *Re Hampstead Garden Suburb Institute* (1995) Times, 13 April, [1996] Conv 63, following *Canadian Pacific Railway Co v R* [1931] AC 414.
9   Originally (see *Kerrison v Smith* [1897] 2 QB 445) a contractual licence was revocable at any time, the licensee not being permitted to enforce the performance of the contract by a decree of specific performance and his remedy lying solely in damages. The modern law stems from the decisions in *Hurst v Picture Theatres Ltd* [1915] 1 KB 1, and *Winter Garden Theatre (London) Ltd v Millennium Productions Ltd* [1948] AC 173, [1947] 2 All ER 331; (M & B).
10 *Hurst v Picture Theatres Ltd,* supra; *Hounslow London Borough Council v Twickenham Garden Developments Ltd* [1971] Ch 233, [1970] 3 All ER 326; (M & B).
11 *Winter Garden Theatre (London) Ltd v Millennium Productions Ltd,* supra.

to compel the licensor to abide by the contract. The decree, being an equitable remedy, is awarded at the discretion of the court.[12]

C. Licences coupled with an interest

If R confers on E a legally enforceable right to take something from his land (whether part of the land, eg sand from a quarry; or a chattel on the land, eg coal in a sack) then the right includes not only the right to take the thing concerned but also the right to enter the land for the purpose of taking that thing. A licence conferred in these circumstances is termed a licence coupled with an interest. Where the right is to take something forming part of R's land then a licence coupled with an interest is anomalous (ie when compared with bare or contractual licences) in that it is enforceable against a purchaser of the land. (Whether or not a licence coupled with an interest to take chattels is enforceable against a purchaser, is uncertain.)

THE CONTRIBUTION OF EQUITY[13]

The position we have explained so far is that which represents the basic principles of English property law. However, during the past century the law relating to licences has been modified by the courts in the exercise of their jurisdiction in equity. The modifications have been made in an attempt to prevent injustices that might result from the application of the common law rules relating to licences. Consider, for example, a situation in which R allows E to occupy his, R's, land under a bare licence. With R's knowledge and encouragement E builds himself a house on the land. A year later R revokes the licence, ousts E, and takes the house for himself. At common law E has no remedy. Again, suppose that R grants E a contractual licence to occupy land. With R's knowledge E builds a house on the land. R then sells the land to P, who is aware of the circumstances in which the house was built. R disappears with the purchase money. P ousts E, who is left without a remedy. Does it not seem unjust, in the first case, that the licence should be revocable by R and, in the second case, that the licence should not be binding on P?

It is in instances such as these that equity has intervened in order to give a remedy to the person adversely affected. But, as we shall see, in the course of so intervening disturbing uncertainties have been introduced into the law.

In dealing with equity's intervention in this sphere we must consider the following. (1) What sets of circumstance have been seen by equity as giving rise to the need for the granting of a remedy where otherwise none would exist? (2) What forms of solution equity has adopted and the characteristics of

---

12 *Thompson v Park* [1944] KB 408, [1944] 2 All ER 477; *Verrall v Great Yarmouth Borough Council* [1981] QB 202, [1980] 1 All ER 839; (M & B).

13 Meagher, Gummow & Lehane *Equity: Doctrine and Remedies*; T. G. Youdan (ed) *Equity, Fiduciaries and Trusts* [1990] Conv 370 (D. Hayton).

each of these? (3) What terms have been used by the courts to describe the remedies they have granted?

The questions are simple to pose. The answers are not always so easy to elucidate. Each may draw his own conclusions, and some may conclude that this field of law is so filled with uncertainties that no satisfactory analysis is possible. But the attempt must be made. However, before this is done, we shall set out the facts and the decisions in a selection of cases which illustrate the topic. The cases are set out in chronological order.

In *Dillwyn v Llewelyn*[14] (1862) a father allowed his son to build himself a house on land which he, the father, owned. It was the understanding that the father would convey the title to the land to the son, and in confirmation of this the father signed the following memorandum: 'H, together with my other freehold estate, are left in my will to my dearly beloved wife, but it is her wish, and I hereby join in presenting the same to my son for the purpose of furnishing him with a dwelling-house.' No conveyance was made. On the father's death, by his will the land was devised to his widow for life, with remainder to the son for life, with remainders over. The son claimed to be entitled to have a conveyance of fee simple. The Court of Appeal in Chancery held that the acts by the son subsequent to the memorandum constituted valuable consideration by the son and therefore converted the transaction from one of imperfect gift into one of binding contract. The son was therefore entitled to have the legal fee simple conveyed to him.

Plimmer v Wellington Corpn[15] (1884) came to the Privy Council on appeal from the Court of Appeal, New Zealand. In 1848 L, as licensee from the government, built a wharf by Wellington Harbour, and, in 1855, a jetty. In 1856, at the request and for the benefit of the government he spent a large sum extending the jetty and erecting a warehouse. The question later arose as to whether L held any interest in the land. The Privy Council held that between 1848 and 1856 L held the land under a revocable licence. By virtue of the transactions in 1856 the licence ceased to be revocable at the will of the government. L acquiring an indefinite right to the jetty. The right was equitable and constituted an 'estate of interest in land' within the meaning of the New Zealand Public Works Act 1882.

Bannister v Bannister[16] (1948) concerned a woman who owned two cottages in Essex. In 1942 she agreed to sell these to her brother-in-law on the basis that he would allow her to remain in the one that had been her home, rent free, for as long as she liked. The cottages were conveyed to the brother-in-law. There was no mention in the conveyance of the woman being permitted to remain in one of the cottages. Later, the brother-in-law, claiming that the woman was no more than a tenant-at-will, gave her notice to quit and sought an order for possession. The Court of Appeal held that the brother-in-law's declaration

---

14   (1862) 4 De GF & J 517.
15   (1884) 9 App Cas 699; (M & B).
16   [1948] 2 All ER 133; (M & B).

gave the woman a life interest in the property , terminable on her ceasing to live in the cottage, and that the brother-in-law held the cottage under a constructive trust for her for his interest.

In *Errington v Errington and Woods*[17] (1952) a father bought a house in 1936 through a building society, to provide a home for his son and daughter-in-law. He retained the title, but promised that if the son and daughter-in-law remained in occupation and paid the mortgage instalments, he would, when the mortgage was paid off, convey the legal fee simple to them. On the father's death, by his will all his property, including the home, was left to his widow. The widow claimed possession. The Court of Appeal held that the couple were contractual licensees and were entitled in equity to remain in occupation so long as the instalments were paid, and that when these were paid they (per Lord Denning LJ) would be, or (per Hodson and Somervell LJJ) might be, entitled to receive the legal title.

Chalmers v Pardoe[18] (1963) came to the Privy Council on appeal from the Fiji Court of Appeal. C held a lease of certain land. P, with the consent of C, built himself a residence on part of the land. The arrangement was that C would seek permission, required under Fiji law, from the appropriate government body to sublet the land to P. Later C and P quarrelled, and C declined to seek the requisite authority. The Privy Council held that equity would intervene to prevent C going back on his word and taking the building for nothing. Since it was not possible to order C to grant P any interest in the land, the court directed that P should have an equitable charge on the land for the money he had expended.

In *Inwards v Baker*[19] (1965) a son wished to build a bungalow as his home but could not afford to buy the land he wanted. His father suggested that he built the bungalow on some land which he, the father, owned. The son did so, and went into occupation of the bungalow and lived there under the impression that he would be allowed to remain there for his lifetime or for so long as he wished. The father died in 1951. In his will the land passed to trustees on trust for persons other than the son. The trustees claimed the bungalow. It was held that the son had a 'licence coupled with an equity'.[20] The son was therefore held to be entitled to remain for as long as he desired.

In *Hussey v Palmer*[1] (1972) W and her husband, H, invited W's elderly mother to go to live with them at their home. A bedroom for the mother was built on to the house and she paid the cost of this, £607. After 17 months, difficulties arose and the mother left. She claimed the £607. In evidence she stated that she had 'lent the money' to H and claimed that H and W had agreed to give her a home for her life, if she so wanted. The Court of Appeal held[2] that the payment to H for the extension of the house was not intended as

17 [1952] 1 KB 290, [1952] 1 All ER 149; (M & B).
18 [1963] 3 All ER 552, [1963] 1 WLR 677.
19 [1965] 2 QB 29, [1965] 1 All ER 446; (M & B).
20 At 37.
 1 [1972] 3 All ER 744, [1972] 1 WLR 1286.
 2 Lord Cairns dissenting.

a gift and since it was unconscionable for H and W to retain the benefit without repayment, the house was held on a constructive trust for the mother, to the extent of the money paid by her.

Binions v Evans[3] (1972) concerned a man, H, who was employed by an estate and lived in a cottage owned by the estate, paying no rent. When H died in 1965, his wife, W continued to live in the cottage. In 1968 the estate made an agreement with W in which the estate agreed to let W occupy the cottage 'as a tenant at will ... free of rent for the remainder of her life or ... ' by W giving four weeks' notice. W, for her part, agreed to keep the cottage in good condition and repair. In 1970 the estate contracted to sell the cottage to P. P was given a copy of the agreement with W, and the contract contained a clause protecting W's right of occupation. As a result, P paid less than the market price for the cottage. In 1971 P gave W notice to quit. W, P claimed, was a tenant at will. Therefore he could terminate the tenancy when he wished. The Court of Appeal held that as W had been given the right to occupy the cottage for her life she could not be a tenant at will. Under the agreement with the estate she was, Lord Denning said, a contractual licensee. The court held that when the cottage was sold to P expressly subject to W's rights, a constructive trust (ie one imposed by law irrespective of the intention of the parties) arose, under which P held the land on trust for W. Only if P had been a purchaser of the land without notice of W's rights would he have taken free of P's equitable interest.

In *Dodsworth v Dodsworth*[4] (1973) H and W accepted an invitation from H's sister to go and live in her bungalow. H and W spent about £711, and H did about £265's worth of work on the bungalow in the expectation, encouraged by H's sister, that they would be able to remain in the bungalow for as long as they wished. A short while later the sister regretted her decision and started proceedings to oust H and W. The Court of Appeal held that H and W were entitled to receive the total of £976, and that possession should be obtained against them on their being paid this sum.

Tanner v Tanner[5] (1975) concerned a man who bought a house in 1970 as a home for his mistress and two children of hers by him. She left her rent-controlled flat and moved into the house with the children. Later the man sought to oust the woman. She declined to leave, claiming that the house was her's and the children's until they left school. The County Court judge made an order for possession against the woman. She moved out and was re-housed by the local authority. The Court of Appeal held that the inference to be drawn from the circumstances was that the woman had a contractual licence to live in the house so long as the children were of school age. The order for possession should therefore not have been made. As the woman did not wish to re-occupy the house, the court ordered that the man should pay her £2,000 by way of compensation for loss of the licence.

---

3   [1972] Ch 359, [1972] 2 All ER 70; (M & B).
4   (1973) 228 Estates Gazette 1115; (M & B).
5   [1975] 3 All ER 776, [1975] 1 WLR 1346; (M & B). Cf *Horrocks v Forray* [1976] 1 All ER 737, [1976] 1 WLR 230; (M & B).

Griffiths v Williams[6] (1977) concerned a woman, W, who had lived most of her life in her parents' home in Hereford. Her work as a teacher took her away for some periods, but since 1950 she lived in the house permanently. W's father died in 1968. Her mother repeatedly assured her that she would be allowed to live in the house for the rest of her life and on the faith of those assurances she spent, in all, about £2,000 of her own money on the property. On the mother's death in 1975, the house was devised not to W, but to K's daughter, G. Possession was claimed by the mother's personal representative from W. The court held that an equity had arisen entitling W to remain in the house for the rest of her life, and as a means of giving effect to the equity the court directed an arrangement, agreed by the parties, under which W should be granted a long lease, terminable upon her death, at a nominal rent of £30 a year, with an absolute covenant against assignment.

In *Hardwick v Johnson*[7] (1978) a mother bought a house in Trowbridge for her son and his fiancée as their home. The house was conveyed into the mother's name. The arrangement was that they should pay her £28 a month. The marriage took place in 1973. Only a few monthly payments were made to the mother. She did not complain when these stopped. Two years later the marriage broke down. The son left the house. His wife remained there with their baby. The mother sought an order for possession of the house. The Court of Appeal held that since under the informal arrangement under which the house had been held no intention had existed as to what was to happen if the marriage broke up, the court had to impute to the parties an intention that had in fact never been formed. In all the circumstances the most appropriate legal relationship to impute in a grant by the mother to the son and his wife (per Roskill and Brown LJJ) a joint contractual licence, or (per Lord Denning MR) a joint equitable licence, to live in the house on payment of £28 a month. The wife and her child were accordingly entitled to remain in the house after the man had left, on payment of the rent due. The mother could not terminate the licence unless some event occurred that would justify bringing it to an end.

In *Chandler v Kerley*[8] (1978) H and W bought a house in 1972 as the matrimonial home. The marriage broke down and H left the home. W became X's mistress. In 1975 H and W sold the property to X. W and her two children continued to live in the house. Shortly afterward the relationship between W and X ended. X served notice on W to quit. W refused to leave. X sought an order for possession. The Court of Appeal held that W had a contractual licence to occupy the house, but this was terminable upon reasonable notice. In the circumstances 12 months was reasonable.

In *Williams v Straite*[9] (1978), after H and W were married, W's parents asked the couple to move into a cottage which the parents owned, next door to the cottage in which the parents lived. H was reluctant to do this, partly because he already had a cottage that went with his job. Eventually, however, on W's

---

6   (1977) 248 Estates Gazette 947; (M & B).
7   [1978] 2 All ER 935, [1978] 1 WLR 683; (M & B).
8   [1978] 2 All ER 942, [1978] 1 WLR 693; (M & B); [1979] Conv 184 (J. M. Masson).
9   [1979] Ch 291, [1978] 2 All ER 928.

parents' assurance that the couple could live in the cottage for as long as they wished, H agreed. He gave up his tied cottage, and moved, with W, next door to the parents. After the parents had died the successors in title to the two cottages sought possession of the cottage occupied by H and W. The Court of Appeal held that H and W had an equitable licence to occupy the cottage for their life time. (The licence had not been terminated by the excessively unneighbourly conduct of H and W towards the successors in title to the parents, their new neighbours.)

In *Pascoe v Turner*[10] (1979) T, a widow, became friendly with a man, P, in 1961. Two years later she moved into his house as his housekeeper. In 1964 they began to live together as man and wife. In 1965 they moved into another house, which P bought. In reliance on P's statement that he had given her the house and its contents, T, with the encouragement or at least the acquiescence of P, spent money on redecorations, improvements and repairs. P said that he had instructed his solicitor to arrange a transfer of the title to T, but he never did so. In 1976, P, who had by then left the house, wrote to T giving her two months' notice to leave. T refused to do so, and P sought an order for possession. The Court of Appeal held that the circumstances between 1973 and 1976 gave no rise to an estoppel (ie that as a result of P's assurances, and actions by T to her detriment carried out on the faith of these, P was estopped from going back on his assurances). The minimum equity to do justice to T was to compel P to give effect to his promises by ordering him to convey the legal title to T.

Greasley v Cooke[11] (1980) concerned a woman who had entered service in 1933 at the age of 16 as a living-in maid with a family, at Riddings, in Derbyshire. She stayed with the family for 43 years, during 29 of which she co-habited with one of the sons, and cared for a mentally ill daughter for 28 years. The father died in 1948, and from this time on she received no wages. When the house was no longer needed by any of the children, certain of them, to whom the house had been devised, sought possession from the servant. She claimed that she had not asked for payment after 1948 because she had been encouraged to believe that she could regard the house as her home for the rest of her life. The Court of Appeal found that her conduct was induced by the assurances given to her, and held that on the grounds of estoppel the woman should be allowed to remain in the house rent-free for as long as she wished. The court held that for estoppel to arise the action by the plaintiff to her detriment, carried out in reliance on the assurances she had received, did not necessarily have to involve the expenditure of money. 'It is sufficient if the party to whom the assurance is given acts on the faith of it in such circumstances that it would be unjust and inequitable for the party making the assurance to go back on it.'[12] The case extended the scope of estoppel in another direction. Previously it had been accepted that for a plaintiff to obtain a remedy based on the principle of estoppel, the onus of proof was on the plaintiff to show that the action to his

---

10　[1979] 2 All ER 945, [1979] 1 WLR 431; (M & B); (1979) 42 MLR 574 (B. Suffirin).
11　[1980] 1 WLR 1306; (M & B).
12　Per Lord Denning, at 1311.

detriment had been carried out in reliance on the assurances given. The Court in *Greasley v Cooke* held that there was no need for the plaintiff to prove that she had acted as she had on the faith of the assurances she had received. It was to be presumed that her actions had been on the faith of the assurances. (The onus of proof is thus on the person contesting the plaintiff's claim to show that the plaintiff's conduct had not been in reliance on the assurances given.)

Re Sharpe (A bankrupt)[13] (1980) concerned a leasehold property in London consisting of a shop with a maisonette above occupied by a man, S, and his aunt, J. The lease was purchased by S in 1975 for £17,000, £12,000 of which was provided by J in reliance on an assurance by S that she would be able to remain in the premises for as long as she liked. In 1978 S went bankrupt. In 1979 S's trustee in bankruptcy contracted to sell the property (ie to assign the lease) to a purchaser for £17,000 with vacant possession. After the date of the contract, J claimed an interest in the property. It was held that the £12,000 provided by J constituted a loan, not a gift. Since it was an essential feature of the loan that J was to make her home in the premises she had a right ('whether it be called a contractual licence or an equitable licence, or an interest under a constructive trust'[14]) to occupy the premises for as long as she liked while the loan remained unpaid. This right of occupation was binding on the trustee in bankruptcy and he was therefore not entitled to an order for possession.

In *Re Basham*[15] (1986) a woman and her husband cared for the woman's step-father, and she bought carpets for his house and helped, without pay, to run his business. At one stage, when the couple were considering moving away, the step-father persuaded them to remain living near him. He assured her that she would lose nothing by these acts, and that his house would be hers at his death. Shortly before his death he indicated that he wished to make a will devising the house to her. He died intestate. It was held that since the woman had established that she had acted to her detriment in reliance on her belief, encouraged by the step-father, that she would ultimately receive his property, the principle of proprietary estoppel entitled her to her step-father's estate, including the house.

These, then, are some instances in which equity has provided a remedy where, if there were only the common law, none would have existed. In analysing these cases, let us consider the types of situation in which, without equity's aid, hardship would exist.

Hardships for which relief has been granted

1. Expenditure on the land of another. The principle here is that 'if the owner of land requests another, or indeed allows another, to expend money on the land under an expectation created or encouraged by the [owner of the land]

13 [1980] 1 WLR 219; [1981] Conv 212 (A. Briggs).
14 At 224.
15 [1987] 1 All ER 405, [1986] 1 WLR 1498; (M & B); [1987] Conv 211 (J. Martin).

that he will be able to remain there, that raises an equity in the licensee such as to entitle him to stay'.[16] For example, it will be recalled that in *Inwards v Baker*[17] a father allowed his son to build a bungalow on his land in the expectation of being able to remain there. Sometimes the expenditure has been on the complete building of a home (or other building) on another's land (as in *Inwards v Baker, Plimmer v Wellington Corpn, Chalmers v Pardoe*), or the expenditure may be on repairs or improvements to an existing building (as in *Hussey v Palmer* and *Dodsworth v Dodsworth*).

2. Conveyance of the title to property from A to B subject to an assurance that A will be allowed to continue in occupation. *Bannister v Bannister*[18] illustrates this. After the plaintiff had conveyed the title to the cottage to the plaintiff, the defendant sought to put her out.

3. Assurance of having a home coupled with contribution to the purchase price. *Re Sharpe*[19] provides an illustration. Here the aunt, J, provided £12,000 towards the purchase of a lease in reliance of an assurance that she would be allowed to remain in the premises for as long as she liked. Later, possession was sought when her nephew went bankrupt.

4. Assurance of having a home, coupled with expenditure on the property. *Griffiths v Williams*[20] comes under this head.[1] The woman teacher spent £2,000 of her own money on improvements and repairs to her mother's house on the faith of assurances that she would be allowed to remain in the house until she died. On her mother's death the house passed to someone else, and the mother's executor claimed possession.

5. Assurance of having a home coupled with action by the plaintiff to his detriment. The previous two heads share with this the feature that action is taken by the plaintiff in reliance on an assurance that he or she could remain on the property. The previous two heads relate to the expenditure of money by the plaintiff. Under the present head are placed instances in which some action is taken by the plaintiff other than the expenditure of money. For example, in

---

16   Per Lord Denning, *Inwards v Barker* [1965] 2 QB 29 at 37; following the principle enunciated in *Ramsden v Dyson* (1866) LR 1 HL 129: 'If a man begins to build on land supposing it to be his own, and the real owner, perceiving his mistake, abstains from setting him right, and leaves him to persevere in his error, a court of equity will not afterwards allow the real owner to assert his title to the land. But if a stranger builds on land knowing it to be the property of another, equity will not prevent the real owner from afterwards claiming the land. So, if a tenant builds on his landlord's land he does not, in the absence of special circumstances, acquire any right to prevent the landlord from taking possession of the land and buildings when the tenancy has determined. If the tenant, being a mere tenant at will, builds on the land in the belief that he thereby acquires a title afterwards to claim a lease of the land, and the landlord allows him so to build, knowing that he is acting in the belief and does not interfere to correct the error, *semble*, that equity will interfere to compel the grant of a lease.' Per Lord Kingsdown, at 170.
17   Supra.
18   [1948] 2 All ER 133; (M & B).
19   [1980] 1 All ER 198, [1980] 1 WLR 219; (M & B).
20   (1977) 248 Estates Gazette 947; (M & B).
 1   See also *Pascoe v Turner* [1979] 2 All ER 945, [1979] 1 WLR 431; (M & B) *Re Basham* [1987] 1 All ER 405 (M & B).

Greasley v Cooke,[2] the servant remained working for the family for many years without wages. Later, after the father's death, when the house was needed by one of the children, and he wanted to sell the property, they sought to put her out.[3]

These five categories are adopted merely for convenience. There may well be instances which have characteristics from more than one of the situations set out. For example, in *Ungurian v Lesnoff*[4] a man bought a house as a home for himself and a woman and her two sons. The woman gave up a flat in Poland and a promising academic career in order to live with the man. She later carried out work on improving the house. The court found that it was not to be inferred that it had been the intention that the woman was to have an interest in the property (ie as a beneficial co-owner) but that there was a common intention, to which the court gave effect through a constructive trust, that the woman should have a right to reside in the house during her life time.[5]

It will be noted that it is on the ground of the equitable principle of estoppel that the court in many instances is able to base its decision: the defendant is estopped from denying that the plaintiff has an entitlement to the land, the estoppel arising as a result of (a) the plaintiff having acted to his detriment, (b) in reliance on assurances by the defendant. (In *Coombes v Smith*[6] it was held that the actions of a woman who had become pregnant by her lover, given birth to the child, redecorated the house, installed decorative beams, and improved the garden, had not been actions to her detriment, with the result that the lover's assurances that she would always have a roof over her head did not give rise to estoppel in her favour (nor, since the couple had never considered the position should the relationship end, to a contractual licence). The woman's claim to the fee simple therefore failed (the lover giving an undertaking that the woman could live in the house until the child was 17).)

Remedies

Having considered the principal categories of circumstances that have been placed before the court by plaintiffs seeking a remedy, we must now examine the remedies that have been granted. These fall under three heads.

1. ENTITLEMENT TO THE FEE SIMPLE

Here the plaintiff is held to be entitled to have the fee simple conveyed to him. Pending the transfer, the fee simple is held on trust for him. This is the highest

---

2 [1980] 3 All ER 710, [1980] 1 WLR 1306.
3 Other examples are provided by *Tanner v Tanner* [1975] 3 All ER 776, [1975] 1 WLR 1346; (M & B); *Hardwick v Johnson* [1978] 2 All ER 935, [1978] 1 WLR 683; and *Binions v Evans* [1972] Ch 359, [1972] 2 All ER 70; (M & B).
4 [1990] Ch 206, [1990] Conv 223 (P. Sparkes).
5 For the effect of the finding, see p 375, *infra*.
6 [1986] 1 WLR 808.

form of remedy. It was the remedy awarded in *Dillwyn v Llewelyn,*[7] *Plimmer v Wellington Corpn,*[8] *Pascoe v Turner*[9] and *Re Basham.*[10]

2.   ENTITLEMENT TO MONEY

Here the plaintiff receives back the money that he has expended. Security for the payment of the money may take the form of a charge on the land (as in *Chalmers v Pardoe*[11]), or by the plaintiff not being required to leave until the money is paid (as in *Dodsworth v Dodsworth*[12] and in *Re Sharp*[13]). In *Hussey v Palmer*[14] the property was declared to be held on a constructive trust to the extent of the sum expended by the plaintiff, with the result that on a sale, the plaintiff would receive this sum.

3.   ENTITLEMENT TO REMAIN ON THE PROPERTY[15]

This has been the most common outcome, but variations exist with regard to the duration of time for which the plaintiff is entitled to remain. Most commonly, the period is the remainder of the plaintiff's life, or until he or she wishes to occupy the property (as in *Bannister v Bannister,*[16] *Inwards v Baker,*[17] *Griffiths v Williams,*[18] *Greasley v Cooke*[19] and *Binions v Evans*[20]), but a shorter period may be decreed, for example in *Tanner v Tanner*[1] entitlement to occupy the house existed for so long as the children were of school age. In *Chandler v Kerley,*[2] the entitlement to occupy lasted until the giving of reasonable notice, the court stating that 12 months would here be reasonable.

It has been suggested[3] that in deciding what form of remedy to grant, the court will take into account the nature of any assurance given. Thus where there is an assurance that the property will be the plaintiff's (as in *Pascoe v Turner* and *Re Basham*), the plaintiff receives the fee simple; where there is an assurance that the plaintiff can remain in the property for as long as he wishes (as in *Inwards v Baker*), then the court so orders. Where the assurance is, in

---

7   (1862) 4 De GF & J 517.
8   (1884) 9 App Cas 699.
9   [1979] 2 All ER 945, [1979] 1 WLR 431.
10   [1987] 1 All ER 405.
11   [1963] 3 All ER 552, [1963] 1 WLR 677.
12   (1973) 228 Estates Gazette 1115.
13   [1980] 1 All ER 198, [1980] 1 WLR 219.
14   [1972] 3 All ER 744, [1972] 1 WLR 1286.
15   See A. R. Everton (1976) Conv (NS) 415.
16   [1948] 2 All ER 133; (M & B).
17   [1965] 2 QB 29, [1965] 1 All ER 446.
18   (1977) 248 Estates Gazette 947; (M & B).
19   [1980] 3 All ER 710, [1980] 1 WLR 1306.
20   [1972] Ch 359, [1972] 2 All ER 70, and in *Matharu v Matharu* (1994) 68 P & CR 93.
1   [1975] 3 All ER 776, [1975] 1 WLR 1346; (M & B). See also *Coombes v Smith,* supra.
2   [1978] 2 All ER 942, [1978] 1 WLR 693; (M & B).
3   S. Moriarty *Licences and Land Law: Legal Principles and Public Policies* (1984) 100 LQR 376. See also [1986] Conv 406 (M. P. Thompson).

effect, that the plaintiff will be able to continue to share in the occup...
the property, then, since this constitutes an informal creation of co-ownership,
and since when a dispute between co-owners arises a sale may be ordered, and
the proceeds distributed according to the co-owners' beneficial entitlements,
effect is given to the arrangement by directing that the plaintiff should receive
in money the equivalent of his interest in the property[4] (short-circuiting, as it
were, an order for sale).

The means adopted

So the plaintiff may receive the title to the property, or receive money, or be
allowed to remain. Next we must ask what have been the means adopted by
the courts to produce each of the three types of outcome we have referred to.
By what routes, in terms of property law, have these ends been achieved? What,
if we may put it this way, have been the labels attached by the court to the
remedies awarded?

The labels have been these:

1. 'Contractual licence' (*Chandler v Kerley, Errington v Errington*[5], *Hardwick
v Johnson*, per Roskill and Brown LJJ, *Tanner v Tanner*).

2. 'Equitable licence' (*Hardwick v Johnson*, per Lord Denning, *Williams v
Staite*[6]).

3. 'Licence coupled with an equity' (*Inwards v Baker*, per Lord Denning).

4. 'Proprietary estoppel' (*Greasley v Cooke, Griffiths v Williams, Pascoe v
Turner, Re Basham*[7]).

5. 'Equitable estoppel' (*Inwards v Baker*, per Dankworth LJ).

6. 'Equitable charge' (*Chalmers v Pardoe*).

7. 'Constructive trust' (*Bannister v Bannister, Binions v Evans, Hussey v
Palmer*, per Lord Denning).

In many judgments the labels attached to a remedy have been specific
(although in the Court of Appeal different labels may be used by different
judges as the basis of the same outcome[8]), but there is no means of predicting,
when an outcome has been determined, what label will be attached to it. We
are left with the feeling that the court, having decided what should happen,
selects the name for the remedy at random. Certainly, no significance (with
rare exceptions) appears to be attached by the court to the mechanics by which
it gives effect to its decisions. For example, in *Re Sharpe*,[9] the court spoke[10] of

4 S. Moriarty, supra.
5 (1981) 97 LQR 513.
6 [1979] Ch 291, [1978] 2 All ER 923. A 'licence to remain' for a person's life or some
   shorter period as she might decide; *Matharu v Matharu* (1994) 68 P & CR 93.
7 See also *Lim Teng Huan v Ang Swee Chuan* [1992] 1 WLR 113, PC. On the nature of estoppel,
   see [1992] Conv 239 (M. Lunney).
8 See *Inwards v Baker*, Lord Denning, 'licence coupled with an equity'; Dankwerts LJ, 'equitable
   estoppel'; *Hardwick v Johnson*, Lord Denning, 'equitable licence'; Roskill and Brown LJJ,
   'contractual licence'.
9 [1980] 1 WLR 219; (M & B).
10 At 224.

the plaintiff having a right to remain on the premises ' ... whether it be called a contractual licence, or an equitable licence, or an interest under a constructive trust', the implications being that the label attached to the remedy was of no import. Thus new remedies have come into existence, but their characteristics have been left indistinct.[11]

Third parties

So far in this chapter we have considered the position of two parties: the grantor and the grantee. But what of third parties? If A confers an entitlement on B to occupy his (A's) land, and A sells the land to P, does B's entitlement bind P? Can B remain on the land, or not?

Originally the answer rested on the distinction between an interest in land and a licence. Only an *interest* was capable of binding a purchaser (ie it did so if the interest was legal or, if equitable, if the purchaser was not a bona fide purchaser). Since, as was held in 1674, a 'licence ... passeth no interest, nor alters or transfers property in any thing, but only makes an action lawful, which without it had been unlawful', a licence was incapable of binding a purchaser, a licensee's remedy lying only against the licensor.

From about the middle of the present century, however, the courts have shown a willingness to find that in certain circumstances an entitlement that the court held to be a licence (not an interest) should nonetheless be capable of binding a purchaser. For example in *Inwards v Baker*,[12] Lord Denning said[13] of the son's interest, described by him as a 'licence coupled with an interest': 'I think that any purchaser who took with notice would clearly be bound by the equity.' In *Re Sharpe*,[14] the aunt's interest was binding on the nephew's trustee in bankruptcy. In *Tanner v Tanner* Lord Denning[15] said in connection with the contractual licence which the court found to exist, the owner, 'could not sell the house over her head so as to get her out'.[16] In *Williams v Staite*,[17] the equitable licence held by the defendants was binding on a purchaser of the property, and in *Errington v Errington*[18] a contractual licence was binding on a devisee. In *Binions v Evans*[19] the plaintiff's contractual licence was made binding on a purchaser with notice by being converted at the moment of transfer to the purchaser into an interest under a constructive trust.

---

11   For endeavours to identify the characteristics of, and to distinguish between, a contractual licence and a licence arising by estoppel, see [1981] Conv 347 (P. N. Todd); [1981] Conv 212 and [1983] Conv 285 (A. Briggs); (1984) 100 LQR 376 (S. Moriarty).
12   [1965] 2 QB 29, [1965] 1 All ER 446; (M & B).
13   At 37.
14   [1980] 1 All ER 198, [1980] 1 WLR 219; (M & B).
15   [1975] 1 WLR 1346.
16   At 1350.
17   [1979] Ch 291, [1978] 2 All ER 928.
18   [1952] 1 KB 290, [1952] 1 All ER 149.
19   [1972] Ch 359, [1972] 2 All ER 70; (M & B).

How a licence could come to be binding on a purchaser was explained by the Court of Appeal in *Ashburn Anstalt v Arnold*.[20] A contractual licence to occupy land was not, standing alone, binding on a purchaser, even if he had notice of the existence of the licence. Where, however, because of the existence of 'appropriate facts',[1] the court was satisfied that the conscience of the purchaser had been so affected that it would be inequitable for him to take the land free from the licence, then the court would compel the purchaser to take the land subject to the licence by imposing a constructive trust.

Thus it has been by invoking the notion of a constructive trust that the court has been enabled to make a licence binding on a purchaser, and this has been so whether what was made binding on the purchaser was a contractual licence (as in *Errington v Errington* and referred to in *Asburn Anstalt v Arnold*) or an equitable licence, ie one imposed by equity because of the circumstances.

The implications of a licence being capable of binding a transferee will be appreciated: if P buys from V, P does not wish to find that he takes the land subject to an incumbrance that reduces the value of his purchase (or even renders it valueless): P knows that if V's document of title is, for example, a vesting deed, he must pay the purchase price to the trustees of the settlement and that equitable interests under the settlement will then be overreached. He knows that inspection of the Land Charges register will reveal most forms of equitable incumbrance likely to affect the land. But unless he makes exhaustive enquiries P may fail to discover the existence of the rights of an equitable licensee – the servant, for example, in *Greasley v Cooke*. Yet he may find himself fixed with constructive notice of the licence, and thus bound by it. (How many purchasers would have thought of asking old Mrs Cooke, when she opened the front door, 'Do you have an equitable licence to occupy this house?') Making equitable licences capable of binding a transferee thus constitutes a step away from the intention of the 1925 legislation that equitable interests should be either registrable or overreachable.[2]

The courts, principally the Court of Appeal, have sought to do justice to an injured plaintiff by finding new equitable bases for the existence of rights, and in so doing have prevented injustice to the plaintiff. Less regard has been had for the injustice done to a purchaser who, through no moral fault, finds himself fixed with constructive notice of one of these new rights. (In *Re Sharpe*,[3] for example, at the time of the trial, the purchaser had been reduced to living, with his wife and two small children, in a small motorised caravan parked in various places on or near Hampstead Heath.[4])

---

20 [1989] Ch 1, [1988] CLJ 353 (A. J. Oakley); (1988) 51 MLR 226 (J. Hill); [1991] Conv 36 (G. Battersby).
1 Per Fox LJ [1989] Ch 1 at 29.
2 See [1981] Conv 347 (P. N. Todd); [1983] (M. P. Thompson); (1984) 100 LQR 376 (S. Moriarty).
3 [1980] 1 WLR 219.
4 At 224.

The following position has therefore been reached:

1. In some reasonably clearly defined circumstances a remedy exists. For example if A allows B to build a house on his, A's, land in the expectation, encouraged by A, that he will be allowed to remain there, then in the event of A seeking to oust B, B will have a remedy.

2. Outside this sphere (*Greasley v Cooke*[5] provides an illustration) we can say that the plaintiff may have a remedy; or, on the other hand, he may not.

3. If equity does provide a remedy, the remedy may take one of about three main forms, to which one of about seven labels may be attached.

4. If a remedy is granted and it is clearly proprietary in nature, eg if a constructive trust exists, then, subject to other relevant rules of law (eg the bona fide purchaser rule) the interest will bind a third party.

5. If a remedy takes the form of a contractual or equitable licence, then if the court holds that third parties are bound, they are bound. If the court does not make any finding on this point, then whether the interest is binding on a third party is unknown, and can only be discovered by further litigation.

The final result, in the words of one commentator, is that, 'What should be a fundamentally simple set of rules has been confused and obscured beyond all recognition, with the result that the simplest of cases now seem difficult.'[6] The courts are not unaware of the quagmire to which the law has been reduced. In *Re Sharpe*[7] Browne Wilkinson J said,[8] 'I reach this conclusion with some hesitation since I find the present state of the law very confused and difficult to fit in with established equitable principles.' (So great, indeed, is the confusion that the uncertainties attaching to equitable licences have begun to seep into the field of express, common law, contractual licences. *Midland Bank Ltd v Farmpride Hatcheries Ltd*[9] concerned an express, written, contractual licence. No question of equity arose. The licensor mortgaged the property to a bank which later claimed possession of the property. The licensee claimed that his licence was binding on the bank. The court determined the matter on the basis of notice. Since, the court held, the bank did not have constructive notice of the licence, it took free. But neither the court, nor counsel for the defendant bank, took note of the fact that notice is relevant when the defence of bona fide purchaser without notice is raised; that this defence is needed against a claim for the enforcement of an equitable interest; and that since the licence was a straightforward common law contractual licence no question of its enforcement against a third party should have arisen.)

5   [1980] 3 All ER 710, [1980] 1 WLR 1306.
6   [1981] Conv 212 (A. Briggs).
7   [1980] 1 WLR 219; (M & B).
8   At 226.
9   (1980) 260 Estates Gazette 493; (M & B).

The Settled Land Act 1925

Until recently this was the end of the matter. Suppose that, as in *Bannister v Bannister*[10] in 1948, the court wished to enable a plaintiff to remain on the property for as long as he wished. The court wanted to ensure that the plaintiff's right to remain on the property was binding on any purchaser. The court decreed that a constructive trust existed, with the property held on trust for the plaintiff for his lifetime, or until he no longer wished to reside on the property, thus giving the plaintiff a determinable life *interest* in the property. Consider the result. The land was held first for the plaintiff, and then, on his death (or when he no longer wished to live on the property) for the defendant. The plaintiff's interest was necessarily (because of s 1 of the Law of Property Act 1925) equitable. The land was not held on trust for sale. Therefore, because there was a trust, and a succession of interests, the land was caught by the Settled Land Act 1925. The plaintiff was entitled to a vesting deed vesting the legal estate in him as Tenant for life, with power under the Act to sell the land.

In *Bannister v Bannister*[11] this can hardly have been the intention of the parties. Yet this was what the court accepted as being the result. In *Binions v Evans*[12] Megaw LJ recognised that the creation of an equitable life interest under a constructive trust created a settlement under the Settled Land Act 1925, a result that might 'produce some odd consequences'.[13] Stephenson LJ concurred in accepting that the land became settled land. The same position was accepted by Russell LJ giving the judgment of the Court of Appeal in *Dodsworth v Dodsworth*:[14] to give the plaintiff an equitable life interest under a constructive trust would 'lead, by virtue of the provisions of the Settled Land Act, to a greater and more extensive interest than was ever contemplated by the plaintiff and the defendants'.[15] These indications that a settlement under the Settled Land Act 1925 arose if an equitable life interest was created under a constructive trust were, however, merely obiter.

The question whether the conferring of a right to occupy premises for life under equitable principles gave rise to a settlement under the 1925 Act was settled in *Ungurian v Lesnoff*[16] when it was held that the succession of interests created did give rise to a strict settlement under the Act, the woman concerned therefore becoming Tenant for life, and so entitled to call for a vesting deed.

The effect of the Trusts of Land and Appointment of Trustees Act 1996 is, it is submitted, as follows.

---

10   [1948] 2 All ER 133; (M & B).
11   [1948] 2 All ER 133; (M & B).
12   [1972] Ch 359, [1972] 2 All ER 70; (M & B). In *Jones v Jones* [1977] 2 All ER 231, [1977] 1 WLR 438; (M & B), the court declined to address the problem.
13   At 370.
14   (1973) 228 Estates Gazette 1115; (M & B).
15   At 1115.
16   [1990] Ch 206; [1990] Conv 223 (P. Sparkes), (1991) 107 LQR 596 (J. Hill), followed in *Costello v Costello* [1994] NPC 32, CA; [1994] Conv 391 (M. P. Thompson); cf *Dent v Dent* [1996] 1 WLR 683.

1. Strict settlements that had arisen prior to the Act as a result of a life interest having been held to exist (as in *Ungurian*), continue to have effect as strict settlements under the Settled Land Act 1925.

2. Where, after the 1996 Act, the application of equitable principles give rise to an equitable life interest:

(a) no strict settlement under the Settled Land Act 1925 comes into existence, (section 2 of the 1996 providing that no settlement under the 1925 Act 'shall be deemed to be made under the Act after the commencement of the Act');

(b) the trust under which the equity is to be presumed to exist comes within the definition of a trust of land under the 1996 Act and so is subject to the 1996 Act; and,

(c) the legal estate, not having been conveyed to trustees, remains with the existing holder of the fee simple, who, as trustee, is bound by the relevant provisions of the 1996 Act.

CHAPTER 21

Covenants between Fee Simple Owners[1]

INTRODUCTION

E (which in this chapter represents 'covenantee'), owns two adjacent plots of land, Redacre and Greenacre. On Redacre he has his house and garden. On Greenacre, a field, he keeps a horse. When the horse dies, E decides to sell Greenacre. R (which in this chapter represents 'covenantor'), wants a piece of land on which to build a bungalow and offers to buy Greenacre. E is reluctant to see Greenacre built on, but is prepared to accept this provided that he does not find that something unacceptable, such as a pig farm, has been built next door to him. So E agrees to sell Greenacre to R, provided that R agrees not to use the land for anything except residential purposes. R agrees to this condition. The sale goes through and the land is conveyed to R in the normal way.

The deed conveying the land to R contains the promise by R which E had required. So the deed is signed not only by E, the person conveying the land, but also by R, the person making the promise. Since R had made his promise in a deed, we say that he had *convenanted* with E. (A covenant is thus a promise made in a deed.) The conveyance thus bears E's signature, as vendor, and R's signature as covenantor. R's covenant constitutes a binding contract enforceable against him (under the ordinary rules of contract). If R is in breach of the covenant, E can sue him and obtain damages[2] for the breach; and, more important, E can seek an injunction ordering him to desist from whatever action had constituted the breach.[3] Whether a breach has occurred is a matter of fact in each case for the court to determine.[4] Whether an injunction will be granted depends, an injunction being an equitable remedy, on the circumstances.[5]

---

1 See Preston and Newsom *Restrictive Covenants* (8th edn, 1991).
2 Damages being assessed by reference to E's loss, not by reference to R's gain. *Surrey County Council v Bredero Homes Ltd* [1993] 3 All ER 705, [1993] 1 WLR 1361, CA; [1994] Conv 110 (T. Ingman), [1994] Conv 329 (J. Martin).
3 See *Remedies for Breach of Restrictive Covenants* [1996] Conv 329 (J. Martin).
4 *C and G Homes Ltd v Secretary of State for Health* [1991] Ch 365, [1991] 2 All ER 841; *Elliott v Safeway Stores plc* [1995] 1 WLR 1396.
5 *Jaggard v Sawyer* [1995] 1 WLR 269 (injury to plaintiff by breach of covenant found to be small; injury adequately compensated by money payment; injunction refused); *Co-operative Insurance Society Ltd v Argyll Stores (Holdings) Ltd* [1996] Ch 286, [1996] 3 All ER 934, CA (order of specific performance granted requiring supermarket to be kept open, notwithstanding practice of the courts not to grant specific performance requiring a business to be carried on, damages not being an adequate remedy); *Brown v Heathlands Mental Health National Health Service Trust* [1996] 1 All ER 133; see p 377.

'Covenantor' and 'covenantee'

In the above example it is the purchaser, R, who makes the covenant: thus R is the *covenantor*; and E, to whom the promise was made, is termed the *covenantee*. But the purchaser is not always the covenantor. For example, suppose that R owned the two plots of land, Redacre and Greenacre; R sold Redacre to E; E was willing to buy Redacre only if R promised not to use Greenacre for anything other than residential purposes; R covenanted accordingly. In this case it is the vendor, R, who is the covenantor.

A common error in studying this topic is to equate purchaser with covenantor, and vendor with covenantee. This may be, but is not necessarily, the position. There is another possibility. This is that there was no sale from E to R or from R to E. R and E may have acquired Greenacre and Redacre respectively from a third person, or from two different persons. Later, in order to preserve the value of Redacre, E may offer R £1,000 if R will covenant that Greenacre will not be used for anything other than residential purposes. R agrees and makes the covenant. Thereupon R's land becomes worth a certain amount less, because it can only be used for residential purposes; but R has £1,000 in hand. E has £1,000 less in cash; but his land, Redacre, is worth more.

Thus, the covenant may have been without any sale being involved between covenantor and covenantee; and, if a sale was involved, the vendor may be a covenantor *or* a covenantee, and the purchaser may be a covenantor *or* a covenantee.

'Burden' and 'benefit' of the covenant

If R, the owner of Greenacre, covenants with E, the owner of Redacre, that, for example, pigs will not be kept on Greenacre, this fact is a disadvantage to R (who may later decide he would like to keep pigs) and an advantage to E (who will not have to suffer the smell of pigs). Hence we speak of R bearing the *burden* of the covenant, and of E having the *benefit* of the covenant.

'Positive' and negative' covenants

In the example at the beginning of this chapter R covenanted not to use the land he bought from E for anything other than residential purposes. Let us suppose that R entered into a number of other covenants, for example:

1. To keep no sheep or cattle.
2. Not to use the premises as the registered office of a company.
3. Not to erect more than a specified number of dwelling-houses on the plot.
4. Not to play musical instruments in the garden.
5. To obtain the approval of Z to any plans for the development of the site before any works are commenced.
6. Not to build any building within 20 yards of the boundary with Redacre.
7. To ensure that any building on Greenacre is below 60 feet in height.
8. To maintain the fence between Greenacre and Redacre.

9. Not to allow Greenacre to become infested with rabbits.
10. To contribute to the cost of clearing the ditch between Redacre and Greenacre.

It will be seen that in 1 to 7 R need not take any positive step in order to comply with the covenant. He can comply by doing nothing. Covenants of this kind are termed *negative* covenants. In the case of 8 to 10, R must, or may have to, take some positive step in order to comply with the covenant. Covenants of this kind are termed *positive* covenants.

It will be seen that the distinction between the two kinds of covenant does not depend on whether the covenant happens to be phrased in a positive or negative way. For example, 9 is phrased in a negative way, but it is clearly a positive covenant. Similarly, 5 is phrased in a positive way, but it is clearly a negative covenant.[6] Thus what matters is not whether the covenant is positive or negative in form, but whether it is positive or negative in substance.[7] Another name for a negative covenant is a *restrictive* covenant, and this term will be used from now on. We shall see later that in certain respects the law concerning restrictive covenants differs from that concerning positive covenants.

Covenants affecting land are, by convention, given as undertakings that the covenant will be observed not only by the covenantor but by his successors in title also.[8] Thus the first covenant in the list above constitutes an undertaking not merely that R will refrain from keeping sheep or cattle, but that sheep or cattle will not be kept. If R makes this covenant and sells the land to S, who buys a cow, then, irrespective of whether (under principles shortly to be discussed) S is liable to the covenantee, R remains personally liable to the covenantee, since the covenant he gave has been breached. (He remains personally liable irrespective of the number of subsequent transfers that take place.)

Practical importance

The ability of one landowner to restrict what is done on adjoining land is of economic importance. If, when E sells part of his land to R he restricts the purposes for which R may use the land to ones that do not adversely affect the land E retains, then the value of E's land is thereby protected from diminution by reason of R's activities. Conversely, if the uses to which R's land may be put are, by a covenant, restricted, the value of the land is thereby reduced.

6 Ie a covenant not to develop without Z's approval (as in *Wrotham Park Estate Co Ltd v Parkside Homes Ltd* [1974] 2 All ER 321, [1974] 1 WLR 798.)
7 *Bridges v Harrow London Borough* (1981) 260 Estates Gazette 284 (covenant to retain trees in a hedgerow held probably to be negative).
8 By LPA 1925, s 79, covenants made after 1925 are deemed to be made (ie without express words to this effect) by the covenantor on behalf of himself and on behalf of his successors in title, and those deriving title under him or them, unless a contrary intention is expressed. See p 386, infra.

In the last century, when the owners of great estates were selling off land to developers for the houses that spread outwards from the cities as populations grew, it was possible for the vendors to impose covenants that (by means that we shall see) bound later holders of individual properties. (And if the original landowners did not impose covenants, developers of the land might do so.) In this way, long before the introduction, in 1949, of a comprehensive system of planning law, means existed by which land use could be controlled, networks of covenants coming to form, in effect, a privately initiated and enforced system of local planning control. The relationship between the law relating to covenants and the modern law of planning will be considered later in this chapter.

Despite the practical importance of covenants, the law on the subject has contained defects that have prevented covenants satisfying needs that have come to be felt in this century. Major changes were proposed[9] by the Law Commission[10] in 1984 that would, inter alia, have prevented the creation of new covenants and, in their place, introduced a new form of proprietary interest in land termed a 'land obligation', a feature of which would be that a positive obligation imposed on land would run with the land burdened. The significance of such a change will be appreciated later in this chapter.

Other forms of covenant

This chapter deals with covenants made between land owners. There are many other situations in which covenants may be made. For example, S may covenant that he will give his daughter £1,000 on her attaining her 21st birthday. This kind of covenant does not come within the province of land law. Or a tenant of a flat may covenant with his landlord not to use the flat for business purposes. Covenants made by a tenant (or by a landlord to his tenant) form part of land law and are considered in the next chapter.

The situations to be considered

We shall discuss the principles of law which arise by considering six situations. In each situation (except the last) we shall use the same starting point. This is that R owns Greenacre, R has entered into a covenant with E; R is thus the covenantor, and R bears the burden of the covenant. E owns Redacre, E is the covenantee, and E has the benefit of the covenant.

---

9   Substantially implementing recommendations of the *Report of the Committee on Positive Covenants affecting Land* (the Wilberforce Committee), 1965 (Cmnd 2719).
10   *Transfer of Land: The Law of Positive and Restrictive Covenants* (Law Com No 127); (1984) 47 LQR 566 (P. Polden); (1984) JPEL 222 (S. B. Edell); (1984) 134 NLJ 481 (H. W. Wilkinson).

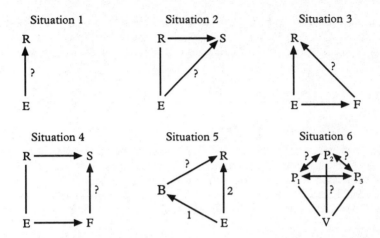

Situation 1

R breaks the covenant. Can E obtain an injunction to restrain R, or obtain damages (or obtain both remedies)? Ie can E enforce the covenant against R? (In this chapter the word 'sue' will be used to mean 'enforce the covenant against'.)

Situation 2

R conveys Greenacre to S. S acts in breach of the covenant. Can E sue S?

Situation 3

E conveys Redacre to F. R acts in breach of the covenant. Can F sue R?

Situation 4

E conveys Redacre to F. R conveys Greenacre to S. S acts in breach of the covenant. Can F sue S?

Situation 5

Before R entered into the covenant with E, E conveyed Blueacre (a plot of land adjacent to both Redacre and Greenacre) to B. After the covenant between R and E has been made, R breaks the covenant. Can B sue R?

Situation 6

V buys a piece of land and divides it into plots. He sells plot 1 to P_1, plot 2 to P_2 and plot 3 to P_3. P_1, P_2 and P_3 all covenant not to keep pigs. If one of the purchasers breaks the covenant can any or all of the others sue him?

THE BASIC SITUATIONS

Situation 1: The original parties

R breaks the covenant. Can E sue R? (Ie can the covenantee sue the covenantor?) Yes. E has a right of action at common law for damages; and in equity he can seek an injunction to restrain R from continuing the breach.

Between E and R there is *privity of contract*. E's action lies in contract and it is the law of contract rather than land law that is primarily concerned here.

In dealing with the position between E and R it is relevant to ask what result ensues if E conveys Redacre to F and then R breaks the covenant. Can E (despite the fact that he no longer occupies Redacre) sue R? (Ie can a covenantee sue the covenantor if the covenantee has parted with the land?)

1. Generally, the answer is, yes. Between E and R privity of contract remains, and R's liability to E continues.

2. If E has leased the land to F, E can recover damages from R in respect of the damage, if any, done to his reversion. He may also be able to obtain an injunction to restrain R's breach.

3. If E has sold the land to F, he can still sue R, but if the covenant had been made for the benefit of E's land (ie and not for the benefit of E personally) then E is unlikely to be awarded more than nominal damages,[11] and equity probably would not grant an injunction.

4. We shall see later than E is able expressly to assign the benefit of the covenant to F. If he has done this, he cannot sue R.

Still dealing with the position between E and R, it is relevant also to ask what result ensues if R conveys Greenacre to S. S then acts in breach of the covenant. Can E sue R? (Ie can a covenantee sue the covenantor if the covenantor has parted with the land?)

The answer generally is, yes. R remains liable to E under the contract between them. More precisely, the position is that if the covenant was made before the end of 1925, R will remain liable if his covenant was in the form of a personal undertaking that neither he nor his successors would act in breach of the covenant, for example by R covenanting 'for himself, his heirs, and assigns and other persons claiming under him'. If the covenant is made after 1925, by virtue of s 79 of the Law of Property Act 1925, R is deemed to have covenanted in this manner unless a contrary intention can be shown. Thus

---

11   *LCC v Allen* [1914] 3 KB 642 at 664.

after 1925, unless the covenant exempts R from breaches of the covenant by his successors in title, he will be liable to E if S acts in breach of the covenant.

So if S acts in breach of the covenant, R may find himself paying damages to E. In order to protect himself against this eventuality, when R conveys Greenacre to S, R may require S to covenant:

(a) that, for example,[12] pigs will not be kept on Greenacre;
(b) that if pigs are kept on Greenacre and if E sues R, and R has to pay damages to E, then S will pay R the sum which he, R, has had to pay E. (S is required to covenant that he will *indemnify* R.)

If S later sells Greenacre to T, S may think – 'If T keeps pigs on Greenacre, E will be able to sue R, and R will be able to claim an indemnity from me, under the covenant which I made with him'. To protect himself, S may require T to enter into the same form of covenant as he himself made with R, ie:

(a) that pigs will not be kept on Greenacre;
(b) that if pigs are kept on Greenacre and if, because of this, S has to indemnify R, T will indemnify S.

When T later sells Greenacre to U, he (T) in his turn may extract the same covenants from U; and so on. In this way a chain of indemnity covenants may come into existence.

Finally, in dealing with the position between E and R, it is relevant to ask what result ensues if E conveys Redacre to F, R conveys Greenacre to S, and then S acts in breach of the covenant. Can E sue R? (Ie can a covenantee sue the covenantor, notwithstanding that they have both parted with their land?) The same principles apply as set out above. R remains personally liable to E under the covenant. If E has sold Redacre to F he will obtain only nominal damages. If E has assigned the benefit of the covenant to F, he cannot sue R at all.

Situation 2: The burden

R conveys Greenacre to S. S acts in breach of the covenant. Can E sue S? (Ie can a covenantee sue an assignee of the covenantor?)

The question here is whether the burden of the covenant runs with the land, ie whether the burden runs with Greenacre into the hands of S. If it does, then E can enforce the covenant against S. If it does not, then he cannot.

In Situation 3 we shall speak of E assigning the benefit to F: we shall be concerned with the benefit of the covenant, which, like the benefit of a contract, is capable of being assigned. But the burden of the covenant, like the burden of a contract, cannot be assigned. So no question of R assigning the burden to S can arise.

In Situation 3 we shall see that it is possible for the benefit to run with the land, ie to run with Redacre into the hands of F. This was recognised both by

---

12   Ie depending on what R had covenanted with E.

common law and by equity (though the conditions in each case differed). When we consider whether the burden can run with the land we find that equity and the common law no longer follow similar paths. We shall consider first the position at common law.

Common law

At common law the burden never ran with the land. If the covenant was against keeping pigs, and S started keeping pigs, at common law E would have no remedy against him.

E might, however, be not entirely without redress. We saw, in Situation 1, that if R conveys Greenacre to S, and S (to continue with the same example) starts keeping pigs, E will be able to sue R, the person who had made the covenant against the keeping of pigs on Greenacre. So E, in the situation we are now dealing with, may be able to obtain damages by suing R.

But E may be more interested in stopping the smell of pigs coming over the fence than in obtaining monetary compensation, and even at common law, although E cannot stop S directly, he may be able to do so indirectly by the following means.

In Situation 1 we saw that when R conveyed Greenacre to S, he might require S to covenant not to keep pigs on Greenacre. If R had extracted this covenant from S, and if S started to keep pigs, then it would be open to E to approach R and say to him 'That man S is keeping pigs. He covenanted with you not to do so. If you don't stop him, I will sue you, R, for damages. And you can stop him, R. Between yourself and S there is privity of contract. You can obtain an injunction to prevent him acting in breach of his covenant with you. You'd better get that injunction, R.' So if he wishes to avoid being sued by E, R will seek an injunction to stop S keeping pigs. By this means E may be able to stop S from keeping pigs as successfully as if he had been able to sue S himself. But there can be snags. For example:

(a) R may have failed to require S to covenant not to keep pigs; or,

(b) R might have required S to make the covenant, but S might have sold Greenacre to T without requiring T to covenant similarly. So there would be no means of bringing pressure on T to make him abide by the covenant.

(c) R might have disappeared; or he might be bankrupt and so indifferent to the threat of being sued for damages.

So for E successfully to stop S by means open to him at common law entails a certain amount of luck and is an unreliable method on which to rely.

We shall see shortly that equity came to E's rescue and, subject to certain conditions being satisfied, enabled E to sue S directly. But before we turn to this aspect of the matter, it must be mentioned that there is one set of circumstances in which, even at common law, E may be able to bring pressure to bear directly on S. Suppose that:

E sold Greenacre to R;

E agreed that R should be entitled to use a road over Redacre leading to Greenacre;

R covenanted, in return, that he would contribute to the upkeep of the road over Redacre;

R sold Greenacre to S;

S refused to contribute to the upkeep of the road over Redacre;

E sued S in an attempt to compel him to contribute to the upkeep of the road.

These were, in essence, the facts in *Halsall v Brizell*.[13] It was held that whilst E had no right of action against S at common law to require him to abide by R's covenant, nevertheless, if S failed to abide by the covenant and make the contribution, then he could not at the same time take advantage of E's covenant, and use the road over Redacre. Thus S did not have to pay; but if he did not pay he could not use the road over Redacre.[14]

For the principle to apply, the rights must relate to the same subject matter and must be reciprocal. (In *Halsall v Brizell*, E's benefit in having the road kept up was reciprocated by R's benefit in using it.) Thus a covenant imposing a positive obligation is not enforceable under the principle in *Halsall v Brizell* where the covenant forms a separate, independent, provision.[15]

EQUITY

Originally equity did not enable E to sue S. By 1848 the position had changed, and subject to certain conditions being satisfied, equity gave a remedy to E against S. The foundations of the modern law on this aspect of covenants were articulated by Lord Cottenham[16] in 1848 in *Tulk v Moxhay*.[17]

The conditions which must be satisfied at the present day[18] in order for the burden to run with Greenacre are as follows:

1. The burden of the covenant must have been intended to run with Greenacre (ie the burden of the covenant must have been intended to run with the covenantor's land).

In the case of a covenant made before the end of 1925 it is necessary to show that the covenant by R was intended to bind not merely R, the covenantor, but also persons to whom the land passed subsequently. In the case of a covenant made after 1925, if the covenant relates to R's land (and not merely to R

---

13 [1957] Ch 169, [1957] 1 All ER 371. Cf *Four Oaks Estate Ltd v Hadley* [1986] LS Gaz R 2326.

14 For a discussion of the principle underlying this decision (the principle of 'benefit and burden') see *Tito v Waddell (No 2)* [1977] 2 WLR 496 at 664–677; and [1985] Conv 12 (E. P. Aughterson).

15 *Rhone v Stephens* [1994] 2 All ER 65, [1994] 2 WLR 429, HL; [1994] Conv 477 (J. Snape); 1994 110 LQR 346 (N. P. Gravells); [1994] CLJ 446 (L. Tee).

16 Developing decisions in *Whatman v Gibson* (1838) 9 Sim 196, and *Mann v Stephens* (1846) 15 Sim 377.

17 (1848) 2 Ph 774; (M & B).

18 For the evolution of the doctrine, see [1981] Conv 55 (C. D. Bell); [1983] Conv 29 (R. Griffiths); [1983] Conv 327 (C. D. Bell).

personally) then by virtue of s 79 of the Law of Property Act 1925, the burden of R's covenant is deemed to have been made by R on behalf of himself, his successors in title, and the persons deriving title under them, unless a contrary intention appears.[19]

2. The covenant must be negative.[20] The meaning of this has been considered.[1] (In *Tulk v Moxhay* the covenant[2] was to maintain the garden in Leicester Square 'in an open state, uncovered with any buildings'.) The reason why equity does not enforce a positive covenant has been explained as being that 'to enforce a positive covenant would be to enforce a personal obligation *against a person who has not covenanted*. To enforce a negative covenant is only to treat the land as *subject to a restriction*'.[3]

3. The covenant must have been made for the benefit of E's land, Redacre (ie the covenant must have been made for the benefit of land held by the covenantee at the time of the covenant[4]). For example, suppose that E had owned only one plot of land, Greenacre, on which stood a house, and suppose that E was willing to sell Greenacre to R, provided that R covenanted not to allow the house to be used for commercial or industrial purposes. In this case the covenant would not be for the benefit of land retained by E (as E, having sold Greenacre would own no land). Therefore, the requirement we are considering (ie that the covenant must have been for the protection of land retained by E) would not be satisfied,[5] and if R sold Greenacre to S, and S failed to abide by R's covenant, E could not enforce the covenant against him.

There are certain exceptions to the rule that the covenant must be made for the benefit of land retained by the covenantee. For example:

(a) If the National Trust sells land to R and requires R to covenant, for example, not to chop down an avenue of trees, if R sells the land to S, the burden of R's covenant binds S, notwithstanding that R's covenant was not made for the benefit of any land retained by the National Trust. This exception to the rule arises by virtue of a provision of statute.[6]

---

19   *Re Royal Victoria Pavilion, Ramsgate, Whelan v FTS (Great Britain) Ltd* [1961] Ch 581.
20   *Austerberry v Oldham Corpn* (1885) 29 Ch D 750; (M & B). Originally, ie from the decision in *Tulk v Moxhay*, supra, the court had recognised the running of the burden of both positive and negative covenants. The restriction of the doctrine to negative covenants was made in *Haywood v Brunswick Permanent Benefit Building Society* (1881) 8 QBD 403. For proposals which would enable positive covenants to be enforced against assignees, see Report of the Committee on Positive Covenants Affecting Land, 1965 (Cmnd 2719).
1   See p 378, ante.
2   Ie the relevant covenant. See R Giffith [1983] Conv 29.
3   *Per* Lord Templeman, *Rhone v Stephens* [1994] 2 All ER 65, at p 71. (The emphasis is added.)
4   *Formby v Barker* [1903] 2 Ch 539; (M & B); *Re Gadd's Land Transfer* [1966] Ch 56, [1965] 2 All ER 800; (M & B).
5   As in *LCC v Allen* [1914] 3 KB 642; (M & B); *Formby v Barker*, supra.
6   National Trust Act 1937, s 8. Another example is provided by the Local Government (Miscellaneous Provisions) Act 1982, s 33 which enabled local authorities in certain circumstances to enforce restrictive covenants notwithstanding that they hold no dominant land. See also Wildlife and Countryside Act 1981, s 39(3); *Peabody Donation Fund Governors v London Residuary Body* (1987) 55 P & CR 355; Town and Country Planning Act 1990, s 106 ('planning obligations' undertaken by developer as condition of grant of planning permission bind subsequent holders of the land).

(b) The requirement we are speaking of does not apply if a Scheme of Development exists.[7]

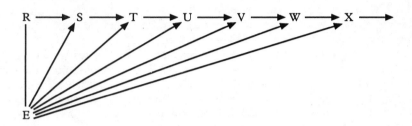

If the above three requirements are satisfied, then E can sue S, and any successor in title to S, as illustrated above.

Thus E's right is no longer purely a personal one against R (though this right against R, as we have seen,[8] continues). E's right to protect Redacre can now be enforced in equity against S, T, U, V, W, X and anyone else in the world who holds Greenacre (whether as purchaser for value, donee, devisee, licensee, squatter, or in any other capacity).

E's right in equity to stop anyone who acquires Greenacre from keeping pigs adds to the value of Redacre. Thus the fact that E is able to enforce the covenant can be regarded as a proprietary interest.[9] Conversely, the fact that in equity the burden of the covenant can be enforced against whoever holds Greenacre entitles us to speak of whoever holds Greenacre as holding it subject to E's equitable interest.

Since E's interest is an equitable one, it is subject to the limitations of any equitable interest. In particular, if R's covenant was made before 1926 (the position was changed by the 1925 legislation), since E's interest was equitable, it did not bind a bona fide purchaser for value of the legal estate (in Greenacre) without notice, actual or constructive, of the existence of the equitable interest held by E.[10] Thus if R sold the legal fee simple to S, and S could show that he had no notice of the covenant, E could not enforce the covenant against him. If S failed to show that he had no notice of the covenant, he would be bound by it.[11] (It was the fact that the transferee had notice that was of particular influence on Lord Cottenham in *Tulk v Moxhay*.)

The change made in 1925 was that under the Land Charges Act 1925[12] a restrictive covenant[13] made after 1925 became registrable under Class D (ii),

---

7 See p 399.
8 See p 382.
9 (1982) 98 LQR 279.
10 *Wilkes v Spooner* [1911] 2 KB 473; (M & B).
11 Similarly, if S held only an equitable interest in the land, he was bound; *London and South Western Rly Co v Gomm* (1882) 20 Ch D 562 at 583.
12 Section 10(1). Now LCA 1972, s 2(5).
13 Other than one made between a landlord and tenant.

Restrictive Covenants. The effect of this is, broadly,[14] that if the covenant was registered, S is deemed to have notice of it, and so is bound by it. If the covenant was not registered, S is deemed not to have notice of it, and so is not bound by it (irrespective of whether S had actual notice of the covenant or not). Since it was E who would be anxious to ensure that S was bound by the covenant, E is the person who would register the covenant. (The Land Charges Act 1925 has now been replaced by the Land Charges Act 1972.[15])

Since E's action against S lies in equity, the remedies available to him are equitable ones. As it happens, the remedy that E probably requires, namely an injunction, is an equitable remedy, but, like all equitable remedies, it is granted at the discretion of the court. The power of the court to award E damages (in addition to or in lieu of an injunction), under the Chancery Amendment Act 1858,[16] is similarly subject to the court's discretion.

So much for the conditions which must be satisfied for the burden of the covenant to run with the land. But before leaving this topic we must mention that there is another way in which it is possible that S may become liable to E, notwithstanding that the conditions for the burden to run with the land have not been satisfied. Suppose that (as in *Tophams Ltd v Earl of Sefton*,[17] a case which concerned this point) R makes a covenant with E that restricts the use of the land to horse racing and agriculture, and suppose that after E sold Greenacre to R, R could show that there had been no intention that the burden of the covenant should run with the land. Furthermore, suppose that E retained no land for the benefit of which R's covenant could be given. In this case when R sells Greenacre to S the burden will not run with the land into the hands of S under the principles we have considered above. But suppose that R had covenanted with E that he would not sell the land during E's lifetime without requiring the purchaser to covenant that the land would not be used otherwise than as R had covenanted. In this case, if R contracted to sell the land to S, but without requiring S to make the covenant, R would be acting in breach of contract. It seems[18] that E could obtain an injunction to restrain R from acting in breach of the covenant with him; and also, if E could show that S was aware of the covenant between himself and R, he (E) could obtain an injunction to restrain S from committing the tort of inducing a breach of contract. If E was unable to apply for and obtain an injunction before the date of the conveyance to S, E could sue R for damages for breach of contract, and S for damages for the tort of inducing a breach of contract. Thus S may find that even though the burden of R's covenant does not bind him under the principles we have considered, he may nevertheless be liable to E for damages in tort. (In *Tophams Ltd v Earl of Sefton*[19] R's covenant was not to 'cause or permit' the land to be

14   Subject to what is said later, Chapter 25.
15   Section 2(5), Class D (ii).
16   Section 2. The Act has been repealed but the jurisdiction is now conferred by Supreme Court Act 1981, s 50.
17   [1967] 1 AC 50, [1966] 1 All ER 1039, HL.
18   See *Tophams Ltd v Earl of Sefton* [1967] 1 AC 50, [1966] 1 All ER 1039, HL.
19   Supra.

used otherwise than for horse racing or agriculture. The House of Lords held that by selling the land to S, R would not be 'causing or permitting' the land to be so used, and therefore E failed in his application for an injunction to restrain the sale.)

In dealing with the position between E and S, it is relevant to ask what result ensues if R conveys Greenacre to S and then E conveys Redacre to F. S acts in breach of the covenant. Can E sue S? (Ie can a covenantee sue an assignee of the covenantor if the covenantee has parted with his land?)

For the burden to be enforceable against S, not only must the covenant have been made by S for the benefit of land retained by E at the time of the covenant, but also the plaintiff seeking to enforce the covenant (E) must show that at the time of the action he retains land for the benefit of which the covenant was given.[20] If E has sold Redacre to F this conditon is not satisfied and so E cannot sue S.[1]

If E had leased Redacre to F, the position might be different. For example, if E had leased Redacre to F for a short lease and the breach of the covenant might damage E's reversion, E might be granted an injunction to restrain the breach.[2] But if the lease had been for, say, 100 years, E might be refused an injunction.

As mentioned earlier in this chapter, in 1984 the Law Commission made recommendations[3] that would create a new interest in land called a land obligation. This would be more akin to an easement than to a covenant, but the effect of the implementation of the recommendation would be to enable a positive obligation to be enforced against transferees of the servient land. Covenants entered into before the introduction of the new provisions would continue to take effect as under existing law.

Situation 3: The benefit

The benefit of a covenant was enforceable by an assignee of the land (F) at common law before it became enforceable in equity; indeed it was enforceable at common law before even the birth of equity. In agreeing to lend its aid to the enforcement of the benefit of a covenant by an assignee of the land equity followed the law; but equity imposed different conditions.

COMMON LAW

The conditions necessary for the benefit of a covenant to be enforceable by F at common law are as follows:

---

20 *Re Union of London and Smith's Bank Ltd's Conveyance* [1933] Ch 611; (M & B).
1 *Chambers v Randall* [1923] 1 Ch 149.
2 See *Hall v Ewin* (1887) 37 Ch D 74.
3 *Transfer of Land: The Law of Positive and Restrictive Covenants* (Law Com No 127), amplifying recommendations in the Commission's *Report on Restrictive Covenants* (Law Com No 11, 1967).

1. The covenant must 'touch and concern' E's land.[4] This means that the covenant must be for the benefit of E's land at the time of the covenant, and not, eg, be merely for the personal advantage of E. 'It is first necessary to ascertain from the deed that the covenant is one which "touches and concerns" the land, that is, it must either affect the land as regards mode of occupation, or it must be such as per se, and not merely from collateral circumstances, affects the value of the land'.[5] Many of the covenants commonly entered into by vendors or purchasers, eg not to use the land for anything other than residential purposes, not to build within a certain distance of the boundary, not to keep certain animals, not to carry on a particular trade or business,[6] 'touch and concern' the land of the person with whom the covenant is made. It is not necessary for the benefit to E's land to be apparent from the wording of the covenant. The benefit can be proved by extrinsic evidence.[7]

2. At the time of the covenant, E must have held a legal estate in the land.[8]

3. In the case of a covenant made before 1926, it is necessary for F to show that he holds the same legal estate as E.[9] This is because before 1926 the benefit was regarded as being attached to the legal estate, not to the land as such.[10] Thus, if the covenant was made before 1926, and F holds merely a lease of the land from E, he cannot enforce the covenant. This requirement does not exist in the case of covenants made after 1925.[11]

4. The land for the benefit of which the covenant was made must be identified, or must be capable of being identified.[12]

5. (a) There must have been an intention that the benefit of the covenant should run with the land:[13] to borrow a word that is normally used in the context of the benefit running in equity, there must have been an intention that the benefit should be 'annexed' to E's land.

(b) Alternatively, E must have expressly assigned the benefit of the covenant to F. But for the benefit to pass to F by express assignment, the assignment

---

4   *Rogers v Hosegood* [1900] 2 Ch 388; (M & B).
5   Per Tucker LJ, *Smith and Snipes Hall Farm Ltd v River Douglas Catchment Board* [1949] 2 KB 500 at 506; (M & B).
6   *Newton Abbot Co-operative Society v Williamson and Treadgold Ltd* [1952] Ch 286, [1952] 1 All ER 279; (M & B).
7   *Smith and Snipes Hall Farm Ltd v River Douglas Catchment Board* [1949] 2 KB 500 at 506.
8   *Webb v Russell* (1789) 3 Term Rep 393.
9   *Smith and Snipes Hall Farm Ltd v River Douglas Catchment Board*, supra, 516; *Westhoughton UDC v Wigan Coal and Iron Co Ltd* [1919] 1 Ch 159 at 170-171.
10 The requirement that F must hold the same legal estate as E was not a feature of the original common law. In an early case in which the benefit passed, E held a fee simple and F held a fee tail; *The Prior's Case* (1368) YB 42 Edw 3 fo 3 pl 14.
11 The change is regarded as having been effected by LPA 1925, s 78; See M & W, p 766. *Smith and Snipes Hall Farm Ltd v River Douglas Catchment Board* [[1949] 2 KB 500, [1949] 2 All ER 179; (M & B).
12 As in *Re Ballard's Conveyance* [1937] Ch 473, [1937] 2 All ER 691.
13 *Rogers v Hosegood* [1900] 2 Ch 388 at 396; (M & B); *Shayler v Woolf* [1946] Ch 320; *Smith and Snipes Hall Farm Ltd v River Douglas Catchment Board* [[1949] 2 KB 500 at 506, [1949] 2 All ER 179 at 183.

must have taken place after 1873,[14] the assignment must have been made at the same time as the transfer of the land, and the assignment must comply with s 136 of the Law of Property Act 1925 (in particular, the assignment must be in writing, signed by E, and notice of the assignment must be given to R). Further, E must have transferred the whole of Redacre to F, not merely part of it.

Looking back over the conditions imposed by common law, it will be seen that the benefit of a covenant is not enforceable where, inter alia, at the time of the covenant E held merely an equitable interest in the land;[15] where, in the case of a covenant made before 1926, F is, eg, merely a tenant of E's; and where E transferred to F only part of the land for the benefit of which the covenant was given.[16]

Since, in order to secure compliance with the covenant, what F is likely to want is an injunction, and since this is an equitable remedy, F will in practice concern himself with whether the benefit has passed to him in equity. Damages, it is true, could be obtainable in an action at common law, but damages can be awarded also by equity (eg coupled with the making of an injunction).[17] So if F is suing R he is unlikely to bother himself with the common law conditions. He will go straight to equity. Another reason why the common law conditions are today of little practical significance is that it is commonly the case that F will be seeking to enforce the covenant not against R, but against a transferee from R, S, and since, as we know, the burden of R's covenant can pass to S only in equity, if F is to sue S his action must lie in equity. So it is a misconception to think in terms of F hoping to enforce the covenant at common law and then, finding that he cannot do so, falling back on an action in equity, as a second best. F, in practice, goes direct to equity and seeks to show that equity's conditions for the benefit to be enforceable by him have been satisfied.

EQUITY

What, then, are equity's conditions? Until relatively recently it was accepted, and established by a long line of cases of high authority, that for the benefit to pass in equity two conditions had to be satisfied, the second condition consisting of two alternatives. The decision of the Court of Appeal in *Federated Homes Ltd v Mill Lodge Properties Ltd*[18] has indicated that the second condition does not, since 1925, need to be complied with. We shall state the conventional view of the law[19] and then deal with *Federated Homes* and its implications.

---

14 Originally the benefit of a covenant could not be assigned at common law. The reason was that the benefit of a covenant is one form of chose in action, and choses in action were not assignable at common law. The Judicature Act 1873, s 25(6), reproduced by the Law of Property Act 1925, s 136, permitted choses in action to be assigned in law.
15 *Fairclough v Marshall* (1878) 4 Ex D 37.
16 *Re Union of London and Smith's Bank Ltd's Conveyance* [1933] Ch 611 at 630.
17 See Chapter 5.
18 [1980] 1 All ER 371, [1980] 1 WLR 594, CA; (M & B).
19 As applied in *Jamaica Mutual Life Assurance Society v Hillsborough Ltd* [1989] 1 WLR 1101 (PC, on appeal from the Court of Appeal of Jamaica).

1. The first condition imposed by equity is that the covenant must touch and concern E's land. The principle here is the same as at common law.

2. The second condition (the condition on which doubts have been cast by *Federated Homes*) is that the benefit will pass to F only[20] if he can show that:

(a) the benefit was annexed to the land at the time of the covenant;[1] or,
(b) the benefit was expressly assigned to him by E.[2]

Annexation

If the benefit becomes annexed to land then it becomes, as it were, dug into the soil, and thus passes with the land into the hands of all subsequent holders.

The conditions for annexation to occur are (according to the traditional view) as follows.

1. R's covenant must show an intention that the benefit should become annexed to the land, so that it runs with the land into whoever's hands the land passes. The necessary intention is shown by the covenant being expressed to be made for the benefit of E in his capacity as owner of Redacre[3] or is expressed to be 'for the benefit' of Redacre.[4] In *Rogers v Hosegood* it was held that a covenant by R 'with intent that the covenants may enure for the benefit of [E] and his successors and assigns and others claiming under him or them to all or any of his land adjoining,' resulted in the benefit of the covenant being annexed to his land, and this form of wording has come to be used by conveyancers as a means of securing annexation.

2. The land for the benefit of which the covenant is taken must be either identified[5] or be capable of identification. Extrinsic evidence is admissible to show the land intended.[6]

3. (i)(a) The benefit which R's covenant confers on Redacre must be capable of benefiting the whole of Redacre (whether it does so will depend on the size of Redacre and on the nature of the covenant[7]), and, (b) the whole of Redacre must have been conveyed to F, or

(ii) if (a) or (b) (or both[8]) is not satisfied, the covenant must be intended to be for the benefit of each and every part of Redacre. If this intention is

---

20 *Reid v Bickerstaff* [1909] 2 Ch 305; (M & B) (no annexation, no assignment; no passing of benefit).
1   As in *Newton Abbot Co-operative Society v Williams and Treadgold Ltd* [1952] Ch 286, [1952] 1 All ER 279; (M & B).
2   As in *Stilwell v Blackman* [1968] Ch 508, [1967] 3 All ER 514.
3   *Osborne v Bradley* [1903] 2 Ch 446 at 450.
4   *Drake v Gray* [1936] Ch 451 at 456.
5   *Renals v Cowlishaw* (1879) 11 Ch D 866.
6   *Newton Abbot Co-operative Society Ltd v Williams and Treadgold Ltd* [1952] Ch 286 at 289.
7   Where the benefit, or lack of benefit, to Redacre cannot be demonstrated decisively, and the matter is one merely of opinion, then the court must decide whether the view that the covenant was and is for the benefit of Redacre as a whole is a view that could reasonably be held: if the court decides that the view is one that could reasonably be held, then the requirement is satisfied; *Wrotham Park Estate Co Ltd v Parkside Homes Ltd* [1974] 2 All ER 321, [1974] 1 WLR 798.
8   Neither (i) nor (ii) was satisfied in *Re Ballard's Conveyance* [1937] Ch 473 and no annexation occurred.

present the benefit then becomes annexed to that part of Redacre that is in fact benefited.[9] If the land which F receives is such a part, he can enforce the covenant. Formerly it was held to be necessary to indicate expressly that the covenant was intended to benefit each and every part of the land, as by the covenant being expressed to be for the benefit of 'the whole or any part of Redacre' or for Redacre 'and every part thereof'.[10] In *Federated Homes Ltd v Mill Lodge Properties Ltd*[11] Brightman LJ (in a part of his judgment subsidiary to the main issue in that case[12]) said[13] 'I find the idea of the annexation of a covenant to the whole of the land but not to a part of it a difficult conception fully to grasp. I would have thought, if the benefit of a covenant is, on a proper construction of a document, annexed to the land, prima facie it is annexed to every part thereof, unless the contrary clearly appears.' It therefore appears that (if the decision is followed on this point) there is no longer any need for the benefit of R's covenant to be expressed to be 'for the whole or any part' of Redacre. There is a rebuttable presumption that such is the intention, but the principle nevertheless remains that if F receives only part of E's land, he cannot enforce the covenant unless the covenant benefits that part of the land which he has received.

It is possible that in some instances annexation may occur without the existence of express words, where it is to be inferred from surrounding circumstances that it was the intention of the parties that the benefit of the covenant should be annexed to the land of the covenantee.[14] Annexation occurs in this way where a building scheme exists. Building schemes are considered later.[15]

Assignment

If the benefit is not annexed to the land, it may pass to F by being assigned to him (as a chose in action) by E.

Whether E transfers the whole or merely part of Redacre to F, if he is to assign the benefit of R's covenant to F, the assignment must be contemporaneous with the transfer of the land.[16]

If the benefit of R's covenant is not annexed to E's land, and E dies, leaving the land to F, then the benefit of the covenant vests in E's personal representative and can (and normally will) be assigned by him to F.[17]

9   *Marquess of Zetland v Driver*, supra.
10   *Re Selwyn's Conveyance* [1967] Ch 674 at 689.
11   [1980] 1 WLR 594; (M & B).
12   See infra.
13   At p 606.
14   In *Shropshire County Council v Edwards* (1982) 46 P & CR 270, it was held that it was to be inferred, despite the absence of express words, that annexation had occurred. See [1984] JPL 847 (G. H. Newsom).
15   See p 399.
16   *Re Union of London and Smith's Bank Ltd's Conveyance* [1933] Ch 611 at 632.
17   *Newton Abbot Co-operative Society v Williams and Treadgold Ltd* [1952] Ch 286, [1952] 1 All ER 279; (M & B); *Earl of Leicester v Wells-next-the-Sea UDC* [1973] Ch 110, [1972] 3 All ER 77.

The difference between the benefit of a covenant having become annexed to the land and the benefit being assigned (by E to F) is illustrated by the position which results if F transfers the land to G. If the benefit of the covenant has been annexed to the land, then the benefit passes automatically to G. But if the benefit has been merely assigned by E to F, when F transfers Redacre to G, the benefit does not pass to G. G does not acquire the benefit of the covenant unless F makes a fresh assignment of the benefit to him. And if G transferred the land to H the position would be the same. Thus annexation indicates that the benefit passes automatically. Assignment indicates that a positive step must be taken to transfer the benefit each time the land changes hands.[18]

Federated Homes Ltd v Mill Lodge Properties Ltd[19]

In dealing with the running of the burden of the covenant we saw that as a result of s 79 of the Law of Property Act 1925, the burden of R's covenant is to be deemed to be intended to run with R's land, unless a contrary intention is shown. Section 78(1) of the Act provides: 'A covenant relating to any land of the covenantee shall be deemed to be made with the covenantee and his successors in title and the persons deriving title under him or them, and shall have effect as if such successors and other persons were expressed.' It might be thought the effect of this section was, if E transferred the land to F, to make R's covenant enforceable by F (and any subsequent transferees of the land) without any need for the covenant to be either annexed to the land, or assigned by E to F. This, however, was never the interpretation placed upon the section. Never, that is, until *Federated Homes*. The Court of Appeal in this case held that the effect of s 78 was to make the benefit of a covenant enforceable at the suit of any successor in title to E, irrespective of annexation or assignment.[20] The facts in the case were these.

In 1970, M Ltd obtained planning permission to build 1,250 houses on land which he owned. In February 1971 he sold part of the land, referred to as the 'blue' land, to the defendant company, requiring the defendant to covenant not to build more than 300 houses (so allowing 950 houses to be built on the land which M Ltd retained). In March 1971 M Ltd sold two plots out of the land it retained (the 'green' land and the 'red' land) to B Ltd. In the case of each transfer M Ltd expressly assigned to B Ltd the benefit of the defendant's covenant. B Ltd conveyed the green land to the plaintiff, the conveyance containing an express assignment of the benefit of the defendant's covenant. Shortly afterwards, B Ltd conveyed the red land to a purchaser, assigning the

---

18   *Re Pinewood Estate, Farnborough* [1958] Ch 280, [1957] 2 All ER 517; (M & B).
19   [1980] 1 All ER 371, [1980] 1 WLR 594; (M & B). (1980) 44 Conv (NS) 216 (A. Sydenham); (1980) 43 MLR 445 (D. Hayton);(1981) 97 LQR 32; (1982) 98 LQR 202; [1980] JPL 371; [1982] JPL 295; (G. H. Newsom)(1982) 2 LS 53 (D. J. Hurst).
20   The precursor of s 78(1), s 58(1) of the Conveyancing Act 1881, having a more limited wording, does not have this effect; *Sainsbury plc v Enfield London Borough Council* [1989] 2 All ER 817, [1989] 1 WLR 590; [1989] Conv 355, 358 (JEM); [1991] Conv 52 (S. Goulding).

benefit of the covenant. In 1975 the purchaser conveyed the red land to the plaintiff, the benefit of the covenant not in this case being assigned. In 1975 the plaintiff discovered that the defendant had obtained planning permission to build an additional 32 houses on the blue land. Since the total of 1,250 houses for the entire estate remained in force, the building of additional houses on the blue land would reduce the density at which the plaintiff could build on the red and the green land. The plaintiff therefore sought an injunction to restrain the defendant from building to a greater density than a total of 300 houses on the blue land. In the High Court the injunction was granted. The Court of Appeal affirmed the grant.

The Court of Appeal held that since, with the conveyances of the green land there had been an unbroken chain of assignments (from M Ltd to B Ltd, and from B Ltd to the plaintiff), the plaintiff was entitled to enforce the covenant against the defendant. This being so, there was no need for the court to consider whether the plaintiff was entitled to enforce the covenant in respect of the red land. The court, however, elected to do so. The benefit of the defendant's covenant, Brightman LJ held, had become annexed to the entire estate (and so including the red land) by virtue of s 78(1). Megaw and Browne LJJ agreed. In the course of his judgment Brightman LJ said:[1] 'If, as the language of s 78 implies, a covenant relating to land which is restrictive of the user thereof is enforceable at the suit of (1) a successor in title of the covenantee, (2) a person deriving title under the covenantee or under his successors in title and (3) the owner or occupier of the land intended to be benefited by the covenant, it must, in my view, follow that the covenant runs with the land, because *ex hypothesi* every successor in title to the land, every derivative proprietor of the land and every other owner and occupier has a right by statute to the covenant. In other words, if the condition precedent of s 78 is satisfied – that is to say, there exists a covenant which touches and concerns the land of the covenantee – that covenant runs with the land for the benefit of his successors in title, persons deriving title under him or them and other owners and occupiers.'

Thus the effect of the decision is that neither annexation nor assignment is needed for the benefit to run. Provided that the benefit touches and concerns the covenantee's land, then, by reason of s 78, the benefit runs with the land. The decision has been both criticised[2] and supported.[3]

Since s 78 (unlike s 79) contains no words permitting the section to be excluded by contrary intention, it seemed from the decision in *Federated Homes*

---

1   At 605.
2   (1981) 97 LQR 32; (1982) 98 LQR 202 (G. H. Newsom); (1980) 43 MLR 445 (D. Hayton). ('It does with respect, seem really quite extraordinary to suggest that s 78 should have effect whether or not the parties intended an annexation when, right back into the last century, annexation has always been said to be a question of intention, and that was reiterated in the Act of 1922. As to s 79 where, with this exception, the wording is substantially identical, it would even be extraordinary if it were correct that it involves merely conveyancing shorthand (which is what the noble and learned Lords said of it), but that s 78, in substantially the same words only the other way round, has an automatic effect of creating an annexation irrespective of intention. Once these facts are analysed and perceived, it really seems almost impossible that the view of Brightman LJ can be correct.' G. H. Newsom, op cit).
3   (1982) 2 LS 53 (D. J. Hurst).

that in the case of covenants entered into after 1925, the benefit runs with the land, irrespective of the wishes of the parties, irrespective even of an intention that the benefit should not run.

That this is not in fact the position was shown in a case heard not long after *Federated Homes*. *Roake v Chadha*[4] concerned a covenant entered into in 1934 against the building of more than one dwelling house on a certain plot. The covenant stated ' ... the purchaser ... covenants with the vendor but so that this covenant shall not enure for the benefit of any owner or subsequent purchaser ... unless the benefit of this covenant shall be expressly assigned ... ' The covenantee's land subsequently passed to a purchaser who sought to enforce the covenant. Paul Baker J held that s 78 could not take effect irrespective of the terms of the covenant. Where, as in the instant case, the covenant stated that the benefit was not to pass unless expressly assigned, then s 78 did not operate to make it so pass. Since the words used showed an express intention that the benefit should not be annexed to the land, and since there had been no assignment, the covenantee's successor in title could not enforce the covenant.

Does *Roake v Chadha* restore the law to the position before *Federated Homes*? By no means. The matter can be summarised by saying before the two decisions, the benefit only passed if, as it were, something was *done*, ie if there was assignment or annexation.[5] After the two decisions, the benefit passes provided that *nothing* is done to stop it passing, as by the inclusion of the words used in *Roake v Chadha*.

Finally in this section we must ask what result ensues if E conveys Redacre to F and then R conveys Greenacre to S. S acts in breach of the covenant. Can F sue R? (Ie can an assignee of the covenantee sue the covenantor, notwithstanding that the covenantor has parted with the land?) The position is that if the benefit of R's covenant has passed to F then it would seem that F can sue R. But his only remedy would be in damages. He would not be able to obtain an injunction against R because, since R no longer holds the land, this remedy would not be appropriate.

Because of the possibility of an action against him, R may, when he parts with the land to S, require S to indemnify him against any damages that he, R, may find himself liable to pay in consequence of a breach of the covenant after he has parted with the land.

Situation 4: Benefit and burden

E conveys Redacre to F. R conveys Greenacre to S. (It is immaterial which conveyance takes place first.) S acts in breach of the covenant. Can F sue S? (Ie can an assignee of the covenantee sue an assignee of the covenantor?)

Consider the diagram of Situation 4 below. It is clear that in order for F to be able to sue S, two conditions must be satisfied:

---

4   [1983] 3 All ER 503, [1984] 1 WLR 40; (M & B); [1984] JPL 847 (G. H. Newsom); [1985] Conv 177 (P. N. Todd).
5   Albeit annexation inferred from the circumstances. See p 393, supra.

(a) the benefit of the covenant must have passed to F; and
(b) the burden of the covenant must have passed to S.

We have already considered the conditions which must be satisfied for the burden and for the benefit to pass to S and F respectively. If both these sets of conditions are satisfied, F can sue S. (And we may note here that the party in the position of F may be not only an assignee of the fee simple, but also a lessee from E, or a mortgagee of the land from E.[6])

But it must be remembered that since the burden can only pass to S in equity, F's action against S can only be in equity. The fact that the benefit of the covenant can pass to F at common law may give F a right of action at common law against R, but it will not give him any right of action at common law against S.

Since F's action against S lies in equity only, it is subject to the same limitations that we considered in connection with E's action against S in Situation 2; in particular, in order to bind S, R's covenant must be registered as a land charge under the Land Charges Act 1972.

So far in this Situation we have spoken of F suing S, but suppose that Greenacre passed from S to T, and then from T to U; and that Redacre passed from F to G, and from G to H, and so to I, and then to J. Can J sue U?

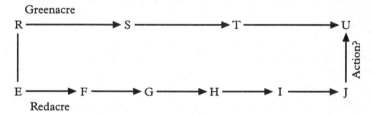

In this case the same principles apply. All we need to know is:

has the benefit passed to J?
has the burden passed to U?

If the answer to both is Yes, J can sue U.

Thus once R and E have parted with Greenacre and Redacre, the number of times that Greenacre and Redacre change hands does not affect the ability of the holder of Redacre to sue the holder of Greenacre. An important corollary follows from this. Suppose that Greenacre had passed from R to S, and then to T; and that Redacre had passed from E to F, and then to G. If the necessary conditions had been satisfied for the burden and the benefit to pass to T and G respectively, then G could sue T, but neither E nor F could sue T, since, having parted with Redacre, they no longer hold land capable of being benefited by the covenant.[7]

---

6   See *Regent Oil Co Ltd v J A Gregory (Hatch End) Ltd* [1966] Ch 402 at 433.
7   *Re Union of London and Smith's Bank Ltd's Conveyance* [1933] Ch 611.

Situation 5: Section 56

Before R entered into the covenant with E, E conveyed Blueacre (a plot of land adjacent to both Redacre and Greenacre) to B. R acts in breach of the covenant. Can B sue R?

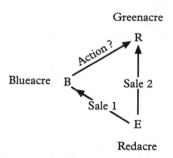

From what has been said so far it would seem that the answer must be, No. For example, let us ask – has the benefit of the covenant passed to B under the principles we have considered? No, because the benefit of R's covenant was not annexed to Blueacre, which E had parted with by the time R made the covenant with E; nor has the benefit of the covenant being assigned by E to B. Is there privity of contract between B and R which would enable B to sue R? It would seem that no such privity exists. The covenant was made between E and R, not between B and R.

It would therefore seem that B cannot sue R. At common law this is in fact the position. It was a rule of common law that only the parties to a deed could sue on it. Thus E, as a party to the deed, could sue R; and B, who was not a party to the deed, could not.

The position is altered by statute. Section 56 of the Law of Property Act 1925[8] provides that a person may take, inter alia, the benefit of any covenant concerning property notwithstanding the fact that he is not named as a party to the instrument. To take advantage of the section the person seeking to enforce the covenant must show that he is the person indicated by the covenant and that he was in existence at the time of the covenant.[9] The learned authors of Megarry and Wade consider that 'The true aim of s 56 seems to be not to allow a third party to sue on a contract merely because it is made for his benefit; the contract must purport to be made *with* him'.[10] This requirement

---

8 Replacing and extending the Real Property Act 1845, s 5.
9 *Re Ecclesiastical Comrs for England's Conveyance* [1936] Ch 430; (M & B).
10 M & W, p 763; *Re Foster* [1938] 3 All ER 357 at 365; *Lyus v Prowsa Developments Ltd* [1982] 1 WLR 1044 at 1049; *Amsprop Trading Ltd v Harris Distribution Ltd* (1996) Times, 13 November (not sufficient for a person in position of B to be named in the covenant, the covenant must purport to be made with him).

would be satisfied if the covenant by R was expressed to be made, not only with E, but also with 'the owners for the time being' of Blueacre.[11] Here B is not a party to the deed (ie he did not sign it) and he is not named personally, but, as he is the owner of Blueacre at the time of the covenant, the covenant does purport to be made with him. The result is that B is enabled, by the section, to sue R.

Thus as a result of s 56, B becomes a covenantee. His status in this respect is no different from that of E. There is an important result of this fact. Since B is a covenantee, if he sells Blueacre to C, then subject to the conditions considered in Situation 3 being satisfied, the benefit of R's covenant will pass from B to C, and C will be able to sue R.

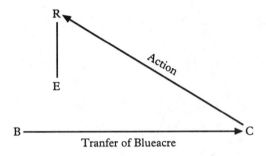

Further, if R conveys Greenacre to S, and if the relevant conditions[12] are satisfied for the burden of the covenant to run with the land into the hands of S, then C can sue S.[13]

Situation 6: Schemes of Development

V buys a piece of land, divides it into plots, and builds a house on each plot. He sells off the houses on the new estate to various purchasers. Each purchaser is required to covenant not to make any alteration to his house which would increase the maximum cubic area by more than 5%; not to use the premises for any purpose other than as a dwelling house; not to keep other than domestic animals on the premises; and not to put dustbins, and not to hang washing, at the front of the house. By this means, V has imposed a set of regulations on the estate. (It will be noted that the first two covenants resemble the kind of controls imposed by a planning authority under the Town and Country Planning Acts.)

11 The requirement was satisfied in *Stromdale and Ball Ltd v Burden* [1952] Ch 223; (M & B); but was not satisfied in *White v Bijo Mansions Ltd* [1938] Ch 351, [1938] 1 All ER 546; (M & B).
12 See p 383.
13 As in *Re Ecclesiastical Comrs for England's Conveyance* [1936] Ch 430; (M & B).

So long as V retains any land on the estate, he can ensure that his intentions with regard to his estate are observed.[14] Let us assume, for simplicity, that there are only three plots on the estate. V sells plot 1 to P_1, plot 2 to P_2 and plot 3 to P_3. V retains no land on the estate. The question we now face is this: if one owner acts in breach of one of the covenants, can another owner enforce the covenant against him?

When a purchaser was considering whether he wanted to live in one of V's houses, he would have taken into account not only its design and appearance, but also the nature of the neighbourhood. There is no use, he would have reflected, in his buying a house if the neighbourhood loses its character. So the amount that he would be prepared to pay to V for a house on the estate would be influenced by whether he could be sure that no one on the estate would be allowed, inter alia, to keep pigs.

V, for his part, will also have been anxious that any purchaser should be able to stop anyone on the estate keeping pigs. V might or might not be interested in his reputation as a builder of select estates, but unless buyers can be assured that the character of the neighbourhood will be preserved, V will not get his money; or, at any rate, he will not get such a good price.

These are the reasons why it is important both to V and to the various purchasers that it should be possible for the owner of any house on the estate to be able to enforce the covenants that protect the character of the neighbourhood against any other owner.

If the conditions are satisfied for a Scheme of Development (sometimes termed a Building Scheme) to exist, then the result is that the owner of any plot on the estate can bring an action against any other owner in order to prevent him breaking covenants entered into by the first purchasers of each plot on the estate. The covenants thus become in effect a set of local by-laws for the estate.

The same result could be achieved by application of the principles considered in Situations 3 and 5, but if a Scheme of Development exists there is no need to show that the conditions in Situations 3 and 5 have been satisfied.

Schemes of Development can be traced back into the last century.[15] The first full statement of the doctrine is in *Elliston v Reacher*.[16] The conditions to be satisfied today are as follows.

1. The area to which the scheme relates must be clearly defined.[17]

---

14 V may impose restrictive covenants (a) to supplement planning controls; or (b) because planning controls would not impose the kind of restriction he intends; or (c) because it may be easier to enforce a covenant than to persuade a local authority to enforce a planning control.

15 *Western v MacDermot* (1866) LR 1 Eq 499; *Nottingham Patent Brick and Tile Co v Butler* (1886) 16 QBD 778.

16 [1908] 2 Ch 374 at 384; affd [1980] 2 Ch 665; (M & B).

17 *Elliston v Reacher*, ante; *Reid v Bickerstaff* [1909] 2 Ch 305 (conditions not satisfied).

2. V must have laid out the estate in plots,[18] or sold off plots of a size which purchasers required.[19]

3. V must have extracted restrictive covenants from P_1, P_2 and P_3.[20]

4. The covenant must have been made by each purchasers on the basis that it was to be enforceable by and against every other purchaser: there must be reciprocity of obligations between the purchasers of the plots.[1] This condition would be satisfied if the covenant stated expressly that this was to be so. But express words to this effect are not essential: it is sufficient if evidence can be adduced to show that a purchaser must have realised, from the circumstances, that it was intended that the covenant should be enforceable by any other purchaser;[2] for example, by showing that the purchaser had seen a plan of the estate on which there was a statement that a covenant by one purchaser was to be enforceable by other purchasers.

5. V must have intended that the restrictions should be for the benefit of all the plots sold.[3] This intention may be expressed, or inferred from the surrounding circumstances.[4]

If these five conditions are satisfied, a Scheme of Development exists and the covenants are mutually enforceable between P_1, P_2 and P_3, and any person to whom a plot, or part of a plot,[5] subsequently passes (irrespective of whether the subsequent holders themselves entered into covenants).

Where the conditions set out above are not satisfied, the same result may nevertheless obtain if conditions analogous to those above are satisfied, the present tendency being to give effect to the intention of the parties. But for a Scheme to exist there must initially have been at least a common intention that the covenants should be mutually enforceable and a common interest in their being so enforceable.[5] For example, in *Re Dolphin's Conveyance*,[6] the covenants were taken not by a common vendor, but by several vendors. Because

18   In *Elliston v Reacher*, ante, Parker J stated that the vendor must have 'laid out his estate ... for sale in lots subject to restrictions intended to be imposed on all the lots, and which ... are consistent ... only with some general scheme of development'. It is difficult to see how the act of laying out an estate (either on the drawing board or on the ground) can be shown to have been done 'subject to restrictions'. From *Baxter v Four Oaks Properties Ltd* (infra) it seems that it is sufficient if the vendor acquired the necessary intention at any time prior to the first sale.

19   *Baxter v Four Oaks Properties Ltd* [1965] Ch 816, [1965] 1 Al ER 906.

20   *Kingsbury v LW Anderson Ltd* (1979) 40 P & CR 136.

1   *Elliston v Reacher*, supra; *Jamaica Mutual Life Assurance Society v Hillsborough Ltd* [1989] 1 WLR 1101; *Emile Elias & Co Ltd v Pine Groves Ltd* [1993] 1 WLR 305 (lack of uniformity in the covenants imposed on lots of similar nature indicated absence of intention to create reciprocally enforceable rights).

2   See *Emile Elias & Co Ltd v Pine Groves Ltd*, supra, (plaintiff seeking to uphold enforceability of building scheme failed to prove that all purchasers aware of all the plots affected; no building scheme created).

3   *Elliston v Reacher*, supra.

4   As in *Eagling v Gardner* [1970] 2 All ER 838.

5   *Brunner v Greenslade* [1971] Ch 993, [1970] 3 All ER 833.

6   *Re Dolphin's Conveyance* [1970] 2 All ER 664 at 670 and 671; (M & B).

there had been the necessary common intention and common interest the covenants were held to be mutually enforceable.

When dealing with Situation 2 we said that for the burden of a covenant to run with the land, the covenant must be made for the benefit of land retained by a covenantee but that this condition did not have to be satisfied if a building scheme existed. We are now in a position to see why this is to. When V sold plot 3 to P_3, V retained no land, but this does not prevent the burden of P_3's covenant from running with the land (ie plot 3) into the hands of P_3's successors in title.

It should be noted that restrictive covenants made after 1925 as part of a Scheme of Development are registrable in the same way as restrictive covenants made outside any such scheme.

This completes our examination of the six situations set out on p 381. We now turn to consider certain matters which concern covenants generally.

COVENANTS WHICH DO NOT CONCERN THE LAND OF ONE OF THE PARTIES

We have seen (Situation 3) that for the benefit of a covenant to run with the land, the covenant must 'touch and concern' E's land. We have seen also that for the burden to run with the land (Situation 2) the covenant must be for the protection of E's land. The consequences of this are as follows.

1. If R's covenant is for the benefit of E personally the result is that:

(a) If E transfers Redacre to F, the benefit of R's covenant does not pass to F.
(b) If R transfers Greenacre to S the burden of R's covenant does not bind S.

2. If R's covenant affects R personally (eg a covenant by R that he will pay for the upkeep of certain property on or adjoining Redacre) the result is that:

(a) provided that R's covenant 'touches and concerns' E's land, the benefit of R's covenant can run with Redacre into the hands of F[7] (this is so at common law[8] as well as in equity);
(b) if R's covenant is positive, the burden of R's covenant will not run with Greenacre into the hands of S. (Even if it is negative it is unlikely to run with Greenacre into the hands of S since, as it is personal to R, it will not be deemed (by virtue of s 79[9]) to have been made by R on behalf of himself, his successors in title and the persons deriving title under him or them.)

POSITIVE COVENANTS[10]

If R makes a positive covenant with E, the consequences are as follows:

---

7   *Shayler v Woolf* [1946] Ch 320, [1946] 2 All ER 54.
8   *The Prior's Case* (1368) YB 42 Edw 3 fo 3 pl 14; *Smith and Snipes Hall Farm Ltd v River Douglas Catchment Board* [1949] 2 KB 500, [1949] 2 All ER 179; (M & B).
9   See p 386.
10   See (1954) 18 Conv (NS) 546 (E. H. Scamell).

1. E can enforce the covenant against R (Situation 1).
2. If E transfers his land to F, F can sue R (Situation 3).
3. If R transfer his land to S, E cannot sue S (Situation 2).
4. If E transfers his land to F, and R transfers his land to S, F cannot sue S (Situation 4).

EXTINGUISHMENT OF RESTRICTIVE COVENANTS

Just as an easement is extinguished where the dominant and servient tenements pass into the hands of the same person, so also a restrictive covenant is extinguished where the fee simple in Redacre and in Greenacre come to be held by the same person.[11] (There is no extinguishment, however, where the covenants exist under a scheme of development.[12])

DISCHARGE OF RESTRICTIVE COVENANTS[13]

Let us suppose that in 1930 E, the owner of two adjacent fields Redacre and Greenacre, sold Greenacre to R, who covenanted that Greenacre would not be used except for residential purposes. By 1990 Greenacre has passed into the hands of V and Redacre has passed into the hands of K. In the years which had elapsed since R's covenant, the nature of the neighbourhood in which Greenacre lay had changed. In 1930 Greenacre had been open farm land on the outskirts of a town. By 1997 the town had expanded. Greenacre Lodge, built by R, stands rotting, surrounded by its high wall, the garden overgrown with weeds. Factories and warehouses lie on all sides. W wants to buy Greenacre in order to build an extension to his factory. If W buys Greenacre, can K stop him building the factory? If the covenant was registered, yes. Is it desirable that because of a covenant made in 1930, K should be able to prevent Greenacre being put to good use? Perhaps not.

In order to resolve this kind of problem (and assuming that K declines to execute a deed discharging the covenant) W may[14] apply to the Lands Tribunal[15] under s 84 of the Law of Property Act 1925[16] for the discharge of the covenant.[17] The Tribunal has power, at its discretion, to discharge the covenant completely, or to modify it. If K would suffer loss by reason of the discharging or

---

11   *Re Tiltwood, Sussex* [1978] Ch 269, [1978] 2 All ER 1091.
12   *Texaco Antilles Ltd v Kernochan* [1973] AC 609, [1973] 2 All ER 118; (M & B).
13   For proposals for reform, see Law Commission, *Transfer of Land: Obsolete Restrictive Covenants*, Law Com No 201.
14   LPA 1925, s 84(1) as amended by LPA 1969, s 28 and Sch 3; (1986) 49 MLR 195 (P. Polden).
15   Lands Tribunal Act 1949, s 3.
16   For proposals for reform, see Law Com No 201, *Transfer of Land: Obsolete Restrictive Covenants*, [1992] Conv 2.
17   For an illustration of such an application, see *Re Bass Ltd's Application* (1973) 26 P & CR 156; (M & B).

modification, the Tribunal has power to require W to pay money to K to compensate him.

The jurisdiction of the Tribunal is confined to the discharge or modification of restrictions on the use of land. It therefore has no power to discharge or modify other forms of covenant, for example ones imposing a positive obligation on a covenantee. (Nor does the jurisdiction extend to the discharge or modification of covenants in leases[18].) The jurisdiction is, however, not confined to restrictions imposed in covenants: it extends to restrictions that are imposed by other means.[19]

In the example above W must[20] satisfy the Tribunal that at least one of the following four grounds exists:

1. That the covenant has become obsolete, because of changes in the character of the property, or of the neighbourhood[1]; or because of other material circumstances.
2. That K has agreed, expressly or impliedly, to the discharge or modification sought. For example, if V, a previous owner of Greenacre, had used Greenacre Lodge as a glue factory, and K had made no objection, K might be taken to have impliedly agreed to the covenant being discharged.
3. That the discharge or modification sought would not injure K.[2]
4. (i) That the continued existence of the covenant would impede some reasonable use of the land for public or private purposes;[3] and (ii) (a) that the covenant does not secure to K any practical benefits of substantial value of advantage,[4] and (b) that money will be an adequate compensation for the disadvantage or loss (if any) suffered by K for the discharge or modification of the covenant.[5]

COVENANTS AND PLANNING CONTROLS

We have noted that a covenant may impose the same type of restriction that is imposed by a local planning authority. If a purchaser is intending to change

18 *Westminster City Council v Duke of Westminster* [1991] 4 All ER 136.
19 Eg under Planning and Compensation Act 1991, s 12. See *Re Barclays Bank plc Application* (1990) 60 P & CR 354 (discharge of planning agreement under Town and Country Planning Act 1990, s 106.)
20 LPA 1925, s 84(1).
1   *Re Wards Construction (Medway) Ltd's Application* LP 49 1992, 12 January 1994.
2   *Re O'Reilly's Application*, Lands Tribunal (Ref No LP 53 1991), (1993) 66 P & CR 485 (continued existence of covenant restricting use of land to car parking secured no practical advantage to persons entitled to benefit of covenant, covenant discharged).
3   *Re Wards Construction (Medway) Ltd's Application,* supra.
4   The Lands Tribunal has indicated that the words 'value or advantage' are not to be assessed in terms of pecuniary value only; *Re Bass Ltd's Application,* supra (a 'resplendent landscape view' from a road adjacent to the objector's land at Heddon-on-the-Wall, Northumberland; *Gilbert v Spoor* [1983] Ch 27, [1982] 2 All ER 576 (evening sunshine in the sun lounge; *Re Bellamy's Application* (1977) JPL 456; all held to be practical benefits of substantial value or advantage.
5   This ground was added by LPA 1969, s 28 and Sch 3. See (1979) 129 NLJ 523 (H.W. Wilkinson) for a survey of cases in which jurisdiction under this head has been exercised.

the use of, or to develop, land it will therefore be necessary for him to consider whether restrictions are imposed under the Town and Country Planning Acts and also whether any covenants affect the use of the land. The acquisition of planning permission to change the use of land does not free a landholder from a covenant prohibiting that use.[6]

Conversely, if an owner obtains planning permission for a certain development this fact is not itself ground, under s 84, for the discharge or modification of a covenant that prevents or impedes the development. It may, however, be of assistance in showing that the proposed user is 'reasonable'[7] (under 4 above).

DECLARATION AS TO RESTRICTIVE COVENANTS

When T is considering purchasing Greenacre from S, he may be uncertain whether he will be bound by R's covenant. There may, for example, be doubts as to whether the benefit of R's covenant was ever annexed to Redacre (or passes under the principle in *Federated Homes Ltd v Mill Lodge Properties Ltd*[8]). In this case, he may[9] apply to the court for a declaration as to whether Greenacre is bound by the covenant. By this means uncertainty as to whether T would be bound by the covenant can be removed.[10]

---

6 *Bell v Ashton* (1956) 7 P & CR 359; *Delyn Borough Council v Solitaire (Liverpool) Ltd* (1995) 93 LGR 614; cf *Brown v Heathlands Mental Health National Health Service Trust* [1996] 1 All ER 133 (injunction to restrain use of land in contravention of covenant refused where land acquired by statutory body under power conferred by statute to enable the body to discharge functions in the public interest with which it had been entrusted).
7 *Re Beecham's Application* (1980) 41 P & CR 369.
8 Supra.
9 Under LPA 1925, s 84(2) as amended by LPA 1969, s 28 and Sch 3.
10 See *Re Gadd's Land Transfer* [1966] Ch 56, [1965] 2 All ER 800; (M & B).

CHAPTER 22

Covenants in Leases

In dealing with the subject of covenants in leases, ie covenants made by a tenant with his landlord or by a landlord with his tenant, three main[1] questions arise.

Suppose that L_1 (L in this chapter representing landlord or lessor) leases land to T_1 (T in this chapter representing tenant or lessee) for 99 years. L_1 and T_1 enter into covenants with each other, for example T_1 covenanting that the rent agreed, subject to increases determined by an agreed procedure, will be paid when due and that the premises will be rendered up at the end of the tenancy in the same condition as at the start; and L covenanting that the grounds around the leased property (eg gardens around a block of flats) will be maintained and kept clear of rubbish.

1. T_1 occupies the premises for ten years and then assigns the lease (ie the unexpired portion of 89 years) to T_2. If the rent is not paid according to the terms agreed with T_1, can L_1 enforce the covenant against T_2? Conversely, if the grounds are not maintained, can T_2 enforce the covenants against L_1? Ie do the burden and benefit of covenants in a lease pass to an assignee of the lease?

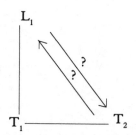

2. After T_1 has been in occupation for ten years, L_1 sells the reversion (ie the fee simple, subject to the lease) to L_2. If T_1 fails to pay the rent according to the terms agreed with L_1, can L_2 enforce the covenant against T_1? Conversely, if L_2 fails to maintain the grounds, can T_1 enforce the covenant against him? Ie do the benefit and burden of covenants in a lease pass with the reversion to an assignee?

---

1   In addition to, eg, the question as to whether a particular covenant is one of a kind that the court is prepared to enforce by decree of specific performance (see *Co-operative Insurance Society Ltd v Argyll Stores Holdings Ltd* [1995] Ch 286, [1996] 3 All ER 934) or injunction.

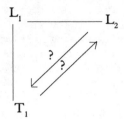

3. T_1 occupies the premises for ten years and then assigns the lease to T_2. T_2 fails to pay the rent due. Can L_1 enforce the covenant against T_2? Ie can a landlord enforce a covenant against a covenantee notwithstanding that the latter has ceased to be the tenant under the lease?

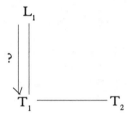

It might seem from the similarity between the diagrams set out under 1 and 2 above and those met in the last chapter (the similarity between, for example, the diagrams under 1 and 2 above and those at Situations 2 and 3 on page 381) that we are treading the same path as in the last chapter and that the answers to the questions posed would be derived by applying the same rules. This is not the case. We are in a different area of law. There are crucial differences. Thus:

(a) In the last chapter we were not concerned with the legal capacity of a party to a covenant (eg whether a party was a purchaser or a vendor), what mattered was whether a person was covenantor or covenantee. In the case of covenants in leases what matters is not whether a party is a covenantor or covenantee, but whether he is the tenant (as covenantor or covenantee) or the landlord (as covenantor or covenantee).

(b) As between lessor and lessee no distinction is drawn between covenants that are negative and those that are positive.

(c) Covenants between lessor and lessee are not registrable as land charges.

(d) The rules relating to whether the benefits and burdens of covenants pass to assignees are , as we shall see, different from those that apply in the case of covenants between fee simple owners.

Before 1996 ...

We have met various instances in this book in which it is necessary to say – 'Before ... ' and 'After ... '; for example, and in particular, 'Before 1926 ... ' and

'After 1925 ... .' We now meet another instance in which the law must be stated in this way. Before the coming into force of the Landlord and Tenant (Covenants) Act 1995 ('the 1995 Act'), the answers to the questions set out at 1-3 above were determined by the application of rules in part settled by the courts in decisions reaching back to the sixteenth century and in part by statute. The 1995 Act, which broadly followed recommendations by the Law Commission,[2] laid down a new set of rules by which the answers are to be determined.

However, the 1995 Act applies, with one exception,[3] only to covenants in a lease that is granted[4] *after* the date when the Act was brought into force, 1 January 1996. Such a lease the Act refers to as a 'new tenancy'. For covenants in leases already in existence at that date (which in this chapter will be referred to as 'old tenancies'), the previously existing law continues to be that applicable.[5] So, since the Act is not retrospective,[6] for many years to come it will very likely be the old law, not that introduced by the 1995 Act, that has to be referred to in determining an outcome.

Where the Act applies, it applies to covenants whether express, implied or (with limited exceptions) imposed by law, and irrespective of whether or not the covenant has reference to the subject matter of the tenancy. The term 'covenant' as used in the Act includes any term, condition, or obligation in a lease (whether or not referred to in the lease as a 'covenant').

The passing of the benefit and the burden

THE POSITION OF THE TENANT

Old tenancies

L_1 grants a lease by deed to T_1. T_1 makes a legal assignment of the lease to T_2. Do the benefit and burden of the covenants made between L_1 and T_1 pass to T_2 under the law as it was before the 1995 Act?

---

2   *Landlord and Tenant Law: Privity of Contract and Estate* 1988, Law Com No 174; [1989] Conv 145.

3   A lease that, although granted after 1 January 1996, if granted in pursuance of an agreement entered into (or an order of the court made) *before* that date is (section 1(3)) excluded from the definition of new tenancy and so counts as an old tenancy and as such is subject to the previous law.

4   'Grant' includes a variation in the terms of a lease that constitutes in law a surrender and re-grant (eg a variation that extends the length of the term of the lease); section 1(5). For the distinction between the variation in a lease and a surrender and re-grant, see *Friends Provident Life Office v British Railways Board* [1996] 1 All ER 336.

5   The determining date is the date of the grant of the lease, not the date on which the lease is stated to commence. Thus a grant of a lease on 1 February 1996, with the commencement backdated to 1 November 1995, is a new tenancy. A grant on 1 December 1995 of a lease to commence on 1 March 1996 is an old tenancy; (1996) SJ 8 March (K. Stepien).

6   With an exception to be noted later.

Under the rule in *Spencer's Case*[7] the benefit and burden of T$_1$'s covenants pass to T$_2$ provided that the covenants 'touch and concern' the land leased to T$_1$. Covenants touch and concern the land if they effect the landlord in his capacity as landlord, and affect the tenant in his capacity as tenant.

For example, covenants by a tenant to pay rent;[8] to repair the property leased;[9] to use the premises as a private dwelling only;[10] to buy beer for the leased public house only from the lessor's brewery;[11] to sell (at a petrol station leased to the tenant) only petrol supplied by the landlord's petrol supply company;[12] and not to assign the lease without the landlord's consent,[13] have all been held to be covenants that touch and concern the land, with the result that the burden will pass under the rule in *Spencer's Case*, to an assignee of the lease (T$_2$).

On the other hand, covenants by a tenant to pay an annual sum to someone other than the landlord;[14] and not to employ persons living in other parishes to work on the land leased,[15] have been held not to touch and concern the land, with the result that the burden will not pass to an assignee of the lease (T$_2$).

Covenants by a landlord to supply water to the property leased,[16] not to build on certain land adjoining the land leased;[17] and to renew the lease,[18] have been held to touch and concern and land, with the result that the benefit passes under the rule in *Spencer's Case* to an assignee of the lease (T$_2$).

On the other hand, covenants by a landlord to repair other houses in the district;[19] to return to the tenant a deposit at the end of the lease;[20] to pay the tenant at the end of the lease for certain chattels not amounting to fixtures;[1] and not to open another public house within half a mile of the public house which was the subject of the lease,[2] have been held not to touch and concern the land with the result that the benefit does not pass to T$_2$. Nor does the benefit of an option granted to the tenant to buy the landlord's freehold (or superior lease) touch and concern the land (and is therefore exercisable by the grantee only).[3]

7   (1583) 5 Co Rep 16a; (M & B).
8   *Parker v Webb* (1693) 3 Salk 5.
9   *Williams v Earle* (1868) LR 3 QB 739.
10   *Wilkinson v Rogers* (1864) 2 De GJ & Sm 62.
11   *Manchester Brewery Co v Coombes* [1901] 2 Ch 608; (M & B).
12   *Caerns Motor Services v Texaco Ltd* [1994] 1 WLR 1249.
13   *Goldstein v Sanders* [1915] 1 Ch 549; *Hemingway Securities Ltd v Dunraven Ltd* [1995] 1 EGLR 61.
14   *Mayho v Buckhurst* (1617) Cro Jac 438.
15   *Congleton Corpn v Pattison* (1808) 10 East 130.
16   *Jourdain v Wilson* (1821) 4 B & Ald 266.
17   *Ricketts v Enfield Churchwardens* [1909] 1 Ch 544.
18   *Muller v Trafford* [1901] 1 Ch 54 at 60; *Weg Motors Ltd v Hales* [1962] Ch 49, [1961] 3 All ER 181; (M & B).
19   *Dewar v Goodman* [1909] AC 72.
20   *Hua Chiao Commercial Bank Ltd v Chiaphua Industries Ltd* [1987] AC 99, [1987] 1 All ER 1110; (M & B).
1   *Gorton v Gregory* (1862) 3 B & S 90.
2   *Thomas v Hayward* (1869) LR 4 Exch 311.
3   *Woodall v Clifton* [1905] 2 Ch 257 at 279.

The rule in *Spencer's Case*, a rule of common law, originally applied only in the case of a lease by deed. As a result of a decision in the Court of Appeal,[4] the rule was extended to cover legal leases for three years or less made merely in writing. (Dicta in the decision[5] suggests that the rule would apply to an equitable lease created by an agreement for a lease.)

The rule in *Spencer's Case* applies in the case of a legal assignment.[6] If the assignment is equitable (eg by the existence of a contract to assign), the burden does not pass to T_2,[7] but T_1 may (under the ordinary rules of contract) expressly assign the benefit to T_2.

EXTENT OF THE ASSIGNEE'S LIABILITY

If T_1 assigns a lease (ie the unexpired position) to T_2 and the burden of T_1's covenants pass to T_2 under the rule in *Spencer's Case*, T_2 is liable for any breach committed while the lease is vested in him. He is not liable for any breach by T_1 (ie committed before the assignment to him) unless the breach is of a continuing nature, eg a failure to repair.

If T_2 commits a breach, he remains liable for this after he has assigned the lease, but he is not liable (unlike the first, covenanting, tenant) for any breach committed by a subsequent assignee after he has assigned the lease.

New tenancies

Under the 1995 Act[8], the burden and benefit of all tenant covenants are annexed to the premises leased.[9] On assignment of the lease, the benefit and burden of all such covenants (except covenants expressed to be personal to any person[10]) pass to the assignees,[11] who thereupon becomes bound by the tenant covenants[12] and entitled to the benefit of the landlord covenants.[13]

---

4   *Boyer v Warbey* [1953] 1 QB 234, [1952] 2 All ER 976; (M & B). Cf *Purchase v Lichfield Brewery Co* [1915] 1 KB 184; (M & B).
5   At 246, (Denning LJ).
6   *Cox v Bishop* (1857) 8 De GM & G 815.
7   *Friary, Holroyd & Healey's Breweries Ltd v Singleton* [1899] 1 Ch 86.
8   [1996] Conv 3; [1996] Conv 432 (P. Walter); (1996) S J March 8 (K. Stepien); (1996) 55 CLJ 313 (S. Bridge).
9   Section 3 (1)(a).
10   Section 3 (6)(a).
11   Section 3(1)(b)
12   Except to the extent that they did not bind the assignor (section 3(2)(a)(i)), or that they relate to a part of the leased premises not comprised in the assignment; section (2)(a)(ii).
13   Except to the extent that they relate to any part of the leased premises not comprised in the assignment; section 3(2)(b).

THE POSITION OF THE LANDLORD

Old tenancies

L_1 leases land to T_1. L_1 assigns the reversion to L_2. Do the benefit and burden of the covenants made between L_1 and T_1 pass to L_2 under the law as it was before the 1995 Act?

The Law of Property Act 1925 (replacing earlier legislation[14]) provides that the benefit (s 141) and the burden (s 142) of L_1's covenants shall pass with the land to L_2, provided that the covenants have 'reference to the subject matter'[15] of the lease.[16] If covenants affect L_1 or T_1 merely personally, and not in their respective capacities as landlord and tenant, the benefit and burden of the covenants do not pass with the reversion to L_2.

If the lease to T_1 includes a forfeiture clause, and L_1 assigns the reversion to L_2, by s 141(3) of the Law of Property Act 1925, the right of re-entry passes with the reversion to L_2, provided that the right has not been waived, expressly or impliedly, by L_1.

If T is in breach of a covenant and L_1 assigns the reversion to L_2 then, as a result of s 141[17] (and subject to any agreement to the contrary[18]) L_1 loses the right to sue T and L_2 acquires this right. Thus if T is in arrears with the rent at the[19] time of the assignment, the arrears are recoverable by L_2, not by L_1.

The provisions in ss 141 and 142 apply irrespective of whether the lease granted was legal or equitable.[20]

New tenancies

Under the 1995 Act[1] the benefit and burden of all landlord covenants and rights of re-entry[2] are annexed to the landlord's reversion. On assignment of

---

14   Commencing with the Grantees of Reversions Act 1540.
15   *Coronation Street Industrial Properties Ltd v Ingall Industries plc* [1989] 1 All ER 979, [1989] 1 WLR 304 (covenant in a lease by a surety with the lessor that in the event of the tenant going into liquidation and the liquidator disclaiming the lease, the surety would accept the lease for the unexpired term; *held* benefit of covenant passed to assignee of reversion; *P A Swift Investments v Combined English Stores Group plc* [1989] AC 632, [1988] 2 All ER 885, HL; (M & B), applied).
16   After the assignment L_2 becomes able to sue in respect of breaches of covenant by T_1, committed before, as well as after, the assignment. (LPA 1925, s 141, replacing CA 1881, s 10, which on this point reversed the effect of *Flight v Bentley* (1835) 7 Sim 149.)
17   Replacing Conveyancing Act 1881, s 10, which reversed the effect of *Flight v Bentley* (1835) 7 Sim 149 on this point.
18   *Re King* [1963] Ch 459, [1963] 1 All ER 781; (M & B).
19   *London and County (A & D) Ltd v Wilfred Sportsman Ltd* [1971] Ch 764, [1970] 2 All ER 600.
20   *Rickett v Green* [1910] 1 KB 253.
1   Section 3(1)(a).
2   Section 4(a).

the reversion, the benefit and burden of all such covenants[3] (except covenants expressed to be personal to any person[4]) and rights of re-entry[5] pass to the assignee of the reversion, who thereupon becomes bound by the landlord covenants[6] and is entitled to the benefit of the tenant covenants.

It will be seen that the 1995 Act introduced uniformity as between tenants' and landlords' covenants with regard to the passing of benefits and burdens to assignees. Thus in the case of new leases the previous tests relating (in the case of tenants' covenants to a covenant 'touching and concerning the land' (under *Spencer's Case*) or (in the case of landlords' covenants) to a covenant 'having reference to the subject matter of the tenancy' (under sections 141 and 142 of the Law of Property Act 1925) are no longer applicable.

The 1995 Act performed a useful function in providing a uniform code with regard to the passing of the benefit and burden of both tenants' and landlords' covenants. In practice, however, it is unlikely to happen often that the effect of this part of the Act will produce a result different from that produced by the old rules. On the other hand, when we come to the next question to be considered – whether the original tenant remains liable after he has parted with the lease – we find that the 1995 Act makes a major change. But since here, as in the matters already considered, the Act does not operate retrospectively, it is the pre-existing law that continues to be applicable to leases in existence at the time of the Act. It is, accordingly, necessary to follow the previous pattern – to deal first with 'old tenancies' and then with 'new tenancies'.

Position after the assignment of the lease

THE POSITION OF THE TENANT AFTER THE ASSIGNMENT OF A LEASE

Old tenancies

In the last chapter we saw that covenants affecting land take the form of undertakings by the covenantor on behalf of himself and on behalf of his successors in title. Covenants in leases follow the same form. Thus a covenant by T_1 to pay rent is commonly given in the form of a covenant by T_1 that the rent due will be paid. Thus, by reason of the privity of contract that exists between L and T_1, if T_1 assigns the lease to T_2 and T_2 fails to pay the rent, T_1 remains liable to L for it (ie notwithstanding that there is no longer privity of

---

3 Section 3(1)(b).
4 Section 3(6)(a).
5 Section 4(b).
6 Except to the extent they did not bind the assignor; section 3(3)(a)(i).

estate between them). (In such a case L can elect to sue either T_2 or T_1, or both of them, but he cannot recover the sum twice.) The original covenanting tenant thus remains personally liable for breaches throughout the period[7] of the lease,[8] irrespective of later assignments of the lease (or of the reversion[9]).[10]

Where T_2 is in breach, and L elects to sue T_1, then, since it is T_2 who is at fault, and since T_1 has, in effect, paid T_2's debt for him, at common law, under the principles of quasi-contract, he is entitled to recover from T_2: he has a right of *indemnity* against T_2.

This right of indemnity exists against the tenant who is in breach.[11] Thus if T_2 assigned the lease to T_3, and T_3 was in breach, and L sued T_1, T_1 could recover from T_3. If T_3 was not worth suing, T_1 has no right at common law to recover from T_2 (unless T_2 had, on the assignment to him, covenanted directly with L to pay rent and observe the covenants[12]). It was for this reason that it became the practice for T_1, when assigning the lease to T_2, to require T_2 expressly to indemnify him (T_1) in the event of his having to pay damages to L by reason of a breach of covenant after he had assigned the lease. Thus if T_2 gave such an indemnity to T_1, and T_2 assigned the lease to T_3, and T_3 was in breach, and L sued T_1, T_1 could recover either (a) by an action at common law based on quasi-contract against T_3, or (b) from T_2, by virtue of the express indemnity given by T_2. T_2 could safeguard himself by taking an indemnity from T_3. Thus a chain of indemnities could come into existence.

The Law of Property Act 1925 provided (and continues to provide for old tenancies[13]) that in any conveyance after 1925 for valuable consideration of land comprised in a lease a covenant indemnifying the assignor should be deemed to be included.[14] Thus only if an assignment was not for valuable consideration did an express indemnity need to be taken.

7   But not during a period extended by the assignee (under the Landlord and Tenant Act 1954) beyond the end of the term specified in the lease; *City of London Corpn v Fell* [1994] 1 AC 458, [1993] 4 All ER 968, HL; [1994] Conv 247 (M. Haley); (1994) CLJ 28 (S. Bridge).

8   *Warnford Investments Ltd v Duckworth* [1979] Ch 127. For the converse position, where L_1 is in breach and T_1 assigns the lease, see *City and Metropolitan Properties Ltd v Greycroft Ltd* [1987] 1 WLR 1085 (L_1 remains liable to T_1 for any loss he suffered before the assignment).

9   *Arlesford Trading Co Ltd v Servansingh* [1971] 3 All ER 113, [1971] 1 WLR 1080.

10 And irrespective of disclaimer of the lease by a liquidator following the insolvency of ultimate assignee; *Hindcastle v Barbara Attenborough Associates Ltd* [1997] Ac 70, [1996] 1 All ER 737, HL; [1997] Conv 24 (T. Tayleur); *March Estates plc v Gunmark Ltd* [1996] 2 BCLC 1; *Re Healing Research Trustee Co Ltd* [1992] 2 All ER 481, [1992] CLJ 425 (S. Bridge).

11 *Moule v Garrett* (1872) LR 7 Exch 101; *Becton Dickinson UK Ltd v Zwebner* [1989] QB 208.

12 Where this occurs, and T_2 assigns the lease to T_3, and T_3 surrenders the lease for consideration to L, and L releases T_3 from his obligations, L thereby releases T_2 from his covenant; *Deanplan Ltd v Mahmoud* [1992] 3 All ER 945, [1992] 3 WLR 467.

13 Section 77(1)(C) and (D). The terms of the covenant are set out in Pt IX of the Second Schedule to the Act. Section 24(1)(b) and (2) of the Land Registration Act 1925 provides that a covenant in similar terms is to be implied in the case of land that is subject to the Act (see Chapter 26); *Re Mirror Group (Holdings) Ltd* (1992) Times, 12 November provides an illustration in which the implied indemnity failed to protect an original tenant. The provisions of the Law of Property Act 1925 and the Land Registration Act 1995 were repealed, with respect to new tenancies, by the 1925 Act, ss 14, 30(2) and Sch 2.

14 *Re Healing Research Trustee Co Ltd*, supra.

THE CASE FOR REFORM

The vulnerability of the original tenant will be apparent. Suppose that T_1 assigns the lease to T_2; T_2 assigns the lease to T_3. T_3 is in arrears of rent and fails to maintain the premises leased. The lease ends. T_1 had covenanted that the premises would be rendered up at the end of the lease in good repair. L sues T_1 for the arrears of rent and for damages for breach of the repairing covenant.

(a) T_1's right of indemnity in quasi-contract against T_3 may be valueless by reason of T_3's bankruptcy.
(b) T_1's right of indemnity under the Law of Property Act 1925 against T_2 may be valueless by reason of T_2's bankruptcy, or his disappearance (or, as a company, its dissolution).

Thus T_1 is liable to L without redress; and, what is more, he is so liable notwithstanding that there have been changes in the terms of the lease to which he had given no consent and of which he had been unaware. Further, he may in certain instances be liable beyond the end of the term specified in the lease. And, it will be appreciated, his liability for damages for breach of the repairing covenant arises from circumstances over which he had no control.

The economic difficulties faced by the property market in the 1980s 'brought into sharp focus the position of the original tenant (and indeed of intermediate assignees who had extended their liability until the end of the term by contract and guarantors). Such tenants who thought that they had disposed of their interests in premises many years previously were being asked by landlords to comply with the covenants. Whilst they would have had some responsibility for the ability of their own assignee to perform the covenants, they would have had no influence over the choice of any subsequent assignees. The perceived injustice of this was exacerbated by the fact that landlords did not owe any "duty of care" to such tenants, in particular, the landlord was not under an obligation to notify the previous tenant when the current tenant began to default under the terms of the lease, was entitled to sue the original tenant before pursuing the current tenant and further the landlord was under no obligation to take steps to minimise the liability of any of the parties against whom he might recover (for example by investigating the financial status of the current tenant prior to the assignment) ... Further, even if the original tenant was aware of this potential liability under the lease, it was a contingent liability which would be very difficult to quantify. This could make the planning and management of business and the winding up of estates problematic.'[15]

In a Working Paper[16] published in 1986, the Law Commission found that the principle of a tenant's continuing liability had been criticised on various grounds: that is was intrinsically unfair, not understood, gave rise to demands which were unexpected, and sometimes caused hardship, afforded undue protection to landlords, and did not allow those who became liable a reasonable

---

15   S. L. Holt and S. Thompson, *Sweet and Maxwell's Legislation Handbook: Landlord and Tenant (Covenants) Act 1995.*
16   Working Paper No 19.

chance of reimbursement by the person primarily liable to perform the covenants. The Commission's recommendation was, broadly, that the principle should be abrogated:[17] that on the assignment of a lease there should be a 'clean break', assignors of leases ceasing to be liable for breaches committed by an assignee. The recommendation was accepted by the government but, as a result of pressure from lessors, the change was not made retrospective. The liability of assignors of leases granted before the Act therefore continues to be governed by the common law. Thus the vulnerability of original tenants noted above will remain a factor of the property market for many years to come. The position in the case of new tenancies is as follows.

New tenancies

Under the 1995 Act, where a lease is assigned and the assignment is not either (a) in breach of a covenant against assignment; or, (b) by operation of law (eg on a tenant's bankruptcy, to the trustee in bankruptcy; or, on a tenant's death, to his executor or administrator), the assignor is released from the tenant's covenants (and ceases to be entitled to the benefit of the landlord's covenants).[18]

Where the assignment is in breach of a covenant against assignment or is by operation of law (such assignments being termed by the Act 'excluded assignments'), the tenant's covenants continue to be binding until the next assignment (if any) which is not an excluded assignment.[19] Thus if (i) T_1 assigns the lease to T_2 in breach of a covenant not to assign without L's consent; (ii) T_2 is in breach of a covenant to pay rent, then since the assignment by T_1 was an excluded assignment, T_1 is liable to L for the duration of the time that T_2 holds the lease; (iii) T_2 later assigns the lease to T_3 with L's consent. The assignment is not an excluded assignment. T_1's liabilty[20] thereupon ends.

GUARANTEE AGREEMENTS

Section 16 of the Act provides that where a tenant covenants not to assign the lease without the landlord's consent, and the landlord's consent is given only on the tenant entering into an agreement with the landlord by which the tenant guarantees the performance by the assignee of the covenants in the lease, then, notwithstanding that the tenant thereby incumbers himself with a continuing liability for breaches committed by the assignee, the agreement is binding on the tenant. It is binding notwithstanding that the agreement has the effect of restricting the release of the tenant from the burden of covenants in the lease and, by reason of having this effect, would otherwise (without section 16) be rendered void by the provision in the Act[1] that makes any agreement relating

---

17 *Landlord and Tenant Law: Privity of Contract and Estate*, Law Com No 174, 1989.
18 Section 5.
19 Section 11.
20 And T_2's liability.
 1 Section 25.

to a tenancy void to the extent that it would have the effect of excluding, modifying or otherwise frustrating the operation of any provision of the Act.

The agreement is binding on the tenant provided that under it the tenant guarantees performance of the covenants (a) by the assignee (ie not performance by any other person); and (b) while the assignee is bound by the covenants, (ie not performance at any later stage). An agreement that complies with these conditions is termed by the Act an 'authorised guarantee agreement'. The effect of the Act is therefore that a tenant can validly guarantee performance of covenants by the person to whom he assigns the lease, but not performance by any subsequent assignee. Thus if, (i) L leases land to T_1 subject to a covenant against assignment without L's consent; (ii) L consents to T_1 assigning the lease to T_2 subject to T_1 guaranteeing performance of the covenants by T_2; (iii) T_2 is in breach of the covenant to pay rent, then, although T_1 is released from the covenant by section 11, he is liable to L under the agreement; (iv) T_2 later assigns the lease to T_3 with L's consent, subject to T_2 guaranteeing performance by T_3 of the covenants in the lease. Thereupon the guarantee agreement made by T_1 terminates. If T_3 is in breach of the covenant, L can enforce the covenant against T_3 or the guarantee agreement against T_2; (v) T_3 assigns the lease to T_4 with L's consent, subject to T_3 guaranteeing performance of the covenants by T_4 *and any subsequent assignee*. The agreement fails to fall within the definition of an authorised guarantee agreement and so is not binding on T_3. If T_4 is in breach of the covenant, L can sue T_4 on the covenant but he cannot sue T_3 on the guarantee.

NOTICE BY LANDLORD OF FIXED CHARGE DUE UNDER GUARANTEE AGREEMENT

Where a tenant assigns a lease and, under an authorised guarantee agreement, he guarantees that the assignee will perform a covenant under which a fixed charge (eg rent[2]) is payable, the Act provides[3] that the tenant is not to be liable under the guarantee unless the landlord gives him notice[4] that the charge is due, that he intends to recover it and specifies the amount.[5]

OVERRIDING LEASE

Suppose that a tenant, T_1, assigns a lease to T_2 under the terms of an authorised guarantee agreement. T_1, as we have seen, is required to guarantee observance of the covenants in the lease by T_2. T_2 fails to pay the rent due. The landlord, L, claims the rent due from T_1. T_1 pays the sum claimed in full. Here, in order to give T_1 a means of recovering from T_2 the sum that T_1 has had to pay, the Act[6] entitles T_1 to require L to grant him, T_1, what the Act terms an 'overriding lease'. This is a lease of the premises containing the same covenant as in the original lease for the same period as the unexpired portion of the original lease plus

---

2 A fixed charge comprises also any service charge as defined by s 18 of the Landlord and Tenant Act 1985 and any liquidated amount payable for breach of covenant, section 17(6).
3 Section 17.
4 The notice must be served within six months beginning with the date when the charge became due.
5 [1996] Conv 324.
6 Section 19.

three days. The effect of the grant is that an intermediate lease arises between L and T_2, T_1 thereby becoming T_2's immediate landlord and by this means able to exercise the remedies available to a landlord against a defaulting tenant, including, in particular, the right to sue for rent and, if the terms of the original lease so provide, to forfeit the lease. Thus if T_2 fails to pay the rent due, and T_1 has to pay L (under the authorised guarantee agreement), T_1 has a means of ensuring that in future T_2 pays the rent due (to T_1 who will pay it to L), or suffer.

The subject of the notice required from a landlord of a fixed charge due under a guarantee agreement and that of the right to require the grant of an overriding lease have been treated under the head of new tenancies. But it must be explained here that under the Act these two measures of protection for a tenant who has assigned a lease apply also to old tenancies, the two relevant provisions of the Act[7] applying retrospectively. In the case of old tenancies, the two measures thus accrue to the benefit of any tenant who, prior to the 1995 Act, had entered into an agreement with his landlord guaranteeing performance of the covenants in the lease by an assignee.

POSITION OF THE LANDLORD AFTER AN ASSIGNMENT OF THE REVERSION

We have seen that with regard to an assignment of the lease, in the case of new tenancies section 5 of the 1995 Act frees T_1 from liability to L_1 from the date of the assignment by T_1. With regard to assignment of the reversion, the Act does not free L_1 from continuing liability under covenants in the lease. But what, instead, it does do, is to provide a procedure under which L_1 can apply to be released from liability for breach of a covenant in the lease.[8]

(i) L_1 serves[9] on T_1 a notice informing him of the assignment of the reversion and requesting release from the covenant.
(ii) If T_1 serves a notice on L_1 consenting to the release, the covenant is released.
(iii) If T_1 lodges an objection, appeal by L_1 against the objection lies to the court which has jurisdiction to make a declaration as to whether it is reasonable for the covenant to be released.

The position of the sub-tenant

If L leases land to T and in the lease T covenants that the premises will not be used except for residential purposes, and L covenants that grounds around

---

7 Sections 17 and 19.
8 Section 8.
9 Before or within 4 weeks of the assignment.

the premises will be cleared and maintained; and T sublets the property (or part of it) to ST; and L fails to maintain the grounds, and ST uses the premises as a betting shop, can ST sue L on the covenant regarding the maintenance of the grounds in the lease from L to T? And can L sue T on the covenant regarding use of property? That is, does a sub-tenant acquire the benefits, and is he faced with burdens, of covenants in the head lease?

Benefits

The benefits of the covenants made by L do not pass to ST under the rule in *Spencer's Case*, since that rule operates only where there is privity of estate between the parties, and between ST and L there is neither privity of contract nor of estate. Nor can the benefit pass to ST under the Landlord and Tenant (Covenants) Act 1995, since the Act deals with the assignment of a lease, not with sub-letting.

It is possible, nevertheless, that ST may be able to proceed against L. Since there is neither privity of contract nor of estate between L and ST, the principles considered in the last chapter apply. In Situation 3 we saw that an assignee of the covenantee could sue the covenantor if the conditions specified were satisfied. Thus:

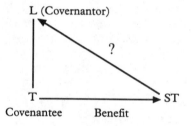

Provided that the necessary conditions are satisfied, the benefit of T's covenant will pass to ST, and ST can sue L. It will be recalled that provided the action is against the original covenantor (ie L) it is immaterial whether the covenant by L was positive or negative.

Burdens

The burden of the covenants made by T do not pass to ST under the rule in *Spencer's Case*, nor do they pass under the 1995 Act, but this does not necessarily mean that ST will be able to disregard with impunity the covenants made by T. There are three ways in which he may be compelled to observe them.

1. Suppose that T covenanted that the premises would be kept in repair. If the premises fall into disrepair, T is in breach and is liable to L. T is therefore likely to require ST to enter into a covenant with him for repair. If he does so, and ST fails to repair, ST can be sued by T.

2. Furthermore, it may be that the lease to T contained a forfeiture clause. In this case if ST fails to keep the premises in repair, the lease to T will become liable to forfeiture. If L forfeits T's lease, this automatically terminates T's sub-lease to ST.

By these two means L can indirectly bring pressure to bear on ST. By the third method he may be able to sue ST directly.

3. We have seen that as there is privity neither of contract nor of estate between L and ST, the principles considered in the last chapter apply. It is therefore possible for the burden of the covenant to pass to ST, and it will do so provided that the conditions set out in Situation 2 in the last chapter are satisfied. Thus:

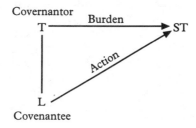

Covenants: privity of contract; privity of estate

In Chapter 21 we saw that when R covenants with E, there is privity of contract between them. If L leases land to T and in the lease T enters into certain covenants with L, then not only would there be privity of contract between L and T but also privity of estate, ie they would be bound together by the relationship created by the lease, by the estate of leasehold.

In Chapter 21 we saw in Situation 2 that if R transfers his land to S, then as between E and S, there is no privity of contract. Since E and R are not linked by the relationship of landlord and tenant, neither is there privity of estate. Similarly, if E transfers his land to F (Situation 3), there is neither privity of contract nor of estate between R and F, and if E and R each transfer their land to F and S respectively (Situation 4), between F and S, here too, there is neither privity of contract nor of estate.

Although in Chapter 21 we discussed the position as between E and R (between whom privity of contract does exist) it was with situations in which there was privity neither of contract nor of estate that we were primarily concerned. We have seen from the present chapter that where there is privity of estate between the parties concerned (eg between L_1 and T_1) then the rules to be applied in determining whether the burden and benefit of covenants pass, are different from those (set out in Chapter 21) where no privity of contract or estate exists.

Covenants on the assignment of a lease

Suppose that L leases adjacent properties, Redacre and Greenacre, to T for 99 years. In the lease T covenants with L that the land will not be used for industrial purposes. After two years T assigns the residue of the lease of Greenacre (97 years) to U. In the assignment, U covenants (with T) that nothing will be constructed on Greenacre that is more than 60 feet in height. Two years later U assigns the residue of the lease (95 years) to V. V proposes to build a factory on Greenacre that will have a chimney 100 feet high. Can L prevent V building the factory? Can T prevent V from building something over 60 feet high?

As between L and V, since there is privity of estate between the two (since L is the landlord and V is his tenant), it will be the principles discussed in this chapter which apply. Thus, in the case of old tenancies, under the rule in *Spencer's Case*, [10] as T's covenant touches and concerns the land he leased, the burden of T's covenant runs with the land (Greenacre) into the hands of V, and, in the case of new tenancies, under section 5 of the 1995 Act, the same result follows. Thus L can enforce the covenant against him.

As between T and V, there is privity neither of contract nor of estate. (It is true that U's covenant was made in the context of a lease, ie on the assignment of a lease, but the covenant was not made *in* a lease: T did not lease (or sublet) the land to U. He assigned an existing lease to U.) Thus, as between T and V, it is the principles in Chapter 21 that must be applied: the principles, in fact, in Situation 2 (relating to the running of the burden of a covenant). If the relevant conditions are satisfied (and if T registered the covenant as a land charge, they are) T can enforce the covenant against V.

Now let us suppose that T assigns the lease of Redacre to Z. Can Z enforce the covenant that U made with T against V? As between Z and V there is privity neither of contract nor of estate. Thus as between Z and V it is again the principles in Chapter 21 that must be applied: the principles in Situation 4. If the conditions necessary for the passing of the benefit to Z have been satisfied, Z can enforce U's covenant against V.

Annexe: commonhold

It will have been noted that whereas in the case of covenants between fee simple owners the burden of a positive covenant does not run with the land of the covenantee, in the case of covenants in a lease the burden of a positive covenant does run with the fee simple reversion. This difference with regard to the running of positive covenant has had a significant bearing on the manner in which properties that physically form part of a large unit (such as flats in a

---

10   See p 409.

block or shops in a mall) have been held.

Suppose that a developer builds a block of flats. He would be more likely to attract people to take one of the flats if he could offer them outright ownership – the fee simple in the flat. But would-be takers are not going to pay for a flat unless they can be sure that the outside of the building, in particular the roof, will be kept in repair; that the common parts (the entrance halls, stairs, lifts, landings) are maintained in a decent condition; and that the surrounding grounds are looked after – the grass cut, litter cleared and so on.

But anyone contemplating purchasing the fee simple in a flat knows that a covenant by the developer that the matters referred to will continue to be attended to is valueless since there is nothing to stop the developer transferring the fee simple in the structure and grounds to a transferee, perhaps a company set up for the purpose, against whom the covenants, being positive, will be unenforceable.

For this reason it has been the practice for properties that form units in a complex to be disposed of by the grant of a long lease, since in this case anyone to whom the developer assigns the fee simple reversion *is* bound by the covenants without which a person would be unwise to take a flat.

However, although the grantee of a lease has the advantage that positive covenants will be enforceable against an assignee from the developer landlord, the fact that person holds only a lease not the fee simple, means that he holds something that each year decreases in value, and that eventually he will have to move out, or be faced with negotiating a new lease. (Worse – as he watches the value of his property decrease, out of the window he sees his neighbour's house increase in value with each year that passes.) Further, the detriment may not be only financial; having paid out what may amount to a substantial sum, people may well want to *own* their home, not be tenants of a landlord.

It was to enable property such as a flat in a block to be owned, while at the same time enabling the owners to be assured that the block would be properly maintained, that in 1996 the government proposed legislation[11] that would have introduced a new system under which the fee simple could be held; a system termed commonhold. Due to the fact that the Opposition indicated that it would oppose certain aspects of the draft bill, the bill was not introduced into Parliament. However, in view of the attention that has been paid to the matter and the announcement in the Queen's Speech in October 1996 that a bill would be introduced, a brief summary of how commonhold, as proposed, would operate is given below.

The scheme in principle can be explained in the context of newly completed block of flats. (The arrangements would also be capable of being applied to premises that are already occupied.)

1. The 'promoter' (normally, and in our example, the developer) applies (by submission of a 'commonhold declaration') to the Land Registry for the land to be registered (in a new register maintained for the purpose) as commonhold.

2. If the necessary conditions are met (eg that the development has reached the required state of development) the land is registered as commonhold.

3. On registration, ownership of those parts of the premises not comprised in units (eg flats) vests in a commonhold association, of which the developer is

the first member.

4. The developer sells off units to purchasers, who acquire the fee simple in the land comprised in each unit.

5. Those who purchase units become (automatically) members of the commonhold association. (After selling off all the units the developer could resign from the association and so cease to have any involvement with the land.)

6. The association, made up of unit holders, becomes responsible for management of the common parts.

7. Members of the association, as unit owners, have rights and are subject to obligations, including a right to vote at meetings and an obligation to pay a service charge set by the association for the repair, maintenance and cleaning of the common parts. Thus the owners of flats in the block become collectively responsible for the management of all those parts other than the separate flats within it.

8. A unit holder can sell his unit, whereupon he ceases to be a member of the association, the purchaser taking his place. A unit can be mortgaged and leased, but not for a period longer than 25 years (to prevent the resurrection of the difficulties that the scheme was designed to overcome).

SUMMARY: CHAPTERS 21 AND 22

See Appendix II, p 568.

---

11   Following recommendation by a Working Group of the Law Commission (the 'Aldridge Report'), 1987, Cm 179 and a Consultation Paper by the Lord Chancellor's Department, 1990, Cm 1345.

CHAPTER 23

Mortgages[1]

Introduction

For many people the biggest financial transaction in their lives is the purchase of a house, a transaction usually made possible by a loan secured by a mortgage of the property purchased. The present century has seen an increase in the proportion of owner-occupied dwellings. In the words of Lord Diplock, in this century we have become a 'real-property-mortgaged-to-a-building-society-owning-democracy'.[2]

In view of the significance of mortgages in the economy it might be expected that mortgages would be subject to statutory control – that, in the same way that we have a Companies Act, a Sale of Goods Act and so on, there existed a Mortgages Act. But this has never come about. As the Law Commission has said, the law of mortgages 'has never been subjected to statutory reform, and over centuries of gradual evolution it has acquired a multi-layered structure that is historically fascinating but', the Commission adds, 'inappropriately, and sometimes unnecessarily, complicated.'[3] To understand the nature of the modern mortgage it is necessary, as so often in English land law, to turn the clock back and see how the present position has been reached. The story involves an interplay of common law and equity that illustrates well how equity has remedied defects and injustices that could arise from the application of the rules of common law.

Creation of mortgages

At the present day there are two ways in which a legal mortgage can be created, both prescribed by the Law of Property Act 1925, but whilst the means by which a legal mortgage can be created were laid down by statute in 1925, the position of the parties continues to be determined, at least in part, by principles established by the courts of common law and equity long before 1925. We must first, therefore, consider what these principles are.

---

1 See P. Fairest *Mortgages*; Fisher and Lightwood *Law of Mortgage*; E. F. Cousins *The Law of Mortgages*. For proposals for reform, see Law Com No 204 (1991).
2 *Pettit v Pettit* [1970] AC 777 at 824.
3 Law Commission Working Paper No 99 (1986), p 1.

Creation of a mortgage before 1926

Before 1926 if R (which in this chapter represents 'mortgagor') held the legal fee simple in Blackacre and he wished to mortgage the land to E (which in this chapter represents 'mortgagee') as security for a loan of, say £1,000, then the normal practice was for R to convey the legal fee simple of E, subject to a covenant by E that he would convey the fee simple back to R if R repaid him the £1,000 on a specified date.[4]

MORTGAGEE TAKING POSSESSION

Under this arrangement E acquired the fee simple in Blackacre and, since he held the fee simple, there was nothing to prevent him from asserting his title and taking possession of the land from R. Indeed, originally it was accepted that this would happen. E was entitled to occupy R's land and take the proceeds of the land. R got the loan he required. E obtained the proceeds of R's land while the loan was outstanding. If R repaid the loan, as agreed, he got his land back; if he did not, E retained R's land free of any obligation to return it to R.

If the proceeds from the land amounted to more than the interest payable by R, originally E was under no obligation to hand over the surplus to R. This might enable E to obtain an unfair advantage. However, in the seventeenth century equity intervened and compelled E (if he had taken possession of the land) to account to R for a full rent of the land; that is, hand over to R the difference between the interest due and whatever would have been a reasonable rent for the land. For example, if R owed E £100 a year interest; E occupied the land and a reasonable rent would have been £130, E would have to hand over to R the difference of £30; and he would have to do this notwithstanding that he might have been able to raise only £80 worth of crops on the land. It will be seen that it would therefore have been safer for E to permit R to remain on the land (and do his own farming) and require R to pay him the interest due, ie £100. Thus, as a result of equity's intervention it ceased, because of the risk involved, to be of any advantage for E to occupy the land. It therefore became the practice for E to allow R to remain in possession of the land, the conveyance of the fee simple by R to E constituting no more than E's security for the loan to R. If R failed to repay the loan or pay the interest due, E could take possession of the land by virtue of the fact that the legal fee simple was vested in him.

FAILURE BY THE MORTGAGOR TO REPAY ON THE DATE FIXED

In describing a mortgage before 1926 we have said that R would convey the fee simple in the land to E subject to a covenant by E that he would reconvey the land to R if R repaid the money on a specified date. Originally, if R failed to repay the money on the date specified, he lost any right to have the land returned to him: since had he failed to make the repayment on the date fixed, the covenant by E was no longer operative; if E had allowed R to remain in

---

4   Originally, in the twelfth and thirteenth centuries, R leased the land to E. Mortgages by a conveyance of the fee simple became normal by the middle of the fifteenth century.

possession of the land, he could take possession of the land from R. Even if the land was worth, say, £1,000, and the loan which R had failed to repay was for £200, E could nevertheless keep the land. The common law gave R no remedy: he lost his land, notwithstanding that its value was worth £800 more than the money he had borrowed. How equity intervened to prevent E taking this unconscionable advantage of R's position, will be explained shortly.

THE EQUITABLE RIGHT TO REDEEM

So, at common law, if R failed to make repayment on the date fixed, E became the unencumbered legal owner: he held the legal fee simple free of the covenant for reconveyance to R. During the seventeenth century, however, equity became prepared to compel E (notwithstanding that the date for repayment had passed) to (1) accept repayment by R of the money due; and (2) reconvey the legal fee simple to him.

When we speak of a mortgage of property being 'redeemed', we mean that the property ceases to be security (as in (2)) on repayment of the money due (as in (1)). We can therefore say that equity gave R a right to redeem his land. This was a valuable right, the value being the value of the land less the amount still owing by R to E.

It should be noted that although R's equitable right to redeem only became *exercisable* after the date for repayment had passed, the right was one which *existed* from the moment of the creation of the mortgage. From the moment the mortgage came into existence R would know that he had a right to redeem not only on the date agreed, but also at any time beyond the date fixed for repayment. He had, from the outset, an equitable right to ignore the date specified in the mortgage as that on which the loan was to be repaid.

From what has been said it might seem that, as a result of equity's intervention, R could delay repaying the loan for as long as he liked, regardless of what had been expressly agreed between the two. E, however, was not without remedy against R if R failed to repay the loan on the date agreed.

THE DECREE OF FORECLOSURE

Equity's aim was not to support R to the disadvantage of E, but merely to prevent E acting unconscionably. If R had failed to repay the loan on the date specified, E might be content to leave the loan outstanding and continue to receive interest on it from R. But if E wanted his money back, and R failed to repay the loan on the date specified in the mortgage, it became established that E could go to Chancery and ask the court to decree that R's equitable right to redeem the property should come to an end. If the court was satisfied that it was equitable that such a decree should be made, for example if the court was satisfied that R had been given a reasonable opportunity to repay the money and that he had unreasonably failed to do so, the court would grant the decree sought. A decree of this nature was termed a decree of foreclosure. The effect of the decree was that, since R's equitable right to redeem was by the decree terminated, E held the legal fee simple free of R's equitable interest. E could then assert his title and take possession of the land.

It will be noted that E could have asserted his legal title at any time (ie before or after the contractual date) and taken possession from R but that if he did so *before* he had obtained a decree of foreclosure, equity would have compelled him to account to R for a full rent of the land. After the granting of the decree, E was freed from his obligation. He took the fee simple free of any obligation to R.

Thus, in practice, if R failed to repay, and E obtained a decree of foreclosure, E got the land. If the value of the land was greatly in excess of the value of the money due to E, equity might couple with the decree of foreclosure an order that the land should be sold. From the proceeds of the sale E would be paid the money owing to him (including any interest due, and his costs) and the balance would go to R.

THE DATE FIXED FOR REPAYMENT

It might seem from what has been said that the date fixed in the mortgage was of no consequence, since R could ignore it. But this was not so. The date was of importance to E in that it was not until this date had been reached that he could seek repayment of the loan and approach Chancery for a decree of foreclosure if R failed to pay. Since E could not get a decree of foreclosure before the date fixed for repayment, it was in E's interest that the date fixed for repayment should be relatively soon after the creation of the mortgage. Once that time had been reached, E had the choice of either calling for repayment (and seeking a decree of foreclosure if R failed to repay) or leaving the money earning interest. It became common, therefore, for the date specified for repayment to be fixed at only six months after the creation of the mortgage.

THE TWO ASPECTS OF THE EQUITABLE RIGHT TO REDEEM

It will be seen that the equitable right to redeem has two aspects:

1. The right was one which enabled R to free his land from the mortgage on repayment of the money due, notwithstanding that the date for repayment has passed.
2. It prevented E (assuming that he was not prepared to run the risks involved in taking possession) from enforcing his security without enlisting the aid of the court of Chancery, and since equitable remedies were discretionary, the court would not grant E a decree of foreclosure if it considered that he had acted unconscionably.

THE 'EQUITY OF REDEMPTION'[5]

We said earlier that when equity gave R a right to redeem the mortgage, he became the holder of an equitable interest in the land. This was an equitable interest in the sense that it was part of R's property and the right might, if the loan had almost been repaid, be nearly as valuable as the land itself.

---

5   B. W. Turner *The Equity of Redemption* (1931).

When speaking of the totality of R's rights, which together constitute his interest in the land, these are referred to as R's 'equity of redemption'. This equity of redemption comes into existence as soon as the mortgage is created.

The equity of redemption is not the same as the equitable right to redeem in that although it includes the latter, it is wider. For example, suppose that R mortgages Blackacre to E for £1,000 on 1 January, the date fixed for repayment being 30 June. R immediately acquires an equity of redemption, which gives him an equitable right to redeem, if he so wishes, after 30 June. But he also immediately acquires an equitable right to require E to account to him if he, E, exercises his legal right to take possession of the land. This additional right also forms part of R's 'equity of redemption'. It is thus the sum of R's equitable rights that constitutes his interest in the land, and which together are termed his 'equity of redemption'. This equity of redemption, being his property, he can deal with like any other form of property; for example, he can sell it, or give it away, or devise it.[6] If he dies intestate it passes to the person entitled under his intestacy.[7] If R transfers his equity of redemption to X, then X obtains all the rights which went to make up R's equity of redemption.

Suppose that R mortgages land worth £4,000 to E as security for a loan of £3,000. At the outset, R's equity of redemption would be worth £1,000. If R repays the loan by instalments the value of the equity of redemption will increase until the point is reached when the value of the equity of redemption reaches the same level as the original value of the land, ie £4,000. However, if, during this time, the value of the land has been rising, the value of the equity of redemption will be more than £4,000. Thus, although E had the fee simple in the land, this gave him no more than security for the loan of £3,000, or for however much was still outstanding. The person who in practice came closest to holding the land was R: not only was he in possession, but he could recover his legal title on repayment of the loan, and any increase in the value of the land belonged to him.

Creation of legal mortgages after 1925

The Law of Property Act 1925 provides[8] that after 1925 a legal mortgage can be created in only one of two ways. These are either:

1. a 'demise for a term of years absolute, subject to a provision for cesser on redemption'; or
2. a 'charge by deed expressed to be by way of legal mortgage'.

We shall consider these in turn, but it should be noted at the outset that neither of the two methods prescribed corresponds with the method used to create a legal mortgage before 1926. Thus after 1925 it was no longer possible to create a legal mortgage by use of the old method of a conveyance of the fee

---

6 *Casborne v Scarfe* (1738) 1 Atk 603 at 605.
7 *Re Sir Thomas Spencer Wells* [1933] Ch 29.
8 Section 85(1).

simple by R to E subject to a proviso for reconveyance. But although after 1925 the methods of creating a legal mortgage were different, the old principles, as will be seen, in the main survived.

The word 'charge' having been introduced, we may explain the difference between a mortgage and a charge. If R mortgages property to E, he conveys some title in the property to E for the purpose of providing security for a loan, subject to a right to the reconveyance of the property on the debt being discharged. If R charges property to E he retains the title, but subjects the property to certain rights exercisable by E as security for a loan. Thus, of the two means of creating a mortgage permitted by the Law of Property Act 1925, the first is a mortgage, the second is a charge. At the present day, however, a charge is generally treated as merely one means of carrying out the transaction known generally as a 'mortgage'.

1.   DEMISE FOR A TERM OF YEAR ABSOLUTE

A 'demise' is a transfer. A 'term of years' is a lease. Thus the first method prescribed consists of a grant by R of a lease of the land to E. The lease is 'subject to a provision for cesser on redemption'. This means that the lease contains a clause providing that the lease is to terminate when R repays E. Thus, by this method, instead of R conveying the legal fee simple to E, as would have been done before 1926, R leases it to E. The Act does not lay down any period for the lease, but the period is usually a long one, eg 3,000 years. E does not pay rent to R under the lease which, like the transfer of the fee simple before 1926, is little more than notional, though it does (like the transfer of the fee simple) provide a means by which E can, if necessary, enforce his security.

The mortgage still specifies a date on which the loan must be repaid and, as before 1926, the date fixed is customarily six months after the creation of the mortgage.

If R fails to repay on the date specified, since the Act does not affect the position in equity, R continues to have an equitable right to redeem notwithstanding that the date specified in the mortgage has passed. R continues, in fact, to enjoy all the rights conferred on him by equity before the Act. For example, E continues to be effectively prevented from taking possession (by virtue of his lease) by the knowledge that if he does so, equity will require him to account to R for a full rent from the land.

A resemblance to the position before 1926 is that it continues to be correct to speak of R holding the equity of redemption. But it is important to remember that whereas, before the Act, the equity of redemption was all that R did hold (the legal fee simple being with E), after the Act R not only holds and enjoys all the rights which go to make up the equity of redemption but, in addition, he retains the legal fee simple (since all he granted to E was a lease). But it is the equity of redemption that matters. Without it (assuming R fails to repay the loan on the date specified) all that R would hold would be the right to get the land back in, say, 3,000 years from the date of the creation of the mortgage; ie the freehold reversion on a 3,000 year lease, and that, in practice, would be valueless. But, by holding the equity of redemption, R's fee simple becomes meaningful; since, by repaying the loan, he can free the land from the incumbrance that the lease constitutes.

The position can be recapitulated like this.

1. Before 1926,
   R held the equity of redemption.
   E held the fee simple (subject to a covenant to reconvey on redemption).
2. After 1925,
   R holds the fee simple and the equity redemption.
   E holds a lease (subject to cessor on redemption).

If, after the Act, R attempts to make a mortgage in the old way, the Act provides[9] that a purported conveyance of a fee simple which is in fact made in order to create a mortgage, operates as a grant to E of a lease for 3,000 years subject to cesser on redemption. Thus the creation of a mortgage in the old form will take effect as a mortgage created by the first of the two methods laid down by the Act.

2. CHARGE BY DEED EXPRESSED TO BE BY WAY OF LEGAL MORTGAGE

In a mortgage created by this means, the mortgage deed must state that the land has been charged with the debt by way of legal mortgage. Here E receives no estate in the land, neither a fee simple (as before 1926) nor a lease (as in the case of the first method of creating a mortgage after 1925, considered above).

When considering the remedies which are open to E if R fails to repay the loan, it will be seen that one of these remedies is for E to take possession of the land. In the case of a mortgage created by way of legal charge, since E has no estate in the land, without special provision he would have no right to take possession. Section 87(1) of the Law of Property Act therefore provides that E (who is termed a 'chargee') should get 'the same protection, powers and remedies' as if he had a lease for 3,000 years. E, therefore, although holding no lease, has the same rights and remedies as if he did.[10]

This second means of creating a mortgage has the advantage of being shorter and simpler than a mortgage created by the first method.

Creation of equitable mortgages

In Chapter 16, on the doctrine in *Walsh v Lonsdale* we saw that,

(a) If X holds a legal fee simple and he transfers his interest to Y by deed,[11] Y receives the legal fee simple.
(b) If X contracts to convey the legal fee simple to Y, then subject to the conditions necessary for the doctrine in *Walsh v Lonsdale* to apply (in particular that the contract is for consideration), Y receives an equitable fee simple.

9   Section 85(2).
10 See *Regent Oil Co Ltd v J. A. Gregory (Hatch End) Ltd* [1966] Ch 402, [1965] 3 All ER 673.
11 Ie before the Law of Property (Miscellaneous Provisions) Act 1989, by a conveyance under seal, after the Act by a transfer that complies with s 1 of the Act.

(c) If X purports to convey the legal fee simple to Y and fails to do so because the transfer is not by deed, but the transaction is of a kind that, had it been a contract to transfer the fee simple to Y, it would have constituted a valid contract,[12] then, as a result of the chain of reasoning set out in Chapter 16, Y receives an equitable fee simple.

(d) If Y holds an equitable fee simple in land and he transfers his interest to Z, Z necessarily receives an equitable fee simple.

The same principles apply in the case of the creation of mortgages. Thus,

1. If R holds the legal fee simple in Blackacre and he mortgages the land to E by legal means (ie before 1926 by conveying the legal fee simple to him subject to a covenant for reconveyance; or after 1925 by one of the two methods prescribed for the creation of a legal mortgage by the Law of Property Act 1925) then E holds a legal mortgage.

2. If R holds the legal fee simple in Blackacre and he mortgages the land to E by a means that is not sufficient (before 1926 or after 1925, as the case may be) to create a legal mortgage, E may nevertheless receive an equitable mortgage, provided that the means used by R is sufficient to satisfy the requirements of the equity in this regard.

3. If R holds an equitable fee simple in Blackacre (eg if R is a beneficiary under a trust) and he mortgages his interest to E, then E necessarily receives an equitable mortgage.

The distinction between 2 and 3 is therefore the distinction between:

an equitable mortgage of a legal interest (2 above);
a mortgage (necessarily equitable) of an equitable interest (3 above).

In the case of both 2 and 3 above, the result will be that E holds an equitable mortgage. In either case it would be correct to speak of an equitable mortgage being made, but it is important to distinguish which form of equitable mortgage is being referred to. These two forms of equitable mortgage must now be considered separately.

A.   EQUITABLE MORTGAGE OF A LEGAL INTEREST (MORTGAGE OF A LEGAL FEE SIMPLE BY EQUITABLE MEANS)

As indicated above, if R holds the legal fee simple in Blackacre and he mortgages the land to E by a means not sufficient to create a mortgage, E will receive an equitable mortgage if the means used by R are sufficient to satisfy the principles of the doctrine in *Walsh v Lonsdale* – with modifications arising from the nature and the circumstances of a mortgage. We must therefore now consider how the principles in *Walsh and Lonsdale* apply to the creation of mortgages.

Before the Law of Property (Miscellaneous Provisions) Act 1989, when a contract for the disposition of an interest in land was, to be enforceable, required to be either in writing, evidenced in writing or evidenced by an act of part

---

12   Ie before the Law of Property (Miscellaneous Provisions) Act 1989 by complying with s 40 of the Law of Property Act 1925; after the 1989 Act by complying with s 2 of the 1989 Act.

performance, an equitable mortgage was, correspondingly, created by the mortgage being in writing (ie and not by deed), or evidenced in writing, or evidenced by an act of part performance. This last was of special importance in the sphere of mortgages since it had for long[13] been accepted that if R deposited the title deeds of Blackacre with E, this was a sufficient act of part performance to constitute evidence of a contract to grant a mortgage, and thus to create an equitable mortgage forthwith. It will be noted that the deposit was made by R, and it might be thought that for this reason the mortgage would not have been enforceable by E. Equity, however, accepted that deposit of title deeds by R with E was a sufficient act of part performance by both parties, and so the mortgage could be enforced by either R or E.[14]

Since the doctrine in *Walsh v Lonsdale* hinges on the transaction being capable of being treated by equity as a valid contract, and since, after the 1989 Act, neither the use of writing signed by one person, nor evidenced in writing, nor an act of part performance are sufficient to constitute a valid contract, the employment of any of these three courses is no longer sufficient for an equitable mortgage to be created. In particular, it is no longer possible for an equitable mortgage to be created merely by the deposit of title deeds.[15]

After the 1989 Act an equitable mortgage can only be created by an instrument that is sufficient to constitute a valid contract for the disposition of an interest in land, ie it must comply with s 2 of the 1989 Act,[16] a requirement of particular relevance being that the instrument must be signed by each party, ie by both R and E.

We may note here that before the Law of Property (Miscellaneous Provisions) Act 1989, the deposit of title deeds by a mortgagor with a mortgagee could fulfil one or other of two functions:

1. The deposit could constitute the act of part performance that resulted in the creation of an equitable mortgage.

2. Even where there was no need for title deeds to be deposited (because the mortgage was by deed and so legal, or a purported mortgage was in writing or evidenced in writing and so equitable without the need for an act of part performance in the shape of deposit of title deeds), it was nevertheless commonly the practice for the mortgagee to require the deposit of the title deeds so as to provide a safeguard against the mortgagor selling or otherwise disposing of the land, thus providing additional security for the mortgagee. (This practice continues after the 1989 Act, for the same reason.)

---

13 *Russel v Russel* (1783) 1 Bro CC 269.
14 Provided that the party seeking to enforce the mortgage was able to show that the deposit was for the purpose of creating a mortgage. If this intention was present it was immaterial that the deposit was to provide security for money owed to E not by R, but by Z, a third party: an equitable mortgage arose; *Re Wallis and Simmonds (Builders) Ltd* [1974] 1 All ER 561, [1974] 1 WLR 391.
15 *United Bank of Kuwait plc v Sahib* [1997] Ch 107, [1996] 3 All ER 215, CA.
16 [1990] 106 LQR 396 (G. Hill); [1991] Conv 12 (J. E. Adams). Cf [1991] Conv 441 (J. Howell).

Recapitulation

Before the Law of Property (Miscellaneous Provisions) Act 1989,

1. A legal mortgage was created by deed, ie a document under seal (together, in practice, for additional security, with deposit of title deeds).
2. An equitable mortgage was most commonly created by deposit of title deeds (together, in practice, to avoid uncertainty as to the purpose of the deposit, with a memorandum signed by the mortgagor, and in some cases also by the mortgagee).

After the Act of 1989,

1. A legal mortgage is created by deed, ie a document complying with s 1 of the1989 Act (together, in practice, for additional security, with deposit of title deeds).
2. An equitable mortgage is created by an instrument signed by both the mortgagor and the mortgagee and complying with the other requirements of s 2 of the 1989 Act, (together, in practice, for additional security, with deposit of title deeds).

When a equitable mortgage is created today what happens may look very much like what happened before the changes made by the Law of Property (Miscellaneous Provisions) Act 1989 – the mortgagor and the mortgagee both sign a document and the mortgagor hands over the title deeds. But what has happened in law is different: before the 1989 Act it was the handing over of the title deeds that created the mortgage; after the Act it is the addition of the second signature that creates it.

B.   MORTGAGE (NECESSARILY EQUITABLE) OF AN EQUITABLE INTEREST

If R holds an equitable interest in Blackacre (eg if R is a beneficiary under a trust) and he wishes to mortgage this interest to E, he transfers his equitable interest to E, subject to a proviso that the interest will be transferred back to him (R) when the loan is repaid. This is the method used both before 1926 and after 1925.

As seen in Chapter 15, under s 53(1)(c) of the Law of Property Act 1925, a transfer of an equitable interest in any form of property must be:

(1) in writing; and
(2) signed by the transferor, or his agent authorised in writing.

Since the mortgage of an equitable interest in the land takes the form of a transfer of the interest from R to E, with a proviso for reconveyance, the mortgage must therefore comply with s 53(1)(c) and be in writing, signed by R or his agent authorised in writing.

When a legal fee simple is mortgaged by equitable means[17] this is sometimes referred to as an 'informal mortgage'. But the mortgage of an equitable interest in land is always termed as an 'equitable mortgage'.

---

17   Ie since the Law of Property (Miscellaneous Provisions) Act 1989, by the execution of a document in conformity with s 2 of that Act.

In 1991 the Law Commission proposed that all existing methods of consensually mortgaging interests in land should be abolished and replaced by two new forms of mortgage, a 'formal land mortgage' and an 'informal land mortgage'.[18]

The mortgagor's right to redeem

Introduction

Equity, having given R a right to free his land of the mortgage (by repaying the loan to E), notwithstanding that the date fixed for repayment had passed,[19] protected the right by preventing E from excluding or restricting R's exercise of it.

But why should E want to prevent R from repaying the loan? Surely, it might be thought, E would be only too glad to get his money back. Why should E attempt to exclude or restrict R's exercise of the equitable right to redeem? In answer to this question, consider this situation.

Suppose that E lends R £10,000 on 1 January, the date fixed for repayment being 1 July, the rate of interest being 7%. In June E finds that the prevailing rate of interest on this type of loan has fallen to 4%. 'If R repays me the £10,000,' E thinks, 'I will only be able to get 4% when I lend the money again. It would be better for me if that money remained loaned to R at 7%.' In these circumstances, therefore, E would want to keep the money on loan to R; and R would want to repay E, thus freeing his land from the mortgage, and enabling him to mortgage the land under a fresh mortgage, on which he would have to pay only 4% interest.[20]

If the position was reversed (ie when R mortgaged the land to E the rate of interest agreed was 4% and later the prevailing rate rose to 7%) E would want to call in the loan, ie get repayment by R, so that he could lend the money afresh at the higher rate. In this case E would be only too glad for R to redeem the mortgage, and, provided that the date fixed for repayment has passed,[1] E can commence proceedings to compel R to redeem.

But in dealing with the rights of a mortgagor, it is with the former situation that we are concerned. A restriction on the right to redeem is termed 'a clog on the equity'. The forms of restriction which E might attempt to impose fall under three heads.

18 Law Com No 204, (HC5), *Transfer of Land Mortgages*; (M & B); [1992] Conv 69 (H. W. Wilkinson).
19 In the case of a mortgage for the purpose of house purchase, when the mortgage is usually repayable by instalments over a period of years, it is customary for the mortgagor to fix a date for repayment, and then go on to provide that E will accept repayment by instalments of a stated amount over a stated period. The equitable right to redeem arises when the (nominal) date fixed for repayment has passed.
20 Another reason why E might want to prevent R from redeeming is the existence of a collateral advantage to E enforceable against R for as long as the mortgage existed. Collateral advantages are dealt with shortly.

Forms of restriction on the right to redeem

1.   COLLATERAL ADVANTAGE TO THE MORTGAGEE

When R mortgages the land to E the arrangement may confer an advantage on E in addition to the payment to him of the interest due on the loan. Such an arrangement is termed a collateral advantage. A mortgagor, owing to his need for money, is in a position of weakness, vulnerable to the demands of a mortgagee who would impose harsh terms as the precondition for the granting of a loan. Equity has for long protected mortgagees from unscrupulous mortgagors and has jurisdiction, in certain circumstances, to strike out a collateral advantage. There are two grounds on which a collateral advantage may be struck out; (a) one is when the collateral advantage is unconscionable; the other, (b) is when it restricts the right to redeem.

(a) If a collateral advantage is unconscionable, it is inoperative from the outset. But the court will not strike out a collateral advantage on this ground merely on the grounds that it is unreasonable. It is for the parties to reach their own agreement and the court will not re-write a contract merely because it transpires that the mortgagor has been improvident in agreeing to its terms.[2] It is only if the collateral advantage is unfair and unconscionable (that is, if it is imposed in a morally reprehensible manner,[2] in the circumstances that indicate that an unfair advantage has been taken of the borrower[3]) that the collateral advantage is struck out from the outset. However, the trend in this century has been for the courts to be slow to interfere with a bargain made by parties who stand on an equal footing, eg if mortgagors are business men, who go in 'with their eyes open with the benefit of independent advice, without any compelling necessity to accept a loan on these terms and without any sharp practice'[4] by the mortgagee.

(b) If R mortgages land to E, and the arrangement is that on the redemption of the mortgage the land will be subject to some disadvantage that did not exist before the creation of the mortgage, then, on the redemption of the mortgage, the arrangement ceases to have effect. The reason is that if the arrangement was allowed to continue to bind R, this would be a factor which that incline R against redeeming the mortgage: it would be a 'clog on the equity'. For example, if R mortgages a public house to E, a brewery, and by a term of the mortgage (as in *Noakes & Co Ltd v Rice*[5]) R covenants only to sell E's beer, when R redeems the mortgage he will cease to be bound by the covenant. If he had continued to be bound by the covenant the result would

---

1   And provided that E has not agreed to accept repayment by instalments. See note 19, supra.
2   *Multiservice Bookbinding Ltd v Marden* [1979] Ch 84, [1978] 2 All ER 489; (M & B) (interest rate fixed by index linking held not to be unconscionable). See also *Nationwide Building Society v Registry of Friendly Societies* [1983] 3 All ER 296, [1983] 1 WLR 1226. (Mortgages with provision for index linking of capital repayments not illegal).
3   *Cityland and Property (Holdings) Ltd v Dabrah* [1968] Ch 166, [1967] 2 All ER 639 (sum due to be repaid substantially higher than value of property at the time of mortgage).
4   *Multiservice Bookbinding Ltd v Marden* [1979] Ch 84 at 110, per Browne-Wilkinson; *J Carrington Ltd v Smith* [1906] 1 KB 79.
5   [1902] AC 24; (M & B).

be that whereas what he mortgaged had been a 'free house', what he redeemed would have been a 'tied house'. During the existence of the mortgage, however (ie until the mortgage is redeemed on the repayment of the loan), the restriction is binding on R.[6]

In some cases the collateral advantage may be brought into existence, perhaps at the same time as the mortgage, but in a separate transaction. In such a situation, if E can satisfy the court that the collateral advantage was secured in a transaction which was distinct from the mortgage (and not, in fact, part and parcel of the mortgage) then the collateral advantage will continue to bind R notwithstanding the redemption of the mortgage by him. Thus if R had mortgaged the public house to E for a loan of a certain sum, and in a separate transaction R had covenanted not to buy beer from any brewery other than E's for 30 years, then provided E can satisfy the court that the two transactions, the mortgage and the covenant, were distinct,[7] the covenant will bind R for the full period irrespective of whether he redeems the mortgage during that time.[8] But if R can show that his covenant was in fact part of the consideration demanded by E for the loan, ie that without the covenant he would not have got the loan, the court will regard the two transactions as interdependent and, in this event, R would cease to be bound by his covenant when he redeemed the mortgage. Whether or not the two transactions are distinct is a matter of fact for the court to decide in each case. 'The question is one not of form but of substance, and it can be answered in each case only by looking at all the circumstances, and not by mere reliance on some abstract principle ...'[9] (Of course, to use the example of the public house, if R had undertaken to sell only E's beer and then, later, R had mortgaged the property to E, the principle with which we are concerned would not arise. The advantage to E would not be collateral to the mortgage. R would have mortgaged a tied house to E, and on redeeming the mortgage, he would hold the property in the same form.[10])

In addition to the grounds so far considered, a mortgage (or a term of a mortgage) may be affected by other factors, for example, by the application of the doctrine of restraint of trade, or by the law of the European Economic

---

6   *Biggs v Hoddinott* [1898] 2 Ch 307; (M & B). Formerly all collateral advantages were struck out (ie from the start) on the ground that they constituted a hidden form of interest payment and as such contravened the laws against usury. (See *Jennings v Wad* (1705) 2 Vern 520 at 521.) The last vestiges of the usury laws were repealed in 1854.

7   As in *De Beers Consolidated Mines Ltd v British South Africa Co* [1912] AC 52; and in *Reeve v Lisle* [1902] AC 461.

8   Provided, of course, that the covenant is otherwise valid (as in *Texaco v Mulberry Filling Stations Ltd* [1972] 1 All ER 513, [1971] 1 WLR 814) and is not struck down, eg as being in restraint of trade (as in *Esso Petroleum Co Ltd v Harper's Garage (Stourport) Ltd* [1968] AC 269, [1967] 1 All ER 699). See also *Alex Lobb (Garages) Ltd v Total Oil Great Britain Ltd* [1985] 1 WLR 173, CA (no restraint of trade found to exist in sale and lease back arrangement); 1985 Conv 141 (P. Todd); (1985) 101 LQR 306.

9   Per Lord Haldane, *Kreglinger v New Patagonia Meat and Cold Storage Co Ltd* [1914] AC 25 at 39; (M & B).

10 *De Beers Consolidated Mines Ltd v British South Africa Co* [1912] AC 52. See also *Re Petrol Filling Station, Vauxhall Bridge Road* (1968) 20 P & CR 1; (M & B).

Community,[11] or by the provisions of the Consumer Credit Act 1974, or by those of the Insolvency Act 1986.[12]

Under the Act of 1974 the court has power to alter or set aside a term of an agreement made between parties of whom one is an individual,[13] where the agreement constitutes an 'extortionate credit bargain'.[14] 'A credit bargain is extortionate if it (a) requires the debtor or a relative of his to make payments (whether conditionally or on certain contingencies) which are grossly exorbitant or (b) otherwise grossly contravenes ordinary principles of fair dealing.[15] Where a mortgagor is a company the court has a jurisdiction under the Insolvency Act 1986[16] similar to that under the Act of 1974, but the jurisdiction is exercisable only where the company goes into liquidation within three years of the execution of the mortgage.

2.   IRREDEEMABLE MORTGAGES

Equity will not countenance any restriction on the right to redeem. Thus a provision that a mortgage is irredeemable is void. Further,[17] a provision restricting the right to redeem to the mortgagor and the heirs male of his body[18] would be void since the right must be freely exercisable by anyone into whose hands the equity of redemption passes. Nor can the exercise of the right be restricted to a certain period of time, eg the life of R.

Further, any term of the mortgage which,[19] though not excluding the right to redeem, may have the effect of preventing R from returning to his original position will be void, since such a term would be inconsistent with R's right to redeem. Thus if the mortgage provides that R mortgages the land to E as security for a loan of £3,000 and that E shall have the option to purchase the fee simple from R for £5,000, then the option is void, even if £5,000 is a fair price.[20]

However, if R mortgages the land to E and then, later, R grants E an option to purchase the land for a specified price at any time within a specified period, in this case, since the option is granted in a separate and independent transaction, it is valid.[1] (The principle is thus similar to that relating to collateral advantages.)

---

11   In particular, EEC Treaty, art 85. See *Esso Petroleum Co Ltd v Kingswood Motors (Addlestone) Ltd* [1974] QB 142, [1973] 3 All ER 1057.
12   Sections 244, 343.
13   Ie the provision does not apply where the agreement is between two companies.
14   See *Davies v Directloans Ltd* [1986] 2 All ER 783, [1986] 1 WLR 823 (interest rate of 21.6%, when 'proper' rate in the circumstances 18%, held not to be extortionate for purposes of the 1974 Act).
15   Section 138(1). Other protection is afforded where the amount borrowed does not exceed £15,000, and where certain other conditions are satisfied, by ss 60, 61.
16   Section 244.
17   *Re Sir Thomas Spencer Wells* [1933] Ch 29 at 52.
18   *Howard v Harris* (1683) 1 Vern 190.
19   *Salt v Marquess of Northampton* [1892] AC 1.
20   *Samuel v Jarrah Timber and Wood Paving Corpn Ltd* [1904] AC 323; (M & B); *Lewis v Frank Love Ltd* [1961] 1 All ER 446, [1961] 1 WLR 261.
1   *Reeve v Lisle* [1902] AC 461.

The reason why equity strikes out an arrangement which is inconsistent with the right to redeem (or which is a collateral advantage if it is part and parcel of a mortgage) but refrains from interfering if it comes into existence subsequently, is that when R is seeking to borrow money from E, his needs may be so urgent that he is obliged to accept whatever terms E dictates. When he is in this position of weakness, equity protects him. But once R has obtained his loan, equity leaves him to make whatever arrangement with E he sees fit.

DEBENTURES

There is one exception to the rule that a mortgage cannot be made irredeemable. If R lends money to E plc, a company registered under the Companies Acts, and E plc gives R a written acknowledgement, this is termed a 'debenture'. Security for such a loan is often provided by a mortgage of land owned by the company. A common arrangement is for the company to mortgage its land to trustees on trust for the debenture holders as security for their loan. If the company fails to repay the loan, the trustees can enforce the mortgage and reimburse the debenture holders from the proceeds of sale. The Companies Act 1980[2] provides that a mortgage to secure debentures can be irredeemable. This form of mortgage is thus a statutory exception to the rule that a mortgage cannot be made irredeemable.

3. UNDUE POSTPONEMENT OF REDEMPTION

As seen earlier, it is not until the date fixed for repayment has been reached that R's right to redeem arises. Until that date is reached R cannot seek to redeem, nor E to claim repayment. E may, however, attempt to restrict R's right to redeem by stipulating that the date for repayment should not be until long after the customary six months. A postponement for a long period[3] may be void on the ground that it unduly hampers the right to redeem. But the decision will depend on the facts of each case. What matters is whether or not the court considers that the postponement is for such a length of time as to make the right to redeem 'illusory'.[4] However, the fact that redemption is postponed for longer than the customary six months will not in itself make the date fixed ineffective, provided that, taking the realities of the transaction into account, the mortgage is not 'oppressive and unconscionable'.[5]

4. DISGUISED MORTGAGES

E may attempt to avoid equity's protection of R's right to redeem by requiring R to enter into a transaction that is not termed a mortgage. For example, suppose that, in order to secure the loan he needs, R has to convey the legal fee

---

2 Section 193, replacing Companies Act 1948, s 89.
3 Eg 19 years, 46 weeks; *Fairclough v Swan Brewery Co Ltd* [1912] AC 565; (M & B). Cf *Santley v Wilde* [1899] 2 Ch 474; (M & B).
4 *Knightsbridge Estates Ltd v Byrne* [1939] Ch 441, [1938] 4 All ER 618; (M & B).
5 Ibid.

simple in Blackacre to E, the conveyance containing a provision that R shall be entitled to repurchase the land at a certain price on a specified date in, say, a year's time. And suppose that this arrangement is in fact security for E for a loan by him to R, the sum fixed for the repurchase of the land by R being the amount of the loan by E to R, plus interest. Here R would get his loan, E would get his security, and if R failed to exercise the option, he would lose the land. Any such attempt by E to side-step equity's protection of the equity of redemption will fail. If R fails to exercise his option (and thus repay the loan) on the date fixed, and he later seeks the aid of equity in order to recover his legal title, equity will look at the substance of the transaction. If it finds that the real intention was for the land to be mortgaged, equity will disregard the cloak under which the true nature of the transaction had been concealed, and will treat the transaction as a mortgage. The rule we have considered relating to mortgages will thereupon become applicable.[6] In the above example, equity will compel E to permit R to exercise the option notwithstanding that the date fixed for exercising it has passed.[7]

'ONCE A MORTGAGE ALWAYS A MORTGAGE'

The principles we have been discussing have been summarised by the maxim 'Once a mortgage always a mortgage'.[8] One meaning of the dictum is that if something is a mortgage, then it is nothing more than a mortgage (thus it is not a means by which collateral advantages to E can be enforced against R after the mortgage has ended). Another meaning is that if something is a mortgage, then that is just what it is: its nature cannot be concealed by dressing it up in other clothes. (The wording of the maxim is unhelpful since, taken literally, the maxim might be thought to indicate a mortgage lasted for ever.)

MORTGAGES AS CONTRACTS

It can be mentioned at this point that just as in its nature a lease is both a contract and an interest in land, so also is a mortgage both a contract and (in the hands of the mortgagee[9]) an interest in land. It follows, therefore, that the general principles of contract law apply to the formation of a mortgage. An aspect of the law of contract, as it affects mortgages, that has been prominent in litigation in recent years has been that concerning the setting aside of a transaction on the ground of undue influence; ie where one co-owner executes a mortgage of the property as a result of undue influence by the other co-owner. This subject will be treated later in this chapter.

---

6 See *Grangeside Properties Ltd v Collingwoods Securities Ltd* [1964] 1 All ER 143, [1964] 1 WLR 139.
7 *Danby v Read* (1675) Cas temp Finch 226.
8 *Seton v Slade* (1802) 7 Ves 265 at 273, per Lord Eldon LC.
9 The equity of redemption retained by the mortgagor is also an interest in land.

Persons entitled to redeem

Any person interested in the equity of redemption may redeem the mortgage. Thus not only R may redeem the mortgage, but, if R sells the land (subject to the mortgage) to S, S can redeem the mortgage.

Or suppose that after mortgaging the land to E_1 R later mortgages the land to E_2. E_2 now has an interest in R's equity of redemption, since if E_1 enforces his security by selling the land, E_2 will want to know whether there will be enough of the proceeds left for him to be repaid after E_1 has taken the amount due to him. Since E_2 thus has an interest in the equity of redemption, he can redeem E_1's mortgage. Thus if R mortgages his land to E_1 and then to E_2, E_1 can be paid off either by R or by E_2. And, whether it is R or E_2 who has paid him, as far as he, E_1, is concerned, his mortgage has been redeemed. The word 'redeem' therefore means 'pay off'.

We may note here that if R mortgages his land to E_1 and the title deeds are deposited with E_1 and then R mortgages the land to E_2, and R redeems the mortgage to E_1, E_1 is under a duty to search the register in order to discover whether any other subsequent mortgage is registered. If, on doing so, E_1 discovers the existence of E_2's mortgage, he, E_1, is under a duty to pass the title deeds to E_2 (ie and not return them to R).

A mortgagee's means of enforcing his security

If R fails to repay the money due to E under a mortgage, provided that the date for repayment has passed, E may sue him for it.[10] The action lies in contract. But an action in contract against R may be of no avail. For example, R may have disappeared, or he may be bankrupt. In this case E will wish to enforce his security against the mortgaged land. A mortgagee has four means of enforcing his security against the land. They are:

1. Foreclosure.
2. Sale.
3. Taking possession.
4. Appointing a receiver.

Certain aspects of the remedies available to a mortgagee under an equitable mortgage differ from those available to a mortgagee under a legal mortgage. The remedies of an equitable mortgagee are treated separately at the end of this chapter.

10   See *Bolton v Buckenham* [1891] 1 QB 278.

Foreclosure

It has already been seen that:

1. Equity gave R a right to redeem the mortgage notwithstanding that the date fixed for repayment had passed.
2. Once the date fixed for repayment had passed, E could apply to the court for a decree of foreclosure which, if granted, terminated R's equitable right to redeem.[11]

The following additional matters now call for attention.

EXERCISE OF THE RIGHT TO FORECLOSURE

If the mortgage does not contain a date for repayment, or if the mortgage provides that the loan is repayable on demand, E may foreclose when he has demanded repayment, and a reasonable time has elapsed after that date.[12] If E undertakes not to foreclose (or to exercise any of the other methods of enforcing his security) until certain conditions are satisfied (eg that he has given specified notice to R, or that R has acted in breach of covenants in the mortgage) E cannot foreclose otherwise than in accordance with his undertaking.[13]

EFFECT OF A DECREE OF FORECLOSURE

Before 1926 the decree of foreclosure, by terminating R's equity of redemption, freed the legal fee simple held by E from R's equitable interest, with the result that E was left holding the legal fee simple absolutely.

Under each of the methods of creating a legal mortgage introduced in 1925, R remains in possession of the legal fee simple. Thus a decree of foreclosure, which merely terminated R's equity of redemption would no longer have the effect of vesting the fee simple absolutely in the hands of E. In order that the decree should continue to have the same effect as before 1926, the Law of Property Act 1925[14] provides that a decree of foreclosure should vest R's fee simple in E. By this means the effect of a decree of foreclosure has been preserved notwithstanding the changes introduced in the methods of creating legal mortgages.

PROCEDURE

Foreclosure proceedings usually take place in the High Court. On E's application the court makes a foreclosure order nisi. This is an order directing the necessary accounts to be taken and directing that unless ('nisi') R repays the money due within a specified period (usually six months from the accounts being agreed by the Master, an official of the court), then the mortgage will be foreclosed. If R fails to repay the money due before the expiry of the time

---

11   *Williams v Morgan* [1906] 1 Ch 804.
12   *Toms v Wilson* (1862) 4 B & S 442.
13   *Ramsbottom v Wallis* (1835) 5 LJ Ch 92.
14   Section 88(2).

allowed, the court makes a foreclosure order absolute which vests the fee simple in E. (The phrase 'to foreclose' usually refers to obtaining a foreclosure order absolute.)

If, after the making of the decree nisi, E, or any subsequent mortgagee, or R, requests the court to order the land to be sold, the court has a discretion to make this order.[15] (There is then no need for a foreclosure decree absolute.) From the proceeds of sale, E is paid the money due to him, and the balance belongs to R.

The mere fact of the vesting of the fee simple in E will not, however, necessarily mean that R leaves the land. If R refuses to go E is not entitled physically to oust him, as this would be a crime under the Criminal Law Act 1977.[16] E must therefore obtain an order for possession from the court. If R refuses to leave the land after the order has been served, the court's bailiffs will put him out. It is therefore common for an application for a decree nisi to be made absolute to be coupled with an application for an order for possession.

When E applies[17] for the decree nisi to be made absolute, if the property mortgaged consists of a dwelling house the court has discretion, conferred by statute,[18] to adjourn the proceedings (or defer for a specified period the coming into effect of an order for possession[19]) if[20] it considers that R is likely to be able within a reasonable period to pay any sums due (or to remedy any default constituting a breach of the mortgage).

What is meant by 'reasonable period'? It has been held that considerations which are likely to be relevant in establishing what constitutes a reasonable period include,

(a) How much could the borrower reasonably afford to pay, both now and in the future?
(b) If the borrower had a temporary difficulty in meeting his obligations, how long was the difficulty likely to last?
(c) What was the reason for the arrears which had accumulated?
(d) How much remained of the original term?
(e) What were the relevant contractual terms and what type of mortgage was it, that is, when was the principal due to be repaid?
(f) Was it reasonable to expect the lender, in the circumstances of the particular case, to recoup the arrears of interest (i) over the whole of the original term, or (ii) within a shorter period, or even (iii) within a longer period, that is, by extending the repayment period? Was it reasonable to expect the lender to capitalise the interest or not?

---

15 LPA 1925, s 91(2). See *Twentieth Century Banking Corpn Ltd v Wilkinson* [1977] Ch 99, [1976] 3 All ER 361; *Palk v Mortgage Services Funding plc* [1993] 2 WLR 415, [1993] 2 All ER 481; [1993] Conv 58 (J. Martin); *Polonski v Lloyds Bank Mortgages Ltd* (1997) 141 Sol Jo LB 114 (court's discretion not limited to purely financial matters).
16 Section 5, 6.
17 With or without an application for an order for possession.
18 Administration of Justice Act 1970, s 36.
19 *Target Home Loans Ltd v Clothier* [1994] 1 All ER 439, CA; *National and Provincial Building Society v Lloyd* [1996] 1 All ER 630, CA.
20 *Cheltenham and Gloucester Building Society v Grant* (1994) 26 HLR 703, CA.

(g) Were there any reasons affecting the security which should influence the length of the period for payment?

It is in the light of answers to these questions that the court will exercise its discretion, taking into account also any further factors that may arise in a particular case. It is, though, not the function of the Court of Appeal to lay down rigid rules as to how judges are to satisfy themselves about the matter.[4]

What is meant by 'sums due'? It sometimes happens that a mortgage that is repayable by instalments contains a provision that if R defaults in paying one instalment on the date due, then the whole of the sum outstanding should immediately become repayable. If R had had difficulty in paying the instalments, it is likely that he would find it impossible to repay the whole of the sum outstanding – perhaps many thousands of pounds. It has therefore been provided[5] that the sum which the court must consider R likely to be able to pay within a reasonable time in order for the court to have discretion to order an adjournment should exclude any sum which the mortgage provides should become payable by R in the event of his defaulting in paying an instalment. The effect is therefore that if the court considers that R can, and will, catch up with his repayments within a reasonable time, it can give him the chance to do so.[6]

To sell

Originally the advantage to E of foreclosure lay in the fact that he might acquire land worth more than the amount which R owed him. With the development of the jurisdiction of the court to order a sale (eg at R's request) this result became less likely. And if E's aim was merely to recover the amount due to him, and not to obtain a profit, for the land to be sold and for E to be repaid out of the proceeds, was, for E, a satisfactory outcome.

It was for this reason that it became the practice for the terms of a mortgage to confer a power on E to sell the land free from R's equity of redemption, provided certain conditions were fulfilled; eg that R had fallen behind in his repayments and E had served notice on R of his intention to exercise the power. Under the terms of the mortgage E would be empowered to recoup himself out of the proceeds of sale, with the balance being handed to R. Equity raised no objection to a mortgage containing such a power of sale, provided that the conditions were reasonable.

---

1   *First National Bank plc v Syed* [1991] 2 All ER 250, CA.
2   *Cheltenham and Gloucester Building Society v Norgan* [1996] 1 All ER 449, [1996] 1 WLR 343, CA.
3   *Per* Evans LJ.
4   *Cheltenham and Gloucester Building Society v Grant* (1994) 26 HLR 703.
5   Administration of Justice Act 1973, s 8(3). See *Habib Bank Ltd v Tailor* [1982] 3 All ER 561, [1982] 1 WLR 1218, CA; (M & B).
6   *Governor and Co of the Bank of Scotland v Grimes* [1985] QB 1179, [1985] 2 All ER 254 (s 8 of 1973 Act held applicable in case of endowment mortgage).

THE STATUTORY POWER

The Law of Property Act 1925 (replacing earlier statutes[7]) now confers on E a statutory power of sale.[8] Thus it is no longer necessary for a mortgage expressly to confer a power of sale on E.

The power can be exercised by E without his having to go to court.

The power is conferred on every mortgagee (unless the mortgage excludes the power) provided that the mortgage is made by deed. Since a legal mortgage must be by deed, the power exists in the case of every legal mortgage (unless it is expressly excluded).

WHEN E CAN SELL THE LAND

In considering when E is able, by virtue of the power, to sell the land it is necessary to distinguish between:

1. E being able to pass a good title to a purchaser (P); and
2. E being able to sell the land without incurring liability to R for selling before he is entitled to do so.

We shall see that E might be able to sell the land to P (ie and pass him a good title), yet nevertheless be liable in damages to R for doing so.

We are concerned with two stages.

1.   THE POWER OF SALE ARISING

When the date fixed for repayment[9] has passed, the power of sale is said to have 'arisen'. The effect of this is that, when this stage has been reached, if E sells the land to P, P will get a good title, ie he receives the legal fee simple free from R's equity of redemption.[10]

E can sell the land to P (even if R is not behindhand in his repayments) in the sense that he can pass a good title to P. But if he does so before one of three specified conditions is satisfied he is liable in damages to R for having sold before he was entitled to do so.

2.   THE POWER OF SALE BECOMING EXERCISABLE

E only becomes able to sell without incurring liability to R when any one of the following three conditions have been fulfilled.[11]

1. Some interest payable under the mortgage is two months or more in arrears; or

---

7   Principally the Conveyancing Acts of 1881 and 1911.
8   Sections 101-107.
9   LPA 1925, s 101(1)(i). See *Twentieth Century Banking Corpn Ltd v Wilkinson* [1977] Ch 99, [1976] 3 All ER 361.
10   LPA 1925, s 104(2). R ceases to be able to redeem the mortgage from the time that E enters into a contract with P for the sale of the land; *Property and Bloodstock Ltd v Emerton* [1968] Ch 94, [1967] 3 Al ER 321. On the background to s 104(2), see [1989] Conv 412 (S. Robinson).
11   LPA 1925, s 103.

2.   E had served notice[12] on R requiring repayment of the loan, and R had failed to repay for three months after receipt of notice; or
3.   R had been in breach of some condition in the mortgage (ie other than the undertaking to repay the loan or interest on it).

When any one of these conditions is fulfilled, the power is then said to be 'exercisable', ie exercisable by E without incurring liability to R.

THE POSITION OF THE PURCHASER

Why does the Act enable E to pass a good title to P if the power has merely 'arisen', ie before R has been in any way at fault? Would it not be fairer to R if E could only pass a good title to P if the power had become 'exercisable', ie if R had been in some way at fault?

The answer is that such an arrangement, whilst it might be fairer to R, would place difficulties in front of an intending purchaser. For example, suppose that R is behindhand in his payment of interest on the loan. E proposes to sell to P. Before P could be sure that E was capable of passing him a good title, he (P) would have to satisfy himself that R was in fact behind in his payment of interest, and it would be understandable if P refused to be drawn into an investigation of the state of the accounts between R and E, particularly if, as is possible, R disputes E's claim that he was behind on his payments. Or P might believe that R was behind in his payments, pay E for the land, and then find later that R had not in fact been behind, with the result that E had not had power to sell the land, and so he, P, had paid his money and received no title.

For P to be willing to buy the land from E, he (P) must be satisfied that E will be able to pass him a good title. Under the provisions of the Act, he can be sure of this. P will know the date fixed for repayment from inspection of the mortgage. If this date has passed he will know that E can pass him a good title. Thus P is not concerned with the state of affairs between E and R.

If the power had not become exercisable (eg if R was not behind in his payment of interest) and R learned that E was proposing to sell the land to P, R could apply to the court for an injunction restraining him from so doing. And there is another safeguard to R's position. Notwithstanding that the power has arisen, P will not take a good title if he 'becomes aware ... of any facts showing that the power of sale is not exercisable'[13] (ie that none of the conditions set out above applies) or even if he becomes aware of facts showing 'that there is some impropriety in the sale',[14] eg that although R had been over two months in arrears in paying interest, he had since tendered repayment of the loan together with all interest due. P does not have to make the same enquiries that a purchaser seeking to take as a purchaser without notice would make, but he should not 'shut his eyes to suspicious circumtances'.[15]

If E sold the land before the power of sale had become exercisable, and passed a good title to P, and R sued him (E) for damages, the damages which

12   See LPA 1925, s 196.
13   *Selwyn v Garfit* (1888) 38 Ch D 273.
14   Ibid.
15   Megarry and Wade, p 938.

R could claim would be the amount which P had paid E, and possibly the additional cost to R of finding and buying another house, and all the costs he had had to bear as a result of being turned out of his house, for example living with his family in a hotel until a new house was available. The prospect of paying such damages as these would thus be likely to make E take care that he did not exercise the power of sale before it had become exercisable.

PROCEEDS OF SALE

1. SALE BY SOLE MORTGAGEE

If E sells the land, then, as regards the proceeds of sale, E holds these as a trustee, on trust:

    1. to pay the expenses of sale;
    2. to recoup the money due to himself;
    3. to pay the balance to R.[16]

2. SALE BY A SUBSEQUENT MORTGAGEE

Let us suppose that R mortgages land first to E_1 for £7,000 and then to E_2 for £6,000. E_2 sells the land to P. As regards E_1, the effect of E_2 exercising his statutory power of sale is to vest the legal fee simple in P, subject to E_1's mortgage. Thus if the land was worth £20,000, P should not (because he would take it subject to E_1's mortgage) pay more than £13,000 for it. (E_2 would recoup the £6,000 due to himself and pass the balance to R.) P would hold the legal fee simple in land worth £20,000 subject to E_1's mortgage of £7,000. If P later redeemed E_1's mortgage by paying off the £7,000 he would hold the fee simple free of encumbrances. P would thus have paid £20,000 for land worth £20,000. R would have received £7,000, the value of the land less the two debts. It is possible, however, for E_2 to sell the land to P free from E_1's mortgage, ie on the basis that E_1's mortgage will be discharged. In this case P will pay E_2 the full value of the land, ie £20,000. E_2 will then hold the £20,000 on trust first to discharge E_1's mortgage, and then to pay the expenses of sale, recoup himself and pay the balance to R.

3. SALE BY A PRIOR MORTGAGE

If it had been E_1 who had sold the land to P, in this case E_1 would hold the proceeds of sale on trust:

    1. to pay the expenses of the sale;
    2. to recoup the money due to himself;
    3. to hand over the balance to E_2.

E_2 would then hold the money he received on trust,
    1. to recoup the money due to himself;
    2. to hand the balance to R.

16   *Halifax Building Society v Thomas* [1996] Ch 217, [1995] 4 All ER 673, CA.

If there had been a further mortgage to E_3, E_2 would have passed the balance not to R but to E_3. E_3 would then have recouped himself and passed the balance to the next mortgagee or, if none, to R, and so on.

If, in the above example, E_2 had passed the balance to R instead of E_3 he would have acted in breach of trust. He can, however, discover E_3's existence by making a search in the Land Charges Registry. If he finds no registration of any subsequent mortgage, he can safely pass the balance to R.[17]

A MORTGAGEE NOT A TRUSTEE OF THE POWER OF SALE

If mortgaged land is sold by the mortgagee, the better the price obtained, the better will the mortgagor's chance be of getting something after the mortgagee has recouped himself (and after any subsequent mortgagees have recouped the money due to them).

The general rule is that while E is under a duty to hold the proceeds of sale on trust for the purposes we have explained, with regard to the sale of the property he is not under the same high duty owed by a trustee in selling trust property – to get the best price reasonably obtainable. The power of sale is conferred on the mortgagee for his own benefit and he may exercise the power accordingly. Thus he is under no obligation to delay the sale until market conditions will enable an improved price to be obtained, or to sell by auction rather than by private treaty.

Nevertheless, a mortgagee is under *some* duty to the mortgagor with regard to the sale. Originally, the duty was considered to be no more than a duty to act in good faith.[18] Latterly, it has been held that more than good faith is required: the mortgagee owes the mortgagor[19] a duty to take reasonable care. For example, in *Cuckmere Brick Co Ltd v Mutual Finance Ltd*[20] it was held that there had been a failure to take reasonable care where the mortgagee had omitted to include on a notice of auction a fact that materially affected the value of the land (viz, that planning permission had been given for building hundred flats), and whilst there is no duty to put the property in a better state of repair before sale,[1] there is a duty to protect the property from vandalism until sale takes place.[2]

Recent cases indicate that the duty of care extends to an obligation to obtain, if not the best price reasonably obtainable, at least the full market value of the property, eg where the property is being sold by private treaty

---

17   Thus no mortgagee should pass a balance of proceeds to R without first searching the register for subsequent mortgagees.

18   *Kennedy v De Trafford* [1897] AC 180.

19   The duty extends to a person who had stood as surety for the mortgage (ie someone who has undertaken that if the mortgagor fails to make the payments due, he will do so); *Standard Chartered Bank Ltd v Walker* [1982] 3 All ER 938, [1982] 1 WLR 1410; but it does not extend to a beneficiary for whom the mortgagor was trustee of the property; *Parker-Tweedale v Dunbar Bank plc* [1991] Ch 12, [1990] 2 All ER 577, CA (M & B); [1990] Conv 431 (L. Bently).

20   [1971] Ch 949, [1971] 2 All ER 633; (M & B); *Downsview Nominees Ltd v First City Corpn Ltd* [1993] AC 295, [1993] All ER 626, PC.

1   *Waltham Forest London Borough v Webb* (1974) 232 Estates Gazette 461.

2   *Norwich General Trust v Grierson* [1984] CLY 2306.

without being put on the open market, the valuation should be based on the price that would have been likely to have been obtainable if the property had been in the hands of estate agents for three months. Thus, although a mortgagee is still not required to obtain the best price reasonably obtained, he must nevertheless obtain a proper one.[3]

By way of an exception, building societies are by statute under an obligation to ensure that when selling mortgaged property they obtain the best price reasonably obtainable.[4]

Can a mortgagee, in exercising his statutory power of sale, sell the property to himself? The general rule is that such a transaction will not be accepted as a true sale, and will be declared void.[5] But a sale to a company in which the mortgagee is a director and principal shareholder may be allowed to stand, provided that the purchaser company can show that steps had been taken to secure the best price reasonably obtainable (as by showing that expert advice had been taken concerning the method and conduct of the sale[6]).

INTEREST TO WHICH A PURCHASER FROM A MORTGAGEE TAKES THE LAND

A mortgagee's statutory power of sale is a power to convey land to a purchaser subject to all interests having priority to the mortgage, but free from all interests over which the mortgage has priority.[7] For example, R holds the legal fee simple in land. He grants a legal lease of part of the land to A and an equitable easement (which is registered as a land charge) to B. He then mortgages the land to E. Later he grants a legal easement to C, and contracts to sell the land to D. R then defaults on his repayments to E. E sells the land to P. P takes the land subject to the interests of A and B, but free from C's easement and D's equitable fee simple.[8] P takes free of D's equitable fee simple irrespective of whether or not D has registered his interest as an estate contract, since R's statutory power to sell the land to P arose before R's contract with D.[9] (Exceptionally, however, P may be required by the court to hold subject to an interest created after the date of the mortgage, where it would be unconscionable for him to do otherwise.[10])

THE SALE MADE OUT OF COURT

The power of sale conferred on E can be exercised by him without the need for him to go to court. This is the main advantage of this remedy over the remedy of foreclosure.

---

3 *Predeth v Castle Phillips Finance Co Ltd* [1986] 2 EGLR 144; [1986] Conv 442 (M. P. Thompson). The duty extends to mortgaged property other than land; *Bishop v Bonham* [1988] 1 WLR 742 (shares).
4 Building Societies Act 1962, s 36, replacing earlier legislation.
5 *Williams v Wellingborough Council* [1975] 3 All ER 462, [1975] 1 WLR 1327.
6 *Tse Kwong Lam v Wong Chit Sen* [1983] 3 All ER 54, [1983] 1 WLR 1349, PC; (M & B); [1984] Conv 143 (P. Jackson).
7 Section 104(1).
8 See Chapter 25.
9 *Duke v Robson* [1973] 1 All ER 481, [1973] 1 WLR 267.
10 *Lyus v Prowsa Developments Ltd* [1982] 2 All ER 953, [1982] 1 WLR 1044; (M & B); [1983] Conv 64 (P. Jackson); (1983) 133 NLJ 188 (D. J. Hayton); (1983) CLJ 54 (E. Harpum); (1983) 46 MLR 96 (P. H. Kenny); (1984) MLR 476 (P. Bennett).

Taking possession[11]

If R fails to repay E, and E either forecloses or exercises his power of sale, then, in either case, R will lose his land. We now turn to consider the position if E does not seek such a drastic remedy as that provided by foreclosure or sale. For example, suppose that R has borrowed money under a mortgage in order to buy land on which to build a block of flats. R falls behind in payment of interest on the loan. E knows that the flats must be producing a good income for R. E does not wish to foreclose or sell, as that would put an end to the mortgage which had been made on terms favourable to E. All that E wants is to ensure that the income from the flats is used to pay him the interest due.

In this situation one or other of the two remaining ways to be considered for a mortgagee to enforce security is likely to be more appropriate than foreclosure or sale. These remedies are taking possession and appointing a receiver. It is with the former that this section is concerned.

It has been seen that under the original form in which a mortgage was created, E had a legal right to take possession of R's land. We have seen, too, that if E did take possession, equity required him to account strictly to R. The right to take possession continues to exist today, and is a means by which E can enforce his security.[12]

THE LEGAL BASIS OF THE RIGHT TO TAKE POSSESSION

Until 1926 E was able to take possession of R's land by virtue of the fact that the legal fee simple in the land was vested in him. After 1925, the legal fee simple remains with R. How, then, can E legally take possession since the introduction of the modern means of creating a mortgage?

One of the two ways in which a legal mortgage may now be created is by means of a term of years, eg for 3,000 years, granted by R to E. If the mortgage is created in this form, E is legally tenant of the land, and he may thus legally take possession of the land by virtue of his lease. If the mortgage was created by legal charge, then, if no statutory provision had been made to cover the point, E would have no right to take possession of the land. However, as has been seen, the Law of Property Act 1925 gives[13] a mortgagee under a mortgage created by legal charge 'the same protection, powers and remedies' as if he had been granted a term of 3,000 years. By virtue of this section such a mortgagee is therefore empowered to take possession of the land.

Thus, unless there is some special clause in the mortgage excluding it, 'possession is a remedy to which a mortgagee is entitled as of right against the mortgagor, whether principal or interest is due or not'.[14] The result, therefore,

---

11   P. Walters and J. Harris, *Claims to Possession of Land.*
12   Ibid.
13   Section 87(1).
14   Per Harman J, *Alliance Perpetual Building Society v Belrun Investments Ltd* [1957] 1 WLR 720 at 722. See also *Birmingham Citizens Permanent Building Society v Caunt* [1962] Ch 883; *Mobil Oil Co Ltd v Rawlinson* (1981) 43 P & CR 221; (M & B); [1982] Conv 453 (P. Jackson); *National Westminster Bank v Skelton* [1993] 1 All ER 242, CA; [1993] Conv 458 (J. Martin).

is that at common law a 'mortgagee may go into possession before the ink is dry on the mortgage'.[15]

TAKING POSSESSION OF LAND THAT HAS BEEN LEASED

If R had granted a lease of a flat to T before the creation of the mortgage then E could not take physical possession of the flat. But he can instead direct T to pay rent to him (E) instead of to R. By this means he will receive the income from the land. And he can, of course, take physical possession of any part of the land which was not let, for example, a room on the ground floor which R used as an estate office for managing the flats and collecting rent.

Indeed, it is more convenient for E if the land is let. If the land is let, E can obtain the income by directing the tenant or tenants to pay their rent to him. If the land is not let, then since, as we saw earlier, E is liable to account strictly to R, he is under a duty to manage the property with due diligence. Thus if E takes possession and grants a lease, and he fails to fix a reasonable rent, he will be liable to R for the difference between the rent fixed and what would have been a reasonable rent.[16] Similarly, if the land or part of it could have been leased and E fails to lease it, he is liable to R for the rent that could have been earned if it had been let. If the land is already let E does not have the responsibility for granting a lease and fixing the rent for it.

APPLICATION OF THE INCOME RECEIVED

After recouping the interest due to him, E is entitled to use any surplus towards paying off the principal debt, but he is not obliged to apply any surplus in this way. He can, if he wishes, pass the surplus to R. This is because he (E) is not obliged to accept repayment in the form of a series of separate sums.

If E takes possession he is under a duty to undertake reasonable repairs. The cost is added to R's debt to E.

PROCEDURE

If the mortgaged land is not let and E wishes to take physical possession, he is not entitled to break into the property and oust R since to do so would be a crime under the Criminal Law Act 1977.[17] E must therefore (unless he is able to take possession peacefully) obtain an order for possession from the court. Since 1926, jurisdiction to hear mortgagees' claims for possession has rested with the Chancery Division. Where the property mortgaged consists of a dwelling house, the court has discretion, conferred by statute,[18] to adjourn the

---

15   Per Harman J, *Four-Maids Ltd v Dudley Marshall (Properties) Ltd* [1957] Ch 317 at 320; (M & B). On the question whether a mortgagee should continue to have a right to possession irrespective of any default by the mortgagor, see [1979] Conv 266 (R. J. Smith); [1979] CLJ 257 (R. A. Pearce).

16   See *White v City of London Brewery Co* (1889) 42 Ch D 237; (M & B).

17   Sections 5, 6.

18   Administration of Justice Act 1970, Pt IV, ss 36-39. Prior to the Act, taking possession could have entailed committing an offence under the Forcible Entry Acts 1381-1623. These Acts were repealed by s 13 of the Act of 1977.

proceedings, provided that the court considers that R is likely to be able to pay the sum due within a reasonable period.[19] As in the case of the discretion conferred on the court to grant an adjournment of an application for a foreclosure decree to be made absolute, the sum that the court must expect R to be likely to be able to pay excludes any sum which, under the mortgage, becomes payable by R in the event of his defaulting in paying an instalment.[20]

TAKING POSSESSION PRIOR TO SALE

Because of the risks incurred by a mortgagee if he exercises his right to take possession, in practice a mortgagee is more likely to appoint a receiver, or to sell the land. But if he is to sell the land, he will only be able to do so if he can sell with vacant possession. It is by exercising his right to take possession that he is enabled to oust the mortgagee and so be in a position to sell the property. Thus today it is normally as an adjunct to the power of sale that the right to take possession is significant.

Appointing a receiver

The remedy of taking possession imposes a heavy burden of responsibility on E. The final remedy to be considered, that of appointing a receiver, enables E to obtain the income from the land without incurring the responsibilities entailed in taking possession. A power to appoint a receiver is now conferred by the Law of Property Act 1925[1] (replacing earlier legislation). Before the existence of the statutory power the terms of mortgages sometimes provided for the appointment of a receiver. The 1925 Act confers a power to appoint a receiver on every mortgagee under a mortgage made by deed.

DUTIES

If a receiver is appointed, his function is to receive all the income from the land and to apply it as follows.[2]

1. To pay rents, rates and taxes due on the land.
2. To pay interest on prior mortgages.
3. To pay the receiver's commission (normally 5% of the gross amount of money he receives).

---

19   On the application of the section and on the execise of the discretion, see *Western Bank Ltd v Schindler* [1977] Ch 1, [1976] 2 All ER 393; (M & B); *Habib Bank Ltd v Tailor* [1982] 3 All ER 561, [1982] 1 WLR 1218; [1983] Conv 80 (P. H. Kenny); *Bank of Scotland v Grimes* [1985] QB 1179, [1985] 2 All ER 254, CA (application of section to an endowment mortgage (see p 462, post)); *Citibank Trust Ltd v Ayivor* [1987] 3 All ER 241, [1987] 1 WLR 1157; *Britannia Building Society v Earl* [1990] 2 All ER 469, [1990] 1 WLR 422; [1990] Conv 450.
20   Administration of Justice Act 1973, s 8. See (1979) 43 Conv NS 266 (R. J. Smith); [1984] Conv 901 (S. Tromans).
 1   Section 109.
 2   Section 109(8).

4. To pay insurance premiums.
5. If E so directs, to pay the cost of repairs.
6. To pay the interest due to E under the mortgage.
7. If E so directs, towards paying off the principal sum outstanding; or, if E makes no such direction, to pay the surplus to the person who would have been entitled to it if the receiver had not been appointed, ie normally R.

APPOINTMENT

E must appoint the receiver in writing. The power to appoint a receiver arises and becomes exercisable in the same circumstances as the statutory power of sale.

Thus once the date fixed for repayment has passed, E has a power to appoint a receiver. But if he does so before the power has become exercisable (ie before R has been at fault in one of the ways explained when dealing with the power of sale), he is liable in damages to R. Once the power has become exercisable, E may appoint a receiver without risk of incurring liability to R.

The reason for the existence of the two stages (ie the power arising and the power becoming exercisable) may be explained by this example. R mortgages land to E to borrow money to build a block of flats. R then lets a flat to T. R fails to keep up his repayment to E. E appoints a receiver. The receiver requires T to pay his rent to him (the receiver) instead of to R. T will want to be satisfied that E had power to appoint a receiver. (Otherwise, if he had not, T may find himself called on to pay the rent over again to R.) The receiver can satisfy T that the power to appoint a receiver had arisen by showing that the date fixed for repayment had passed. T therefore does not have to determine whether R had or had not been at fault, ie whether one of the three conditions on which the power becomes exercisable had been fulfilled.

POSITION OF THE RECEIVER

If E appoints a receiver who collects the income from the land, the receiver, as agent of E, in effect enters into possession of the land. Without special provision this would involve E with the liabilities that this means of enforcing a mortgage entails. This possibility is, however, avoided by the provision of the Law of Property Act 1925[3] that (notwithstanding that he is appointed by E) the receiver is to be deemed to be the agent of R, unless the mortgage provides otherwise. Thus if the receiver was negligent in his handling of the property he could be sued by R, but R could not sue E.

---

3   Section 109(2)

Priorities

R mortgages Blackacre, which is worth £20,000 to E as security for a loan of £3,000. R sells the fee simple in Blackacre to P for a price of £17,000. E claims repayment of the loan. R remains personally liable to E. If E fails to obtain repayment, he can enforce the mortgage by exercising any of the methods available to a mortgagee, provided that the mortgage is *enforceable* against P. If P paid R only £17,000 for land that was worth £20,000, it is clear that it was intended that P was to take the land subject to the mortgage and therefore assume responsibility for repaying the £3,000 to E. This might well have been the arrangement as between R and P (and R may have accordingly taken an indemnity from P for £3,000). However, the terms on which the land was conveyed by R to P is a matter which is distinct from the question whether or not E can, in fact, enforce the mortgage against P.

Suppose that the mortgage to E was made in 1920 and was equitable. E unwisely permits R to retain the title deeds. R conveys the legal fee simple to P for £17,000. P is able to show that he is a bona fide purchaser for value of the legal estate without notice. As such he takes free from the equitable mortgage to E. E therefore cannot enforce the mortgage against P. He thus loses his security and unless he can find R, and make R pay, he loses his money.

We shall shortly consider the principles which determine whether a mortgage is enforceable against a later purchaser of the mortgaged land, but at this point certain preliminary matters must be explained.

Successive mortgages

Suppose that R mortgages Blackacre, which is worth £20,000, to E_1 as security for a loan of £5,000. Later, R mortgages the land again, this time to E_2 as security for a loan of £10,000. R can make the second mortgage by the same methods that he can use to make a first mortgage. If the mortgage is to be legal it will have to be by deed and in the form of a term of years or a legal charge. If the mortgage to E_1 is in the form of a term of 3,000 years, the mortgage to E_2 will be in the form of a term of 3,000 years plus a day (or it could be in the form of a legal charge). Alternatively, the second mortgage could be equitable.

Where there are successive mortgages to E_1 and E_2, then as regards whether the mortgages are legal or equitable there are the following possibilities:

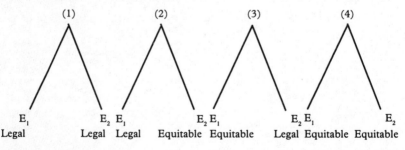

	(1)	(2)		(3)		(4)	
	E_1	E_2	E_1	E_2	E_1	E_2	E_1	E_2
	Legal	Legal	Legal	Equitable	Equitable	Legal	Equitable	Equitable

This is the position at the present day, assuming that the interest mortgaged is itself legal, eg a legal fee simple in land. If the interest mortgaged is equitable, eg a life interest under a strict settlement, then each of the two successive mortgages will be equitable (as in (4) above).

Before 1926, however, the position shown at (1) would not normally exist, because before 1926 a legal mortgage was usually created by R conveying the legal fee simple to E (subject to a proviso for reconveyance on redemption). Since the legal fee simple would be with E_1, R could not convey the fee simple to E_2. The positions shown at (2), (3) and (4) were, however, all met before 1926.

'Priority'

Suppose that R mortgages Blackacre to E_1 for a loan of £5,000, and then to E_2 for a loan of £10,000. R fails in his repayment to E_1. E_1 exercises his statutory power of sale and the land is sold for £20,000 to P. Out of the proceeds, E_1 retains £5,000 and passes the balance to E_2. E_2 retains £10,000 and passes the balance of £5,000 to R. Here no problem arises since the value of the land was more than sufficient to provide security for the loans to E_1 and E_2. But suppose that the value of the land had fallen to £7,000. The value of the land will then no longer provide adequate security for both E_1 and E_2. In the event of R failing in his repayments to E_1 and E_2 (or to both of them), and E_1 and E_2 (or both of them), seeking to enforce their security, the problem arises as to how the £7,000 is to be applied. One solution would be to divide the value of the land between E_1 and E_2 equally. Another solution would be to divide the value of the land between E_1 and E_2 in proportion to the debts due to each. English and Welsh law accepts neither of these solutions and instead adopts the principle that either E_1 or E_2 takes 'priority'; that is, one or other will have first claim. Thus, if E_2 has priority, he will take the whole £7,000 and E_1 will receive nothing.

This, of course, assumes that R has no other property. When we say that if E_2 takes priority he will take the whole £7,000, we mean that he will take not less than that amount. He, E_2, can sue R in contract for the balance of £3,000 due to him. Similarly E_1 can sue R in contract for the debt of £5,000 owed to him. But E_2 has no security for the balance of £3,000 owed to him, and E_1 no security for the £5,000. If R had no other property apart from the land, there would be no point in E_1 and E_2 suing him in contract for these sums. Or it may be that R does have other property, but that he is bankrupt, with other creditors besides E_1 and E_2 claiming payment of debts. Suppose that R's assets, apart from Blackacre, total £5,000 and that one creditor, C_1, claims a debt of £4,000 and C_2, another, a debt of £8,000. R's debt will total £20,000 and, since his assets (other than the land) total £5,000, R's trustee in bankruptcy will declare a dividend of 25%. E_1, E_2, C_1 and C_2 will receive 25% of the sums owed to them, ie E_1 receives £1,250; E_2 receives £750; C_1 receives £1,000 and C_2 receives £2,000. (E_2 receives £750 under his action in contract against R, plus the value of Blackacre, £7,000, by virtue of the security which the mortgage constitutes.)

What has been said has been based on the assumption that E_2 took priority over E_1. If E_1 had taken priority, the mortgage of Blackacre would have ensured that he received the amount owed to him (£5,000) in full. The balance of £2,000 would go to E_2 who would in this case have to claim £8,000 in contract from R; or, if R was bankrupt, from his trustee in bankruptcy. A dividend of 25% would then give E_2 £2,000.

It is clear, therefore, that unless R has sufficient assets to meet his debts, it is important to E_1 and E_2 which of them has priority. The rules that determine the priority of successive mortgages are, broadly, the same rules which determine the question referred to at the beginning of this section – whether a mortgage by R to E is enforceable against P, a purchaser of the land from R.

PRIORITY RULE BEFORE 1926

Before 1926 the order of priority was determined in accordance with the doctrine of legal and equitable interests. It will be recalled that there are two aspects of this doctrine, namely:

1.   Legal interests are valid against all the world.
2.   Equitable interests are valid against all the world except a bona fide purchaser for value of the legal estate without notice.

Before 1926 these were the principles which determined both the question whether a mortgage of realty was enforceable against a subsequent purchaser, and also the question, in the case of two successive mortgages of realty, which mortgage took priority. (Since a mortgagee is a purchaser *pro tanto*, it is to be expected that the same rules should apply in both situations.)

The 1925 legislation altered the previous position by providing that certain mortgages had, in order to be enforceable against a subsequent purchaser (and to take priority over a subsequent mortgage), to be registered. What forms of mortgage were made registrable we shall consider shortly, but first the operation of the pre-1926 rules must be examined.

Consider the situations set out at (1), (2), (3) and (4) on p 452.

1.   We saw that this position would normally not exist before 1926.
2.   Here the first mortgage is legal. Legal interests are binding against all the world. Therefore E_1 takes priority over E_2.[4] Only in certain exceptional instances would E_1 lose his priority to E_2. Thus, if,
     (a) E_1, by fraud,[5] helped to deceive E_2 that there was no prior mortgage; or
     (b) E_1, by gross negligence, failed to obtain the title deeds; or
     (c) E_1 did some act or made some representation which gave R apparent authority to deal with the property free of the mortgage (as by E_1 endorsing a receipt on the mortgage, thus acknowledging that the mortgage had been redeemed),
     E_1 would lose the priority which his legal interest would otherwise have given him over E_2's equitable mortgage. E_2 would therefore take priority.

---

4   *Walker v Linom* [1907] 2 Ch 104; (M & B).

3   Here the first mortgage to E_1 is equitable and the second mortgage to E_2 is legal. If E_2 can prove that he took the mortgage bona fide and without notice of E_1's equitable mortgage (we already know that he is a purchaser for value of the legal estate) then, under the normal rule, he takes priority over E_1.[6] If he cannot show this, E_1 takes priority.

    If E_2 asks R to let him see the title deeds and R, knowing that the title deeds are deposited with E_1, gives some excuse to E_2 for not being able to produce them which E_2 accepts, then if the court accepts that R's explanation was reasonable, E_2 is not fixed with notice (and therefore retains his property). The courts, in this context, appear to have accepted some weak excuses as being reasonable (for example that R was busy and would produce the deeds later[7]).

4.   Here both mortgages are equitable. Here the rule was 'first in time, first in right'. Thus E_1 would take priority, but the rule applied only where 'the equities were equal'. This meant that it was possible for E_1, by his conduct to lose priority to E_2. For example, if E_1 failed to ask R for the title deeds, or returned the deeds to R, thus enabling E_2 to be deceived into believing that there was no prior mortgage, E_1 lost his priority to E_2.[8]

These were the rules for determining priority between successive mortgages of land before 1926. In some respects they were unsatisfactory. For example, whilst normally E_1 took priority, in some circumstances he lost priority to E_2. E_1 would usually (though not always[9]) be safe if he required R to deposit the title deeds with him.

    E_2 would usually take this mortgage without fear of an earlier mortgagee taking priority if R could produce and hand over the title deeds. The moral for any mortgagee was thus not to lend money unless R could produce the title deeds. But even if the title deeds were produced, a mortgagee would not necessarily be certain of taking priority. For example, suppose that R mortgages Blackacre, which is worth £20,000 to E_1 by legal mortgage, for a loan of £6,000. R later seeks a loan of £11,000 from E_2. On E_2's request for the title deeds, R tells him of the mortgage to E_1. E_1 confirms that R owes him £6,000. E_2 makes the loan in the security of an equitable mortgage. R then seeks a loan of £7,000 from E_3. On E_3's enquiry about the title deeds R tells him of the mortgage to E_1. E_1 confirms to E_3 that R owes him £6,000. E_3, not knowing of the mortgage to E_2, lends R £7,000 on the security of an equitable mortgage. R fails in his repayments. E_1 sells the land. E_1 takes priority over E_2. As between E_2 and E_3 each holding equitable mortgages, E_2, being first in time, takes priority. Thus, E_1 receives £6,000, E_2 £11,000 and E_3 the balance of £3,000. (For the balance of £4,000 E_3 has to take his place in the queue with R's other creditors.) E_3, it

5   *Northern Counties of England Fire Insurance Co v Whipp* (1884) 26 Ch D 482, CA; (M & B).
6   *Pitcher v Rawlins* (1872) 7 Ch App 259; (M & B).
7   *Hewitt v Loosemore* (1851) 9 Hare 449; (M & B); cf *Oliver v Hinton* [1899] 2 Ch 264; (M & B).
8   *Rice v Rice* (1853) 2 Drew 73.
9   As where the mortgage to E_1 was equitable and the mortgage to E_2 legal, and E_2 was able to show that R had given a reasonable excuse for not producing the title deeds. See ante.

will be noted, had had no means of learning of the prior mortgage to E_2. Thus a mortgagee could generally learn of a first mortgage, but had no means of discovering whether other prior mortgages, after the first, had been made.

PRIORITY RULES AFTER 1925

Registration

This problem the 1925 legislation overcame by providing that if the title deeds were not deposited with the mortgagee when a mortgage was made, then the mortgage was registrable as a land charge in the Land Charges Registry. This provision was contained in the Land Charges Act 1925,[10] and is now contained in the Land Charges Act 1972.[11]

Consider the position if the facts in the last example occurred in 1988.

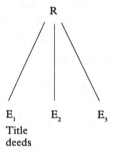

The mortgage to E_1 is not registrable, since the title deeds were deposited with E_1. The mortgages to E_2 and E_3 are not so protected, and are therefore registrable. Thus when E_3 is considering whether to lend money to R he can discover the existence of the mortgage to E_2 by inspecting the register. If E_2 has failed to register his mortgage, then, under the Land Charges Act 1972,[12] it is void as against E_3 (and any other later mortgagee), ie E_3 takes priority over E_2. If E_2 failed to register his mortgage, but E_3 in fact had notice of E_2's mortgage, this is irrelevant. What matters is registration. If E_2 wishes to protect his priority, he must register his mortgage. (If E_2 fails to register his mortgage, this does not affect the position between himself and R. It merely affects his priority as regards E_3.)

In the example, E_3's mortgage is also registrable. If he fails to register the mortgage, then, as between himself and E_2 his failure to register is irrelevant. His failure to register would only matter if there was a further mortgage to E_4. In this event (if E_2 and E_3 failed to register) the order of priorities would be E_1, E_4, E_3 (who loses priority to E_4), and finally E_2 (who loses priority to E_3 and E_4).

10   Section 10(1).
11   Section 2(3).
12   Section 4(6).

It should be noted that both legal *and* equitable mortgages without deposit of title deeds are made registrable by the Act, though the two kinds are registered under different classes. Legal mortgages without deposit of title deeds are registrable (as what the Act terms 'puisne', ie lesser, mortgages) under Class C (i) of the Register; equitable mortgages without deposit of title deeds are registrable under the heading of 'General Equitable Charges' in Class C (iii) of the Register.

Non-registrable mortgages

R mortgages land to E_1 and deposits the title deeds with him. The mortgage is therefore not registrable. Suppose that R then mortgages the land to E_2. The question arises as to how priority is to be determined between E_1 and E_2 in view of the fact that E_1's mortgage is not registrable. The answer is that where the first mortgage is not registrable, the old pre-1926 rules apply. In this case it will therefore be necessary, in order to apply the old rules, to consider whether the mortgages were legal or equitable.

Application of the rules after 1925

MORTGAGES OF A LEGAL INTEREST IN LAND

The position after 1925 may therefore be summarised as follows with regard to the mortgage of a legal interest in land.

1. If the first mortgage is registrable, priority depends on whether it is registered. If it has been registered, E_1 takes priority. If it has not been registered, then, as a result of the Land Charges Act 1972,[13] E_2 takes priority.
2. If the first mortgage is not registrable, the old rules apply.

Here are four examples.

1. In 1990 R mortgaged the legal fee simple in Blackacre by an equitable mortgage to E_1, and deposited the title deeds with him. In 1995 R mortgaged the land to E_2 by a legal charge. The mortgage to E_2 was not registered.

(a) The mortgage to E_1 was not registrable. The mortgage to E_2 was registrable.
(b) As between E_1 and E_2, E_2's failure to register is irrelevant.
(c) As E_1's mortgage was not registrable the old rules apply. Under the old rules E_2 having a legal mortgage would take priority over E_1's equitable mortgage if he could show that he was a bona fide purchaser without notice. The fact that R cannot produce the title deeds fixes E_2 with constructive notice of E_1's mortgage. Thus, E_1 takes priority.[14]

---

13   Section 4(6); replacing LCA 1925, s 13(2).
14   If R gave E_2 what the court accepted as a reasonable excuse for not producing the title deeds, then E_2 is not fixed with constructive notice and, by establishing his claim to be a bona fide purchaser without notice, takes priority. See p 454.

2. In 1985 R mortgaged the legal fee simple in Blackacre to E$_1$ by a legal charge and deposited the title deeds with him. In 1990 R mortgaged Blackacre to E$_2$ by an equitable mortgage, which E$_2$ registered. In 1995 R mortgaged Blackacre to E$_3$, by a legal charge. Who has priority as between E$_2$ and E$_3$?

(a) The mortgage to E$_2$, not being protected by deposit of title deeds (which were with E$_1$), was registrable.

(b) Since E$_2$ registered the mortgage before the creation of E$_3$'s mortgage, he, E$_2$, takes priority over E$_3$. (E$_1$ takes priority over both E$_2$ and E$_3$.) (It will therefore be seen that if the first of two mortgages is registrable, it is immaterial whether the two mortgages were legal or equitable. All that matters is whether or not the first was registered.)

3. In 1990 R mortgaged the legal fee simple in Blackacre to E$_1$ by a legal mortgage for a loan of £10,000, and deposited the title deeds with him. In 1995 R sought a loan from E$_2$ and told him of the mortgage to E$_1$. In reply to an enquiry from E$_2$, E$_1$ by error informed him that the mortgage had recently been redeemed. In fact none of the £10,000 had been repaid. E$_2$ lent money to R on the security of an equitable mortgage.

(a) The mortgage to E$_1$ was not registrable since it was made with deposit of title deeds. The pre-1926 rules therefore apply in determining priority.

(b) E$_1$ takes priority unless the application of the pre-1926 rules gives priority to E$_2$. Under the pre-1925 rules, as E$_1$'s mortgage is legal this will bind E$_2$ unless the matter falls within one of the exceptional instances when E$_1$, by his conduct, loses his priority. In representing to E$_2$ that the mortgage had been redeemed, E$_1$ would bring himself within an exception,[15] and E$_2$ would thus take priority.

4. In 1985 R mortgaged the legal fee simple in Blackacre to E$_1$ by a legal mortgage, and deposited the title deeds with him. In 1990 R mortgaged the land to E$_2$, by an equitable mortgage, and in 1995 to E$_3$ by a legal charge. None of the mortgages was registered. Who has priority, E$_2$ or E$_3$?

(a) The mortgage to E$_2$, not being protected by deposit of title deeds, was registrable.

(b) Since E$_2$ failed to register the mortgage, it is void as against E$_3$ who thus takes priority. (It is irrelevant here that E$_3$'s mortgage is registrable and had not been registered.)

SECTION 4(5) OF THE LAND CHARGES ACT 1972,[16] AND S 97 OF THE LAW OF PROPERTY ACT 1925

At this point it will be convenient to consider the position if:

R mortgages Blackacre to E$_1$ (there being no deposit of title deeds);
R mortgages Blackacre to E$_2$ (there being no deposit of title deeds);

---

15   See p 455.
16   Replacing s 13(2) of the Land Charges Act 1925.

E_1 registers his mortgage;
E_2 registers his mortgage.

According to s 4(5) of the Land Charges Act 1972, since E_1 had failed to register his mortgage when R mortgaged the land to E_2, it is void as against E_2's mortgage, with the result that E_2 takes priority. However, s 97 of the Law of Property Act 1925 provides that every registrable mortgage shall rank according to its date of registration.

Since E_1 registered his mortgage before E_2 registered his, the effect of s 97 would be to give priority to E_1. The two sections thus produce different results. The better view is that s 4(5) prevails and that E_2 therefore takes priority notwithstanding s 97.

MORTGAGES OF AN EQUITABLE INTEREST

On p 456 were stated the rules after 1925 relating to mortgages of a legal interest in land. Now consider this situation.

S devises the legal fee simple in Blackacre to T_1 and T_2 on trust for sale for his widow, R, for her life, with remainder to his daughter. R wishes to borrow money. E_1 lends her £3,000 on the security of a mortgage of her life interest. Later, R makes a second mortgage of her life interest, this time to E_2, as security for a loan of £2,000.

It will be seen here that R has mortgaged property which consists of an equitable, not a legal, interest. After 1925, in the case of successive mortgages of an equitable interest in any form of property, priority among the mortgagees depends on the order in which notice of the mortgages is received by the appropriate[17] trustees.[18] This is the rule in *Dearle v Hall*.[19] (Under the Law of Property Act 1925,[20] in order to establish priority under this rule the notice must be in writing.) Thus if E_2 gave notice of his mortgage to T_1 and T_2 before notice was received by them of the mortgage to E_1, then E_2 takes priority. It is therefore in E_1's interest to give notice to T_1 and T_2 immediately the mortgage to him has been made.

Before 1925 the rule in *Dearle v Hall* governed the order of priority of mortgages of equitable interests in pure personalty. The Law of Property Act 1925 made the rule applicable to *all* equitable interests (in land or personalty).

SUMMARY OF CHANGES MADE BY THE LAW OF PROPERTY ACT 1925

The changes made by the Land Charges Act 1925 and the Law of Property Act 1925 as regards the rules relating to the priority of mortgages of land can be summarised in the following way:

---

17   Eg in the case of a mortgage of an equitable interest under a strict settlement, the appropriate trustees are the trustees of the settlement, ie the Settled Land Act trustees.
18   Section 137.
19   (1828) 3 Russ 1; (M & B).
20   Section 137(3).

The property mortgaged	Before 1926	After 1925
Legal interests in land	The doctrine of legal and equitable estates (subject to special rules, eg as to a 'reasonable excuse'[1])	Registration or where the first mortgage is not registrable, the pre-1926 doctrine of legal and equitable estates (subject to special rules, eg as to 'reasonable excuse'[1])
Equitable interests in land	The doctrine of legal and equitable estates (subject to special rules, eg as to 'reasonable excuse'[1])	The rule in *Dearle v Hall*.

It will be seen that after 1925 the question of whether an interest is legal or equitable arises in two ways in the context of priorities.

1. It is necessary to know whether property mortgaged consists of a legal or an equitable *interest* in order to know which rule to apply.

2. If it is found that it is a legal interest in land that has been mortgaged, and it is found that the first mortgage is not registrable then, in order to determine who has priority, it is necessary to know whether the *mortgages* were legal or equitable.

SEARCHING THE REGISTER

It will be seen from what has been said in this chapter that there will be three occasions when, in the context of mortgages, it will be necessary to search in the register of land charges for the existence of a mortgage.

1. Before making a loan a potential mortgagee needs to search the register to ascertain whether any prior mortgage exists. (See p 456.)

2. A mortgagee who has exercised his power of sale must search the register to ascertain whether any subsequent mortgage exists before he can safely hand any surplus proceeds of sale to the mortgagor. (See p 445.) (There is no need for such a mortgagee to concern himself with the existence of any prior mortgagee, since the purchaser will take the land subject to the prior mortgage. It will be for the purchaser to find the existence of this mortgage by searching the register, as part of his searches generally into any possible encumbrances on the land.)

3. A mortgagee who is repaid must search the register to discover whether any subsequent mortgage exists. If it does, he must pass any title deeds deposited with him to the subsequent mortgagee, not to the mortgagor. (See p 439.)

1   See p 455.

Mortgages of leaseholds

We have considered mortgages in the context of a mortgage of a fee simple in land. But it may be that R holds, not the fee simple in Blackacre, but a lease of Blackacre for, say, 99 years, and it is this that he mortgages to E. The principles relating to the mortgage of leaseholds are essentially the same as in the case of a mortgage of the fee simple, but the following matters call for attention.

Creation of a legal mortgage of a lease

Before 1926, if R wished to mortgage his lease of Blackacre to E he could either:

1. grant to E a sub-lease of the land for a period at least one day less than the unexpired portion of his own lease, with a proviso for cesser on redemption; or
2. assign the lease to E with a covenant for re-assignment on redemption.

The second was the method most commonly employed.

After 1925, only the following two methods of mortgaging a lease may be employed:

1. by R granting E a sub-lease at least one day shorter than the unexpired portion of his own lease, with a proviso for cesser on redemption; or
2. by R charging the land to E by deed expressed to be by way of legal mortgage (ie by 'legal charge').[2] (This method has the advantage that it probably does not constitute a breach of a covenant against sub-letting.)

Creation of an equitable mortgage of a lease

The same principles apply as in the case of a mortgage of a fee simple. Thus before the Law of Property (Miscellaneous Provisions) Act 1989:

1. if the mortgage was in writing, signed by R; or
2. if the mortgage was evidenced in writing, signed by R or his agent; or
3. if the mortgage was oral, and was supported by an act of part performance by E;

under the doctrine in *Walsh v Lonsdale*, E acquired an equitable mortgage of the lease.

After the 1989 Act, for the doctrine in *Walsh v Lonsdale* to apply the mortgage must be in writing and be signed by both R and E.

---

2   LPA 1925, s 86.

Equity of redemption

The same principles apply in the case of mortgages of leases as in the case of mortgages of the fee simple. Thus R has an equitable right to redeem the mortgage notwithstanding that the date fixed in the mortgage for repayment has passed.

Building society mortgages and other considerations

In recent times the most common form of mortgage has been that in which a house-buyer mortgages the property to a building society. It has been the availability of loans from building societies which has permitted the growth in home ownership during this century. (Certain aspects of the operations of building societies are regulated by statute.[3])

It is the practice for mortgage agreements with building societies to provide that the rate of interest on loans should be variable at the discretion of the society. The need for such a provision is apparent: societies need to be able to adjust their interest rates in accordance with the fluctuations of the money market. The legality of such a provision has never been tested. The inclusion of such an arrangement in a mortgage other than with a building society might in some circumstances be held by the court to be unconscionable.[4]

If R wishes to borrow, say, £80,000 from a building society (or other lender, for example, a bank) there are today two main ways in which the loan can be repaid. The most common way is for R to make monthly payments, each payment consisting partly of interest on the loan, and partly of repayment of capital. As the capital is paid off, the amount of interest decreases, and the proportions of each instalment consisting of capital repayment therefore increases.

Alternatively, under what is termed an 'endowment mortgage', R takes out an insurance policy on his own life, under which the insurer agrees to pay (to continue our example) £80,000 on R attaining, say, the age of 60, or on his death under that age. R assigns his right under the policy to the building society. Until he reaches 60, R pays, usually each month, interest on the £80,000 to the building society, and a premium to the insurance company. When R attains 60 the company pays the £80,000 to the building society, and the mortgage is redeemed. The principal advantage[5] of this method is that it provides security for R's wife (or other dependant): if R dies before he reaches 60, the mortgage is paid off.

If, while a mortgage[6] is being paid off, R wishes to move, on the sale of his house the purchase money will go to pay off whatever is outstanding on the

---

3   Building Societies Act 1986.
4   The matter is discussed by Wurtzburg and Mills, *Building Society L:aw* (14th edn, 1976) p 165; see also Law Commission Working Paper No 99, *Land Mortgages*, pp 80-83.
5   There may also be tax advantages.
6   Whether taken out as an endowment mortgage or as a mortgage repayable by instalments.

mortgage.[7] If his house has been increasing in value there is likely to be a surplus after the redemption of the mortgage. This will go to R, and he can use the money for the purchase of his new house. But in addition he may need a fresh loan in order to buy his new house. He should not, however, assume that the building society from whom he borrowed money previously will automatically grant him a loan towards the cost of another house (and he should certainly not imagine that a mortgage from a building society is in some way transferable from one house to another). Since building societies are normally more favourably disposed to those who have been regular savers with the society (eg by making monthly deposits), while R is paying off the mortgage on his first house, he would be well advised to make regular savings with the society in case he ever has to move, and needs to apply for a fresh loan to enable him to obtain the new house.

Mortgage of land held by co-owners: undue influence

If land is owned by co-owners, for example a husband (H) and wife (W), we know (from Chapter 11) that H and W hold the legal estate on trust for themselves beneficially (as joint tenants or tenants in common, as the case may be). If H and W wish to borrow money on the security of the property they can mortgage the legal estate by jointly executing a mortgage deed.

If one of the co-owners, say H, acting alone, purports to mortgage the property (for example, by forging W's signature), he is treated as having mortgaged his equitable interest in the property (ie the extent of his share).[8]

If two co-owners both execute a mortgage, but one of them signs without knowing the nature or the full terms[9] of the transaction, and only as a result of pressure from the other co-owner, pressure that amounts in law to undue influence, what result follows – specifically, does the fact that the signature of one mortgagor was given without genuine consent invalidate the mortgage, with the result that mortgagee loses his security? The matter has been the subject of considerable litigation, culminating in the decision of the House of Lords in *Barclays Bank plc v O'Brien*.[10]

---

7 If the mortgage had been an endowment mortgage, the building society will re-assign to R the benefit of the insurance policy on his life.

8 *Thames Garanty Ltd v Campbell* [1985] 1 QB 210, 219.

9 Eg that the liability is unlimited and not, as understood by the co-owner misled, limited to a specific sum; *TSB Bank plc v Camfield* [1995] 1 WLR 430, CA.

10 [1994] 1 AC 180, [1993] 4 All ER 41; [1994] Conv 140 (M. P. Thomson); [1994] Conv 241 (M. Dixon and C. Harpum); [1995] Conv 250 (P. Sparkes); *Midland Bank plc v Massey* [1994] 2 FLR 342; [1995] Conv 148 (J. Mee); *Banco Exterior Interacional v Mann* [1995] 1 All ER 936 (bank not fixed with constructive notice); *TSB Bank plc v Camfield* (bank fixed with constructive notice); *Midland Bank plc v Serter* (1995) 71 P & CR 264 (bank not fixed with constructive notice).

In this case a husband (H) and wife (W) agreed to take out a second mortgage of their home as security for an overdraft from a bank, on the account of a company in which H (but not W) had an interest. H falsely represented to W that the overdraft was limited to £60,000. In reliance on this W signed the mortgage. When the overdraft had exceeded £154,000 the bank sought to enforce the mortgage and obtained an order for possession so that the house could be sold. W appealed against the order for possession. The House of Lords held that (i) where a wife was induced to stand surety for her husband's debts (ie including acting as co-mortgagor of jointly owned property) by the husband's misrepresentation, undue influence or other legal wrong, the wife had a right in equity to set aside the transaction; (ii) this right against the husband was enforceable not only against him but also against a third party who had notice, actual or constructive, of the circumstances that had given rise to the wife's right to set the transaction aside (or a third party for whom the husband had been acting as agent); (iii) where a wife agreed to provide security for her husband's debts in a transaction that was not in her financial interests and the circumstances were such that there was a substantial risk of the husband acting in a way that would give the wife a right in equity to set the transaction aside, then, unless the third party had taken steps to satisfy himself that the wife's agreement had been properly obtained, he would be fixed with constructive notice of the wife's right to set the transaction aside, and his right to enforce the mortgage therefore lost.

When the overdraft arrangements were being made, the relevant bank official was instructed to ensure that both the husband and the wife were fully aware of the nature of the transaction and to advise them that if they were in any doubt they should consult their solicitor before signing. These instructions were not carried out, the wife signing solely in reliance on what her husband had told her. In these circumstances, the House of Lords held, the bank was fixed with constructive notice of the wife's right to set the transaction aside. The mortgage was therefore not enforceable by the bank and the order for possession was set aside. (This would not necessarily have been the end of the story.[11] The debt remained outstanding. If the bank sued H, and H was unable to pay, and was declared bankrupt, the bank would be able to seek an order that the property should be sold so that H's share of the proceeds of sale could be applied towards the repayment of the sum owing to the bank. If a sale was ordered, the wife would, by virtue of her beneficial interest in the property, receive her share of the proceeds, but the home would be lost.)

In *O'Brien* the parties were man and wife. Lord Browne-Wilkinson (who gave the sole speech in the Lords) indicated[12] that the principles enunciated in the case would apply also to all cases where one cohabitee stood surety for the other cohabitee's debts and the lender was aware that an emotional relationship existed between the cohabitees.[13]

11　[1994] Conv 140, 145 (M. P. Thompson).

12　At pp 185, 198, 199.

13　See also *Credit Lyonnais Bank Netherland NV v Burch* [1997] 1 All ER 144 (employer and employee in close personal relationship, employee's mortgage of her property to bank as surety for employer's debts set aside as transaction in the category of ones that 'shock the conscience of the court'); (1997) 113 LQR 10 (H. Tjio). Cf *Banco Exterior Internacional SA v Thomas* [1997] 1 WLR 221 (transaction not set aside; cohabitee had had independent legal advice that she chose to ignore).

On the same day that the House of Lords delivered judgment in *O'Brien*, the House delivered judgment also in another case, *CIBC Mortgages plc v Pitt*[14] in which the same issue arose. In the *CIBC* case the mortgage of the home was obtained on the basis that the money lent was for the purpose of the purchase of a second property. In fact, the money was obtained, and applied, for the purchase of shares, the value of which subsequently fell. The wife knew of the purpose behind the mortgage. But her agreement was given reluctantly and only due to pressure from her husband. When repayments fell into arrears, the lender sought an order for possession of the home. The House of Lords held that whilst the wife had a right against the husband to set the transaction aside on the ground that the husband had exercised undue influence, this right did not bind the lender since the lender had no actual notice of the undue influence nor were there any circumstances to indicate to the lender that the transaction was anything other than a normal loan to a husband and wife for their joint benefit. (Nor was the husband regarded as having acted as agent of the lender.) Thus, not being fixed with constructive notice of the wife's right to have the transaction set aside, the lender took free of this right and so was entitled to enforce the mortgage (ie by an order for possession, so that the property could be sold).

Remedies available to a mortgagee under an equitable mortgage

1. FORECLOSURE

A decree of foreclosure[15] awarded to an equitable mortgagee directs the mortgagor to convey the land to the mortgagee unconditionally.

2. SALE

The statutory power of sale conferred by the Law of Property Act 1925 exists where the mortgage is by deed.[16] Thus where the mortgage is equitable (ie not by deed but in a form that satisfies s 2 of the 1989 Act), the mortgagee does not have the statutory power of sale that is conferred on a mortgagee where the mortgage is legal. An equitable mortgagee does, however, have a right conferred by statute[17] to apply to the court which has power (a) to order a sale, or (b) to vest a legal term of years in E, so as to give E power to sell the land as if he were a mortgagee under a legal mortgage. But in either case E cannot sell without application to the court.

---

14 [1994] 1 AC 200, [1993] 4 All ER 433. See also *Dunbar Bank plc v Nadeem* [1997] 2 All ER 253.
15 See p 440.
16 LPA 1925, s 101(1).
17 LPA 1925, s 91(2); *Arab Bank plc v Mercantile Holdings Ltd* [1994] Ch 71.

3.   TAKING POSSESSION

It is sometimes said that a mortgagee under an equitable mortgage has no right to take possession. The better view,[18] however, is that since such a mortgagee should, under the doctrine in *Walsh v Lonsdale*, have the same rights as a mortgagee under a legal mortgage, he should therefore have the same right to take possession of the land.

A mortgagee under an equitable mortgage has no right, however, to collect rent from tenants if the land is let, but he may obtain such a right by an order of the court.

4.   APPOINTING A RECEIVER

The statutory power to appoint a receiver exists only[19] where a mortgage is made by deed.

An equitable mortgagee may, however, apply to the court for an appointment, and if, eg interest is in arrears, the court has jurisdiction to appoint a receiver.

SUMMARY

A mortgagee's right to redeem is the right to repay the money owed notwithstanding that the contractual date for repayment has passed.

A mortgagee's right of redemption is the totality of his rights.

After 1925 a legal mortgage is created either by a (long) lease with a condition for termination on the repayment of the money lent, or by a charge.

An equitable mortgage arises from either the mortgage of a legal interest by informal means under the principle in *Walsh v Lonsdale*, or by the mortgage of an interest that is itself equitable.

For added security the title deeds may be deposited with the mortgagee.

Restrictions on the right to redeem are resisted by equity.

A mortgagee may enforce his security by foreclosure, sale, taking possession or appointing a receiver.

After 1925 the priority of successive mortgages of land is determined:

where it is a legal interest that is mortgaged;

if the first mortgage was registrable, according to whether it was registered;

if the first mortgage was not registrable, by application of the old rules;

where it is an equitable interest that is mortgaged, by the application of the rule in *Dearle v Hall*.

---

18   (1995) 71 LQR 204 (H. W. R. Wade).
19   LPA 1925, s 101(1)(iii).

CHAPTER 24

Limitation and Adverse Possession[1]

Introduction

Suppose that in 1965 O (which in this chapter represents 'owner') buys a piece of land, Greenacre, which he uses as a market garden. In 1975, S (which in this chapter represents the term 'squatter'), noticing that the land is no longer cultivated, resolves to use it and proceeds to plant cabbages there. O makes no objection. S continues to use the land until his death in 1980. After S's death his wife, T, continues to use the land. In 1985 T makes a will in which she purports to leave Greenacre to her nephew, U. On T's death in 1990, U builds a house on Greenacre, which he lets to V for 99 years. In 1995, O returns to Greenacre, discovers the house and claims possession of the land from V. Who in this situation has the better claim? O has the better title, but it would inflict hardship on V if O were to succeed. Both O and V it will be noted, are innocent of any fraud. Who, we must ask, bears the greater responsibility for this conflict of interests? It would probably be agreed that the greater fault lies with O, since it has been his failure to claim the land for so long a period after S took possession that has been the cause of the difficulty. In the words of Best CJ in 1825, 'Long dormant claims often have more of cruelty than justice in them'.[2]

Limitation of actions

Statute has for long provided that if a person wishes to bring an action for recovery of land he must do so within a certain period; the *'period of limitation'*. At the present day the relevant period is 12 years. This is laid down by the Limitation Act 1980,[3] which consolidated the Limitation Acts 1939-1980.[4] At the end of 12 years if an owner has brought no action to recover land from a squatter (a person who has taken possession without title to do so) he is barred from bringing an action and the squatter has the right to remain in possession, having now acquired what is termed a good *'possessory title'* – not, be it noted, as a result of some kind of 'statutory transfer' from the owner to the squatter, but as a result of *'adverse possession'*.

---

1   See A. M. Pritchard, *Squatting*; P. Walters and J. Harris *Claims to Possession of Land*.
2   *A'Court v Cross* (1825) 3 Bing 329.
3   Section 15.
4   Ie Limitation Act 1939, Limitation Act 1963, Limitation Amendment Act 1980. The period of 12 years was introduced by the Real Property Limitation Act 1874. Previously, under the Real Property Limitation Act 1833, the period was 20 years.

Possession

In order to understand the nature of adverse possession we must first examine the significance of the fact of possession in English law. Possession is important in English law since the fact of possession of land entitles a person to retain the land against anyone in the world except someone who has a better title. Thus if C, an owner, is dispossessed by D, and D in turn is dispossessed by E, then D, having a good title against the whole world except C, can claim possession from E. It is important to note that E cannot plead that D has no title since he (D) has dispossessed C. He cannot, we say, plead '*jus tertii*' (the right of a third person). He must rely on the strength of his own title, not on the weakness of D's.[5]

If E is dispossessed by F, E can claim from F, and so on. But if F could show that the land had been, for example, devised to him by D then since D's title would be better than E's; F would be able to defeat E's claim. But he would be relying on the strength of his own title, not on the weakness of E's.

If, however, E could show that what F claimed could not be true by proving, for example, that during his lifetime D had sold the land to Z, in this case since E would have defeated F's attempt to rely on the strength of his own title, and since, as between E and F, E has the better title (by virtue of his prior possession) E would succeed.[6] E would, in a sense, be pleading *jus tertii* – the right of Z, which although not available to F to defeat E's claim, is available to E to defeat F's claim that he has a better title than he, E, does. The *jus tertii* may thus be pleaded in support of a person (E), claiming by virtue of prior possession but not against such a person. This is really no more than an illustration of the operation of the principle that the law upholds the entitlement of the person who had prior possession as against a subsequent holder.[7]

Extinguishment of previous title

Suppose that D occupies C's land for 12 years. C's right to bring an action against D is then barred. Later D allows C to return to the land. C then refuses to give up possession. D sues C for recovery of the land. Can C plead 'I am retaining possession in reliance on my better title'? The answer is that he cannot do so since the Limitation Act 1980 provides[8] that at the end of the period of limitation not only is C's right of action barred, but also his very title is extinguished.[9] D's action against C for the recovery of the land will therefore succeed.

---

5   *Asher v Whitlock* (1865) LR 1 QB 1; (M & B).
6   *Culley v Doe d Taylerson* (1840) 3 Per & Dav 539.
7   For the effect of s 8 of the Torts (Interference with Goods) Act 1977 on the *jus tertii* principle as it applies to actions in conversion in respect of personal property, see [1992] Conv 100, (G. Battersby).
8   Section 17, following the principle that first appeared in the Real Property Limitation Act 1833, s 34.
9   For an exception that was held to have arisen under the principle of estoppel, see *Colchester Borough Council v Smith* [1992] Ch 421, [1992] 2 All ER 561. The decision of Ferris J has been criticised, [1991] Conv 397 (A. H. R. Brierley); [1992] CLJ 420 (M. Dixon)(' ... a truly remarkable decision.') It is submitted that it is unfortunate that there was no appeal.

Titles to land relative

It will be seen from what we have said that the titles of C, D, E and F are not absolute, but merely relative. F's title is not as good as that of C, D or E, but it is better than that of anyone else in the world except those three.[10] D's title is better than that of E or F, but not as good as that of C. Even C's title is relative: it is better than those of D, E and F but it will be defeated by anyone who can show a title better even than his (for example, if B can show that A devised the land to him, not to C, as C claims). It is true that it is common to speak of an 'owner' of land, but since all titles are relative, 'owner' can mean no more than 'the person with the best ascertained right of possession'.[11]

The principle that all titles in English law are not absolute but merely relative is the framework within which the law relating to the limitation of actions operates.

Adverse possession[12]

NATURE

We have said that if S takes possession of O's land and retains possession of it for 12 years, then O's title is barred and S acquires a good title to the land. But this clearly would not be the result if S had taken possession of the land by virtue of his having been granted a lease (or a licence) of the land by O. If O's title is to be barred after 12 years, S's occupation must have been without O's authority: his possession must have been '*adverse possession*', ie adverse to O's title. If S occupied the land as a tenant or licensee[13] (express or implied) of O,[14] then S's possession would not have been inconsistent with O's title, and therefore not adverse possession.

In *Wallis's Cayton Bay Holiday Camp Ltd v Shell-Mex and BP Ltd* Lord Denning expressed the opinion that the basis of a squatter's possession was attributable to the grant of an implied licence by the owner.[15] This view (which has been described as 'clumsy, unreal and unnecessary'[16]) would, of course, prevent possession from ever being adverse. The notion was rejected when the Limitation Amendment Act 1980[17] provided that,

'For the purpose of determining whether a person occupying any land is in adverse possession of the land it shall not be assumed by implication of law that his

---

10   Or any one having a title better even than that of C.
11   Megarry and Wade (4th edn) p 1009.
12   M. Dockray, *Why do we need adverse possession?* [1985] Conv 272.
13   *Hughes v Griffin* [1969] 1 All ER 460.
14   Or if he occupies land as a purchaser under an uncompleted contract for the sale of land; *Hyde v Pearce* [1982] 1 All ER 1029, [1982] 1 WLR 560, CA; (1983) 46 MLR 80 (M. Dockray). For possession by a person who claims to hold, or is held by the court to hold, an equitable licence, see [1991] Conv 280 (M. Welstead).
15   [1975] QB 94, [1974] 3 All ER 575. The principle was followed by Slade J in *Powell v McFarlane* (1977) 38 P & CR 452; (M & B). See (1980) 96 LQR 333 (P. Jackson).
16   (1975) 38 MLR 354 at 358.
17   Section 4, now consolidated in the Limitation Act 1980, Sch 1, para 8(4).

occupation is by permission of the person entitled to the land merely by virtue of the fact that his occupation is not inconsistent with the latter's present or future enjoyment of the land.

'This provision shall not be taken as prejudicing a finding to the effect that a person's occupation of any land is by implied permission of the person entitled to the land in any case where such a finding is justified on the actual facts of the case.'

It will be noted that the section preserves the principle that where the evidence indicates that in fact S[18] occupied the land under an implied licence from O, then S's occupation will not be adverse.

THE FACT OF POSSESSION

In order that S's possession should amount to adverse possession, S must show the fact of his possession. Factual possession signifies an appropriate degree of physical control.[19] For example, if S built and occupied a house on the land, or if he ploughed up and cultivated agricultural land, or if he placed a notice on the land warning intruders to keep out and enforced the notice by blocking up entrances, these are all acts that would constitute physical possession by S. But if S merely made occasional use of the land, for example, for parking a car, or if he allowed his children to play on a field adjoining his house,[20] these acts might constitute a series of trespasses, but not possession of the land.

In order to amount to possession (and so be capable of being adverse possession) S's use of the land must to some material extent have the effect of excluding O from the land: S's use must be 'sufficiently exclusive' of O. For example, in a case[1] where S turned heifers on to O's land to graze, it was held that this action by S did not sufficiently exclude O to amount to adverse possession by S. On the other hand, S's possession need not necessarily be such as totally to exclude O. It may be sufficient if the possession is as exclusive as the nature of the situation permits. For example, where S laid buoys in O's creek and made a charge to those using the moorings, this was held to be sufficiently exclusive to constitute possession of the creek by S.[2]

Enclosure of the land by S is normally 'the strongest possible evidence of adverse possession'.[3] But enclosure is not a prerequisite of adverse possession (nor is it necessarily conclusive evidence of adverse possesion[4]). Further, for S to establish that he has had possession of an area of land, he does not necessarily

---

18 As in *Gray v Wykeham-Martin* [1977] Bar Library Transcript 10A, CA (S used O's land 'for letting hens run there, keeping a few rabbits, drying her washing, and the like'; S held to have used the land under an implied licence from O).
19 Per Slade J, *Powell v McFarlane* (1977) 38 P & CR 452; (M & B).
20 *Tecbild Ltd v Chamberlain* (1969) 20 P & CR 633.
1 *Bligh v Martin* [1968] 1 All ER 1157, [1968] 1 WLR 804.
2 *Fowley Marine (Emsworth) Ltd v Gafford* [1968] 2 QB 618, [1968] 1 All ER 979.
3 *Seddon v Smith* (1877) 36 LT 168 at 169; *Williams v Usherwood* (1983) 45 P & CR 235; [1983] Conv 398 (M. Dockray)(acts of adverse possession consisted of fencing, paving, and parking car on, the land claimed). Cf *Marsden v Miller* (1992) 64 P & CR 239 (fence enclosing land in position for only 24 hours).
4 *George Wimpey & Co v Sohn* [1967] Ch 487, [1966] 1 All ER 232.

have to show that he has made physical possession of the whole.[5] But the acts done must constitute the taking possession of the land, not merely acts done on, over, or under[6] O's land. In the latter case, S denied that the use of a sewage pipe under O's land for 12 years gave S a good possessory title to the space within the pipe. The claim failed. S had not sufficiently possessed the relevant land. A right to use the pipe, if such a right existed (eg after 20 years' use) constituted the exercise of an easement against another's land, not possession of it.

Clearly, if O recovers possession by re-entering[7] the land, S ceases[6] to have adverse possession and the time that was running in his favour ceases.

AN INTENTION TO POSSESS

In addition to the need to show the *fact* of possession S must show an *intention* from the start of the limitation period to take possession: he must show what has come to be termed 'animus possidendi'. Thus to adverse possession there is both a physical and a mental element. It is immaterial that in taking possession S did so in the mistaken belief[8] that he was the owner of the land.[9] And it seems that it is not necessary that he must have had a conscious intention of excluding O, provided that he intended to exclude everyone, including O.[10] Thus what S must show is that what he did, he did with the intention of taking *possession*, not with some other object, short of this, in mind; for example, making use of the land for some purpose that happened to be convenient to him.[11]

IS THE OWNER'S INTENDED USE OF THE LAND OF ANY RELEVANCE?

According to decisions in certain cases, given support during one period by the Court of Appeal, a further requirement for possession to be adverse was regarded as being that not merely had S to show the *fact* of possession, and an intention to possess, but, further, that the use to which S put the land had to be inconsistent with O's enjoyment of the land for the purpose for which O intended to use it.[12] For example, in *Leigh v Jack*[13] in 1879 O owned a strip of land which he intended eventually to dedicate as a highway. S used the land for dumping old metal and other refuse. It was held that since this use by S did not substantially interfere with O's intended plans for the land, it did not amount

---

5   *Higgs v Nassauvian Ltd* [1975] AC 464, [1975] 1 All ER 95.
6   As in *William Sindall plc v Cambridgeshire County Council* [1994] 3 All ER 932.
7   The sending of a letter by O demanding that S delivers up possession of the land does not amount to re-entry by O unless S gives a written acknowledgment of O's title. *Mount Carmel Investments Ltd v Thurlow* [1988] 1 WLR 1078.
8   *Littledale v Liverpool College* [1900] 1 Ch 19; *Powell v McFarlane* (1977) 38 P & CR 452 at 472; (M & B).
9   *Pulleyn v Hall Aggregates (Thames Valley) Ltd* (1993) 65 P & CR 276, CA; *Hughes v Cork* [1994] EGCS 25, CA (S mistakenly believed that a plot of land was part of land that he had purchased from O).
10   *Ocean Estates Ltd v Pinder* [1969] 2 AC 19, [1969] 2 WLR 1359, PC.
11   As in *R v Secretary of State for the Environment, ex p Davies* (1990) 61 P & CR 487.
12   (1974) 38 Conv (NS) 172 (J. A. Omotola).
13   (1879) 5 Ex D 264; (M & B).

to adverse possession. The same principle was applied by the Court of Appeal in 1957,[14] 1974[15] and 1976.[16] (It will be recognised that under the law produced by the Court of Appeal, the question of who held the title to land could turn on evidence as to what was in a landholder's mind, perhaps many years earlier.) The validity of the principle was questioned[17] and criticised[18] (and there was comment on the way in which it seemed that judges 'openly exult in the defeat of squatters' claims'[19]). In 1977 the Law Reform Committee[20] expressed the view that acceptance of the principle amounted, in effect, 'to a judicial repeal of the statute'.[1]

In 1989, however, in *Buckinghamshire County Council v Moran*,[2] the doctrine that a squatter's possession was not adverse if the acts done by the squatter did not substantially interfere with any plans the owner might have for the future use of undeveloped land, was held by the Court of Appeal to have been abrogated by para 8(4) of Sch 1 to the Limitation Act 1980 (set out on p 469): provided that the squatter had both factual possession and an intention to possess, any plans that the owner might have had for the future use of the land were irrelevant.

Where, however, the acts relied on by S as evidence of the dispossession of O are in accordance with O's *present* purpose for the land, the court may conclude that the acts by S are not sufficient to constitute dispossession of O: that S has not obtained possession of the land. For example where S relied on the fact that he had authorised a sailing club to use a strip of land for standing boats on as evidence of his possession of the strip, and this use of the land was that which O himself intended for the land, the Court of Appeal held that S had not sufficiently ousted O for his claim based on adverse possession to succeed.[3]

HOW ADVERSE POSSESSION MAY BE TAKEN

So far we have envisaged the position where (1) O abandons the land and S enters into possession of it. Adverse possession will also be taken by S if (2) S drives O out of possession (if S 'ousts' O) and takes possession himself; (3) O fails to take possession of land and S takes possession (eg where T devises Greenacre to O, O fails to take possession of the land, and S does so); (4) O gives S a licence to occupy the land; subsequently the licence either expires or is revoked; and S remains in possession; (5) S holds a determinable fee simple and O the possibility of reverter, the determining event occurs, S remains in

14   *Williams Bros Direct Supply Ltd v Raftery* [1958] 1 QB 159, [1957] 3 All ER 593; (M & B).
15   *Wallis's Cayton Bay Holiday Camp Ltd v Shell-Mex and BP Ltd* [1975] QB 94, [1974] 3 All ER 575 (Stamp LJ dissenting).
16   *Treloar v Nute* [1977] 1 All ER 230, [1976] 1 WLR 1295; (M & B). Cf *Williams v Usherwood* (1981) 45 P & CR 235; [1983] Conv 398 (M. Dockray).
17   (1970) 38 Conv (NS) 172.
18   (1978) 42 Conv (NS) 2.
19   (1980) 96 LQR 333 (P. Jackson).
20   Final Report on Limitation of Actions (1977) Cmnd 6823.
 1   Page 45; para 3.50.
 2   [1990] Ch 623, [1989] 2 All ER 225 (M & B); [1989] Conv 211 (G. McCormack); [1990] CLJ (C. Harpum).
 3   *Pulleyn v Hall Aggregates (Thames Valley) Ltd* (1993) 65 P & CR 276, CA.

possession;[4] (6) O grants S a lease of the land; the lease expires, and S remains on the land without O's consent.[5] (Although in this situation S is a 'tenant at suffrance',[6] his possession is nevertheless adverse.)

If S remains in possession of the land after the expiry of his lease with O's consent, S is a tenant at will,[7] and since he is on the land with O's consent, his possession is not adverse possession. He is therefore in the same position as a licensee, and can never acquire a possessory title (unless O withdraws his consent, and S remains on the land for the requisite period after the date of the withdrawal of consent[8]).

EFFECT OF ACKNOWLEDGEMENT OF O's TITLE

If S, being in adverse possession of O's land, acknowledges that O is the owner of the land (either expressly or impliedly, eg by offering to buy the land or to pay rent) and the acknowledgement is in writing, signed by S and addressed to O (or his agent),[9] then S's period of adverse possession ends.[10]

If S thereafter remains in possession, O's title will become statute barred at the expiry of 12 years from the date of the acknowledgement. Once O's right to recover the land becomes statute barred, an acknowledgement by S of O's title (ie made after the expiry of the 12 years) does not revive O's title.[11]

PERMISSION

If S enters O's land with O's permission, then, as we have seen, and as stands to reason, time does not begin to run in his favour under the Limitation Act 1980 since his possession is not adverse possession. If S obtains possession of O's land and the possession *is* adverse, the twelve year period begins to run in his favour. According to established principles, once S is in adverse possession of O's land, the only two occurrences that will stop time running in his favour are (a) an acknowledgement by S of O's title, or, (b) the commencement of legal proceedings by O to recover the land. If S is in adverse possession of O's land O informs S that he, O, gives S permission to be on the land and S acknowledges O's communication then the acknowledgement is treated as constituting acknowledgement by S of O's title to the land with the result that (as seen above) the twelve year period that had been running in his favour ends. If, on the other hand, S ignores O's communication, according to the established principles, the nature of his possession, ie that it is adverse possession, is not affected, with the result that the twelve year period continues to run.

4   *Re Peel's Release* [1921] 2 Ch 218.
5   See *Long v Tower Hamlets London Borough Council* [1996] 2 All ER 683, [1996] 3 WLR 317 (O's right of action accrues on date of last receipt of rent, not on expiry of notice to quit).
6   See *Hayward v Chaloner* [1968] 1 QB 107, [1967] 3 All ER 122; (M & B).
7   See Chapter 17.
8   Section 9(1) of the Limitation Act 1939, which made special provision for tenants at will, was repealed by the Limitation Amendment Act 1980, s 3(1).
9   Limitation Act 1980, s 29.
10 See *Browne v Perry* [1991] 1 WLR 1297, PC.
11 *Sanders v Sanders* (1881) 19 Ch D 373; *Nicholson v England* [1926] 2 KB 93.

In *BP Properties Ltd v Buckler*,[12] however, the Court of Appeal held that the communication to a person who had no title to land that he was permitted to remain on the land as licensee halted time running under the Act. The effect of the decision is, it has been observed, 'that unilateral communication from a documentary owner to a squatter giving him permission to continue his occupation of disputed property prevents his subsequent possession from being adverse for the purposes of the Limitation Act even if, as in *Buckler*, that permission was neither sought, acknowledged nor accepted'. Dillon LJ, in delivering the judgment of the court, recognised that the finding that the grant of a unilateral licence could stop time running was a new one, and could have the result that 'it would enable a person who is not prepared to incur the obloquy of proceedings for possession, or of enforcing a possession order, to keep his title alive for many years until it suits him to evict'. The judge recognised that the finding ran counter to the Act, but did not consider it necessary to justify the court's disregard for the intention of the legislature. It is submitted that it is to be hoped that the decision will be regarded as having been reached on the particular, and somewhat exceptional, facts of the case and not as establishing as law a principle that is contrary both to the previous rational development of the law and the clear intention of the legislature.

SUCCESSIVE PERIODS OF ADVERSE POSSESSION

In the illustration at the beginning of this chapter, S took adverse possession of the land from O. The adverse possession was continued first by T, and then by U, and then by V. The subsequent periods of possession by T, U and V may be added to that by S in reckoning the 12-year period. Thus if S and T together had been in possession for, say, ten years, O's title would be extinguished two years later.

Where one squatter is dispossessed by another squatter, as where C was dispossessed by D, and D by E, and E by F, the effect of the successive periods of adverse possession can be shown thus:

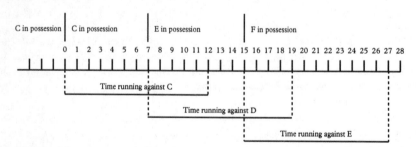

Five years after E has been in possession, C's title is barred. But at that point D can still claim possession from E (and can continue to do so throughout

---

12   (1987) 55 P & CR 337. For criticism of the decision and an analysis of the nonsensical corrolaries that flow from it, see H. Wallace *Limitation, Prescription and Unsolicited Permission* [1994] Conv 196.

the period of E's possession). When F has been in possession for four years, D's title becomes barred; but E can still claim possession from F. When 12 years have elapsed since F took possession, E's title becomes barred. Thus time begins to run against each successive holder from the date on which he was dispossessed.

The estate held by a squatter

Suppose that P, the holder of a fee simple absolute in possession is dispossessed by S. S also holds the land for an estate of fee simple absolute in possession, but one that is liable to be defeated if O brings an action for recovery of the land. It might be thought that S held a conditional fee simple[13] but this is not so: he holds a fee simple absolute in possession. Thus there can be two (or more) conflicting fee simple estates existing in the same land, the validity of each being relative to the others. It follows that a squatter who sells the land will convey to the purchaser a fee simple absolute in possession, though one that is liable to be defeated. (After 12 years of adverse possession he can pass a fee simple that is indefeasible by the previous holder.)

It may happen that a squatter who acquires an indefeasible title by adverse possession holds the land subject to an easement in favour of the former owner,[14] the easement arising in a manner analogous to that in which an easement may, on a grant of land, be impliedly reserved under the doctrine[15] in *Wheeldon v Burrows*.[16]

Adverse possession against land held on trust

Suppose that T_1 and T_2 hold land on trust for A for life with remainder to B in fee simple. A occupies the land, but is later ousted by S. An action can be brought either by T_1 and T_2 as the trustees, or by A (or, after A's death, by B). A has 12 years in which to bring an action, and in general[17] this period applies as much to recovery of equitable interests as to that of legal titles.

B, however, as remainderman, is permitted by the Act to bring an action either within six years of his interest falling into possession, or within 12 years of S taking possession, whichever is the longer period. Thus if S took possession one year before A's death, B would have eleven years in which to sue; if S had taken possession 14 years before A's death, B would have only six years in which to sue.

The trustees' title is not extinguished until the title of all the beneficiaries is extinguished.[18] Suppose that T_1 and T_2 hold land on trust for A for life with

---

13 Ie on condition that O does not claim possession.
14 *Williams v Usherwood* (1981) 45 P & CR 235; [1983] Conv 398 (M. Dockray).
15 See Chapter 18.
16 (1879) 12 Ch D 31; (M & B).
17 Subject to what is said below on remaindermen.
18 Limitation Act 1980, s 18.

remainder to B, and S occupies the land for 12 years without any action being brought against him, A's title is barred. Can T_1 and T_2 then sue for recovery of the land? The answer is that they cannot, because this would have the effect of restoring A's title. Although T_1 and T_2's legal title is not extinguished, they cannot bring an action between the time when A's title is extinguished and his death. During this time S holds a legal fee simple in the land, but one which is subject to the legal fee simple held by T_1 and T_2 on trust for sale for B's interest. When A dies then either B or T_1 and T_2 can bring an action against S for the recovery of the land. When B's equitable title becomes extinguished (ie six years after A's death or 12 years after S took possession, whichever period is the longer), at the same moment, the legal title of T_1 and T_2 becomes extinguished also.

Suppose that B had been an infant, say seven years old, at A's death. Under the rule[19] relating to remaindermen, his title would become extinguished while he was still under age. Special rules apply, however, in the case of a person who is under a disability (ie a person who is an infant or a mental patient[20]) at the time when his right of action accrues.[1]

Persons under a disability

If S dispossesses O when O is an infant, an action must be brought either within the normal period of 12 years from the dispossession, or within six years of his coming of age or within six years of his dying,[2] whichever is the longer period. Thus if S took possession when O was 16, O's right of action would not be barred until O was 28 (ie 16+12). If S took possession when O was two, O's right of action would not be barred until O was 24 (ie 18+6). If S took possession when O was two, and O died at, say, 17, the right to sue for recovery of the land (by O's estate) would become barred six years after O's death.

In the example above, where T_1 and T_2 held land on trust for A for life with remainder to B, if B was an infant at A's death, his right of action would become barred (and therefore that of the trustees also) either within 12 years of the dispossession or six years of B attaining 18 or dying, whichever was the longer. When B's right of action becomes barred, the right of action of T_1 and T_2 is barred also.

The same principles apply in the case of a person who is a mental patient, the date of ceasing to be a mental patient taking the place of the date of attaining the age of majority.

The alternative periods available to a person under a disability are subject to a maximum of 30 years from the date when the person's right of action accrues. This is likely to be relevant only in the case of a mental patient.[3] For example, S dispossesses O, who is at that time a mental patient. Twenty-six

---

19   See ante.
20   LA 1980, s 38(3).
 1   LA 1980, s 28.
 2   The action in this case being brought by his estate.
 3   An action can be brought on a mental patient's behalf by the Court of Protection; Mental Health Act 1959, s 103(1)(h).

years later O recovers his sanity. O has four years (not six) in which to bring an action. If he had remained a mental patient for 30 years, his right of action would have been lost at the expiry of that period.

Adverse possession by trustees

Trustees can obtain a title to land by adverse possession. If they do so, they hold the land on the trust for which they are trustees.[4] But a trustee cannot acquire a beneficial title against a beneficiary by adverse possession.

Leaseholds

ADVERSE POSSESSION AGAINST A TENANT

Suppose that L (a landlord) leases land to T (a tenant) for 21 years. A year later S ousts T and remains in occupation of the land for 12 years without any action having been brought against him. S acquires an indefeasible title against T, but not against L. T had 12 years from the dispossession in which to sue: after which his title was barred. L, on the other hand, has 12 years from the expiry of the lease in which to sue.

During the interval between the barring of T's title and the expiry of the lease, S does not become L's tenant. The mere fact of dispossession creates no such relationship and since there is privity neither of contract nor of estate between L and S, the covenants in the lease (including a covenant, if any, to pay rent) are not enforceable against S.[5] However, because of the factors set out below, L is likely to be far from powerless against S.

1. If L retained a right of re-entry exercisable in the event of breach of a covenant (eg a covenant that rent would be paid) and S fails to pay rent to L, then although L cannot sue S for breach of the covenant, he can threaten to exercise the right of re-entry and by this means induce S to pay the rent due. (L can use the same threat to compel S to observe the other covenants in the lease provided that a right of re-entry exists in relation to those covenants.)

2. If S pays rent to L and this is measured with reference to a specific period (eg £500 pa) then at common law S becomes a periodic tenant.[6]

3. If S accepts any benefit provided in T's lease, then S is estopped from claiming that he does not hold under the lease, and by this means becomes bound by all the terms of the lease.[7]

---

4   *Churcher v Martin* (1889) 42 Ch D 312 (conveyance to trustees for charitable purposes; conveyance ineffective owing to absence of compliance with formalities required by law; trustee remained in possession for the statutory period; held, trustees acquired possessory title, holding on the trusts declared in the conveyance.)

5   *Tichborne v Weir* (1892) 67 LT 735 (M & B).

6   See Chapter 17.

7   *Ashe v Hogan* [1920] 1 IR 159.

4. If the covenants in T's lease are restrictive, the burden of the covenants may pass to S under the principles explained in Chapter 21.
5. If, in the case of land the title to which is not registered,[8] S occupies the land leased to T for the statutory period, and T then surrenders his lease to L, it has been held that L acquires a right of action for possession of the land against S.[9] (By this decision, the 'operation of the Limitation Act 1980 in respect of leaseholds is thus substantially curtailed'.[10])

ADVERSE POSSESSION BY A TENANT AGAINST HIS LANDLORD

If L leases land to S, and S encroaches (from the land leased to him by L) on to land belonging to O, and O's title to the land encroached on by S becomes statute barred, the presumption is that the benefit accrues to L, ie L acquires a good title to the fee simple in the land on which S encroached and, at the expiry of S's lease, can enter into possession of it.[11]

On the other hand, if L leases land to S, and S encroaches on the other land belonging to L, then if, on the evidence, the court finds as a matter of fact that S occupied the land adversely to L, after 12 years L's title to the land encroached on will become statute barred so as to give S a good possessory title to it. However, if the court finds on the facts that S's occupation was not adverse to L's title and that S occupied the land 'as a mere extension of the *locus* of his tenancy',[12] ie that he occupied the land encroached on (along with the land in the lease) as a *tenant*, L's title will not become statute barred.[13] But, although he can claim no possessory title to the fee simple, S will be able to retain his occupation of the land encroached on until the end of the period of the lease since, it has been held, he occupies it as a tenant along with the land originally leased to him.[14]

Rights of third parties

Suppose that S occupies O's land, Greenacre. At the time of dispossession by S,

(a) Greenacre was mortgaged by a legal mortgage without deposit of title deeds, to A;
(b) B had a legal easement across Greenacre;
(c) C had an equitable easement across Greenacre;
(d) Greenacre was subject to a restrictive covenant made in 1920.

---

8   For the position where the title is registered, see p 491.
9   *Fairweather v St Marylebone Property Co Ltd* [1963] AC 510, [1962] 2 All ER 288; (M & B). In the case of registered land (see Chapter 26) where S is registered as proprietor of the lease, the surrender of the lease by T to L will not entitle L to claim possession from S; *Spectrum Investment Co v Holmes* [1981] 1 All ER 6, [1981] 1 WLR 221; (M & B).
10 Megarry and Wade, p 1052.
11 *Kingsmill v Millard* (1855) 11 Exch 313.
12 Per Lord Russell CJ, *Lord Hastings v Saddler* (1898) 79 LT 355 at 356.
13 *Lord Hastings v Saddler*, ante.
14 *Smirk v Lyndale Developments Ltd* [1975] Ch 317, [1975] 1 All ER 690; (M & B).

These rights all bind S; and they do so both before and after the time when O's title is extinguished. The reason why S is bound is explained in the next chapter.

Other actions relating to land

We have said that the limitation period for actions for the recovery of land is 12 years. The period of 12 years also applies to certain other actions relating to land. Thus a mortgagor (R) mortgages land to a mortgagee (E), and (a) E takes possession of the land and remains in possession for 12 years without giving any written acknowledgement of R's title or of his equity of redemption, and without receiving interest or repayment of principal, then R's right to redeem is barred,[15] or (b) R fails to make a repayment due under the mortgage, and E fails to sue for repayment of the principal, fails to sue for possession, and fails to foreclose, then 12 years after the repayment became due, these rights of E are barred (and E thus loses the right to claim any money outstanding).[16]

Other limitation periods of recovery of land

In certain circumstances the limitation period for an action of the recovery of land is longer than 12 years. Thus, if a subject takes possession of land belonging to the Crown, the Crown's title to the land is not barred until the expiry of 30 years.[17]

If the Crown land consists of foreshore, the Crown's title is not barred until the expiry of 60 years.[18] (If the Crown takes possession of a subject's land, the subject's land is barred after the normal period of 12 years.)

Limitation periods for actions in contract

The Limitation Act 1980 provides[19] that an action founded on contract shall not be brought after a period of six years from the date on which the action accrued. Thus where an action concerns land, but the action is founded on contract, as where V contracts to sell land to P, or S contracts to grant D an easement, the six-year period applies. The six-year period is applicable also to actions for arrears of rent.[20] However, in the case of a covenant by deed seal

---

15 LPA 1980, s 16. This is so notwithstanding that E's possession was not adverse possession. This is therefore an exception to the general rule that for time to run possession must be adverse possession.
16 LA 1980, s 20.
17 LA 1980, s 15(7), Sch 1; *Secretary of State for Foreign and Commonwealth Affairs v Tomlin* (1990) Times, 4 December.
18 Ibid.
19 Section 5.
20 LA 1980, s 19.

(eg a covenant between two fee simple owners, or a covenant in a conveyance or in a lease) the Act provides that the period is to be 12 years.[1]

'Legal interests are valid against all the world'

In conclusion it should be noted that this dictum has no place in the context of conflicting legal fee simple estates where, as we have seen, what matters is the relative strength of each title. It is a common misapprehension to think that the dictum means that if A is the legal owner of Blackacre no one can take it away from him (they can, if they have a better title). The 'legal interests' referred to in the dictum are the legal interests in land the legal estate in which belongs to another, eg A's legal easement over B's land; T's legal lease in L's land. The words 'valid against all the world' refer not to validity against the grantor of the legal interest (eg B, the grantor of A's easement, or L, the grantor of T's lease) but against persons who *subsequently* hold the land (eg a purchaser from B or from L).

The maxim might thus more aptly be phrased, 'Legal interests bind land irrespective of whoever in the world acquires it'.

SUMMARY

A person seeking to recover land from a squatter has twelve years in which to do so. At the expiry of this period his action is statute barred and the squatter acquires a good possessory title, by adverse possession.

To acquire title by adverse possession the squatter must show the fact of possession and an intention to possess.

A person seeking to counter a claim by adverse possession must rely on the strength of his own title not on the weakness of the claimant's.

Due acknowledgement of the owner's title stops time running.

Particular rules apply in the case of life tenant and remaindermen and infants.

The title of trustees is barred when the last beneficiary's entitlement to sue ends.

A dispossessed tenant has twelve years in which to sue; a landlord has twelve years from the end of the lease.

Interests in land at the date of the dispossession bind a squatter.

---

1   Section 8.

CHAPTER 25

Registration of Incumbrances

We know from earlier chapters[1] that the Land Charges Act 1925 made certain matters registrable. In this chapter we shall examine a number of these matters in more detail and consider the effect of registration more precisely. We shall also consider the registration of local land charges.

Matters registrable

Between the passing of the Land Registry Act 1862 and the Land Registration Act 1925 various matters were by various statutes made registrable at the Land Registry established by the 1862 Act.

The Land Charges Act 1925 repealed some of the provisions of earlier statutes, amended others, and increased the number of matters that were registrable. Except for certain provisions relating to local land charges, the Land Charges Act 1925 was repealed and replaced by the Land Charges Act 1972, which consolidated the Act of 1925 and subsequent amendments[2] which had been made to it.

The Act of 1925 imposed, and the 1972 Act continues to impose, on the Chief Land Registrar a duty to keep at the Land Registry the following five registers:

(a) a register of land charges;
(b) a register of pending actions;[3]
(c) a register of writs and orders affecting land;
(d) a register of deeds of arrangement affecting land;
(e) a register of annuities.

The Act also made provision for the registration of local land charges.

The registers are maintained at the Land Charges Department of the Land Registry at Plymouth.

It will be noted that each of the last four items above is a 'land charge' in the sense that it is registrable in the Land Charges Department of the Land

---

1 Eg Chapters 5, 16, 18, 21 and 23.
2 Eg in the Land Registration and Land Charges Act 1971, Administration of Justice Act 1977, s 24.
3 [1995] Conv 309 (J. Howell).

Registry; but it is not a 'land charge' in the narrower sense of being an item registrable in the first register. The term 'land charge' is thus both a genus and a species.

The largest number of land charges are registered in the first register, and it is the matters registrable in this register with which this chapter will be concerned (but noting here, that it is in the third register, the register of writs and orders affecting land, that an access order made by the court under the Access to Neighbouring Land Act 1992 must be registered[4]).

In every instance registration must be made 'in the name of the estate owner whose estate is intended to be affected'.[5] Thus if R enters into a restrictive covenant in favour of E, the covenant must be registered under R's name, and not E's. (If the estate owner dies before the registration is made, registration may nonetheless be made under his name[6].)

Contents of the register of Land Charges

The register is divided into six[7] Classes.

CLASS A[8]

Certain statutes authorise or require certain categories of land holder to incur certain expenses in connection with the land and, in order to provide security for the recovery of such expenses, provide for the land to be charged, on the application of the land holder, with the sum concerned. Such charges are registrable under this head.

CLASS B

Under this head are registrable any charges imposed automatically by statute[9] (ie not on the application of any person) other than charges registrable in the local land charges register.[10]

---

4   See p 495.
5   LCA 1972, s 3(1). For the position where registration is made against the estate owner, but under a name that differs from his formal name, see *Oak Co-operative Building Society v Blackburn* [1968] Ch 730, [1968] 2 All ER 117; and p 494, infra.
6   Law of Property (Miscellaneous Provisions) Act 1994, s 15, giving effect to the recommendation of the Law Commission in Working Paper No 105, *Transfer of Land: Title on Death* (1987); [1995] Conv 476 (L. Clements).
7   The sixth Class was added by the Matrimonial Homes Act 1967, s 2(6), replaced by the Matrimonial Homes Act 1983, s 2, and now contained in the Family Law Act 1996, Part IV.
8   The matters registrable in the first four Registers and in Class A of the fifth Register were registrable under legislation prior to 1925. The Land Charges Act 1925 amended and consolidated the previous legislation relating to matters previously registrable, and grouped the matters concerned into the first four Registers, and the first Class of the fifth Register. The matters contained in the remaining Classes of the fifth Register were not registrable until made so by the Land Charges Act 1925 or subsequent legislation.
9   Eg under the Agricultural Holdings Act 1986.
10   See end of this chapter.

CLASS C

This Class is divided into four sub-classes.

(i)   PUISNE MORTGAGES

As we saw in Chapter 23 a puisne mortgage is a mortgage which (a) is legal; and (b) is not protected by deposit of the title deeds.

(ii)   LIMITED OWNERS' CHARGES

If land is settled under a settlement on A for life with remainder to B for life with remainder to C in fee simple and on the death of A inheritance tax is payable in respect of the land, the tax due is found from capital money or from sale of part of the land. If B pays the tax out of his own pocket he is entitled to recover the sum concerned from the settled property. As security for the recovery of this money, the Inheritance Tax Act 1984[11] imposes a charge on the settled land for the amount concerned. Such a charge on the settled land is registrable as a limited owner's charge.

(iii)   GENERAL EQUITABLE CHARGES

A general equitable charge is defined[12] as 'any equitable charge which:

(a) is not secured by a deposit of documents relating to the legal estate affected; and
(b) does not arise or affect an interest arising under a trust of land or a settlement; and
(c) is not a charge given by way of indemnity against rents ...; and
(d) is not included in any other class of land charge'.

The matter most frequently registered under this residuary class of equitable charges is an equitable mortgage which is not protected by deposit of title deeds.[13]

The effect of the exclusion under (b) is to exclude, for example, a mortgage by a tenant for life of his equitable interest under a settlement.

(iv)   ESTATE CONTRACTS

The meaning of an estate contract was explained in Chapter 16. The definition[14] of an estate contract can be broken into the following two parts. An estate contract is either:

---

11   Originally the charge was for estate duty under the Finance Act 1894, s 2(2), 237, 238.
12   LCA 1972, s 2(4), as amended by the trusts of Land and Appointment of trustees Act 1996, Sch 1.
13   See Chapter 23.
14   LCA 1972, s 2(4).

1.   'a contract by an estate owner ... to convey or create a legal estate',[15] or
2.   'a contract by ... a person entitled at the date of the contract to have a legal estate conveyed to him, to convey or create a legal estate ...'

Under (1) would be included a contract by A to sell Blackacre to B, or to lease Blackacre to B, or to mortgage Blackacre to B.

Regarding (2), suppose that V contracts to sell land to P. This gives P the right to call on V to convey the legal estate to him. P then contracts to sell the land to Q. Q's (equitable) interest in the land is registrable as an estate contract since P, although not yet an 'estate owner', is 'a person entitled at the date of the contract' (with Q) 'to have the legal estate conveyed to him'. Since Q is required to register the interest against the name of the (legal) 'estate owner', he must register the estate contract against the name of V, not that of P.[16] (If he registers against the name of P, the registration is ineffective against any person to whom P (in breach of his contract with Q) subsequently sells the land.[17])

OPTIONS[18]

Suppose that A is intending to sell Blackacre and B is interested in buying the land. B has not made up his mind and wants A to keep the offer to him open (ie and not part with the land to anyone else). B offers to pay A £100 if A will keep the offer to him open for, say, a month. A agrees. This contract confers an *option* on B to buy the land. (An option may equally relate to the granting of a lease, the renewal of a lease[19] (including an option to renew contained in a covenant in an existing lease[20]) or the granting of any other interest.)

As a contract for the disposition of an interest in land (one conditional on B's exercise of the option), the instrument in which the option is granted, to be enforceable (by B against A, or by A against B in the event of B exercising the option but failing to complete) must comply with s 2 of the Law of Property (Miscellaneous Provisions) Act 1989.[1]

If B exercises the option, this brings into being an unconditional contract for the sale of the land. A contract for the sale of land is, as an estate contract,

---

15   Since 'legal estate' refers to a legal estate in land, a contract for the purchase of the equitable interest of a beneficiary under a trust for sale, being (by the doctrine of conversion, before its abolition, qv, see Chapter 8), personalty, was held not to be registrable; *Re Raleigh Weir Stadium* [1954] 2 All ER 283, [1954] 1 WLR 786; see also *Taylor v Taylor* [1968] 1 All ER 843, [1968] 1 WLR 378; *Thomas v Rose* [1968] 3 All ER 765, [1968] 1 WLR 1797.
16   LCA 1972, s 3(1); *Barrett v Hilton Developments* [1975] Ch 237, [1974] 3 All ER 944; (1975) 39 Conv (NS) 65 (F. R. Crane).
17   For the possibility that, although ineffective in property law, registration against the name of P might (from the discovery by the purchaser from P of the registration of the P–Q contract) render the purchaser from P liable in tort for procuring a breach of contract, see [1989] Conv 232 (JEA).
18   (1977) NLJ 18 August (K. Davies); (M & B); [1984] CLJ 55 (S. Tromans); R. Castle, *Barnsley's Land Options* (1992).
19   *Beesly Hallwood Estates Ltd* [1961] Ch 105, [1961] 1 All ER 90; *Phillips v Mobil Oil Co Ltd* [1989] 3 All ER 97, [1989] 1 WLR 888; [1990] Conv 168 and 250 (J. Howell).
20   As in *Phillips v Mobil Oil Co Ltd*, supra.
1   *Spiro v Glencrown Properties Ltd* [1991] Ch 537, [1991] 1 All ER 600; [1991] Conv 140 (P.F. Smith); [1993] Conv 13 (P. Jenkins).

registrable. Does this mean that for B's interest to bind a purchaser from A (ie A thus being in breach of contract), B must register the grant of the option *and* its exercise? It has been held that this is not the case. An option is a contract for the sale of land subject to a condition precedent, namely, the exercise of the option. The exercise of the option fulfils the condition and the contract thereupon becomes (to borrow language from the fee simple[2]) absolute. Thus the grant of the option and the fully-fledged contract that results from its exercise are part and parcel of the same legal entity. Thus the registration of the grant of the option is sufficient to protect both the option (pending its exercise) and the contract that becomes absolute on its exercise.[3]

If the price at which B should be allowed to purchase the land is not specified in the option, there is an implied term that the sale should be at a fair and reasonable price.[4] If the parties specify machinery how this price is to be fixed (eg by the appointment of a valuer), this machinery is to be followed. If one party prevents the operation of the agreed machinery (eg by refusing to agree to the appointment of a valuer) or if a specified means of determining the price is not available,[5] the court will, if necessary after directing an enquiry, determine the price.[6]

The granting of the option to B confers on him an interest in the land,[7] since by holding the option B has a right that will enable him (by exercise the the option) to bring into being a contract that will entitle him to acquire the land.

The definition of an estate contract given on page 484 continues, '... including a contract conferring either expressly or by statutory implication a valid option to purchase, a right of pre-emption or any other like right'. An option is thus registrable as an estate contract. So, if A grants the option to B, B registers the option, and A then sells the land to P, B can enforce the option against P.[8] (Since, as stated earlier, registration of a land charge is made against the name of the estate owner whose estate is intended to be affected, the option must be registered against the name of A, not of B.)

RIGHTS OF PRE-EMPTION

Suppose that A owns Blackacre. B would like to buy the land. A is not certain whether he will sell, but he agrees with B that if he does decide to sell, he will offer the land first to B. A and B enter into a contract giving effect to this agreement. Here A grants B what is termed a *right of pre-emption* or, colloquially, a right of 'first refusal'. The following matters call for attention.

---

2 See Chapter 4.
3 *Armstrong and Holmes Ltd v Holmes* [1994] 1 All ER 826, [1993] WLR 1482; [1994] Conv 483 (N.P. Gravells).
4 *Sudbrook Trading Estate Ltd v Eggleton* [1983] 1 AC 444, [1982] 3 All ER 105, HL; (M & B); (1983) 46 MLR 493 (P. Robertshaw).
5 *Re Malpass* [1985] Ch 42, [1984] 2 All ER 313; [1984] Conv 439.
6 Ibid.
7 *London and South Western Rly Co v Gomm* (1882) 20 Ch D 562 at 581; *Mountford v Scott* [1975] Ch 258, [1975] 1 All ER 198.
8 *Beesly v Hallwood Estates Ltd*, supra.

(a) A right of pre-emption is not precluded from being valid by reason of the fact that the agreement does not specify the price at which the land would be sold to B. In the absence of reference to a price, the agreement is to sell at a fair and reasonable price. Thus (where no price is fixed) an offer by A to B to sell at an extravagant price does not constitute observance of the agreement.

(b) Under an option, one condition must be satisfied for the grantee to obtain the fee simple: the exercise of the option by the grantee. Under a right of pre-emption, two conditions must be satisfied, the grantor must decide to sell, and the grantee must decide to buy. Thus under an option the grantee can have the land if he wants it; under a right of pre-emption, whether the grantee can obtain the land depends on the grantor's volition.

(c) Does the grant of a right of pre-emption give the grantee an interest in the land, with the result that if the grantor sells the land to a purchaser, the right of pre-emption is capable of being enforced against the purchaser? Or does the grant of a right of pre-emption create no interest in land, with the result that if the grantor sells the land without offering it to the grantee, the grantee's only remedy lies against the grantor, for damages for breach of contract? In *Pritchard v Briggs*,[9] the Court of Appeal by a majority[10] (Templeman and Stephenson LJJ) held[11] that the answer lay between these two poles: if A grants B a right of pre-emption, B receives no interest in the land. But if A takes some step indicating an intention to sell, then at that point B's right crystallises into an interest in land, in the form of an option, and if, prior to this point, the right of pre-emption has been registered as a land charge, it will bind a purchaser.[12]

The facts in *Pritchard v Briggs*,[13] in essence, were these. A granted X a right of pre-emption to buy certain land for £3,000. The right was to endure until either A or X died. X registered the right of pre-emption as a land charge. A then granted to Y an option to buy the land for £3,000 at any time during the three months following A's death (the intention being that if X did not

---

9   [1980] Ch 338, [1980] 1 All ER 294; *Kling v Keston Properties Ltd* (1983) 49 P & CR 212; (M & B).

10   Goff LJ held (following *Manchester Ship Canal Co v Manchester Racecourse Co* [1901] 2 Ch 37 and *Murray v Two Strokes Ltd* [1973] 3 All ER 357, [1973] 1 WLR 823) that a right of pre-emption was not, and never became, an interest in land, and so was not capable of binding a purchaser, even if registered as a land charge, and this was so, he said, notwithstanding that the Land Charges Act 1972, after defining an estate contract, adds '... including a contract conferring ... a valid option to purchase, a *right of pre-emption* or any other like right'. The property legislation of 1925 had, he said, proceeded on the mistaken assumption that a right of pre-emption was an interest in land. This error could not alter the law. (The Perpetuities and Accumulations Act 1964, s 9(2) also assumes that a right of pre-emption is an interest in land.)

11   Reversing the decision of Walton J [1980] Ch 338, [1978] 1 All ER 886.

12   The decision in *Pritchard v Briggs* does not alter the principle that where statute provides that a right of pre-emption is to bind third parties, then the right constitutes an interest in land; eg in the case of the right of pre-emption reserved by local authorities on the sale of council houses under s 104(3) of the Housing Act 1957; *First National Securities Ltd v Chiltern District Council* [1975] 2 All ER 766, [1975] 1 WLR 1075.

13   [1980] Ch 338, [1980] 1 All ER 294.

want the land, Y should have the opportunity of acquiring it). Y registered the option as a land charge. A sold the land to X for £14,300. Later, A died. Did X take the land subject to Y's option (with the result that Y could require X to sell him the land for £3,000) or free from it? The Court of Appeal held that since the option granted to Y was not exercisable until after the expiry of the right of pre-emption granted to X, the grant of the option to Y did not constitute a step which caused X's right of pre-emption to crystallise into an interest in land. Thus when A granted the option to Y, X's right was not capable of binding Y. Thus Y took the option free from X's right. When A sold the land to X, since Y's option had been registered, it bound X. Thus Y could call on X to sell him the land for £3,000 (£11,300 less than he had paid A for it). As was later observed[14] 'With the costs of the case added (including nine days' argument on appeal), the disaster for X was of some magnitude. It belongs to the class of disasters which a sound system of property law ought to strive at all costs to avoid: the defeat of a prior interest by a later purchaser taking with notice of the conflicting prior interest. The rigour of the system of registration has increased the risk of this occurring, but there was no such complication in the present case since the prior claimant had duly registered his interest before the later claimant came on to the scene'. The injustice wrought on X, and the contradictions and anomalies inherent within the decision, have been the subject of comment.[15] None of the difficulties raised by the decision of the Court of Appeal would have existed if the decision of Walton J at first instance had been confirmed (that a right of pre-emption was an interest in land and, if registered, bound any subsequent holder of the land).

Class D

(i) When a person dies, if his estate is valued at more than a certain sum, tax may be payable. If the deceased's property includes freehold land the duty payable becomes a charge on land: ie if the duty is not paid, the Crown (through the Inland Revenue) may proceed against the land.

Estate duty in respect of a death occurring after 1925 which became a charge on freehold land was registrable under Class D (i).[16] Registration is in practice unlikely to be entered under this head unless the estate is insolvent.

Until August 1949 two other forms of death duty existed, viz, succession duty and legacy duty. These were registrable under this head in the case of any death occurring after 1925.

(ii) Restrictive covenants

A restrictive covenant runs with the land of the covenantor, provided that the necessary conditions[17] are satisfied and provided, if the covenant was made after 1925, that the covenant was registered. Such covenants are registrable

---

14   (1980) LQR 488 (HWRW).
15   (1980) 97 LQR 488 (HWRW); [1980] CLJ 35 (C. Harpum); [1980] Conv 433 (J. Martin).
16   Inheritance tax is now registrable under this head under the Inheritance Tax Act 1984.
17   See Chapter 21.

under Class D (ii). The definition[18] of a restrictive covenant expressly excludes any such covenant between a lessor and a lessee. Restrictive covenants contained in leases are therefore not registrable.

It should be noted that a restrictive covenant (eg between two fee simple owners) is only registrable if entered into after 1925. Whether a covenant made before 1926 binds a purchaser depends on whether or not the purchaser had notice of the covenant.[19]

(iii)   EQUITABLE EASEMENTS

The Act defines[20] an equitable easement as 'Any easement right or privilege over or affecting land created or arising after the commencement of this Act, and being merely an equitable interest'. Although not mentioned specifically, equitable profits à prendre are thought to be included within the definition.'[1] In Chapter 18 we saw that in *ER Ives Investment Ltd v High*[2] it was held that easements arising under principles of estoppel are not registrable as land charges.

It is anomalous that it is easier to discover (by inspecting the register) the existence of (registrable) equitable easements than legal ones (which are not registrable). It has been recommended[3] that equitable easements should cease to be registrable. Legal and equitable easements would then be on the same footing, and it would be up to a purchaser to ascertain the existence of any easement by an examination of the land and by making enquiries from the vendor.[4]

CLASS E ANNUITIES

Annuities registrable in this Class are those created before 1926 but not registered until after 1925. This Class (like the second Register) will eventually become obsolete.

CLASS F CHARGES AFFECTING ANY LAND BY VIRTUE OF THE FAMILY LAW ACT 1996

Under Part IV of the Family Law Act 1996[5] (replacing earlier legislation[6]), if the legal title to a matrimonial home[7] is vested in one spouse alone, the other

---

18   LCA 1972, s 2(5). *Dartstone Ltd v Cleveland Petroleum Co Ltd* [1969] 3 All ER 668, [1969] 1 WLR 1807 (covenant, the benefit of which was annexed to the leasehold interest, but the burden of which was not annexed to the reversion, held to be between lessor and lessee within the meaning of s 2(5) and so not registrable).
19   See Chapter 21.
20   LCA 1972, s 2(5).
1   M & W, p 1043.
2   [1967] 2 QB 379, [1967] 1 All ER 504; (M & B).
3   Report of the Roxburgh Committee on Land Charges, 1956, Cmnd 9825, which recommends the abolition of Class D(iii) Land Charges; (para 16).
4   Another suggestion has been that easements which are continuous and apparent should not be registrable; and that those which are not continuous and apparent should be registrable. See 88 LQR 336, 337. (P. V. Baker).
5   Section 30.
6   Matrimonial Homes Act 1967; Matrimonial Proceedings and Property Act 1970; Matrimonial Homes and Property Act 1981; Matrimonial Homes Act 1983.
7   The Act applies to any 'dwelling house'.

spouse, although not having any legal title to the property, has a right to occupy[8] the home. This statutory right of occupation, now termed a matrimonial home right, confers a right not to be evicted from the home except with the leave of the court.

Under the Land Charges Act 1972,[9] a spouse who has a right of occupation under the Act can register the right as a land charge under Class F (a class added by the Act of 1967).

Let us suppose that a matrimonial home is vested in a husband (H) alone, and that his wife (W) has the statutory right of occupation. If W registers this right and H sells the land to P, P would not be able to put W out of the house. For this reason P would decline to buy the house unless the charge was cancelled. W will be unlikely to cancel the charge unless she is satisfied that H has provided alternative accommodation for her.

If P, despite the registration, purchases the house, he can apply to the court for an order determining W's right of occupation.[10] The order of the court on such an application can require W to make periodical payments to P and can allocate between P and W the costs of maintenance and repair. In making an order the court is required[11] to consider 'all the circumstances of the case' (which include the circumstances of P[12]).

The right of occupation conferred on W by the Act ends on the termination of the marriage, by the death of H or by divorce.[13] In this event, if the right has been registered, registration is cancelled.[14]

The following matters should be noted.

(i) The right conferred by the Act is valid as against H whether registered or not. It is as against a purchaser that failure to register renders the right void.

(ii) If W has an equitable interest in the property this will give her a right of occupation (a proprietary right) which is distinct from, and in addition to, the statutory right of occupation conferred on her by the Act. (It is the statutory right that is registrable, not any proprietary interest she may have.)

(iii) If W has an equitable interest in the property, and H dies, her statutory right of occupation ends, but her proprietary right remains.

8   *Barnett v Hassett* [1982] 1 All ER 80, [1981] 1 WLR 1385.
9   Section 2(7).
10 Family Law Act 1996, s 49.
11 Section 1(3).
12 *Kaur v Gill* [1988] Fam 110, [1988] 2 All ER 288, CA; [1988] Conv 295 (M. Welstead); [1988] CLJ 355 (C. Harpum); (1989) 52 MLR 110 (P. Sparkes).
13 Section 31(8).
14 Schedule 4, para 4.

Effects of registration and non-registration

In earlier chapters we have indicated that where a matter is registrable under the Land Charges Act 1972 then, if it is registered, it binds a subsequent purchaser; and that if it is not registered, it does not. This is broadly so, but the position must now be considered more precisely.

EFFECT OF NON-REGISTRATION

The Act provides[15] that the effect of failing to register a registrable interest shall be as set out in the following table.

Register	Class			If not registered does not bind
1		Pending actions	Pending actions other than bankruptcy petitions	Any purchaser for value without express notice
			Bankruptcy petitions	Any purchaser of the legal estate in good faith for money or money's worth without notice of an act of bankruptcy[16]
2			Annuities created before 1926[17]	Any purchaser for value
3			Writs and orders	Any purchaser for value[18]
4			Deeds of arrangement	Any purchaser for value
5	A		Charges imposed by statute, on application	Any purchaser for value
	B		Charges imposed by statute automatically	Any purchaser for value
	C (i)		**Puisne mortgages**	**Any purchaser for value**
	(ii)		Limited owners' charges	Any purchaser for value
	(iii)		**General equitable charges**	**Any purchaser for value**
	(iv)		**Estate contracts**	**Any purchaser of the legal estate for money or money's worth[19]**
	D (i)		Inheritance tax	Any purchaser of the legal estate for money or money's worth
	(ii)		**Restrictive covenants made after 1925**	**Any purchaser of the legal estate for money or money's worth**

---

15   LCA 1972, s 4.
16   For present bankruptcy procedure, see Insolvency Act 1986.
17   Annuities created before 1926 and registered before 1926 are entered in the Second Register; those registered after 1925 are registrable in Class E of the Fifth Register.
18   Receiving orders, registrable as writs and orders, are void against the same persons as are Bankruptcy petitions.
19   If the estate contract was made before 1926 it is void against a purchaser for value.

(iii)		Equitable easements created after 1925	Any purchaser of the legal estate for money or money's worth
E		Annuities created before 1926	Any purchaser for value
F		Rights under the Matrimonial Homes Act 1983	Any purchaser for value

The word 'purchaser' means any person (including a mortgagee or lessee) who, for valuable consideration, takes any interest in land or a charge on land.[20]

The operation of the above provisions can be illustrated by two examples. Suppose that A, the holder of the legal fee simple in Blackacre, grants an equitable easement to B. B fails to register his interest. A then conveys the legal fee simple in the land to his fiancée, C, as part of an ante-nuptial marriage settlement. The Act provides that if the easement is not registered, it will not bind (in the words of the Act,[1] it is 'void as against') a purchaser of the legal estate for money or money's worth. C, although a purchaser for value (ie her promise of marriage), is not a purchaser for money or money's worth, and so does not come into this category. So she cannot avail herself of the protection afforded by the Act. Since the Act does not, in her case, apply, the old rules[2] are brought into operation. C will take free of B's equitable easement only if she can show that she is a bona fide purchaser for value of the legal estate without notice. Thus, if she can show that she had no notice, actual or constructive, of B's equitable easement, then she will take free of it. If she cannot, she is bound.

Consider another example. R mortgages land to E by a legal mortgage. There is no deposit of the title deeds. The mortgage is registrable under Class C (i). E fails to register. R subsequently gives the land to Z. Under the Act, if the mortgage is not registered it will not bind any purchaser for value. Z is not a purchaser for value. So the Act does not apply. So the old rule that legal interests bind all the world is brought into operation. Since E's mortgage is legal it binds Z, notwithstanding its non-registration.

It is therefore not correct to say that if an interest is not registered, it will not bind a subsequent holder of the land. However, in practice, it will only be in exceptional cases that a subsequent holder will be bound by an interest which is registrable but not registered.

If R enters into a restrictive covenant in favour of E, and E fails to register it, as between R and E the non-registration is immaterial and E can enforce the covenant against R. The original parties (eg covenantor and covenantee, vendor and purchaser, mortgagor and mortgagee) are not affected by registration or non-registration.[3] Only third parties (eg a purchaser from R) are affected by whether or not a matter has been registered.

---

20   LCA 1972, s 17(1).
1   LCA 1972, s 4.
2   Ie legal interests bind all the world, equitable interests bind all the world except a bona fide purchaser for value of the legal estate without notice.
3   *Hollington Bros Ltd v Rhodes* [1951] 2 All ER 578n; *Markfaith Investments Ltd v Chiap Hua Flashlights Ltd* [1991] 2 AC 43, PC.

It must be stressed that if an interest is registrable and it is not registered, it is not binding on a purchaser[4] who is protected by the Act, irrespective of whether the purchaser had notice of the interest.[5] Even if he had actual notice, he is not bound.[6]

An illustration of the principle that an unregistered land charge is not binding on a purchaser is provided by *Midland Bank Trust Co Ltd v Green*.[7] In 1961 a father, W, who owned a 300-acre farm in Lincolnshire (Gravel Hill Farm, Thornton-le-Moor) granted a lease of the farm to his son, coupled with an option, lasting for ten years, entitling G to purchase the farm at £75 an acre. The option was not registered as a land charge. Later, in 1967, W decided that he did not wish G to be able to buy the farm. In order to nullify G's option, W conveyed the farm (then worth about £40,000) to his wife, E, for £500. The matter was done quickly. When, shortly afterwards, G found out about the sale he registered the option as a land charge and sought to enforce it against E. Was the option void against E? As the option had not been registered it was void against a purchaser 'for money or money's worth'. But, with the land being worth £40,000, was the consideration given by E, £500, 'money or money's worth'—particularly when seen against the fact that the purchaser, E, was aware of G's option, and that the sale was specifically for the purpose of rendering the option void? At first instance Oliver J held[8] that E was a purchaser for 'money or money's worth', and that the option was therefore void against E. The Court of Appeal[9] held[10] that in determining whether a purchaser was a purchaser 'for money or money's worth' the court could inquire into the adequacy of the consideration and the genuineness of the transaction and that in the circumstances of the case E was not a purchaser 'for money or money's worth'. The option was therefore not void for non-registration, and so could be enforced by G against E. The House of Lords[11] reversed the decision of the Court of Appeal. The wording of the section was not, the House held, qualified by any requirement that, in order to take free of an unregistered land charge, a purchaser must not only be one 'for money or money's worth' but must also act in good faith and that the money paid must not be nominal. Therefore E was a purchaser 'for money or money's worth' and so took free of G's option. (In later litigation E's executor successfully sued for negligence the firm of solicitors which had drawn up, but failed to register, the option.[12])

There is only one, limited, exception to the rule that failure to register renders a registrable land charge void. It is possible that in some circumstances

4   Ie who is a purchaser for value, or a purchaser of the legal estate for money or money's worth, as the case may be, according to the type of land charge in question.
5   *Lloyds Bank plc v Carrick* [1996] 4 All ER 630140 Sol Jo LB 101; [1996] Conv 295.
6   The modern foundation for this principle is *Re Monolithic Building Co* [1915] 1 Ch 643 (concerning the registration of an incumbrance under s 93 of the Companies (Consolidation) Act 1908).
7   [1981] AC 513, [1981] 1 All ER 153, HL; (M&B); [1981] CLJ 213 (C. Harpum).
8   [1980] Ch 590, [1978] 3 All ER 555.
9   [1980] Ch 590, [1979] 3 All ER 28.
10 Sir Stanley Rees dissenting.
11 [1981] AC 513, [1981] 1 All ER 153.
12 *Midland Bank Trust Co Ltd v Hett, Stubbs and Kemp* [1979] Ch 384, [1978] 3 All ER 571; cf *Bell v Peter Browne & Co* [1990] 2 QB 495, [1990] 3 All ER 124.

the principle of proprietary estoppel may save an unregistered land charge from being void. For example, L grants a lease to T for 21 years, with an option to renew for a further period. The option is not registered. L sells the freehold to M. T, with the encouragement, or perhaps even with merely the knowledge, of M undertakes work on the land in the belief, created, encouraged or permitted,[13] by M that the option would be accepted as binding by M. Here M may be estopped from relying on the non-registration of the option.[14]

Finally, it will be convenient to note at this point that if T holds an equitable lease from L for, say, five years, and T fails to register the lease, and T pays rent to L at, say '£1,000 per annum', then, as seen in Chapter 17, at common law a periodic, yearly, lease arises. If L sells the fee simple to P, then, whilst T's equitable five-year lease is not binding on P, his legal yearly lease is. (This fact may be of particular importance if T's yearly lease is protected under the Rent Acts.)

EFFECT OF REGISTRATION

The Act does not expressly provide that if a registrable interest is registered it binds any subsequent holder of the land. This, nevertheless, is the result produced.

The Law of Property Act 1925, s 198(1), provides that registration under the Land Charges Act 1925 is to be deemed to constitute notice of the matter registered 'to all persons and for all purposes'. The result is that if it is an equitable interest which is registrable, then since registration constitutes notice to all the world, including a subsequent holder of the land, the latter cannot show that he is a bona fide purchaser without notice, and so is bound. If it is a legal interest that is registrable, then registration removes the penalty which failure to register brings (eg making the interest not binding on a purchaser for value) and thus leaves the way clear for the old rule to apply, namely that legal interests bind all the world. So a subsequent purchaser is bound. But this is not the same thing as saying that the fact of registration makes it binding on a subsequent purchaser. Thus even in the case of matters which are registrable, the system does not abolish the old rules[15] but merely builds on them.

SEARCHES[16]

P has contracted to buy V's house. Before he signs the conveyance he needs to know whether any land charges have been registered against the land. He

13 *Willmott v Barber* (1880) 15 Ch D 96. Here the defendant was not aware that the plaintiff had acted in ignorance of his legal rights and therefore the plaintiff's claim failed.
14 See *Taylor Fashions Ltd v Liverpool Victoria Trustees Co Ltd* [1982] QB 133n, [1981] 1 All ER 897; (M & B).
15 See n 4, p 492.
16 F. Silverman *Searches and Enquiries* (1985).

therefore makes a search in the Land Registry. He can do this by completing a form asking for a search to be made. He sends the form together with the appropriate fee[17] to the Land Registry at Plymouth. Staff at the Registry search the registers. If any entries affect the land, details are entered on a Search Certificate which is returned to P. If no entries are found, the Search Certificate is returned to P with a statement to this effect. (P is said to receive a 'nil' or 'clear' certificate.)

A search in this form is termed an official search.[18] It is the most common form of search. Alternatively P (or, eg, his solicitor) can visit Plymouth and search the Registers personally.[19]

The entries on a Search Certificate are conclusive.[20] Thus if V contracts to sell the land to X; X registers the estate contract against V's name; V later proposes to sell to P; P searches in the land charges register; the Registry, in error, send P a 'nil' certificate; and P buys the land, the result is that X's estate contract is void against P. X's only remedy is against V for breach of contract; or against the Registry for negligence (or against both).

Registration against the name of estate holders

It would be convenient when searching in a register to be able to discover all the charges registered against a certain piece of land by referring to its location, eg Derbyshire, Youlgreave, Church Street, number 12. Unfortunately this is not how the Land Charges Register is maintained. Entries are registered not against the land (ie according to the address or map reference) but (as noted earlier[1]) against the name of the holder of the legal estate at the time of registration.[2] Thus suppose that before 12 Church Street, Youlgreave, had passed into the hands of V, it had been owned, as in the example above, by C, D and E. P would have to request the Land Registry to make a search against the names of each of these persons (and against the name of V). Before he can make the search P will thus have to ascertain who were the previous holders of the land.

However, when D bought the land from C, D will have made a search and obtained a search certificate, and so will E and V when they in turn acquired the land. In this case the earlier certificates will reveal any entries against the names of earlier owners. If the earlier certificates have been retained, and V lets P inspect these, P will need only to make a search against the name of V. This will save him both time and Land Registry fees. He will, in addition, need to inspect the title deeds to ensure that the search certificates cover all the

---

17   Section 10(2). A search may also be made by the requisition for the search being sent by telephone or fax, provided that the searcher maintains a credit account at the Registry, s 10(1).
18   Section 10.
19   Section 9.
20   Section 10(4).
1   See p 482.
2   Section 3(1).

previous owners. It will be noted that this inspection of the title deeds is necessary in connection with the search for incumbrances, and is distinct from the verification of V's title to the land, though P may do this at the same time.

Errors as to the name of the estate owner

Under the Act,[3] registration must be made against 'the name of the estate owner whose estate is intended to be affected'. In the event of a dispute as to the correct name for this purpose, the court will assume, in the absence of evidence to the contrary, that the correct name is that used in the document by which the land was conveyed to the estate owner.[4]

Disputes can arise as a result of an incorrect name, in the form of a variation of the correct name, being used (a) by the person registering the charge; (b) by the Land Registry; or (c) by a would-be purchaser (in making a search).

Let us suppose that land is conveyed to (and conveyed into the name of) John Stuart Frost who mortgages the land without deposit of title deeds to X. Then,

(a) X sends the appropriate form to the Registry to register the mortgage (as a Class C (i) land charge) against the name of John Stewart Frost. The land is later sold to P. Is P bound by X's mortgage? The answer is that (i) if P had searched in the correct name and obtained a 'nil' certificate from the Registry he is not bound;[5] (ii) if he failed to search,[5] or if he failed to search in the correct name,[6] then the fact that X had not used the correct version of the name does not invalidate the mortgage as against P, and P is bound.

(b) X applies for registration of his mortgage against the (correct) name of John Stuart Frost. The Registry, by error, registers the charge against the name John Stewart Frost. The land is sold to P. P searches and obtains a nil certificate. Here, since the Act provides[7] that a search certificate is to be conclusive, P takes free of X's mortgage, and X's remedy lies against the Registrar for negligence.

(c) X applies for registration (correctly) against the name John Stuart Frost, and the Registry enters the charge correctly against this name. In his application for a search, P requests a search against the name of John Stewart Frost. He receives a nil certificate and purchases the land. Here P is bound by X's mortgage.[8] (In such circumstances the Registry may draw attention to the entry under John Stuart Frost, thus warning X to check the correct name and, if necessary, make a fresh search.)

3   LCA 1972, s 3(1).
4   *Diligent Finance Co Ltd v Alleyne* (1971) 23 P & CR 346; [1987] Conv 135 (JEA).
5   *Oak Co-operative Building Society v Blackburn* [1968] Ch 730, [1968] 2 All ER 117.
6   Ibid.
7   LCA 1972, s 10(4).
8   *Du Sautoy v Symes* [1967] Ch 1146 at 1168: a purchaser is entitled to rely on a nil certificate only where his application for a search gives 'no reasonable scope for misunderstanding in the Land Registry.'

In *Oak Co-operative Building Society v Blackburn*[9] land was held by (and in the name of) Francis David Blackburn, (B), who carried on business as an estate agent under the name of Frank D Blackburn. In 1958 B contracted to sell the land to C. In 1959 C registered the estate contract against the name of 'Frank David Blackburn'. In 1962, B approached a building society for a loan on the security of the land. The society applied for a search against the name of 'Francis Davis Blackburn', received a nil certificate, and advanced money to B under a mortgage of the land. Here, it will be seen, errors had been made both by the person registering the charge (as in (a) above), and the person making the search (as in (c) above). The court held that registration in names that might fairly be described as a version of the proper names was not a nullity and constituted an effective registration against a person who failed to apply for an official search or who applied in the wrong name. The registration would, however, be ineffective against a person who obtained a nil certificate after searching in the correct name. Since the building society had searched in the wrong name, C's registration was effective against the society. (Thus C's estate contract took priority over the society's mortgage.)

Land charges discovered after the date of the contract

It is not the practice for purchasers to search for land charges until after the contract for the sale of the land has been signed. What if P signs the contract and, on searching, discovers an incumbrance the existence of which he was not aware and the existence of which, had he known of it, might have decided him against contracting to buy the land? In *Re Forsey and Hollebone's Contract*[10] it was held that in the circumstances given P was, by s 198 of the Law of Property Act 1925, precluded from refusing to complete the purchase. To remedy this defect, the Law of Property Act 1969[11] provides that in the circumstances given above, P should, as against V, only be bound by those incumbrances of which he had actual notice at the date of the contract. The effect is to give P the right to rescind the contract on discovery, after the date of the contract, of a land charge the existence of which has not been revealed to him.

Non-registrable interests

Matters which are not registrable include the following.

---

9   [1968] Ch 730.
10   [1927] 2 Ch 379.
11   Section 24, enacted following the recommendations of the Report of the Committee on Land Charges, 1956 (the Roxburgh Committee), Cmnd 9825, and of the Law Commission *Report on Land Charges affecting Unregistered Land*, 1965 (Law Com No 18).

1. Legal interests, except a legal mortgage not protected by deposit of title deeds.
2. The following equitable interests:
   (a) restrictive covenants entered into before 1926;
   (b) certain equitable rights of re-entry, as in *Shiloh Spinners Ltd v Harding*[12] (this case is set out on p 502);
   (c) equitable rights arising under the principle of estoppel, as in *ER Ives Investments Ltd v High*[13] (this case is set out on p 348);
   (d) equitable interests arising from a contribution to the purchase of property (or from the improvement of property) the legal title of which is vested in another, eg the equitable interest in a matrimonial home held by a wife[14] as a result of her having contributed to the purchase price of the property, the title to which is in the name of her husband alone (the husband thus holding the land on trust for himself and his wife[15]).

In the case of matters which are not registrable, the old rules apply.[16] Thus non-registrable legal interests (eg a legal lease) bind any subsequent holder of the land. In the case of non-registrable equitable interests, eg a restrictive covenant entered into before 1926, if a purchaser has notice actual or constructive of the interest concerned, he is bound.[17]

From this it might be thought to follow that if a covenant was contained in a conveyance by A to B in 1920, since the existence of the covenant could be discovered from an examination of the title deeds, a purchaser would at least have constructive notice of the covenant, and so would be bound. But this is not necessarily so. The reason is that a person is deemed to have notice only of those matters which he would have discovered if he had investigated the vendor's title back to the 'root of title'. In order to understand the meaning of this statement we must first explain the meaning of the term 'root of title'.

Root of title

Suppose that in 1997 P wishes to buy a house occupied by V (the title to which is not registered. Registration of *title* is treated in the next chapter). V is willing to sell. Before P can safely complete the purchase he will need to satisfy himself as to what incumbrances, if any, affect the land. P will also need to ascertain whether the land is V's to sell: he will need to investigate V's title to the land.

---

12 [1973] AC 691, [1973] 1 All ER 90; (M & B).
13 [1967] 2 QB 379, [1967] 1 All ER 504; *Crabb v Arun District Council* [1976] Ch 179, [1975] 3 All ER 865; (M & B).
14 And, it would seem, the interest held by a husband who contributes to the purchase of a home conveyed into the name of his wife alone, as in *Falconer v Falconer* [1970] 3 All ER 449, [1970] 1 WLR 1333.
15 See Chapter 5.
16 *Caunce v Caunce* [1969] 1 All ER 722, [1969] 1 WLR 286; (M & B).
17 Provided that the interest is of a nature that is capable of binding a purchaser; *Bristol and West Building Society v Henning* [1985] 2 All ER 606, [1985] 1 WLR 778.

How far back in time will V be called upon to produce evidence of the ownership of the property? He may have title deeds in his possession dating back to 1983, but will this be far enough back to satisfy P? It is up to P, if he wishes, to specify in the contract the length of period for which he requires V to produce evidence of title. If the contract is silent, statute provides[18] that the period is to be 15 years.[19]

Consider these transactions:

1920	1940	1969	1983	1989	1997
A sells	B sells	C sells	D sells	E sells	V proposes to
to B	to C	to D	to E	to V	sell to P

The conveyance of 1983 will not be a sufficient root of title, since the document does not establish who was the owner at the beginning of the 15-year period, ie in 1982. (The conveyance does not establish that D was owner in 1982, merely that D was owner in 1983.) In order to show who was owner in 1982, V must produce the conveyance of 1969 from C to D. This, coupled with the later documents of title, establishes the chain of title for the statutory period. Thus the document starting the chain must be *at least* 15 years old and may, as in our example, be considerably older.

The conveyance of 1969 is termed the 'root of title'. A root of title need not be a conveyance. It can, for example, be a deed of gift, or an assent.[20] But to be a good root of title it must be a document that deals with the whole legal and equitable interest in the land and gives an adequate description of the property. (A legal mortgage fulfils these requirements.)

We can now return to the question whether a covenant in a conveyance from A to B in 1920 binds a purchaser of the land in 1997. A purchaser has constructive notice of all matters back to the root of title.[1] If the root of title was dated before 1920 (or if the root of title was the conveyance of 1920 containing the covenant) then P is bound. If the root of title is dated after the date of the covenant, P is not bound. In our example, since the date of the covenant was before the date of the root of title, P is not bound (unless he had actual notice of the covenant, eg as a result of examining the conveyance of 1920).

(If an interest is registrable, and is registered, it binds a purchaser irrespective of whether the registration occurred before or after the date of the root of title. This fact may lead to a problem that is considered later.[2])

---

18   LPA 1969, s 23, amending LPA 1925, s 44(1) under which the period was 30 years. Before 1926 the period was 40 years, under the Vendor and Purchaser Act 1874, s 2. Before the 1874 Act the period was, by the general practice of conveyancers, 60 years.
19   As recommended by the Law Commission, *Transfer of Land: Interim Report on Root of Title to Freehold Land* (Law Com No 9, 1967).
20   Provided that the assent was made after 1925.
1   Determined in accordance with the statutory period (notwithstanding that the purchaser may have agreed to accept a root of title of a later date than this); *Re Nisbet and Potts' Contract* [1906] 1 Ch 386; (M & B).
2   See infra.

UNDISCOVERABLE LAND CHARGES

INTERESTS REGISTERED BEFORE THE ROOT OF TITLE

Suppose that, as in the example above, V produces title deeds starting with a good root of title dated 1945. This will tell P the holders of the land since that date, but he will not know who held the land before then, and V is not obliged to ascertain this for him, as a root of title dated 1945 is earlier than the commencement of the statutory period. Yet an incumbrance might have been registered against the name of an earlier holder, say B, in 1928. Since it is registered, it will bind P. But P cannot discover its existence, because he cannot know that B held the land in 1928. A purchaser may thus have no means of discovering an incumbrance registered before the date of the root of title, and, if the root of title is after 1925, he may find himself bound by an incumbrance the existence of which he has no means of finding.

In order to meet such a situation the Law of Property Act 1969[3] provides[4] that where a person suffers loss as a result of being bound by a registered land charge of which he had no actual notice, and which was not registered against the name of a person who was a party to the transaction (V) or of a person whose name appeared on the relevant documents of title (C, D and E), then the person who suffers the loss shall be entitled to claim compensation from the Chief Land Registrar. He is, nevertheless, still bound by the incumbrance.

LESSEES: SECTION 44

By s 44(2)–(4) of the Law of Property Act 1925, if L contracts to grant a lease to T, then unless the contract provides to the contrary, T has no right to require L to prove his title to the land. If L declines to allow T to see his title deeds, T has no means of knowing who were the previous owners of the land. So he cannot discover the existence of incumbrances affecting the land (other than those registered against the name of L).

The position with regard to whether incumbrances affecting leased land bind a tenant is as follows.

1. In the case of unregistrable equitable interests (eg a restrictive covenant made before 1926, or an equitable mortgage protected by deposit of title deeds), if T is not able to discover the existence of the incumbrances by reason of the provision of s 44(2)–(4), and if he has no actual notice of the incumbrances, then by s 44(5) he is deemed to take without notice of them. Thus, as a bona fide purchaser of the legal estate without notice, he takes free of the interests

---

3   Section 25 replacing Vendor and Purchaser Act 1874, s 2 as amended by the Conveyancing Act 1881, ss 3, 13.

4   As recommended by the Law Commission, *Transfer of Land, Report on Land Charges affecting Unregistered Land* (Law Com No 18, 1969).

concerned. This is just to T, but unjust to the holder of the equitable interest (particularly, for example, an equitable mortgagee).[5]

2. In the case of unregistrable legal interests, notice is irrelevant, and T is bound.

3. In the case of registrable interests, if these are registered, then, since registration is deemed to constitute actual notice,[6] T is bound by the interests concerned (whether legal or equitable). This is just to the holder of the interest, but is unjust to T. He is bound by an interest the existence of which he has no means of discovering[7] (and, unlike the purchaser of a fee simple in these circumstances, he is not able to claim compensation under the Law of Property Act 1969[8]). Thus if T is considering taking any substantial leasehold interest from L he will ensure that the contract confers on him a right to call on L to show his title to the land. By this means he will be able to search for land charges that will be binding on him.

RIGHTS OF THIRD PARTIES AGAINST A SQUATTER

In Chapter 24 we said that rights of third parties bind a squatter (S). Consider the four interests set out on p 478.

(a) If the mortgage was registered, it binds S. If it was not registered it is void only as against a purchaser for value. S is not a purchaser for value. It is therefore not void as against him for non-registration. Under the old rules,[9] since it is legal, it binds him.

(b) The easement is not registrable. Under the old rules, being legal, it binds S.

(c) If the easement was registered, it binds S. If it was not registered it is void only as against a purchaser for value of the legal estate for money or money's worth. S is not such a person. It is therefore not void as against him for non-registration. Under the old rules S will only take free if he can show that he is a bona fide purchaser for value of the legal estate without notice. He is not such a person. He is therefore bound.

(d) The interest is not registrable. The old rules apply. S is not a bona fide purchaser for value; he is therefore bound.[10]

If S sells the land to a purchaser (P) the normal rules apply in determining whether or not P is bound, eg in the case of (a) above, if the mortgage is registered, P is bound; if it is not, he is not bound.

---

5   Prior to the enactment of s 44(5), under the rule in *Patman v Harland* (1881) 17 Ch D 353, a lessee was deemed to have notice of all matters that he would have discovered if, under the contract, he had been entitled to inspect the lessor's title deeds. This was just to the holder of the interest, but unjust to T. Thus s 44(5) did not remove injustice; it merely changed the person who suffered it. See *Shears v Wells*[1936] 1 All ER 832; (M & B).

6   LPA 1925, s 198.

7   *White v Bijou Mansions Ltd* [1938] Ch 351, [1938] All ER 546; (M & B).

8   Sections 25(9).

9   See n 4, p 492.

10   *Re Nisbet and Potts' Contract* [1906] 1 Ch 386; (M & B).

ILLUSTRATION

We have seen that if a matter is registrable, then whether it binds a purchaser of the land depends (broadly[11]) on whether it is registered. If it is not registrable, then whether it binds a purchaser depends, if it is equitable, on the outcome of the application of the bona fide purchaser rule. Let us consider an illustration of how these principles are applied in the case of an equitable interest.

Suppose that A holds the interest, and it constitutes an incumbrance on Blackacre. The interest is not registered. Blackacre passes into the hands of Z. A wishes to show that his interest binds Z. Z, for his part, wishes to show that he holds the land free of A's interest. In this situation A will seek to show (1) that the matter was not registrable (so that his failure to register it has not rendered it void as against Z), and (2) that Z has notice, actual or constructive, of the interest; so that, under the old principles, Z is bound by it. Z, for his part, will seek to show either (a) that the matter *was* registrable with the result that, as it was not registered, it does not bind him; or (b) (more difficult) if he is driven to accept that the matter was not registrable, that he had no notice, actual or constructive, of the interest, and so is not bound by it. The conflict between A and Z can be illustrated by two cases.

In *Greene v Church Commissioners for England*[12] a company leased a flat to S for seven years. In the lease S covenanted not to assign the lease without the company's consent, and in a proviso it was stipulated that if S wished to assign the lease he must first offer to surrender the lease to the company without consideration, and that the company could accept the surrender if it so wished. In 1972 the company assented to an assignment of the residue of the term of the lease by S to G, and the assignment to G was made. G had carpets fitted in the flat and spent money on various other fixtures and fittings. In 1973 the company transferred the reversion to the Church Commissioners (who thus became G's landlord). Later in 1973 G wished to assign the lease to K, who was prepared to pay G £3,000 for the carpets and other items. G asked the Commissioners for consent to assign the lease. The Commissioners replied stating that they would want to take a surrender of the lease and would not consent to an assignment. Thus G had the choice of staying in the flat (which he did not want to do) or of surrendering the lease to the Commissioners. If he surrendered the lease, he would have had to take out the fitted carpets, etc (and in so doing would have suffered a loss). The right of the Commissioners to decline consent to an assignment and to require the tenant to offer to surrender the lease without consideration was thus an incumbrance attaching to the land, ie to G's leasehold interest in the land. (If G had in fact been aware of the incumbrance he would probably either not have taken the assignment from S, or not had the carpets fitted and the other fixtures and fittings installed.) Could G escape the restriction which the covenant imposed on him? He argued that the covenant which S had made with the company was a contract to convey a legal estate (ie a contract to surrender the lease back to the company)

---

11 See p 490.
12 [1974] Ch 467, [1974] 3 All ER 609.

and as such was registrable under Class C (iv) (Estate contracts) of the Land Charges Acts 1925 and 1972. Since it had not been registered, he argued, it did not bind him. The Court of Appeal upheld his contention:[13] the interest was registrable under Class C (iv); it had not been registered and so did not bind him.[14]

Now consider *Shiloh Spinners Ltd v Harding.*[15] In this case L leased land to S. In 1961 S assigned part of the land to T. In the assignment T made certain covenants, some positive, some negative. S reserved a right of re-entry if the covenants were not observed. In 1965 T assigned the land he held to H. H failed to observe the covenants. Because of the terms of the assignment by S to T, T was not liable for H's breach. S therefore sought to proceed against H. He could not enforce the positive covenants against H, because the burden of positive covenants does not run with the land of the covenantor.[16] He could not enforce the negative covenants against H as these had not been registered as restrictive covenants.[17] So S sought to enforce the right of re-entry against H. H claimed that the right of re-entry was not binding on him on the ground that the interest was registrable and had not been registered. His argument was as follows: (1) the right of re-entry, although arising in the context of a lease, had not come into existence on the grant of the lease (by L to S); (2) it had merely been reserved when an existing lease was assigned (by S to T); (3) the right of re-entry was therefore not a right of entry 'exercisable over or in respect of a legal term of years absolute' under s 1(2) of the Law of Property Act 1925. (4) Thus, the right of re-entry, not being capable of being legal, must be equitable. (5) The equitable right of re-entry was an interest registrable as a 'right' under Class D (iii) – 'an easement, right or privilege over or affecting land and being merely equitable'. Since it had not been registered, he said, it did not bind him. S claimed that the right of re-entry was not registrable and that since H had notice (at least constructive) of the interest, he was bound. The House of Lords accepted H's arguments down to and including (4) above, but held that the right of re-entry was not registrable under Class D (iii) since the word 'right' under that head was not intended to have a meaning so different from easement and privilege as to include a right of re-entry. Therefore, since the interest was not registrable, and H had notice of it, he was bound.

Thus in *Greene* the person holding the benefit of the incumbrance lost, since the incumbrance was registrable and had not been registered. In *Shiloh Spinners Ltd v Harding*, the person holding the benefit of the incumbrance succeeded, since the incumbrance was not registrable, and the person against whom it was sought to be enforced had notice of it.

We may note here that, in the light of the intention of the 1925 legislation to avoid where possible the need for a purchaser to show that he is a bona fide

---

13   The Court therefore did not have to decide whether, as G further argued, the proviso was void as being contrary to s 19 of the Landlord and Tenant Act 1927. See Chapter 17.
14   See also *Lloyds Bank plc v Carrick* [1996] 4 All ER 630, 140 Sol Jo LB 101; [1996] Conv 295.
15   [1973] AC 691, [1973] 1 All ER 90; (M & B).
16   See Chapter 21.
17   Ibid.

purchaser without notice, the continued existence of non-registrable interests such as that in *Shiloh Spinners Ltd v Harding* might seem to be anomalous. In 1925 it was perhaps thought that with the passage of time the significance of such interests would decrease. In recent years, however, the cases have shown that non-registrable equitable interests of much importance can come into existence.[18] The old bona fide purchaser rule thus still looms larger in English land law than those who drafted the legislation of 1925 perhaps expected or intended.

LOCAL LAND CHARGES[19]

In addition to, and distinct from, the registry of land charges maintained at Plymouth by the Land Charges Department of the Land Registry, local authorities maintain registers of Local Land Charges.[20]

Matters registrable as local land charges consist, in the main, of disadvantages attached to the land as a result of a decision of a public body, usually that of a local authority. For example, if P is considering buying V's house he may discover on inspecting the local land charges register that three trees in the garden cannot be felled because they are the subject of a Tree Preservation Order; that a 'planning obligation'[1] imposed by a local planning authority on the grant of a planning permission imposed certain obligations, or placed restrictions, with regard to the use of the land; that money is owed (by instalments) by whoever owns the house to the local authority to pay for making up the road in front of the house, and that this sum is a charge on the land; that a strip of land at the end of the garden is the subject of a compulsory purchase order made by the local authority; that he cannot make any extension to the front of the house because of the existence of a 'building line' prescribed by the local authority; that land within the grounds lies within an area designated as an area of special scientific interest[2] (with the result that restrictions exist with regard to certain operations on the land). It is disadvantages such as these which are registrable as local land charges. Responsibility for registration generally rests with the local authority.

If a local land charge is not registered it nonetheless binds any person who acquired the land. However, if a purchaser obtains an official search certificate which does not reveal the existence of the charge, he is entitled to compensation from the authority on whom rested responsibility for registering

---

18 As in *ER Ives Investment Ltd v High* [1967] 2 QB 379, [1967] 1 All ER 504; (M & B); and *Shiloh Spinners Ltd v Harding*, ante.

19 J. F. Garner *Local Land Charges*; Law Commission: *Transfer of Land – Report on Local Land Charges* 1974 (Law Com No 62).

20 Local Land Charges Act 1975. (The Act repealed those parts of the Land Charges Act 1925 not repealed by the Land Charges Act 1972.) The Local Government (Miscellaneous Provisions) Act 1982, s 34, permits the register to be kept in a computerised form.

1 Town and Country Planning Act 1990, s 106 as amended by Planning and Compensation Act 1991, s 12.

2 Wildlife and Countryside Act 1981, s 28(10). Such areas have come to be termed Sites of Special Scientific Interest (SSSIs).

the charge.[3] (It will be noted that the fact that a local land charge binds a purchaser notwithstanding its non-registration constitutes a significant difference between the effect of failure to register a central land charge and the effect of failure to register a local land charge.)

Unlike the registers maintained in the Land Charges Department of the Land Registry, local land charges are registered against the land. Thus it is necessary to supply only the address of the land concerned when making a search.

SUMMARY

See Appendix II, p 569.

3   Local Land Charges Act 1975, s 10.

CHAPTER 26

Registered Land: Registration of Title[1]

Introduction

The verification of a vendor's title is generally a more complex job than searching for land charges. To search for land charges, normally all one has to know is the county[2] in which the land falls, the names of the persons to be searched against and the years between which they were involved with the land. The relevant forms can be completed and sent off by a 16-year-old typist. But to verify a title needs a knowledge of law and considerable care.

A solicitor acting for a purchaser[3] must be on the watch for any possible defects in the vendor's title; for any possible weakness, or missing links, in the chain of title leading to the vendor. For example, if V sells land to P, P will need to satisfy himself that V has a good title to the land. V may produce as a root of title a conveyance by Q to R. P examines the conveyance from Q to R, a grant of probate to S (the executor appointed by R in his will), an assent by S to T (to whom R had devised the land), a deed of gift by which T gave the land to U, and a conveyance on sale from U to V. Only after all these documents have been scrutinised and found to be in order could P safely buy the land.

Let us suppose that three months after purchasing the land P wishes to sell the land to X. X must verify P's title, and X's solicitor will inspect the same series of documents, this time including the conveyance by V to P. Each time the land changes hands (at any rate, on every transfer for value) the same costly and time-consuming procedure must be followed.

Would it not be sensible, it might be asked, if the State once and for all officially verified who was the owner of the land and recorded this fact in a central register – a register showing who was the owner of every plot of land in the country? If P wished to buy land from V, all he would have to do would be to check this register. If he found V registered as the owner, he could safely buy the land. V's name could then be struck out and P's name substituted.

In fact a land register has been in existence for over 100 years, although even now it is a long way from covering every plot of land in the country. Originally set up by the Land Registry Act 1862, the system proved unworkable and an entirely different system was established by the Land Transfer Acts of

---

1   Ruoff and Roper *Law and Practice of Registered Conveyancing*; S.R. Simpson *Land Law and Registration*; D. J. Hayton *Registered Land*, T.B.F. Ruoff and E. J. Pryer *Land Registration Handbook: Forms and Practice*.
2   Or former county.
3   The same considerations apply as between, for example, a mortgagor and mortgagee, the latter needing to ensure that the former has a good title to the land to be mortgaged.

1875 and 1897. In general this is the system which operates today, its present statutory basis being the Land Registration Acts 1925 to 1997,[4] as supplemented by the Land Registration Rules 1925, as amended, and by later statutory rules.

Proposals that would make significant changes to the system have been made by the Law Commission.[5] The Commission is working on proposals that would entail a complete overhaul and updating of the system.[6]

The system of registration

Section 1 of the Act of 1925 provides: 'There shall continue to be kept at His Majesty's Land Registry a register of title to ... land'. When the title to a piece of land has been entered on this register the land concerned is termed 'registered land'.

It will be noted that it is the Land Registry, under the Chief Land Registrar,[7] which is responsible for maintaining both the Register of Land Charges (treated in the last chapter) and the register of title, which for convenience is maintained, not at the headquarters of the Land Registry in London, but on a geographical basis at nineteen District Land Registries.

The Act did not introduce registration at once, a period of ten years intervening until specified areas were made within which registration, when land changed hands on sale, became compulsory. As time passed more areas were added to those within which registration was compulsory, urban areas being given priority. In 1990 the process was completed, and the whole of England and Wales is now subject to compulsory registration.[8]

When title becomes registrable

Under the 1925 Act, the title to land was required to be registered on the first occasion that land in an area of compulsory registration changed hands on sale; it was only sale that, as the matter is colloquially expressed, 'triggered' registration.

---

4   Land Registration Acts of 1925, 1936, 1966, 1986, 1988 and 1997 and Pt 1 of the Land Registration and Land Charges Act 1971.
5   Culminating in Law Com No 173 (1988). See *First Report of a Joint Working Group on the Implementation of the Law Commission's Third and Fourth Reports on Land Registration*, Law Com No 235 (1995).
6   See Law Commission, Annual Report for 1995, Law Com No 239, p 40.
7   Section 126(1).
8   Compulsory registration was first introduced, for dealings with land in the County of London, by the Land Transfer Act 1897. Compulsory registration was not introduced from the date of the Act due to opposition from the Law Society, the system drastically reducing the amount of work needing to be undertaken by solicitors. See C. Harpum [1990] CLJ at 277, 287, 304.

The Land Registration Act 1997[9] extends the transactions that require the title to be registered by providing that the title to land is to be registered:

(a) on the conveyance of the fee simple, for consideration or by gift;
(b) on the grant of a lease of more than 21 years, for consideration or by gift;
(c) on the assignment of a lease with more than 21 years to run, for consideration or by gift;
(d) on the making of an assent disposing of a fee simple, or a lease with more than 21 years to run;
(e) on the mortgage, with deposit of title documents, of a fee simple or a lease with more than 21 years to run, the mortgage having priority over other mortgages affecting the land (ie, normally a first mortgage).

Procedure

When land to which the title is not yet registered is subject to a transaction that triggers registration (most commonly, on sale) the new holder (or in the case of (e) above, the mortgagor) is required to send (in practice usually through his solicitor) the title deeds together with an application for registration to the appropriate District Land Registry. If on examination the land can be satisfactorily identified on the ordnance Survey map and the title is found to be satisfactory, certain information relating to the land was (prior to computerisation) entered on a sheet of blue card[10] measuring 11 inches by 9 inches. This card, and now its computer equivalent, is termed a 'register'.[11] The register for each particular piece of land is divided into three sections, viz: A. Property Register; B. Proprietorship Register; and C. Charges Register. (It is therefore necessary to distinguish between three separate ways in which the noun 'register' is used. It may mean (i) the register required to be kept by s 1 of the Act of 1925 (ie comprising all registered land); (ii) the register relating to one particular piece of land; or (iii) a section of that register. (The meaning intended when used in the Act or the Rules made under the Act has to be decided from the context.[12])

The three registers

A. PROPERTY REGISTER

This gives the county or other administrative area and the parish or place where the land is situated and provides a brief description (eg '12 West Hill Avenue' or; land to the north of Tilehouse Lane') augmented by reference to a

---

9 Section 1, substituting a new s 123 in the Land Registration Act 1925.
10 Or if necessary, a number of such cards held together with binding tape.
11 The Administration of Justice Act 1982, s 66 provides that the register need not be kept in documentary form (thus permitting computerisation). Computerisation of the system is expected to be complete in every District Registry by the end of 1993.
12 *A J Dunning & Sons (Shopfitters) Ltd v Sykes & Son (Poole) Ltd* [1987] Ch 287, [1987] 1 All ER 700, CA; [1987] Conv 214 (A. Sydenham).

plan on which the land is shown, usually edged in red. It is prepared on an extract from the published Ordnance Survey map.

The Property Register also contains details of any rights over other land of which the registered land has the benefit (eg a right of way) and particulars of any matters which might be expected to be included with the land but are not. (For example if the registered land is a flat it is necessary to say that the parts of the building above and below it, although within the red edging on the plan, are not included.)

B.   PROPRIETORSHIP REGISTER

This gives the name and address of the land owner and contains details of any limitation on his powers of dealing with the land. An example of such a limitation is given later.

C.   CHARGES REGISTER

Under the system described so far, if P was buying land from V, P could satisfy himself that V had a good title to the land by searching at the Land Registry, but it would still be necessary for him to find if there were incumbrances attaching to the land by searching in the Land Charges Registry. In order to avoid the need for a separate search, the Land Registration Act 1925[13] provides for registration of land charges to be made, where the title to the land affected is registered, by an entry in the register of the land concerned. Where the incumbrance takes the form of what, under the unregistered system, would be protected by registration of a land charge (eg the burden of a restrictive covenant), it is in the Charges Register that the entry is made.[14] Local land charges[15] relating to registered land continue to be registrable in the appropriate Local Land Charges Registry and a separate search must therefore be made for these land charges.

Certain other matters[16] are recorded in the Charges Register and these will be mentioned later.

---

13   Section 59(2).
14   Where the incumbrance is protected by a caution, inhibition or restriction (see pp 523–525), the entry is made in the Proprietorship Register.
15   See Chapter 25.
16   Particulars of the following matters are entered in the Charges Register:
    1.   Registered charges, with the name and address of the chargee. (See p 544.)
    2.   Leases for over 21 years. (See p 544.)
    3.   Restrictive covenants, estate contracts and all other matters, which in the unregistered system would need to be protected by the registration, under the Land Charges Act 1972, of a land charge. (See p 544.)
    4.   Easements and other similar interests (eg profits) to which the land is subject, and which are apparent from the title deeds at the date of first registration. (See pp 530 and 543.)
    5.   Easements and other similar interests (eg profits) granted by the registered proprietor. (See p 512.)
    6.   Minor interests protected by the entry of a notice other than those at 3 above.

The land certificate

If P becomes the registered proprietor of land, he is given a Land Certificate.[17] This contains the same details as those recorded in the register and is divided into the same three sections. It also contains a copy of the plan indicating the location of the land. If P sells the land to Q, P completes a form of transfer[18] and sends this together with the Land Certificate to the appropriate District Land Registry. There Q's name is entered in the Proprietorship Register (below that of P, which is deleted). Q thereupon becomes the registered proprietor of the land. An identical entry is made on the land Certificate which is then sent to Q. No conveyance of the land from P to Q is required. The fee simple becomes vested in Q by his registration as proprietor.[19] (P can dispose of the fee simple in no other manner.[20])

The Land Certificate thus resembles Q's deeds of title,[1] but it is the register at the Land Registry, not the Land Certificate, which is conclusive as to entries on the register. Thus if Q wishes to sell the land to R, R will have to enquire from the Land Registry whether any entry has been made on the register which is not shown on Q's Land Certificate.

Registration of leasehold titles

Suppose that L grants T a lease for 999 years. If T assigns the lease to U, and U assigns it to V, each successive assignee will need to verify the assignor's title. Such verification can be as time-consuming, and hence as costly, as verifying a title on the conveyance of a fee simple.

For this reason, the Land Registration Act 1925 provides for the tenant of certain legal leases to be registered as proprietor of the lease. The tenant receives a Land Certificate as evidence of his title to the lease. The Property Register states that the proprietor holds a leasehold estate. (In the case of the title to a freehold, the Property Register states that a freehold estate is held.) Brief details of the lease, including its date, duration and rent payable are also included in the Property Register. If the lease is later assigned the name of the assignee is entered in the Proprietorship Register at the Land Registry (and on the land Certificate) as the new proprietor.

The Charges Register sets out any incumbrances that affect the leasehold estate and[2] also incumbrances which have been entered in the Charges Register of the freehold (since these will also bind the land leased).

It should be noted that throughout the remainder of this chapter, where we refer to a lease (or a tenant), this includes, where such exists, a sub-lease

---

17 Section 63(1).
18 This must be executed as a deed.
19 Section 69(1).
20 Section 69(4).
1 See the reproduction of a Land Certificate in M & B.
2 Provided that the lease is registered with 'absolute title'. The meaning of this term is explained later.

(or a sub-tenant). Thus this section, headed 'Registration of leasehold titles' refers also to the registration of titles to sub-leases.

If L holds the legal fee simple in Blackacre and he is registered as proprietor of the land, and he grants a registrable lease to T, and T grants a registrable sub-lease to ST, it will be seen that there will be three separate Land Certificates relating to the same piece of land; and there will correspondingly be three separate title registers at the Land Registry.

Where the title to a freehold is registered, the former title deeds cease to be of any relevance.[3] (They are returned to the person registered as proprietor, stamped in a way to prevent their being passed off as title deeds of continuing validity.) But where the title to a lease is registered, the lease continues to be a document of title as it may (and generally will) contain terms of the lease which are not set out in the property Register.

The Act provided for the registration of only those leases which were, inter alia, legal,[4] and for a term over 21 years[5] The provisions of the Act with regard to the registration of the title to leases were complex, six factors needing to be taken into account in determining into which category, as regards registration, a lease fell. Further complexity was added by the provisions of two subsequent statutes that in one case restricted and in the other case extended the types of lease that were registrable, the Land Registration Act 1966[6] and the Housing Act 1980[7] respectively. In 1983 the Law Commission made recommendations[8] for simplifying and rationalising the position, and these were implemented by the Land Registration Act 1986.[9]

The position was further simplified when all of England and Wales became an area in which registration became (on the occurrence of a 'triggering' transaction) compulsory. Following the Land Registration Act 1997,[10] the position is that all legal leases granted for a term of over 21 years are registrable; others (ie leases for a term of 21 years or less and equitable leases) are not.

When the title to a lease is registered, if the title to the reversion happens also to be registered, a note of the principal terms of the lease is entered in the Charges Register of the register of the title to the reversion.[11]

Registration of the title to rentcharges

Under the Act[12] not only is the title to a legal fee simple and to certain leases registrable, but also the title to a legal rentcharge. Thus if (before the

---

3 Unless they contain personal covenants or similar matters not entered on the title register; or a question of rectification arises (see p 535).
4 Section 2(1).
5 Section 19(2), provso (a).
6 Section 1(2).
7 Section 20(1). Any lease of a flat for 125 years or more granted by a local authority or other body under Pt 1 of the Housing Act 1980.
8 *Property Law: Land Registration* (Law Com No 125, 1983).
9 Sections 2–4.
10 Section1, adding s 123A to the Land Registration Act 1925.
11 See n 16, (2), page 508
12 Sections 2, 3(viii).

Rentcharges Act 1977[13]) A, the holder of a fee simple in an area of compulsory registration, granted a rentcharge to B, B's title to the rentcharge had to be registered. A separate title register was opened at the Land Registry and B received a Rentcharge Certificate, which contained a copy of the information on the title register of the rentcharge.

Extent of registration

Since, prior to the Land Registration Act 1997, land was only registrable compulsorily when it changed hands on *sale*, or a lease satisfying certain conditions was granted, the compilation of the register has been essentially sporadic. Thus what we have had, and still have, is a system of 'creeping' registration. (Out of an estimated 22 million properties in England and Wales, in 1995 the titles to approximately 14 million had been registered.)

Effect of registration

Application to register must be made within two months of the triggering transaction.[14] Pending registration, ie during the two months permitted, the transaction takes effect in the normal way, eg in the case of the sale of the fee simple, the legal title vests in the purchaser.

If registration has not been applied for by the end of the two months, the disposition becomes void. Thereupon, in the case of a transfer of the fee simple or the assignment of the lease, the legal title reverts to the transferor who holds it on a bare trust for the transferee. In the case of the grant of a lease or the creation of a mortgage, the disposition takes effect as a contract to grant the lease or to create the mortgage.

Privacy

Under the 1925 Act, information on the Register could not be disclosed to the public.[15] The registered proprietor was entitled to inspect the Register relating to his land and he could authorise the Registry to allow any person (eg a potential purchaser) to inspect the Register of his title. In 1985 the Law Commission recommended that the Register should be open to inspection by the public.[16] Effect was given to this recommendation by the Land Registration Act 1988. (A fee is payable.)

---

13   See Chapter 3.
14   Land Registration Act 1925, s 123, as substituted by the Land Registration Act 1997, s 1.
15   LRA 1925, s 112.

Dispositions of registered land

A registered proprietor of freehold land may carry out the same transactions with regard to the land as a fee simple owner under the unregistered system; thus he may lease the land, grant easements and profits, make covenants for the benefit of other land, receive the benefit of covenants made by the holders of other land, mortgage the land, give the land to a donee, transfer it to trustees on trust, enter into a contract to sell (or otherwise deal with) the land, and so on. Any transaction that can be effected by an unregistered fee simple owner can be effected by a registered proprietor. (Similarly, any transaction that can be carried out by a leaseholder under the unregistered system can be carried out by the registered proprietor of a lease.[16])

Certain transactions, however, can be carried out only if the registered proprietor executes them in accordance with the provisions of the Act. These transactions (termed by the Act[17] 'dispositions') are:

1.   the transfer of the legal fee simple (or lease) in the land (by sale or gift);
2.   the grant of any legal lease for a term of over 21 years;
3.   the grant (before the Rentcharges Act 1977) of a legal rentcharge;
4.   the grant of a legal easement or other right (eg a profit);
5.   the grant of a legal mortgage.

In the case of (1) above, the disposition is effected by the proprietor completing the statutory form of transfer and sending it with the Land Certificate to the Land Registry. No special form is required to be completed in respect of the other transactions, but the document concerned must in each case be sent to the Land Registry.

In the case of each transaction, the grantee receives a legal interest only when the disposition is registered.[18]

With regard to what 'registration' consists of, in the case of (1) above, registration consists of the entering of the name of the transferee as the proprietor in the Proprietorship Register.

In the case of (2) and (3) above, registration consists of:

(a)   the substantive registration of the title to the lease or (before the Rentcharges Act 1977) the rentcharge (by the opening of a new title register); and
(b)   the entering of a Notice[19] in the Charges Register of the register of the freehold, giving the principal particulars of the lease or (before the Rentcharges Act 1977) the rentcharge.

---

16   Sections 21, 22.
17   Section 18.
18   LRA 1925, ss 19(1), 22(1); *Brown and Root Technology Ltd v Sun Alliance and London Assurance Co Ltd* (1997) 141 Sol Jo LB 38, CA. For the position pending registration see *Mascall v Mascall* (1984) 50 P & CR 119; *Re Rose* [1952] Ch 499, [1952] 1 All ER 1217.
19   The nature of a Notice is explained later.

In the case of (4) and (5) above, registration consists of entering particulars of the easement or mortgage in the Charges Register of the land affected. (The benefit of the easement may also be entered in the Property Register of the title register of the dominant land.)

From what has been said above it will be noted that there is a difference between the first *title* being registered and a subsequent *disposition* being registered.

Registered interests

When one of the interests set out above (eg the fee simple of the new owner; a lease; an easement; a mortgage) has been registered in whatever is the appropriate way, as just explained, then the interest of the grantee becomes a 'registered interest'. It should be noted that a registered interest may be (a) one in respect of which the *title is registered* (eg in the case of a freehold); or (b) one in respect of which registration consists of the *making of an entry* on the title register of the land affected (eg in the case of easements); or (c) one in respect of which registration consists of both the substantive registration of the title *and* the making of an entry in the register of the land affected (eg in the case of registrable leases).

It will be noted that only a legal interest may be a registered interest.

Interests in registered land

In dealing with land law under the unregistered system we saw that estates and interests could be classified into the following categories.

1. Legal estates and interests that are not registrable under the Land Charges Act 1972 (eg a legal lease, a legal easement).
2. Legal interests that are registrable under the Land Charges Act 1972 (eg a legal mortgage without deposit of title deeds).
3. Equitable interests that are registrable under the Land Charges Act 1972 (eg an estate contract, an equitable lease, an equitable easement).
4. Equitable interests that are not registrable under the Land Charges Act 1972 but which are overreachable (eg the interests of beneficiaries under a trust of land).
5. Equitable interests that are not registrable under the Land Charges Act 1972 and which are not overreachable (eg a restrictive covenant entered into before 1926).

Under the registered system any interest in land falls under one of three heads.

1. Registered interests

The nature of registered interests has been considered above.

A registered interest binds any subsequent holder of the land.

2. Overriding interests

Overriding interests are defined in s 70 of the Land Registration Act 1925. They include, inter alia, the following:

'(a) Rights of common ... public rights,[20] profits à prendre ... rights of way ... rights of water, and other easements not being equitable easements required[1] to be protected by notice on the register';

'(f) ... rights acquired or in course of being acquired under the Limitation Acts';

'(g) The rights of every person in actual occupation of the land or in receipt of the rents and profits thereof, save where enquiry is made of such person and the rights are not disclosed';

'(i) Local land charges';

'(k)[2]Leases granted for a term not exceeding 21 years'[3].

The nature of overriding interests will become apparent during the course of this chapter. For the moment, it should be noted that their essential characteristic is that they bind any holder of the land irrespective of whether he has notice of them or not.

3. Minor interests

Any interest in land that is not a registered interest or an overriding interest is a minor interest.[4] Minor interests do not, like registered interests and overriding interests, automatically bind a purchaser: they require protection by the making of an entry on the title register of the land affected. An entry protecting a minor interest may take one of four forms. The entry may be in the form of a notice, a caution, a restriction or an inhibition. The nature of each of these is considered later.

Minor interests[5] fall into two categories.

(a) Interests that are not capable of being overreached. The principal matters in this group comprise all matters that are registrable under the Land Charges Act 1972 (eg restrictive covenants, equitable easements, estate contracts, access orders made under the Access to Neighbouring Land

---

20   Rights exercisable by any person by virtue of being a member of the public; *Overseas Investment Services Ltd v Simcobuild Construction Ltd* [1996] 02 EG 107, CA, (rights arising under agreements made under Highways Act 1980, s 38, for the carrying out of highway works held not to be 'public rights' and so not overriding interests).

1   In *Celsteel v Alton House Holdings Ltd* [1985] 2 All ER 562, [1985] 1 WLR 204; (M & B), Scott J expressed the view (at 220) that 'required to be protected' meant 'needed to be protected'. There remains uncertainty, however, as to what kinds of easement are excluded by the proviso.

2   As substituted by LRA 1986, s 4(1).

3   Including statutory tenancies that come into existence on the termination of a protected contractual tenancy (under s 1 of the Rent Act 1977); *Pourdanay v Barclays Bank plc* (1996) Times, 12 November.

4   Section 3(xv).

5   Ibid; *Clayhope Properties v Evans* [1986] 2 All ER 795, [1986] 1 WLR 1223 (receiving order registrable under LCA 1925, s 6(1)(b) and so capable of protection as a minor interest under the Land Registration Act 1925 (under s 54)).

Act 1992 and a spouse's right of occupation of the matrimonial home conferred by the Matrimonial Homes Act 1983, now conferred as 'matrimonial home rights' under the Family Law Act 1996 (the last being registrable, it will be recalled, as a Class F land charge under the unregistered (ie unregistered title) system). Also falling within the group are other matters that are equitable proprietary interests in land under the general law. (There is uncertainty as to how rights arising from equitable doctrines such as estoppel[6] are to be treated under the registered system.[7])

(b) Interests that are capable of being overreached,[8] eg the interests of beneficiaries under (i) a strict settlement in existence on 1 January 1997; (ii) prior to the Trusts of Land and Appointment of Trustees Act 1996, a trust for sale; and (iii) after the 1996 Act, a trust of land as defined by the Act.

An interest under (a) above can be protected by entering a Notice in the Charges register of the title register of the land concerned. The effect of entering a Notice is that if the interest to which it relates is itself valid and effective it becomes binding on every subsequent holder of the land. If not so protected, the interests will not bind a subsequent purchaser for value of the land. Thus if R, the registered proprietor of Greenacre, covenants for the benefit of Redacre, held by E, that pigs will not be kept on Greenacre, for the covenant to bind a purchaser from R, E must enter a Notice in the Charges Register of the title register of Greenacre. (The entering of the Notice thus corresponds to registration of the covenant under the Land Charges Act 1972 under the unregistered system.)

Regarding (b) above, suppose that in 1995 (ie before the 1996 Act) A, the registered proprietor of Blackacre, created a settlement under the Settled Land Act 1925 for the benefit of B for life with remainder to C. D and E were appointed the trustees of the settlement. A transferred the land to B (the Tenant for life) who was registered as the proprietor. B proposes to sell the land to P. In order to ensure that P does not pay the purchase money to B, P must be made aware that he will only take free of the equitable interests of B and C if he pays his money to the trustees, D and E. To achieve this, an entry, which in this case takes the form of a Restriction, was made on the proprietorship register of Blackacre.[9] This prohibits any disposition of the land by B (i) not authorised by the Settled Land Act 1925, and (ii) unless any capital money arising has been paid to the trustees, being at least two in number, or a trust corporation. If A creates a trust of land under the 1996 Act, the Restriction may further prohibit the registration of any dealing unless specified consents have been obtained. The Restriction thus provides the warning that, in unregistered conveyancing, is provided by the contents of the vesting deed (or vesting assent) or the deed creating a trust of land.

---

6 See Chapter 20.
7 See [1983] Conv 99 (T. Bailey).
8 *Elias v Mitchell* [1972] Ch 652, [1972] 2 All ER 153, (interest in the proceeds of sale under a trust for sale held to be a minor interest in land by virtue of LRA 1925, s 3(xv)). See also *Bird v Syme Thomson* [1978] 3 All ER 1027, [1979] 1 WLR 440.
9 A Notice may not be entered in respect of a beneficiary under a strict settlement or a trust of land under the Trusts of Land and Appointment of Trustees Act 1996, except pending the appointment of trustees, s 49(2).

The classification of interests into overriding interests and minor interests is not mutually exclusive. An interest can at one and the same time be a minor interest and an overriding interest, eg the interest of a beneficiary under a trust of land who is in actual occupation of the land (under s 70(1)(g)).[10]

OVERRIDING INTERESTS[11]

We have seen that overriding interests bind a holder of the land without any protection (eg in the form of a Notice) being required, and irrespective of whether or not the holder of the land has notice of them. The following points now call for attention.

1. In the above respect overriding interests resemble non-registrable legal interests under the unregistered system (eg a legal lease). They resemble such interests also in that they are of the kind about which a purchaser is expected to learn by inspecting the land and by making inquiries. As would therefore be expected, there is a substantial overlap between the interests which come into these two categories. For example, some easements come into both categories. But the two categories are not identical, eg some interests which are non-registrable legal interests under the unregistered system are not overriding interests, eg a legal lease exceeding 21 years, the tenant not being in occupation.

2. Some matters which are overriding interests in the context of the registered system, and so under that system do not require any form of protection, are registrable under other legislation, for example, local land charges (s 70(1)(i)) are registrable under the Local Land Charges Act 1975 in the local land charges register.[12]

3. Notwithstanding that an overriding interest binds a holder of the land without the interest being protected by the making of an entry on the register, a note of the existence of certain overriding interests is nonetheless in certain circumstances entered by the Registrar, in the form of a note (ie a record, not a Notice) in the Charges Register of the land affected. Thus if at the time of first registration it is apparent from the title deeds that an easement or profit adversely affects the land, the Registrar must[13] note this fact on the register. Further, the Registrar has discretion to make a note on the register of the existence of any overriding interests, the existence of which is proved (or admitted) to him (ie easements and other overriding interests coming into

10   *Williams and Glyn's Bank Ltd v Boland* [1981] AC 487, [1980] 2 All ER 408; see p 546, infra.

11   For proposals for reform, see Law Commission, *Property Law, Third Report on Land Registration*, Part A (Law Com No 158, 1987) recommending, inter alia, that the number of overriding interests should be reduced to five: legal easements and profits à prendre not expressly created after first registration; rights acquired by adverse possession; leases for 21 years or less; rights of persons in actual occupation; customary rights (eg the right of fishermen inhabitants of a parish to dry their nets on the land of a private owner). See [1987] Conv 334 (R. Smith); [1987] Conv 328 (A. M. Pritchard).

12   See p 503.

13   Section 70(2); *Re Dances Way, West Town, Hayling Island* [1962] Ch 490 at 508.

existence prior to first registration the existence of which is not apparent from the title deeds, and overriding interests coming into existence subsequently to first registration).

4. Section 70 begins 'All registered land shall ... be deemed to be subject to such of the following overriding interests as may be for the time being subsisting in reference thereto ...' In Chapter 8 we saw that the interests of a beneficiary were, prior to the Trusts of Land and Appointment of Trustees Act 1996, by the doctrine of conversion, personalty, not realty. This fact did not prevent the interest of a beneficiary under a trust for sale from being capable of being an overriding interest, the interest of such a beneficiary, it was held, being one 'subsisting in reference' to land.[14]

5. The relevant date for determining the existence of an overriding interest is the date of registration, not the date of the transfer (or creation) of the legal estate.[15] (But in order to establish the existence of an overriding interest under s 70(1)(g), considered below, the claimant must show that he was in actual occupation at the date of the transfer[15].)

6. RIGHTS OF PERSONS 'IN ACTUAL POSSESSION'

(a) Section 70(1)(g) makes into an overriding interest 'the rights of every person in actual occupation of the land or in receipt of the rent and profits thereof, save where enquiry is made of such person and the rights are not disclosed'. Under the unregistered system, the fact that a person is in actual occupation may be relevant in that the fact of occupation may in certain circumstances constitute notice to a purchaser of the occupier's equitable interest in the property. Under the registered system, s 70(1)(g) can operate to convert an interest that is not otherwise binding on a purchaser without some step being taken (eg entry of a Notice) into one that, as an overriding interest, is automatically binding on a purchaser.[16]

(b) For an overriding interest to bind a purchaser under s 70(1)(g), two conditions must be satisfied:

(i) The plaintiff must be in actual occupation. The plaintiff is in actual occupation if he is in physical possession[17] of the land. But his occupation must have some degree of permanence and continuity. Acts of a preparatory character such as those done prior to moving into a house, eg laying carpets and unloading furniture, are not sufficient.[18] A person is in actual occupation also if he is in receipt of rents and profits from the land (but not if he merely

---

14 *Williams and Glyn's Bank Ltd v Boland* [1981] AC 487, [1980] 2 All ER 408 (disapproving *Cedar Holdings Ltd v Green* [1981] Ch 129, [1979] 3 All ER 117).
15 *Abbey National Building Society v Cann* [1991] 1 AC 56, [1990] 1 All ER 1085, HL; (M & B).
16 *London and Cheshire Insurance Co Ltd v Laplagrene Property Co Ltd* [1971] Ch 499, [1971] 1 All ER 766. (The lien was held not to be registrable under s 95 of the Companies Act 1948 (now replaced by Companies Act 1985, ss 295–297).)
17 *Strand Securities Ltd v Caswell* [1965] Ch 958, [1965] 1 All ER 820, CA; (M & B); see also *Chhokar v Chhokar* [1984] FLR 313, [1984] Fam Law 269; (M & B).
18 *Abbey National Building Society v Cann*, supra.
19 *Strand Securities Ltd v Caswell*, supra.

allows another to occupy the premises, rent free[19]). Whether a plaintiff is held to be in 'actual occupation' will depend on the circumstances. For example, in *Epps v Esso Petroleum Co Ltd*[20] it was held that the parking of a car on an unidentified part of disputed land for an undefined time did not constitute 'actual occupation' under the section.

(ii)   The interest must be proprietary in nature: it must be an interest that is 'capable of enduring through different ownerships of land according to the normal conceptions of title of real property'.[1] Thus rights of a merely personal nature cannot be overriding interests. (As a result of the decision in *Pritchard v Briggs*[2] that a right of pre-emption is not an interest in land, it seems that rights of pre-emption cannot be overriding interests.)

(c) Section 70(1)(g) concludes '... save where enquiry is made of such person and the rights are not disclosed'. Thus if land is held by H on trust for H and W, and W is in actual occupation and H sells the land to P, W's equitable interest is binding as an overriding interest on P only if: (1) P makes no enquiries from W as to whether she has any interest in the land; or (2) he makes such enquiries and W fails to disclose the existence of her interest. Thus to guard against being bound by an interest of which he would otherwise have no knowledge, P will wish to ascertain whether any person besides the vendor is in occupation (if necessary by inspecting the property[3]); and, if the existence of such a person is revealed, to enquire from this person whether he or she has any interest in the property. Only if the other occupant disclaims any interest in the property can P safely proceed with the purchase. (Further, P may be wise to ensure that the other occupier has independent legal advice, so as to avoid a claim made subsequently by the other occupier that his denial of an interest was secured by undue influence.[4]) How institutional lenders deal with this matter in practice is treated later in this chapter.[5]

(d) An understanding of interests under s 70(1)(g) may be assisted by some illustrations. In *Bridges v Mees*[6] A contracted orally to sell B certain land, and allowed B into possession. B did not register his interest as an estate contract. Later the land passed into the hands of A's liquidator who sold it to C, who was registered as the first proprietor. It was held that B's equitable fee simple (arising from the contract) was, by virtue of B's occupation of the land, binding on C as an overriding interest.

In *Grace Rymer Investments Ltd v Waite*,[7] L, in October 1956, leased property to T for three years. At the time of the lease L did not own the property. On 6

---

20   [1973] 2 All ER 465, [1973] 1 WLR 1071; (M & B).
1   Per Russell LJ, *National Provincial Bank Ltd v Hastings Car Mart Ltd* [1964] Ch 665 at 696, [1964] 1 All ER 688 at 701, approved [1965] AC 1175, [1965] 2 All ER 472, HL. (E), followed in *Webb v Pollmount Ltd* [1966] Ch 584 at 596.
2   [1989] Ch 338, [1980] 1 All ER 294.
3   The nature of the inspection required in a case concerning unregistered land was considered in *Kingsnorth Trust v Tizard* [1986] 2 All ER 54, [1986] 1 WLR 783; [1986] Conv 283 (M. P. Thompson); see p 198, supra.
4   As was found to be the case in *Kingsnorth Trust Ltd v Bell* [1986] 1 All ER 423, [1986] 1 WLR 119.
5   Page 552, infra.
6   [1957] Ch 475, [1957] 2 All ER 577.
7   [1958] Ch 831, [1958] 2 All ER 777; (M & B).

January 1956 L was registered as proprietor of the property, and on the same day a charge on the property in favour of P was registered. L failed to keep up the mortgage repayments. P sought possession from T (in order to be able to sell). T resisted. It was held that at the time of the granting of the lease, T acquired a tenancy by estoppel.[8] When L was registered as a proprietor the estoppel was fed, and L acquired a legal lease. Since T was in actual occupation of the property at the time when P's charge was registered, T's lease was binding on P as an overriding interest under s 70(1)(g).[9]

In *Webb v Pollmount Ltd*,[10] in 1961 L leased land to T for seven years. The lease contained a clause giving T an option to purchase the reversion at a specified price. The option was not registered as a land charge. In 1962 the freehold was conveyed to P, subject to the lease. P was registered as proprietor. In 1963 T sought to exercise the option against P. P declined to sell. T sought an order for specific performance. It was held that as T was in actual occupation of the land at the time of the transfer to P, his option was binding on P as an overriding interest. (It will be recognised that if T had not been in actual occupation at the time when P was registered as proprietor, the option would have been binding on P only if it had been protected by a Notice in the Charges Register of the land.)

In *London and Cheshire Insurance Co Ltd v Laplagrene Property Co Ltd*[11] the plaintiff was in occupation of land as a tenant under a lease. The interest which was binding as an overriding interest on a subsequent purchaser was an unpaid vendor's lien. In *Hodgson v Marks*,[12] P was in occupation of the land as a lodger. The interest which was binding as an overriding interest was her equitable interest under the constructive trust which the court held to exist.

In *Blacklocks v J.B. Developments (Godalming) Ltd*,[13] V conveyed to P two plots of land, plot A and plot B. It had been the intention of both V and P that only plot B should be the subject of the sale, plot A being conveyed to P in error. V remained in occupation of plot A. P sold both plots to Q. V applied to have the register rectified so as to have Q's name as proprietor of plot A removed and his own name substituted. It was held that V had a right to rectification in the sense of having an equitable right to have a document rectified on the ground that it failed to represent the intention of the parties.[14] By virtue of his occupation of Plot A this was an overriding interest and so binding on Q. Thus V was entitled to an order requiring the Registrar to rectify the register by restoring his, V's, name as proprietor of plot A.

In *Celsteel v Alton House Holdings Ltd*[15] the plaintiff was in occupation of a flat as a tenant under a lease. The interest which was binding as an overriding

---

8   See Chapter 17.
9   It was binding on P also as an overriding interest under s 70(1)(k).
10 [1966] Ch 584, [1966] 1 All ER 481; (M & B); *Kling v Keston Properties Ltd* (1983) 49 P & CR 212; [1984] LS Gaz R 1683; (M & B).
11 [1971] Ch 499, [1971] 1 All ER 766.
12 [1971] Ch 892, [1971] 2 All ER 684.
13 [1982] Ch 183, [1981] 3 All ER 392.
14 [1983] Conv 169, [1983] Conv 257 (D. Ritchie); cf [1983] Conv 361 (D.G. Barnsley) (equitable right of rectification probably not a proprietary right, so burden not capable of passing, so right not capable of being an overriding interest; same result could have been achieved by rectification of the register under LRA 1925, s 82(1)(a), (b) or (c)).
15 [1985] 2 All ER 562, [1985] 1 WLR 204; (M & B).

interest was an equitable easement giving access from the street to a basement garage demised with the flat.

These illustrations of the operation of s 70(1)(g) demonstrate that the interests which may be protected include an equitable fee simple, a legal lease, an option, an unpaid vendor's lien, an interest under a constructive trust, a right to rectification of a conveyance, and an equitable easement; and that the capacities in which a person may be in actual occupation include that of a purchaser allowed into possession, a tenant under a lease, a beneficiary under a constructive trust, and a vendor who has remained in possession of disputed land. A further, and important, illustration of an overriding interest (the equitable interest of a wife in the matrimonial home) is provided by *Williams and Glyn's Bank Ltd v Boland*.[16] This case is treated at the end of this chapter.

(e) It should be noted that s 70(1)(g) does not *create* any new right or interest. It does not, in particular, create any right of occupation. Its effect is that *if* an interest exists, and *if* the holder of the interest is in occupation, then the interest is an overriding interest (and so binding on a purchaser).

(f) The right of a spouse to occupy the matrimonial home conferred by the Family Law Act 1996 cannot be an overriding interest. This is because (i) the Act so decrees,[17] and (ii), in any case, the right conferred by the Act is not a proprietary *interest*. (But if the spouse has a proprietary interest in the property, then this can be an overriding interest.)

(g) A minor interest can be binding on a purchaser either because it is protected by entry of a Notice on the register of the land affected, or because the person entitled to the benefit of the interest is in 'actual occupation' of the land with the result that the interest is an overriding interest under s 70(1)(g) (or for both reasons).

(h) Further, if L grants a lease to T, and the lease is registrable, and if L allows T to go into occupation before the lease is registered, and L sells the reversion to P, then notwithstanding the non-registration of the lease, P is bound by the lease, since T's interest is an overriding interest under s 70(1)(g).[18] (Once the lease is registered, T's interest ceases to be an overriding interest and becomes a registered interest.) All registrable interests may in this way rank as overriding interests pending registration if the holder of the interest is in actual occupation of the land.

Suppose that a husband and wife, H and W, buy a house from V. They agree that the property should be transferred into the name of H alone. The purchase price is provided by money paid by H and by W with the balance being obtained by a loan from E, secured by mortgage of the house. Completion is fixed for 1 May. On 1 April, with V's permission, H and W, move into the house. On the morning of 1 May, H and W, E, and V meet for the completion

16   [1981] AC 487, [1980] 2 All ER 408. Cf *Winkworth v Edward Baron Development Co Ltd* [1987] 1 All ER 114, [1986] 1 WLR 1512, HL (no equitable interest in home held to have been acquired by wife, hence no interest in wife capable of existing as overriding interest).
17   Section 31(10)(b), replacing Matrimonial Homes Act 1983, s 2(8)(b).
18   *Strand Securities Ltd v Caswell* [1965] Ch 958, [1965] 1 All ER 820; (M & B); *Skipton Building Society v Clayton* (1993) 66 P & CR 223.

of the transaction. V signs the form of transfer. H then signs the mortgage of the property to E. The transfer is registered at the Land Registry on 1 June. H later ceases to be able to continue making the mortgage repayments. In order to exercise his power of sale, E seeks an order for possession. W opposes the granting of the order. W's argument is this. (i) By contributing to the purchase price, she acquired an equitable interest in the property. (ii) The date when it is necessary to be in occupation to have an overriding interest is the date when the legal interest is transferred. (iii) She was in actual occupation at this date (ie when V signed the transfer). (iv) Thus her equitable interest (by virtue of which she was entitled to occupy the property) was protected as an overriding interest under s 70(1)(g) against all subsequent purchasers. (v) Thus when, a moment after the transfer by V, H signed the mortgage to E, E took the mortgage subject to her equitable interest. Does W's argument succeed? The success of her argument hinges on there being an interval, however fleeting, a mere *scintilla temporis*, between the transfer to H and the mortgage to E. In *Church of England Building Society v Piskor*[19] in 1954, a case concerning land to which the title was not registered, it was held that such an interval between the two transactions did exist, with the result that, in the example above, W's argument would have succeeded.

The issue arose again in 1991, in *Abbey National Building Society v Cann*,[20] a case concerning land the title to which was registered, and in which the facts were in essence those set out above. The House of Lords upheld W's contention at (ii) above, that the time when a person had to be in actual occupation in order to claim that an interest was an overriding interest under s 70(1)(g) was the time of the transfer of the legal estate.[1]

But the House of Lords nonetheless rejected W's claim. Her argument had depended on the transfer to H and the mortgage to E being distinct transactions separated by a *scintilla temporis*, at the beginning of which, with the transfer to H, W's interest crystallised, and ending with the signing of the mortgage to E, at which point E took the mortgage subject to W's overriding interest (her equitable interest in the property). The Lords held that (at least where, as had occurred, W had previously agreed to the mortgage) the transaction of transferring the legal estate to H and the mortgage to E were not separate. They were one and indivisible, no *scintilla temporis* separating them: the two transactions were 'not only precisely simultaneous but indissolubly linked together'.[2] Thus the mortgage to E was not subject to the overriding interest claimed by W, and E was entitled to an order for possession. (Even if the *scintilla temporis* argument had not been rejected, W's claim would, the Lords held, have failed, since, on the facts, W had not been in actual occupation within the meaning of section 70(1)(g) at the time of the transfer

19   [1954] Ch 553, [1954] 2 All ER 85, CA.
20   [1991] 1 AC 56, [1990] 1 All ER 1085, HL; (M & B); [1991] Conv 116 (S. Baughen); [1990] Conv 155 (P.T. Evans); (1990) 106 LQR 545 (R.J. Smith); [1990] CLJ 397 (A.J. Oakley), [1994] Conv 242 (J de L).
 1   Confirming on this point, *Lloyd's Bank plc v Rosset* [1991] 1 AC 107, [1990] 1 All ER 1111, HL; (M & B); [1991] CLJ 38 (M. Dixon); [1991] Conv 314 (M.P. Thompson).
 2   Per Lord Oliver, at p 1853; [1990] Conv 155, 164 (P.T. Evans).

to H, W having done no more than have contractors move in furniture and begin laying carpets 35 minutes before the transfer was signed, actions that were no more than preparatory to taking up actual occupation.)

(i) Significant as is the effect of s 70(1)(g), three limits should be noted. First, an interest does not become bigger merely because the holder of the interest is in occupation of land. In *Paddington Building Society v Mendelsohn*[3] a mother (M) and son (S) agreed to buy the leasehold interest in a flat for £32,500. M provided £15,500 and the balance was raised by mortgage. In view of the mother's age it seemed unlikely that she would obtain a mortgage and M and S therefore agreed that the property should be conveyed into S's name alone. The interest was conveyed to S and the mortgage executed, the Society having no notice, actual or constructive, of M's interest. M moved into the flat. Soon afterwards the mortgage was registered at the Land Registry. S fell into arrears with the mortgage repayments and the Society sought an order for possession. M claimed that her equitable interest was binding on the Society as an overriding interest under s 70(1)(g). The Court of Appeal held that the nature of M's interest depended on the intention to be imputed to both M and S at the time when the mortgage was executed. Since M knew that without the mortgage the flat could not be obtained, it must have been the intention of both S and M that the Society's mortgage should take priority over M's equitable interest. Thus the nature of her equitable interest was not one that would take priority over the Society's mortgage. The fact that she was in actual occupation did not affect the matter.

(j) Secondly, the principle of overreaching takes precedent over the principle of overriding interests. If T_1 and T_2 hold land on trust for a beneficiary, B, B is in occupation of the land, and the trustees sell the land to P who pays the purchase money to the trustees and obtains a receipt signed by both of them, then B's equitable interest is overreached and attaches to the proceeds of sale. Notwithstanding that he is in actual occupation, B has no overriding interest binding on P. This is because once the sale to P has occurred B ceases to have any interest under the trust and so holds nothing capable of being an overriding interest. This principle was upheld in *City of London Building Society v Flegg*,[4] a case that will be considered later in this chapter.

(k) Thirdly, a minor cannot be in actual occupation for the purpose of section 70(1)(g).[5]

PROTECTION OF MINOR INTERESTS

We have seen that minor interests may be protected by the entry of a Notice, Caution, Restriction or Inhibition on the title register of the land affected.

---

3   [1987] Fam Law 121, 50 P & CR 244.
4   [1988] AC 54, HL.
5   *Hypo-Mortgage Services v Robinson* (1997) Times, 2 January, [1997] Conv 84, (no inquiry of kind contemplated by the section can be made of a minor.

Notices[6]

A Notice is the entry appropriate for the protection of a minor interest that takes the form of an interest registrable under the Land Charges Act 1972 under the unregistered system (eg the benefit of a restrictive covenant, an equitable easement or a spouse's matrimonial home rights under the Family Law Act 1996.[7] Further, where a registered proprietor grants a registrable lease, or a legal easement, or charges the land under s 25 (registered charge), then the disposition, being a registrable disposition,[8] entails the entering of a Notice in the register of the land affected. So too does the creation of a lien by deposit of the Land Certificate.[9]

Notices are entered in the Charges Register of the land affected.

The effect of the entry of a Notice is that any subsequent dealing with the land takes effect subject to the matter in respect of which the Notice has been entered.[10]

A Notice may, however, only be entered if the Land Certificate of the land affected is produced to (or is already lodged with) the Land Registry.[11] Thus, if the Certificate is not already at the Registry (eg because the land has been charged[12]), a Notice may only be entered if the registered proprietor is willing to co-operate by producing the Land Certificate. Thus if V sells land to P, subject to a covenant by P in favour of land retained by V, V faces no problem in entering a Notice since prior to the disposition he himself will hold the Land Certificate, but if V enters into a contract to sell land to P, and P wishes to enter a Notice to protect his equitable interest (ie the estate contract) and V (perhaps hoping to sell to Q) refuses to produce the Certificate, then P cannot enter a Notice. The requirement serves no useful purpose since the entry itself is made on the register, and the Certificate, on which a corresponding entry is made, is no more than a copy of the register. (Removal of the requirement has been recommended by the Law Commission.[13])

Where a person wishes to enter a Notice on the register of certain land and the proprietor declines to produce the Certificate, the only course available is for a Caution to be entered instead. The protection afforded by a Caution is, however, as we shall see, weaker.

---

6   LRA 1925, ss 48–52.
7   Section 31(10)(b).
8   See p 511.
9   Section 66. See p 545. By Rule 239(4) of the Land Registration Rules 1925 a Notice of deposit takes effect as a Caution. For Cautions, see below.
10 Cf the position in the case of non-registration of a matter registrable under the Land Charges Act 1972 under the unregistered system. See Chapter 23.
11 Section 64(1). The Land Certificate need not be produced in order to enter a Notice protecting a matrimonial home right under the Family Law Act 1996.
12 In which case the Land Certificate is held by the Registry. See p 490.
13 *Property Law: Third Report on Land Registration* (Law Com No 158, 1987).

Cautions[14]

A Caution may be entered by any person having an interest in registered land, and whose interest is not registered, or protected by a Notice or Restriction. As we saw above,[15] a Caution is the entry available when the Land Certificate cannot be produced by the person who wishes to have the entry made.

Cautions are entered in the Proprietorship Register. The effect of entering a Caution is as follows. If A enters a Caution on the register of land of which B is the registered proprietor:

1. B is notified of the entry. B is then entitled to require the Registry to give notice to A requiring him to substantiate the interest he claims to have protected by the Caution. If A defends his claim to the satisfaction of the Registrar, the Caution remains on the register of B's land. If he fails to do so, it is removed. This process is termed 'warning off': B 'warns off' A's Caution.

Alternatively, B may apply to the court for the removal of the Caution, and the court has jurisdiction to order that the Caution be vacated.[16]

2. If B applies for some dealing with the land to be registered (eg a sale to P), the Registry must notify A.[17] A then has 14 days in which to produce evidence substantiating his interest to the Registrar. If A fails to do so, the Caution is removed, and the disposition by B is registered, free from the matter in respect of which the Caution was lodged. If, within the 14 days, A substantiates his interest, the Caution remains on the register of B's land. If the disponee (eg a purchaser or chargee) chooses to proceed with the transaction, the disposition by B is registered, and the disponee takes subject to A's interest.[18]

Inhibitions[19]

An Inhibition may be entered by the Registrar on the application of any person interested, or on the order of the court. An Inhibition prohibits any dealing, either absolutely or until a specified condition is satisfied. Inhibitions are employed when no other method of protecting an interest exists. Their use is rare.[20]

---

14   LRA 1925, ss 53–56.
15   Page 423.
16   For an example of the exercise of the jurisdiction, see *Clearbrook Property Holdings Ltd v Vernier* [1973] 3 All ER 614, [1974] 1 WLR 243; and *Tiverton Estates Ltd v Wearwell Ltd* [1975] Ch 146, [1974] 1 All ER 209.
17   LRA 1925, s 55(1).
18   The entering of a Caution does not of itself, ie with out the notification to A, and the substantiation by A of the interest, secure priority for the matter in respect of which the Caution was entered; *Clark v Chief Land Registrar* [1994] Ch 370, [1994] 4 All ER 96.
19   LRA 1925, s 47.
20   For an example, see *Ahmed v Kendrick and Ahmed* [1988] 2 FLR 22, CA, inhibition entered by wife to prevent sale by husband who had forged wife's signature on contract and transfer.

If a receiving order is made against a registered proprietor then, in order to prevent him from disposing of the land, a special form of Inhibition, a Bankruptcy Inhibition, is entered on the title register of the land.

Inhibitions are entered in the Proprietorship Register.

Restriction[1]

We have already met circumstances in which a Restriction is entered, ie in connection with the machinery of a strict settlement or trust for sale.[2]

The effect of a Restriction is that no disposition may be registered unless specified conditions are satisfied. Thus in the case of a trust of land under the Trusts of Land and Appointment of Trustees Act 1996, a condition will require the purchase money to be paid to the trustees being two in number or a trust corporation (ie and not to a sole trustee). Another will provide that only a disposition authorised by the Settled Land Act 1925 may be registered.

A Restriction may be entered by a settlor, or trustees of a trust of land, or by any other person interested, eg the beneficiaries. In practice, the Registry ensures that when it is evident that a Restriction is required, one is entered in suitable terms.

It will be apparent that it is vital for the protection of beneficiaries under a trust of land under the 1996 Act that a Restriction should be entered: if none is entered, a disponee who is registered as proprietor takes free of their equitable interest, even if he has notice of them.[3]

Restrictions are entered in the Proprietorship Register.

Interests to which a registered proprietor is subject

Much of the law under the unregistered system is concerned with the question: if A holds the fee simple in Blackacre and various interests in the land are created (eg a legal lease, an equitable mortgage, an estate contract), and A then sells the land to P, subject to what interests does P hold the land? The same question arises, of course, under the registered system, but in setting out the position it is necessary to distinguish between the position of the first registered proprietor and subsequent holders of the land. It is also necessary to determine whether or not the latter are purchasers for value in good faith.

---

1 LRA 1925, s 58.
2 See p 515.
3 Section 74.

First registered proprietor

Let us suppose that A holds the fee simple in Blackacre, the title to which has not been registered. The land is subject to a legal easement (which arose by prescription) held by B, a legal easement (which was reserved for the benefit of other land at the time of a previous sale) held by C, an equitable mortgage without deposit of title deeds (which has been registered as a Class C (iii) land charge) held by D. A contracts to sell the land to E, who does not register the estate contract. A then, in breach of contract, sells the land to F. The purchase money is provided by F and his wife G. F thus holds the legal fee simple on an implied trust for himself and G. The title to the land is registered with F as the first proprietor. Under the Act,[4] F, as first registered proprietor, takes the fee simple:[5]

1. Subject to overriding interests (unless the contrary is expressed on the register). Thus F takes the land subject to B's easement.[6]
2. Subject to all entries 'on the register'[7].[8] The Registry will have recorded a note of the existence of C's easement on the title register of the land, and will have entered a Notice in respect of D's mortgage in the Charges Register. Thus F will hold the land subject to C's and D's interests.
3. Where the first registered proprietor is not entitled 'for his own benefit' to the land (ie where he holds the land on trust for some other person or persons), he takes subject to the interests of those persons of which he has notice.[9] Since F has notice of G's equitable interest, he holds the land subject to her interest.

Since E's equitable interest was not protected by an entry in the Land Charges Register, F takes free of it.

A first registered proprietor does not take subject to an interest on the register if the interest is itself void. For example, in *Kitney v MEPC Ltd*,[10] in 1933 A granted B an option with regard to land the title to which was not registered. B did not register the option as a land charge. A sold the land to C in 1947. C was registered as proprietor. A Notice in respect of B's option appeared in the Charges Register. B later sought to exercise the option. It was held that he was not entitled to do so. On the sale to C in 1947 the option became void under s 13(2) of the Land Charges Act 1925. Its appearance on the title register did not cause it to be resurrected.

---

4   Section 59.
5   Where the title registered is title to a leasehold interest the first registered proprietor takes the land subject to the same interests as does the first registered proprietor of a fee simple, together with all express and implied covenants, obligations and liabilities incident to the land, s 9.
6   Section 5(b).
7   The word 'register' here refers to the register of the land affected, not to the global register of all registered land; *A J Dunning & Sons (Shopfitters) Ltd v Sykes & Son (Poole) Ltd* [1987] Ch 287, [1987] 1 All ER 700.
8   Section 5(a). See *Kitney v MEPC Ltd* [1978] 1 All ER 595, [1977] 1 WLR 981.
9   Section 5(c).
10 [1978] 1 All ER 595, [1977] 1 WLR 981.

Subsequent registered proprietors

A subsequent registered proprietor of a fee simple[11] holds the land subject to:

1. overriding interests (unless the contrary is expressed on the register);[12]
2. all entries 'on the register'[13] at the moment of his registration as proprietor.[14]
   It will be noted that such entries may relate to;
   (a) matters which are recorded on the register at the first registration, eg the fact that the land is subject to a particular easement created before first registration;
   (b) matters which are entered as a result of a registrable disposition by a previous proprietor, eg a registered charge[15]; or a substantively registered lease;[16]
   (c) minor interests in respect of which a notice,[17] caution, restriction or inhibition has been entered. (He takes subject to such interests notwithstanding that by error of the Registry he was informed that there was no entry on the register.[18])

Unprotected minor interests

A subsequent registered proprietor who is not a purchaser for valuable consideration (eg a donee or a devisee) takes the land subject to all minor interests,[19] whether or not protected by entry of a Notice, etc, on the register.

A subsequent registered proprietor for valuable consideration in good faith takes the land free from minor interests[20] that are not protected by entry on the register.[1] (The fact that he has notice of the existence of the interest will not of itself cause him to be regarded as lacking good faith.)

There has been uncertainty, however, as to whether a subsequent registered proprietor for valuable consideration who does not take in good faith, takes subject to, or free from, unprotected minor interests: if good faith is lacking, is he bound by such interests? The uncertainty stems from a seeming conflict

---

11 A subsequent registered proprietor of a lease takes subject to the same interests, together with all express and implied covenants, obligations and liabilities incident to the estate transferred or created, s 23(1).
12 Section 20(1)(b).
13 Section 20(1)(a).
14 *Freer v Unwins Ltd* [1976] Ch 288, [1976] 1 All ER 634.
15 See p 544.
16 As in *Strand Securities Ltd v Caswell* [1965] Ch 958, [1965] 1 All ER 820; (M & B).
17 As in *Re White Rose Cottage* [1965] Ch 940, [1965] 1 All ER 11; (M & B).
18 *Parkash v Irani Finance Ltd* [1970] Ch 101, [1969] 1 All ER 930; (M & B).
19 LRA 1925, s 20(4).
20 Including minor interests that should have been on the register at the time of his registration but which (due to an error by the Registry) were not on the register at that time and which are entered by rectification of the register subsequently; *Freer v Unwins Ltd* [1976] Ch 288, [1976] 1 All ER 634.
 1 *De Lusignan v Johnson* (1974) 230 Estates Gazette 499; *Miles v Bull (No 2)* [1969] 3 All ER 1585.

between two sections of the Act. Section 20(1) provides that a transferee for valuable consideration shall take subject to the matters set out at 1 and 2(a), (b) and (c) above but 'free from all other ... interests whatsoever'. It would seem to follow that as an unprotected minor interest falls outside the list, any purchaser for valuable consideration with or without good faith, would take free from such an interest.

However, it is also necessary to consider s 59(6). This speaks of 'a purchaser' not being 'concerned with' certain matters. Section 3(xxi) defines a 'purchaser' as a 'purchaser in good faith for valuable consideration'. Inserting this definition into s 59(6), the latter reads 'a purchaser in good faith for valuable consideration ... shall not be concerned with any matter ... which is not protected by a caution or other entry on the register, whether he has or has not notice thereof, express, implied, or constructive'. It would seem to follow, as a corollary, that a purchaser (for valuable consideration) who is *not* in good faith *shall* be concerned (ie take subject to) an unprotected minor interest. This result would be contrary to that produced by s 20(1) in which, it will be noted, a 'transferee' is not required to be in good faith in order to take free from unprotected minor interests.

So the question is, does s 20(1) stand on its own; or is it to be read in conjunction with, and subject to, s 59(6)? In *Peffer v Rigg*[2] Graham J adopted the latter view: a purchaser was required to have acted in good faith before he was entitled to take free from unprotected minor interests. In *Lyas v Prowsa Developments Ltd*[3] Dillon J followed the same tack. V, a company, owned an estate divided into plots on which it was building houses. V mortgaged the estate to a bank by a legal charge. Later, V contracted to sell one of the plots to P. P did not protect the estate contract by entry of a Notice in the register of the land. V went into liquidation. The bank, as mortgagee, in exercise of its statutory power of sale, contracted to sell the estate to D. The bank elected to insert in the contract a clause that provided that the land was sold 'subject to and with the benefit of' P's contract. D was registered as proprietor of the land. Did D take subject to or free from P's unprotected minor interest? According to s 20(1) he would take free. Dillon J held, however, that D, having accepted the land subject to P's interest, took the plot subject to a constructive trust in favour of P. For D to seek to renege on the stipulation in favour of P would be a fraud on the part of D, and since the Land Registration Act 1925 was not to be used as an instrument of fraud,[4] D could not rely on s 20 of the Act to defeat P's interest. Dillon J's decision did not rest on s 59(6), but the outcome was in accord with the decision of Graham J in *Peffer v Rigg*.[5]

2   [1978] 3 All ER 745, [1977] 1 WLR 285; (M & B); (1977) 41 Conv (NS) 207 (F. R. Crane); (1978) 42 Conv (NS) 52 (J. Martin); following *Jones v Lipman* [1962] 1 All ER 442, [1962] 1 WLR 832; *Orakpo v Manson Investments Ltd* [1977] 1 All ER 666, [1977] 1 WLR 347.
3   [1982] 2 All ER 953, [1982] 1 WLR 1044; (1983) 46 MLR 96 (P. H. Kenning); (1984) 47 MLR 476 (P. Bennett); [1983] Conv 64 (P. Jackson).
4   Following the principle in *Bannister v Bannister* [1948] 2 All ER 133, CA; (M & B).
5   Supra.

The dilemma before the court in the last two cases was a perennial one – should the court set its sights on justice, or on certainty?[6] In both cases, the court opted for justice, but the consequence is uncertainty, for who can tell what is lack of good faith? In *Smith v Morrison*[7] it was held that the expression 'in good faith'[8] meant 'honestly and with no ulterior motive.' In *Jones v Lipman*[9] good faith was held to be lacking where a sale was a sham, the purchaser being merely the vendor in the guise of a limited company (with a token capital). The decisions in *Peffer v Rigg*[10] and *Lyas v Prowsa Developments Ltd*[10] suggest that for good faith to be lacking some element of fraud must be present, fraud sufficient to constitute the purchaser a constructive trustee of the interest from which he seeks to take free.

To remove the uncertainty as to the correct interpretation of sections 20 and 59 the Law Commission has recommended[11] that it should be a statutory requirement that all transferees and other purchasers who wish to take free from unprotected minor interests must take 'in good faith and for valuable consideration'. The Commission saw no need to propose a statutory definition of 'good faith' but recommended, for the avoidance of doubt, that it should be enacted that a transferee or purchaser should not be deemed dishonest merely because he had actual knowledge of the unprotected minor interest in question.

Equitable interests

It will now be seen that an equitable interest may be binding on a subsequent proprietor as a result of:

(i)   the holder's interest being an overriding interest under s 70(1)(g);[12]
(ii) the holder of the interest having protected his interest by entering a Notice (or Caution, etc) on the register of the land; or
(iii) the subsequent proprietor being:
  (a) not a purchaser for valuable consideration (eg a donee or devisee); or
  (b) a purchaser for value, but not in good faith.

Priorities[13]

Any person who acquires a registered *interest* in land, eg a registered chargee, takes subject to the same matters as a subsequent registered proprietor, ie he

6   See [1985] CLJ 280 (M. P. Thompson).
7   [1974] 1 All ER 957, [1974] 1 WLR 659.
8   In the Land Registration (Official Searches) Rules 1969.
9   [1962] 1 All ER 442, [1962] 1 WLR 832.
10 Supra.
11 Law Com No 158 (1987), supra, Part C, para 415.
12 As in *Woolwich Equitable Building Society v Marshall* [1952] Ch 1, [1952] 2 All ER 769.
13 For proposals for reform, see Law Com No 158, supra, Part C.

takes subject to overriding interests and interests 'on the register'. Thus a chargee will take subject to the equitable lease of a tenant in actual occupation of the land (the tenant holding an overriding interest under s 70(1)(g)[14]); and to the equitable fee simple of a beneficiary under an implied trust, the beneficiary being in actual occupation of the land (the beneficiary here also holding an overriding interest under s 70(1)(g)[15]), and such a person takes free from the same matters as does a subsequent registered proprietor, ie he takes free from minor interests not protected by entry on the register.[16]

Any person who acquires a *minor* interest in land takes subject to overriding interests and interests on the register and, in addition, to all prior minor interests, even though these are not protected by an entry on the register.[17] This is because minor interests are equitable,[18] and as between competing equities, the rule (which applies under the registered system, since it is nowhere ousted by the Land Registration Acts) is that where the equities are equal, the first in time prevails. This principle applies notwithstanding the fact that the second minor interest has been protected by an entry (eg a Notice) on the register: this is because an entry may protect a minor interest against subsequent dealings, but it cannot obtain for the minor interest priority over an earlier minor interest.[19] Thus as between an unregistered legal mortgage (which, being unregistered, is a minor interest) and a subsequent estate contract, the former prevails, with the result that the mortgage binds the proposed purchaser.[20]

Illustration

At this point it may be helpful to give an illustration of the operation of registered, overriding, and minor interests.

Event	Remarks
1. A, the owner of Greenacre Farm, by deed grants to B, the owner of Redacre, a right of way across Greenacre. The area was not one in which registration of title was compulsory.	A memorandum should properly be endorsed on the conveyance of Greenacre to A stating the terms of the grant (or a copy of the deed put with A's title deeds). Due to carelessness this is not done.
2. A conveys Greenacre to C reserving to himself an easement across Greenacre, for the benefit of his adjoining land Blackacre.	The easement in favour of Blackacre will thenceforward be apparent from an examination of the title deeds of Greenacre.

---

14   *Grace Rymer Investments Ltd v Waite* [1958] Ch 831, [1958] 2 All ER 777; (M & B); *Woolwich Equitable Society v Marshall* [1952] Ch 1, [1951] 2 All ER 769.
15   *Hodgson v Marks* [1971] Ch 892, [1071] 2 All ER 684; *Williams and Glyn's Bank Ltd v Boland* [1981] AC 487, [1980] 2 All ER 408.
16   *De Lusignan v Johnson* (1973) 230 Estates Gazette 499.
17   (1977) 93 LQR 541 (R. J. Smith).
18   LRA 1925, s 2.
19   *Barclays Bank Ltd v Taylor* [1974] Ch 137, [1973] 1 All ER 752; (M & B); *Mortgage Corpn Ltd v Nationwide Credit Corpn Ltd* [1993] 4 All ER 623, [1993] 3 WLR 769, CA (as between two unregistered charges, first in time prevailed).
20   *Barclays Bank Ltd v Taylor*, supra; cf *Clark v Chief Land Registrar* [1993] Ch 294.

Event	Remarks
3. The area becomes one of compulsory registration.	
4. C sells Greenacre to D.	D is registered as the proprietor. A note of the easement in favour of Blackacre is entered on the register of Greenacre. Since the easement in favour of Redacre is not disclosed by the title deeds to Greenacre, no note of the existence of the easement is made on the register of Greenacre.
5. D, by deed, grants a right of way across Greenacre to E, the owner of Whiteacre.	E does not acquire a legal easement until the grant is completed by the registration of the disposition in the (Charges) register of Greenacre. The easement thereupon becomes a registered interest.
	If the title to Whiteacre is registered it is desirable that the benefit of the easement should be entered on the register of Whiteacre as being appurtenant to the land.
6. D grants F (owner of Brownacre) in writing, not by deed, a right to lay pipes beneath Greenacre for a sum of £100.	F's equitable easement is a minor interest and requires protection by entry of a Notice in the Charges register of Greenacre.
7. D by deed grants G a lease of field X of Greenacre Farm for 25 years.	The title to the lease is registrable. G becomes the registered proprietor of the lease. A note of the lease is entered in the Charges register of Greenacre. G receives a Land Certificate as evidence of his title.
8. D grants H a lease in writing not by deed of field Y of Greenacre Farm for 12 years. H sublets the field to I at £300 a year.	H's lease is not registrable. Since H is in receipt of rent, H's lease is an overriding interest under s 70(1)(g).
9. D covenants with J for the benefit of J's land Blueacre that no building will be erected on Greenacre within a certain distance of the boundary with Blueacre.	The restrictive covenant is a minor interest and requires protection by the entry of a Notice in the Charges register of Greenacre.
10. D makes a contract to sell Greenacre to K. K takes no step to protect his interest.	K acquires an equitable fee simple in Greenacre.
11. Before the completion date, D allows K to go into possession of Greenacre.	K's right becomes an overriding interest under s 70(1)(g).
12. D (in breach of contract with K) sells Greenacre to L.	L is registered as proprietor of the land.

Subject to what interests does L take the land? The answers are set out below. The result if the land had not been registered land is given for the purpose of comparison in the third column.

Interest	Result if the land is registered	Result if the land is unregistered
1. B's legal easement	L takes subject to B's easement because it is an overriding interest. L can learn of the easement only by inspecting the land.	L takes subject to B's easement because it is a legal interest and is not registrable. L can learn of the easement only by inspecting the land.
2. A's legal easement	L takes subject to A's easement because it is an overriding interest. L is aware of the easement because of the note on the register.	L takes subject to A's easement because it is legal and not registrable. L can learn of the easement from an inspection of the title deeds.
5. E's legal easement	L takes subject to E's easement because it is a registered interest. L is aware of the easement because of the entry on the register.	L takes subject to E's easement because it is legal and is not registrable. L can learn of the easement only by inspecting the land or making enquiries from D.
6. F's equitable easement	If F entered a Notice in the Charges register of Greenacre, L is bound. If he has not, L is not bound.	This is registrable as a Class D (iii) Land Charge. If F has registered the interest in the Land Charges Registry, L is bound. If he has not, L is not bound.
7. G's legal lease	G's lease, being a registered interest, binds L. L is aware of the lease from the note on the register of Greenacre.	L is bound by G's lease because it is legal and is not registrable. L can discover the lease only from inspecting the land or from making enquiries from D.
8. H's equitable lease	H's lease, being an overriding interest under s 70(1)(g), binds L. L can discover the lease only by inspecting the land or making enquiries.	H's lease, being equitable, is registrable as a Class C(iv) Land Charge. If H has registered the interest, L is bound. If he has not, L is not bound.
9. J's benefit of D's covenant	This is a minor interest. If J has entered a Notice in the Charges Register of Greenacre, L is bound; if he has not, L is not bound.	This is registrable as a Class D(ii) Land Charge. If J has registered the interest, L is bound. If he has not, L is not bound.
10. K's equitable fee simple	Before K goes into possession, this is a minor interest and can be protected by entry of a Notice in the Charges Register of Greenacre. When K goes into possession his interest becomes an overriding interest and as such binds L.	This is registrable as a Class C(iv) Land Charge. If K has registered the interest, L is bound. If he has not, L is not bound (notwithstanding that he has notice of the contract).

Classes of title[1]

Freehold titles

ABSOLUTE TITLE

If a landowner, A, applies to be registered as the proprietor of his land, and if the Land Registry is satisfied that A has a good title to the land, then (and this is the position in the majority of cases) A is registered as having an 'Absolute' title. The statement that A has an Absolute title is made in the Proprietorship Register of the title register.

If A is registered as having an Absolute title and it later appears that A was not entitled to be registered as proprietor, for example because B proved that he has a better title to the land, then subject to what is said below, the register will be rectified so as to register B as proprietor, but compensation will be paid to A for the loss of the land.

POSSESSORY TITLE

It may happen that when, after a transfer on sale, a landholder applies for first registration of the land he is unable to produce any document of title other than the conveyance to himself. This may be because the earlier title deeds have been destroyed, or because the vendor was a squatter. In such circumstances, the applicant may be registered as having a 'Possessory' title to the land. The effect of such registration is that the proprietor's title is guaranteed but he and subsequent proprietors take the land subject to the interests existing at the date of registration.[2] Thus if O holds a fee simple in land, S occupies the land for five years and then sells the land to P, and P is registered as having Possessory title, P will take subject to the right of O to claim the land at any time until the expiry of 12 years from his dispossession. If (within the 12 years) the register is rectified to make O the proprietor, P receives no compensation.

If the Registrar is satisfied that P in fact has a satisfactory title to the land (eg if S and P have together been in possession for more than 12 years; or if the applicant can produce evidence of title deeds that have been destroyed) the Registrar may, and on the application of the proprietor must, register the applicant as having an Absolute title.[3]

---

1   Proposals for reform, including a reduction in the number of forms of title and modification of the system of conversion (ie up-grading) titles, made by the Law Commission (*Property Law Land Registration* (Law Com No 125)), were implemented by the Land Registration Act 1986, s 1.
2   LRA 1925, s 6.
3   Section 77, as amended by LRA 1986, s 1; (1986) 130 Sol Jo 579 (D. C. S. Phillips).

Leasehold titles

ABSOLUTE LEASEHOLD TITLE[4]

If a tenant is registered as having an Absolute Leasehold title, the effect is to guarantee both that the proprietor is the holder of the lease, and also that the lessor had the right to grant the lease, ie the lessor's title is also guaranteed.

GOOD LEASEHOLD TITLE[5]

The Law of Property Act 1925[6] provides that a lessee shall not, in the absence of agreement to the contrary, have any right to call on the lessor to prove his title. If a lessor declines to permit examination of his title, if a lessee is to obtain a lease he must take the risk that there may be a defect in the lessor's title (which might invalidate the lease, leaving the lessee merely to claim damages for breach of contract against the lessor). If a lessee of a registrable lease applies for registration and (as is commonly the case) he cannot, for the reason given, produce proof of the lessor's title, the Registrar can register the tenant as proprietor of the lease with Good Leasehold title. The effect is that no guarantee is given as to the right of the lessor to grant the lease, but otherwise the guarantee is the same as that given where a tenant is registered as having an Absolute Leasehold title.[7]

If the title to the freehold is registered, then notwithstanding that the lessor declines to permit the lessee to investigate his title, the Registrar will be able to examine the lessor's title by inspecting the register and, if he is satisfied, he will register the tenant as having an Absolute Leasehold title.

POSSESSORY LEASEHOLD TITLE[8]

If T_1 assigns a lease to T_2, and on assignment the lease is registrable, but T_2 is not able to produce the lease (for example, because while in T_1's hands it had been lost or destroyed), then the Registrar has discretion to register T_2 as holding a Possessory Leasehold title. A Possessory Leasehold title may also arise by virtue of the leaseholder acquiring other land by adverse possession as an accretion to his lease.[9]

---

4   Section 9.
5   Section 10.
6   Section 44(2).
7   Section 10.
8   Section 11.
9   LRA 1925, s 77, as amended by LRA 1986, s 1, makes provision for the conversion of possessory leasehold title to good leasehold title.

Rectification[10]

Effect of registration

In 1990 T dies leaving certain land (which did not lie in an area of compulsory registration) to his son A. He appoints X his executor. X makes an assent of the land to A, thus vesting the legal fee simple in him. Later, by error, X makes an assent of the same land in favour of B. A and B are unaware of the error and both think that the land has been left to B. B goes into occupation. The area becomes one of compulsory registration. B, by deed, conveys the land to C. C applies for registration and is registered as the freehold proprietor of the land.[11] The effect of registration is to vest the fee simple in C. This is so notwithstanding that the registration of C has been made possible by the error of X and that hitherto the fee simple had been vested in A, the person entitled to the land under T's will. The effect of registration is thus to vest the legal fee simple in the registered proprietor[12] regardless of whether or not, according to the principles of common law, he is properly entitled. This vesting occurs 'by a kind of statutory magic entirely regardless of the facts which have led up to registration'.[13] Even if a person becomes registered as proprietor as a result of some fraud or forgery, once his name is on the register, the legal estate is vested in him.

Rectification

In the facts we have described, if the area had not become one of compulsory registration, A could have asserted his title by claiming possession from C and, provided that his title had not become statute barred,[14] he would have had a claim as of right to an order for possession from the court against C.

Under the system of registered land A has no title to the legal estate to assert. This is vested, by the fact of registration, in C. A can, however, seek to have the register rectified by the entry of his name as proprietor in place of C. Jurisdiction to rectify the register is conferred on the court and on the Chief Land Registrar, subject to appeal to the court (except in the case of 1 below, where only the court has jurisdiction).[15] There is no claim of right to rectification; the Act confers discretion as to whether the register should be

---

10 [1983] Conv 361 (D. G. Barnsley). For proposals for reform, see Law Commission, *Property Law, Third Report on Land Registration*, Part B (Law Com No 158, 1987); [1987] Conv 334 (L. Smith).
11 This example is based on the facts in *Epps v Esso Petroleum Co Ltd* [1973] 2 All ER 465, [1973] 1 WLR 1071; (M & B) (though in this case rectification was refused under s 82(3)(c)).
12 LRA 1925, s 5.
13 Ruoff and Roper, p 70.
14 See Chapter 24.
15 LRA 1925, s 82(1).

rectified and, furthermore, the Act provides[16] that the register may be rectified only[17] in one of eight situations. These include, inter alia:

1. Where the court decides that any person (eg A) is entitled to 'any estate, right or interest' (eg A's fee simple estate) 'in or to any registered land' and that in the opinion of the court rectification is therefore required.[18]

2. Where the court or the registrar is satisfied that an entry in the register has been obtained by fraud.[19]

3. Where two or more persons are, by mistake, registered as proprietors of the same land.[20]

4. Where a legal estate has been registered in the name of a person who, if the land had not been registered, would not have been the estate owner.[1]

5. Where, by reason of any error or omission in the register, or by reason of any entry made under a mistake, it is deemed just to rectify the register.[2]

6. Where all parties interested consent to the rectification.[3]

The discretion of the court to order rectification is further limited by the provision[4] that where a registered proprietor is in possession[5] of the land, the register may not be rectified:

(1) unless it is to give effect to an overriding interest[6] (or an order of the court). (Eg in the example above, after C has been registered as proprietor, D occupies the land for 12 years. The right which D has acquired under the Limitation Act 1980 is an overriding interest.[7] D can seek to have the register rectified by having his name entered as proprietor in place of C, notwithstanding that C has regained possession at the time of the application.); or,

(2) unless the proprietor caused, or substantially contributed, to the error or omission by fraud or lack of proper care;,[8]

(3) unless for any other reason it would be unjust not to rectify the register by removing the name of the registered proprietor;[9]

(4) unless it is to give effect to an order of the court.

---

16   Section 82(1).
17   *Norwich and Peterborough Building Society v Steed (No 2)* [1993] Ch 116, [1993] 1 All ER 330; [1992] Conv 293 (C. Davis).
18   Section 82(1)(a).
19   Section 82(1)(d). See *Re Leighton's Conveyance* [1936] 1 All ER 667; *Argyle Building Society v Hammond* (1984) 49 P & CR 148; (M & B) (forgery); (1985) 101 LQR 79 (R. J. Smith).
20   Section 82(1)(e).
 1   Section 82(1)(g).
 2   Section 82(1)(h); *Cambro Contractors Ltd v John Kennelly Sales Ltd* (1994) Times, 14 April.
 3   Section 82(1)(c).
 4   Section 82(3) as amended by the Administration of Justice Act 1977, s 24.
 5   Including in receipt of rents and profits, LRA 1925, s 3(xviii).
 6   LRA 1925, s 82(3); *Bridges v Mees* [1957] Ch 475, [1957] 2 All ER 577.
 7   Section 70(1)(f).
 8   *Re No 139 High Street Deptford, ex p British Transport Commission* [1951] Ch 884, [1951] 1 All ER 950; (M & B). The contribution to the mistake consisted of a purchaser putting forward (innocently) a misleading description of the property for the purposes of registration. See also *Re Sea View Gardens* [1966] 3 All ER 935, [1967] 1 WLR 134; (M & B).
 9   See *Hodges v Jones* [1935] Ch 657 at 671; *Epps v Esso Petroleum Co Ltd* [1973] 2 All ER 465, [1973] 1 WLR 1071; (M & B).

We envisaged rectification being necessary as a result of an error (in our example by an executor) prior to first registration. A claim for rectification may also arise from an error by the Registry. For example, the error may relate to the fact that the plan filed at the Land Registry (and the plan attached to the Land Certificate) did not correctly represent land which had been the subject of a contract of sale and which had been correctly set out in the plan attached to the form of transfer.[10] Or the error may consist of the failure of the Registry to enter a Notice of the burden of a restrictive covenant in the Charges Register of land at the time of first registration. (Here the claim would be to have the register rectified so as to include the Notice.[11]) Or the error may be made by the Registrar in noting on the title register of freehold land the existence of a lease with, according to the entry, 50 years unexpired, whereas in fact 80 years were unexpired.[12]

The distinction should be noted between the equitable right to rectification (eg of a conveyance) and the right conferred by the Land Registration Act 1925 to seek rectification of the title register of registered land. The former may be a ground for seeking the latter.[13]

Relative titles under the system of registered land

A registered proprietor who is in possession[14] of the land has the most secure title to land in the country. Next in order of security is a registered proprietor who is not in possession. But even such holders will lose their interest in the land if the register is rectified so as to remove their name as proprietor. Thus the principle that all titles to land are relative does not cease to apply merely because a title to land is registered, although its operation is restricted by the fact that the conditions set out above must be satisfied before the register can be rectified.

Compensation

The Act[15] provides[16] that if a person suffers loss through rectification of the register he may be compensated. (The Act speaks of his being 'indemnified'.) Compensation ('indemnity') is paid by the Chief Land Registrar and comes from the Consolidated Fund from which all government expenditure is met.

For example, in the example at the beginning of this section, if the register is rectified so as to remove C's name and replace it with that of A, C suffers a loss and (subject to what is said below) has a right to compensation up to the

10   *Lee v Barrey* [1957] Ch 251, [1957] 1 All ER 191.
11   *Freer v Unwins Ltd* [1976] Ch 288, [1976] 1 All ER 634.
12   Ruoff and Roper.
13   As in *Blacklocks v J B Developments (Godalming) Ltd* [1982] Ch 183, [1981] 3 All ER 392.
14   Including in receipt of rents or profits, LRA 1925, s 3(xviii).
15   As amended by the Land Registration Act 1997, s 2, which substitutes a new s 83 in the 1925 Act, following proposals for reform by the Law Commission, Law Com No 125 (1995).
16   LRA 1925, s 83(1).

value of the land immediately before the date of rectification.[17] Reasonable costs and expenses may also be claimed.[18]

Further, compensation is payable where the claim for rectification arises from an error by the Registry, eg in the making of boundaries,[19] or in stating the unexpired period of a lease on the title register of freehold land. (In the last instance, compensation could be claimed by a purchaser of the freehold who discovered, for example, that 80 years were unexpired, not 50 years as incorrectly stated on the register, and who had paid a higher price for the reversion than he would have done had he known the correct position.[20])

Compensation is payable also where rectification is made on the grounds of forgery.[1] For example, O is registered as proprietor of property. F obtains O's land certificate and forges a transfer of the land to P who has no knowledge of F's dishonesty. P is registered as proprietor. O seeks, and obtains, rectification[2] restoring his name as proprietor. P can claim compensation for his loss. (If P had charged the land to E as security for a loan, and E had registered the charge, and O had sought and obtained rectification restoring his name as proprietor and deleting the charge,[3] E could claim compensation for his loss, eg, in the event of P defaulting.)

Conversely, the Act provides[4] that where an error or omission has occurred but the register is *not* rectified, then any person who suffers loss is entitled (again subject to what is said below) to receive compensation. Thus, in the example used on page 535, if the register is not rectified A is entitled to be compensated for the loss of the fee simple to which, had it not been for the error of X, he would have been entitled. The maximum amount payable is the value of the land at the time when the error or omission which caused the loss was made.[5] Thus the sum which A receives will not include any appreciation in the value of the land since the date of the assent by X to B.

No compensation is, however, payable on account of any loss suffered by a claimant wholly or partly as a result of his own fraud or wholly as a result of his own lack of proper care.[6] Thus if A seeks rectification and rectification is ordered, and C claims compensation, then if B and C had known of the assent to A, and C had bribed B not to remind X of the earlier assent, C would be debarred from claiming compensation. Similarly, if rectification is not ordered and A claims compensation, then if it is shown that A had been aware of the

---

17   LRA 1925, 83(8)(b).
18   LRA 1925, s 83(9) and (5)(c)
19   Eg compensation was payable following the decision in *Lee v Barrey* [1957] Ch 251, [1957] 1 All ER 191.
20   Ruoff and Roper, Chapter 40.
 1   LRA 1925, s 83(4). See 'Forgeries and Land Registration' (1985) 101 LQR 79 (R. J. Smith).
 2   LRA 1925, s 82(1)(h).
 3   As in *Argyle Building Society v Hammond* (1984) 49 P & CR 148; (M & B); [1985] Conv 135 (A. Sydenham).
 4   LRA 1925, s 83(2).
 5   LRA 1925, s 83(8)(a).
 6   LRA 1925, s 83(5)(a).Where any loss is suffered by a claimant partly as a result of his own lack of proper care any compensation paid to him is reduced to such extent as is fair and reasonable having regard to his share in the responsibility for the loss (s 83(b)).

later assent to B, and of C's application for registration, but had taken no steps to bring these matters to the notice of the Registrar, then, because of his lack of care, he would not be entitled to compensation.

There are certain other grounds on which a claimant may be debarred from receiving compensation. For example, since fraud or lack of proper care by a person from whom the claimant claims title is, by the Act,[7] to be treated as if it were fraud or lack of proper care by the claimant, no compensation is payable to a claimant who derives his title from a person who has caused the loss by fraud or by lack of proper care, unless he gave valuable consideration and his interest has been registered.[7] Thus if B had known of the earlier assent to A but had not notified X, and C had been a donee from B, and the register was rectified in favour of A, compensation would not be payable to C

Nor, it has been held, is compensation payable where rectification places the applicant in no worse a position than he was in before. For example in *Re Chowood's Registered Land*,[8] L acquired a title by adverse possession to a strip of woodland, the fee simple to which had previously been in V. V, unaware of the title which L acquired, sold the land to C Ltd which was registered as proprietor. L applied to have the register rectified so as to have herself registered as the proprietor in place of C. This was done.[9] C Ltd applied for compensation. It was held that (i) when C Ltd was registered as proprietor it took the land subject to overriding interests; (ii) these interests included L's interest (under s 70(1)(f)); (iii) so the rectification of the register placed C Ltd in no worse position than before rectification; (iv) so no compensation was payable.[10]

Further, no compensation is payable if more than six years have elapsed since the claimant knew, or but for his own default might have known, of the existence of his right to claim.[11]

The security accorded to a registered proprietor thus arises not only from the fact that rectification will only be ordered if certain conditions are fulfilled but also from the fact that if a registered proprietor is deprived of his title he may be entitled to up to the value of the land by way of compensation. Thus when a landowner becomes a registered proprietor the fee he pays to the Land Registry may be regarded as being, in part, in the nature of premium under a policy of insurance under which the state guarantees to compensate the proprietor in the event of his loss of the land by reason of rectification being ordered against him.

A registered proprietor who acquired his interest for valuable consideration and who has not been guilty of any fraud or lack of proper care can thus be certain of enjoying either the land or, if this is lost to him by reason of rectification, monetary compensation in its place. Such a proprietor comes closest in English law to holding an indefeasible title to land.

---

7   LRA 1925, s 83(7).
8   [1933] Ch 574; (M & B).
9   Under LRA 1925, s 82(g) and (h); *Chowood Ltd v Lyall* [1929] 2 Ch 406; (M & B).
10   See also *Re Boyle's Claim* [1961] 1 All ER 620, [1961] 1 WLR 339.
11   LRA 1925, s 83(2).

Parties to an action concerning rectification

It will be noted that in a claim for rectification, the plaintiff is normally the 'true owner' and the defendant the registered proprietor. In a claim for compensation the applicant may be either the 'true owner' (whose claim for rectification has been rejected) or the (former) registered proprietor (against whom rectification has been ordered).

Fraud

It will be noted that in the context of rectification fraud may be relevant in three ways.

1. Fraud is one of the grounds on which rectification may be ordered.
2. Rectification may be ordered against a registered proprietor notwithstanding that he is in possession if he has been guilty of fraud.
3. Compensation is not payable to any claimant who has been guilty of fraud.

A DIFFERENT SYSTEM OF LAW?

The system of registration of title was engrafted onto the existing land law and the majority of principles of land law still apply to both registered and unregistered land. For example, the law relating to settlements, perpetuities, covenants,[12] easements, and adverse possession[13] apply equally under each system.

On the other hand, as seen earlier in this chapter, in some instances the outcome of a particular situation may differ according to whether the land is registered or unregistered.[14] Of particular relevance here is the fact that the principle inherent in section 70(1)(g) of the Land Registration Act 1925 has no place in the unregistered system. Thus if (i) V contracts to sell Blackacre to P (and the contract complies with section 2 of the 1989 Act) and P gives consideration; (ii) P goes to live on Blackacre; (iii) P takes no step to protect his equitable fee simple (arising under the principle in *Walsh v Lonsdale*); (iv) V mortgages the land to E; the result is that if the title to Blackacre is registered, E's mortgage is subject to P's equitable fee simple (since, by virtue of being in occupation, P's interest is an overriding interest under section 70(1)(g)); if the title to Blackacre is not registered, E takes his mortgage free from P's equitable fee simple by reason of the fact that P failed to protect his interest by registering it as an estate contract in the register of land charges, the fact that he is in occupation of the land being of no relevance.[15] Thus, on identical facts, the

---

12   Eg as in *Cator v Newton and Bates* [1940] 1 KB 415, [1939] 4 All ER 457.
13   Eg as in *Bridges v Mees* [1957] Ch 475, [1957] 2 All ER 577; *Chowood Ltd v Lyall* [1929] 2 Ch 406; (M & B).
14   See (1977) 41 Conv (NS) 405.
15   *See Lloyds Bank plc v Carrick* [1996] 4 All ER 630, [1996] 140 Sol Jo LB 101; [1996] Conv 295; [1997] Conv 10.

priority differs according to whether the system of registration of title applies, or it does not.

Differences between the two systems have also been created by the fact that some statutes apply to one or other system only. For example, the Law of Property (Joint Tenants) Act 1964 does not apply to registered land.[16]

It cannot be denied, therefore, that in certain respects a different system of land law does operate where land is registered. And even to the substantial extent that the two systems attain the same ends, the systems are so different in their operation (and in their terminology[17]) that someone attempting to understand the two systems may at the outset find it more useful to think of the two as distinct rather than seeking to be able to switch mentally from one to the other at random. Certainly, to understand the registered system (to some the most difficult area of any in English and Welsh property law) it is necessary to become 'registration minded'.[18]

Application of the Land Registration Act 1925

In the section that follows we shall set out the principal aspects of land law covered in earlier chapters, and, after recalling how they are treated under the unregistered system, consider how they are treated under the system of registered land.

Strict settlements (Chapter 7)

Section 119(3) of the Settled Land Act 1925 provided, and in relation to settlements in existence at the date of the Trusts of Land and Appointment of Trustees Act 1996, continues to provide: 'This Act, as regards registered land, takes effect subject to the provisions of the Land Registration Act 1925.' Under the registered system the holder of the legal estate, whether the Tenant for life or the statutory owner, is registered as the proprietor.

The interests of the beneficiaries under settlement are minor interests.[19] They can be protected by the entry of a Restriction in the proprietorship register.[20] The Restriction will (a) order that no disposition giving rise to capital money (eg a sale of the land) is to be registered unless the money is paid to specified trustees or into court; (b) prohibit the registration of any disposition other than one authorised by the Settled Land Act 1925.

---

16   Section 3.
17   The terminology of the registered system (with its 'registered interests' and 'interests on the register', which sound the same but are not; its 'minor interests', which are far from minor; and its 'overriding interests' which do not ride over anything) certainly makes it a strange world to the newcomer.
18   (1978) 94 LQR 239 at 254 (D. C. Jackson).
19   See p 514.
20   See p 525.

Trusts for sale (Chapter 8)

Trustees of a trust for sale created prior to the Trusts of Land and Appointment of Trustees Act 1996 were registered as proprietors of the land. The interests of the beneficiaries of such a trust for sale are minor interests. On an application by the trustees the Chief Land Registrar placed a Restriction in the proprietorship register prohibiting the registration of any dispositions by a sole proprietor (ie by the survivor of two or more trustees), not being a trust corporation, except under the order of the registrar or of the court.[1] If the trustees failed to apply, the beneficiaries were able to protect their interests by lodging a Caution.[2] Trusts for sale created after the 1996 Act are trusts of land under the Act and treated accordingly.

Trusts of land under the 1996 Act (Chapter 10)

The trustees are registered as proprietors of the land. The interests of the beneficiaries are capable of being protected in the same manner as were those of beneficiaries of a trust for sale created before the 1996 Act,[3] as set out above. Thus any limitation of the trustees' powers or imposition of a duty to obtain consents, will be recorded by entry of a restriction in the Proprietorship Register.

Co-ownership (Chapter 11)

Where the legal estate is vested in two or more trustees on trust for the beneficial co-owners, the arrangements just mentioned for trusts of land apply.

Where the legal estate is vested in a sole trustee, on trust for the beneficial co-owners (eg where H holds the title to the matrimonial home on trust for himself and W) if W can produce the Land Certificate (or if it is already at the Land Registry) she can enter a Restriction to protect her interest. If the Land Certificate cannot be produced (eg because H declines to give it up) W can enter a Caution. If no Restriction or Caution is entered, and H sells to P, and W is in actual occupation, her equitable interest in the property is an overriding interest under s 70(1)(g)[4] and so binds the purchaser; if she is not in occupation, the purchaser takes free from her interest.

The right of a spouse to *occupy* the matrimonial home conferred by the Family Law Act 1996[5] is not (even if the spouse is in actual occupation) an overriding interest. This statutory right *of* occupation (ie as distinct from the right, if any, of a person *in* occupation under section 70(1)(g)) is protected by the entry of a Notice in the Charges Register.

---

1   Section 49(1)(d).
2   Section 54. See (1990) CLR 277, 306 (C. Harpum).
3   Ibid.
4   *Williams and Glyn's Bank Ltd v Boland* [1981] AC 487, [1980] 2 All ER 408. See p 546.
5   Section 31(10)(b), replacing Matrimonial Homes Act 1983, s 2(8)(b).

Leases (Chapter 17)

The position is as set out on p 509.

Easements[6] (Chapter 18)

If a legal easement comes into being (by grant or by prescription) before the date of first registration, and the existence of the easement is apparent from the title (ie from the title deeds delivered to the Land Registry at first registration), the Registrar enters a note of the easement on the register of the servient land at the time of first registration of the servient land. Since the easement is then 'on the register' it binds subsequent purchasers (see p 527). If the existence of the easement is not apparent from the title, and so is not noted on the register at first registration, it nevertheless binds a purchaser as being an overriding interest.[7]

If a legal easement is granted after the date of first registration of the land, then the grant is a registrable disposition (see p 512) and must be treated accordingly: a note of the benefit may, and generally will, be entered in the property register of the title register of the dominant land and, if the title to the servient land is registered, a Notice of the burden will be entered in the Charges Register of the title register of the servient land.

If an equitable easement[8] comes into existence before first registration, and is protected by registration as a land charge under the Land Charges Act 1972, then on the registration of the title of the servient land the Registrar enters a Notice in respect of the easement in the Charges Register, and the easement thereby binds a purchaser. If the easement was registrable but had not been protected by registration as a land charge then no Notice is entered at first registration and the easement does not bind a purchaser.

If an equitable easement comes into existence after first registration and it would, under the unregistered system, be registrable as a land charge, it is a minor interest and, to bind a purchaser, must be protected by entry of a Notice[9] on the register of the servient land. Where an equitable easement is found by the court to have arisen under an equitable principle such as estoppel,[10] it would seem that effect would be given to the court's decision by the making of the appropriate entries in the registers of the dominant and servient land.

An equitable easement may also be binding on a purchaser as being an overriding interest under s 70(1)(g).[11]

6 'Easements in Registered Land' (1985) 82 LS Gaz R 337 (P. H. Kenny).
7 Section 70(1)(a).
8 'Equitable Easements in Registered Land' [1986] Conv 31 (M. P. Thompson).
9 Or Caution see p 524.
10 See p 347 et seq.
11 *Celsteel v Alton House Holdings Ltd* [1985] 2 All ER 562, [1985] 1 WLR 204; (M & B).

Covenants between fee simple owners (Chapter 21)

The benefit of a restrictive covenant is a minor interest (since, under the unregistered system, it is registrable as a land charge under the Land Charges Act 1972). The appropriate means of protection is therefore by means of the entry of a Notice in the Charges register of the servient land. It has been the practice of the Registrar not to enter a Notice unless he is satisfied that the benefit runs with the land. If the decision in *Federated Homes Ltd v Mill Lodge Properties Ltd*[12] holds its ground, the Registrar may come to accept the entry of Notices in respect of the benefit of restrictive covenants as a matter of course. At the discretion of the Registrar the benefit of a restrictive covenant may be entered in the Property Register of the dominant land (but such entry is no guarantee of the enforceability of the covenant).

Covenants in leases (Chapter 22)

Since covenants between lessor and lessee are not registrable as land charges under the Land Charges Act 1972 under the unregistered systems, such covenants are not required to be protected by any entry under the system of registered land. Whether such covenants are binding on assignees from the lessor and the lessee is determined by the principles set out in Chapter 22, unaffected by any matter relating to registration of title.

Mortgages (Chapter 23)

Whilst in general the principles relating to mortgages set out in Chapter 23 (eg regarding the mortgagor's right to redeem) operate under the registered system as they do under the unregistered system, differences exist under the registered system with regard to the method by which a mortgage may be made.

If a registered proprietor, R, wishes to mortgage his interest in his land to E the following methods are open to him.

1.   REGISTERED CHARGE: SECTION 25

A deed charging the land to the mortgagee (strictly a 'chargee'), E, is drawn up and executed by R and E. The deed, together with R's Land Certificate, and an application for registration are sent to the Land Registry. Here the charge is registered by the making of an entry in the Charges Register of the title register of R's land, giving the date of the charge. A further entry names E as proprietor of the charge and gives his address. A Charge Certificate which contains a copy of the entries on the title register of the land is sent to E. Attached to the Certificate is the original mortgage deed. The Registry retains R's Land Certificate until the mortgage is redeemed.[13] When the Charge

---

12   [1980] 1 All ER 371, [1980] 1 WLR 594; (M & B). (See Chapter 21).
13   LRA, s 65.

Certificate is lodged with a Deed of Discharge at the Land Registry, the entries in the Charges Register are deleted, the Charge Certificate cancelled, and the Land Certificate, made up to agree with the register, is returned to R.

It should be noted that the creation of a registered charge is a 'registered disposition'.[14] Thus E does not obtain a legal interest until the registration has been made.[15]

On the registration of the charge, E, the registered chargee, has all the powers of a legal mortgagee.[16]

2. DEPOSIT OF THE LAND CERTIFCATE: SECTION 66

Under section 66 R may, by depositing the Land Certificate with E, create a 'lien' on the land in his, E's, favour. E may have a 'Notice of Deposit' entered on the Charges Register of the title register of the land. This has the effect of a Caution.[17] The execution of a document is not necessary for the creation of the lien, but it is desirable, and usual, for a document containing the details of the transaction to be drawn up and signed by the parties. This form of mortgage is cheaper to carry out than the creation of a registered charge, as the fee payable on the creation of the latter is avoided; but for E the method has the disadvantage that he does not have a power of sale. If he wishes to exercise the statutory power of sale he must have the mortgage registered,[18] thus converting it into a registered charge.

Where co-owners, A and B, are registered as proprietors of land, holding on trust for themselves in equity, and A, without the consent of B, deposits the Land Certificate by way of security for a loan, no charge of the fee simple is created. The lender acquires, however, a charge on A's equitable interest, unless the court finds that a charge on A's interest would so prejudicially affect B's equitable interest (as by exposing B to the risk of ceasing to be able to occupy the property in the event of A defaulting and the lender seeking possession in order to sell) that the hardship on B would outweigh any hardship to the lender by the absence of a charge.[19]

3. MORTGAGES CREATED OUTSIDE THE LAND REGISTRATION ACT 1925

The most common types of mortgage of registered land are those set out at 1 and 2 above, but the methods of mortgaging registered land provided by the Act are in addition to, not in substitution for, those which exist in the unregistered system.[20]

---

14 Section 18(4). A registered charge of a leasehold interest is a registered disposition under s 21(4).
15 *Grace Rymer Investments Ltd v Waite* [1958] Ch 831, [1958] 2 All ER 777.
16 LRA s 27(1).
17 Rule 239(4) of the Land Registration Rules 1925. For Cautions, see ante.
18 Ibid.
19 *Thames Guaranty Ltd v Campbell* [1985] QB 210, [1984] 1 All ER 144.
20 Section 106(1), as amended by s 26 of the Administration of Justice Act 1977. It is no longer possible to protect such mortgages by the entry of a Caution in a specially prescribed form (called a 'Mortgage Caution') and the Chief Land Registrar has power to convert existing mortgages protected by Mortgage Cautions into registered charges.

Thus there can[1] be a legal or an equitable mortgage of registered land outside the Act.[2] (In either case there can be no deposit of title deeds since, the land having been registered, the original title deeds no longer have effect as such.) The Act decrees that until a mortgage created outside the Act (whether legal, ie by deed or equitable) is converted into a registered charge, it takes effect only in equity and ranks (ie with regard to priorities) as a minor interest.[3] Protection (eg against a subsequent registed charge) is secured by entry of a Notice on the title register of the land.[4]

As in the case of a lien created by deposit of the Land Certificate, E has no power of sale unless the mortgage is converted, by registration, into a registered charge.

Limitation (Chapter 24)

In general, the principles of law relating to adverse possession apply in the case of registered land as they do under the unregistered system.[5] One difference, however, is that whereas under the unregistered system, if S occupies O's land for 12 years, S acquires the fee simple, under the registered system, on the expiry of the 12-year limitation period, O continues to hold the fee simple, but on trust for S.[6] S can apply to the Registrar to have his name substituted for that of O as proprietor of the land.[7] S takes the land subject to the same interests as if he were the first registered proprietor.[8]

Suppose that S occupies O's land and O later sells the land to P who is registered as proprietor. Here S has a right that is 'in the course of being acquired under the Limitation Acts', an overriding interest under s 70(1)(f). As such, it is binding on P. If later P's title becomes statute barred, S can call on the Registrar to register his name as proprietor in place of P.

Williams and Glyn's Bank Ltd v Boland[9]

The facts

Mr and Mrs Boland were married in 1959. Their first home was in Epsom. They both contributed to the purchase of the house, which was in their joint

1 Section 106(1).
2 Further, a mortgage can arise by estoppel, with legality subsequently being fed through; *First National Bank plc v Thompson* [1996] Ch 231, [1996] 1 All ER 140, CA.
3 Section 106(2).
4 Section 106(3).
5 Section 75(1); *Spectrum Investment Co v Holmes* [1981] 1 All ER 6, [1981] 1 WLR 221; [1982] Conv 201 (P. H. Kenny).
6 Section 75(1).
7 Section 75(2).
8 Section 75(3).
9 [1981] AC 487, [1980] 2 All ER 408; (M & B); (1980) 44 Conv (NS) 361 (J. Martin); (1980) 44 Conv (NS) 427 (C. Sydenham); (1980) 43 MLR 692 (S. Freeman); (1980) 39 CLJ 243 (M. J. Pritchard); (1981) 97 LQR 12 (R. J. Smith).

names. In 1969, they sold the house in Epsom and with the proceeds bought a house in Purley. The title was registered in Mr Boland's name alone. Mrs Boland did not know that the property had been registered in this way. Mr Boland expanded his building business and it came to employ 60 people. He had the business incorporated as Epsom Contractors Ltd, with himself and his brother as directors. To expand further, the firm wanted to borrow money. Mr Boland approached Williams and Glyn's Bank, and the bank agreed to lend money. As security, the bank took a mortgage on Mr Boland's house.

Later, the business went downhill. The money was not repaid, and the company went into liquidation. The yard was sold, but a substantial deficit remained. The bank claimed possession of Mr Boland's house. Mrs Boland resisted the bank's claim on the ground that her equitable interest (arising from her contribution to the purchase of the property) gave her a right to occupy the premises. Unless the bank could obtain vacant possession, it could not exercise its statutory right to sell. The case came before Templeman J. Following a case he had decided four days earlier (*Bird v Syme-Thomson*[10]), his judgment was for the bank: Mrs Boland would have to leave her home. She appealed to the Court of Appeal, and from there the case went to the House of Lords. Before dealing with the Lords' decision let us consider how the matter would be dealt with under the unregistered system. The husband held on a trust for himself and his wife.[11] As they were co-owners, a trust for sale existed.[12] By s 26(3), H, as trustee, ought not to have dealt with the land without the consent of the other co-owner, W, his wife. If she had agreed to the sale of the land, H could have appointed another trustee, and when H and the new trustee had sold the land, and the purchaser had obtained a receipt signed by both of them, he would have taken free of W's equitable interest, which would have been overreached. If H had not consulted W, and had not appointed a second trustee, but had sold the land (holding himself out to be the sole beneficial owner), then since the overreaching provisions of the Law of Property Act 1925 would not apply, the old principles would come into play: if the purchaser was a bona fide purchaser for value without notice he would take free of the wife's equitable interest. Otherwise, he would not.

How the bona fide purchaser rule should be applied in circumstances corresponding to those in *Boland* was the question in an unregistered title in *Caunce v Caunce*,[13] in 1969. The question here was whether a mortgagee bank had notice of a wife's equitable interest by reason of her presence in the house. Stamp J decided in the bank's favour. He said[14] of the wife that her presence was 'wholly consistent with the title offered by the husband to the bank'. Thus the bank did not have constructive notice of her interest. Then, about a year later, came *Boland*.

---

10   [1978] 3 All ER 1027, [1979] 1 WLR 440.
11   See Chapter 5.
12   See Chapter 11.
13   [1969] 1 All ER 722, [1969] 1 WLR 286; (M & B).
14   At 293.

The arguments

For Mrs Boland it was argued that (1) the Land Registration Act 1925 provided that a purchaser should take land subject to overriding interests; (2) overriding interests, as set out in s 70(1), included the rights of persons in 'actual occupation'; (3) she as in 'actual occupation' – she *lived* there; (4) she did have a 'right' – namely her equitable interest, derived from her contribution to the purchase of the property. So her equitable interest in the house was binding on the bank.

The bank contended that the argument for Mrs Boland ran counter to the whole logic of the 1925 Act. The Act provided, the bank pointed out, three types of interest: (1) registered interests; (2) overriding interests, and (3) minor interests. These three, the bank claimed, were mutually exclusive. In defining minor interests the Land Registration Act 1925 laid down that minor interests were to include all interests capable of being overreached by trustees for sale.[15] Mrs Boland's interest under the trust for sale was capable of being overreached. Therefore she held a minor interest. And so s 70(1)(g) did not apply, and the question of 'in actual occupation' therefore did not arise. As she had a minor interest, this would only bind a purchaser if the interest was protected by an entry on the register. There was no entry. So the bank took free. The contention must be correct, the bank argued, since s 3(xv), which defines minor interests, expressly excludes overriding interests.

The decision[16]

Lord Wilberforce said that he found the bank's argument formidable. But this did not prevent him from rejecting it. True, he said, Mrs Boland's interest under the trust for sale was a minor interest, but when we speak of her interest under the trust for sale what we are speaking of is (ie under the doctrine of conversion, prior to its abolition by the Trusts of Land and Appointment of Trustees Act 1996) her interest in the *proceeds of sale*. But, he said, we have to look also at her interest pending sale. Her interest pending sale included a right to occupy the land, and he cited *Re Warren*[17] and *Bull v Bull*[18] in support of this. Before the Law of Property Act 1925 people who were co-owners were entitled to concurrent rights of occupation, and in the two cases he had cited the court had held that the conversion of the legal interests of co-owners into equitable ones at the end of 1925 did not affect the rights of occupation that existed before 1926. So, he said, Mrs Boland had two interests – that in the proceeds of sale, which was a minor interest, and her right of occupation, which was, or could be, an overriding interest. (Lord Scarman agreed with this view. He said that the critically important right of the wife was the right of occupation. This right, if unaccompanied by actual occupation, was a minor

---

15   Section 3(xv) (prior to its amendment by the Trusts of Land and Appointment of Trustees Act 1996, Sch 3).
16   [1981] AC 487, [1980] 2 All ER 408.
17   [1932] 1 Ch 42.
18   [1955] 1 QB 234, [1955] 1 All ER 253.

interest. But once this right became associated with actual occupation, the wife's right became an overriding interest.)

Lord Wilberforce said that he rejected the argument that there was a 'firm dividing line' or 'an unbridgeable gulf' between minor interests and overriding interests. Mrs Boland *was* capable of having an overriding interest, if she was in actual occupation.

Whether Mrs Boland was in actual occupation was a further point at issue. The bank argued that even if she was capable of having an overriding interest under s 70(1)(g), she was not in actual occupation, because it was her husband who was in *actual* occupation, not her. She was only there, the bank contended, by virtue of his occupation. The bank supported this contention by referring to the decision in *Caunce v Caunce*,[19] (seeking to draw an analogy with unregistered land), and the decision in *Bird v Syme-Thomson*.[20] But the Lords found little difficulty in rejecting the bank's argument. Lord Wilberforce said that in reply to the question – 'was Mrs Boland in actual occupation?' he would reply, 'Why not?' Mrs Boland was living in the house, she was physically present, so she was in actual occupation. So, Lord Wilberforce said, any notion that the wife's occupation was 'but a shadow of her husband's' – the words of Templeman J at first instance – this notion was, he said, 'heavily obsolete'.[1]

So Mrs Boland had been in actual occupation; she had an overriding interest; and therefore this was binding on the bank.

The implications

It seemed, perhaps, that justice had been done. As Lord Denning had said in the Court of Appeal:[2] 'Anyone who lends money on the security of a matrimonial home nowadays ought to realise that the wife may have a share in it. He ought to make sure that the wife agrees to it, or to go to the house and make inquiries of her. It seems to me utterly wrong that a lender should turn a blind eye to the wife's interest or the possibility of it – and afterwards seek to turn her and the family out – on the plea that he did not know she was in actual occupation. If a bank is to do its duty, in the society in which we live, it should recognise the integrity of the matrimonial home. It should not destroy it by disregarding the wife's interest in it – simply to ensure that it is paid the husband's debts in full – with the high interest rate now prevailing. We should not give monied might priority over social justice.'[3]

The decision was inconvenient for those who lent money, because the decision meant that the interest of any person, not just that of a husband or a

19 Supra.
20 Supra.
1   He said that the word 'actual', if it added anything, was intended to emphasise the fact of occupation. He said that the use of the word 'actual' seemed to have emerged from its use in the phrase 'actual possession', where the word was used to distinguish between a person who was in physical possession, and a person who was technically 'in possession' by virtue of his being entitled to receive rents and profits. 'Actual occupation' indicated the former.
2   [1979] Ch 312.
3   At 332.

wife, who is in actual occupation is binding on a purchaser. And it is well established that the principle that a person who contributes to the purchase or improvement of a property acquires an equitable interest in the property is not confined to man and wife.

So, whenever a house is in the name of one person, and the title is registered,[4] a purchaser (including here a lessee and a mortgagee) must find out (1) who else is in actual occupation and (2) whether they have any interest in the property. The inconvenience of this was recognised by the House of Lords and it is worth noting Lord Scarman's words, 'While the technical task faced by the courts, and now facing the House, is the construction to be put upon a sub-clause in a subsection of a conveyancing statute, it is our duty, when tackling it, to give the provision, if we properly can, a meaning which will work for, rather than against, rights conferred by Parliament, or recognised by judicial decision, as being necessary for the achievement of social justice. The courts may not, therefore, put aside, as irrelevant, the undoubted fact that, if [Mrs Boland succeeds], the protection of the beneficial interest which English law now recognises that a married woman has in the matrimonial home will be strengthened whereas, if they lose, this interest can be weakened, and even destroyed, by an unscrupulous husband. Nor must the courts flinch when assailed by arguments to the effect that the protection of her interest will create difficulties in banking or conveyancing practice. The difficulties are, I believe, exaggerated: but bankers, and solicitors, exist to provide the service which the public needs. They can – as they have successfully done in the past – adjust their practice if it be socially required.' (As Lord Denning had said, 'Let the conveyancers look after themselves'.[5])

The decision, as *The Conveyancer* put it, 'sounded alarm bells in the office of every solicitor in the land' – seemingly, the journal said, to send them out to play at private detectives. The difficulty is that however full the enquiries made by a purchaser's solicitor, the enquiries may not discover every fact that is relevant. The purchaser's solicitor could formulate pre-contract enquiries asking the names of people in occupation, and if a vendor failed to disclose the name of someone in residence, the purchaser would have a remedy against the vendor. But this would be a personal one (for misrepresentation) and if the purchaser was a mortgagee, a personal remedy would be of no use, since the mortgagor will have no money (or not enough) – the reason why the claim for the house will have been made against him. And even if the purchaser does find out the names of all the people in actual occupation – by enquiries or inspection or both – he still has the problem of finding out if they have a beneficial interest in the property. And an occupier may not know whether he or she has such an interest. (For example, if a person in occupation, say a wife, has made an indirect contribution to the purchase of the house, for example, by going out to work, using her money for the house-keeping, so enabling her husband to

---

4   If *Caunce v Caunce* is not followed where the title is not registered, the same will apply under the unregistered system.
5   *Brikom Investments Ltd v Carr* [1979] 2 All ER 753 at 760.

pay off the mortgage more quickly, it may take a court decision to determine whether she *has* an equitable interest.) Another solution which has been suggested is that if H is proposing to sell or mortgage a house, and the purchaser or mortgagee has any doubts whatsoever, he should require H to appoint a co-trustee, so that any equitable interests that do exist are overreached. (This, of course, is the position in both registered and unregistered land – the registered land system having no overreaching machinery of its own, and adopting that of the unregistered system.)

We have spoken of the problems facing a purchaser. It is worth mentioning that matters are not necessarily satisfactory for a wife who has an equitable interest. First, if enquiries are made of her, and she does not disclose her interest, it does not bind a purchaser. Secondly, the fact that she has an overriding interest does not mean that she can be sure of remaining in continued occupation of the property. Even if she successfully upholds her claim to remain in possession against the mortgagee (which will in practice prevent him exercising the statutory power of sale), the mortgagee could initiate bankruptcy proceedings and let the trustee in bankruptcy take steps to sell the property.[6] And there is a line of cases which show that as between the interest of a wife in staying put, and the interests of her husband's creditors, it is the latter which prevail.[7] Even if there are children, the decision will not necessarily be any different.[8] As Walton J said in *Re Bailey*, 'The voice of the trustee in bankruptcy, reminding the debtor of the obligation to pay one's debts, should prevail as compared with one's obligations to maintain one's wife and family. This may be yet another case where the sins of the father have to be visited on the children, but that is the way in which the world is constructed, and one must be just before one is generous.' Generally, the most that a wife will be able to obtain is a postponement of the order for sale.[9]

The decision in *Williams and Glyn's Bank Ltd v Boland* was the subject of much debate[10] and the problems raised were referred to the Law Commission.

The Commission reported in 1982[11] but its recommendations were not found generally acceptable. Instead, in 1985, a Bill[12] was introduced that would have adopted an alternative solution. But parts of the Bill proved controversial and, owing to shortage of parliamentary time, the Bill was withdrawn.

---

6   The proceeds of sale in this case being divided between the wife (according to her beneficial interest, eg one-half) and the husband's creditors.
7   *Re Solomon* [1967] Ch 573, [1966] 3 All ER 255; *Re Turner* [1975] 1 All ER 5, [1974] 1 WLR 1556; *Bird v Syme-Thomson* [1978] 3 All ER 1027, [1979] 1 WLR 440.
8   *Re Bailey (A bankrupt) (No 25 of 1975)* [1977] 2 All ER 26, [1977] 1 WLR 278.
9   *Re Holliday* [1981] Ch 405, [1980] 3 All ER 385; *Burke v Burke* [1974] 2 All ER 944, [1974] 1 WLR 1063; *Re Turner* [1975] 1 All ER 5, [1974] 1 WLR 1556.
10 (1979) 95 LQR 501; [1980] Conv 361 (J. Martin); [1980] Conv 427 (C. Sydenham); (1980) 43 MLR (S. Freeman); [1980] Conv 313; (1980) 130 NLJ 896 (R. L. Deech); [1981] Conv 19 (S. M. Clayton); [1981] Conv 84 (J. Martin); [1981] Conv 219 (J. Martin); (1981) 97 LQR 32 (R. J. Smith).
11 *Property Law: The Implications of Williams and Glyn's Bank v Boland* (Law Com No 115, 1982); (1983) 46 MLR 330 (W. T. Murphy). Further recommendations have been made by the Commission: *Third Report on Land Registration* (Law Com No 158, 1987).
12 Land Registration and Law of Property Bill.

As time passed, however, it became clear, as Lord Scarman had forecast, that the difficulties foreseen proved to have been exaggerated, and mortgagees successfully adapted their procedures to take account of the decision,

It has since become the practice that when a sole owner applies for a mortgage, he is required to state (on the mortgage proposal form) whether any other person over 18 is resident in the property offered as security (and to acknowledge that his reply to this question constitutes a representation). If the reply to the question reveals the existence of another adult resident, this person is required to acknowledge on the mortgage deed that he disclaims, as against the mortgagee, any beneficial interest in the property.

The procedure is not watertight: if the mortgagor fails to disclose the existence of a person in occupation, the mortgagee will be bound by any equitable interest in the property that that person holds, and the mortgagee's only remedy for any resultant loss will lie against the mortgagor merely in contract (for misrepresentation); further the procedure will not protect a mortgagee against a claim by an infant.[13] However, the number of instances in which the big institutional lenders (principally building societies and banks) have suffered loss as a consequence of being bound by an undiscovered overriding equitable interest has not been large enough to have had any discernible effect on the economics of the mortgage market.

So, after the dust has settled, matters proceeded once more on an even keel. At least until 1985, when litigation in a case that reached the House of Lords as *City of London Building Society v Flegg*[14] caused conveyancers another jolt.

City of London Building Society v Flegg[14]

The case concerned a house in Kent – Bleak House, in Gillingham. In 1977 the house was conveyed to a Mr and Mrs Brown in fee simple on trust for sale for themselves as beneficial joint tenants. They intended the house to be a home for themselves and Mrs Brown's parents and the latter, Mr and Mrs Flegg, contributed £18,000 towards the purchase price of £34,000. Later, money was borrowed from a building society by the Browns on the security of the property. In all, a total of £37,500 was raised. Mr and Mrs Brown subsequently defaulted in the mortgage repayments and the society sought an order for possession. The Fleggs resisted the granting of the order. They had, they claimed, an equitable interest in the property by reason of their contribution to the purchase price. When the money had been borrowed by the execution of a legal charge on the house they had been in occupation. The society had made no enquiries of them as to any interest of theirs in the property. Thus, they

---

13   No purpose would be served by requiring the revelation of the existence of infants resident at the property since their signature would not be sufficient (because of the law relating to infants contracts) to deprive them of their interests.

14   [1988] AC 54; (M & B); [1987] Conv 451 (W. J. Swadling); (1987) 103 LQR 520 (R. J. Smith); [1988] Conv 141 (P. Sparkes); [1988] Conv 188 (M. P. Thompson). Applied in *State Bank of India v Sood* [1997] 1 All ER 169, [1997] 2 WLR 421, CA (overreaching occurred notwithstanding that no capital money arose); [1996] Conv 134 (M.P. Thompson).

claimed, they had an interest that, under *Williams and Glyn's Bank Ltd v Boland*,[15] was binding on the society as an overriding interest under s 70(1)(g). At first instance their claim was rejected: they did have an interest, the court held, but the interest was overreached by the charge having been executed by trustees for sale, and the mortgagee society having obtained a receipt signed by two trustees.[16] The Court of Appeal allowed the appeal: the Flegg's equitable interest was an overriding interest under s 70(1)(g) and as such binding on the society.[17]

The society appealed to the Lords. The issue seemed to be this. Two separate parts of the 1925 legislation appeared to be in conflict. According to the overreaching principles of the Law of Property Act 1925,[18] the interests of Mr and Mrs Flegg should be overreached (and attach to the money raised) and the society therefore take free. According to the Land Registration Act 1925, it seemed that the interests of Mr and Mrs Flegg were binding on the society as overriding interests under s 70(1)(g). Which should prevail? The House of Lords found for the society. In the course of so doing, speeches in the House demonstrated that in fact no conflict existed. The reasoning was this. The Fleggs had an equitable interest in the proceeds of the property. The interest entitled them to occupy the property. The fact of their occupation made their equitable interest an overriding interest. But the right of occupation was not separate from their equitable interest: the right of occupation was one 'that stems from, depends upon and is co-terminus with the interest in the rents and profits'[19] arising under the trust for sale. 'Actual occupation is not an interest in itself.'[20] When the Browns executed the legal charge, and as trustees for sale gave the society a receipt for the money advanced, under s 27 of the Law of Property Act the Flegg's equitable interest was overreached. At this point they ceased to have any interest that was capable of being an overriding interest by virtue of their occupation.[1] Thus no conflict existed between the principles of overreaching and those governing overriding interests. As Lord Oliver said,[2] '... the philosophy behind both the Land Registration Act 1925 and the Law of Property Act was that they should operate in parallel and it would, therefore, be surprising if it were found that the two systems were not constructed so as to dovetail into one another. In fact they do.'[3] The decision in *Boland* had been reached because the mortgage had been executed by a sole trustee; thus the equitable interest of Mrs Boland had not been overreached; thus her interest was still subsisting and, by virtue of her occupation, was an overriding interest under s 70(1)(g), and as such, binding on the mortgagee bank. Where, on the other hand, a receipt was obtained from two trustees for sale, a purchaser took

15   Supra.
16   See Chapter 8.
17   For criticism see [1986] Conv 131 (D. J. Hayton).
18   Section 27(1).
19   Lord Oliver of Aylmerton, at 74.
20   Lord Templeman at 70.
 1   At 70.
 2   At 84.
 3   Instances exist, however, in which the two systems fail to dovetail into one another. See p 540; and (1977) 41 Conv (NS) 405 (J. G. Riddall).

free. So the law was confirmed as being what, until the Court of Appeal's decision in *Flegg*, it had, since 1925, been understood to be.[4]

The House of Lords' decision in *Flegg* demonstrated a refusal to extend the effect of the *Boland* decision. Two other, earlier, cases showed an important restriction on the effect of the *Boland* decision. In *Paddington Building Society v Mendelsohn*,[5] a mother and son agreed to purchase property as their home. The mother provided £15,500, and £17,000 was to be raised by a mortgage. As the mother was too old to be likely to be granted a mortgage it was agreed between her and the son that the property should be registered in the son's name alone. This was done, and on the same date a mortgage was executed. The mother and son moved in. Some time later, with the mother's agreement, the son executed a further mortgage. He subsequently failed in the repayments and the mortgagee sought an order for possession. The mother resisted the order, claiming that she had an equitable interest in the property, and that this was, following *Boland,* binding on the mortgagee as an overriding interest under s 70(1)(g). The Court of Appeal held that there was no doubt that since the mother was in occupation, the society took the land subject to her rights in the property. But the question was, the Court said, what *were* her rights? Since there had been no express declaration of trust or agreement as to the beneficial interests of the mother and son at the time of the acquisition of the flat, the nature of the mother's equitable interest had to depend on the intention to be imputed to the son and the mother at the time. Since the mother had known and intended that the flat was to be mortgaged to the society and that without the mortgage the property could not have been acquired, the only possible intention to impute to the parties was an intention that the mother's rights were to be subject to the rights of the society.[6] Thus, the inherent quality of the mother's entitlement was that it was an equitable interest to which the mortgage was intended to take priority. The fact that the mother was in occupation did not, under s 70(1)(g), make her interest a bigger one than it already was – it could not convert her interest into one that took priority over that of the mortgagee. Thus the mother's interest was not binding on the society, which was therefore entitled to an order for possession.

We may mention here that the outcome in *Paddington* was the same in a case, *Bristol and West Building Society v Henning*[7] (judgment in which was delivered on the same day as *Paddington*), which concerned land the title to which was not registered. In this case also it was held that a mortgage executed

---

4   Cf [1986] Conv 379 (W. J. Swadling).
5   (1985) 50 P & CR 244; [1986] Conv 57 (M. P. Thompson). The grounds for the Court of Appeal's decision were the same in dismissing the claimant's appeal in *Abbey National Building Society v Cann* [1991] 1 AC 56, [1990] 1 All ER 1085 (see p 469 supra). The decision of the Court of Appeal was upheld by the House of Lords on different grounds, but not dissenting from the Court of Appeal's reason.
6   At 247.
7   [1985] 2 All ER 606, [1985] 1 WLR 778; [1985] Conv 361 (P. N. Todd); [1986] Conv 57 (M. P. Thompson); applied in *Equity and Law Home Loans Ltd v Prestidge* [1992] 1 All ER 909, [1992] 1 WLR 137, CA; [1992] Conv 206 (M. P. Thompson); (1992) 108 LQR 371 (R. J. Smith); [1992] CLJ 223 (M. Dixon).

by a man who was the sole legal owner of land in which a woman had an equitable interest was to be regarded as having been made with the common intention of the man and the woman that the mortgage should have priority over any equitable interest of the woman. Thus after the man had defaulted in the mortgage repayments, the woman's claim that her interest was binding on the mortgagee failed, and an order for possession was granted.

To what extent has the decision in *Paddington* nullified the effect of that in *Boland?* It is likely to be common that, when a home is purchased by a couple, say H and W, by means of a mortgage and the property is conveyed into the name of H alone, it will be the couple's understanding of the matter, and hence their common intention, that the mortgage should have priority over any equitable interest of W. From this it might seem that a mortgagee has less need, as a result of *Paddington*, to fear that he will be bound, as was the bank in *Boland*, by an equitable interest. This may well be the position where a mortgage is taken out on the occasion of an initial purchase of a home, when it is likely that, following *Paddington*, W's interest may be, because of the common intention, not of a quality to bind the mortgagee. But there is no certainty that the common intention found in *Paddington* will always be found to have been present. (W might satisfy the court that she had had no knowledge that a loan was required for the purchase of the property.) So a mortgagee cannot rely on the outcome being the same as in *Paddington*. (And, in any case, institutional lenders would not wish to be faced with the possibility of Supreme Court litigation every time they sought possession against a defaulting mortgagor.)

Where a mortgage is taken out subsequently to the initial purchase of a property (as in *Boland*), then there is all the more reason for a mortgagee to make the now customary enquiries, since it may very well be that the mortgagor sought the loan without the knowledge of an equitable owner in occupation, with the consequence that, no common intention as to priority having been present, the equitable interest would bind the mortgagee as an overriding interest in the event of his seeking possession. (That the inquiries by the mortgagee must (for the mortgagee not to be bound) be proper ones is illustrated by *Kingsnorth Finance Ltd v Tizard*[8] a case concerning unregistered land considered in Chapter 12.)

Thus, whilst, in law, *Paddington* marks an important restriction on the effect of *Boland*, in practice mortgagees will have been wise not to relax their safeguards.

SUMMARY

See Appendix II, p 570.

---

8   [1986] 2 All ER 54, [1986] 1 WLR 783; [1986] Conv 283 (M. P. Thompson).

CHAPTER 27

Conclusion

In Chapter 6 we learned that the Law of Property Act 1925 reduced to two the number of estates which could exist as legal estates (and to five those interests which could exist as legal interests).

The reduction in the number of legal estates was one part of the means adopted by the 1925 legislation to achieve its major aim. The major[1] aim is sometimes described as having been to simplify conveyancing. Anyone who has read so far might be surprised to learn that the legislation of 1925 simplified anything. However, although the legislation of 1925 certainly added greatly to the volume of land law, it did resolve many difficulties which previously existed. These difficulties were not so much those confronting the conveyancer himself, but were rather those which might confront a person wishing to transfer land. The principal difficulties that existed before 1925 were as follows:

1. If V sold land to P, P could never be certain,

(a) that someone would not later appear and show that he had a legal interest in the land (eg a legal mortgage) which would therefore bind him;

(b) that someone would not later appear and show that he had an equitable interest in the land that he, P, would be unable to show that he was a bona fide purchaser without notice, and so would be bound by the equitable interest.

2. If S granted land in 1881[2] to A for life with remainder to B, an infant, then notwithstanding that A did not want the land, and P wanted to buy it, the land could not be sold.

3. If G granted land to A and B as tenants in common, and A died intestate leaving 47 next of kin, then notwithstanding that B wanted to sell the land and P wanted to buy it, then, as we learned in Chapter 11, there could be insuperable difficulties.

4. Before he could safely buy land, a purchaser might have difficulty, or at least be involved in much trouble, in verifying the vendor's title to the land.

The problem referred to in 1(a) above was tackled (i) by reducing the number of interests that could exist as legal interests; (ii) by restricting those that could exist as legal interests to ones which it would normally be possible for a vendor to discover from the title deeds or by inspecting the land; and (iii)

---

1 Other aims included the assimiliation of the law of real property to that of personal property and the abolition of anachronisms (eg the abolition of copyhold tenure and the repeal of the Statute of Uses 1535).

2 Ie before the Settled Land Act 1882. See Chapter 7.

by making a legal mortgage not protected by deposit of title deeds (ie a legal interest which a purchaser might not readily be able to discover) registrable as a land charge.

The problem referred to in 1(b) above was tackled in part by making a large number of equitable interests registrable as land charges. In the case of these interests a purchaser could therefore discover by what interests he would be bound.

Regarding the problem set out at 2 above, it will be noted that one reason for the difficulty was that it was possible for the legal fee simple to be carved up into chunks of 'time'; into, for example a series of life estates followed by a fee simple in remainder. The difficulty was overcome by making it impossible for the legal fee simple to be so divided up; life interests, fee tails and determinable and conditional interests could exist only as equitable interests. So the fee simple absolute in possession (and the term of years absolute) stood inviolate. Thus if, after 1925, G grants land to A for life with remainder to B, A's and B's interests are equitable and the legal fee simple remains intact. A, as Tenant for life, has a statutory power of sale, and so the land can be sold. If the settlement took the form of a trust for sale, the trustees could sell by virtue of the duty imposed on them. The equitable interests of A and B were in either case thus kept 'off the title', ie separate from the legal fee simple[3] which could be sold free of the equitable interests, these being overreached and attached to the purchase money.

Regarding the problem considered at 3 above, here the difficulty arose from the fact that there was nothing to prevent the ownership of the legal fee simple becoming shared between an unlimited, and perhaps ever-increasing, number of persons. As we saw in Chapter 11, this problem was resolved by the impositions of a statutory trust for sale whenever land is held by more than one person. Since the trustees held (and still hold) as joint tenants, the number of persons in whom the legal fee simple is vested can never exceed the statutory limit of four. The fact that the trustees held the land on trust for sale enabled the land to be sold.

Regarding the difficulties arising in connection with verifying a vendor's title (4 above), we saw in Chapter 26, that registration of titles to land at the Land Registry has, where land is registered, now removed such difficulties.

The 1925 legislation was intended to enable English land law to fulfil its proper role in the twentieth century. The success of the draftsmen[4] in achieving this end constituted a very great accomplishment. But the draftsmen, being practical men, cannot have supposed that their work would be flawless and, as we have seen in earlier chapters, defects remained.

Some defects were caused by the basis adopted for certain parts of the machinery. For example, in Chapter 25 we saw the difficulties produced by the fact that land charges are registrable against the names of landholders.

---

3 Before 1925 the power being conferred by the Settled Land Act 1882 on whoever was the Tenant for life.
4 The architect of the 1925 reforms was William Wolstenhome. The principal draftsman was Sir Benjamin Cherry. For the history of the legislation see (1977) 40 MLR 5 (A. Offer).

Other defects were due to a failure to realise the effect that one part of an Act would have on another. For example, in Chapter 23 we saw the conflict which can arise between s 97 of the Law of Property Act 1925 and s 4(5) of the Land Charges Act 1972. Other failings were due to a failure to take account of the fact that the correction of one defect could lead to the introduction of another in its place. For example, in Chapter 25 we noted how s 44(5), and the rule that an unregistered land charge does not bind a purchaser even if he has actual notice, each has this effect.

To the extent that criticism of the legislation itself is warranted, it is against the Land Registration Act 1925 that it must be directed. We have already noted certain substantive defects in the machinery of the Act and the confusion that can be caused by the terminology of the Act. But the failing of the Act lies deeper than any flaws such as these. It lies in the absence from the Act of guidelines indicating the purpose and methods of the system which the legislation introduced, an absence reflected by the lack of any ordered arrangement of the Act's provisions. The high priests of the system, the civil servants who administer the scheme, find their way about the Act with a marvellous facility, but to the outsider, the Act with its 'obscurities, defective definitions and unsuitable rules'[5] is not easy to follow. There is indeed a need for a 'thorough revision, rationalisation and simplification of the law.'[6]

A defect of a more fundamental nature was the failure of the legislation to bring the bare trust within what was intended to be an all inclusive scheme under which all trusts of land were either strict settlements or trusts for sale. How the Trusts of Land and Appointment of Trustees Act 1996 achieves the object sought by the 1925 legislation (by bringing trusts of land under one umbrella) was seen in Chapter 10.

So much for the defects of the legislation itself. The aim of the legislation was, as we have said, to enable the land law to play its proper part in the twentieth century. In what ways did the legislation of 1925 failed to cater for the needs of more recent times?

One deficiency of the 1925 legislation was its failure to anticipate the position where a sole trustee holding on an implied trust for himself and another sells the land to a purchaser. The nature of this problem was considered in dealing with *Caunce v Caunce*[7] in Chapter 12; the solution adopted (where the title to the land is registered) by the House of Lords in *Williams and Glyn's Bank Ltd v Boland*[8] was examined in Chapter 26.

The shortcomings of the legislation must, however, be set against its achievement. In the seventy-two years between 1925 and 1996 only two amendments of any substance (those in 1969[9] and 1986[10]) were made.[11] In

---

5   M & W p 1153.
6   Ibid.
7   [1969] 1 All ER 722, [1969] 1 WLR 286; (M & B).
8   [1981] AC 487, [1980] 2 All ER 408.
9   Law of Property Act 1969. See Chapter 25.
10   Land Registration Act 1986. See Chapter 26.
11   The Perpetuities and Accumulations Act 1964, the Rentcharges Act 1977 and the Law of Property (Miscellaneous Provisions) Act 1989 implemented changes in policy, not changes required by defects in the machinery established in 1925.

the light of the complexity of the changes carried out in 1925, and the volume of the legislation required to achieve them, the cause for wonder is that the machinery in general worked so well, and not that here and there imperfections – and minor imperfections at that – came to be seen as needing attention.

The 1925 legislation was (like the Act of 1996) in essence, *conveyancing* legislation. It was concerned with the machinery with which lawyers carried out standard transactions – the creation of settlements, the granting of leases, the execution of mortgages, the conveyance of land to co-owners. It was concerned with the bread and butter of real property as it had long been familiar to conveyancers. The problem which has bedevilled the land law in recent times is one that has arisen outside the world of routine conveyancing. It concerns entitlements recognised by equity which have come into existence otherwise than by express grant.

We first met these entitlements in Chapter 5 when we saw that if A provides the purchase price for land that is conveyed into the name of B, then B is presumed to hold the land on trust for A. We saw in Chapter 12 how this principle is relevant with regard to the matrimonial home – that if a wife provides part of the purchase price of a house that is conveyed into the name of her husband alone, the husband holds on trust for both of them. We saw, too, that an equitable beneficial interest could arise from an indirect contribution such as by carrying out improvements. Then in Chapter 20 we learned that a beneficial entitlement could be acquired in a whole variety of other ways, for example by acting to one's detriment in reliance on an assurance with regard to certain property. These beneficial entitlements were examined in two separate chapters, Co-ownership and Licences, because there *is* such a thing as co-ownership, with its own body of law, and there *are* such things as licences, because the courts say there are; and it is convenient to follow the customary divisions of the law. It will be appreciated, though, that the subject matter of certain aspects of co-ownership merges with that of licences – throughout the question being, in what circumstances will a person with no legal title to property come to acquire an entitlement to the property? We have now had sufficient cases to have a fair idea of the kind of circumstances that will give rise to such an entitlement, but we do not know what other (if any) kinds of circumstances will be regarded as doing so. And, most important, we are still in the dark as to the precise nature of these acquired entitlements (the use of the word 'entitlement', it will be noted, avoids the begging of the question entailed in using 'interest', or 'licence', words that carry their own pre-existing connotations). Are these entitlements *interests* in property or do they rest on no more than a *licence* to occupy land for some specified period (commonly the lifetime of the person entitled). Since a licence is not binding on a purchaser of the land the court, to provide security for the person entitled, has in some instances held that the person entitled has an interest (eg a life interest) in the property, so that, if the land is sold, the equitable interest will be capable of binding a purchaser. But such a finding resulted, before the Trusts of Land and Appointment of Trustees Act 1996, in the creation of a strict settlement and results, after the 1996 Act, in the creation of a trust of land, in either case with consequences far removed from what is likely to have been in the mind of the parties.

The Trusts of Land and Appointment of Trustees Act 1996 accomplished a major and much needed reform of the law (and, bearing in mind the distance that the ripples in the pond extend, in a remarkably small compass). It would be unfair to criticise the Act for not dealing with a matter it did not set out to tackle. But the nature and effect of equitable entitlements to occupy land are matters that may nevertheless at some stage come to be considered as requiring attention from those charged with reviewing the operation of the law.

Public rights of way[1] and certain other public and semi-public rights

An individual may acquire a right:

(1) to cross another's land by virtue of a licence or an easement;
(2) to roam on another's land by virtue of a licence, and, it seems, at least if the land is not of an unduly large area, by virtue of an easement;[2]
(3) to take something from another's land by virtue of a licence or a profit;
(4) to use another's land for some other specific purpose by virtue of a licence or an easement.

Here we consider whether:

A. a member of the public;
B. a member of a group whose membership fluctuates (eg the inhabitants of a parish),

may acquire the rights listed under 1-4 above, and, if so, what form in each case the right takes.

1.   THE RIGHT TO CROSS ANOTHER'S LAND

A.   The public

A member of the public has the right to cross another's land if there is a public right of way over the land. The surface of the land over which a public right of way exists is termed a highway. A highway is not necessary metalled: an unmade track may be as much a highway as a motorway.

The existence of a highway gives a member of the public the right to pass and repass along it. The manner in which he may do so (eg on foot, on horseback, by a horse-drawn or mechanically propelled vehicle) depends on the nature of the highway. A highway which falls into the category of a footpath entitles a member of the public to walk on it. A highway which falls into the category of a bridleway entitles him to walk or ride a horse on it. A highway which falls into the category of a carriageway entitles him to walk, ride, or

---

1   S. J. Sauvain *Highway Law* (1989); *Rights of Way: A Guide to Law and Practice* (2nd edn, 1992), J. G. Riddall and J. Trevelyan.
2   *Re Ellenborough Park* [1956] Ch 131, [1955] 3 All ER 667, where a right to 'the full enjoyment of the pleasure ground' (a park) was held to be capable of existing as an easement.

drive vehicles on it. These common law principles are in some instances varied by regulations made under statutory powers, eg a regulation excluding learner drivers from using motorways.

CREATION OF PUBLIC RIGHTS OF WAY

1.   *By dedication by the owner of the land and acceptance by the public*

Dedication may be express or implied. If there has been user as of right by the public for such a period of time that the user must have come to the notice of the owner of the land, and he has taken no steps to interrupt the user, then at common law these facts raise a presumption that the owner intended to dedicate the way as a public right of way. The length of user that needs to be shown depends on the circumstances. It may be as little as 18 months where the circumstances point to an intention to dedicate.[3]

In order to remove uncertainty as to the period necessary to raise a presumption of dedication, the Rights of Way Act 1932 provided that proof of user as of right by the public without interruption for 20 years established a good claim unless the landowner could prove that there was no intention on his part to dedicate the way. The Act of 1932 has now been replaced by provisions in the Highways Act 1980.[4]

The provisions of the Acts of 1932 and 1980 do not prevent the making of a claim at common law based on user for a shorter period than 20 years, but to succeed, the circumstances must have indicated an intention to dedicate by the owner.

2.   *By statute*

Several statutes provide for the creation of highways. The most important is the Highways Act 1980.

EXTINGUISHMENT

At common law the principle is 'once a highway, always a highway'. Thus, once a highway has come into existence, the fact that the public has not used the way (whether due to lack of need or because the owner has blocked the route or for any other reason) does not extinguish the public right of way, however long the period of non-use.

The only way in which a public right of way can be extinguished is if the way is closed or diverted by an order made under a statutory provision.[5] For example the Highways Act 1980[6] confers power on certain authorities to close (or divert) certain types of highways in specified circumstances.

---

3   *North London Rly Co v St Mary, Islington, Vestry* (1872) 27 LT 672.
4   Sections 31, 32.
5   See *Sstonleigh Nomineees Ltd v A-G* [1974] 1 All ER 734, [1974] 1 WLR 305.
6   Sections 116, 118, 119.

B. Fluctuating bodies

A fluctuating body of persons (such as the inhabitants of a parish) cannot claim a right of way[7] as an easement. There are two reasons for this. 1(a) Easements must be capable of being granted. (b) For an easement to be granted the grantee must be a legal person. (c) A fluctuating body cannot be a legal person.

2. There is no certainty that all the inhabitants will be owners of land capable of forming dominant tenements to which the right would be appurtenant.

A fluctuating body may, however, be able to claim a right of way as a local custom. For such a custom to be valid at common law (and so enforceable under common law) the following conditions must be fulfilled.

1. The custom must be 'ancient'. This requirement is satisfied by showing user since 1189. Proof of user for a long period raises a presumption of user since 1189.
2. User must have been continuous.
3. The custom must be certain. Thus the custom must be confined to an area known to the law, for example a parish.
4. The custom must be reasonable.

An example of the right of members of a fluctuating body to cross the land of another by virtue of a local custom is provided by a right which the inhabitants of a parish were held to have to use a path in order to reach the parish church.[8]

2. THE RIGHT TO ROAM ON ANOTHER'S LAND

A. The public

No form of right exists at common law which can given members of the public a right to roam at will (a 'ius spatiando) on the land of another.[9]

Various statutes contain provisions that can lead to the public acquiring the right to roam on another's land, whether in ownership of a private person, or of a local authority, or other body. For example, the National Parks and Access to the Countryside Act 1949 enables local planning authorities to make access agreements with landowners or, in the absence of agreement, access orders.[10] The effect of such agreements or orders is to give members of the public specified rights of access to privately owned land.

In 1997 a government was elected whose pre-election pledges included a commitment to introduce legislation that would confer a statutory right to

---

7 Or any other right; eg to enter land for the purpose of holding horse races; *Mounsey v Ismay* (1865) 3 H & C 486.
8 *Brocklebank v Thompson* [1903] 2 Ch 344.
9 *A-G v Antrobus* [1905] 2 Ch 188. But a right may exist that entitles the public to take recreation, a right which will presumably include the right to roam. See under 4A, infra.
10 Sections 51-55.

roam on uncultivated countryside such as mountain, moor and common, subject to restrictions to protect legitimate interests.[11]

B.   Fluctuating bodies

Just as members of a fluctuating body may, as we have seen, acquire a right of way across the land of another by virtue of a local custom, so may they acquire a right by virtue of local custom to roam on the land of another. For example, the inhabitants of a parish[12] may, by custom, have rights of recreation,[13] including the right to roam, on a village green[14] (often formerly part of the waste land of a manor).

The right of inhabitants of a particular locality to access to land may in some cases be based on an Inclosure Act. As part of the rearrangement and redistribution of land under an award made under such an Act, inhabitants were sometimes given rights over certain land set aside for their benefit. The land concerned was commonly allotted to the churchwardens or overseers of the poor for, eg the benefit of the poor (eg for collecting fuel[15]) or as a place for exercise or recreation for the inhabitants. The latter right might include a right to roam at will over the land.

3.   THE RIGHT TO TAKE SOMETHING FROM ANOTHER'S LAND

A.   The public

No right can be created at common law which entitles members of the public to take something from a person's land.

B.   Fluctuating bodies

One of the reasons why an easement cannot be granted to a fluctuating body is that such a body is not capable of being the grantee of an easement. For the same reason a profit à prendre cannot be granted to a fluctuating body. Nor can a fluctuating body successfully claim the right by virtue of a local custom, because such a custom would not be 'reasonable'[16] since it 'might leave nothing

---

11   T. Blair (10 October 1995); A. Taylor (25 January 1996); C. Smith (26 September 1994); F. Dobson (24 September 1995); E. Morley (8 May 1996); J. Ruddock (21 May 1996). For the story of the fight to secure access to open land see H. Hill, *Freedom to Roam.*

12   But not 'all persons for the time being, being in the' parish; *Fitch v Rawling* (1795) 2 Hy Bl 393.

13   Eg the right to indulge in lawful 'sports and pastimes'; *New Windsor Corpn v Mellor* [1975] Ch 380, [1975] 3 All ER 44.

14   Town and village greens were made registrable under the Commons Registration Act 1965, ss 1, 22. See *New Windsor Corpn v Mellor*, ante.

15   See *Re Turnworth Down, Dorset* [1978] Ch 251, [1977] 2 All ER 105.

16   See p 563.

for the owner of the soil' and so would be 'wholly inconsistent with the right of property in the soil'.[17]

However, although a right to take something from another's land cannot be claimed by virtue of a local custom it may nevertheless be possible for a fluctuating body effectively to acquire the benefit of such a right by one or other of two means which the courts have accepted in order to uphold practices which have existed for a long period.

1. PRESUMPTION OF INCORPORATION AND GRANT BY THE CROWN

We have said that a fluctuating body cannot acquire a profit as it is not a legal person. But there would be no problem if the fluctuating body was a corporation, since a corporation is a legal person. A corporation can be created under statute or by royal grant. This is the basis which the courts have used to construct the following fiction.

If it can be shown that:

(1) members of a fluctuating body, eg a 'Company or fraternity of Free Fisherman'[18] or the inhabitants of a certain parish[19] have enjoyed the benefit of a certain practice, eg dredging for oysters in the water and creeks of a manor[18] or lopping branches for fuel on the waste land of a manor;[19] and,
(2) the benefit has been enjoyed for a long period; and,
(3) those claiming the right have always regarded themselves as forming a corporation for the purpose of administering the practice and have acted as such in the regulation of the practice, eg by holding meetings; and
(4) the subject matter of the benefit lay in the grant of the Crown, eg because the manor from the waste of which the branches of tree were lopped belonged to the Crown,[19] then the court may be prepared to presume that the Crown had granted the right to the body concerned, which the Crown had at the same time incorporated for the purpose of the grant.

2. PRESUMPTION OF A GRANT BY THE CROWN TO AN EXISTING CORPORATION

In *Goodman v Saltash Corporation*[20] the free inhabitants of Saltash claimed the right to fish for oysters from the estuary of the river Tamar between Candlemas and Easter Eve each year. Evidence showed that the right claimed had been exercised for 200 years but there was no evidence that the claimants had ever had any vestige of a corporate character. The House of Lords therefore declined to presume incorporation and grant by the Crown. There was evidence, however, that the right claimed had been shared by the Corporation of Saltash, which owned the bed of the estuary. The Lords held that it was to be presumed that the Corporation enjoyed the right concerned by virtue of a grant from the Crown; and (2) the right concerned had been granted to the Corporation not

---

17 *Race v Ward* (1855) 4 E & B 702 at 709; *Wolstanton Ltd v Newcastle-under-Lyme Borough Council* [1940] AC 860, [1940] 3 All ER 101.
18 *Re Free Fisherman of Faversham Co* (1887) 36 Ch D 329.
19 *Chilton v London Corpn* (1878) 7 Ch D 735.
20 (1882) 7 App Cas 633.

only for its own benefit but also on trust for the free inhabitants of the town. By this means the right claimed was upheld.

4. THE RIGHT TO USE THE LAND OF ANOTHER FOR SPECIFIED PURPOSES OTHER THAN THOSE UNDER 1-3 ABOVE

A. The public

No rights exist that entitle members of the public to use the land of another for any purpose other than those set out under 1 and 2 above, except, possibly, a right to take recreation.[2]

B. Fluctuating bodies

We have noted that members of a fluctuating body may be able to claim a right by virtue of a custom to cross land or to roam on land, provided that the necessary conditions are satisfied (eg the custom is 'ancient', etc).

The rights which members of a fluctuating body may claim by virtue of a custom extend to other forms of use of land. For example, fishermen of a parish were held to have a right by custom to dry their nets on private land near the sea;[3] inhabitants of a parish to have a right by custom to hold a fair on a certain day each year on a certain part of the waste land of the manor;[4] inhabitants of a borough to have certain rights of recreation on a piece of land owned by the borough;[5] and, as noted above, inhabitants of a locality may have rights to recreation or exercise on a village green; including for example, the right to 'to dance on the freehold of another, and spoil his grass'.[6]

1   Cf *Alfred F Beckett Ltd v Lyons* [1967] Ch 449, [1967] 1 All ER 833.
2   *R v Doncaster Metropolitan Borough Council, ex p Braim* (1986) 85 LGR 233 (grant presumed of right for public to take recreation in a defined area).
3   *Mercer v Denne* [1904] 2 Ch 534.
4   *Wyld v Silver* [1963] Ch 243, [1963] 3 All ER 309.
5   *New Windsor Corpn v Mellor* [1974] 2 All ER 510, [1974] 1 WLR 1504.
6   *Abbot v Weekly* (1665) 1 Lev 176.

Summaries

Chapter 5

A trust is created by the transfer of property to a trustee to hold for the benefit of a beneficiary, or by a person who holds property declaring himself trustee of a property for another.

The interests of beneficiaries came to be enforceable against trustees through applications to the Lord Chancellor's Court, the Court of Chancery, during the fifteenth century.

Chancery applied to equitable interests the rules relating to estates that had been evolved by the common law courts for legal estates.

Under the rule in *Saunders v Vautier*, where trustees hold property on trust for a beneficiary who is of full age and absolutely entitled, the beneficiary can call on the trustees to transfer the legal estate to him, thus ending the trust.

A beneficiary is one who holds under a trust. A beneficial owner is one who is entitled to the benefit of property.

A bare trust is one under which the beneficiaries are of full age and absolutely entitled and the trustees have no specified duty to perform.

The bona fide purchaser rule is that which (subject to the intervention of statute) determines whether a purchaser from trustees takes the property subject to or free from equitable interests.

Legal interests to which land is subject bind (subject to the intervention of statute) a purchaser of the land.

As between the holders of equitable interests, the rule is first in time, first in right.

The bona fide purchaser rule applies to purchasers pro tanto.

Equity acts in personam.

Equity's remedies are discretionary.

An implied trust is one that arises from what is inferred to have been the parties' intention.

A constructive trust is one imposed by the court.

Chapter 6

Prior to the Law of Property Act 1925, any form of interest in land could exist in a legal or an equitable form.

After the Act, the only estates in land that can exist as legal estates are the fee simple absolute in possession and the term of years (together with, after the Law of Property (Amendment) Act 1926, a fee simple subject to a legal or equitable right of entry or re-entry).

After the Act, the only interests that can exist as legal interests are the five listed in the Act; of special importance being easements and mortgages.

Chapter 17

A lease is an interest, a proprietary interest, in land. A licence is not. It is from this distinction that most of the differences between a lease and a licence stem.

For a lease to exist there must be certainty of duration and the tenant must have exclusive possession.

In deciding whether an arrangement is a lease or a licence the court looks primarily to intention.

Leases may be for a fixed period; or periodic; or at will or at suffrance; or by estoppel.

A deed is required to create a legal lease unless the lease is for a period not exceeding three years, et cetera.

An equitable lease can arise under the doctrine in *Walsh v Lonsdale*.

A legal lease can be assigned only by deed.

A legal lease may be assigned in equity under the doctrine in *Walsh v Lonsdale*.

The assignment of an equitable lease must be in writing under section 53(1) of the Law of Property Act 1925.

A contract to grant or assign a lease must (with exceptions) comply with section 2 of the Law of Property (Miscellaneous Provisions) Act 1989.

Obligations of a tenant or landlord may arise at common law, under the 'usual covenants' or by statute.

Leases may be terminated by notice, surrender, merger, disclaimer, or forfeiture.

Chapters 21 and 22

A.   If the parties are the original parties to the covenant, there is privity of contract and a covenant is enforceable accordingly.

B.   If the parties are not the original parties to the covenant (ie if one or both are assignees),

1.   if there is privity of estate (ie a landlord and tenant relationship),
(a)   as regards the position between the current landlord and tenant,
    (i)   in the case of old tenancies
       – whether the tenant can sue and be sued depends on the rule in *Spencer's Case*;
       – whether the landlord can sue and be sued depends on respectively sections 141 and 142.
    (ii)   in the case of new tenancies, the tenant can sue and be sued and the landlord can sue and be sued;
(b)   as regards the liability of a tenant after the assignment of the lease,
    (i)   in the case of old tenancies, the tenant remains liable;
    (ii)   in the case of new tenancies, the tenant is not liable (subject to guarantee agreements).

2. if there is no privity of estate (eg as between fee simple owners (Chapter 21),

(a) if there is a scheme of development, the covenants are mutually enforceable (page 399);

(b) otherwise,
   - whether the burden passes depends on the principles in *Tulk v Moxhay*;
   - whether the benefit passes now hinges on the principles in *Federated Homes* and *Roake v Chadha*.

Chapter 25

Certain matters, to bind a purchaser, must be registered in the Land Charges Department of the Land Registry.

The matters of most importance that require registration lie in the first of five registers, Land Charges. These are:

1 A legal mortgage without deposit of title deeds, registrable in Class C(i), puisne mortgages.
2 An equitable mortgage without deposit of title deeds, registrable in Class C(iii), general equitable charges.
3 A contract for the disposition of a legal interest in land, registrable in Class C(iv), estate contracts.
4 An option, registrable in Class C(iv), estate contracts.
5 A restrictive covenant made after 1925, registrable in Class D(ii), restrictive covenants.
6 An equitable easement, registrable in Class D(iii), equitable easements.
7 A right arising under the Family Law Act 1996, registrable in Class F, as a charge affecting any land by virtue of the 1996 Act.

Legal and equitable mortgages not protected by deposit of title deeds and rights under the 1996 Act, if not registered, are void against a purchaser for value.

Estate contracts and restrictive covenants made after 1925, if not registered, are void against purchaser of the legal estate for money or money's worth.

The matters of most practical importance that are not registrable include:

1 Legal interests (except puisne mortgages).
2 Restrictive covenants made before 1926.
3 Equitable interests arising from a contribution to the price of property.

Whether a purchaser is bound by a non-registrable interest is determined by the old rules.

A purchaser is not bound by an interest registered before the date of the root of title unless he had notice of it. A person who suffers loss from this is entitled to compensation.

A lessee who is bound by a registered interest the existence of which he has no means of discovering without examining his landlord's title is not entitled to compensation.

Interests in the land of another bind a squatter, irrespective of registration.

Local land chanrges bind a purchaser even if not registered. A person who suffers loss from this is entitled to compensation.

Chapter 26

When, in the case of land the title to which is not yet registered, one or other of certain specified transactions take place (for example on the sale of the land) the new holder of the land must apply to the Land Registry to have himself registered as the owner (as the 'registered proprietor') of the parcel of land concerned.

If he fails to do so, after two months, the title reverts to the previous holder.

If the Registry is satisfied, from an examination of the title deeds, that the applicant has a good title to the land, the Registry opens a 'register' (the 'title register' for the parcel of land, which is identified by a map.

On the title register (in one or other of three sub-divisions, the Property register, the Proprietorship register and the Charges register) the Registry enters the name of the holder; what kind of interest he has (ie the fee simple); benefits attaching to the land apparent from the title deeds; and disadvantages attaching to the land, in particular, matters registered under the Land Charges Act 1972 (Chapter 25) prior to the title being registered.

The proprietor receives a Land Certificate.

A proprietor can carry out the same transaction as the holder of unregistered land, but some transactions ('registrable dispositions') can only be effected by being registered at the Land Registry.

The grant of a lease for over 21 years is a registrable disposition. A title register is opened for the lease. The tenant becomes the proprietor of the leasehold title. The tenant receives a Land Certificate. A Notice is entered in the Charges register of the the freehold.

Interests *in* registered land consist of, (a) registered interests (ie interests in respect of which a registrable disposition has been registered); (b) overriding interests, set out in section 70; and (c) other interests, which are termed 'minor interests'.

Interests *on* the register consist of (a) matters recorded at first registration; (b) matters registered in respect of subsequent registrable dispositions; (c) minor interests that have been protected by the entry of a Notice, etc.

A subsequent proprietor for consideration takes subject to overriding interests and interest on the register (see above). He takes free from unprotected minor interests.

A subsequent proprietor not for consideration takes subject to overriding interests, interests on the register, and all minor interests (ie including unprotected minor interests).

A person who acquires a registered interest in land takes subject to overriding interests and interests on the register.

A person who acquires a minor interest in land takes subject to overriding interests, interests on the register and all prior minor interests whether protected or not.

In specified circumstances, the Registrar has jurisdiction to rectify errors, etc, in the Register. A person who suffers loss as a result of the rectification (or non-rectification, as the case may be) can claim compensation.

A spouse who is in occupation of a home in which she has an equitable interest, the legal title being in the other spouse, has an overriding interest under section 70(1)(g) (*Boland*) unless the inherent nature of her interest is such that it was not intended to take priority over a particular prior interest (*Mendelsohn*).

Index